D0788553

Judah and the Judeans in the
Fourth Century B.C.E.

Judah and the Judeans
in the
Fourth Century B.C.E.

edited by

ODED LIPSCHITS, GARY N. KNOPPERS,
and RAINER ALBERTZ

L.C.C.C. LIBRARY

Winona Lake, Indiana
EISENBRAUNS
2007

© Copyright 2007 by Eisenbrauns.
All rights reserved.
Printed in the United States of America.

www.eisenbrauns.com

Cataloging in Publication Data

Judah and the Judeans in the fourth century B.C.E. / edited by Oded
Lipschits, Gary N. Knoppers, and Rainer Albertz.
    p. cm.
    Includes bibliographical references and indexes.
    ISBN 978-1-57506-130-6 (hardcover : alk. paper)
    1. Judaea (Region)—History—Congresses. 2. Yehud (Persian
province)—Congresses. 3. Jews—History—586 B.C.–70 A.D.—
Congresses. 4. Judaism—History—Post-exilic period, 586 B.C.–210
A.D.—Congresses. 5. Bible. O.T.—Criticism, interpretation, etc.—
Congresses. I. Lipschits, Oded. II. Knoppers, Gary N., 1956–
III. Albertz, Rainer, 1943–
    DS110.J78J82 2007
    933—dc22

        2007028004

The paper used in this publication meets the minimum requirements of the
American National Standard for Information Sciences—Permanence of
Paper for Printed Library Materials, ANSI Z39.48-1984.♾™

Contents

12-10-08 59.50

v

PART 3

Edom and Samaria:
Judah's Neighbors in the Late Persian
and Early Hellenistic Periods

PART 4

Biblical Literature in the Late Persian
and Hellenistic Periods

Abbreviations

General

col(s).	column(s)
D	Deuteronomy (pentateuchal source)
DNb	inscription on tomb of Darius at Naqš-i Rustam
DSS	Dead Sea Scrolls
Dtr	Deuteronomistic historian
ET	English translation
Eth	Ethiopic
fem.	feminine
frg.	fragment
LXX	Septuagint
masc.	masculine
MS(S)	manuscript(s)
MT	Masoretic Text
Mur	Murabbaʿat
P	Priestly writer/source
P./Pap.	papyrus
pl.	plural
RS	field numbers of tablets excavated at Ras Shamra
SamP	Samaritan Pentateuch
sing.	singular
Syr	Syriac

Museum Sigla

AO	tablets in the collections of the Musée du Louvre
Ash.	tablets in the collections of the Ashmolean Museum, Oxford
BRM	Babylonian Records in the Library of J. Pierpont Morgan

Reference Works

AASOR	Annual of the American Schools of Oriental Research
AB	Anchor Bible
ABD	Freedman, D. N., editor. *The Anchor Bible Dictionary.* 6 vols. Garden City, NY: Doubleday, 1992
ABRL	Anchor Bible Reference Library
ADPV	Abhandlungen des Deutschen Palästinavereins
AJSL	*American Journal of Semitic Languages and Literature*
AJSR	*Association for Jewish Studies Review*
AOAT	Alter Orient und Altes Testament

AoF   *Altorientalische Forschungen*
AP   Cowley, A. E., editor. *Aramaic Papyri of the Fifth Century* B.C. Oxford:
           Clarendon, 1923
ATD   Das Alte Testament Deutsch
BA   *Biblical Archaeologist*
BAR   *Biblical Archaeology Review*
BASOR   *Bulletin of the American Schools of Oriental Research*
BBB   Bonner biblische Beiträge
BEATAJ   Beiträge zur Erforschung des Alten Testaments und des antiken
           Judentum
BeO   *Bibbia e oriente*
BETL   Bibliotheca ephemeridum theologicarum lovaniensium
Bib   *Biblica*
BibOr   Biblica et Orientalia
BJRL   *Bulletin of the John Rylands University Library of Manchester*
BJS   Brown Judaic Studies
BKAT   Biblischer Kommentar: Altes Testament
BN   *Biblische Notizen*
BO   *Bibliotheca Orientalis*
BWANT   Beiträge zur Wissenschaft vom Alten und Neuen Testament
BZ   *Biblische Zeitschrift*
BZAW   Beihefte zur Zeitschrift für die Alttestamentliche Wissenschaft
CAH   *Cambridge Ancient History.* 3rd ed. London: Cambridge University
           Press, 1970–
CBQ   *Catholic Biblical Quarterly*
CRAIBL   *Comptes rendus de l'Académie des inscriptions et belles-lettres*
CT   Cuneiform Texts from Babylonian Tablets in the British Museum
DJD   Discoveries in the Judaean Desert
DS-NELL   *Dutch Studies—of the Near Eastern Languages and Literatures*
           Foundation
EBib   Études bibliques
ErIsr   *Eretz-Israel*
FAT   Forschungen zum Alten Testament
FB   Forschung zur Bibel
FOTL   Forms of the Old Testament Literature
FRLANT   Forschungen zur Religion und Literatur des Alten und Neuen
           Testaments
GCS   Griechischen christlichen Schriftsteller
GKC   Kautzsch, E., editor. *Gesenius' Hebrew Grammar.* Translated by A. E.
           Cowley. 2nd ed. Oxford: Oxford University Press, 1910
HALOT   Koehler, L.; Baumgartner, W.; and Stamm, J. J. *The Hebrew and*
           Aramaic Lexicon of the Old Testament. Translated and edited under
           supervision of M. E. J. Richardson. 5 vols. Leiden: Brill, 1994–2000
HAR   *Hebrew Annual Review*
HAT   Handbuch zum Alten Testament
HBS   Herders biblische Studien

HBT	*Horizons in Biblical Theology*
HeyJ	*Heythrop Journal*
HKAT	Handkommentar zum Alten Testament
HSM	Harvard Semitic Monographs
HSS	Harvard Semitic Studies
HTKAT	Herders theologischer Kommentar zum Alten Testament
HTR	*Harvard Theological Review*
IDBSup	Crim, K., editor. *Interpreter's Dictionary of the Bible Supplementary Volume.* Nashville: Abingdon, 1976
IEJ	*Israel Exploration Journal*
JAOS	*Journal of the American Oriental Society*
JBL	*Journal of Biblical Literature*
JCS	*Journal of Cuneiform Studies*
JDS	Judean Desert Studies
JJS	*Journal of Jewish Studies*
JHS	*Journal of Hellenic Studies*
JNES	*Journal of Near Eastern Studies*
JNSL	*Journal of Northwest Semitic Languages*
JPS Torah Commentary	Jewish Publication Society Torah Commentary
JQR	*Jewish Quarterly Review*
JRAS	*Journal of the Royal Asiatic Society*
JSJ	*Journal for the Study of Judaism*
JSOT	*Journal for the Study of the Old Testament*
JSOTSup	Journal for the Study of the Old Testament Supplement Series
JSPSup	Journal for the Study of the Pseudepigrapha Supplements
JSS	*Journal of Semitic Studies*
KAT	Kommentar zum Alten Testament
LAPO	Littératures anciennes du Proche-Orient
LASBF	*Liber annuus Studii biblici franciscani*
LCL	Loeb Classical Library
NCB	New Century Bible
NEAEHL	Stern, E., editor. *New Encyclopedia of Archaeological Excavations in the Holy Land.* 4 vols. Jerusalem: Israel Exploration Society and Carta / New York: Simon & Schuster, 1993
NTL	New Testament Library
NTS	*New Testament Studies*
OBO	Orbis biblicus et orientalis
OBT	Overtures to Biblical Theology
OEANE	Meyers, E. M., editor. *The Oxford Encyclopedia of Archaeology in the Near East.* 5 vols. New York: Oxford University Press, 1997
OIP	Oriental Institute Publications
OIS	Oriental Institute Seminars
OLA	Orientalia Lovaniensia Analecta
OLZ	*Orientalistische Literaturzeitung*
OTL	Old Testament Library
OtSt	Oudtestamentische Studiën

PTMS   Pittsburgh Theological Monograph Series
RAcc.   Thureau-Dangin, F. *Rituels accadiens*. Osnabrück : Zeller, 1975
RB   *Revue biblique*
ResQ   *Restoration Quarterly*
SBLDS   Society of Biblical Literature Dissertation Series
SBLMS   Society of Biblical Literature Monograph Series
SBLSS   Society of Biblical Literature Semeia Studies
SBLSymS Society of Biblical Literature Symposium Series
SBS   Stuttgarter Bibelstudien
ScrHier   Scripta hierosolymitana
SEG   *Supplementum epigraphicum graecum*
Sem   *Semitica*
SIG   Dittenberger, W., editor. *Sylloge inscriptionum graecarum*. 4 vols. 3rd
          ed. Leipzig: Hirzel, 1915–24
SJOT   *Scandanavian Journal of the Old Testament*
STDJ   Studies on the Texts of the Desert of Judah
TA   *Tel Aviv*
TAD/*TADAE*   Porten, B., and Yardeni, A., editors. *Textbook of Aramaic
          Documents from Ancient Egypt*. 4 vols. Jerusalem: Hebrew University
          Dept. of the History of the Jewish People, 1986–99
TDOT   Botterweck, G. J., and Ringgren, H., editors. *Theological Dictionary of
          the Old Testament*. Grand Rapids, MI: Eerdmans, 1974–
Transeu   *Transeuphratène*
TRu   *Theologische Rundschau*
TTZ   *Trierer theologische Zeitschrift*
TUAT   Kaiser, Otto, editor. *Texte aus der Umwelt des Alten Testaments*. 3 vols.
          Gütersloh: Mohn, 1982–2001
TZ   *Theologische Zeitschrift*
UF   *Ugarit-Forschungen*
VS   Vorderasiatische Schriftdenkmäler der Königlichen (Staatlichen)
          Museen zu Berlin
VT   *Vetus Testamentum*
VTSup   Vetus Testamentum Supplements
WBC   Word Biblical Commentary
WHJP   World History of the Jewish People
WMANT Wissenschaftliche Monographien zum Alten und Neuen Testament
WUNT   Wissenschaftliche Untersuchungen zum Alten und Neuen
          Testament
ZA   *Zeitschrift für Assyriologie*
ZABR   *Zeitschrift für altorientalische und biblische Rechtsgeschichte*
ZAW   *Zeitschrift für die Alttestamentliche Wissenschaft*
ZPE   *Zeitschrift für Papyrologie und Epigraphik*

Introduction

GARY N. KNOPPERS, ODED LIPSCHITS,
and RAINER ALBERTZ

The group of essays included in this volume originated in an inter-national conference entitled "Judah and the Judeans in the Fourth Century B.C.E.," held at the University of Münster, 12–15 August 2005. The international meeting at Münster follows two similar earlier con-ferences: "Judah and the Judeans in the Neo-Babylonian Period," held at the University of Tel Aviv in 2001 (Lipschits and Blenkinsopp 2003) and "Judah and the Judeans in the Persian Period," held at the Univer-sity of Heidelberg in 2003 (Lipschits and Oeming 2006).

The academic study of fourth-century Judah presents some special challenges. In modern historical research, the fourth century B.C.E. along with the third century B.C.E. are traditionally known as the "Dark Ages" of ancient Judean history. Why such a negative assess-ment? There are a number of factors and causes. To begin with, this was a neglected period in biblical and archeological research. For genera-tions, the research focus of many scholars was on topics such as the an-cestral age, the origins of Israel, the Exodus, the so-called Conquest, and Israel's emergence in the land. Compared with the glorious events of the Exodus, Sinai, and Conquest, the Persian period was a "time of small things." Happily, generations of neglect have given way in the past few decades to a more concerted scholarly effort to grapple with the importance of this age in the history of the people of Israel. Indeed, many scholars now see the Achaemenid age as a pivotal one for the composition and editing of many works in the biblical corpora (e.g., Al-bertz 1994: 437–38).

But the lack of attention given to the late Persian period in past gen-erations has to do with more than scholarly neglect. There were other factors and causes. Interestingly, the reasons for viewing the fourth and third centuries B.C.E. as "the Dark Ages" do not have to do with a rash of terrible, devastating, and catastrophic events occurring during this period. To be sure, there were some monumental events in the fourth century. Chief among these was the conquest of the southern

1

Levant by Alexander the Great and his armies in 332 B.C.E. Yet, few historians would view the campaigns of Alexander, however much destruction they may have wrought, as major catastrophes or as a time of great decline for the peoples living in Palestine. Indeed, as the lead essay by Josef Wiesehöfer ("The Achaemenid Empire in the Fourth Century B.C.E.: A Period of Decline?") in this volume demonstrates, much of the fourth century was not even a time of great economic recession or societal disintegration for the central Achaemenid administration.

Rather than being tied to a series of terrible historical tragedies, the traditional assessment of the fourth through third centuries as constituting the "Dark Ages" is, in some respects, tied to the nature and extent of the ancient historical sources pertaining to this epoch in Judean history. The historical writings of the Hebrew Bible do not directly deal with the period in question. The book of Ezra-Nehemiah ends with Nehemiah's frustration in confronting (what he regards as) regression in the Jerusalem community in the latter part of the fifth century (Neh 13:6–31).[1] Unfortunately, there is no other biblical book that begins where Ezra-Nehemiah ends and attempts to give some sort of account of events in the fourth and third centuries B.C.E. The book of Chronicles has a few genealogies that may extend into the Hellenistic age (e.g., 1 Chr 3:22–24), but most of the book deals with the long-gone monarchic age (Knoppers 2004: 317–36). The apocryphal (or Deuterocanonical) book of 1 Esdras revisits the time of Josiah, the return under Cyrus, and the exploits and reforms of Zerubbabel but ends with the reforms of Ezra. The books of 1 and 2 Maccabees provide fascinating, albeit very disparate, perspectives on the Judean uprising of the second century B.C.E., but these works, for the most part, neither address nor reflect on the historical context in the southern Levant during the late Achaemenid period and the early Hellenistic epoch. The later writings of Josephus are, as most contemporary scholars acknowledge, of uneven value in treating the Persian and early Hellenistic periods.

What holds true for the region of Yehud in the late Persian period also holds true unfortunately for the regions north and south of Yehud —Samaria and Edom/Idumea. Ancient historical documentation that directly addresses developments in these two important areas during the late Achaemenid and early Hellenistic period is lamentably not what ones hopes it could be. There are, of course, some important ac-

---

1. We are assuming the traditional order of the missions of Ezra and Nehemiah, but our generalization would not be materially affected if Ezra actually came after Nehemiah in the time of Artaxerxes II Mnemon (ca. 398 B.C.E.).

counts and historical records that pertain to this period, such as the Zenon archive, the *History* of Herodotus, and the *Bibliothēkē* ('Library') of Diodorus Siculus.[2] When handled carefully and critically, sources of this sort can be immensely helpful in understanding larger historical movements and even certain specific events and conditions during these times. Nevertheless, much of the information gleaned from these sources insofar as they pertain to the regions of Samaria, Judah, and Edom is indirect, scattershot, and incidental.

One of the aims of the Münster conference (and the present volume) was to rectify, however partially, the traditionally dismal historical assessment of the fourth century as part of the "Dark Ages" by exploring and exploiting newly available sources of information. The historical sources we have in mind are not long-lost or hidden ancient books that have been suddenly and dramatically recovered from antiquity but, rather, the valuable new information that is slowly becoming available through the disciplines of archaeology, epigraphy, historical linguistics, numismatology, and ancient Near Eastern history. Archaeological and epigraphic data can be extraordinarily difficult to gather, decipher, analyze, and employ in the service of larger historical reconstructions. Nevertheless, there can be no doubt that the accumulation, analysis, and publication of these data offer distinct benefits to the reconstruction of societal relations, demography, settlement patterns, and economic conditions in Judah, Samaria, and Edom during the fourth century. Indeed, the last few decades have witnessed an unprecedented number of archaeological, epigraphic, and numismatic discoveries that are proving to be quite useful in better understanding the fourth and third centuries B.C.E. in the southern Levant.

Some of these recent discoveries are published, synthesized, and assessed for the first time in this volume. The essays by André Lemaire ("Administration in Fourth-Century B.C.E. Judah in Light of Epigraphy and Numismatics"), Amos Kloner and Ian Stern ("Idumea in the Late Persian Period [Fourth Century B.C.E.]"), Esther Eshel ("The Onomasticon of Mareshah in the Persian and Hellenistic Periods"), Oded Lipschits and David Vanderhooft ("Yehud Stamp Impressions in the Fourth Century B.C.E.: A Time of Administrative Consolidation?"), and Yitzhak Magen ("The Dating of the First Phase of the Samaritan Temple on Mount Gerizim in Light of the Archaeological Evidence") stand out in this respect.

---

2. For a recent assessment of these and other relevant ancient sources, see Grabbe 1992: 1–212; 2004: 322–49.

Lemaire's detailed analysis sheds new light not only on economic and social conditions during an obscure century but also on the transition from the Persian period to the Hellenistic period in Palestine. The careful study of Kloner and Stern has two components. One deals with the existing evidence for the borders of and site distribution in Idumea in the fourth century B.C.E. The other identifies and examines the epigraphic evidence for a mixed population in Idumea during the same period. The kind of specialized ethnographic study of E. Eshel, based on an in-depth analysis of proper names found in the approximately 1,600 Aramaic inscriptions stemming from the region of Idumea, could scarcely have been imaginable even two decades ago. That she is able to provide her readers with such a precise and revealing breakdown of the onomasticon in these texts is testimony to the kind of detailed data now available to scholars. The essay of Lipschits and Vanderhooft draws on their thorough and still ongoing study of the Yehud stamp impressions over the *longue durée* of the Achaemenid era to query whether the formulas employed in these impressions enable any larger generalizations to be made about the changing nature and extent of Persian administrative practices in Yehud. Magen's study revisits the remarkable results of his many years of excavations at Mt. Gerizim (Magen, Misgav, and Tsfania 2004) to deal with specifically the Persian period remains from the site. The main focus of his essay lies with the fifth- and fourth-century evidence relating to the Samari(t)an temple found at this location.

How the results of archaeology and epigraphy function in the service of historical reconstruction varies quite widely, depending on the assumptions and questions of the investigators, the research methodologies employed, and the range of available data. In some cases, archaeological and epigraphic finds allow scholars to track long-term settlement patterns, linguistic trends, administrative developments, and ethnographic changes in a given society or societies. The essays of Oded Lipschits and Oren Tal ("The Settlement Archaeology of the Province of Judah: A Case Study"), Ingo Kottsieper ("'And They Did Not Care to Speak Yehudit': On Linguistic Change in Judah during the Late Persian Era"), and Hanan Eshel ("The Governors of Samaria in the Fifth and Fourth Centuries B.C.E.") are good case studies of such types of thoughtful interdisciplinary analysis.

The database for the study of Lipschits and Tal includes both excavations of individual sites and larger settlement surveys. The broad chronological range of their analysis extends from the Neo-Babylonian age to the Hasmonean period. The interesting research questions they pose have to do with continuity, discontinuity, and growth in patterns of settlement with a special focus on the end of the Persian period and the beginning of the Hasmonean period (fourth to mid-second centuries B.C.E.). The specialized studies of Kottsieper and H. Eshel focus on the written remains from the Achaemenid era in the southern Levant. Kottsieper draws on a variety of Aramaic inscriptions dating to the Neo-Babylonian, Persian, and Hellenistic periods to contend that the use of Hebrew was limited largely to elite scribal and priestly contexts. Eshel draws on epigraphic, biblical, and numismatic evidence to propose a new reconstruction of the succession of Persian-period Samarian governors.

On some occasions, the evidence provided by newly discovered material remains and inscriptions compels scholars to revisit old issues and to ask new questions about traditional reconstructions of the past. The essays by Bob Becking ("Do the Earliest Samaritan Inscriptions Already Indicate a Parting of the Ways?") and Lester Grabbe ("Archaeology and *Archaiologias*: Relating Excavations to History in Fourth-Century B.C.E. Palestine") serve as examples of this sort of rethinking. Taking a close look at the inscriptions recently published in the first volume of the Mt. Gerizim excavations, Becking draws some tentative conclusions about what this evidence may indicate about possible strains in Judean-Samarian religious relations. Grabbe's essay addresses a different set of Persian-period issues—the theories of a "Megabyzus rebellion," a "Tennes rebellion," and a "Revolt of the Satraps"—and inquires as to whether there is any solid archaeological evidence to support these claims.

The treatment of recently-discovered material and literary remains is one important area of concentration in this volume. Another critical area of focus is the history of biblical literature pertaining directly or indirectly to the late Persian and early Hellenistic periods. Some readers may be surprised to find essays on the Pentateuch and Joshua in a book dedicated to the history of Judah and the Judeans in the fourth century B.C.E. A brief explanation may be helpful. There have been a number of consequential developments in the study of the Pentateuch and the Hexateuch in the past two decades.[3] Many recent studies locate the compilation (however this may have occurred) and editing of the books in the Pentateuch in the postexilic era. Indeed, some scholars view the distinctive endings of the books of Deuteronomy and Joshua

---

3. The recent treatments of Thomas Römer (2005) and Jean-Louis Ska (2006) provide helpful overviews of these new scholarly developments.

as reflecting, in part, a postmonarchic debate about whether the foundational document of the Judean community should constitute a Pentateuch (Genesis through Deuteronomy) or a Hexateuch (Genesis through Joshua).

One of the aims of the conference organizers was to bring some of the scholars involved in this recent line of research into conversation with scholars whose research focuses on the biblical literature more traditionally viewed as stemming from the Persian period (for example, Haggai, Zechariah, Chronicles, Ezra-Nehemiah). A related aim was to bring both groups of biblical scholars into more sustained conversations with archaeologists, historians, and epigraphers. The essay by Konrad Schmid ("The Late Persian Formation of the Torah: Observations on Deuteronomy 34") is a new contribution to the study of how the Pentateuch eventually emerged triumphant in the long literary debate between the proponents of a Hexateuch and the proponents of a Pentateuch. The essay of Reinhard Achenbach ("The Pentateuch, the Prophets, and the Torah in the Fifth and Fourth Centuries B.C.E.") also contributes to the ongoing scholarly discussion by tying the different stages in the redaction of the Hexateuch and the Pentateuch to evolving concepts of prophecy in the history of the postexilic Judean community. The essay by Rainer Albertz ("The Canonical Alignment of the Book of Joshua") addresses a related issue, namely, whether (and how) the Priestly-style passages in the book of Joshua are dependent on and pertain to specific injunctions, declarations, and prophecies found within the Pentateuch. In Albertz's view, the Priestly passages in Joshua reflect the process of the canonization of the Pentateuch at a very significant stage. The text of the Pentateuch has become authoritative to such a degree that the book of Joshua must be aligned with it.

Whereas some of these essays in this volume situate the formation and editing of the Pentateuch in the fourth century, others discuss specific problems in the historical literature that stems from this general era—Chronicles and Ezra-Nehemiah. Each of the essays in this section of the book attempts to integrate the understanding of the postexilic historical books with a better understanding of the material remains relating to the Persian and Hellenistic periods. Working against the background of recent studies on ethnicity on the one hand and the material culture of Samaria on the other hand, Gary Knoppers ("Nehemiah and Sanballat: The Enemy Without or Within?") examines the conflict between Nehemiah and Sanballat. His study investigates the degree to which the tensions between Sanballat and Nehemiah, as portrayed in the book of Ezra-Nehemiah, reflect an inner-Judean community struggle as much as they reflect a Judean-Samarian leadership rivalry. In his essay ("Rebuilding Identity: The Nehemiah Memoir and Its Earliest Readers—A New Model for the Composition of Ezra-Nehemiah"), Jacob Wright revisits the compositional history of Ezra-Nehemiah. Drawing upon his recent monograph (Wright 2005), he contends for a multistage, complex compositional process that took as its initial point of departure Nehemiah's building report (now embedded in Nehemiah 1–13). Major later additions in this process were the temple foundation narrative of Ezra 1–6 and finally the so-called Ezra memoir of Ezra 7–10.

Two essays in the book focus specifically on the book of Chronicles. In his study ("Who Knew What? The Construction of the Monarchic Past in Chronicles and Implications for the Intellectual Setting of Chronicles"), Ehud Ben Zvi explores the communal (postexilic) relevance of two puzzling features: characters in the book who (a) know a variety of biblical texts, including some that are explicitly set at a time later than their own putative time, and (b) exhibit knowledge about future events. The research focus of John Wright is somewhat different ("'Those Doing the Work for the Service in the House of the Lord': 1 Chronicles 23:6–24:31 and the Sociohistorical Context of the Temple of Yahweh in Jerusalem in the Late Persian/Early Hellenistic Period"). By means of a comparative form-critical analysis, he develops the sociohistorical implications of a previously unknown parallel he has discerned between an early-Seleucid-period temple duty roster and the temple duty roster attributed to the administration of David in Chronicles. The concluding essay by Joseph Blenkinsopp ("The Development of Jewish Sectarianism from Nehemiah to the Hasidim") follows a strategy of reading back from the "symbolic historiography" of the second and first centuries B.C.E. (Daniel, *Jubilees, Animal Apocalypse, Apocalypse of Weeks, Testament of Levi, Damascus Document*) and forward from Ezra-Nehemiah and the late prophetic texts. In so doing, he establishes some connections between the 'children of the exile' (*běnê haggôlâ*) of the sixth century and sectarian groups reflected in certain texts from the Hasmonean and Roman eras.

The conference organizers, participants, and volume editors would be remiss if they did not express their profound thanks to the generous sponsors of this special academic meeting: the Deutschen Forschungsgemeinschaft, the Universität Münster, the Evangelisch-Theologische Fakultät, and the Old Testament Department (Alttestamentliches Seminar). These sponsors were essential partners in making this conference a tremendous success. Thanks also go to Tel Aviv University for supporting the international cooperative effort to hold the Judah and the Judeans in the Fourth Century B.C.E. conference in Münster. We hope that the essays in this volume reflect the good results of the fruitful discussions that these institutions made possible. Special gratitude is due to Prof. Dr. Rainer Albertz and also to Prof. Dr. Rüdiger Schmitt for all of their diligent work in planning, organizing, and managing the conference.

Finally, the editors of this book would like to express their sincere thanks to the publisher of all the "Judah and the Judeans" volumes: Eisenbrauns. Publisher Jim Eisenbraun, Mrs. Beverly McCoy, and the rest of the Eisenbrauns staff are unflinching in their commitment to quality and incredibly resourceful in tackling all kinds of challenges in the process of copy editing. They are unfailing enemies of all error and inexactitude. To them we owe a debt of gratitude.

Bibliography

Albertz, Rainer
  1994   *A History of Religion in the Old Testament Period.* 2 vols. OTL. Louisville: Westminster John Knox.
Grabbe, Lester L.
  1992   *Judaism from Cyrus to Hadrian.* 2 vols. Minneapolis: Fortress.
  2004   A *History of the Jews and Judaism in the Second Temple Period.* Library of Second Temple Studies 47. London: T. & T. Clark.
Knoppers, Gary N.
  2004   *I Chronicles 1–9.* AB 12. New York: Doubleday.
Lipschits, Oded, and Blenkinsopp, Joseph (eds.)
  2003   *Judah and the Judeans in the Neo-Babylonian Period.* Winona Lake, IN: Eisenbrauns.
Lipschits, Oded, and Oeming, Manfred (eds.)
  2006   *Judah and the Judeans in the Persian Period.* Winona Lake, IN: Eisenbrauns.
Magen, Yitzhak; Misgav, Haggai; and Tsfania, Levana
  2004   *Mount Gerizim Excavations, 1: The Aramaic, Hebrew and Samaritan Inscriptions.* Judea and Samaria Publications 2. Jerusalem: Israel Antiquities Authority.
Römer, Thomas C.
  2005   *The So-Called Deuteronomistic History: A Sociological, Historical, and Literary Introduction.* London: T. & T. Clark.
Ska, Jean-Louis
  2006   *Introduction to Reading the Pentateuch.* Winona Lake, IN: Eisenbrauns.
Wright, Jacob L.
  2005   *Rebuilding Identity: The Nehemiah Memoir and Its Earliest Readers—A New Model for the Composition of Ezra-Nehemiah.* BZAW 348. Berlin: de Gruyter.

PART 1

The History of the Fourth Century: A View from the Center

The Achaemenid Empire in
the Fourth Century B.C.E.:
A Period of Decline?

JOSEF WIESEHÖFER

Christian-Albrechts-Universität Kiel

The book of Daniel reports that King Nebuchadnezzar of Babylon dreamed of an immense statue whose head was made of pure gold, with breast and arms of silver, body and hips of bronze, and legs and feet of iron or a mixture of iron and clay. Through no fault of human beings, this statue was crushed by a stone, a stone that turned into a large mountain and filled the entire earth. In emulation of Daniel (Dan 2:37–44), who interpreted the parts of the sculpture for the king as the great historical empires of the Babylonians, Medes, Persians, and Greeks and the destruction by the stone as the advent of the kingdom of the Messiah, the sequence of the empires (which goes back originally to a concept of Herodotus and Ctesias; Wiesehöfer 2003; 2005a) was viewed up until early modern times as the principal order of world history. It was not only an order to which political events and the history of ideas were tied chronologically but also an order that would become the widely understood vehicle of eschatological ideology. And like the Jews of the Hellenistic epoch, people of all times have been concerned with the question why the empire of iron, the empire of Alexander and his successors, was able to "defeat and destroy" the empire of bronze, the Persian Empire, as the book of Daniel relates.

Three models for explaining the downfall of the Achaemenid Empire are referred to frequently. The first model sees the cause of the end of Persian sovereignty in the moral or physical defects of the Persians. The moral defects can be of various kinds and for various reasons. The second model assumes that there were problems inherent in Achaemenid rule right from the start (or beginning with a certain period) that

---

Author's note: I wish to thank my friend Reinhold Bichler (Innsbruck) for many valuable comments on this essay. A rather similar approach, as far as the Greek sources are concerned, can be found in Briant 2002a.

proved to be insurmountable. Finally, the third model, of a more recent date, emphasizes by contrast the remarkable vitality of the Empire until shortly before its downfall. Accordingly, it speaks about a rather surprising end to Persian rule. Perhaps one could best call these three types of interpretation a "decadence or decline model," a "structural weaknesses model," and a "catastrophe model."

The first model is not really a modern attempt at explanation; unlike the others, it has its roots in the tradition of classical antiquity and thus also in the Greeks' self-image and in their perception of what was "foreign" or "non-Greek" in that period. Plato, in the third book of his *Laws*, his last and most extensive dialogue, also discusses the Persian Empire in his review of the historical development of existing forms of state. For him, it embodied an order of state that did not ensure that there was a balance of reason, freedom, and harmony for its citizens, as was the case in Sparta or Crete. This balance would have ensured its survival. Instead, the Persian form of government increased sovereign power excessively. Thus, an oppressive despotism developed out of a monarchy founded by its judicious ruler, Cyrus, already during the reign of his son, Cambyses, a mistake that, by the way, was repeated in the reigns of Darius and his son, Xerxes. The dialogue partners in Plato presume that the cause of this fatal development lay in the education of the kings' sons by the women (and eunuchs) of the royal house, an education that was said to have produced effeminate, undisciplined, dissolute persons of them (*Leg.* 695a–b).[1]

This image of the negative influence of the women of the royal house and of life at court on the whole had appeared already in the beginning of the fourth century B.C.E. in Ctesias, who was said to have been the Greek personal physician to the Persian Great King Artaxerxes II, but who may never have resided in Iran. However, Ctesias had taken the liberty of freely revising his predecessor Herodotus's royal history of the Persians by retaining the order of the rulers but changing the characters and the deeds of the kings from Cyrus to Xerxes in an astonishingly malicious and witty manner (Bichler 2004). His Cyrus seems a great deal nastier than the Cyrus portrayed by Herodotus, while Cambyses' evil is played down so that it lacks the madness of a despot. Even Darius cuts a rather dull figure compared with Herodotus's dazzling royal Darius, and Xerxes is turned into a rather honest family man concerned about the honor of his daughter at precisely the moments in Herodotus in which he drifts along in a quag-

---

1. For Plato, see Schöpsdau 1990.

mire of intrigue and cruelty at the mercy of female moods. For Ctesias, however, the real reason for the instability of Persian sovereignty was not the education of the kings' sons but the political intrigues of the women and eunuchs.[2]

The concept of the degeneration of Persian character and the resulting decline of Persian power that can be detected in the Greek literature of that time is particularly noticeable in Xenophon and Isocrates. The last chapter of the eighth book of Xenophon's *Cyropedia* (8.1ff.) refers to education by contrasting the manners and customs in Persia in the grand period of Cyrus, the founder of the Empire, with the manners of his Persian contemporaries. However, Xenophon considers the main cause of the decline to lie in a change in the educational curriculum, which lacked real instruction, riding, and hunting. Moreover, Xenophon argues that the reason for negative developments were the fickleness of the kings in keeping agreements, their wickedness and iniquity, and especially their effeminacy (Greek *thrypsis*). The rhetorician Isocrates does not stop there; in his great appeal for an all-Greek undertaking against the Great King, he also refers to the military weakness of the Persian Empire in the fourth century, the reason for which was the effeminacy and servility of the Persians (see primarily *Paneg.* 144ff.).

Indeed, others before these authors had already seen signs of a threat to the powerful Persian Empire. The idea of the Great King as a despot, for example, in contrast to whom even the highest dignitaries appear as slaves, has its roots as early as in the fifth century (Bichler forthcoming). Already in Aeschylus's *Persians*, the image of the Great King Xerxes is defined by the negative idea of a tyrant that was forming at that time due to certain elementary analogies, such as immense personal power, being above the law, lack of accountablility, and growing ostentatiousness. Aeschylus's drama, in turn, also shaped this idea to a great extent. From this time onward, the Persian king was considered a tyrant *par excellence* (*Pers.* 242, among others). In addition, the reason for the astonishing victories of the Greeks was found to be the decisive independence and strength of the Greeks, which grew out of the knowledge of their own individual and collective freedom.

The thought that power could entice a ruler to luxury and the pursuit of pleasure to such an extent that it softened him and that, consequently, a ruling people sooner or later would lose its ability in combat

---

2. Lenfant (2004: cxxxvi) shows that Ctesias is not exactly presenting a decadent empire but an empire "marqué par la récurrence de scénarios toujours identiques (rébellions, complots, vengeances)."

and be defeated by the undiminished energy of poor but pure people was not a new one. In the fifth century, this idea was tied to social-medical theories that set up a direct link between climate, fertility, and the breed of people in a region—as in the Hippocratic text *On the Environment*, for example (*De aere locis aquis* 23). It can be deduced from this theory that a change in the conditions of people affects their character and way of life. Herodotus, in an anecdote at the end of his work, gives impressive evidence of this idea: Cyrus is pestered by his Persian subjects to allow them to move from their small, uneconomical native region to settle in one of the richer countries—having first conquered it, as befits a ruling people. The king , however, is able to talk his soldiers out of these plans, pointing out to them the corrupting effect of luxury and opulence (9.122). The Persians conquer rich countries, but they do not give up their rugged country. The Persian Empire remains powerful. Only Xerxes and his court succumb to the temptations that come with power, and his defeat by the Greeks, a poor people in a similarly rugged country, is the consequence of this royal "decadence." This, at least, is how Herodotus interprets the deeper meaning of the historical events.

Thus, the concepts of rise and decline were in no way new to the Greek literature of the fourth century—not even the idea of the corrupting effect of luxury on victorious peoples or the identification of the Great King as a tyrant or slave-driver. What was new, however, was the depiction in Ctesias of the royal court as a petticoat government, a place of vice, intrigue, and sycophancy; in Plato, the significance of educational failure in the decline of the Empire; and in Xenophon and Isocrates, the general scant regard for Persian combat strength. Many things coalesced to form an outright contempt for barbarians in the work of the great rhetorician, Isocrates. In Greece, the term "barbarians," which (based on a pattern widespread among many peoples) was intended to keep one's own culture distinct from the outside world, was narrowed to refer specifically to the Persians, as early as the middle of the fifth century; it also began to take on noticeably pejorative traits. Isocrates used this mainly Attic image of the enemy as barbarian caricature but coarsened and simplified it even more. The war he envisaged was intended to be directed against the "enemies of nature" and thus have a moral justification. The barbarians, because of their inferiority, deserved nothing less than to become Greek subjects. And, while Herodotus had determined that the reason for the epochal contrast between the world of the barbarians and the world of the Greeks was that the area of their habitat overlapped geographically and, logically, had advocated their physical separation, even if it meant the Greeks' abandoning Asia Minor, Isocrates in contrast called for the conquest of the Asian barbarian country (Herodotus, passim; Isocr. *Phil.* 121–23; cf. Heinrichs 1989: 129ff.).

How can such Greek images of "Persian decadence" be explained, and what support do they find in Iranian tradition? Common to all records is the idea of the effeminacy of the Persians due to the influx of luxury. Irrespective of the stock rhetorical character of this reproach, however, the fact of the display of riches by the king cannot be denied. Admittedly, Greek contemporaries missed its deeper meaning, or they suppressed it for reasons of argumentation. Gifts to and from the king in the form of luxury articles were especially important in the Persian royal system. On the one hand, they made differences in status clear; on the other hand, they established an advantageous relationship between the king and his subjects (Wiesehöfer 2001). Banquets played an important role in the exchange, which is only touched upon here and which is usually referred to as "redistribution," to use a term from ethnology (Vössing 2004: 38–51). On these occasions, which were designed to express the power of the king both symbolically and materially, the ruler showered gifts on the people who had themselves given gifts to the king or had distinguished themselves with special loyalty.

The alleged decline of Persian education and the postulated negative influence of the women of the royal house must also be questioned as signs of decline. In this connection, Herodotus's remark is well known, that Persians taught their sons "only three things from the age of five up to the age of twenty: riding, archery and telling the truth" (1.136). This quotation is similar to Xenophon's remarks in his *Anabasis* (1.9.3) and in the first book of the *Cyropedia* (1.2.2ff.) about education during Cyrus's reign. Now it is quite obvious that the description of the education of early Persian times that was handed down by Herodotus and Xenophon reflected a "behavior code"—in other words, a set of rules that was *supposed* to characterize a sovereign. This is exactly how Darius understood the rules according to the lower register of one of his tomb inscriptions (DNb 5–45), and he claimed to embody them. Such a code, such a self-characterization naturally does not tell us anything about the actual conduct of the ruler, and justice and honesty are defined as virtues by each person who uses them. When Xenophon in his *Cyropedia* laments the loss of these virtues immediately after the death of Cyrus, he does not do it to inform the reader about historical facts but does it as a man of letters. The extraordinary qualities of his ideal ruler and the necessity of these qualities even in his own time become much clearer through this account. The parks and hunting grounds (Greek *paradeisoi*) and the numerous images on coins, seals, and reliefs in the fourth century (indeed even after that) that depict the king as an archer or during a hunt all indicate that military prowess and proving one's worth during a hunt were considered virtues for Persian royalty right up to the end. The testing of weapons and the chase were symbols of royal and aristocratic daily life. The pictorial and epigraphic self-portrayal of local princes in Persian-period Asia Minor (for example, Arbinas in Lycia; cf. *SEG* XXVIII 1245, 14–15) are also evidence of the influence of these motifs.

Similarly, Plato's comments on the causes of Persian despotism must not be taken as historical statements or as descriptions of Persian reality in the fourth century. They stem from the political theory of the philosopher—his thoughts about the best or, in his *Laws*, at least a well-governed state in which a decent life for the citizens comes first. According to Plato, this requires a radically reformed education, and so it is no surprise that he also sees the main reason for the decline of order in the Persian state to be the wrong education of the kings' sons.

The pernicious role assigned to the women of the court by Ctesias should, again, not be understood as a historical fact but as a literary cliché. The misogynous tendency of some Greek literature in the fifth and fourth centuries is reflected in these stories. Women are perceived as being a threat to a world of politics dominated by men. If there is a historical core to the stories of plotting and scheming women, then it is that political marriages for preserving loyalty were very important in a monarchic system that was originally a tribal society. The question of a successor in the polygamous Persian royal house could at times be a grave question indeed. The "divided loyalties" of women, so to speak, may be describing these tensions in the royal system. Set in a historical context, however, they can hardly be used as reliable portraits of female figures.

We come across female relatives of the royal house even on the small Elamite administrative clay tablets from early Persepolis (Persepolis Fortification Tablets), our most important records of that time from the central country of the Empire. On these tablets, they appear to be extremely attractive, active, and used to making decisions. They participate in royal festivities and banquets or hold their own feasts; they travel across the country and give instructions, as well as check their goods and work force. Historians of Alexander also mention them as being in the train of the king during his campaigns.[3] No won-

---

3. On the topic of Persian royal women, see Brosius 1996.

der Greeks who paid homage to an ideal woman of unblemished rep-
utation who lived a secluded life also perceived the women of the
Persian royal house as being "at home" (cf. Plut. *Them.* 26). The tablets
prove that the life they led had nothing to do with seclusion. It is no
surprise, then, that Persian women appeared both attractive and dangerous to these Greeks. If Persian women also became politically active
behind the palace walls, then this could only be detrimental to the
house! These sorts of opinions, coupled with Western ideas about Oriental life in a palace (in a "harem") have survived until recent times.

How is it that the idea of "Persian decadence" and scheming women
could command such fascination? In Germany, for one thing, this concept is rooted in the ancient records just presented; for another thing, it
has to do with the way classical antiquity was viewed in the nineteenth
century. Many readers undoubtedly know that the Neoclassical scholars' rediscovery and idealization of Greek culture and the attempt to
connect its achievements and merits with the nature of the Greeks was
the first step toward comparing their own time with the Greeks'. The
notion that developed was that Germans were especially close to the
Greeks of ancient times because of their intellectual and natural affinity with them. This was one of the starting points for Romantic *Volksgeistlehre* and German national consciousness.

It was the concept of the unbridgeable contrast between the highly
esteemed Greeks' love of freedom and Persian despotism that, in its
wake, had a decisive influence on how the ancient Iranians were regarded in Germany (Wiesehöfer 1988; 1990; 1992; 2005b: 83–110). This
concept had already existed from ancient times but now had become
even more pointed. In addition (or in its stead), the differences between the cultural achievements of the Greeks and the achievements
of their Eastern neighbors were stressed. The Greek achievements
were said to have been based on the free development of the individual
and the unimpeded development of intellectual powers, while Persian
culture was said to have been based on the theocratic and authoritar-
ian "power of the priests." Basically, nothing changed in this antinomy
even after the kinship between the Iranian (Aryan) and "Germanic"
languages was recognized. However, soon after, as part of Romantic
Volksgeistlehre, the view that "Indo-Germanic" primitive peoples were
culturally superior and that a similarity of character existed among the
Indo-Germanic peoples (both Eastern and European) gained in emphasis. This resulted in a more positive appraisal of the ancient Persians and set them apart from other Oriental peoples, but it still did not
change the Germans' preference for Greek (that is, mostly Athenian)

approach to art, culture, and politics. This approach is still reflected in the textbooks of modern times.

I turn now to the second model, the "structural weaknesses" model. In past decades, scholars increasingly came to believe that causes other than ethical or moral causes were to blame for the downfall of Persian rule. Scholars now spoke of an irreversible crisis—a kind of political, military, economic, and social quagmire—into which the Empire fell during the reign of Xerxes and his successors. Several causes of the crisis were mentioned repeatedly in these analyses: the inability of Persian rulers to shape the Empire into one organic entity and to prevent separatist tendencies in parts of the Empire; the tensions in the royal house and between kings and provincial governors who were throwing off the shackles of central government; the increasing dependency on foreign mercenaries coupled with a loss of combat strength among units drawn from the Empire; and, finally, economic stagnation due to massive hording of precious metal resources, exhaustion of the soil, excessive tax pressure, and, as a consequence of all this, a heightening of social disparities.

To record and describe the relations between the Persian king and his subjects requires, however, that we abandon two concepts as uncharacteristic of the Achaemenid Empire. One concept understands the Empire as a modern, centrally controlled nation that attempts to monitor and regulate the affairs of its population right down to its daily life. Local autonomy, political, linguistic, cultural, and religious heterogeneity of the Empire, the lack of an imperial community of values at the level of popular culture appear to have been signs of the increasing inability of the central authority to shape the Empire into one organic entity or to maintain it as a whole. Many a classical literary document about the control mechanisms applied by the Great King or the considerable power of the satraps is used first as an argument for a "centralist" view of the organization of the Empire and then secondly for the concept of a "weak (Persian) state." In reality, however, these mechanisms (besides imperial ideology) are the usual forms of making sure that an empire holds together. Other scholars proceed precisely from the heterogeneity of conditions just described and emphasize the astonishing amount of local autonomy and structural tolerance observable in the royal inscriptions and reliefs. They rightly consider all of this to be desirable and normal but at the same time believe they have to deduce a lack of central authority. The reason for the "weak Empire" in this case was a well-meaning concept of sovereignty that nevertheless endangered the unity of the Empire. The Persian influence on the material culture of the provinces that can be seen only on a very small scale in archaeological discoveries outside Persis plays a considerable role in this thesis.

Numerous regional studies have been able to prove, however, that in the Achaemenid Empire local autonomy and royal control indeed were able to complement one another, well after initial difficulties, and to guarantee stable conditions (Briant 2002b: passim). In this case, one only needs to think of the reforms of Artaphernes in 492 B.C.E. (Herodotus 6.42–43), the mediation of the border dispute between Myus and Miletus by the satrap Struthas in 390 B.C.E. (*SIG* I 34, 31–44), and the famous case of Elephantine. The Persian kings showed political foresight and flexibility not only in legal matters and political questions relating to religion; in their own interest and in the interests of the provincial populations, they adapted their authority to the royal traditions of formerly independent regions. They granted a wealth of tax privileges, concluded contracts with politically and militarily inferior neighbors, and took into account local and regional conditions when setting up and filling official posts. What may be very surprising at first glance is the fact that certain groups in the population were obviously able to maintain very relaxed relations with the state authorities, and others, primarily the tribes of the Zagros Mountains, even received gifts from the king instead of paying tribute themselves (Wiesehöfer 2004). As for the Greeks, it should be remembered that a great number of them lived as expatriates in the Persian Empire next to mercenaries, physicians, artists, and other employees of the Great King. By contrast, there was a much smaller number of Persian immigrants in Greece.

The generosity shown by kings to their loyal subjects on their numerous travels, the timeless idea propagated in epigraphs and pictures of a universal, cosmic order that was supposedly due to divine assistance, and the mutual loyalty of king and subjects impressed many inhabitants, visitors, and neighbors of the Achaemenid Empire. The "universal world" ideology emanating from the political center and the "flawless sovereign" ideology flowing toward this center combined with tolerance of local and regional traditions paid dividends to the end. Nevertheless, structural weaknesses and temporary crises in Persian rule cannot be left unmentioned. Despite all efforts of the Great King to continue indigenous traditions and respect old institutions and privileges in the formerly independent regions of the Empire, far-reaching changes in the status of these areas and their inhabitants could not be avoided. Although Egypt and Babylon, for example, may have had special rank in the overall Empire, they did, nevertheless, lose their freedom in foreign trading, were obliged to pay tributes and be part of the army, and were governed by foreign kings. The fiscal and political reorganization of the Empire by Darius I, with its greater systemization of legal and financial relations between king and provinces (Herodotus 3.89), contributed to the fact that in certain cases anti-Persian parties of native elites attempted to restore indigenous sovereignty.[4] In the case of Egypt, its border position must be added to this consideration—that is, its proximity to powers in the Mediterranean that were hostile to Persia. However, resistance by forming coalitions was only successful in Egypt and, even there, only for two generations.

The Persian concept of preserving sovereignty was marked by limited access of the elitist culture to lower echelons and by the lack of a plan for absorbing the aspirations of the subjects or forcing them to become "Iranian" or "Persian," as was the case with the later phenomenon of Romanization with which we are all familiar. In other words, there was no integration of subjects into the Persian political and social world view; it was neither desired by the provincial elite nor implemented by the political center. It is true that Persian lifestyle (that is, the lifestyle of the royal family and aristocracy) was exemplary and worthy of imitation for some subjects of the Great King, but not to the extent of later Roman acculturation, which extended to the details of everyday life. On the contrary, the regional and local elite of the Achaemenid Empire had limited access to the highest offices, which were reserved predominantly for members of the Persian aristocracy. To be a Persian and to come from Persia distinguished an inhabitant of this Empire as someone special. The *koinonia* between Persians and loyal Greeks, for example, was indeed evident and cultivated, but the gratitude of the Great King for favors and loyalty demonstrated was expressed in the granting of honorary titles or material gifts rather than in access to political and military decision-making. At the same time, the Persians strived to stand out clearly from the other inhabitants of the Empire. Furthermore, the script, language, and religion(s) of the Persians, in contrast to their Roman counterparts, were hardly attractive or open enough to tighten the bond between Persians and non-Persians.

Without a doubt, the prestige of the Great King was particularly great in the provinces of the Iranian highland, and the special place

---

4. For the problem of the historicity of these imperial reforms, see Wiesehöfer forthcoming.

held by the Persians, Elamites, Medes, and Bactrians was·known throughout the Empire. Nevertheless, relations between the Great Kings and the Iranian elite in the Empire were strained. Conflicts could arise between the Persian satraps, their families, and the elite of their provinces. That is, relations that the king also regarded as desirable were not used for the purpose of maintaining the *pax Achaemenidica* but for founding and securing local or regional positions of power. The Great Kings tried to counteract these tendencies at all times by means of the royal *polydoria*—that is, the generous granting of titles, offices, property, fortune, and honorary gifts—by which the recipients were bound to absolute loyalty. Another technique was to admit loyal aristocrats into a circle of so-called "benefactors" of the king who were noted in a special registry, along with the special privileges granted to them. The education of the sons of aristocrats was centered on loyalty to the king, temporary command posts were established that frequently consulted with the court, and relatives of the satraps were situated near the king. These policies were additional guarantees that separatist tendencies in the border regions would remain limited in time and space. Moreover, being near the king, which was important for furthering one's career, gave rise to a kind of "staff nobility" at court. For these people, loyalty to the king, if the need arose, was more important than loyalty to one's clan. Competition for offices, benefits, and the king's favor also made it more difficult for aristocrats to join together against the sovereign. The miserable failure of the satraps' rebellions of the fourth century in the west was largely due to rivalries among the people involved.

A fourth and final structural weakness in Persian rule is still to be examined, a weakness that is characteristic of all empires with a monarchic head. Although neither the monarchy as such nor its assignment to the Achaemenid clan was disputed in Iran, there were repeated conflicts over the throne and crises in the dynasty. In this respect, it was primarily the brief period between the death of a king and the accession to power by his successor that was important for all Achaemenids and for all who believed they had a voice in the matter (Briant 1991). This was because a legitimate successor to the throne did not accede immediately but only after a required period of mourning and "suspension of the laws" (Greek *anomia*), as well as the fulfillment of certain duties (burial of the predecessor, execution of the provisions of his "will") and the observance of special rituals. Ambitious princes such as Cyrus the Younger and Secyndianus, queens such as Amestris and Parysatis who wanted to secure the throne for their sons, and

influential persons at court such as Bagoas who wanted to retain or extend their position played a part in the fact that successions to the
Achaemenid throne could escalate and turn into extremely serious crises. The fact that private relations and dependencies within the royal
house and in court society could not help becoming political issues lay
in the nature of the autocratic system itself. As I have mentioned
above, this has just as little to do with "harem intrigues" as with the
moral decadence of the people involved.

And what about the decline of Persian power in combat observed by
Isocrates? One should be careful not to see the engagement of mercenaries as a sign of the decline of Persian power and military art (as Isocrates did and as many do even today). Historical facts contradict this
idea: for example, the reconquest of Egypt shortly before Alexander's
campaign; and what is known as the "Great Satraps' Rebellion," which
was revealed to be a phantom but had been regarded as a great threat
to the Great King (Weiskopf 1989; Briant 2002b: passim). The use of
mercenaries was, moreover, a general phenomenon of the fourth century and only shows the capability and combat strength of the Greek
hoplites and their motives for service under the Great King. The Persian monarch had good reason (and, above all, the necessary means)
for enlisting mercenaries instead of the rural population, which could
not both cultivate the land and also provide military service. What is
more, the mercenaries were in service mainly in the coastal region of
Asia Minor, where Greek influence had manifested itself for a long
time anyway. They were hardly stationary, nor were they permanent
residents in the interior of the Empire. It is not surprising that Isocrates
was so concerned about the lack of Persian combat strength. It was precisely by stressing the weaknesses of the Persian Empire that he aimed
to encourage Athens, Sparta, and, later, Philip of Macedon to attack the
barbarian country. In this "ideology of pan-Hellenic war on the barbarians," as it was called, references to the Great King as a militarily powerful man or to his soldiers and mercenaries as brave men who were
loyal to the king were totally out of place.

The idea of the economic decline of the Achaemenid Empire in the
late fifth and fourth century is also farfetched. It is true that texts from
Babylonia, at least (only in Babylonia is there enough evidence available to clarify our problem), show changes in the economic system and
shifts in the significance of certain parts of the country, but they indicate economic growth rather than an economic standstill or regression.
The fact that the Achaemenids were judged rather favorably in the
historical tradition of Seleucid Babylonia is further proof of our thesis

(Wiesehöfer 2002). The motive imputed to Alexander in older works of achieving a rapid increase in the amount of money in circulation and thus boosting the entire economy through the coinage of precious metal resources hoarded by the Persian kings is an application of modern economic insights to ancient times. However, Alexander's main reasons were clearly of a more pragmatic nature. He required substantial numbers of minted coins for the campaigns planned for the following years. He may also have been aware of the effect that his name on the coins would have; by contrast, the economic results of his coin policy likely were unintended effects. The fact that the hoarding policy of the Great Kings was economically unsound, although totally in keeping with the ideology of the Achaemenid monarchy, should not lead us to postulate an economic decline or widening socioeconomic gaps. There are no indications of such developments—not in the Western portion of the Empire, which traded in coins; not in the regions of Mesopotamia and western Iran, where cut pieces of silver were used for trading; and not in the barter economy of the East.

Thus, there was no downhill slide and no existential crisis of authority, but there were tensions in the imperial structure that in certain circumstances could grow into regional instability or temporary weakness of royal power. None of these crises threatened the existence of the Achaemenid Empire. Even the loss of Egypt for approximately 60 years did not really change anything with regard to the excellent position of the Great King in the power structure of the eastern Mediterranean and the Near East. On the contrary, the times during the reign of Artaxerxes II and his son, Artaxerxes III—with the "King's Peace," the suppression of the Phoenician rebellion, and the winning back of Egypt—could only be regarded as steps in the decline of Persian power by people such as Isocrates, who wished to put an end to the inability of motherland Greeks to act jointly by propagating distorted pictures of this sort, and by others, such as some later contemporaries, who attempted to explain the sudden collapse of Persian power in the battles against Alexander—after the event.

It is precisely this surprising end that is, in my opinion, the only apt way of defining the end of the Achaemenid dynasty. How can the success of Alexander be explained in view of a Persian authority that was by no means unstable, in view of an impressive Persian military power, that, after all, was capable of recovering Egypt for the Empire shortly before? In recent years, it has become clear just how long the Macedonian king was in a precarious military situation after crossing over to Asia Minor. He had precious metal reserves for a bare three months before conquering Sardis. For a long time, he had to rely on supplies from the conquered country because the Persian fleet controlled the eastern Mediterranean, and he needed to attempt, at all costs, to obtain control of the bases of the Persian fleet in Cilicia and Phoenicia. His victories at Granicus and Issus, the approximately simultaneous triumphs of Antigonus in Asia Minor and of the king himself at Tyre and Gaza were for Alexander of vital importance and crucial for survival. He could not have afforded a defeat. Without a doubt, Alexander was an excellent military leader. His army was not superior to the enemy in numbers and morale but in training, tactics, and military techniques (especially the siege of cities [*poliorcetics*]).

But does this alone explain his triumph? If one believes Arrian and the majority of modern scholars, then Alexander was faced with a Great King, Darius, who was politically and militarily totally out of his depth, a king who for no reason prematurely abandoned the field at Issus and Gaugamela. A closer look at tradition provides a different picture.[5] The common tradition (cf. Diod. 17.6.1–3) describes the last Great King before his accession to the throne as brave and highly qualified. His forceful personality enabled him to end the confusion over the throne after the murder of Arses. He selected, not really by chance, the name Darius in memory of his great-grandfather, or Darius I, and his military operations and defense tactics have just recently been acknowledged as being guided by expertise and logic. And what about his flight from the battlefields of Issus and Gaugamela? Proving one's worth in battle was indeed an important aspect of Achaemenid imperial ideology, but there is much to be said for the fact that the death or even capture of the king, who was selected by the gods and the guarantor of world order (in contrast to the later Hellenistic rulers, whose charisma depended directly on their active participation in battle), would have been considered a trauma rather than a mark of distinction by his subjects. Darius left the battlefield because only he could restore order and only he could organize further resistance.

The failure to block the Hellespont in 334 B.C.E. and the very late formation of the imperial army are the only issues remaining to be discussed. Only in retrospect and from the viewpoint of the historians of Alexander does it become clear how significant Alexander's crossing over to Asia Minor was. For Darius, this was just another attempt of the kind undertaken unsuccessfully by Agesilaus and Parmenion. The attempt to repulse him could be left to the combined units of the Asia

---

5. See the impressive study of Briant (2003).

Minor satraps. Furthermore, mustering the entire imperial force was a measure that was taken only in an emergency, was extremely time-consuming, and up to that point had seldom been required.

Did Alexander, then, also prove to be a liberator to the majority of the Persian subjects in, for example, Asia Minor, Egypt, and Babylon? Doubts are also in order about this widespread thesis. The privileges that were bestowed in Asia Minor if one surrendered voluntarily were impressive only verbally, but effective at least for the moment. The Lydians, for example, could now reinstate their old laws and were free and autonomous—but what did this mean? The "tributes" that the Greeks had been required to pay to the Persians were abolished and replaced by "contributions" to the king. Occupation forces as such were not planned but were used when it appeared appropriate to the king for military reasons. Other than this, nothing changed, with Alexander installing Macedonian instead of Persian satraps in office in the existing administrative districts. The Egyptians accepted Alexander without any difficulty less because he had driven out the Persians and more because he deliberately presented himself as ruler in Egyptian clothing and conscientiously fulfilled his royal duties to the gods and sacred objects. Otherwise, his policy in this country differed very little from his predecessors'. Finally, in Babylon, the Persian satrap Mazaeus, who was later left in office, and the civilian and religious authorities of the city received Alexander and organized his triumphal entrance into the city (Curt. V 1, 17–23), to which the king responded with worship of the gods and the restoration of places of cultural importance, which, by the way, had not been destroyed by Xerxes (Kuhrt and Sherwin-White 1987). This ceremony and these royal actions, which conformed to the usual Babylonian custom, illustrate the unchallenged position of Alexander in Mesopotamia and his knowledge of the duties of a legitimate king of Babylon. However, they do not reveal how unsatisfied (or satisfied) the Babylonians were with the Achaemenid predecessors (Kuhrt 1990; Briant 1999; van der Spek 2003).

The following facts must also be taken into consideration. Along with the rehabilitation of Darius, the degree to which Alexander acted in Achaemenid fashion even before the death of his opponent is becoming clear (Briant 2003; cf. Wiesehöfer 1994: 23–49). He behaved as an Achaemenid not to his fellow Macedonians or to the Greeks but to the subjects and officials of the Great King and to Darius himself. Well versed in the prerequisites of the Persian Empire and benefiting from his successes, he attempted to outdo his opponent in the virtues of a Great King, to let the splendor of the founder of the Empire, Cyrus, shine on himself, and to draw high Persian dignitaries over to his side. He was able to offer positions to all who changed sides, as well as benefices comparable with their previous privileges. His successes lent him and his policy the necessary charisma. Alexander's efforts did not work in every case. At times, he proceeded with immense brutality against those who were not prepared to follow him unconditionally, but it was his long-term policy of understanding and working together with the Iranians that gained him recognition in the east, even after his death.

Finally, we must consider the reaction of the subjects to the ideology and practical policy of the Great Kings. On the one hand, the writings of the Achaemenid kings presuppose that subject loyalty is the norm, and they consider it a divine command and royal resposibility to provide justice, "truth," and well-being for all inhabitants of the Empire. In turn, the well-being of the inhabitants is also desired by the gods, and Ahura Mazda qualifies the king specifically for these tasks. However, the inscriptions are very clear about the threat of sanctions that must be borne in mind by those who do not wish to follow divine or royal commands. Furthermore, Greek tradition as well as the Persian royal statements (such as DB) both refer to the merciless revenge inflicted on rebels and insurgents and their punishment (even though kings such as Cambyses and Xerxes, who are said to have been especially merciless in this respect, must be exonerated from some of the atrocities imputed to them and even though their action in this case hardly differs from that of their popular fathers, Cyrus and Darius). A stick-and-carrot guarantee of well-being (though part of an "unbalanced" economic and social mix according to Greek tradition) *and* graveyard silence after the suppression of rebellions were the two sides of the *pax Achaemenidica* at all times. This must be emphasized, because the opinions of victims of Achaemenid imperial education and power, with the exception of a few rebels (literally, "liar kings" in Persian royal diction), are only seldom found in our records. Furthermore, the importance given to imitation of a royal lifestyle and adoption of royal images and messages by the elite of the Empire should be reconsidered in the light of more recent studies, for example, on Augustan culture (Hölscher 1999). Would not the propaganda and pragmatism of the system have prevented any possible counter or alternative ideology? Must we explain imperialism's expansion right into the private sphere only by the recipients' happily accepting it, or would it not also be possible that their acceptance was to some extent a "noncommittal political applause," an expression of a rather opportunistic mentality? Might not the spectators and listeners of that period also have been weary of the constant repetition and ubiquity of the pictorial motifs and inscriptional language used by the Great Kings on their monuments, even though they seem attractive to us today with their emphasis on peace and order and their renunciations of images of war and combat—not to speak of the problem that the political reality was not as peaceful as was proclaimed?

To the present, the positive image that the Persian kings drew of themselves and their policy still exerts an influence, if we disregard the practically based Greek/Occident portrayal of the Persian conflict with the Greeks. The tolerance of the Persian kings has been emphasized time and again, especially in comparison with their precursors in power, the Assyrians. This tolerance is supposed to be in sharp contrast to the severity and harshness—indeed brutality—of Sargon, Senacherib, and Assurbanipal. In particular, the difference in tenor of the Assyrian and Achaemenid royal self-representations is adduced in support of this thesis, both epigraphic and pictorial. However, three points are forgotten in this context. First, the Achaemenids must have borne in mind the Assyrian example of the foundation, preservation, and decline of an empire when they themselves founded, expanded, and secured their Empire. Second, Cyrus and his successors indeed followed Assyrian example in word (for example, the famous Cyrus Cylinder from Babylon in which Assurbanipal is named), image (for example, the sculptures and images on the palaces that demonstrate Assyrian influence), and deed (deportation, suppression of rebellions). Cyrus and his successors also made it quite plain that their Empire was founded by means of war. Third, Achaemenid handcraft (glyptics, etc.) often had totally "unpeaceful" themes, and the Achaemenid images of imperial peace are found on the exteriors of the palaces. By contrast, the Assyrian images of conquest and subjection appear on the interior, in the palace rooms (Kuhrt 2001).

Moreover, there is evidence that the Persians learned from the example of Assyrian sovereign ideology and practice and undoubtedly also from the (Neo)Babylonians, and thus they (1) created an imperial ideology that placed more emphasis on the reciprocity of royal welfare and loyalty of the subjects; (2) showed greater flexibility in the administration of the Empire (generally avoided provincializing conquered areas and practiced a greater acceptance and support of local autonomy); (3) renounced a hierarchical structure of the divine, sacral sphere (the local gods were not described as inferior to Ahura Mazda); and (4) turned away from mass deportations as a means of pacification and securing royal power.

Even though the extent of the acceptance, resignation, or rejection of the royal Achaemenid "order of peace" by its subjects cannot actually be determined, the Achaemenid Empire ultimately did not end due to a lack of inner unity or due to administrative or economic crises, thanks to the royal ideology regarding the well-being of its subjects, thanks to the astonishing extent of autonomy and structural "tolerance" granted by the imperial government and, not least, thanks to its strict surveillance. The fall of the Empire was mainly due to the outstanding military and tactical skill of its military opponent. The fact that the Achaemenid Empire seemed exemplary and worthy of imitation in some institutions even to its conqueror earned Alexander the title of "the last Achaemenid" (Briant). It also explains the emulation of the Achaemenids by later empires of the Near East.

References

Bichler, R.
  2004	Ktesias "korrigiert" Herodot: Zur literarischen Einschätzung der *Persika*. Pp. 105–16 in *Ad Fontes! Festschrift für G. Dobesch zum 65. Geburtstag*, ed. H. Heftner and K. Tomaschitz. Vienna: Im Eigenverlag der Herausgeber.
  Forthcoming	Der "Orient" im Wechselspiel zwischen Imagination und Erfahrung: Zum Typus der "orientalischen Despotie," in *Getrennte Wege? Kommunikation, Raum, und Wahrnehmung in der Alten Welt*, ed. R. Rollinger, A. Luther, and J. Wiesehöfer. Oikumene 3. Frankfurt: Antike.
Briant, P.
  1991	Le roi est mort: Vive le roi! Remarques sur les rites et rituels de succession chez les Achéménides. Pp. 1–11 in *La religion iranienne à l'époque achéménide: Actes du colloque de Liège, 11 décembre 1987*, ed. J. Kellens. Iranica Antiqua Supplement. 5. Gent.
  1999	Alexandre à Babylone: Images grecques, images babyloniennes. Pp. 23–32 in *Alexandre le Grand dans les littératures occidentales et proche-orientales*, ed. L. Harf-Lancner, C. Kappler, and F. Suard. Nanterre: Centre des sciences de la littérature de l'Université Paris X.
  2002a	History and Ideology: The Greeks and "Persian Decadence." Pp. 193–210 in *Greeks and Barbarians*, ed. T. Harrison. Edinburgh Readings on the Ancient World. Edinburgh: Edinburgh University Press.
  2002b	*From Cyrus to Alexander: A History of the Persian Empire*. Winona Lake, IN: Eisenbrauns.
  2003	*Darius dans l'ombre d'Alexandre*. Paris: Fayard.
Brosius, M.
  1996	*Women in Ancient Persia (559–331 B.C.)*. Oxford: Clarendon.

Heinrichs, J.
1989   *Ionien nach Salamis: Die kleinasiatischen Griechen in der Politik und politischen Reflexion des Mutterlands.* Antiquitas 1; Abhandlungen zur alten Geschichte 39. Bonn: Habelt.
Hölscher, T.
1999   Augustus und die Macht der Archäologie. Pp. 237–73 in *La révolution romaine après Ronald Syme: Bilans et perspectives.* Entretiens sur l'Antiquité Classique 46. Vandoeuvres: Fondation Hardt.
Kuhrt, A.
1990   Alexander and Babylon. Pp. 121–30 in *The Roots of the European Tradition: Proceedings of the 1987 Groningen Achaemenid History Workshop,* ed. H. Sancisi-Weerdenburg and J. W. Drijvers. Achaemenid History 5. Leiden: Nederlands Instituut voor het Nabije Oosten.
2001   The Persian Kings and Their Subjects: A Unique Relationship? *OLZ* 96: 165–73.
Kuhrt, A., and Sherwin-White, S.
1987   Xerxes' Destruction of Babylonian Temples. Pp. 69–78 in *The Greek Sources: Proceedings of the Groningen 1984 Achaemenid History Workshop,* ed. H. Sancisi-Weerdenburg and A. Kuhrt. Achaemenid History 2. Leiden: Nederlands Instituut voor het Nabije Oosten.
Lenfant, D.
2004   *Ctésias de Cnide. La Perse. L'Inde. Autres Fragments. Texte établi, traduit, et commenté.* Paris: Les Belles Lettres.
Schöpsdau, K.
1990   Persien und Athen in Platons Nomoi. Pp. 25–39 in *Pratum Saraviense: Festgabe für P. Steinmetz,* ed. W. Görler and S. Koster. Palingenesia 30. Stuttgart: Franz Steiner.
Spek, R. van der
2003   Darius III, Alexander the Great and Babylonian Scholarship. Pp. 289–302 in *A Persian Perspective: Essays in Memory of H. Sancisi-Weerdenburg,* ed. W. Henkelman and A. Kuhrt. Achaemenid History 13. Leiden: Nederlands Instituut voor het Nabije Oosten.
Vössing, K.
2004   *Mensa Regia: Das Bankett beim hellenistischen König und beim römischen Kaiser.* Beiträge zur Altertumskunde 193. Munich: Saur.
Weiskopf, M.
1989   *The So-Called "Great Satraps' Revolt," 366–360* B.C.*: Concerning Local Instability in the Achaemenid Far West.* Historia-Einzelschriften 63. Stuttgart: Franz Steiner.
Wiesehöfer, J.
1988   Das Bild der Achaimeniden in der Zeit des Nationalsozialismus. Pp. 1–14 in *Sources, Structures and Synthesis: Proceedings of the Groningen 1983 Achaemenid History Workshop,* ed. A. Kuhrt and Heleen Sancisi-Weerdenburg. Achaemenid History 3. Leiden: Nederlands Instituut voor het Nabije Oosten.

1990 Zur Geschichte der Begriffe "Arier" und "arisch" in der deutschen Sprachwissenschaft und Althistorie des 19. und der ersten Hälfte des 20. Jahrhunderts. Pp. 147–63 in _The Roots of the European Tradition: Proceedings of the 1987 Groningen Achaemenid History Workshop_, ed. H. Sancisi-Weerdenburg and J. W. Drijvers. Achaemenid History 5. Leiden: Nederlands Instituut voor het Nabije Oosten.

1992 "Denn es sind welthistorische Siege . . .": Nineteenth and Twentieth-Century German Views of the Persian Wars. _Culture and History_ 12: 61–83.

1994 _Die "dunklen Jahrhunderte" der Persis: Untersuchungen zur Geschichte und Kultur von Fārs in frühhellenistischer Zeit (330–140 v.Chr.)._ Zetemata 90. Munich: Beck.

2001 Gift-Giving, II: In Pre-Islamic Persia. Pp. 607–9 in vol. 10 of _Encyclopaedia Iranica_. New York: Bibliotheca Persica.

2002 Kontinuität oder Zäsur? Babylonien unter den Achämeniden. Pp. 29–48 in _Religion und Religionskontakte im Zeitalter der Achämeniden_, ed. R. G. Kratz. Gütersloh: Chr. Kaiser.

2003 The Medes and the Idea of the Succession of Empires in Antiquity. Pp. 391–96 in _Continuity of Empire (?): Assyria, Media, Persia_, ed. G. Lanfranchi, M. Roaf, and R. Rollinger. Padua: S.a.r.g.o.n.

2004 Bergvölker im antiken Nahen Osten: Fremdwahrnehmung und Eigeninteresse. Pp. 11–26 in _Die Kurden: Studien zu ihrer Sprache, Geschichte, und Kultur_, ed. S. Conermann and G. Haig. Asien und Afrika 8. Schenefeld: EB-Verlag.

2005a Daniel, Herodot und "Dareios der Meder": Auch ein Beitrag zur Abfolge von Weltreichen. Pp. 647–53 in _Von Sumer bis Homer: Festschrift für M. Schretter zum 60. Geburtstag am 25. Februar 2004._ AOAT 325. Münster: Ugarit-Verlag.

2005b _Iraniens, Grecs et Romains._ Studia Iranica, Cahier 32. Paris: Association pour l'avancement des études iraniennes.

Forthcoming Ein König erschließt und imaginiert sein Imperium: Persische Reichsordnung und persische Reichsbilder zur Zeit Dareios' I. (522–486 v.Chr.). In _Raumwahrnehmung und Raumerfassung in der Antike_, ed. M. Rathmann. Mainz: von Zabern.

PART 2

Judah in the Late Persian and Early Hellenistic Periods

The Settlement Archaeology
of the Province of Judah:
A Case Study

ODED LIPSCHITS AND OREN TAL
Tel Aviv University Institute of Archaeology

This essay assesses changes in settlement archaeology in the "heart" of the province of Judah (*Yehud*) under Achaemenid and Ptolemaic rule. Using the results of archaeological excavations and surveys, we will try to reconstruct settlement changes between the end of the Persian period and the Hasmonean period (fourth to mid-second centuries B.C.E.), with a focus on the contribution of the fourth century to the process. Judah and especially Jerusalem, owing to their role in biblical literature and their religious impact on Western civilizations, have long been important in archaeological research. However, the research directed at the region's first-millennium B.C.E. history was mostly focused on the periods that preceded and succeeded the one under discussion—that is, it was mostly focused on the First Temple period and the latter part of the Second Temple period—times when the country was a small but independent political entity. In the last few years, there has been growing interest in the settlement archaeology of the Neo-Babylonian and Persian (Achaemenid) periods. The early Hellenistic period, however, has largely been ignored, partly because of the methodological problems that we will discuss below and partly because of its intermediate nature as a transitional period between the domination of the region by Eastern and Western powers.

The available data seem at first glance to be sufficient to tackle the problem at hand. However, they are actually quite problematic. In many of the large-scale excavations carried out in archaeological sites in Judah, the strata pertaining to the late Persian and early Hellenistic (Ptolemaic and Seleucid) periods were meager; some revealed few architectural remains with unclear building plans or pits (silos, refuse, etc.), while others yielded pottery at best, which was in some cases not classified by strata and did not represent proper occupation layers.

Suffice it here to mention sites such as Bethel, Tell en-Naṣbeh (biblical Mizpah), Gibeon, Tell el-Fûl (biblical Gibeah of Saul), Nabi Samwil, Anathoth, Bethany, Ramat Raḥel, and Jericho.[1] In the case of Jerusalem, the Persian period city shrank back to its pre-eighth-century B.C.E. size, and the western hill was empty until the second century B.C.E. (Geva 2003: 521–24; Lipschits and Vanderhooft forthcoming).[2] Even this small city was apparently sparsely settled and mostly confined to the southern part of the City of David near the Pool of Siloam (Reich and Shukron 2007: 64–65). The most impressive building plan of the period under discussion in Judah was discovered at En Gedi (Building 234) and dated to the Persian period (see now Stern 2007). The stratigraphic relationship of the first fortress at Beth-zur to occupational layers of Persian date is questionable, and therefore we cannot assign its building plan to the Persian period with certainty (cf. Stern 1982: 31–40; 2001: 428–43, for a review of these sites). Other late Persian and early Hellenistic buildings were documented in non-urban sites. Worthy of mention are the fortress and agricultural estate of Har Adar (Dadon 1997) and the agricultural estates of Qalandya (Magen 2004) and Aderet (Yogev 1982).[3]

Methodological Notes

Using the results of archaeological excavations and surveys, we will compare the number and character of settlements in three areas that can safely be considered within the borders of the province of Judah during the late Persian and early Hellenistic periods.[4] These include the hill country of Benjamin, the area around the Old City of Jerusalem, and the area south of Jerusalem—west of Bethlehem and Ramat Raḥel. In the hill country of Benjamin, 59 sites were attributed to the Persian period and 123 to the Hellenistic (Finkelstein and Magen 1993; fig. 3 below). In Jerusalem, 15 sites were attributed to the Persian period and 37 to the early Hellenistic period (Kloner 2000–2003; fig. 4 below). In the survey map of Nes Harim, 12 sites were attributed to the Persian period and and 35 to the Hellenistic period (Weiss, Zissu, and

---

1. See Stern 2001: 428–43; Betlyon 2005: 20–26; Lipschits 2005: 154–81; Tal 2006: 15–163 (and index).

2. We find it difficult to accept the renewed "maximalist opinion" recently advanced by Ussishkin (2006), in which "Nehemiah's wall" follows the line of the late Iron Age wall, even though most of the delimited area remained unoccupied.

3. For a list of sites of early Hellenistic date, see Tal 2006: 125–29, 145–54.

4. For a recent survey of the borders of Judah between the end of the seventh century and the second century B.C.E., see Lipschits 2005: 154–81.

Solimany 2004; fig. 5 below); and in the survey map of Deir Mar Saba, only 1 site was attributed to the Persian period and 10 to the Hellenistic period (Patrich 1994; fig. 6 below).

Another reason for focusing on these areas is the similar method of surveying and publishing the different maps within the Israel Antiquities Authority series entitled Archaeological Survey of Israel. For the purpose of this essay, we did not include the data of survey-oriented Ph.D. dissertations on the region under discussion (for example, A. Ofer's 1993 survey of the Judean Hills) or outside the region under discussion (Y. Dagan's 2000 survey of the Judean Shephelah). We also took no notice of the data given in the so-called "emergency survey" carried out in 1968 as an outcome of the Six-Day War. The reasons for excluding these sources were mainly because of the overlapping that these data produce with the Archaeological Survey of Israel, the different methods of surveying, the absence of some of the main periods from the publications (Ph.D. dissertations that are either First-Temple or Second-Temple-period oriented), and the fact that we have no way to check the results of these surveys.

For the sake of comparison and as a means of control, we also included surveys carried out in regions adjacent to the province of Judah that are both just outside its borders and surveyed and published employing a similar method. These include the map of Lod, which basically corresponds to the southwestern part of the province of Samaria, where 28 sites were attributed to the Persian period and 19 to the Hellenistic period (Gophna and Beit-Arieh 1997; fig. 7 below); the map of Lachish, which basically corresponds to the northwestern part of the province of Edom, where 11 sites were attributed to the Persian period and 25 to the Hellenistic period (Dagan 1992; fig. 8 below); and the map of Naḥal Yattir, which corresponds to the southern part of the province of Edom, where 7 sites were attributed to the Persian period and 6 to the Hellenistic period (Govrin 1991; fig. 9 below).

Most late Persian and early Hellenistic sites surveyed are basically rural in nature, not exceeding 5 dunams in size, and normally located in rocky terrains next to agricultural terraces. Jerusalem—as the temple city of Judah—was thus flanked by villages and agricultural estates that formed the predominant type of settlement. Results from both excavations and surveys show a sharp decrease not only in the total number of settlements (as opposed to the late Iron Age) but also in the size of settlements in which late-Iron-Age, Persian-period, and Hellenistic-period occupation appears. These data allow us to define three types of settlements in the province of Judah: (1) centralized—

sites that functioned as administrative centers; (2) martial—military strongholds; and (3) rural—villages and agricultural estates. Centralized sites together with military strongholds were established at key junctures on roads of strategic and political importance and served as the seats of representatives of the ruling powers.

Unlike the pottery of the coastal regions of the country, the pottery of Persian and early Hellenistic period Judah mainly continued the ceramic tradition of the late Iron Age (Lipschits 2005: 192–206). In terms of morphology, many of the table and storage vessels shared similar forms with the vessels of the late Iron Age. Thus, in cases in which small fragments are involved (as is usual in surveys), it is sometimes difficult to decide whether a given piece belongs to the late Iron Age, the Persian period, or even the early Hellenistic period. Furthermore, many of the Persian types are similar to early Hellenistic types.[5] Early and late pottery types within the Persian or early Hellenistic period can thus scarcely be defined due to the continuous tradition of late Iron Age types and the absence of excavations with a stratigraphic sequence within each period. The frequent appearance of brownish-gray ware in both Persian and early Hellenistic period sites is not confined to Judah but also appears in Samaria and Edom. Nonetheless, several pottery vessels such as certain types of bowls, kraters, and lamps from the Persian period can be differentiated from late Iron Age forerunners and early Hellenistic predecessors. However, most of the Persian and early Hellenistic Judean vessels share similar morphological and fabric characteristics. This datum alone raises doubts about the credibility of the attribution of Judean sites to either the Persian or the early Hellenistic period. Moreover, the reliability of the surveyed pottery sampling has been questioned (Redman and Watson 1970; Schiffer, Sullivan, and Klinger 1978). For our purposes, it is important to emphasize that the appearance of Persian and early Hellenistic pottery in Judean sites does not necessarily testify to a clear continuity between the two periods, since sites can be occupied intermittently. However, in this essay, continuity is our preferred explanation, given the historical and political realia of the province of Judah.

Stamped seal impressions contribute much to helping us define the border of the province of Judah (Stern 2001: 545–51; 2004: 14). This is

---

5. For example, Tushingham's Persian and Hellenistic pottery from the "early Jewish fills" in the Armenian Garden (e.g., 1985: figs. 12–19, passim) can hardly be morphologically attributed to either period alone. The same holds true for many of the locally manufactured vessel types retrieved from Lachish Level I (Fantalkin and Tal 2004).

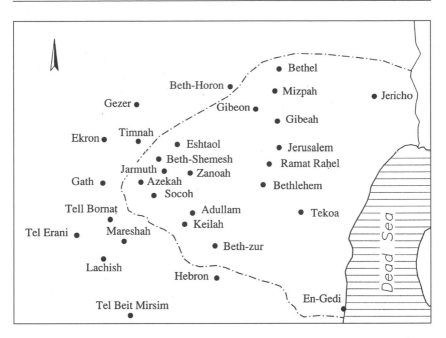

Fig. 1. Suggested Borders of the Province of Judah in the Persian Period (from Lipschits 2005: 183, map 6; reprinted courtesy of Eisenbrauns).

evident by the fact that storage vessels with Judahite seal impressions were circulated almost exclusively within the province. Up till now, more than 500 *Yehud* stamp seal impressions are known, as well as about 150 *lion* stamp seal impressions. New evidence will most likely be forthcoming due to the high number of archaeological excavations underway in Judah. First and foremost are the recent excavations at Ramat Raḥel. Lipschits and Vanderhooft suggest that there are three stages represented in the production of Judahite stamped seal impressions: the first stage was the late sixth and fifth centuries B.C.E., the second was the fourth and third centuries, and the third was the second century (Lipschits and Vanderhooft, in this volume, pp. 75–94; Vanderhooft and Lipschits 2007).

Another indicator of the province's borders that meshes well with the above consideration is the distribution of the *Yehud* coins. Their geographical distribution is restricted mainly to within the borders of Judah, with the exception of a few coins that were found at Tell Jemmeh, Mount Gerizim, and Ḥorvat ʿEtri (Ariel 2002: 287–94, esp. table 3). The small number of Yehud coins retrieved from controlled archaeological excavations (a mere 23 coins) is supplemented by the many examples with supposed Judahite find-spots that came from the antiquities market. Yehud coins can thus be seen as currency that mostly belonged to an "inner-provincial monetary system" that operated under a Jerusalemite minting authority. The small number of Yehud coins found as strays or in excavations outside Judah lends support to our understanding that their primary use was as a local currency. In cases where Yehud coins were discovered outside Judah, they were either used at their nominal value or, if unacceptable as currency in the local market, at bullion value.

The Database and Discussion

In what follows we will consider the data collected from the relevant survey maps by means of graphs.

When the evidence from the surveys in the geographical region of Judah is considered as presented above, we note a sharp increase in the number of the Hellenistic sites (fig. 2). This growth represents an increase of about 126% according to the cited survey maps. In fact, in all cited survey maps that are located within our defined limits of the province of Judah, the main conclusion is that the number of Hellenistic sites is more than double, if the results are accepted as provided. In the hill country of Benjamin (fig. 3), an increase of about 109% can be observed; in the survey map of Jerusalem (fig. 4), an increase of about 147% can be observed; in the survey map of Nes Harim (fig. 5), an increase of about 192% can be observed; and in the survey map of Deir Mar Saba (fig. 6), an increase of about 900% can be observed! This evidence, however, referring to some 87 Persian sites and 205 Hellenistic sites is misleading. This is because only in the survey of Jerusalem (Kloner 2000–2003: 3.30*–32*) was an attempt made to distinguish early from late Hellenistic (namely, Hasmonean) sites—albeit, even with these attempts, the multiple site number trend remains the same! However, it should be pointed out that this distinction was made with many limitations, because of the nature of the finds (as discussed above), in that most Hellenistic sites without Persian occupation reflect Hasmonean settlement activity rather than Ptolemaic or Seleucid settlement activity. This view is supported by the results of many Second Temple period excavations in Jerusalem and its environs. In most sites, the earliest Hellenistic stratum is normally attributed to the second half of the second century B.C.E. or the first half of the first century

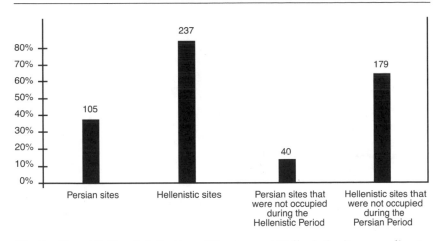

Fig. 2. Quantitative distribution of Persian and Hellenistic sites according to surveys carried out in the province of Judah and bordering regions.

Survey Maps	Persian sites	Hellenistic sites	Persian period sites that were not occupied during the Hellenistic period	Hellenistic sites that were not occupied during the Persian period
Map of the hill country of Benjamin:[a]				
Beit Sira (south)	8	16	1	9
Ramallah (south) el-Bireh (south) En Kerem (north)	33	70	8	51
Wadi el-Makukh	3	10	1	9
Jerusalem (east)	15	27	9	21
Map of Jerusalem[b]	15	37	5	27
Map of Nes Harim[c]	12	35	6	29
Map of Deir Mar Saba[d]	1	10	—	9
Map of Lakhish[e]	11	25	7	21
Map of Naḥal Yattir[f]	7	6	3	2
Map of Tel Malḥata[g]	—	1	—	1
Total	105	237	40	179

a. See Finkelstein and Magen 1993.
b. See Kloner 2000–2003.
c. See Weiss, Zissu, and Solimany 2004.
d. See Patrich 1994.
e. See Dagan 1992.
f. See Govrin 1991.
g. See Beit-Arieh 2003.

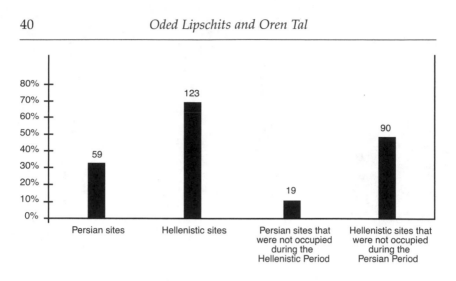

Fig. 3. Quantitative distribution of Persian and Hellenistic sites according to the survey maps of the hill country of Benjamin.

Survey Maps	Persian sites	Hellenistic sites	Persian period sites that were not occupied during the Hellenistic period	Hellenistic sites that were not occupied during the Persian period
Map of the hill country of Benjamin:[a]				
Beit Sira (south)	8	16	1	9
Ramallah (south) el-Bireh (south) En Kerem (north)	33	70	8	51
Wadi el-Makukh	3	10	1	9
Jerusalem (east)	15	27	9	21
Total	59	123	19	90

a. See Finkelstein and Magen 1993.

B.C.E.—a period, when Judah as a political entity was in firm Hasmonean control. Notable among these is the recently published final report of Avigad's excavations of the Jewish Quarter (Geva 2003: 524–26). The same holds true for the numerous Second Temple period tombs excavated and documented in Jerusalem (Kloner and Zissu 2003: 67–68). It thus appears that Jerusalem and the "province of Judah" during

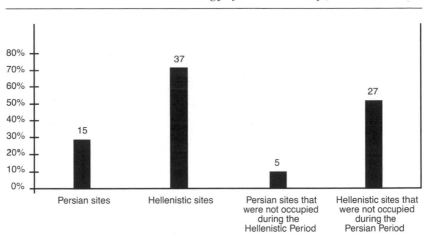

Fig. 4. Quantitative distribution of Persian and Hellenistic sites according to the survey map of Jerusalem.

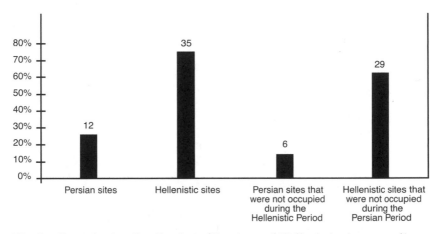

Fig. 5. Quantitative distribution of Persian and Hellenistic sites according to the survey map of Nes Harim.

the late fourth, third, and early second centuries B.C.E. did not witness major changes in size and number of sites in comparison with the Persian period (Bahat 1990: 36).[6]

---

6. The indirect evidence on the size of Jerusalem (as a prosperous urban center) from the *Letter of Aristeas* is most likely related to its Hasmonean past, because most scholars tend to attribute this source to the late second century B.C.E. (cf. Honigman 2003: 128–30).

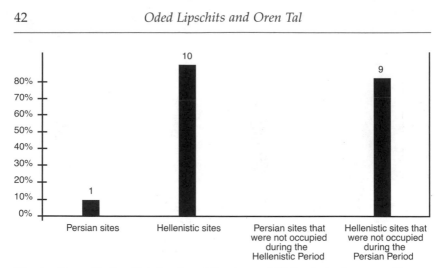

Fig. 6. Quantitative distribution of Persian and Hellenistic sites according to the survey map of Deir Mar Saba.

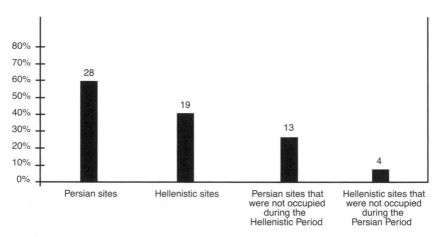

Fig. 7. Quantitative distribution of Persian and Hellenistic sites according to the survey map of Lod.

The Dead Sea region may present what may be termed as a radical case study for this phenomenon, because both excavations and surveys on the western shores of the Dead Sea yielded no early Hellenistic finds.[7] The same picture emerges from the excavations of ʿAin ez-Zâra (Clamer 1997) and from surveys conducted on the eastern shores of the

---

7. See Bar-Adon 1972; see also "Operation Scroll," in *ʿAtiqot* 41 (2002), esp. the papers on Regions XI, XII, XIII, XIV, XV.

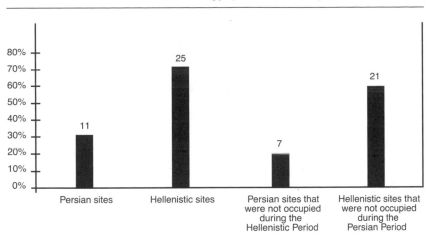

Fig. 8. Quantitative distribution of Persian and Hellenistic sites according to the survey map of Lachish.

Dead Sea (Mallon 1924; ʿAmr et al. 1996). Finds from En Gedi (Tel Goren) Stratum III (Mazar, Dothan, and Dunayevsky 1966: 39–44) and the forts of Miṣpe En Gedi and Rosh Maʿale En Gedi (Ofer 1986), although they include a few Ptolemaic and Seleucid coins, should be attributed to activity during the Hasmonean occupation.[8] The lack of Ptolemaic and Seleucid coins in Regions XI, XII, XIII, XIV, and XV of "Operation Scroll" (Ariel 2002: table 1) corresponds well with this conclusion. Other "Hellenistic" remains, such as tombs (Hadas 1994),

8. In the publication of the first two seasons of excavation in En Gedi (Tel Goren), Stratum III was "dated with a great degree of certainty to the . . . 3rd–2nd centuries B.C.E." (Mazar, Dothan, and Dunayevsky 1966: 39). This dating was based on stratigraphy (between Persian [V] and Hasmonean [II = Alexander Jannaeus] strata), pottery, out-of-context coins ("one Seleucid and several Ptolemaic"), and a reference to En Gedi in Sirach (24:6–15), which the excavators date to the first half of the second century B.C.E. In the publication of the fourth and fifth seasons, Stratum II was down-dated to the Herodians, and Stratum III was subsequently "stretched" down to the Hasmoneans (Mazar and Dunayevski 1966: 192). In the final excavation report of En Gedi, it was stated that "The Stratum III fort are [sic!] undoubtedly later than Stratum IV (Persian period) and are [sic!] earlier than the fort of Stratum II (the Hasmonean period, especially the reign of Alexander Jannaeus)"; the report then adds: "A fairly large quantity of the Hellenistic pottery was found in a stratigraphic context to be assigned to Stratum III, especially in Locus 2 . . ." (Stern and Matskevich 2007: 271), yet not a single fragment was published. Given the site and the region's character, it is safe to assume that the fort of Stratum III is of Early Hasmonean date (John Hyrcanus?). The forts of Miṣpe En Gedi and Rosh Maʿale En Gedi guarded the routes that led to En Gedi and are connected with the site's Hasmonean occupation.

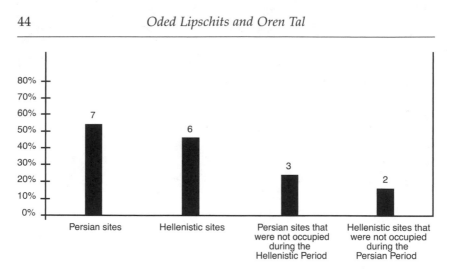

Fig. 9. Quantitative distribution of Persian and Hellenistic sites according to the survey map of Naḥal Yattir.

anchoring tracts (Hadas 1993), and anchors (Hadas 1992) are preferably dated to the Hasmonean period (and to later times), because of
geopolitical and archaeological evidence (Fischer, Gichon, and Tal
2000: 139–42). A similar phenomenon is evident from the survey maps
carried out to the south, north, and east of Jerusalem, parts of which
are adjacent to the northwestern sections of the Dead Sea region. Some
of these areas (Hirschfeld 1985; Syon 1994: 50) yield no documentation
on Hellenistic sites; in other cases (Patrich 1994; Syon 1997: 91; Kloner
2000–2003: 1.11*; vol. 2; 3.30*–32*), the Hellenistic sites should be
mainly attributed to the Hasmonean period. The same settlement activity can be discerned in regions south of this area, in the Negeb and
Araba. Hellenistic or, preferably, Nabatean sites were documented in
all survey maps (Sedé-Boqer, Har Nafḥa, Har Ḥamran, Miẓpé Ramon,
Har Ramon, Makhtesh Ramon, Har Saggie). Although the surveyors
treated (in some maps) the Nabatean period as contemporaneous with
the Hellenistic and early Roman periods, most sites should be dated
to the first century B.C.E. onward. It is important to mention that the
few Persian sites discovered in the region show no continuing Hellenistic occupation.

Thus, tracking the settlement archaeology of the province of Judah
in Persian and early Hellenistic times cannot be based on surveys
alone, because there is a clear contradiction between the evidence of

excavations and the survey finds. This contradiction is also apparent in survey maps of adjacent regions. The map of Lod, for example, shows an opposite trend: the number of Persian sites is far higher (by about 47%) than the number of Hellenistic sites (fig. 7). In contrast, on the map of Lachish, the same Judahite trend is apparent and an increase of about 127% is noted (fig. 8). A different trend is apparent on the map of Naḥal Yattir, where the number of Persian sites is almost equal to the number of Hellenistic sites (fig. 9). All of the above factors compel us to inquire further into the nature of our database by means of more "delicate" archaeological tools.

It was Stern (2001: 580–82) who, basing his argument on the administrative-oriented archaeological finds of the Persian period, suggested that the provinces of the country and their major administrative units became functional largely during the latter part of the Persian period. This view was recently corroborated for the inland regions of southern Palestine after studying the Lachish Level I finds of the renewed Israeli excavations. It became clear that the "substantial architectural remains" of Level I should be down-dated by about 50 years (Fantalkin and Tal 2004). In a subsequent study, Fantalkin and Tal (2006) argued for a reorganization of the southern frontier of the Fifth Satrapy by means of a "new" arrangement of the provinces' boundaries, in about 400 B.C.E., once Egypt became independent, as is evident from the monumental building activities in a series of "southern" administrative and military sites. Among the administrative-oriented sites are Lachish, Tell Jemmeh, Tel Seraʿ, Tel Haror, Tel Ḥalif, Beth-zur, Ramat Raḥel, and En Gedi (Tel Goren), whereas the military-oriented sites are Ḥorvat Rogem, Ḥorvat Ritma, Meṣad Naḥal HaRoʿa, Ḥorvat Mesora, Arad, Beer-sheba, Tell el Farah (South), and possibly Kadeshbarnea and En Ḥazeva. It is clear that this new architectural landscape should be seen as a response to a new political reality: Egypt was no longer a part of the Persian Empire or subject to Achaemenid rule. Southern Palestine became one of the frontiers of the Persian Empire (see also Lipschits 2006: 35–38). Thus we suggest that only after this date should one look for established boundaries for the provinces of Yehud or Edom (and consequently of Philistia and Samaria as bordering centers). It seems that before this date the Persian authorities deliberately permitted a certain degree of independence with regard to the resettlement of the area. It is no coincidence that signs of autonomy, such as "municipal coin issues" of Jerusalem (Yehud) and "standardized" Aramaic seal impressions on local storage jar handles do not appear (in all probability) before the fourth century B.C.E.[9] The same holds true for the several thousand Idumean ostraca that allegedly come from the site of Khirbet el-Kom (Lemaire 1996; 2002; 2006; Eph'al and Naveh 1996, all with additional bibliography) and the many dozens that came from Tel Arad (Naveh 1981) and Tel Beer-sheba (Naveh 1973; 1979). Southern Palestine experienced a significant transformation in its political organization: a higher level of direct imperial involvement in the local administration is apparent. What one can observe here is a completely different level of Achaemenid involvement in local affairs that most likely included a fixed arrangement of district boundaries, garrisoning of the frontiers, and, most of all, tight Achaemenid control and investment, as is witnessed by the unprecedented construction at many sites in southern Palestine (Fantalkin and Tal 2006; Lipschits 2006).

Persian domination over Egypt was reestablished for a short period between 343 and 332 B.C.E., prior to the Macedonian conquest (Briant 2002: 685–88, with further references). As a result, the frontier shifted once more, leaving Palestine deep in Achaemenid territory. In this context, for levels attributed to the late Persian periods, it is abandonment rather than destruction that we witness in southern Palestine. Some sites were never resettled after this abandonment (Tel Haror, Tell el Farah, Ḥorvat Rogem, Ḥorvat Ritma, Meṣad Naḥal HaRoʿa, Ḥorvat Mesora), while others were occupied at various times in the Hellenistic period (Lachish, Tell Jemmeh, Tel Seraʿ, Tel Ḥalif, Beth-zur, Ramat Raḥel, En Gedi, Arad, Beer-sheba), a few of which preserved the administrative character of their Achaemenid predecessors (Tell Jemmeh, Beth-zur, Ramat Raḥel, En Gedi—the latter two most likely only during the Hasmonean period). The archaeological evidence allows us to argue that during the early Hellenistic period Judah experienced a smooth shift from its Persian (Achaemenid) past. In the case of Jerusalem, both Yehud coins and Yehud seal impressions are worthy examples.

As clearly demonstrated in this volume (Lipschits and Vanderhooft, pp. 75-94), the Yehud stamp impressions went through a fundamental change in form, style, paleography, and orthography at the end of the

9. On the chronology of the Yehud coins, see Ariel 2002: 287–94, with additional references. On the Aramaic stamped seal impressions, see Ariel and Shoham (2000), where Persian types are differentiated from Hellenistic counterparts on the basis of contexts, comparisons, and paleography. See also Lipschits and Vanderhooft, in this volume, pp. 75–94.

fifth or beginning of the fourth century B.C.E. The new system, pointing to a simplification or consolidation of previous practices, persisted through the first half of the second century, when it underwent additional modification during the Hasmonean period.

The Hellenistic Yehud coins continued to be used in the same late-Persian-period denominations—quarter-obols in the main, weighing 0.18 gram on average. In both the late Persian and early Hellenistic periods, these coins were produced with a high elemental silver value of about 97%, a suitable currency for Temple payments. In other words, these coins were regarded as "pure silver issues" (Ronen 1998: 125 n. 5; Gitler and Lorber 2006: 19–25). In both periods, preference for Paleo-Hebrew over Aramaic is much evident. Early-Hellenistic-period coins demonstrate artistic ability on a similar level as their Persian counterparts, being influenced by monetary centers (Alexandria in the early Hellenistic period and Athens in the late Persian period). Early Hellenistic coins were, in fact, minted until the late 260s, during the reign of Ptolemy II (on their chronology, see Gitler and Lorber 2006: 6–16).

Summary and Further Thoughts

When we compare the number of settlements in late Persian period Judah to the number in late Iron Age Judah, we note a sharp decrease not only in the total number of settlements but also in the amount of administrative-oriented sites. In other words, late Persian period Judah as a political entity may be defined, according to data retrieved from both excavations and surveys, as a rural province with no more than half the number of settlements as the late Iron Age. By contrast, methodical analysis of the late Persian and early Hellenistic sites reveals continuity of the settlement pattern and model from the Persian period in most centralized, rural, and military sites (Tal 2006: 15–163 [and index]). Moreover, there is no distinct increase in the territory of the province between the two periods or in the territory of the city of Jerusalem, which covered, roughly, the Temple Mount and the City of David. Furthermore, the military pattern has only a few examples, and in these there appears to be settlement continuity from Persian times. Thus a change between the two periods cannot be demonstrated. Our conclusion is strengthened by administrative-oriented finds, such as coins and seal impressions. This evidence suggests that the organization of the administrative system was continuous from the last days of the Achaemenids to the early days of the Lagids and Ptolemies.

The general trend of continuity in the settlement pattern and model is not confined only to Judah but is evident in to other regions of Palestine as well. This continuity could imply a similar administrative system in both the late Persian and early Hellenistic periods. However, within this continuity of settlement, we note marginal types of settlement change that occurred for local social, political, and economic reasons. One must emphasize, of course, that the evidence is limited, because short occupational gaps are barely traceable. However, with no finds to contradict this assumption, continuity still remains the logical explanation.

A broader look at the evidence collected here must take into consideration the so-called Hellenization process that the country underwent after the Greco-Macedonian conquest—that is, the alleged absorption of Greek cultural customs, spiritual and material, by the local populations. In the historical and archaeological research of the Hellenistic East, the term *break* is often used as a synonym for the Hellenization process, and *continuity* is often used as a synonym for local traditionalism. The province of Judah, based on our understanding of the archaeological data, retained traditional cultural patterns during the transition between the Persian and Hellenistic periods. The archaeological data provide evidence for the superiority of local traditions over foreign traditions and for continuity of settlements and of political organization. Partial and limited Hellenization did occur at a later stage but was mainly visible in the archaeological record in things related to the royal administration; but this is beyond the purpose of our study (Tal 2006: 323–35).

References

'Amr, K.; Hamdan, K.; Helms, S.; and Mohamadieh, L.
    1996   Archaeological Survey of the East Coast of the Dead Sea Phase 1: Suwayma, az-Zāra and Umm Sidra. *Annual of the Department of Antiquities of Jordan* 40: 429–49.
Ariel, D. T.
    2002   The Coins from the Surveys and Excavations of Caves in the Northern Judean Desert. *'Atiqot* 41/2: 281–304.
Ariel, D. T., and Shoham, Y.
    2000   Locally Stamped Handles and Associated Body Fragments of the Persian and Hellenistic Periods. Pp. 137–71 in *Excavations at the City of David 1978–1985, VI: Inscriptions,* ed. D. T. Ariel. Qedem 41. Jerusalem: Institute of Archaeology, Hebrew University of Jerusalem.

Bahat, D.
   1990   *The Illustrated Atlas of Jerusalem.* Jerusalem: Carta.
Bar-Adon, P.
   1972   The Judaean Desert and Plain of Jericho. Pp. 91–149 in *Judaea, Samaria and the Golan: Archaeological Survey 1967–1968*, ed. M. Kochavi. Jerusalem: Carta. [Hebrew]
Beit-Arieh, I.
   2003   *Map of Malhhata (144).* Archaeological Survey of Israel. Jerusalem: Israel Antiquities Authority.
Betlyon, J. W.
   2005   A People Transformed: Palestine in the Persian Period. *Near Eastern Archaeology* 68: 4–58.
Briant, P.
   2002   *From Cyrus to Alexander: A History of the Persian Empire.* Translated by P. T. Daniels. Winona Lake, IN: Eisenbrauns.
Clamer, C.
   1997   *Fouilles archéologiques de ʿAïn ez-Zâra/Callirrhoé villégiature hérodienne.* Bibliothèque Archéologique et Historique 147. Beirut: Institut Français d'Archéologie du Proche-Orient.
Dadon, M.
   1997   Har Adar. *ʿAtiqot* 32: 63–79. [Hebrew; English abstract, pp. 39*–40*]
Dagan, Y.
   1992   *Map of Lakhish (98).* Archaeological Survey of Israel. Jerusalem: Israel Antiquities Authority.
   2000   *The Settlement in the Judean Shephela in the Second and First Millenium B.C.: A Test-Case of Settlement Processes in a Geographic Region.* Ph.D. Dissertation, Tel Aviv University.
Ephʿal, I., and Naveh, J.
   1996   *Aramaic Ostraca of the Fourth Century B.C. from Idumaea.* Jerusalem: Magnes.
Fantalkin, A., and Tal, O.
   2004   The Persian and Hellenistic Pottery of Level I. Pp. 2174–94 in *The Renewed Archaeological Excavations at Lachish 1973–1994*, ed. D. Ussishkin. Monograph Series of the Institute of Archaeology 21. Tel Aviv: Tel Aviv University.
   2006   Redating Lachish Level I: Identifying Achaemenid Imperial Policy at the Southern Frontier of the Fifth Satrapy. Pp. 167–97 in *Judah and the Judeans in the Persian Period*, ed. O. Lipschits and M. Oeming. Winona Lake, IN: Eisenbrauns.
Finkelstein, I., and Magen, Y., eds.
   1993   *Archaeological Survey of the Hill Country of Benjamin.* Jerusalem: Israel Antiquities Authority.
Fischer, M.; Gichon, M.; and Tal, O.
   2000   *ʿEn Boqeq: Excavations in an Oasis on the Dead Sea, Volume II: The Officina—An Early Roman Building on the Dead Sea Shore.* Mainz: von Zabern.

Geva, H.
  2003   Summary and Discussion of Findings from Areas A, W, and X-2. Pp. 501–52 in *Jewish Quarter Excavations in the Old City of Jerusalem Conducted by Nahman Avigad, 1969–1982, Volume II: The Finds from Areas A, W, and X-2—Final Report*, ed. H. Geva. Jerusalem: Israel Exploration Society.
Gitler, H., and Lorber, C.
  2006   A New Chronology for the Ptolemaic Coins of Judah. *American Journal of Numismatics* n.s. 18: 1–41.
Gophna, R. and Beit-Arieh, I.
  1997   *Map of Lod (80)*. Archaeological Survey of Israel. Jerusalem: Israel Antiquities Authority.
Govrin, Y.
  1991   *Map of Naḥal Yattir (139)*. Archaeological Survey of Israel. Jerusalem: Israel Antiquities Authority.
Hadas, G.
  1992   Stone Anchors from the Dead Sea. *ʿAtiqot* 21: 55–57.
  1993   Where Was the Harbour of ʿEn-Gedi Situated? *Israel Exploration Journal* 43: 45–49.
  1994   *Nine Tombs of the Second Temple Period at ʿEn Gedi*. ʿAtiqot 24. Jerusalem: Israel Antiquities Authority. [Hebrew; English abstract, pp. 1*–8*]
Hirschfeld, Y.
  1985   *Map of Herodium (108/2)*. Archaeological Survey of Israel. Jerusalem: Israel Antiquities Authority.
Honigman, S.
  2003   *The Septuagint and Homeric Scholarship in Alexandria: A Study in the Narrative of the Letter of Aristeas*. London: Routledge.
Kloner, A.
  2000–2003   *Survey of Jerusalem: The Southern Sector; The Northeastern Sector; The Northwestern Sector. Introduction and Indice*s. 3 vols. Archaeological Survey of Israel. Jerusalem: Israel Antiquities Authority.
Kloner, A., and Zissu, B.
  2003   *The Necropolis of Jerusalem in the Second Temple Period*. Jerusalem: Yad Ben Zvi. [Hebrew]
Lemaire, A.
  1996   *Nouvelles inscriptions araméenes d'Idumée au Musée d'Israël*. Transeuphratène Supplement 3. Paris: Gabalda.
  2002   *Nouvelles inscriptions araméenes d'Idumée*, vol. 2: *Collections Moussaïeff, Jeselsohn, Welch et divers*. Transeuphratène Supplement 9. Paris: Gabalda.
  2006   New Aramaic Ostraca from Idumea and Their Historical Interpretation. Pp. 413–56 in *Judah and the Judeans in the Persian Period*, ed. O. Lipschits and M. Oeming. Winona Lake, IN: Eisenbrauns.
Lipschits, O.
  2005   *The Fall and Rise of Jerusalem: Judah under Babylonian Rule*. Winona Lake, IN: Eisenbrauns.

2006 Achaemenid Imperial Policy, Settlement Processes in Palestine, and the Status of Jerusalem in the Middle of the Fifth Century B.C.E. Pp. 19–52 in *Judah and the Judeans in the Persian Period*, ed. O. Lipschits and M. Oeming. Winona Lake, IN: Eisenbrauns.

Lipschits, O., and Vanderhooft, D. S.
forthcoming Jerusalem in the Persian and Hellenistic Periods in Light of the *Yehud* Stamp Impressions. *Eretz-Israel* 28 (Teddy Kolek volume). [Hebrew]

Magen, Y.
2004 Qalandiya: A Second Temple-Period Viticulture and Wine-Manufacturing Agricultural Settlement. Pp. 29–144 in *The Land of Benjamin*, by Y. Magen et al. Judea and Samaria Publication 3. Jerusalem: Israel Antiquities Authority.

Mallon, A.
1924 Voyage d'exploration au sud-est de la Mer Morte. *Biblica* 5: 413–55.

Mazar, B.; Dothan, T.; and Dunayevsky, I.
1966 *En-Gedi: The First and Second Seasons of Excavations 1961–1962.* ʿAtiqot 5. Jerusalem: Israel Antiquities Authority.

Mazar, B., and Dunayevski, I.
1966 The Fourth and Fifth Seasons of Excavations at En-Gedi. *Yediot* 30: 183–94. [Hebrew]

Naveh, J.
1973 The Aramaic Ostraca. Pp. 79–82 in *Beer-Sheba I: Excavations at Tel Beer-Sheba 1969–1971 Seasons*, ed. Y Aharoni. Tel Aviv: Tel Aviv University Institute of Archaeology.
1979 The Aramaic Ostraca from Tel Beer-Sheba (Seasons 1971–1976). *TA* 6: 182–85.
1981 The Aramaic Ostraca from Tel Arad. Pp. 153–76 in *Arad Inscriptions*, by Y. Aharoni. Jerusalem: Bialik Institute / Israel Exploration Society.

Ofer, A.
1986 ʿEn Gedi. *Excavations and Surveys in Israel* 5: 27–28.
1993 *The Highland of Judah during the Biblical Period.* Ph.D. Dissertation, Tel Aviv University.

Patrich, Y.
1994 *Map of Deir Mar Saba (109/7).* Archaeological Survey in Judea and Samaria. Jerusalem: Israel Antiquities Authority.

Redman, C. L., and Watson, P. J.
1970 Systematic Intensive Surface Collecting. *American Antiquity* 35: 279–91.

Reich, R., and Shukron, E.
2007 The Yehud Seal Impressions from the 1995–2005 City of David Excavations. *TA* 34: 59–65.

Ronen, Y.
1998 The Weight Standards of the Judean Coinage in the Late Persian and Early Ptolemaic Period. *Near Eastern Archaeology* 61: 122–26.

Schiffer, M. B.; Sullivan, A. P.; and Klinger, T. C.
 1978   The Design of Archaeological Surveys. *World Archaeology* 10: 1–28.
Stern, E.
 1982   *Material Culture of the Land of the Bible in the Persian Period 538–332 B.C.*
         Warminster: Aris & Phillips / Jerusalem: Israel Exploration Society.
 2001   *Archaeology of the Land of the Bible, Volume II: The Assyrian, Babylonian
         and Persian Periods 732–332 B.C.E.* Anchor Bible Reference Library. New
         York: Doubleday.
 2004   The Distribution of the Yehud Stamp Impressions and the Borders of
         the Yehud Province. P. 14 in *New Directions and Fresh Discoveries in the
         Research of the Yehud Stamp Impressions (Abstracts from a Conference Held
         at Tel Aviv University, January 2004)*, ed. O. Lipschits. Tel Aviv. [Hebrew]
 2007   Stratum IV—The Persian Period. Pp. 193–270 in *En-Gedi Excavations I
         (Final Report 1961–1965)*, by E. Stern. Jerusalem: Israel Exploration So-
         ciety / Institute of Archaeology, Hebrew University of Jerusalem.
Stern, E., and Matskevich, S.
 2007   Stratigraphy of Stratum III. P. 207 in *En-Gedi Excavations I (Final Report
         1961–1965)*, by E. Stern. Jerusalem: Israel Exploration Society / Insti-
         tute of Archaeology, Hebrew University of Jerusalem.
Syon, O.
 1994   Survey Map of Wadi el-Qilṭ. *Excavations and Surveys in Israel* 12: 50–51.
 1997   Survey Map of Qalya. *Excavations and Surveys in Israel* 16: 90–91.
Tal, O.
 2006   *The Archaeology of Hellenistic Palestine: Between Tradition and Renewal.*
         Jerusalem: Bialik Institute. [Hebrew]
Tushingham, A. D.
 1985   *Excavations in Jerusalem 1961–1967, Volume I.* Toronto: Royal Ontario
         Museum.
Ussishkin, D.
 2006   The Borders and *De Facto* Size of Jerusalem in the Persian Period. Pp.
         147–66 in *Judah and the Judeans in the Persian Period*, ed. O. Lipschits and
         M. Oeming. Winona Lake, IN: Eisenbrauns.
Vanderhooft, D. S., and Lipschits, O.
 2007   A New Typology of the *Yehud* Stamp Impressions. *TA* 34: 12–37.
Weiss, D.; Zissu, B.; and Solimany, G.
 2004   *Map of Nes Harim (104)*. Archaeological Survey of Israel. Jerusalem: Is-
         rael Antiquities Authority.
Yogev, O.
 1982   Aderet. *Excavations and Surveys in Israel* 1: 1.

Administration in Fourth-Century B.C.E. Judah in Light of Epigraphy and Numismatics

ANDRÉ LEMAIRE
École Pratique des Hautes Études, The Sorbonne

During the last 20 years, many new Palestinian Aramaic Inscriptions and coins from the fourth century B.C.E. have been published, and several hundred Aramaic ostraca from Idumea are still to be published.[1] This new documentation comes either from Judah itself or from the neighboring provinces, mainly Samaria and Idumea, and sheds some (direct and indirect) light on the organization of the administration of fourth-century B.C.E. Judah.

In addition to my recent overview of the epigraphic documentation published before about 2000 (Lemaire 2002b), I only need to present here the major (recent) numismatic publications of the late Leo Mildenberg (2000a; 2000b; 2000c) and of the late Yaakov Meshorer (2001; cf. Meshorer and Qedar 1999), as well as a few more detailed studies (Gitler 2000; Gerson 2001; Ariel 2002; Elayi and Lemaire 2003; 87–90; Fried 2003; Gitler and Lemaire 2003: 153–55). Of the newly published epigraphic documents, allow me to mention the official publication of the Samaria papyri by Gropp (2001: 1–116), the Persian-period Jerusalem ostraca (J. Naveh in Ariel 2000: 9–12) and seal impressions (Ariel and Shoham in Ariel 2000: 137–94), the papyrus from Ketef Jericho (Eshel and Misgav 2000), and more than 400 Aramaic ostraca from Idumea, probably from the area of Khirbet el-Kom near Idnah (Lemaire 2002a: Porten and Yardeni 2003; 2004; Aḥituv and Yardeni 2004).

All these new publications reveal that the fourth century B.C.E. need no longer be considered a "dark age." Any study of Judah during this period has to take into account the new documentation. This is especially true if we are to understand the nature of the Judean administration. Let me mention here two aspects especially illuminated by epigraphy and numismatics: the officials and the taxes.

---

1. For a preliminary *status quaestionis*, see, for instance, Lemaire 2006; Porten and Yardeni 2006.

Officials

When we study the Judean administration during the Persian period, one of the classic problems is the succession of the governors heading the province. I do not intend to discuss the topic here in detail, because it is somehow connected with the succession of governors in the neighboring province of Samaria (see already Cross 1975), a subject that is presented in detail by H. Eshel in this volume (pp. 223–234), as well as in Jan Dušek's study (2005). I shall mention only the names of the governors attested in epigraphic sources (Kratz 2004: 93–106):

1. "Bagavahya/Bagôhî, governor of Yehud (*pḥt yhwd*)," is attested in the Aramaic petition of Yedoniah and his colleagues in Elephantine papyrus *Cowley* 30, written in November 407 B.C.E. (Cowley 1923: 108–19; Grelot 1972: no. 102,1; Porten and Yardeni 1986: 68–71, A4.7,1) as well as in the reply memorandum (*Cowley* 32,1). These references indicate that he may still have been governor of Yehud/Judah in the early fourth century B.C.E. Identification of this name with the Bagoses of Josephus, *Ant.* 11.297–301 is more uncertain and is still a subject of discussion (e.g., Williamson 1998: 163; 2004: 22, 74–89).

2. "Yehizqiyah, the governor," is written as a Paleo-Hebrew legend on fractional Judean coins (Meshorer 2001: 15–16, no. 22). Unfortunately, these coins (see more below on fractional coins, pp. 57ff.) have been diversely dated from 378–368 to 340–333 (Fried 2003: 67, table 1). It is not impossible that Bagavahya and Yehizqiyah were the only governors of Judah in the pre-Alexandrian, fourth-century period (Fried 2003: 85), but it is far from certain, and other scenarios are possible.

The same kinds of documents also attest to only one name for a high priest in Jerusalem:

1. "Yehôhanan the high priest (*yhwḥnn khnʾ rbʿ*)" is mentioned in the Aramaic petition sent to Bagavahya in 407 (*Cowley* 30,18; 31,17), and he could well have been still in office in the early fourth century B.C.E.

2. "Yôhanan the priest (*ywḥnn hkwhn*)" is mentioned as a Paleo-Hebrew legend on a (so far) unique fractional Judean coin (Meshorer 2001: 14, no. 20). Unfortunately, its date is also approximate and much discussed: from 378–368 to 335–333 (Fried 2003: 67, table 1). It is not impossible that this last Yôhanan is the same as the person mentioned in *Cowley* 30,18; 31,17 (Fried 2003: 85; 2004: 227–31; pace Kratz 2004: 107), but this is far from certain. It is also possible that this Yôhanan/Johanan is the person mentioned in Neh 12:22 and, in this case, his successor could well have been Jaddua (Neh 12:10–11, 22), a priest under Darius (II or III?) and perhaps the last of a complete list (VanderKam

1991). According to the Darius III interpretation (*Ant.* 11.302)[2], Yad-dua/Jaddua could well have also been mentioned by Josephus as welcoming Alexander in "Saphein" (see *Ant.* 11.326), even though this story presents many legendary motifs. According to Josephus (*Ant.* 11.346–47), this Yaddua/Jaddua died before Alexander's death and was succeeded by his son Onias (Ḥoniah).

Besides the governor, the Samaria papyri mention at least two high civil officials of the province, a 'prefect' (*sgn*: WDSP 7,17; 8,12; 10,10) and a 'judge' (*dyn*: WDSP 2,11; 3,10). These officials are also attested at Elephantine (*Cowley* 8,13; 10,13.18–19; *Kraeling* 1,6; 12,28 = Porten and Yardeni 1989: B2.3,13; B3.1,13.18–19; B3.2,6; 12,28). Although some-times misunderstood, the "judges" are also mentioned in an Aramaic document quoted in Ezra 4:9 (Williamson 1985: 54). In Elephantine, the papyri mention the 'judges of the king' (*dyny mlkʾ*; *Cowley* 1,3) and the 'judges of the province' (*dyny mdntʾ*; *Cowley* 16,7; Porten 1968: 48–49; Greenfield 1990: 89–90). When named, most (if not all) of these judges had Persian names (*Cowley* 6,6; 17,6; WDSP 2,11; 3,10). One explanation is that they were appointed as "judges of the king" and had life tenure, but they faced a possible death penalty if they were found guilty of misconduct while in office (Herodotus 5.25; 7.194). The other phrase, "judges of the province," may have indicated local judges, and this type of judge may be alluded to in Ezra 7:25. Actually, one of the pur-poses of Ezra's mission in 398 (Lemaire 1995: 56–61; Becking 2003: 25–26; Fried 2003: 63 n. 2; 2004: 212; Abbadie 2004: 19–23) seems to have been the appointment of new "judges" (Fried 2001; 2004: 217) in charge of the application of the new "law," a judicial synthesis of the various Jewish traditions.

As for the 'prefect' (*sgn*)— the Persepolis tablets often mention this official together with the *gnzbrʾ* 'treasurer' and the *ʾpgnzbrʾ*, 'subtrea-surer' (Bowman 1970: 25–32), but the prefect is always the first listed. In this context, the *segan* was probably the superior of the *ganzabaraʾ* and in charge of the economic administration of the province, primar-ily the collection of taxes (Greenfield 1984–86: 153–54). In the Bible, *segan* is always plural, both in Aramaic (Dan 2:48; 3:2, 27; 6:8) and in Hebrew (Isa 41:25; Jer 51:23, 28, 57; Ezek 23:6, 12, 23; Ezra 9:2; Neh 2:16; 4:8, 13; 5:7, 17; 7:5; 12:40; 13:11). On the basis of Neh 2:16 and Ezek 23:6, 12, 23, one can say that the *segan*s were probably the highest-ranking officials under the governor.

---

2. For a discussion of Josephus, showing that "all the possibilities are open," see Schwartz 1990: 193.

The *gnzbr*> 'treasurer' was probably under the orders of a *segan*. Note that this official is attested in two Aramaic ostraca from Idumea: Arad ostracon no. 37,1 and Tell ʿIra ostracon no. 1 (Lemaire 2002a: 227–28), apparently in connection with the collection of the capitation (see below). This official also appears in Ezra 7:21. The *ganzabara*> was probably responsible for money collecting; another official, mentioned several times in the Aramaic ostraca (GB>, GB">, GBY> 'tax collector': EN 187,2; 199,6; AL 116,2), may have been responsible for collecting taxes in kind. Actually, the verb GBY 'collect' is already well attested in the Egyptian Aramaic custom account C3.7 (AR 2,1 . . . , etc.) in the formula MNDT> ZY GBY MNH WʿBYR ʿL BYT MLK> 'the duty that was collected, counted, and turned over to the storehouse of the king' (Porten and Yardeni 1993: 85ff.; cf. Albertz 2003: 343).

Taxes

Because I have recently published a preliminary study of the various taxes in southern Palestine (Lemaire 2004), I shall not delve into all of the issues here except to stress the contribution that the new documents make to our understanding of several aspects of tax collecting in fourth-century Judah (Heltzer 1989; 1992a; 1992b; 1995; Albertz 2003: 350–56). The Aramaic ostraca from Idumea have revealed that, apparently, the system of tax collecting did not change with the arrival of Alexander. The documentation of the Khirbet el-Kom ostraca is clearly dated to at least ca. 362–312 and apparently to 373–306 B.C.E. (Aḥituv and Yardeni 2004: 8), and we can see that the same formulas were used before and after Alexander. I only note that in the dating formula the rarely used eponym for magistrates changed. Instead of "Artaxerxes," we have "Alexander," "Philippos," "Antigonos," or "Ptolemaios." The tax-collecting practices before and after Alexander probably remained the same in Judah as well.

Of the various taxes collected in Idumea, the Aramaic ostraca most often refer to the collection of agricultural products—most likely a land tax in kind. The various fields were registered in a cadastre of sorts (Briant 1996: 424–26, 960–61, 1056) with a certain quantity of grain (apparently mostly barley but perhaps also wheat). The products themselves were most often registered after the harvest and, besides barley, wheat, and various kinds of flour, there were also oil and, more rarely, wine. Furthermore, the Aramaic ostraca contain a few possible references to livestock farming (cattle, sheep . . .) as in Deut 12:17. This kind of land tax may have been called *>škr* 'tribute' (EN 98,4; 168,2; cf. Ezek

27:15, Ps 72:10); the phrase *'škr šnt* . . . 'tribute of year . . .', is well attested in the Aramaic texts from Persepolis (Bowman 1970: 53–55,
no. 1,1; 2,5; 3,5 . . .); more conjecturally, RB' means 'quarter' (EN 189,3?;
AL 129,2).

Actually, the "quarter" tax seems to be attested in the ancient Near
East toward the turn of the era, while a "fifth" tax is mentioned in Gen
47:24, 26. Furthermore the use of a fraction to indicate a tax can be
compared with the word 'tithe' (*ma'ăśēr*), apparently absent from the
Aramaic ostraca but well attested in the Bible for Persian-period Judah, as we can see from Neh 10:38, 39; 12:44; 13:5, 12, as well as from
Gen 14:20; Lev 27:30–32; Num 18:21–28; Mal 3:8, 10; and 2 Chr 31:5, 12.
As several times specified, this (Judean) tithe had to be paid in kind
and collected from all the products of the earth (Lev 27:30): "grain,
new wine, and oil" (Neh 13:12, 2 Chr 31:5), and the men in charge of
the collections were the priests or, for the most part, the Levites. They
were authorized to collect a tithe of the tithe for themselves (Num
18:21–28, Neh 10:38–39). Moreover, according to Ezra 7:24, the employees of the temple (priests, Levites . . .) were tax exempt (Albertz
2003: 332). In exchange for these advantages, these men had to be
"trustworthy" (Neh 13:3).

On one hand, this land tax apparently continued during the Hellenistic period (Mittwoch 1955). On the other hand, some of the biblical
references to the "tithe" may go back to the First Temple period (especially Deut 12:6–17; 14:23, 28; 26:12), and a Paleo-Hebrew ostracon
from the Ophel excavations in Jerusalem seems to confirm the existence of this "tithe" during this period (Lemaire 1978: 159–60; Renz
1995: 195–96). Furthermore, the "tithe" is also attested in the Egyptian
account of imported and exported duties (Porten and Yardeni 1993:
C3.7: KR 2,19; Fr 2,12; GR 3,2.9 . . .). However, the best epigraphic parallels to the Judean "tithe" in the fourth century B.C.E. are probably
some six Phoenician fiscal seals from the Kingdom of Tyre dating to the
second half of the fourth century B.C.E. (Bordreuil 1988: 302; Lemaire
1991: 140–45; in press).

It is clear that collecting a land tax in kind presupposed a good material infrastructure to stock grain, oil, wine, and so forth in good condition. From the Aramaic ostraca from Idumea, we learn that these
products of the earth were probably put in 'the storeroom of Makkedah' (*msknt mnqdh*; cf. especially L 32!; EN 81; AL 14, 35, 85), where they
were probably stocked in jars (ḤBYH: L 28,3!; EN 57,2; GRB: AL 299). In
AL 259,3, the reading and interpretation of the phrase BYT MLK'
'house of the king', a possible synonym of 'WṢR MLK' 'storehouse of

the king' in Ezra 6:4 and in Egypt (Albertz 2003: 342), remains unfortunately somewhat uncertain.

For Persian-period Judah, the Bible gives some indication that these "tithes" were stocked in special rooms (*liškâ/niškâ*) of the temple in Jerusalem (Neh 12:44, 13:7; 2 Chr 31:11) or in the (house of the) treasury/storeroom(s) (*'ôṣār*, Neh 12:44, 13:12; Mal 3:10). These storerooms/treasuries were apparently part of the Second Temple complex, but we have no indication that the storeroom of Makkedah had any connection with any of the various temples there (Lemaire 2001).

From the Aramaic ostraca from Idumea, we may have some indication of the existence of taxes on craftsmen and on trade, especially on slave trade. The slave trade is also clearly attested by the Samaria papyri, which are mostly contracts for the conveyance of slaves (Gropp et al. 2001: 1–116). Furthermore, the taxation of slave sales is well attested in contemporaneous Babylonia (Stolper 1989). So far, we do not have similar evidence from Judah, but we have to be careful not to use the argument *a silentio,* because the absence of evidence is not evidence of absence! Actually, the existence of Judean slaves is generally attested in the census of Ezra 2:65 and Neh 7:67; and enslavement for debts is clearly mentioned in Nehemiah. Either to eat or to pay the king's tax (*middat hammelek*), people were mortgaging (*'orbîm*) their fields, vineyards, and houses, giving their sons and daughters as pledges for debt, and finally, selling them as slaves (Neh 5:2–5). We may note here that from Aramaic ostracon AL 365, we learn that the guaranteeing or mortgaging ('RB) of silver (KSP), like the drinking of wine, was probably typical of the Canaanite and Aramaic (see also Porten and Greenfield 1969) way of life and was practiced by only one part of the population of Makkedah, apparently not by the North Arabian people living there.

In Neh 5:4, the literally translated sentence 'we borrow money (*lāwînū kesep*) to (pay) the king's tax' presumes that the king's tax is to be paid in silver. As I have already tried to show (Lemaire 2004: 139–40), the Aramaic ostraca from Idumea probably reveal the existence of a poll tax, because a few ostraca manifest a list of personal names followed by "R II" (= '2 qu[arters of a shekel]' = half a shekel = a didrachm) or a multiple of half a shekel. This is particularly the case in ostracon AL 255 (= EN 184) with a list of 8 personal names followed by "R II/2 qu(arters of a shekel)," and of the Arad ostracon no. 41 with a list of the names of 6 people "who brought silver," each one: "R II/2 qu(arters of a shekel)" (Lemaire 2002a: 226–27). They can also be compared with L 5 (Lemaire 2002a: 224), EN 140 (Lemaire 2002a: 225), and

EN 180, while Tel 'Ira ostracon no. 1 probably mentions the 'treasurer' (GZBR') registering the poll tax brought by 2 people (Lemaire 2002a: 227–28).

These lists of persons bringing the same amount of money or a multiple thereof can be compared with the Elephantine papyrus *Cowley* 22, a list of more than 100 people "who gave silver/money to the god Yâhô, each one the sum of 2 shekels" (line 1, probably in 400 B.C.E.; Porten and Yardeni 1993, 224). As for Judah, the poll tax of "2 qu(arters of a shekel)" is probably attested by the Ketef Jericho papyrus (Eshel and Misgav 1988; 2000), which has a list of 23 personal names followed by an amount of money: except for the last one, this amount is "R II" or a multiple of "R II," that is, "1" or "2 sh(ekels)." Though the *editio princeps* proposed interpreting this list as a list of loans (Eshel and Misgav 2000: 22–23), the length of the list and the amounts of money sound very much like the collection of a poll tax of "2 qu(arters of a shekel)" by person, and eventually of 1 or 2 shekels per household (Heltzer 1992a: 174–75; Lemaire 2004: 140). Paleographically, this papyrus should probably be dated to the last third of the fourth century, or around 300 B.C.E., after Alexander's arrival, and the amounts of money indicated on the papyrus can be illustrated by a coin found in the same area, apparently a silver Alexander drachma from the Colophon mint dating to 323–319 B.C.E. (H. Eshel and Zissu 1995: 295; 2000: 11; 2002: 163; E. Eshel 1997: 49; Ariel 2002: 284).

This Judean poll tax probably has a long history, which we can trace, from the Bible, for about five centuries:

1. When the covenant was renewed under the governor, Nehemiah, people explicitly undertook "the duty of giving yearly one-third of a shekel for the service of the house of our God" (Neh 10:33). Although the historicity of this *miṣwâ* has been debated, it is probably historical because it does not correspond precisely to anything in the Pentateuch. Furthermore, the amount of one-third of a shekel does not correspond to the drachma monetary system, the drachma being the equivalent of a "quarter of a shekel," not a "third of a shekel."

2. In Exod 30:13 and 38:26, the poll tax for the sanctuary is "half a shekel by the sacred standard" or "a *beka*, that is, half a shekel." The identification of this tax as a poll tax is well indicated by Exod 30:14–15: "Everyone from twenty years old and upward . . . shall give a contribution to the LORD. The rich man shall give no more than a half shekel, and the poor man shall give no less." Now, because it is more than a "third of a shekel," "half a shekel" fits the drachma system very well because it is the equivalent of 2 drachms or one "didrachm." As

we have just seen, the amount was apparently levied in Judah and Idumea during the fourth century. Because it is higher than the poll tax levied at the time of Nehemiah, one can propose that it was prescribed in Judah by the new "law" introduced by Ezra in 398.

3. This poll tax continued throughout the Second Temple period until the temple's destruction in 70 C.E. as shown, for instance, by Matt 27:4: "[at] Capernaum, the collectors of the didrachm came up to Peter and asked, 'Does your master not pay the didrachm?' 'He does,' said Peter." (On this, see also the rabbinic tradition.)

The institution of this poll tax of a didrachm in fourth-century B.C.E. Judah had two important consequences:

1. It developed the use of coins, and Judah adopted a monetary system connected with the drachma system, as shown by the small Judean coinage of this period (drachma; see below). As shown by the various lists of payment, during the fourth century, the main unit was apparently the "qu(arter of a shekel)" because it was the equivalent of a drachma.

2. This poll tax was collected at the temple of Jerusalem, and thus Jerusalem was at once a kind of "public treasury," "national bank," and "monetary workshop." No wonder the high priest appears also to be a minting authority, as shown by the Paleo-Hebrew legend "Yôhanan, the priest" (see above). More precisely, the role of the Jerusalem temple in the transformation of silver (pieces and coins) into silver smelt that was poured into jars, as described in Herodotus 3.96 (Zournatzi 2000), to be sent as a tribute to the great king, may be alluded to in jar inscription AL 254 and in Zech 11:13 in reference to the *yôṣer* 'caster/founder?' (Torrey 1936; Schaper 1995: 530–31; Briend 2000), while Neh 13:13 and Ezra 8:33–34 probably refer to a small committee of two priests and two Levites in charge of the treasury funded by the collection of silver and taxes in kind (Schaper 1997). The role of the temple as the center of the collection of taxes is apparently connected to the origin of the economic and political power of the Jerusalem high priest during the Hellenistic period.

Several Aramaic ostraca from Idumea mention 'workers/laborers' (PʿLN). Porten and Yardeni (2006: 474–75) have counted no less than 44 ostraca mentioning from 1 to 8 workers, which they thought were "day-laborers in the field" (2006: 477). There are several lists of personal names without any indication of quantities that may have been compiled for the same reason. However, this remains conjectural, because they may also have been written for census purposes and eventually used for collecting poll tax or for the requisition of forced labor.

Whatever the use of these lists of persons was, the registration of a certain number of "workers" was most likely connected with forced labor or *corvée*. Actually, *hălak* (Ezra 4:13, 20; 7:24) was probably the Aramaic word for *corvée* (see *Driver* 8,5; Porten and Yardeni 1986: A6.11, 5), probably corresponding, at least partly, to Akkadian *ilku*. The existence of an imperial *corvée* in the fourth-century Persian Empire seems to be confirmed by the Bagawant leather manuscripts from Afghanistan (probably near Khulmi: Shaked 2003: 1521–22): apparently manuscript 14 reports a problem with building a wall and a moat around a town by a troop (ḤYL), probably a troop of *corvée* people, because they wanted to work in their own fields to harvest them as soon as possible, before the grasshoppers arrived (Shaked 2004: 28–32).

Although so far we have no definite example of *corvée* in fourth-century Judah, we probably have a good example dated to 445 B.C.E., in Nehemiah's organization of the "rebuilding" of the city wall of Jerusalem in 52 days (Neh 6:15; Heltzer 1989: 340). In this context, we see that *corvée* individuals were probably called *sabbāl* in Hebrew (Neh 4:4; cf. 4:11; 1 Kgs 5:29, etc.), while Hebrew *pelek*, probably corresponding to Akkadian *pilku*, indicated a group of *corvée* people, especially when they were working in construction (Demsky 1983; Janzen 2002: 155).

Thanks to the 445 B.C.E. *corvée*, the walls of Jerusalem were rebuilt and the city became a *bîrâ*/*birtā'* (Lemaire and Lozachmeur 1987; 1995). Although one can say that Mizpah (Lemaire 2003: 291–94) was probably the previous seat of the governor from an allusion in Neh 3:7 (Blenkinsopp 1998: 29, 42 n. 48), Jerusalem now became the administrative capital of Judah and the seat of the provincial government again, as well as the seat of the royal treasury/storeroom (cf. Albertz 2003: 339 and 342). Its temple could now become not only the center of the cult but also the center of tax collection. Note that Aramaic was used as the administrative language, as shown by the Aramaic documents quoted in the book of Ezra. Unfortunately, apart from Hananiah, the brother of Nehemiah (Neh 7:2), we do not know the names of the Jerusalem officials with the position of *śar habbîrâ* during the fourth century.

Finally, if we compare the Judean administration with the Idumean administration, we see many similar aspects as well as clear differences:

1. *The role of wine in the land tax.* Under the influence of the North Arabian culture, Idumean local wine seems to have almost disappeared. Wine was apparently imported from Phoenicia, as shown by a few Phoenician jar inscriptions found together with the Aramaic ostraca. In Judah, local wine was apparently still playing an important role, as probably shown by seal impressions on jars (Ariel 2000: 137–94),

especially seal impressions with the abbreviation Ṭ (Delavault and Lemaire 1975; Lemaire 1991: 138 and 140).

2. *The role of the Y*ʜᴡ(ʜ) *Temple.* In Idumea, a province in which
several cultures coexisted, the Makkedah Temple of YHW was probably only significant for the small Yahwist minority. There were temples
of other deities for the Edomite and North Arabian people, and the
storeroom used to collect the local taxes does not seem to have had any
direct connection with this temple. However, in fourth-century Judah,
the Jerusalem temple was apparently the main (and perhaps the only)
temple for the whole local population: it played a capital role in the
collection of taxes. No wonder that its head, the high priest, played an
increasingly important political role.

Excursus:

Ten New Aramaic or Phoenician Inscriptions from Idumea[3]

1. A clear brown sherd from the surface of a jar, measuring 77 × 54 ×
8/9 mm. It is inscribed on the convex side at about –60° in relation to
the potter's wheel traces. The script is very cursive (see especially the
letters D, L, N, and ʿ).

Transcription

   1. QWSḤNN GRGRN XX X III
   2. L*BNY* QWṢY ʿL *YD* HLL

Translation

   1. Qôshanan *shriveled olives* 33
   2. (*Belonging*) to *the sons* of Qôṣî by (*the intermediary*) of Hillel.

Commentary

QWSḤNN is very well attested in this collection of ostraca (at least
19 times; cf. also Porten and Yardeni 2004). GRGRN is also mentioned
quite often (at least 17 times). Its precise meaning remains uncertain
(Lemaire 2002a: 77). What is clear is that whatever it was could be
counted with numerals as high as "53" (EN 163,2).

The phrase BNY QWṢY is also attested several times (EN 92,2; 93,1;
119,2[!]; AL 82,2; 150,1–2; 184,1; 185,2; ISAP 616; cf. BNY QṢY: EN
94,1). At the end of line 2, the cursive D of ʿL YD could also be read as

3. This excursus is a kind of continuation of Lemaire 2006 (with previous bibliography). The first seven inscriptions belong to the collection of M. Welch, and the last three
inscriptions appeared on the antiquities market.

N or W; because of the ligature with the preceding Y, YD could also be confused with a Ṣ. The final name, HLL, is apparently new in these ostraca but is already attested in Nabatean (Negev 1991: 22, no. 303), in North Arabic (Harding 1971: 622), and in Biblical Hebrew (Judg 12:13, 15).

2. A clear brown sherd from the thin surface of a jar, measuring 73 × 63 × 5 mm. It is inscribed on the slightly concave, wavy side at about −5° in relation to the potter's wheel traces. The inscription is well preserved and was written in formal script with many straight strokes and approximate right angles (see especially ', D/R, Ḥ, Y, L, and M; see also the formal shape of the S in lines 1 and 2). This formal script is rare on ostraca but appears quite often on jar inscriptions (see, for instance, AL 336 for the L; AL 344 and 345 for the S and the M).

Transcription

1. QWSYD/R MŠḤ
2. S II Q III R III
3. LŠ'D/R'L

Translation

1. Qôsyad, oil:
2. s(eah) 2, q(ab) 3, qu(arter) 3,
3. (*Belonging*) to Sha'adel.

Commentary

The personal name QWSYD/R is already attested in EN 85,1(!); AL 211,2; and Lemaire 2006: no. 22,1. It could well be an abbreviation of QWSYD' (L 165,1; AL 132,2?). MŠḤ 'oil' is a well-attested product in these ostraca. It was relatively expensive, and the quantities are generally smaller than for wheat or barley. As an abbreviation for RB' 'quarter', R may be used for a qu(arter) of qab of fine flour (EN 6,2), wheat (EN 106,3; 179,1.3), or oil (EN 11,3 with a precise indication of "One-eighth [of qab]," and 115,3, with exactly the same quantity as in our ostracon [see also AY 12,2]. In another context, R may also be an abbreviation for a "qu(arter)" of a shekel (EN 140,2; AL 255,1–8).

In line 3, the long tail of the D/R could indicate a R rather than a D. However, because of the onomastic parallels, D is probably to be preferred. Š'D'L is already attested at least 7 times in these ostraca, especially as a kind of signature (EN 2,4; 6,4; 28,4; 54,4; AL 82,4).

3. A brown sherd from the surface of a jar, measuring 83 × 80 × 9 mm. It is inscribed on the slightly concave, wavy side, approximately

following the potter's wheel traces. The blurred inscription, apparently of two lines, is very difficult to decipher, and any reading is conjectural. At the beginning of line 1, one imagines the word *QWS . . .*, *'Qôs . . .'*, and at the beginning of line 2, *Ḥ S . . . 'w(heat): s(eah). . . .'*

4. A small sherd from the surface of a jar, brown/orange on the outside and gray on the inside, measuring 51 × 55 × 7 mm. It is inscribed on the inside, a practically flat side, approximately following the potter's wheel traces. The erased inscription is very difficult to decipher. Actually, the existence of lines 2 and 3 remains uncertain and, in line 1, one can only propose as a conjecture: *?L-S/Q−W/D/R?*

5. A small brown sherd probably from the surface of a jar, measuring 50 × 65 × 7 mm. It is inscribed on the slightly convex side at about −5/10° in relation to the potter's wheel traces. It could well be part of an inscription on a jar, and the reading of this fragmentary inscription remains very uncertain.

1.　　*?]Q III I[?*
1.　　*?]q(abs) 4[?*

6. A large orange/clear brown triangular sherd from the surface of a jar, measuring 190 × 210 × 11 mm. It is inscribed with 2 lines of cursive Phoenician script following the potter's wheel traces. It is clearly a well-preserved inscription on a jar (first publication: Lemaire and Yardeni 2006: 222–23).

Transcription

1.　　'BD'RŠ
2.　　BN 'BMLK

Translation

1.　　'Abdarish
2.　　son of Abimilk

Commentary

In line 1, the long tail of the third letter could indicate an R but, because of the context and the somewhat different shape of the R (two letters on the left), a reading of D is preferable. The first and last letters are noticeably smaller: ' and Š. 'BD'RŠ 'servant of Arish'—Arish probably being a theonym (Lipiński 1995: 111–12) or a divine appellative (perhaps for Baal?)—is a well-known Punic name (Benz 1972: 149, 276).

In line 2, the second B is smaller than the first one. However, the reading is clearly 'BMLK 'the father is king' which is a name already attested at least once in Punic (Benz 1972: 54). It is also known in Ugaritic (*abimilku* / *ʾbmlk*: Gröndahl 1967: 86, 315, 360) and in the Hebrew Bible, where it is the name of a king of Philistia (Gen 20:21, 26), a king of Shechem (Judges 8–9), and a priest under David (1 Chr 18:16).

Paleographically, this cursive Phoenician script fits well with a date in the fourth century B.C.E., contemporaneous with the Aramaic ostraca. Actually, other Phoenician inscriptions on jars of the same type (orange/clear brown) have already been published (L 203; AL 349, 393, 394; Lemaire 2006: no. 29).

7. A clear brown/slightly orange rectangular sherd from the surface of a jar, measuring 74 × 145 × 9 mm. It contains traces of two cursive Phoenician inscriptions following the potter's wheel traces and is very difficult to decipher:

(A) Close to the top of the sherd and at about –5/10° in relation to the potter's wheel traces, one can see traces of a word that probably has 3 or 4 letters, the last one being perhaps a K.

(B) About the middle of the sherd, one can see faint traces of two lines following the potter's wheel traces. The ink inscription is worn away, however, and its reading remains conjectural.

Tentative transcription

1. ʿBDM/ŠH/G?
2. . [BN] MTN II

Tentative translation

1. ʿAbd . . . .
2. [*son of*] Mattan 2

Commentary

This reading is so uncertain that it suffices to say that we may have a personal name followed by its patronym.

8. An almost flat beige sherd from the surface of a jar, measuring 42 × 55 mm. It is inscribed perpendicularly in relation to the potter's wheel traces and reveals three short lines in good condition.[4]

Transcription

1. BYT ʿZH
2. ʿBDʾD/RH
3. MTRN

---

4. See *Archaeological Center: Ancient Coins and Antiquities Auction* no. 31, 7 April 2004, Tel Aviv: no. 425.

Translation

1. House of ʿUzzah
2. ʿAbduṛah
3. Mataran

Commentary

The script used on this ostracon is very cursive, as shown by the shapes of Z (line 1); D, practically without a head (line 2); and the looped ʾ (line 2) that appears in a few ostraca of this lot and becomes classic in the Nabatean script. The reading, however, is certain.

In line 1, BYT ʿZH 'house of ʿUzzah' is somewhat ambiguous. ʿUzzah may be a personal name. Even though, so far, it does not seem to appear in these ostraca, it could be compared with ʿZY (L 94,3; AL 164,2). Furthermore, ʿUzzah is known in the Bible as a spelling variant of ʿUzzaʾ (2 Sam 6:6–8, 1 Chr 6:14). According to this interpretation, BYT ʿZH could be compared with other syntagms with BYT attested in these ostraca: BYT BʿLRY/WM (EN 87,2; AL 28,2; 29,1–2; 30,2; 32,3; 33,1–2; ISAP 1739), BYT GWR (AL 23,5; EN 196,4?; ISAP 432), BYT YHWKL (EN 106,2; AL 83,2; cf. BYT YʾKL: AL 243,1; Porten and Yardeni 2003), BYT ʿLBʿL (EN 76,1; AL 99,2), BYT QWSY (Lemaire 2006: no. 6,6), and BYT QWṢY (L 28,2; EN 131,2?; AL 94,2; 130,1–2; 244,2), which may also be compared with many similar syntagms with BNY 'sons of'. In this case, the personal names of lines 2 and 3 would probably be the names of two brothers (cf. AL 216,1) or, at least, of two members of the same "house."

ʿUzzah may also be the name of a goddess and BYT ʿZH compared with BYT ʿZʾ in AL 283, where it probably means 'the Temple of ʿUzzaʾ', a well-known North Arabian deity (Macdonald and Nehmé 2000: cols. 967–68; Lemaire 2001: 1157–58), even though it is difficult to pinpoint her individual characteristics. In this case, the personal names of lines 2 and 3 could be names of people connected to the Temple of ʿUzzaʾ, perhaps as a kind of employee(s). Because of the present state of the documentation, it is difficult to choose between these two possibilities for the name ʿUzzah.

In line 2, ʿBDʾD/RH is already attested elsewhere in these ostraca (L 121,1; EN 46,1; 50,2; 55,2; 56,2; 58,2; 59,2; 102,2; 126,1; 179,2; AL 42,2; 210,1; 255,7). One may hesitate in reading the theophorous element as either ʾDH (as proposed by Naveh and Ephʿal) or ʾRH (as I have proposed), because ʾRH could be connected with the meaning 'light'.

Line 3, MṬRN is already attested twice in these ostraca (L 78,3; AL 255,4). It may designate someone born on a rainy day and may be compared with Biblical Hebrew *Māṭrî* (1 Sam 10:21), Safaitic and Sabean MṬRN (Harding 1971: 551), and the Greek transcription *Mataranès* (Wuthnow 1930: 74, 147).

9. A gray/beige sherd from the surface of a jar, in the shape of a parallelogram, measuring 100 × 50 mm. It is inscribed at +5/10° in relation to the potter's wheel traces. The ostracon is complete and contains four lines.[5] Unfortunately, the end of the inscription is partly blurred and worn away.

Transcription

1. *B* XX III III III *LSYWN* ŠNT II
2. ʾ*ḤYW* BR MRṢʿT Š S XX
3. III III Q III II P ʿL *YD* ---?
4. -------- ?

Translation

1. On the 29th of S*iw*an, year 2,
2. ... ? ... son of Marṣeʿat: b(arley) s(eah) 26,
3. q(ab) 5, h(alf), by *(the intermediary of)* ... ? ...
4. ...... ? ......

Commentary

In line 1, the first letter, probably a B, and the letters YW in SYWN remain uncertain.

At the beginning of line 2, the reading ʾ*ḤYW* 'Ahyaw' (Lemaire 2006: no. 1,5?; 6,4) is conjectural. The rest of the line is clear except the ʿ*ayin*, which is difficult to decipher because of the long tail of the N in line 1. MRṢʿT is already attested in these ostraca as a personal name (L 95,1! = EN 159,1; L 109,1; EN 49,1; 172,1; 175,2; AL 174,1; 181,1?).

In line 4, the inscription is worn away: there are traces of 7 or 8 letters; one is tempted to read, conjecturally: ZBDW ḤNN or ZBWD ḤNN.

10. A large brown sherd from the surface of a jar, measuring 138 × 107 mm. It presents the remains of an ink inscription of 7 lines, partly worn away.

Transcription

1. ʾŠL –ʿ---- *S* XX ------ ? *S*
2. *Y/S* XX III –SN------ ? *MRṢ*ʿT

---

5. See *Archaeological: Center, Ancient Coins and Antiquities Auction* no. 33, 4 October 2004, Tel Aviv: no. 290.

3.   *–T* . . . . *ʿZ*ʾ
4.   ----- *?ʿ ḤLT Š S III III* ---ʾ
5.   *–Lʿ X WRQQH ZY TḤ[T] MN KPR*ʾ
6.   *XX X* --- *? ʾŠL Š S XX ?----L*
7.   *? QWSYD/R S XX III II*

Tentative translation

1.   Rope: . . . . *s(eah)* 20 . . . .
2.   *s(eah)* 23 . . . . *Marṣeʿat*
3.   . . . . *ʿUzza*ʾ
4.   . . . . *sandy field: b(arley) s(eah)* 6 . . . .
5.   . . . . *10 and the pool* that *is belo[w] the tomb/village*
6.   *30* . . . . *Rope: b(arley) s(eah)* 20 . . . .
7.   *? Qôsyad: s(eah)* 25

Commentary

In line 1 and probably line 6, we come across ʾŠL, literally, 'rope', a term that is well attested in these ostraca (L 100,3; EN 189,3; 191,1.3; 195,1; AL 258,2.4.7; 262,2.3; 280,3; 309,3?; Lemaire 2006: 24,2). It is probably a surface measure (compare *ašlu* in Akkadian) and may well have been the approximate size of a field.

In line 4, the term ḤLT is also well attested in these ostraca (L 87,1; 188,2[!]; EN 192,6[!]; A 2.8; AL 265,1; 268,4; 269,1; 271,3 [bis]) and probably indicates a kind of field, maybe some kind of sandy field (Lemaire 2002a: 140) or a field in a valley (compare *ḥlḥ* in 4Q205 1 xii 5, 7).

In line 5, the word RQQ/RQQH is already attested in EN 191,4 and AL 283,5, and probably indicates a shallow pool or a swamp/marsh (Lemaire 2002a: 151–52). The phrase ZY TḤT MN 'that is below' is already attested in A1. At the end of line 5, KPR, already attested in AL 283,4.6 and Lemaire 2006: no. 23,3, may mean 'village' or 'tomb' (as in the Nabatean funerary inscriptions).

In line 7: for the name QWSYD/R, see above, no. 2, line 1.

Though this inscription is partly worn away, the presence of ʾŠL, ḤLT, RQQH, and KPRʾ indicates that it was a list of various kinds of fields with quantities of barley, probably a draft for a cadastre (Lemaire 2002a: 133–56, 205–7; 2004: 136–37), and the fixing of the land tax to be paid in kind.

Abbreviations

A	Aḥituv 1999
AL	Lemaire 2002a
AY	Aḥituv and Yardeni 2004
Cowley	Cowley 1923
Driver	Driver 1954
EN	Ephʿal and Naveh 1996
ISAP	Institute for the Study of Aramaic Papyri
Kraeling	Kraeling 1953
L	Lemaire 1996
WDSP	Wadi ed-Daliyeh Samaria Papyri

References

Abbadie, S.
  2004   Esdras, prêtre et scribe. *Transeu* 28: 13–31.
Aḥituv, S.
  1999   An Edomite Ostracon. Pp. 33–38 in *Michael: Historical, Epigraphical and Biblical Studies in Honor of M. Heltzer*, ed. Y. Avishur and R. Deutsch. Tel-Aviv–Jaffa: Archaeological Center Publications.
Aḥituv, S., and Yardeni, A.
  2004   Seventeen Aramaic Texts on Ostraca from Idumea: The Late Persian to the Early Hellenistic Periods. *Maarav* 11: 7–23.
Albertz, R.
  2003   *Geschichte und Theologie: Studien zur Exegese des Alten Testaments und zur Religionsgeschichte Israel.* BZAW 326. Berlin: de Gruyter.
Ariel, D. T. (ed.)
  2000   *Excavations at the City of David 1978–1985 Directed by Yigal Shiloh, VII: Inscriptions.* Qedem 41. Jerusalem: Institute of Archaeology, Hebrew University.
  2002   The Coins from the Surveys and Excavations of Caves in the Northern Judean Desert. *ʿAtiqot* 41: 281–304.
Becking, B.
  2003   Law as Expression of Religion (Ezra 7–10). Pp. 18–31 in *Yahwism after the Exile*, ed. R. Albertz and B. Becking. Studies in Theology and Religion 5. Assen.
Benz, F. L.
  1972   *Personal Names in the Phoenician and Punic Inscriptions.* Studia Pohl 8. Rome: Pontifical Biblical Institute.
Blenkinsopp, J.
  1998   The Judaean Priesthood during the Neo-Babylonian and Achaemenid Periods: A Hypothetical Reconstruction. *CBQ* 60: 25–43.
Bordreuil, P.
  1988   Du Carmel à l'Amanus: Notes de toponymie phénicienne II. Pp. 301–14 in *Géographie historique du Proche-Orient (Syrie, Phénicie, Arabie, grecques, romaines, byzantines)*, ed. P. L. Gatier et al. Paris: CNRS.

Bowman, R.
1970　*Aramaic Ritual Texts from Persepolis.* OIP 91. Chicago.
Briant, P.
1996　*Histoire de l'Empire Perse, de Cyrus à Alexandre.* Paris: Fayard. [ET: *From Cyrus to Alexander: A History of the Persian Empire.* Winona Lake, IN: Eisenbrauns, 2002.]
Briend, J.
2000　Le trésor de Yʜᴡʜ en Jos 6,19.24b. *Transeu* 20: 101–6.
Cowley, A. E.
1923　*Aramaic Papyri of the Fifth Century* ʙ.ᴄ. Oxford: Clarendon. [Repr. Osnabrück: Otto Zeller, 1967.]
Cross, F. M.
1975　A Reconstruction of the Judean Restoration. *JBL* 94: 4–18.
Delavault, B., and Lemaire, A.
1975　La tablette ougaritique RS 16 127 et l'abréviation 'Ṭ' en nord-ouest sémitique. *Sem* 25: 31–41.
Demsky, A.
1983　*Pelekh* in Nehemiah 3. *IEJ* 33: 242–44.
Driver, G. R.
1954　*Aramaic Documents of the Fifth Century* ʙ.ᴄ. Oxford: Clarendon.
Dušek, J.
2005　*Les manuscrits araméens du Wadi Daliyeh et la Samarie vers 450–332 av. J.C.* Thesis École Pratique des Hautes Études, Sciences historiques et philologiques. Paris. [Forthcoming, Leiden: Brill.]
Elayi, J., and Lemaire, A.
2003　Numismatique. *Transeu* 25: 63–105.
Ephʿal, I., and Naveh, J.
1996　*Aramaic Ostraca of the Fourth Century* ʙᴄ *from Idumaea.* Jerusalem: Magnes.
Eshel, E.
1997　Some Paleographic Success Stories. *BAR* 23/2: 48–49.
Eshel, H., and Misgav, H.
1988　A Fourth Century ʙ.ᴄ.ᴇ. Document from Ketef Yericho. *IEJ* 38: 158–76.
2000　Jericho papList of Loans ar. Pp. 21–30 in *Miscellaneous Texts from the Judaean Desert,* ed. J. Charlesworth et al. DJD 38. Oxford: Clarendon.
Eshel, H., and Zissu, B.
1995　Ketef Yericho, 1993. *IEJ* 45: 292–95.
2000　Jericho: Archaeological Introduction. Pp. 3–20 in *Miscellaneous Texts from the Judaean Desert,* ed. J. Charlesworth et al. DJD 38. Oxford: Clarendon.
2002　The Excavations of Cave VIII/9 ('The Large Cave Complex'). *ʿAtiqot* 41: 151–66.
Fried, L. S.
2001　"You Shall Appoint Judges": Ezra's Mission and the Rescript of Artaxerxes. Pp. 63–89 in *Persia and Torah,* ed. J. W. Watts. SBLSymS 17. Atlanta: Society of Bibilical Literature.

2003 A Silver Coin of Yohanan Hakkohen. *Transeu* 26: 65–85.

2004 *The Priest and the Great King: Temple-Palace Relations in the Persian Empire.* Biblical and Judaic Studies from the University of California, San Diego 10. Winona Lake, IN: Eisenbrauns.

Gerson, S. N.

2001 Fractional Coins of Judea and Samaria in the Fourth Century B.C.E. *Near Eastern Archaeology* 64/3: 106–21.

Gitler, H.

2000 Achaemenid Motifs in the Coinage of Ashdod, Ascalon and Gaza from the Fourth Century B.C. *Transeu* 20: 73–87.

Gitler, H., and Lemaire, A.

2003 The Levant. Pp. 151–75 in *A Survey of Numismatic Research 1996–2001.* International Association of Professional Numismatics Special Publication 14. Madrid.

Greenfield, J. C.

1984–86 Notes on the Early Aramaic Lexicon. *Orientalia Suecana* 33–35: 149–55.

1990 The Aramaic Legal Texts of the Achaemenian Period. *Transeu* 3: 85–94.

Grelot, P.

1972 *Documents araméens d'Égypte.* LAPO 5. Paris: Cerf.

Gröndahl, F.

1967 *Die Personennamen der Texte aus Ugarit.* Studia Pohl 1. Rome: Pontifical Biblical Institute.

Gropp, D. M., et al.

2001 *Wadi Daliyeh II: The Samaria Papyri from Wadi Daliyeh and Qumran Cave 4. XXVIII. Miscellanea, Part 2.* DJD 28. Oxford: Clarendon.

Harding G. L.

1971 *An Index and Concordance of Pre-Islamic Arabian Names and Inscriptions.* Toronto: University of Toronto Press.

Heltzer, M.

1989 The Social and Fiscal Reforms of Nehemiah in Judah and the Attitude of the Achaemenid Kings to the Internal Affairs of the Autonomous Provinces. *Appolinaris* 62: 333–54.

1992a Again on Some Problems of the Achaemenid Taxation in the Province of Judah. *Archaeologische Mitteilungen aus Iran* 24: 173–75.

1992b The Provincial Taxation in the Achaemenid Empire and "Forty Shekels of Silver" (Neh 5,15). *Michmanim* 6: 15*–26*.

1995 Zu einem Verwaltungsproblem in den Provinzen der V. Satrapie des Achämenidenreiches. *AoF* 22: 70–72.

Janzen, D.

2002 *Witch-Hunts, Purity and Social Boundaries: The Expulsion of the Foreign Women in Ezra 9-10.* JSOTSup 350. New York: Sheffield Academic Press.

Kraeling, E. G.

1953 *The Brooklyn Museum Aramaic Papyri.* New Haven: Yale University Press.

Kratz, R. G.
2004 *Das Judentum im Zeitalter des Zweiten Tempels.* FAT 42. Tübingen: Mohr Siebeck.
Lemaire, A.
1978 Les ostraca paléo-hébreux des fouilles de l'Ophel. *Levant* 10: 156–61.
1991 Le royaume de Tyr dans la seconde moitié du IVe siècle av. J.-C. Pp. 131–50 in vol. 1 of *Atti del II Congresso Internazionale di Studi Fenici e Punici.* Rome: Consiglio Nazionale delle richerche.
1995 La fin de la première période perse en Égypte et la chronologie judéenne vers 400 av. J.-C. *Transeu* 9: 51–62.
1996 *Nouvelles inscriptions araméennes d'Idumée au musée d'Israël.* Transeu Supplement 3. Paris: Gabalda.
2001 Les religions du sud de la Palestine au IVe siècle av. J.-C. d'après les ostraca araméens d'Idumée. *CRAIBL* 1141–58.
2002a *Nouvelles inscriptions araméennes d'Idumée II: Collections Moussaieff, Jeselsohn, Welch et divers.* Transeu Supplement 9. Paris: Gabalda.
2002b Das Achämenidisch Juda und seine Nachbarn im Lichte der Epigraphie. Pp. 210–30 in *Religions und Religionskontakte im Zeitalter der Achämeniden,* ed. R. Kratz. Gütersloh: Chr. Kraiser.
2003 Nabonidus in Arabia and Judah in the Neo-Babylonian Period. Pp. 285–98 in *Judah and the Judeans in the Neo-Babylonian Period,* ed. O. Lipschits and J. Blenkinsopp. Winona Lake, IN: Eisenbrauns.
2004 Taxes et impôts dans le sud de la Palestine (IVe s. av. J.-C.). *Transeu* 28: 133–42.
2006 New Aramaic Ostraca from Idumea and Their Historical Interpretation. Pp. 413–56 in *Judah and the Judeans in the Persian Period,* ed. O. Lipschits and M. Oeming. Winona Lake, IN: Eisenbrauns.
In press Nouveau sceau fiscal phénicien et la Galilée au IVe s. av. J.-C. In *Adam Zertal Volume,* ed. M. Heltzer and D. Eitam. Haifa.
Lemaire, A., and Lozachmeur, H.
1987 *Bīrāh/birtā'* en araméen. *Syria* 64: 261–66.
1995 La *birta* en Méditerranée orientale. *Sem* 43–44: 77–78.
Lemaire, A., and Yardeni, A.
2006 New Hebrew Ostraca from the Shephelah. Pp. 195–223 in *Biblical Hebrew in Its Northwest Semitic Setting: Typological and Historical Perspectives,* ed. S. E. Fassberg and A. Hurvitz. Jerusalem: Magnes / Winona Lake, IN: Eisenbrauns.
Lipiński, E.
1995 *Dieux et déesses de l'univers phénicien et punique.* OLA 64. Leuven: Peeters.
Macdonald, M. A., and Nehme, L.
2000 ʿUzzâ. Cols. 967–68 in vol. 10 of *Encyclopaedia of Islam.* Leiden: Brill.
Meshorer, Y.
2001 *A Treasury of Jewish Coins.* Jerusalem: Yad Ben-Zvi / Nyack, NY: Amphora.

Meshorer, Y., and Qedar, S.
1999 *Samarian Coinage*. Numismatic Studies and Researches 9. Jerusalem: Israel Numismatic Society.
Mildenberg, L.
2000a Über das Kleingeld des 4. Kahrhunderts im Perserreich. Pp. 137–57 in *Pour Denise: Divertissements numismatiques*, ed. S. M. Burner and C. Arnold-Biuchi. Bern.
2000b On Fractional Silver Issues in Palestine. *Transeu* 20: 89–100.
2000c Über die Munzbildnisse in Palästina und Nordwest Arabien zur Perserzeit. Pp. 376–91 in *Images as Media: Sources for the Cultural History of the Near East and Eastern Mediterranean (First Millennium* B.C.E.*)*, ed. C. Uehlinger. OBO 175. Fribourg: Universitätsverlag / Göttingen: Vandenhoeck & Ruprecht.
Mittwoch, A.
1955 Tribute and Land-Tax in Seleucid Judaea. *Bib* 36: 352–61.
Negev, A.
1991 *Personal Names in the Nabatean Realm*. Qedem 32. Jerusalem: Institute of Archaeology, Hebrew University.
Porten, B.
1968 *Archives from Elephantine: The Life of an Ancient Jewish Military Colony*. Berkeley: University of California Press.
Porten, B., and Greenfield, J. C.
1969 The Guarantor in Elephantine-Syene. *JAOS* 89: 153–57.
Porten, B., and Yardeni, A.
1986 *Textbook of Aramaic Documents from Ancient Egypt 1: Letters*. Jerusalem: Hebrew University.
1989 *Textbook of Aramaic Documents from Ancient Egypt 2: Contracts*. Jerusalem: Hebrew University.
1993 *Textbook of Aramaic Documents from Ancient Egypt 3. Literature, Accounts, Lists*. Jerusalem: Hebrew University.
2003 In Preparation of a Corpus of Aramaic Ostraca from the Land of Israel: The House of Yehokal. Pp. 207–23 in *Shlomo: Studies in Epigraphy, Iconography, History and Archaeology in Honor of Shlomo Moussaieff*, ed. R. Deutsch. Tel Aviv–Jaffa: Archaeological Center.
2004 On Problems of Identity and Chronology in the Idumaean Ostraca. Pp. 161*–83* in *Teshûrôt LaAvishur: Studies in the Bible and the Ancient Near East in Hebrew and Semitic Languages*, ed. M. Heltzer and M. Malul. Tel Aviv–Jaffa: Archaeological Center.
2006 Social, Economic, and Onomastic Issues in the Aramaic Ostraca of the Fourth Century B.C.E. Pp. 457–88 in *Judah and the Judeans in the Persian Period*, ed. O. Lipschits and M. Oeming. Winona Lake, IN: Eisenbrauns.
Renz, J.
1995 *Die althebräischen Inschriften 1*. Handbuch der althebräischen Epigraphik 1. Darmstadt: Wissenschaftliche Buchgesellschaft.

Schaper, J.
  1995   The Jerusalem Temple as an Instrument of the Achaemenid Fiscal Administration. *VT* 45: 528–49.
  1997   The Temple Treasury Committee in the Time of Nehemiah and Ezra. *VT* 47: 200–206.
Schwartz, D. R.
  1990   On Some Papyri and Josephus' Sources and Chronology for the Persian Period. *JSJ* 21: 175–99.
Shaked, S.
  2003   De Khulmi à Nikhšapaya: Les données des nouveaux documents araméens de Bactres sur la toponymie de la région (IVe siècle av. n. è.). *CRAIBL* 1517–35.
  2004   *Le satrape de Bactriane et son gouverneur: Documents araméens du IVe s. avant notre ère provenant de Bactriane.* Persika 4. Paris: de Boccard.
Stolper, M. W.
  1989   Registration and Taxation of Slave Sales in Achaemenid Babylonia. *ZA* 79: 80–101.
Torrey, C. C.
  1936   The Foundry of the Second Temple at Jerusalem. *JBL* 55: 247–60.
VanderKam, J. C.
  1991   Jewish High Priests of the Persian Period: Is the List Complete? Pp. 67–91 in *Priesthood and Cult in Ancient Israel*, ed. G. A. Anderson and S. M. Olyan. JSOTSup 125. Sheffield: JSOT Press.
Williamson, H. G. M.
  1985   *Ezra, Nehemiah.* WBC 16. Waco, TX: Word.
  1998   Judah and the Jews. Pp. 145–63 in *Studies in Persian History: Essays in Memory of David M. Lewis*, ed. M. Brosius and A. Kuhrt. Achaemenid History 11. Leiden: Brill.
  2004   *Studies in Persian Period History and Historiography.* FAT 38. Tübingen: Mohr Siebeck.
Wuthnow, H.
  1930   *Die semitischen Menschennamen in griechischen Inschriften und Papyri des Vorderen Orients.* Leipzig.
Zournatzi, A.
  2000   The Processing of Gold and Silver Tax in the Achaemenid Empire: Herodotus 3.96.2 and the Archaeological Realities. *Studia Iranica* 29: 241–71.

Yehud Stamp Impressions
in the Fourth Century B.C.E.:
A Time of Administrative Consolidation?

ODED LIPSCHITS and DAVID VANDERHOOFT

Tel Aviv University and Boston College

The Yehud Stamp Impressions (YSI) represent one of the most important sources of administrative data for Judah (Yehud) in the Persian and early Hellenistic periods. These impressions were most often stamped on the handles of various types of jars, in a few cases on the bodies of jars. In an ongoing project by the two authors to collect and publish a comprehensive catalog of these stamp impressions, we offer here new evidence pertaining to the administration of Yehud in the Persian and early Hellenistic periods.

Distribution

We have examined or recorded 570 stamp impressions of different types; about 150 of these were not previously published. However, 38 stamp impressions that were originally published as YSIs have proved upon closer inspection not to belong to the corpus, so we are now dealing with a total of 532 seal impressions.[1] At Ramat Raḥel, 4 km south of the City of David, 257 YSIs were found (48% of the total number). In the area of the ancient city of Jerusalem, 162 YSIs (30% of the total) were found; of these, 135 are from the City of David and the area of the Ophel (25% of the total), and 27 YSIs (5% of the total, all of them very late types) were discovered in various areas of the Western Hill and its immediate vicinity. Outside these two main centers of YSIs, 79 were found in six secondary centers (15% of the total number): 20 were found in Tell en-Naṣbeh, 16 in Nebi Samwil, 8 in Gezer, 10 in En-gedi, 7 in Rogem Gannim, and 18 in Jericho. An additional 21 YSIs (4% of the

---

1. This number includes nearly all known stamp impressions, including those recently published in *TA* 34/1 (2007).

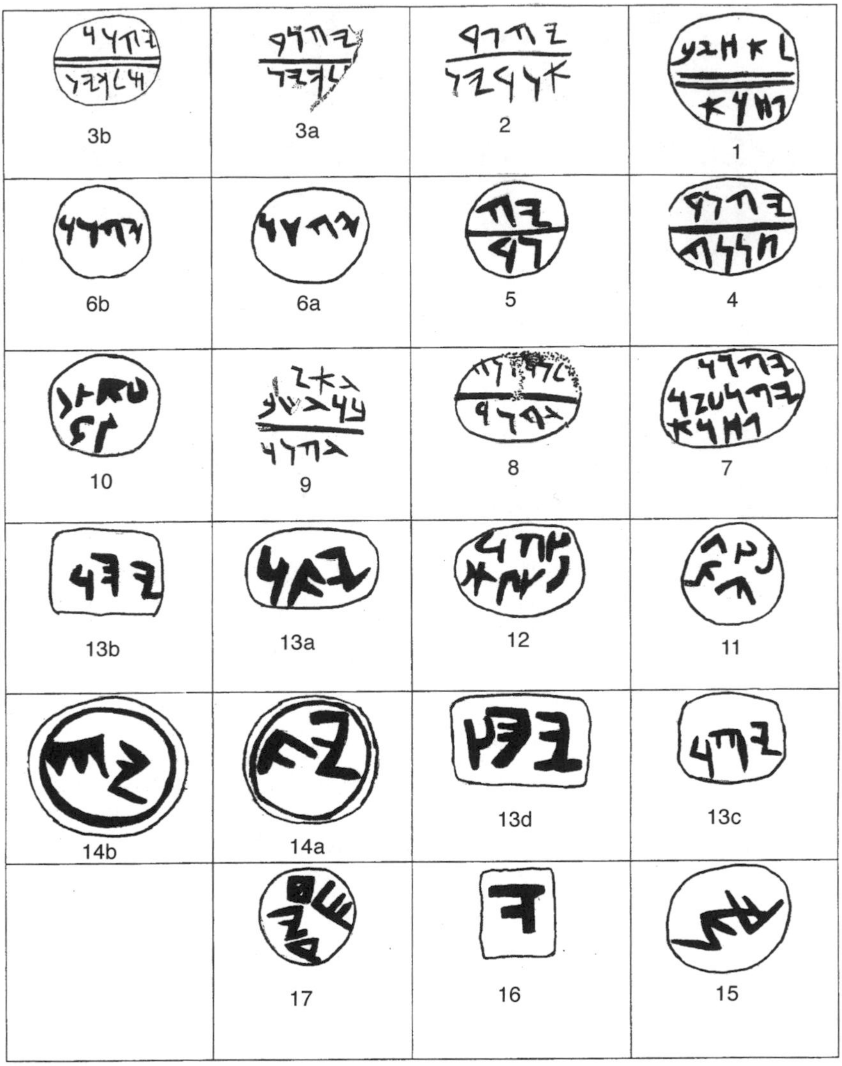

Fig. 1. Yehud stamp impressions: Types 1–17.

total number) were found in small sites (with 1 or 2 in each site, except for Khirbet Nisya, where 3 YSIs were found). The source of 13 YSIs (2.5% of the total number) is not known.

These distribution data show that 80% of the YSIs were found in Ramat Raḥel and Jerusalem. About 95% of the entire corpus was found

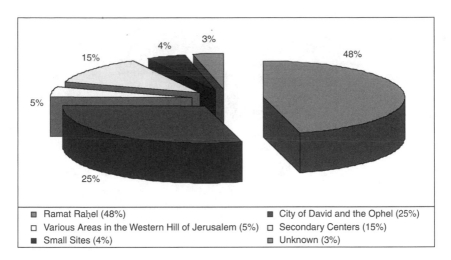

Fig. 2. Sites where YSIs were found.

in a small circle between Tell en-Naṣbeh in the region of Benjamin and Ramat Raḥel. Only about 5% were found outside this circle, including at Gezer and Tel Harasim in the west, and En-gedi and Jericho in the east. A few were found farther afield, including 1 each in Kadesh-barnea, Tel Nimrin (east of the Jordan), and in the city of Babylon.

Overview of Typology

Content, paleographic typology, form, and stratigraphic data permit grouping of the large number of YSI types into three chronologically defined groups: early, middle, and late (Vanderhooft and Lipschits 2007). Within these groups, there are 12 early types (fig. 1: types 1–12), 3 middle types (fig. 1: types 13–15), and 2 late types (fig. 1: types 16–17). We date the 12 early types to the late sixth and fifth centuries B.C.E. In total, 108 YSIs belong to the "early group," about 20% of the total number of YSIs. Three types, with at least 16 subtypes (that is, different seals with the same readings), belong to the middle group, dated to the fourth–third centuries B.C.E. In total, 283 YSIs belong to this "middle group," 53% of the total number of YSIs. Two types (with many different subtypes) were defined as late types, dated to the second century B.C.E. In total, 141 YSIs belong to the "late group," 27% of the total number of YSIs.

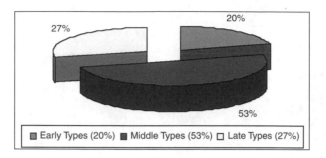

27%

20%

53%

☐ Early Types (20%) ■ Middle Types (53%) ☐ Late Types (27%)

Fig. 3. Relative dates of YSI types.

Early Types

The main characteristic of the early group is the diversity among the different types. Many of the different stamp types belonging to the early group are known from only a few impressions each.[2] It is interesting to note that of the 6 early types from which we have only a few exemplars each—types 2, 3, 5, 8, 9, and 11 have yielded 15 YSIs in total—only 3 were found in the City of David and one in Ramat Raḥel. These types may have been used in an ad hoc manner in very local contexts, perhaps for occasional purposes. From the 6 types that produced slightly more exemplars—types 1, 4, 6, 7, 10, and 12 (see fig. 1) have yielded 93 YSIs in total—68 were found in Ramat Raḥel, 14 in the City of David, and only 11 in other sites. These types may represent formal provincial seals, and their use on different types of jars could mean that the seals were used over a longer period of time.

Several overlapping criteria place these stamp impressions in the early group of YSIs:[3] all of the seals were incised in lapidary Aramaic; only a few examples of cursive Aramaic letter forms appear; and no Paleo-Hebrew letter forms appear. Paleo-Hebrew letter forms begin to appear in coins and epigraphs of the fourth century.[4] The absence of Paleo-Hebrew forms from the early types is, therefore, an important chronological criterion. Also, 9 of the 12 early types contain the geographical name יהוד, always spelled fully with the *waw* as a *mater lectionis*, never as יהד, which is more common in later stamps and in Yehud

---

2. Four of the types are known from only 1 or 2 exemplars; 4 types are known from between 4 and 7 exemplars; 2 types have 11 or 13 exemplars, while 1 type has 16 exemplars. Only 1 type has produced a significant number (42 exemplars).

3. A fuller presentation and analysis of these early stamp types will appear in the completed catalog. See also Vanderhooft and Lipschits 2007.

4. Naveh (1998: 91 n. 5) has remarked that the script should more properly be called "Neo-Hebrew," but we retain the traditional terminology for the sake of simplicity.

coins. The spelling יהוד does appear occasionally in later stamps (as it does on coins), but in those stamps the script is Paleo-Hebrew. The full spelling יהוד in Aramaic script appears to be an early characteristic.[5]

Three of the early types also contain the title פחוא 'governor'.[6] Two of the governors are named: אחיב 'Aḥiab[7] and יהועזר Yehoʿezer.[8] No personal names appear in the middle or late groups of YSIs, which possess Paleo-Hebrew script and the defective form of the province name, יהד, or its abbreviated form, יה. In fact, 9 of the early stamp types contain personal names (in one case also a patronym). This phenomenon resembles the "private" seal impressions from the end of the Iron Age, but it disappears in the later groups of YSIs. Among the early stamps, 7 possess line dividers between the fields of text, most commonly one line but occasionally two. This feature, especially the double line divider, is also in continuity with late Iron Age sealing practices and is also attested among the so-called *mwṣh* stamp impressions. The *mwṣh* impressions are likewise incised in lapidary Aramaic, while one *mwṣh* type has a single-line field divider between two rows of letters. All of these characteristics argue in favor of assigning the stamps of the early group to the sixth–fifth centuries B.C.E.

Secure stratigraphic information for YSIs in this early group remains difficult to ascertain. Although almost all known YSIs come from licit excavations, few sites possess Persian-period stratigraphy sufficiently precise to do more than assign the stamps to the general era (Stern 2001: 549). The best data come from the City of David exemplars, where excavators have securely dated numerous stamps to stratum 9 from the Persian period. Some of the early types were found in an early phase of stratum 9: a יהוד חננה stamp was discovered in an

---

5. The use of the Aramaic toponym, Yehûd, for the former Kingdom of Judah is an Achaemenid period innovation. Naveh (1996), among others, explained the origin of the Aramaic toponym as originating secondarily from the gentilic by analogy. Of course, biblical sources in the Persian era also refer in Aramaic to the former kingdom as יהוד מדינתא, 'the province of Judah' (Ezra 5:8). Use of the Aramaic toponym could conceivably date from the period of the Neo-Babylonian dynasty after the fall of the Kingdom of Judah (586–539 B.C.E.), but other evidence argues for the emergence of the Aramaic form of the toponym as a designation for the distinct province of Judah in the Persian era.

6. This office was not established before the demise of the Judean kingdom; it never appears in Iron Age Hebrew seals or epigraphs. It was probably introduced as an imperially sanctioned office in the Achaemenid era (Petit 1988). There is as yet no clear philological evidence that the Babylonians installed governors of this sort in the southern Levant (Vanderhooft 1999; Lipschits 1998; 2005).

7. The reading אחיב is new (Vanderhooft and Lipschits 2007: 14–16).

8. We have not included Elnathan among the governors or in the corpus, primarily because the bullae and seals associated with this name came from unprovenanced sources (Avigad 1976: 6).

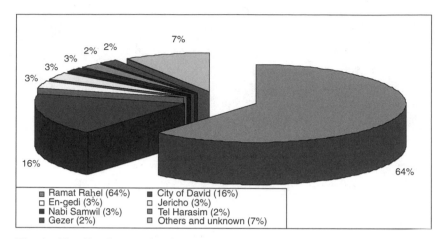

Fig. 4. Site distribution for the early group.

early subphase together with a *mwṣh* stamp impression; a לאחיב פחוא stamp was in a later subphase. The early types, in any case, were found under the YSIs of the later types, which were excavated in the second or the third phases of stratum 9 (DeGroot and Ariel 2004). More important is the total absence of the early and middle groups from the second-century stratum in the Western Hill of Jerusalem, where only YSIs from the late types were found, together with well-known pottery from this period and 10 *yršlm* seal impressions (Geva 2004; 2007). An identical second-century date for the late types is now supported by the excavations of Zubah (Finkielsztejn and Gibson 2007). We can therefore conclude that the early and late groups do not overlap, and we can date the late group fairly securely to the second century. Thus, considerable time elapsed between the first and third groups, and it is to the interval between them, roughly the fourth and third centuries, that we must assign the middle group.

In sum, the early stamp types show considerable uniformity in their Aramaic lapidary script, significant diversity in content, and relatively restricted distribution. They most often specify the toponym, Yehud, and either the personal name or the official title, "governor," of the seals' owners.

Middle Types

The profusion of types and subtypes characteristic of the early group disappears in the middle group. Three main types of stamps now occur, types 13–15 (see fig. 1). These stamps were produced from seals reading simply יהד (in three letters, type 13) or from seals with the abbreviated writing יה (in two letters, types 14–15). Among the 246 seal impressions belonging to the middle types—more than 50% of the total YSI corpus—personal names no longer appear. The toponym is now uniformly spelled יהד, or it is abbreviated to יה. No official titles appear in any stamps from the middle group (or among later stamps). Furthermore, new shapes appear among the stamp types: many of the יהד stamps come from rectangular seals with rounded corners or from square seals, while the יה stamps come from round seals set in a ring. The early types were uniformly round or oval stamp seals.

Our relative chronology for the YSIs is not precise enough to associate the changes in form and content between the early and middle types with a single historical catalyst. How can we be sure that our proposed middle types really do belong to the fourth and third centuries, as we suggested above? Paleography of the middle types is helpful in this respect and shows several important changes, even though the number of letters relevant for paleographic analysis is small. The letter *he* in particular deviates substantially from the lapidary Aramaic model that prevailed in the early types. Now, *he* often appears with three bars joining the main stroke, and its orientation varies widely. Occasionally the *he* is inscribed in reverse and sometimes upside down. This "three-bar" *he*, in any case, is not Aramaic and appears to reflect Paleo-Hebrew influence (Vanderhooft and Lipschits 2007). This type of *he* also appears on pre-Macedonian יהד coins that have Paleo-Hebrew legends (Meshorer 2001: nos. 2, 3 [retrograde], 4 [retrograde], 5 [retrograde], 6, 9, 10 [retrograde], 13, 15, 16, 17 [retrograde], and 18 [retrograde]). These fourth-century coins with Paleo-Hebrew script may have provided the model for this style of *he* in the יהד stamps. The same may be true for the *yod* in several of the יהד stamp subtypes. If this is correct, the evidence supports a fourth-century date for our middle יהד stamp types.

Other comparative material for our middle stamp types includes coins from Yehud and Samaria and the so-called Philisto-Arabian coins. The famous large-denomination drachma with a male figure seated above a winged wheel possesses the legend יהד.[9] Paleography, as Cross argued (1969: 142), indicates that the lapidary Aramaic script of the coin is characteristic of the fifth century and later. According to

---

9. The most recent full catalog of the Yehud coins was published by Meshorer (2001); the coin in question is no. 1 (pp. 2–6).

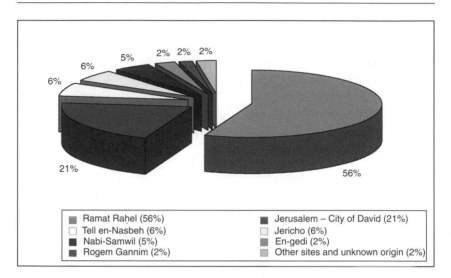

Fig. 5. Site distribution for the middle group.

Mildenberg (1979), stylistic indications date the coin more precisely to the period between about 380 and 360 B.C.E. Its date in the late Persian period is, in any case, well established (Barag 1986–87: 6; Naveh 1998: 92). The orthography, without *waw*, is the same as the YSIs of our proposed middle group. In the corpus of יהד coins, Meshorer dates the coins in which the toponym is spelled without the *mater lectionis*, whether in Aramaic or Paleo-Hebrew script, to the pre-Macedonian era. Coins with the toponym spelled יהוד or יהודה in Paleo-Hebrew characters are later. Thus, the יהד stamp impressions of our middle group find a fairly good parallel in this coin.

A second important comparative example is another fourth-century Yehud coin, a silver obol (Meshorer 2001: no. 12, p. 198, and pl. 2:12; cf. Meshorer 1990–91: pl. 17:2), which preserves a legend that is very close to our יהד subtype 13*a* (Vanderhooft and Lipschits 2007). The coin legend reads יהד in retrograde Aramaic script. The *yod* on the coin could be Aramaic or Paleo-Hebrew. The letter *he* is, however, close to the *he* on the יהד subtype *a*. Meanwhile, the *dalet* of the coin is the usual open Aramaic lapidary form.

Another Yehud silver obol from the fourth century bears an inscription that also deserves mention as an excellent parallel to our יהד subtype 13*f* (Vanderhooft and Lipschits 2007). Meshorer (2001: no. 9, pl. 1: 9) suggested that this coin was inscribed in Paleo-Hebrew, but close analysis reveals that, although the *he* is Paleo-Hebrew, the *dalet* is a reverse Aramaic exemplar with an open head formed with two lines, while the *yod* is not determinative. The form and stance of the letters on this coin parallel almost exactly the script of our יהד stamp subtype 13*f* (Vanderhooft and Lipschits 2007). Both have an upright *yod* (with an admittedly uncharacteristic breakthrough of the foot in the stamp); the *he* is the three-bar Paleo-Hebrew type, while the *dalet* is a reverse Aramaic type with open head. The fact that both the coin and the stamp have the Paleo-Hebrew *he* and the reverse Aramaic *dalet* leads to the suspicion that the seal and coin engravers shared a very similar model. These fourth-century Yehud coins in particular provide, therefore, close orthographic and paleographical parallels for our יהד sub-types. These parallels support the proposed fourth–third-century date for the YSIs of our middle type.

The second type of YSI in our middle group has only the abbreviated יה. The phenomenon of abbreviated spellings of geographical names, such as יה, proliferated in the regional mints of the southern Levant beginning in the fourth century. Several different coin issues from Judah and nearby regions have abbreviated spellings of toponyms. Examples include: יד from Judah (Meshorer 1982: pl. 56:1); ש, שמר, שן, שם, from Samaria (Meshorer and Qedar 1999: 17); אן from Ashkelon; and עז from Gaza (Meshorer 1982: pl. 56:1; Meshorer and Qedar 1991: 14). The phenomenon in the stamps thus has a parallel development in the fourth-century coins, giving additional evidence to support a fourth- and perhaps third-century date for the middle YSI types.

One of the יה stamp types, 15, is newly deciphered by us, based on the finds from Ramat Raḥel. It is formed by an overlapping *yod* and *he*. The letters of the seal were not incised in the correct orientation or stance. In the impressions, the *yod* appears on the left and the *he* to its right. The *yod* is also retrograde, which means that the engraver inscribed the *yod* in positive, instead of negative. If this interpretation is correct, stamps of this type may represent a transitional type between *yh* stamps and the later, so-called *yh*-ligature stamps (type 16). Reliable stratigraphical information is lacking for this type, but if we are correct to see it as transitional between the יה stamps of the middle group and type 16 (Vanderhooft and Lipschits 2007), then a fourth- or third-century date seems suitable.

If the proposed date for the middle group in the fourth–third centuries B.C.E. is correct, it argues for administrative continuity between the Persian and the Macedonian-Ptolemaic periods. Similar continuity can be seen in the use of local coinage in Judah, as well as in Samaria (Meshorer 2001: 11, 22). It may also be noted that the prominence of Jerusalem increases somewhat among YSIs from the middle group. As against 16% of YSIs from Jerusalem in the early group, now 21% come from Jerusalem, all of them from the City of David and none from the Western Hill. Meanwhile, the number of stamps excavated at Ramat Raḥel decreases from 64% in the early group to 56% of the middle types, although Ramat Raḥel remains the best represented administrative center. Tell en-Nasbeh and Nabi Samwil possibly served as secondary centers, connected perhaps to administrative activity about which no further information can be recovered.[10]

Although there are at least 9 subtypes (that is, distinct seals) among the type 13 יהד stamps and several subtypes among the type 14 יה stamps, the question remains: what does the relatively rapid consolidation of types mean for reconstructing the administrative system of Yehud in the fourth century?

Administrative Consolidation in the Fourth Century B.C.E.

Before we can answer this question, we may restate the main conclusions that derive from the above discussion about the early and middle groups of Yehud stamp impressions:

1. Clear continuity exists in form, style, content, paleography, and other characteristics between seals and stamp impressions of the late Iron Age and the early group of Yehud stamp impressions; the early group dates to the late sixth and fifth centuries B.C.E.
2. A fundamental change occurs between this early group and the second, or middle, group of YSIs. Differences include form, style, paleography and, importantly, the orthography of the province name, now in three letters, including Paleo-Hebrew letter forms. If our dating is right, the changes between the early and middle groups occurred around the end of the fifth or the beginning of the fourth century B.C.E.
3. Continuity existed in the provincial administration between the late Persian period and the Macedonian and Ptolemaic periods.

---

10. These finds indicate that Tell en-Naṣbeh did continue to function as an administrative center throughout the Persian period, even if it was eclipsed in importance by Jerusalem and Ramat Raḥel.

The characteristics of the second group of YSIs, and even the places where those stamped handles were found, demonstrate that during the fourth and third centuries a slow and gradual development occurred in Judah, during which no fundamental change can be detected. The same phenomenon of continuity can be detected in the coins of this period.

4. The next change occurs in the late stamp types, probably during the second century B.C.E. Again, the differences include form, style, paleography and, importantly, the orthography of the province name, now with *yod* and *he* written together as a digraph (type 16) or in three letters plus *ṭet* (type 17), all in Paleo-Hebrew. These changes may pertain specifically to the Hasmonean period, during which other administrative changes also took place.

The first point has been much discussed in recent years (see the summary in Lipschits 2005: 185–271) and is beyond the chronological horizons of the current volume. The fourth point has not received sufficient attention and deserves a separate discussion. However, it is also beyond the chronological horizons of the current volume.[11] Scholars have discussed the third point as well, especially in connection with the coins (Meshorer 2001: 22); it argues in favor of administrative continuity after the end of the Persian period into the Hellenistic. In what follows, however, we wish to focus on the second point in order to outline and assess administrative changes that accompanied the fundamental shift between the first and second groups of the Yehud stamp impressions around the end of the fifth or the beginning of the fourth centuries B.C.E.

In the foregoing discussion, we emphasized six fundamental changes between the early and middle types:

1. The disappearance of the profusion of types and subtypes characteristic of the early group and the emergence of two main stamp types, יהד and יה, each with different subtypes (that is, different seals cut according to two main "models").

2. A change in the way the name of the province was written: from יהוד, always spelled in Aramaic characters, to the defective יהד and יה in the second group.

3. Unlike in the early group, in which personal names appear in 9 of the 12 types, personal names no longer appear in the second group.

---

11. We will discuss these points further in our future volume, *The Yehud Stamp Seal Impressions: A Corpus of Inscribed Stamp Seal Impressions from the Persian and Hellenistic Periods in Judah* (forthcoming at Eisenbrauns).

4. Unlike in the early group, no official titles appear in any stamps from the second group or the late group.
5. Unlike the early group, which had uniformly round or oval stamp seals, new shapes appear among the second group. Many of the יהד stamps are from rectangular seals with rounded corners or from square seals, while many יה stamps come from round seals set in a ring.
6. The paleography of the second group shows several important changes from the lapidary Aramaic model, especially the introduction of non-Aramaic letter forms such as the Paleo-Hebrew *he*.

These six changes point to a disjunction in administrative habits: the early group of stamps from the late sixth and fifth centuries B.C.E. shows substantial continuity with techniques of the late Iron Age, even allowing for differences in script and language. The second group, from the fourth and third centuries B.C.E., points to a much more consolidated system. The provincial administration moved in the direction of unification and consolidation. These later habits of the last century of Persian control in Palestine continued beyond the Persian period into the Macedonian, Ptolemaic, and possibly the early Seleucid period. After that, a major change evidently occurred under the Hasmoneans in the second century B.C.E.

Historical Context

We suggest that the administrative consolidation in Yehud during the fourth and third centuries was one of numerous changes in the administration of Palestine in the Persian period, especially in its southern part, that occurred around the beginning of the fourth century B.C.E. Scholars have already linked other social, economic, and military changes during this period to the more robust Persian interest in the area after 404 B.C.E., when the Egyptians sought to free themselves from the Persian yoke.[12] In 398 B.C.E., Pharaoh Nepherites, founder of the XXIXth Dynasty, entered into a coalition with Sparta against Arta-

---

12. On the beginning of the rule of King Amyrtaeus (probably the grandson of Amyrtaeus I, mentioned by Herodotus [3.15]) in the delta region of Egypt, see Porten 1990: 19; cf. Briant 2002: 619, with bibliography on pp. 989–90. On the significance of the new situation for both Persian and Egyptian affairs, see Lloyd 1994; Briant 2002: 663–66; and Ray 1987. We cannot accept, however, the terminology of Betlyon (1986: 636), who connected one of the changes (the appearance of the first Jewish coins) with the "decadence" of the Persian Empire (cf. Briant 2002: 992). For specific changes in Palestine affected by these developments, see Graf (1993: 160); Eph'al (1998: 108–9, 117–19); and Fantalkin and Tal (2006: 186–89).

xerxes II (Memnon, 404–359 B.C.E.; Briant 2002: 634–35). In 380 B.C.E., Nekhtenebef (Greek Nectanebo I, 380–363 B.C.E.) was recognized as pharaoh and founder of the XXXth Dynasty. He perpetuated an anti-Persian policy focused on fortifying the Delta region, on blocking future Persian attacks, and on initiating an active policy in Asia in coalition with potential allies. The Persians did not forego their attempts to reconquer Egypt, because an independent Egypt (preserved until 343 B.C.E.) was a threat to Persian control in the Levant and a natural ally to any future anti-Persian coalition (Briant 2002: 652). Palestine, and especially its southern part, therefore became one of the most important border zones of the Empire for more than 50 years. After "the peace of Antalcidas" (386 B.C.E.), when Artaxerxes II ended a long period of instability in Asia Minor (begun with the formation of the Delian League, 478–477 B.C.E.) and along the eastern Mediterranean (Briant 2002: 648–49), Egypt remained the lone enemy of Persia outside Europe.[13] Even if unrest in the eastern Mediterranean continued during the following years, the description of Justin (6.6.2) may indicate that the possibility of war against Egypt was the main reason for Artaxerxes II to impose peace during this time (Briant 2002: 649).

Few historical sources illuminate Persian activities in Egypt, but we know that huge Persian armies attacked Egypt probably in 385–384 B.C.E. and again probably in 374–373 B.C.E. (Briant 2002: 652–55, 992, with additional references). Large numbers of Persian troops were stationed in Palestine after the withdrawal from Egypt, preparing for a new assault on the country. Persians and Egyptians may have encamped face to face during the years between the Persian attacks, although no historical sources prove this (Briant 2002: 655). The next clash between the two sides attested in historical sources occurred in 359 B.C.E. Under the leadership of Tachos, along with many Greek mercenaries and Sparta as its ally, the Egyptian army attempted to attack the coastal region of Phoenicia or Palestine. This war ended with no real results, possibly because of a conspiracy against Tachos (Briant 2002: 663–65, 993–94, with additional literature). The Persians may have reacted with an attack of their own in that same year, led by Artaxerxes Ochus (Artaxerxes III, 359–338) just before he became king (Briant 2002: 665). We then have no clear evidence about Persian attacks on Egypt until 351 B.C.E., when Artaxerxes III was defeated in his attempt to gain a foothold in Egypt (Briant 2002: 682–83, 1004, with

---

13. On the chronology of this period, see Shrimpton 1991; van der Spek 1998. For literature on the King's Peace, see Briant 2002: 991.

bibliography). In the next years we learn only about the suppression of revolts in Cyprus and Sidon (the famous "Tennes rebellion") but with no real knowledge about its extent or its effect in Judah and Samaria (Stern 1982: 242, 255; Elayi 1990: 182–84; Briant 2002: 683–85). Egypt was reconquered in 343–342 B.C.E. (Bickerman 1934), about 60 years after it had begun to seek independence from Persian domination. During that period, order was restored in Phoenicia. However, a short time later the king was poisoned and Egypt revolted again. The last two Persian kings—Arses (338–336) and Darius III Codoman (336–331)— did not have sufficient time to prepare the Persian army for another expedition to Egypt before Alexander defeated Darius III and brought the Achaemenid Empire to an end.

For the military expeditions just described, the Persian army had to requisition ships in Phoenicia and control logistic bases along the coast. They also needed a sufficient agricultural supply and at least a basic administration to organize all of this. Palestine, especially the southern Shephelah, served as an important station in the Persian network on the way to and from Egypt until Persia lost its hold in Egypt. It was important for military and civilian officials, for military units, and for commercial traveling caravans (Naveh 1981: 171–74; Eph'al and Naveh 1996: nos. 11, 28; Eph'al 1998: 117–19). Palestine was also important for the Arabian trade that arrived from the east and was concentrated in Gaza.[14]

After the loss of its hold in Egypt, Palestine became an especially important border area of the Persian Empire, particularly its southern parts (Briant 2002: 646–55, 663–66, 991–92; Lipschits 2006: 38). Palestine no doubt underwent a transformation in its administrative and probably also its political organization, possibly as a result of direct imperial involvement (Fantalkin and Tal 2006: 180–81).[15] This was probably the period when the Idumean provincial district was created, or at least when its population began to crystallize (de Geus 1979–80:

---

14. In our opinion, this is probably the reason for the linear setting of many of the Persian fortresses along the Beer-sheba–Arad valley (Ḥorvat Rogem, Arad, Beer-sheba, and probably Tell el-Farah [S]), and along the Negeb highlands, about 30 km to the south (Meṣad Naḥal Haro'a, Ḥorvat Ritma, and Ḥorvat Mesora). Kadesh-barnea and En Haseva were probably important stations on the southern roads and not parts of the military defensive line against Egypt, as Fantalkin and Tal (2006: 184–86, in many respects following the suggestion of Graf 1993: 160) have indicated.

15. We will not deal here with the various theories connecting Ezra's mission to the seventh year of Artaxerxes II (398 B.C.E.). See Cazelles 1954; cf. Lemaire 1995; 1992: 88–93, with additional literature).

62; Eph'al 1982: 197–201). The Achaemenids evidently entrenched their rule and reorganized the administration and security along the roads in the southern parts of Palestine, including along the southern part of the coastal area, the southern Shephelah, and throughout the Beer-sheba–Arad valleys. This was also the probable date for the erection of the main administrative center in Lachish (Level Ib; Fantalkin and Tal 2006: 167–77) along with other administrative centers and Persian forts in the Negeb (Stern 2001: 420–21, 577–79) and the southern Shephelah, along the main roads adjacent to the coast, in the Shephelah, and along the central mountain ridge (Tal 2005; Fantalkin and Tal 2006: 181–83). During this period, the Persians allowed the local cities and regions, including Yehud and Samaria, Gaza, Ashdod, and Ashkelon, to start minting their own coins (Betlyon 1982; 1986; Meshorer 1989: 287–91; 2001: 1–17; Mildenberg 1990; Machinist 1994; Meshorer and Qedar 1999; Eph'al 1998: 111–13). Many unprovenanced Aramaic ostraca from the southern Shephelah come from this period (Lemaire 1996; 2002; Eph'al and Naveh 1996; see recently, Lemaire 2006; Porten and Yardeni 2006, with additional literature), along with ostraca from the Beer-sheba–Arad valleys. Taken together, these data point to the importance of the southern Shephelah and the Beer-sheba–Arad valleys for local Persian economic, military, and administrative interests.

Summary

In this essay, we have presented a new thesis about the development of the YSIs. A fundamental change in the form, style, paleography, and orthography occurred at the end of the fifth or the beginning of the fourth century B.C.E. This change resulted in the consolidation of stamping practices connected with the Yehud jars. We have also suggested a possible link between this fundamental change and the historical circumstances of the Persian Empire during the same period. When the Persians lost control over Egypt, the significance of the southern Levantine coast as a border zone increased. This, in turn, may account for greater Persian involvement and influence in the southernmost reaches of the eastern Mediterranean littoral.

The consolidation in stamping practices in Yehud is apparently one of numerous other changes that occurred in the southern Levant after the Achaemenid loss of control in Egypt. We can hypothesize that Achaemenid authority over populations in the border region was tightened. The Aramaic ostraca from the southern Shephelah point in this direction, as does the date of the establishment of the palace in Lachish and probably some other forts in the Judean Hills, the Shephelah, and the Negeb area. The use of natural resources in the area, including agricultural products such as grain, wine, and oil became much more critical for the Persian army as a consequence of the presence of large contingents of Persian troops stationed in the area, as well as the presence of administrators. Persian forces must have assembled and passed through the border region before and after the numerous expeditions to Egypt or as part of the defensive battles against Egyptian and allied assaults.

The changes that occurred in the YSIs of the middle period, in any case, point to a simplification or consolidation of previous practices connected with collecting agricultural products, perhaps as taxes. This could have resulted from tighter control—possibly tighter Persian control—in the administration of the distribution system, which the stamps reflect. The province name, or its abbreviated form, becomes the only necessary piece of information in the stamps. This suggests that the names of local administrators, whether governors or not, were no longer relevant for the system. Only the source of the product was significant. Given that the jars were not designed for export and were found almost exclusively within a small radius in the heart of Yehud, we may conclude that the system functioned on the basis of a simple binary opposition: there were jars stamped with the name of the province and jars that were not stamped. We may hypothesize about why the jars were stamped at all: they may have been marked for official consumption (whether local or imperial); they may have been marked as taxes; the volume or quality of the produce in the jars may have been verified by the stamp; or perhaps the product originated from official estates. We cannot know, however, whether Persian administrators had a direct role to play in the consolidation reflected by the middle types or whether it was an indirect consequence of the increased Persian presence in the region.

We may note, finally, that the system represented by the middle YSI types was quite durable and evidently persisted through the first half of the second century, when it underwent additional modification during the Hasmonean period. Even then, however, continuity with the middle types is discernible, because only the name of the province appears in the late stamps, either abbreviated with the *yh* symbol or in Paleo-Hebrew with the *ṭet* symbol. Thus, the new system, created around 400 B.C.E., continued until the first half of the second century B.C.E. and was changed only during the Hasmonean period.

References

Aharoni, Y.
  1956 Excavations at Ramat Raḥel, 1954: Preliminary Report. *IEJ* 6: 137–55.
  1962 *Excavations at Ramat Rahel: Seasons 1959 and 1960.* Rome: Università Degli Studi; Centro di Studi Semitici.
  1964 *Excavations at Ramat Rahel: Seasons 1961 and 1962.* Rome: Università Degli Studi; Centro di Studi Semitici.
Ariel, D. T., and Shoham, Y.
  2000 Locally Stamped Handles and Associated Body Fragments of the Persian and Hellenistic Periods. Pp. 137–69 in *Excavations at the City of David 1978–1985 Directed by Yigal Shiloh, 6: Inscriptions*, ed. D. T. Ariel et al. Qedem 41. Jerusalem: Institute of Archaeology, Hebrew University of Jerusalem.
Avigad, N.
  1957 A New Class of *Yehud* Stamps. *IEJ* 7: 146–53.
Barag, D.
  1986–87 A Silver Coin of Yohanan the High Priest and the Coinage of Judea in the Fourth Century B.C. *Israel Numismatic Journal* 9: 4–21, and pl. 1.
Betlyon, J. W.
  1982 *The Coinage and Mints of Phoenicia: The Pre-Alexandrine Period.* HSM 26. Chico, CA: Scholars Press.
  1986 The Provincial Government of Persian Period Judea and the Yehud Coins. *JBL* 105: 633–42.
Bickerman, E. J.
  1934 Notes sur la chronologie de la XXXᵉ dynastie. Pp. 77–84 in vol. 1 of *Mélanges Maspero*. Mémoires publiés par les membres de l'Institut français d'archéologie orientale du Caïre 66. Cairo: L'Institut Français d'Archéologie Orientale.
Briant, P.
  2002 *From Cyrus to Alexander: A History of the Persian Empire.* Winona Lake, IN: Eisenbrauns.
Cazelles, H.
  1954 La mission d'Esdras. *VT* 4: 113–40.
Cross, F. M.
  1969 Judean Stamps. *ErIsr* 9 (Albright Volume): 20*–27*.
DeGroot, A., and Ariel, D.
  2004 *Yehud* Stamp Impressions from Shiloh's Excavations in the City of David. P. 15 in *New Directions and Fresh Discoveries in the Research of the Yehud Stamp Impressions: Abstracts from a Conference Held at Tel Aviv University, January 2004*, ed. O. Lipschits. Tel Aviv: Tel Aviv University. [Hebrew]
Elayi, J.
  1990 *Sidon, cité autonome de l'Empire perse.* 2nd ed. Paris: Idéaphane.

Eph'al, I.
1982   *The Ancient Arabs: Nomads on the Border of the Fertile Crescent, 9th–5th Centuries B.C.* Leiden: Brill, 1982.
1998   Changes in Palestine during the Persian Period in Light of Epigraphic Sources. *IEJ* 48: 106–19.

Eph'al, I., and Naveh, J.
1996   *Aramaic Ostraca of the Fourth Century BC from Idumaea.* Jerusalem: Israel Exploration Society.

Fantalkin, A., and Tal, O.
2006   Redating Lachish Level I: Identifying Achaemenid Imperial Policy at the Southern Frontier of the Fifth Satrapy. Pp. 167–97 in *Judah and the Judeans in the Persian Period,* ed. O. Lipschits and M. Oeming. Winona Lake, IN: Eisenbrauns.

Finkielsztejn, G., and Gibson, S.
2007   The Retrogade-F-Shaped *yh(d)* Monogram: Epigraphy and Dating. *TA* 34/1: 104–13.

Geva, H.
2007   A Chronological Reevaluation of Yehud Stamp Impressions in Palaeo-Hebrew Script, Based on Finds from Excavations in the Jewish Quarter of the Old City of Jerusalem. *TA* 34/1: 92–103.

Geus, C. H. J. de
1979–80 Idumaea. *Jaarbericht van het Vooraziatisch-Egyptisch Genootschap ex Oriente Lux* 26: 53–72.

Geva, H.
2004   The Jewish Quarter Excavations: New Chronological Conclusions for the Dating of the Late *Yehud* Stamp Impressions. P. 16 in *New Directions and Fresh Discoveries in the Research of the Yehud Stamp Impressions: Abstracts from a Conference held at Tel Aviv University, January 2004,* ed. O. Lipschits. Tel Aviv: Tel Aviv University. [Hebrew]

Grabbe, L. L.
1992   *Judaism from Cyrus to Hadrian, I: Persian and Greek Periods.* Minneapolis: Fortress.

Graf, D. F.
1993   The Persian Royal Road System in Syria–Palestine. *Transeu* 6: 149–66.

Lemaire, A.
1991   Le royaume de Tyre dans le second moitie du IV av. J.C. Pp. 132–49 in *Atti del II Congresso internazionale di studi fenici e punici: Roma, 9–14 novembre 1987,* ed. Enrico Acquaro. Collezione di studi fenici 30. Rome: Consiglio nazionale delle ricerche.
1995   La fin de la période perse en Égypte et la chronologie judéenne vers 400 av. J.C. *Transeu* 9: 51–61.
1996   *Nouvelles inscriptions araméennes d'Idumée du Musée d'Israël.* Transeu Supplement 3. Paris: Gabalda.
2002   *Nouvelles inscriptions araméennes d'Idumée du Musée d'Israël,* vol. 2: *Collections Moussaïeff, Jeselsohn, Welch et divers.* Transeu Supplement 9. Paris: Gabalda.

2006 New Aramaic Ostraca from Idumea and Their Historical Interpretation. Pp. 413–56 in *Judah and the Judeans in the Persian Period*, ed. O. Lipschits and M. Oeming. Winona Lake, IN: Eisenbrauns.

Lipschits, O.
1998 Nebuchadrezzar's Policy in Hattu-Land and the Fate of the Kingdom of Judah. *UF* 30: 467–87.
2005 *The Fall and Rise of Jerusalem: Judah under Babylonian Rule*. Winona Lake, IN: Eisenbrauns.
2006 Achaemenid Imperial Policy, Settlement Processes in Palestine, and the Status of Jerusalem in the Middle of the Fifth Century B.C.E. Pp. 19–52 in *Judah and the Judeans in the Persian Period*, ed. O. Lipschits and M. Oeming. Winona Lake, IN: Eisenbrauns.

Lipschits, O., and Vanderhooft, D.
Forthcoming *The Yehud Stamp Seal Impressions: A Corpus of Inscribed Stamp Seal Impressions from the Persian and Hellenistic Periods in Judah*. Winona Lake, IN: Eisenbrauns.

Lloyd, A. B.
1994 Egypt, 404–332 B.C. Pp. 337–60 in vol. 6/2 of *CAH*.

Machinist, P.
1994 The First Coins of Judah and Samaria: Numismatics and History in the Achaemenid and Early Hellenistic Periods. *Achaemenid History* 8: 365–80.

Meshorer, Y.
1982 *Ancient Jewish Coinage*. 2 vols. Dix Hills, NY: Amphora.
1989 The Mints of Ashdod and Ascalon during the Late Persian Period. *ErIsr* 20 (Yadin Volume): 287–91 [Hebrew, with English summary, *205].
1990–91 *Ancient Jewish Coinage*: Addendum I. *Israel Numismatic Journal* 11: 105–32.
2001 *A Treasury of Jewish Coins*. Nyack, NY: Amphora.

Meshorer, Y., and Qedar, S.
1991 *The Coinage of Samaria in the Fourth Century B.C.* Beverly Hills, CA: Numismatics Fine Arts International.
1999 *Samarian Coinage*. Numismatic Studies and Researches 9. Jerusalem: Israel Numismatic Society.

Mildenberg, L.
1979 Yehud: A Preliminary Study of the Provincial Coinage of Judaea. Pp. 183–96 in *Greek Numismatics and Archaeology: Essays in Honor of Margaret Thompson*, ed. O. Mørkholm and N. M. Waggoner. Wetteren, Belgium: NP.
1990 Gaza Mint Authorities in Persian Time [*sic*]: Preliminary Studies of the Local Coinage in the Fifth Satrapy, Part 4. *Transeu* 2: 137–46.

Naveh, J.
1970 *The Development of the Aramaic Script*. Proceedings of the Israel Academy of Sciences and Humanities 5/1. Jerusalem.

1981   The Aramaic Ostraca from Tel-Arad. Pp. 153–76 in *Arad Inscriptions*, ed. Y. Aharoni. Judean Desert Series. Jerusalem: Israel Exploration Society.

1996   Gleanings of Some Pottery Inscriptions. *IEJ* 46: 44–51.

1998   Scripts and Inscriptions in Ancient Samaria. *IEJ* 48: 91–100.

Petit, T.

1988   L'évolution sémantique des termes hébreux et araméenes *phh* et *sgn* et accadiens *pāḫatu* et *šaknu*. *JBL* 107: 53–67.

Porten, B.

1990   The Calendar of Aramaic Texts from Achaemenid and Ptolemaic Egypt. Pp. 13–32 in vol. 2 of *Irano-Judaica: Studies Relating to Jewish Contacts with Persian Culture throughout the Ages*, ed. by S. Shaked and A. Netzer. Jerusalem: Ben-Zvi.

Porten, B., and Yardeni, A.

2006   Social, Economic, and Onomastic Issues in the Aramaic Ostraca of the Fourth Century B.C.E. Pp. 457–88 in *Judah and the Judeans in the Persian Period*, ed. O. Lipschits and M. Oeming. Winona Lake, IN: Eisenbrauns.

Ray, J. D.

1987   Egypt: Dependence and Independence (425–343 B.C.). Pp. 79–95 in *Sources, Structures and Synthesis: Proceedings of the Groningen 1983 Achaemenid History Workshop*, ed. H. Sancisi-Weerdenburg. Achaemenid History 1. Leiden: Brill.

Shrimpton, G.

1991   Persian Strategy against Egypt and the Date of the Battle of Cition. *Phoenix* 45: 1–20.

Spek, R. van der

1998   The Chronology of the Wars of Artaxerxes II in the Babylonian Astronomical Diaries. Pp. 239–56 in *Achaemenid History XI: Studies in Persian History—Essays in Memory of David M. Lewis*, ed. M. Brosius and A. Kuhrt. Leiden: Brill.

Stern, E.

1982   *The Material Culture of the Land of the Bible in the Persian Period: 538–332 B.C.* Jerusalem: Israel Exploration Society.

2001   *Archaeology of the Land of the Bible, II: The Assyrian, Babylonian, and Persian Periods (732–332 B.C.E.).* ABRL. New York: Doubleday.

Tal, O.

2005   Some Remarks on the Coastal Plain of Palestine under Achaemenid Rule: An Archaeological Synopsis. Pp. 71–96 in *L'archéologie de l'empire achéménide, nouvelles recherches: Actes du colloque organisé au Collège de France par le "Réseau international d'études et de recherches achéménides," GDR 2538 CNRS, 21–22 novembre 2003*, ed. Pierre Briant and Rémy Boucharlat. Persika 6. Paris: De Boccard.

Vanderhooft, D. S.

1999   *The Neo-Babylonian Empire and Babylon in the Latter Prophets.* HSM 59. Atlanta: Scholars Press.

Vanderhooft, D. S., and Lipschits, O.

2007   A New Typology of the Yehud Stamp Impressions. *TA* 34/1: 12–37.

"And They Did Not Care to Speak Yehudit": On Linguistic Change in Judah during the Late Persian Era

INGO KOTTSIEPER

Universität Göttingen

Introduction

It is well known that during the Persian era Aramaic gained a strong influence in Judah. Thus it was not only used in official documents, as was usual in the western Achaemenid Empire, but also, for "those who returned after Cyrus' edict and for the groups which returned later, Hebrew was no longer a mother tongue; they were surely Aramaic speakers" (Naveh and Greenfield 1984: 119). Because Aramaic was still used as a spoken language after the end of the Persian era, the question about the role and function of Hebrew has arisen in modern scholarship. Was it also still used as a spoken language? Or was it completely superseded by Aramaic as a spoken language? And if it was superseded, when did this happen? If it was not superseded, where was Hebrew spoken and within which groups? Were its speakers multilingual, thus using Hebrew and Aramaic on different occasions and in different environments? And was the language choice based on social or ideological factors?[1]

---

1. For example, a choice of this sort can be based on different social environments. Thus, in multilingual societies, often one language is taken as the standard, used in public and with foreigners, while other languages are used in private communication at home or with friends. A language can also be bound to a social group. Thus, in some villages of North Frisia, the Frisian language is used by women in some families, while the men (and women speaking with men) use the local German dialect. But as an official language and in communication with foreigners, they all use standard German. An ideological use is found when a certain language or dialect is used deliberately or propagandized as a sign of the membership of a certain group. Thus the question about which language to use played an important role in nationalistic ideologies of the 19th and 20th centuries (and still does even today). And the refusal to use one language can be also grounded in ideology as, for example, the refusal to use Modern Hebrew by some ultra-orthodox groups in Israel shows.

It was the common opinion in the 19th century that Hebrew had been totally superseded by Aramaic at the end of the Persian era or during the early Hellenistic period. Thus, Mishnaic Hebrew (MH) was deemed to be an artificial language, created from Biblical Hebrew (BH) with strong Aramaic influence. But since the groundbreaking works of Segal (e.g., 1909; 1927: 5–20), the notion that Hebrew survived as a spoken dialect that later served as a base for MH has steadily gained influence (e.g., Naveh and Greenfield 1984: 118–22; Barr 1989: 82–90). The main argument was that most of the innovations found in MH could not be explained as depending directly on BH or on Aramaic influence. Thus they must show the development of vernacular Hebrew, traces of which could even be found in Late Biblical Hebrew (LBH). The Hebrew documents and texts found during the 20th century were taken as a further proof of this assumption, because they include some elements that can also be found in later MH. But the texts from Qumran, in particular, are much closer to (L)BH than to MH. This was explained either by the assumption that they were partially written in "a last offshoot of Late Biblical Hebrew" (Barr 1989: 88) or that "the full emancipation of MH" as the language of the people "was the result of a social upheaval, viz., the break between Pharisaism and the Qumran Sect," which still tried to use the traditional Hebrew literary language of the higher educated classes.[2] A third solution—which takes into account the fact that even the grammar of the late Bar-Kokhba letters differs from MH—is to assume different spoken Hebrew dialects, of which the Jerusalem version influenced Qumranic Hebrew (QH), the Copper Scroll, and the Bar-Kokhba letters, while a different one was the dialect used by the later rabbis (Qimron 2000).

But other scholars, such as Beyer (1984: 55–58; 2004: 34–36), are still convinced that Hebrew died out as a spoken language in the fourth century B.C.E., because there are almost no Hebrew documents dealing with daily life after 300 B.C.E. and, aside from taking into consideration the great influence of Aramaic, some grammatical innovations could only have developed if the language was no longer spoken. Thus no one would have spoken Hebrew as a mother tongue after 300 B.C.E.

In this essay, I will mainly analyze the picture given by the biblical and epigraphic sources about the linguistic situation in Judah during the late Persian era. Because they appear to demonstrate that Hebrew was indeed superseded by Aramaic as the commonly spoken language during this time, the question arises whether this continued to hold

---

2. See Rabin 1958: 161. See also the overview provided by Morag (1988: 148).

true in later times, given the evidence of later sources, or whether the sources can *prove* that Hebrew was still spoken as a common language or was revived. I will show that they corroborate the conclusion that Hebrew indeed was no longer used as a commonly spoken language. But they also demonstrate that Hebrew was used as a kind of religious lingo in religious circles, which of course had its own development, leading to the later MH.[3]

The Biblical Account

Nehemiah 13:23–24

The most interesting note about the linguistic situation in Judah during the Persian era is found in Neh 13:23–24. According to the traditional interpretation, v. 23 deals with Nehemiah, who saw "the" Judeans, who married women from Ashdod, Ammon, and Moab. Verse 24 has been understood in the sense that half the children of these mixed marriages spoke Ashdodit, the language of the other people, and were unable to speak Yehudit. Verses 25–27 describe Nehemiah's hostile reaction to this phenomenon. Because the reference to the Ammonite and Moabite women is added without a copula and only Ashdodit is explicitly mentioned in v. 24, עמוניות מואביות is commonly taken as a gloss. Moreover, the reference to the language of various peoples at the end of v. 24, which is missing in the LXX and would be more appropriate after v. 24aα, is deemed to be a later addition (e.g., Myers 1965: 216; Williamson 1985: 393, 397; Blenkinsopp 1988: 362; Pakkala 2004: 218–19).

A more radical interpretation was recently proposed by Wright (2005: 245–46), who takes only v. 23 (probably without עמוניות מואביות) and v. 25 as the oldest text. Thus, the question of language would be part of a very late *relecture* "in order to demonstrate the consequences of this *connubium* for the solidarity of the Judean people, which required a common language" (Wright 2005: 246). But Pichon (1997: 180–81) has observed that v. 25b, which alludes to Deut 7:3 and Ezra 9:12, does not fit the case given in vv. 23–24. Consequently, vv. 26–27 are also secondary because, without v. 25b, an introduction to the speech would be missing and because these verses, like v. 25b, allude to other biblical

---

3. I am fully aware that my conclusion contradicts the view of the history of Hebrew held by the majority of modern scholars. But we must keep in mind that "collating the new data that keep coming to light is like working on a puzzle with an irregular supply of pieces. These have to be fitted together carefully and a constant re-examination of the data must be accompanied by the re-evaluation of accepted views" (Naveh 1982: vii).

texts (2 Sam 12:24; 1 Kgs 3:7, 8:20, and especially 1 Kgs 11). Thus vv. 25b–27 are "une veritable 'exégèse' de l'Ecriture qui tend à motiver une dècision" (Pichon 1997: 184), added as a short treatise about mixed marriages by a learned scribe who knew his Scripture well.

But the crucial point is the correct understanding of v. 24. Because מדבר is singular, חצי cannot be taken as an adverb (Gesenius 1987–2005: 385a) but must be the subject of מדבר. And because the suffix of ואינם probably points back to בניהם and not to the singular חצי, one has to ask with Wright (2005: 245) which language(s) the other half spoke, if one takes מכירים as meaning 'to be able'.[4] A closer look at the meanings of נכר (*Hiphil*) solves this problem. It denotes an attitude toward something or someone, to examine it and to get to know the facts (Gen 31:32; 37:32, 33; 38:25, 26; Sir 15:19; 1QSb 3:19 (?); 4Q427 frg. 11:3). Comparable to ידע, especially the perfect of נכר may mean also 'to have recognized' and *only* in this way 'to know (a fact)'.[5] Further, it connotes 'to take into account something or someone' (Deut 1:17; 16:19; Job 34:25; Prov 24:33; 28:21; Sir 38:10, 20 [B$_{Marg.}$]; 11QT 51:12), 'to accept it as it is' (Deut 21:17, Jer 24:5, Dan 11:39), and 'to take care of someone or something' (Isa 63:16; Ps 142:5; Job 24:13; Ruth 2:10, 19). Finally, it can mean just 'to pay attention to' or 'to take notice of something' (1QH^a 6:30 [14:19]; 13:15 [5:13]). Thus, though this word shows a broad range of meanings, the connotation 'to be able to do something' is elsewhere not to be found.[6]

Consequently, to translate v. 24aβ 'and they were not able to speak Yehudit' would not only force the question of what language they spoke but also introduce an otherwise unattested meaning of the verb. However, the connotations cited above allow us to understand מכיר as 'directing one's attention to something in order to deal with it or to accept it'. Thus, the translation 'and they did not care to speak Yehudit' would not only be in accord with the use of נכר (in *Hiphil*) found elsewhere but would also avoid the problem with regard to which languages besides Ashdodit and Yehudit were spoken.[7] Consequently,

---

4. Note also the comment of Gunneweg (1987: 172): "Der . . . Passus ist allerdings sprachlich . . . eine Crux."

5. Genesis 27:23; 42:7, 8; Deut 33:9; Judg 18:3; 1 Sam 26:17; 2 Sam 3:36; 1 Kgs 18:17; 20:41; Isa 61:9; Ps 103:16; Job 2:12; 4:16; 7:10; 24:17; Ruth 3:14; Ezra 3:13; Neh 6:12; 1QH^a 15:16 (7:13), 16:14 (8:13); 25x:34 (frg. 7 ii 9 ‖ 4Q427 frg. 7 ii 15); 4Q318 frg. 13:2; frg. 45a + b:2; 4Q398 frg. 11–13:3.

6. Furthermore, the other Semitic languages do not show this meaning.

7. This is also in accord with the etymology of the root. Its basic meaning is probably 'to be strange, different' (Kottsieper 1990: 218), which developed the meaning 'to deal

v. 24aβ describes a linguistic situation in which Yehudit had lost its role as the main spoken language. This is fully in accord with the preceding sentence, which states that "half" did speak Ashdodit.

The reference to the children also fits very well in this picture, because the generation growing up would naturally not learn the old language alongside the new one if there was no need to do so—and obviously there was no need, if nobody cared to speak Yehudit. Thus, one should follow Pichon's observation that vv. 25b–27, mentioning the mixed marriages, is a secondary addition. And because v. 24a only mentions Ashdodit and v. 23aβ is syntactically difficult to connect with the preceding sentence, the traditional view of v. 23aβ as a gloss is also convincing. But the question remains whether the motif of marriages with the Ashdodites is original, which Pichon (1997: 194) also denies. The secondary character of vv. 25b–27 alone would not be a sufficient reason for this view, because it would be understandable that a later editor added these verses, if in v. 23 a mixed marriage was mentioned. But if it was part of the original text, then one must assume either that the fact of a mixed marriage did not bother Nehemiah (or the author of the passage) very much but the linguistic evolution caused by it did bother him, or else that the phrase "Ashdodite women" must be understood as "women from the area of Ashdod" and that these women were Jewish. This possibility cannot be ruled out, because we now know of Jews who lived in the coastal plain outside Judah.[8]

But there is a more convincing reason to take the allusion to the Ashdodite women as a later addition. There are two ways to analyze the syntax of the verse. Thus, the sentence beginning with הֹשִׁיבוּ could be an asyndetic clause relative to הַיְּהוּדִים. But the expression "I saw *the* Judeans who had married Ashdodite women" would normally refer to a known fact and not to something new.[9] However, this fact was not previously mentioned. If the point of the story was to inform us that Nehemiah saw some Judeans who had married these women, one

with as strange, different' and thus 'to examine it' and 'to devote attention to it', from which other connotations can easily be deduced but not the connotation 'to be able to do'. Thus, in Tazerwalt, a Berber language, *enker* means 'sich an etwas machen, auf etwas losgehen' (Rössler 1952: 373). But even if one takes 'to inspect' as the basic meaning with the positive connotation 'to recognize, acknowledge' (*HALOT* 699b), it would be a very big leap to the meaning 'to be able to do' but a small step to 'pay attention to something'.

8. See the essay by E. Eshel about the documents from Maresha in this volume (pp. 145–156) and Naveh and Greenfield 1984: 124. Note also Zech 9:5–7.

9. One should not overlook the fact that הַיְּהוּדִים is a plural form. Thus, the use of the article cannot be explained according to GKC (§126q–t), as proposed, for example, by Williamson (1985: 393).

would expect יהודים instead of היהודים. The second way to analyze the sentence would be to take . . . השיבו as a second object to ראיתי.[10] Then Nehemiah would have seen "the Judeans that they had married. . . ." But in this case, one would also expect the form יהודים.

If one leaves out the note about the marriage with the Ashdodite women, these problems are solved. Verses 23aα*, 24 tell us that Nehemiah observed the Judeans and their children: "In those days I observed the Judeans and their children: half spoke Ashdodit, and they did not care to speak Yehudit."[11] Thus it would indicate that Nehemiah realized a linguistic evolution had happened in Judah, especially with the younger generation—the loss of Yehudit as a spoken language. Because no one cared to speak Yehudit and it was possible for half the population, especially the children, to speak just Ashdodit, the reaction of Nehemiah to the Judeans is quite understandable. Only if those who could still speak Yehudit (but had not been careful to do so) changed course and altered their behavior would the next generation be able to speak the Yehudit language.[12]

Two questions remain: What language was Ashdodit? And why did Nehemiah struggle to retain Yehudit? Ashdodit must have been not only a very commonly spoken language in Judah but also a language that was understood by everyone. Otherwise it would be impossible for it to have been spoken as the only language, especially by the younger members of the population. Thus, it must have been an Aramaic dialect. And because the Judeans coming back from the Exile spoke Aramaic as their mother tongue, we can understand why this language became common in Judah. It was not only a language shared by most of the neighbors, but it was now also used by members of the new upper class that had gained great influence in the society. This is a typical situation in which a new language supersedes a traditional one. But why then is it not called ארמית? The reason is easy to determine. Apparently, ארמית was the name given to the Aramaic dialects

---

10. For ראה governing two objects, see, for instance, Gen 7:1 and especially Judg 9:48 (מה ראיתם עשיתי 'what you saw me do').

11. By the way, the writer of the gloss in v. 24b (וכלשון עם ועם) probably understood the sentence in this way: "but like the language of any other people (they did care to speak Yehudit)." Thus, there is no need to place the gloss after אשדודית. For the meaning of עם ועם, see Waltke and O'Connor 1990: §7.2.3.c.

12. The argument by Wright (2005: 246) that Nehemiah should have persuaded the Judeans "that they should organize *ulpanim* throughout Judah" cannot be taken seriously, because *ulpanim* of this sort had not yet been invented. To expect such courses in a society that did not even know of public schools would be anachronistic.

used in Mesopotamia (2 Kgs 18:26//Isa 36:11, Dan 2:4) and to Imperial Aramaic, derived mainly from these dialects and used in official documents during the Persian era (Ezra 4:7). Undoubtedly, however, the dialects spoken in Judah and the neighboring areas were different.[13] Thus, probably Ashdodit was a name for these vernacular dialects of Aramaic, which were also spoken elsewhere, especially in the coastal plain of Ashdod.[14] But the possibility cannot be ruled out that the author used this designation deliberately to mark this new language as foreign.

Even if the above is true, the opposition to this linguistic evolution was certainly not grounded in a nationalistic attitude supporting the concept of a monolingual society, following the ideology of modern nationalists that a nation should have one and only one language. On the contrary, the text deals not with an evolution of bilingualism but with the evolution from bilingualism to monolingualism. The fact that there were other languages spoken is not what bothers the author but the fact that Yehudit had ceased to be spoken.[15]

But there is another reason that is even more convincing. It was the Persian era in which the written Hebrew Torah became the basis for Judaism. Even though the returnees from the Exile probably spoke Aramaic, they obviously belonged, for the most part, to the better-educated upper classes. For this reason, they could understand and deal with traditional Hebrew texts. But the Judeans who lived in the land and were mostly not well educated would lose their ability to understand the Torah and the old traditions entirely if they grew up monolingual, using only Aramaic dialects as their mother tongue. Thus, for those who wished to ground their society on the Hebrew Torah, the common ability to understand Hebrew had great value. It is understandable that they were upset by their observation that the Judeans were not careful to speak their Hebrew dialects, to such an

---

13. That the western Aramaic vernacular differed from Imperial Aramaic is not only a likely assumption but is proved, for example, by the fact that traits of it are even found in the Aramaic of the later sections of Pap. Amherst 63, written at the end of the fourth century B.C.E. (Kottsieper 2003: 106–7, 112–13).

14. Thus even in the seventh century B.C.E., Aramaic was known on the coastal plain, as TAD A:1.1 shows. Even in the later rabbinic tradition, the Palestinian Aramaic dialects could be called לשון סורסי (*Sipre* to Deut 11:19) in contrast to the Aramaic dialects of Mesopotamia, which are called לשון ארמי (*b. B. Qam.* 83a).

15. By the way, this even holds true if one follows the traditional interpretation of the text. Even if the children learned Ashdodit because their mothers spoke it, they surely would have had to learn and use Yehudit when they were old enough to go out and communicate with other Judeans, if Yehudit was still the common language in Judah.

extent that their children, especially, only spoke Aramaic vernacular. There were two ways to deal with the problem. Either one could try to stop this evolution (this is what Nehemiah did, according to our text) or one could develop the tradition of translating the Torah (hence, the Targumim). Judging by later history, this is obviously what happened.

Nehemiah 8:1–8

Nehemiah 8:1–8 presents the public reading of the Torah by Ezra. The story is divided into two parts. Verses 1–4 center on Ezra, who did the reading alone, but in vv. 5–8 he is accompanied by certain Levites, who explain the reading to the people (vv. 7–8). But most interesting are the various descriptions of the people. Verses 2–3 stress that the people consist of men, women, and 'all who could hear' (וכל מבין לשמע, v. 2) and 'understand' (ומבינים, v. 3). Apparently the latter group are adolescents. Because Neh 12:23–24 states that especially with respect to children Nehemiah observed the loss of the capability to *speak* Yehudit, we cannot rule out the possibility that the reference to those "who could *hear*" refers to a younger generation, out of which only some were able to follow the public recitation of the Hebrew Torah. Meanwhile, the older ones, though not being careful to *speak* Yehudit, could still understand a Hebrew reading. But of course, the traditional interpretation is also possible, that the younger, not fully grown persons were meant, who were nevertheless intelligent enough to get the sense of the reading.[16]

Whatever the case, vv. 1–4 clearly presuppose that normal men and women understood the reading of the Torah. But vv. 5–8 do not share this view. In this context, מבינים are also mentioned (v. 7), but now they are the Levites who made the reading understandable to all the people. Thus, the conclusion is inevitable that a later author was of the opinion that normal people could not follow a plain reading of the Hebrew Torah.[17] If one does not want to presume that the people lost their intellectual capabilities, one has to assume that they lost the ability to

---

16. See, for example, Rudolph (1949: 144) and Blenkinsopp (1988: 283, 287). Thus, in 10:29 the phrase כל יודע מבין is added to the list of the participants in the contract after the mention of people coming from other nations, their women and children. But because there they are referred to as 'knowing to understand' (cf. Rudolph 1949: 174), and this phrase probably is not only speaking about children but also about the women and maybe even all the Jews, this reference should not be taken as decisive. Less convincing is the assumption that this expression just wants to assure that the Judeans could understand the reading (Pakkala 2004: 147).

17. For the assumption that vv. 5–8 are a later layer, see also Blenkinsopp 1988: 286–88. Pakkala (2004: 146–49) assumes that vv. 4–8 are later.

understand Hebrew. Probably the author of this later part of the story did not understand the meaning of מבין in the earlier text. And obviously, knowing the rite of reading the Torah part by part,[18] which was followed by an explanation that was surely given in a language people would understand, he probably interpreted the מבינים of the first part as the people who explained the reading. Thus, he explains how this reading in front of "men, women, and all מבין לשמע" was carried out. Ezra started it, but there were also people "who made (people) capable of hearing."

Conclusion

The biblical verses analyzed witness a linguistic process from a bilingual situation in which Hebrew and Aramaic were spoken in Judah to a basically monolingual situation, in which Hebrew was no longer spoken by ordinary people and, as a consequence, no longer understood. As every linguist knows, a change of this sort happens step by step. First, members of the population, especially the younger ones, lose the capability of speaking one of the languages, and this is, of course, the one that the others do not cultivate. Real bilingualism is only maintained in a society in which either (1) different ethnic or social groups live apart from each other, and thus different environments exist in which different languages are used; or (2) a traditional language is cultivated deliberately. But, in the latter case, special effort is needed to keep both languages alive.[19] Obviously, an attempt of this sort is recorded in Neh 13:23aα*, 24a, 25a. But because Neh 8:4–8 depicts a situation in which the common people lost their ability to understand Hebrew, it is obvious that "Nehemiah" did not succeed in his protest against the loss of Hebrew as a spoken language.

By the way, this explains quite easily why Neh 13:23–25* was later interpreted as dealing with mixed marriages. Because speaking only Aramaic was obviously not a problem for later readers (the problem had been solved by the intervention of Aramaic translations and interpretations of the Hebrew Torah during its public reading, a process that led to the later targumic literature), this interpretation was very close at hand, especially because the text called the Aramaic vernacular Ashdodit. In later times, when Aramaic was the common language

---

18. Thus, the probable meaning of מפורש.

19. Thus most dialects in Germany have almost died out altogether, and only in the cases in which older speakers of a dialect or people really interested in preserving a dying dialect intervene can this process be stopped or at least delayed. But to keep a dialect alive, adults have to persuade younger people to learn both languages and to use them.

of Judah, this term easily could be (mis-)understood as referring to the
language of a heathen people.

The Epigraphic Sources

The Documents

Only a few ostraca and papyri have been found in the province of
Judah that can be dated to the Persian era. Because of the scarcity of
finds, one should not overrate the picture given by these sources. One
also has to keep in mind the fact that judicial, official, and most economic texts were written in Aramaic during the Persian era, because
Aramaic was the language used in the realm of administration. Nevertheless, the fact that there is no Hebrew text and that even short notes,
consisting of just a name, are written in Aramaic[20] shows the heavy influence of Aramaic and the willingness of the people to use it. [21]

The Seals and Stamp Impressions

Any analysis of seals and stamp impressions encounters certain difficulties.[22] First, the provenance and date of many are unknown or in
dispute. In particular, the authenticity of the collection edited by Avigad (1976), which probably includes most of the Hebrew examples
that stem from Persian-period Judah, is questioned by some scholars.[23]
Thus, I shall deal with these examples separately. Second, how to determine whether a text is Hebrew or Aramaic is a question that must
be answered. Although there is no problem if a text shows clear Hebrew or Aramaic words or forms, a seal or stamp with just a name
provides no information about the language used. Even the script may
be misleading in this situation. Thus, the well-known *Yehud* stamps
use either Aramaic or Hebrew script. But because *Yehud* was the Aramaic name for the Persian province, one should hesitate to assume
that people who used Hebrew script were Hebrew speakers. The seal-

---

20. Thus, an ostracon from Jerusalem, dating to the fourth century B.C.E., reads יחזקיה
בר שמעיה (Yardeni 2000: A 360).

21. This is in accord with the picture given by the hundreds of ostraca found in
southern Palestine outside the province of Judah, which "attest to the extent of Aramaic
penetration in Palestine—down to the local rural population. These sources were written
in vulgar script by people who, although literate, can hardly be classified as professional
scribes—they made spelling errors that a professional would surely have avoided"
(Eph'al 1998: 116).

22. If a seal or stamp impression can be found in Avigad and Sass 1997, it is cited here
as WSS followed by the number given to it in this corpus. The number given to it in the
collection of Röllig 2003 is added in square brackets.

23. Thus, they are not included in Avigad and Sass 1997.

cutters tended to use the lapidary script or more archaic sign forms. Thus, we may assume that the Hebrew-written *Yehud* stamps simply followed the traditional *script* used by the early stone-cutters. These are probably earlier stamps, while the later stone-cutters gradually turned to the Aramaic script. Only at a very late state were they obviously influenced by the book script. Thus many undoubtedly Aramaic seals still show the lapidary form of the *yod*, while the one seal that manifests a cursive *yod* is probably a very late one (Millard 1989: 61).[24]

Except for the disputed items published by Avigad (1976), there are no clearly Hebrew seals or stamps (impressions)[25] that can be dated indisputably to the late Persian era and that originated from the Persian province of Judah.[26] The same holds true for the questionable items published by Avigad, who dated them mostly on paleographic grounds to the late sixth century B.C.E. (Avigad 1976: 13–18).[27] That

---

24. For the corrected reading as יאז/בר ישב/יהוד, see Naveh 1996: 45.

25. The stamp reading שלמי/העד, which Cross (1969: 27) interpreted as a Hebrew stamp from the fourth century, must be excluded for two reasons. First, its provenance is highly debated. For example, it was also taken to be an Edomite or Ammonite stamp (Hübner 1992: 112 n. 290). Second, the interpretation of העד or עד as the Hebrew word for 'witness' is highly improbable, because such a *title* is unknown. Of course, עד could follow a name in the list of witnesses to a contract, but there it designated the person as a witness for that contract only. There were no professional witnesses or notaries in ancient Israel or in its neighboring countries, as Garbini (1974: 166) rightly argued. Thus, either העד should be interpreted as a name (cf. Garbini 1974: 166–167, who points to the Qatabanian name *h'd* and to the fact that the stamp's design resembles a South Arabian stamp found at Beitin), or the inscription should be read as שלם/יהעד taking יהעד as a biform of the name יועד. Though this form of the name is otherwise unattested, one could compare, for instance, the name יהאר (Röllig 2003: 435 [50.1]).

26. Thus there are only a few items dated by Sass (Avigad and Sass 1997) to the sixth century (WSS 180 [10.38], 220 [11.5], 223 [11.13]), but it is not clear whether they were made after 538 B.C.E. or not. Even WSS 305 [16.31] cannot be dated with certainty to a postexilic setting (Röllig 2003: 339: sixth century). Furthermore, WSS 102 [2.6] and 336 [17.40] would belong to the early Persian era, if Sukenik (1945: 8–9) is right, but Sass (Avigad and Sass 1997) and Röllig (2003) date WSS 102 [2.6] to the seventh or early sixth century, and 336 [17.40] is not dated by Sass but is ascribed to the seventh century by Röllig (2003).

27. Though no. 12 (למיכה) shows a script with no specific Aramaic signs, most of the seals are written in an Aramaic script with clear archaic or Hebrew influence. Because one has to ask how the cutter could have come to know the archaic lapidary Aramaic script, signs such as a closed *ʿayin* (nos. 7, 9, 11), *bet* (nos. 7–10), or *reš* (nos. 7–9, 11), a w-shaped *šin* (nos. 7, 10, 14), a *mem* with an upper-left zig-zag line (nos. 9–10), a *kap* with two fingers (no. 7), and a *taw* written crosswise (nos. 5, 14) advocate more for influence by the traditional Hebrew script, used by the cutters until the Persian era. Though the *dalet* in no. 3 is open, its left finger turns to the right and thus shows a transitional form from the archaic/Hebrew closed *dalet* to the later open *dalet*. Only one seal in this collection is written in purely Aramaic script, though giving the Hebrew text לירמי/הספר (no. 6). Assuming

they belong to the early Persian period if they are authentic is also corroborated by the fact that their cutters used the same design, which
was common in pre-Persian times.[28] However, later Aramaic seals often show a different design.[29]

Thus, the seals and stamp impressions fit the analysis of the biblical
texts and the other documents. Aramaic was the language used for
them at least in the later Persian era, and Hebrew was used, if ever,
only at the beginning of this period. Because the bearer of the seals or
those who used stamps obviously belonged to the leading groups or
the higher classes of society, one should of course be careful not to take
this inference as proof that Hebrew died out as the vernacular language of the people. But it illustrates again the influence of Aramaic.
The willingness of the higher classes to adopt it is illustrated by the
fact that the use of Aramaic was obviously not mandatory for seals and
stamps in the Persian era. In fact, there did exist a purely Hebrew
stamp impression of a son of the governor Sanballat from Samaria.[30]
And, keeping in mind that most of the leading members of this group
were returnees from the Exile, we should not find it surprising that
they used Aramaic as their mother tongue. But, likewise, this shows
that they had no interest in changing their language.

The Coins

Most of the coins just bear the Aramaic name of the Persian province *Yehud*, though mostly in Hebrew script. However, on two coins,
personal names are given together with a Hebrew title: יוחנן הכוהן and
יחזקיה הפחה, though the latter name also appears without the title. Finally, there is one coin with יהודה written beside יהד (Meshorer 2001: 2–
16). These last three coins are suspicious, because other coins from the

---

that the seal is authentic, this fact could be explained by the assumption that a scribe
would probably take care that his seal was written well and not in a mixture of different
forms—and he would have been able to show the cutter the right way to do it.

28. Thus no. 3 and no. 7 show design B2, nos. 4–5 design A2, no. 6 design A3, no. 8
design B3, no. 10 design B4, no. 11 design A1, and no. 12 design B1, according to the
overview of the designs of pre-Persian seals given by Röllig (2003: 99). For no. 9, see WSS
34, and for no. 14, see WSS 22.

29. Note especially the clearly late Aramaic seal impression published by Millard
(1989: 61; cf. n. 31 and the related text), which was obviously made by a round seal divided by a stroke into two parts. In contrast to the "traditional" design, the first part has
a name on two lines without a dividing stroke. Furthermore, the (probably) later seal
bearing the inscription יהוד/יהועזר/פחוא (Avigad 1976: 22 [no. 7], fig. 17,7) shows no
strokes between the lines, though it is oval.

30. WSS 419. Note also WSS 1206 (עשניהו עבד המלך) from Tell Qasile, which Stern
(1982: 207) dated to the fourth century, but this is probably a forgery (WSS).

Persian Empire do not give titles after personal names or a name beside the name of the province. That they show a deviation from the common style of coinage in the Persian era leads us to wonder whether they are dated correctly. Though this is likely for the coin mentioning יוחנן הכוהן,[31] the claim that the coins bearing the title הפחה should also be dated to the end of the Persian era is less convincing (Meshorer 2001: 16). Aside from the fact that this title would be very uncommon on a Persian coin, one must keep in mind that there was no such person as "the governor" in the Persian Empire but only "governors" of a certain province. Thus, the word פחה as a title is always connected to the name of the province in all other documents from Persian times (TAD A4.7:1, 29; C2.1:31 [VII 3]; WDSP 7:17; 8:10).[32]

There are three ways to explain the conspicuous הפחה: (a) Yeḥezqiyah was the governor of *Yehud* who held this office at the very end of the Persian era, and the use of the title is a Judean innovation, perhaps influenced by the priest coins minted a short time before. The coins with his name but without the title could have been minted after the end of the Persian dominion. But one cannot exclude the possibility that they just followed the "traditional" form of other Persian coins. (b) The coins with the title were issued by the above-mentioned Governor Yeḥezqiyah, but after the end of Persian domination. This is quite possible, because פחה was a well-known title in Hebrew, not just for the governor of a Persian province. Because Yeḥezqiyah was obviously a political leader in Judah even after the end of the Persian dominion, it would be quite understandable if he still used this title.[33] After all, what other title would have been appropriate? But because Judah was no longer even a province of the Persian Empire, there was no need to call himself "governor of *Yehud*" and thus to keep the full official Persian title.[34] (c) The coins with הפחה were issued by a minor

---

31. Probably he has to be identified with Jehochanan II; thus the coin should be dated in the mid-fourth century (Meshorer 2001: 14).

32. This holds true even for seal inscriptions, as WSS 419 shows. The seals with the Aramaic title פחוא are no counterargument, because this is a different title from פחה, the determinative form of which is פחתא. Probably פחוא deviated from the plural פחות 'governors, officials' and does not designate the "governor" of a province but a minor official. See, for example, Naveh and Greenfield 1984: 123.

33. Thus, he should probably be identified with "Ezekias, a 'high priest' of the Jews" mentioned in Josephus, *Ag. Ap.* 1.187 [22]. See, for instance, Meshorer 2001: 15–16 and Josephus (ed. Labow) 2005: 197–98.

34. By the way, this would explain why, in what is probably a late addition to Neh 12:26 (Rudolph 1949: 195), Nehemiah is just called הפחה. If in the post-Persian era the political leader could have been called הפחה, then this addition would reflect this later use of the word.

official and not by the governor himself. Thus they would have been a local edition, not an "official" coin, and thus, like a minor official's stamp, using פחוא as the title. However, it is hard to believe that a minor official would issue coins, and so this solution is less convincing. The second solution (b) seems to me to be the most likely, though the first suggestion (a) cannot be ruled out.

The third coin mentioned above also presents a problem. Should we take יהודה as a personal name or as the Hebrew name of the province of Judah? Meshorer (2001: 15) argued for the first solution, "since it is unreasonable that anyone would be troubled to provide such unimportant information as two variants of the province's name on such a small coin with a limited area. . . . However, we know of no high priest or satrap from the Persian period who was so called." The reason that in contrast to other coins from the Persian era the name of the province is also given on this coin could have been to make it clear that יהודה was a personal name and not the name of the province. But because the Aramaic name יה(ו)ה for the province was well known and used on all other coins, there was only a slight chance that a person would misunderstand יהודה. Thus, the second solution is most likely. The coins of the Ptolemaic period show the Aramaic provincial name יה(ו)ה or the Hebrew יהודה. Consequently, it is possible that shortly after the end of the Persian era coins were minted that carried the same impression as the existing coins, still using the "Persian" design but replacing the Aramaic יה(ו)ה with the Hebrew יהודה,[35] thus reflecting the new political situation. However, because this name was not common on coins during the transitional time, the "traditional" יהד was added to clarify that the name of the province was meant. Thus, only the priest's coin can be dated with high probability to the Persian era, and the other coins probably belonged to the transitional phase that followed.

The fact that in contrast to the documents and the seal or stamp impressions the coins of the late Persian era or the time following it use Hebrew is not enough evidence to discount the arguments presented so far. Two facts must be borne in mind. Minting coins was an innovation in the Persian era and, as the design of most of the Judean coins shows, they normally followed the Greek, especially the Athenian tradition. It had the most influence on the design traditions used in southern Palestine (Hendin 2001: 96). Outside Judah, local forms of the

---

35. The word יהודה is written before the Athenian owl, in the same place where on the Persian coins the word יהד appears.

Phoenician script have been found on these coins from southern Palestine (Hendin 2001: 82, 85). Thus, the appearance of Hebrew script can easily be explained as the southern Palestine tradition of using the local script on coins.

Second, it is not by chance that the coins that use the Hebrew language were minted by a priest or by a (former) governor who was also a priest. Obviously, the temple economy was involved in issuing coins. The temple played a prominent role in the economy and fiscal transactions of Judah, so this is no great surprise. Hebrew surely was used in the cult and thus probably was also the language used in the temple, so its use on coins poses no problem, especially if the use of Hebrew script on coins was traditional. Thus we may assume that especially coins issued by the temple or high priest used not only Hebrew script but also the Hebrew language and retained this practice on coins issued after the Persian era. And thus it is also understandable that Hasmonean coins and others minted during the later Jewish revolts continued the practice of using Hebrew.

The Use of Hebrew in the Persian Era: Conclusions

There can be little doubt that Hebrew was superseded by Aramaic as the commonly spoken language in Judah during the Persian era. The fact that there are no Hebrew documents and probably only very early Hebrew seals and stamp impressions shows that Hebrew was not used in everyday life by people who could write or use written documents. As stated above, this is probably due to both the use of Aramaic as the common language in the western parts of the Persian Empire and the influence of the Aramaic-speaking returnees from the Exile (see also Polak 2006: 591–92). The analysis of the biblical evidence shows that Aramaic gained status as a commonly spoken language throughout Judah in addition to Hebrew, thus creating a bilingual society. Because the majority of Judeans were not careful to continue speaking Hebrew, Aramaic began to supersede Hebrew as the spoken language— an evolution criticized by Nehemiah (Neh 13:23–25*). As the various layers of Neh 8:1–8 show, this evolution could not be prevented, and thus the tradition of interpreting the reading of the Torah for the common people arose; the later addition of Neh 8:1–4 presupposed this later tradition.

Summing up the evidence, the evolution of a bilingual society should be dated to the end of the sixth or, at the latest, the beginning of the fifth century. The phase in which Aramaic began to supersede Hebrew was probably the end of the first half of the fifth century; it probably was completed during the fourth century, which led to the tradition of interpreting and (finally) translating the Torah (and other books) into Aramaic at the end of fourth and during the third centuries.[36]

These observations lead to two more conclusions: (1) the linguistic development from Hebrew to Aramaic as the commonly spoken language was not reversed in the Hellenistic era; (2) the main reason for the opposition to this evolution of language in the Persian period was not a nationalistic but a religious reason. The loss of ability to understand Hebrew would separate the uneducated people from the Hebrew Torah, which had just been propagated as the unifying document for the Jewish people. However, as Neh 8:1–8 shows, a different solution was found. One should be very careful not to read a nationalistic-language ideology into the texts; this ideology did not arise until the 19th century C.E.[37] Thus, there are only two realms in which Hebrew was still used. It was retained as the language of the cult and the language of literature—which were both basically religious. It was also used on coins, probably due to the economic influence of the temple.

---

36. Thus, the picture given by texts such as Ezra 10; and Neh 5, and 8, that people conversed with Ezra or Nehemiah in Hebrew, *could* be historically correct. One may assume that these conversations were held with elders and leaders, who were probably still able to speak Hebrew in the second half of the fifth century or even around 400 B.C.E., and they spoke with people who had been careful to retain Hebrew (see Neh 13!). But, given the fact that in Ezra 1:1–4 and Neh 2:2–6, Cyrus and Artaxerxes are also quoted as delivering Hebrew speeches, which surely does not mean that they spoke Hebrew, one should not give this argument too much weight. The same holds true regarding the observation made by Polak (2006: 606–11) that the quoted speeches show the style "of spontaneous spoken language . . . : short simple clauses with only a few arguments, a small number of subordinate clauses, and only a few noun groups" (Polak 2006: 607). The same style is also used in the Hebrew quotations of Artaxerxes' conversation with Nehemiah in Neh 2:2–6. Thus it is clear that the author could deliberately choose this style of spontaneous spoken language for quotations, as any good author would do. And though it is true that "quoted discourse of this type is to a certain extent representative of the vernacular," the fact that it "fits the cross-cultural typology of spontaneous spoken language" (2006: 607) even allows for the possibility that an Aramaic-speaking author, who used Hebrew only as a literary language could have mimicked this style for quotations in his Hebrew texts. Thus, these texts and observations cannot prove that Hebrew was still commonly used as a vernacular at the end of the fifth century or even later.

37. Even the rabbis did not share this sort of ideology. Thus *b. B. Qam.* 83a || *b. Soṭah* 49b argue against the use of Aramaic (but not of Hebrew) as a national language; they believed one should use either the "Holy tongue" or Greek or Persian.

The Use of Hebrew after the Persian Era

The ongoing production of Hebrew (religious) literature found in the later biblical books and especially at Qumran illustrates the use of Hebrew as the language of the cult and religion. Not only were older works being transmitted and expanded but also new works were being written, and thus Hebrew must still have been a "living" language in the sense that it could be developed and expanded. Especially when new literary forms such as halakic texts were created, the language used for them needed to be developed to fit the new situation. Thus, it is not surprising that 4QMMT, especially, with its halakic orientation, reveals a language that deviates more from Biblical Hebrew than the bulk of the Qumranic texts do (Qimron 1994: 65–108). The fact that 4QMMT obviously is some sort of letter or treatise from a religious group (maybe under the guidance of the Teacher of Righteousness) to a leader of Judah (perhaps Jonathan), dealing with Halakah, is an argument that Hebrew was used as the main language in these sorts of religious and learned groups to discuss religious themes and issues. Although even a literary language can undergo linguistic changes independently from a spoken language (Blau 2000), it is quite possible that in religious circles such as the community of Qumran and the temple community of Jerusalem Hebrew was still spoken. Thus the common argument that the development of Hebrew proves its ongoing use as a vernacular is not convincing. Developments of this sort can also be explained by the ongoing use of Hebrew as a religious lingo and are even possible in a language still used only for literature. I do not find Schniedewind's statements (2006: 137, 141, 143) convincing that the Hebrew scribal tradition came to an end in the Persian era and was revived in the third century. A language can survive as a scholarly or religious lingo. This is a well-known phenomenon as is shown, for example, by the use of Akkadian in literary texts and some official inscriptions up to the first century C.E. and the use of Latin as a scholarly and religious language even up to today.

It is likely that CD 14:10 reflects this situation. It requires the inspector of all the camps to know not only the secrets of men but also all their languages. Though the next word is obviously corrupt, in the context of the community of which CD is speaking, the inspector would apparently also use languages other than Hebrew to call the members to order and to discuss matters with them (CD 14:10–11). Members who had just entered the community or were not well educated (yet) were in special need of someone with whom they could discuss problems in their own language. Because it seems to be unlikely that vernacular Hebrew dialects differed from each other or from the "literary" Hebrew used in the community to such an extent that members could not understand each other, the easiest explanation is that the ordinary people spoke different languages, such as Aramaic or even Greek, and thus their leaders had to use these languages as well. Consequently, Hebrew was not a language spoken by everyone in the community, though it was the language of the texts and probably of the community itself.

It is relevant to observe that 1QH^a 10:20–21 (2:18–19) speaks about those who understood but had changed something "into an uncircumcised lip and a different language for a people without knowledge to be ruined by their mistake." Obviously, this passage is a short commentary on the preceding section. Note that it not only changes from 1st-person to 3rd-person singular, but it also shows no *parallelismus membrorum*. The speaker praises God for giving him "the answer of the tongue to his uncir[cumcised] lips" (10:9 [2:7]) so that he can teach those who repent and offend those who mediate error. The claim that this alludes to the use of vernacular Hebrew in place of the Hebrew used in the community is not convincing (contra Rabin 1958: 146; Schniedewind 2000: 246). Rather, this is probably an attack on the Aramaic translations or Aramaic interpretations of the Torah that were given to the common people, who spoke Aramaic. Thus, it reflected the linguistic ideology of the Qumran community, that true doctrine should be transmitted in Hebrew and not in Aramaic. This would be in accord with the fact that the literature composed at Qumran was written in Hebrew.[38]

The only nonliterary document from the Hellenistic period that evinces Hebrew influence is an ostracon from Jerusalem that dates to the last decades of the fourth or the beginning of the third century B.C.E.: בצק / ככרן 1 לף לחנניה] (Naveh 2000: 9–10).[39] Naveh interpreted ככר as 'loaf (of bread)', and thus this text would not only show the Hebrew word for 'dough' (בצק) but also a second Hebrew word with ככר:

---

38. Obviously Hebrew is called "the holy language" in 4Q464 frg. 3 i 8. The fact that there are also Aramaic texts and even some Targumim found at Qumran is not a counterargument. The library of Qumran included many non-Qumranic works—even Greek texts. One should not confound such a linguistic ideology with fundamentalism. If my interpretation is right, then it proves only that Hebrew was the language of the community; it does not necessarily follow from this that other languages were condemned. Books in Aramaic—even Targumim—could be used, for example, as an aid to understanding Scripture (Beyer 1984: 273). But the doctrine of the community was obviously taught in Hebrew.

39. For the reading, see Yardeni 2000: A 361.

'Loaves (of bread): 1 thousand; for Ḥananiah dough'. Speaking of the 1,000 loaves and dough, Naveh states "that this ostracon served as a label in a public (probably military) bakery, where Hebrew was presumably the spoken language" (Naveh 2000: 10). But one must keep in mind that ככר has the feminine-plural form, when it is used with the meaning 'loaf'.[40] Because, the form used is ככרן instead of ככרות,[41] the language is clearly Aramaic. Though the writer used some traditional Hebrew *termini technici*, he was writing Aramaic, and Hebrew was obviously not his spoken language![42] While it is easy to use the traditional names for things, such as certain forms of bread or dough, the real language of a speaker is revealed by the grammar he uses.[43]

Moreover, the interpretation of the ostracon as a label from a military bakery is unconvincing. It mentions two different things, bread and dough—the latter obviously being designated for Ḥananiah. The word בצק is not written at the beginning of the line but under לחנניה, and לחנניה is written a little bit lower than ככרן 1 לך, with a different slant. This probably means that the ostracon served as a notepad. Thus, the writer probably made a note about an order or delivery of 1,000 loaves of bread and indicated that Ḥananjah received or should receive dough. Moreover, one must ask whether there was a large enough garrison in Jerusalem to need 1,000 loaves of bread.[44] Possibly this ostracon belonged to the realm of the temple. During the feasts especially, when people were coming to Jerusalem from other places, there was a need to provide hundreds or maybe even thousands of pilgrims with fresh bread. Thus, it seems plausible to connect this note with the temple. This theory easily explains the use of the Hebrew terminology, because Hebrew was still the language used in the temple and for the cult. A worker or administrator of a bakery surely would have known these *termini*[45] and might have used them in his own

---

40. See Judg 8:5, 1 Sam 10:3. In the rabbinic texts as well, the plural of ככר denoting 'loaves' is feminine, while the dual is ככרים (thus, also in *m. Ṭehar.* 1:7, ככרים should be taken as a dual, which makes good sense when speaking of two loaves sticking together).

41. And not ככרים, as Schniedewind (2006: 43) assumes.

42. Thus Yardeni (2000: A 361 + B 120) correctly places these texts under the heading "Selected Aramaic Documents."

43. Thus, there is no need to assume that the use of these words "indicates the continuation of some type of vernacular Hebrew" (Schniedewind 2006: 143).

44. As Naveh (2000: 9) notes, a loaf of bread was adequate for two meals; thus it was a daily ration for one person (cf. also Jer 37:21).

45. The use of ככר for 'loaf' is also found in *Tg. Neof.* on Exod 29:23, which shows that such Hebrew words were still understandable (and usable) for Aramaic-speaking people in later times.

colloquial Aramaic language when the items were ordered by the temple administration.

As is well known, some Hebrew documents and letters are preserved that date to the first and second centuries C.E. But all datable legal documents belong to the time of the Jewish War or the Bar Kokhba Revolt and none to the time in between. Obviously, the use of Hebrew was part of the ideology of the rebels (Cotton 1999: 225). But because this usage ceased after the rebellions, it must have been an innovation rather than evidence of the linguistic situation in Judah. This conclusion is corroborated by the observation that even in the Hebrew documents from the Jewish War all men are named x בר x.[46] Thus they probably spoke Aramaic and referred to themselves in this language. Though the writers of the Hebrew documents during the Bar Kokhba Revolt normally used בן instead of בר, XHev/Se 8 clearly reveals the prevalence of Aramaic. The text of the document is given twice, the outer (lower) version in Hebrew but the more important, inner (upper) version, which was legally binding, in Aramaic (Cotton 1999: 225). Moreover, the Hebrew text is based on the Aramaic text, even giving the number 'three' in the Aramaic form ת [תל (line 8). This document also shows that in the documents from the time of the Bar Kokhba Revolt (in contrast to documents from the time of the Jewish War) the use of בן or בר is dependent on the language of the text and does not reflect the language of the people. Thus בר is used in the Aramaic part, the only exception being שמעון בן כוסבה (line 1), who, as the leader of the revolt, was the promoter of the use of Hebrew. However, in the Hebrew part, בן is also used for other names (frgs. e–k 3).

It was under the administration of Simeon that the attempt to establish Hebrew as the language of the people was made, which is illustrated by the fact that most of the Hebrew documents deal with leases given out by the administration itself.[47] The only other Hebrew documents are the above-mentioned Aramaic-Hebrew XHev/Se 8 (year three) and Mur. 22 (year four; Yardeni 2000: A 47). It is probably not by chance that these two documents date to the last period of the revolution. Obviously, first the administration of Simeon began to issue He-

---

46. Mur. 22, 29, 30. Probably also the woman mentioned in Mur. 29:18 is called ברת and not בת, as read by Milik (1961: 142) and Yardeni (2000: A 50). The sign before the *taw* resembles the ligature for בר more than it resembles a normal *beth*.

47. Mur. 24; P. Yadin (NH) 44, 45. Though P. Yadin (NH) 46 does not mention the administration of Simeon, it was obviously written under his administration. This is proved by the fact that it was written by the same scribe who wrote 44 and 45 and at the same date as 45, which also names the same persons.

brew documents and use Hebrew in letters if the writers or addressees were able to deal with them;[48] this innovation gradually led to the use of Hebrew in nonadministrative documents, first bilingually and then solely.

We know that priests were the primary leaders behind the use of Hebrew, based on findings from Masada. "Among the inscriptions designating priestly shares . . . , Hebrew distinctively prevails. . . . Hebrew was the language of the priests in the Temple, in particular, and the tongue used to describe religious rites, in general" (Yadin and Naveh 1989: 9). Because there was priestly influence on the groups at Massada, and because during the Jewish War Hebrew was promoted by the rebels as shown by the use of Hebrew in legal documents, one should hesitate to take Hebrew names with בן, Hebrew nicknames, or some other Hebrew notes found at Massada as a clear sign of the use of Hebrew as a spoken language outside the priestly and religious circles, as proposed by Yadin and Naveh (1989: 8–9). Such Hebrew notes may also have been "priestly" texts; furthermore, it would not be surprising if in a group of rebels to which priests belonged some people decided to Hebraize their names or take Hebrew nicknames. These (nick)names are mainly found at Massada, but even at Massada Aramaic was used for letters and dockets. Thus, even the (very few) inscriptions and fragmentary texts that show Hebrew names and words, which are not precisely datable but belonged to the first century C.E., are not proof that Hebrew was used as a spoken language by ordinary people. They could either belong to members of priestly or religious circles or show the influence of language politics during the Jewish War.[49] Moreover, family documents such as marriage contracts (Mur. 20 [66/117 C.E.]; Mur. 21 [first century C.E.]; Naḥal Ṣelim 11 [first–second century C.E.]; P. Yadin [NḤ] 10 [122/125 C.E.]), bills of divorce (Mur. 19 [72 ?] C.E.), and a waiver given by a woman to her previous husband (Naḥal Ṣe'elim 13 [134/135 C.E.]) were written solely in Aramaic even during the time of the revolts. This means that Aramaic was probably spoken on the family level.[50] It is hard to imagine that Aramaic would have

---

48. See especially P. Yadin (NḤ) 52, a letter written in Greek because the writer could not handle Hebrew (lines 11–15). There are nearly the same number of Aramaic letters as Hebrew. This shows that only some of the rebels could read or write Hebrew.

49. Thus, for instance, 4Q348 probably was a deed written in Hebrew, but even this text shows the Aramaic name in the form of x בר x (line 15) as in the legal documents from the time of the Jewish War, and furthermore, it mentions the כוהן גדול (line 13).

50. Thus it is probably not by chance that the legal documents concerning transactions from one member of a family to another are also in Aramaic; see P. Yadin (NḤ) 7 (120 C.E.), 8 (122 C.E.).

remained the language of such private documents through the centuries if people had not spoken it on the common level. After the end of the Persian era, there was no need to do so unless people demanded it.[51] They could also use Greek for these documents, but they apparently did not use Hebrew.

The prevalence of Aramaic as the commonly spoken language is also revealed by some linguistic data. Though there was Hebrew influence on the Palestine Aramaic dialects, it affected only the lexicon. This is not surprising. In a society where Hebrew was used in the cult and for religious matters by educated people, borrowings into the common language would be quite natural.[52] On the other hand, Aramaic influence on Hebrew went far beyond borrowed words and clearly affected the syntax and morphology as well. For example, the later Hebrew verbal system—with its perfect as the main narrative tense, the participle for the present, the imperfect for the future, and the periphrastic combination of a form of היה with a participle to express ongoing actions—clearly evolved from an earlier Aramaic verbal-syntactical system.[53] The use of earlier uncommon noun patterns such as *paʿlān* is also easily explained by Aramaic influence (Beyer 1984: 442).

One also must keep in mind that the nature of Hebrew as a Semitic language facilitates the creation of new nouns by applying a noun pattern to a root. Indeed, it is even easier to apply a new stem to a root. Educated people using a particular lingo, such as priests or members of a religious community, would easily be able to create and understand neologisms. However, when a language is commonly spoken, the innovation of professional neologisms is a bit more restricted be-

---

51. Thus the claim is unconvincing that "Aramaic was the natural choice . . . because this was the language of legal documents from time immemorial in this part of the world" (Cotton 2005: 151). It is true that Aramaic was the language of legal documents in the Persian era, but why would it have been retained in documents dealing with family affairs if all the participants spoke Hebrew? One would expect that at least during the time of the Hasmoneans, who also revived the use of Hebrew on coins, Hebrew would have been used for legal documents if it had been possible.

52. That Hebraisms of this sort also occur in Christian Palestinian and Samaritan Aramaic is no indication that Hebrew was a commonly spoken language. Late Christian Palestinian Aramaic is based on the earlier Palestinian Aramaic, which obviously contained some Hebrew words, and early Palestinian Christians surely took over the language and terminology of their Jewish forefathers. Hebrew was also used by the Samaritans, not only in their cult (as, for example, the Hebrew prayers show), but probably also by the elite at least until the end of the Persian era (see the seal of Sanballat's son, WSS 419). Thus, a lexical Hebrew influence on Samaritan Aramaic is also no surprise.

53. One morphological Aramaism is, for example, the ending -*āt* for the 3rd fem.-sing. perfect of roots *tertia infirma*.

cause common people have more problem understanding them. Thus, the fact that innovations of this sort occur and that they often show parallels in Aramaic implies that Hebrew was not a common language but the lingo of religious groups that was influenced by Aramaic (the commonly spoken language).[54]

This discussion sheds new light on the character of MH. As Qimron has shown, Mishnaic Hebrew grammar differs conspicuously from the dialect used at Qumran and in the documents written during the Bar Kokhba Revolt.[55] Moreover, his assumption is probably correct that the language of the Qumranic texts and the epigraphic sources is based on the Hebrew used in Jerusalem, especially at the temple. This comports with the facts that (1) the community at Qumran was subject to strong priestly influence and (2) Jerusalem played an important role in the ideology of the Bar Kokhba Revolt, in which priests had an important function—at least in the beginning.[56] But there is no need to assume that these "dialects" were based on colloquial Hebrew dialects. The rabbis who compiled the Mishnah and used its language for other texts were not primarily priests but came from various religious groups that had developed their own religious traditions. It is no surprise that their Hebrew shows different developments from the Hebrew of the religious groups in the temple or communities such as Qumran. Especially after the destruction of the temple, the influence of "cultic" Hebrew decreased, opening the way for developments in the language of other religious circles.

Conclusion

From all the evidence discussed above, there can be little doubt that Hebrew was superseded by Aramaic as the commonly spoken language in Judah during the Persian Era. Nevertheless, Hebrew was still in use in religious circles and in the realm of the temple, not only for traditional texts, but also for new texts and probably also as the lingo

---

54. Contra Bar-Asher (2000: 16), who argued that Aramaicized neologisms "certainly belonged to a living dialect or perhaps dialects of Hebrew." By the way, we must of course keep in mind that we do not know the complete lexicon of Hebrew as a spoken language in the pre- and early Persian period. Thus some "new" words may actually have been old but not used in the sources that we possess.

55. Qimron (2000) is quite right to stress the picture given by the grammar because the real nature of a dialect is revealed by its grammar. Words can easily be borrowed or transmitted.

56. This influence is shown, for example, by the coins of Bar Kokhba, which in the first year mention a priest and in every year mention Jerusalem (Kottsieper 2005: 328–30).

of these communities. Consequently, Hebrew experienced its own evolution(s), as every language (even a literary one) does that is still productive. However, Aramaic, as the commonly spoken language, had a special influence on this evolution not only as a source of new words but also as a source of grammatical and syntactical change.

Appendix:
The Rabbinic Sources

In the discussion about the use of Hebrew as a common vernacular, scholars sometimes quote various rabbinic sources. Though these late texts cannot be taken as direct evidence, one should not wholly discount them. However, they need to be read carefully. In this appendix, I will treat some of the most interesting statements. Because Hebrew was the religious language of the early sages and most of the prayers, it is understandable that occasional admonitions to teach children Hebrew appear, especially in the context of learning the Torah. Thus *t. Ḥag.* 1.2 states that a father should teach the Shemaʿ, the Torah, and the "holy language" to his son when he "knows how to speak."[57] The context, which deals with the time when a child should be obligated to observe certain laws, makes it clear that this is not meant as an instruction for teaching Hebrew as the normal vernacular but as a religious language. The mother tongue of the child who at this time already "knows how to speak" is obviously not the "holy language," which also connotes MH (Segal 1927: 2). Thus, when R. Meir states that a person who lives in Israel, recites the Shemaʿ twice a day, and speaks the "holy language" is a son of the world to come *(Sipre Deut.* 32:43 [333]), he is obviously not describing the common linguistic situation of Judah but Israel as a religious society in which the "holy language" should be used.

The same is true of the saying of Rabbi (R. Yehuda ha-Nasi) in *b. B. Qam.* 83a ‖ *b. Soṭah* 49b: "Why Aramaic (לשון סורסי) in the land of Israel? The holy language or Greek!" First of all, this shows that Aramaic was the common language spoken in Israel at his time. However, it does not prove that in addition to Aramaic Hebrew was used as a vernacular outside the religious groups of the sages. Thus, it is followed by a parallel saying of R. Yose: "Why Aramaic (לשון ארמי) in Babylonia? The holy language or Persian!" It is obvious that in Babylonia Hebrew was not used as a vernacular but as a language of the sages and their

---

57. Compare *Sipre Deut.* 11:19 (46) and *Sipre Zuṭah Šallaḥ* 38.

religious community. Because according to *b. Sanh.* 22a, Hebrew was
chosen for the Torah while Aramaic was for the הדיוטות during the time
of Ezra, Aramaic was probably understood by sages such as Rabbi and
R. Yose as the language of the unlearned people and was not to be used
by the ideal Jew, who learned Torah and "the holy language." Thus, the
best course of action is to interpret these sayings in connection with the
well-known antagonism between the sages and the common people,
or the עם הארץ.

The fact that Hebrew was the language used by the early sages in
their religious communities, such as the court of the rabbis, but Aramaic was the vernacular of the unlearned people is illustrated by a
story about an exceptional maid of Rabbi, who received some sages
coming to visit Rabbi and ushered them in.[58] She conversed with them
in MH and knew it even better than they did. Thus, even the sages had
problems with MH. This is evidence against the assumption that MH
was based on a common Hebrew dialect. One should also note that,
when the maid spoke to another maid, she used Aramaic.

In this context, we should also be very careful about not placing too
much weight on the language in which a person is quoted in talmudic
literature. It is well known that one and the same sage was sometimes
quoted in Hebrew and sometimes in Aramaic. Obviously, the choice
depended either on the language of the sources the redactors were using or on their own decision for each passage. For example, the above-
mentioned maid of Rabbi is quoted speaking Aramaic both to the
sages and to Rabbi himself in *b. ʿErub.* 53b.

On the other hand, Hebrew was chosen as the language for the quotation of a Judean in *b. ʿErub.* 53b, which exemplifies the way Judean
scholars were careful in their speech and used mnemonics (cf. *b. ʿErub.*
53a). Asked which color a cloak had that he wanted to sell, he answered: כתרדין עלי אדמה, 'like chard, leaves of the ground'. In contrast
to this, a story is told about a "stupid Galilean," who according to
b. ʿErub. 53a was not careful in his speech and did not use mnemonics.
He asked just for a donkey, which led to the question whether he
wanted חמר למירכב או חמר למשתי עמר למילבש או אימר לאיתכסאה 'an ass for
riding or wine to drink, wool for clothing, or a lamb for killing'. Apparently, the main point is not the sloppy pronunciation of the guttur-
als by the Galilean but the fact that, if he had used an additional

---

58. See *y. Meg.* 2.2 (73a); cf. *b. Meg.* 18a and *b. Roš Haš.* 26b. That the maid of Rabbi was
not deemed by the sages to be an ordinary maid but a well-educated maid is illustrated
by *b. Moʾed Qaṭ.* 17a.

description, he would have made his wish clear and thus would have not been deemed stupid. This passage is not intended to contrast different languages used by the Judeans and the Galileans but to illustrate how the clever Judeans solved the problem of the ambiguity of words. By doing this, they showed themselves to be a better source for deciding the correct reading of a discussion in the Mishnah. This view is corroborated by the fact that the answer of the Judean without the apposition would be ambiguous only in an Aramaic conversation or with Aramaic speakers: תרדין could be taken as תור דין 'a bull of judgment', as the wordplay by R. Yose b. Asiyan that is quoted in 53b shows.[59] Moreover, in contrast to the Aramaic example of the Galilean, the Hebrew example seems to be a bit farfetched, which indicates that it may have been invented just for its purpose. Thus, the fact that the Judean is quoted in Hebrew does not prove that the Judeans actually spoke Hebrew in the market; instead, it is probably either based on a Hebrew source and used by the redactor of this passage to illustrate how the Judean scholar managed to avoid ambiguities or chosen deliberately to broaden the contrast between the learned Judean and the "stupid" Galilean.

---

59. He used to say במשפט שור instead of תרדין in a wordplay. By the way, this corroborates the vocalization of תרד with an *o*-vowel in the first syllable, as proposed by Löw (1928: 347).

Bibliography

Avigad, Nahman
  1976   *Bullae and Seals from a Post-Exilic Judean Archive.* Qedem 4. Jerusalem: Hebrew University.
Avigad, Nahman, and Sass, Benjamin
  1997   *Corpus of West Semitic Stamp Seals.* Jerusalem: Israel Academy of Sciences and Humanities, Israel Exploration Society, and Institute of Archaeology, The Hebrew University of Jerusalem.
Bar-Asher, Moshe
  2000   A Few Remarks on Mishniaic Hebrew and Aramaic in Qumran Hebrew. Pp. 12–19 in *Diggers at the Well: Proceedings of a Third International Symposium on the Hebrew of the Dead Sea Scrolls and Ben Sira,* ed. Takamitsu Muraoka and John F. Elwolde. STDJ 36. Leiden: Brill.
Barr, James
  1989   Hebrew, Aramaic and Greek in the Hellenistic Age. Pp. 79–114 in vol. 2 of *The Cambridge History of Judaism,* ed. by W. D. Davies and L. Finkelstein. Cambridge: Cambridge University Press.

Beyer, Klaus
1984   *Die aramäischen Texte vom Toten Meer: Samt den Inschriften aus Palästina, dem Testament Levis aus der Kairoer Genisa, der Fastenrolle und den alten talmudischen Zitaten.* Göttingen: Vandenhoeck & Ruprecht.
2004   *Die aramäischen Texte vom Toten Meer.* Vol. 2. Göttingen: Vandenhoeck & Ruprecht.

Blau, Joshua
2000   A Conservative View of the Language of the Dead Sea Scrolls. Pp. 20–25 in *Diggers at the Well: Proceedings of a Third International Symposium on the Hebrew of the Dead Sea Scrolls and Ben Sira,* ed. Takamitsu Muraoka and John F. Elwolde. STDJ 36. Leiden: Brill.

Blenkinsopp, Joseph
1988   *Ezra-Nehemiah.* OTL. London: SCM.

Cotton, Hannah M.
1999   The Languages of the Legal and Administrative Documents from the Judean Desert. *ZPE* 125: 219–31.
2005   Language Gaps in Roman Palestine and the Roman Near East. Pp. 151–69 im *Medien im antiken Palästina,* ed. Christian Frevel. FAT 2/10. Tübingen: Mohr Siebeck.

Cross, Frank Moore, Jr.
1969   Judean Stamps. *ErIsr* 9 (Albright Volume): 20–27.

Eph'al, Israel
1998   Changes in Palestine during the Persian Period in Light of Epigraphic Sources. *IEJ* 48: 106–19.

Garbini, Giovanni
1974   Ammonite Inscriptions. *JSS* 19: 159–68.

Gesenius, Wilhelm
1987–2005   *Hebräisches und Aramäisches Handwörterbuch über das Alte Testament,* ed. R. Meyer, H. Donner, and U. Rüterswörden. 3 vols. 18th ed. Berlin: Springer.

Gesenius, Wilhelm, and Kautzsch, E.
1909   *Wilhelm Gesenius Hebräische Grammatik.* 28th ed. Leipzig: Vogel.

Gunneweg, Antonius H. J.
1987   *Nehemia.* KAT 19/2. Gütersloh: Mohn.

Hendin, David
2001   *Guide to Biblical Coins.* 4th ed. New York: Amphora.

Hübner, Ulrich
1992   *Die Ammoniter: Untersuchungen zur Geschichte, Kultur und Religion eines transjordanischen Volkes im 1. Jahrtausend v. Chr.* ADPV 16. Wiesbaden: Harrassowitz.

Josephus, Flavius
2005   *Contra Apionem I: Einleitung, Text, Textkritischer Apparat, Übersetzung und Kommentar* by Dagmar Labow. BWANT 167. Stuttgart: Kohlhammer.

Kottsieper, Ingo
1990   *Die Sprache der Aḥiqarsprüche.* BZAW 194. Berlin: de Gruyter.

2003   Zum Hintergrund des Schriftsystems im Pap. Amherst 63. *DS-NELL* 5: 89–115.
2005   *Nordwestsemitische Texte (8. Jh. v.Chr. 3. Jh. n.Chr.)*. Pp. 307–30 in *Staatsverträge, Herrscherinschriften und andere Dokumente zur politischen Geschichte*. *TUAT* 2. Gütersloh: Gütersloher Verlaghaus.

Löw, Immanuel
1928   *Die Flora der Juden I.* Vienna: Loewit.

Meshorer, Yaakov
2001   *A Treasury of Jewish Coins: From the Persian Period to Bar Kokhba.* Jerusalem: Yad Ben-Zvi / New York: Amphora.

Millard, Allan
1989   Notes on Two Seal Impressions on Pottery. *Levant* 21: 60–61.

Morag, Shelomo
1988   Qumran Hebrew: Some Typological Observations. *VT* 38: 148–64.

Myers, Jacob M.
1965   *Ezra-Nehemiah.* AB 13. New York: Doubleday.

Naveh, Joseph
1982   *Early History of the Alphabet: An Introduction to West Semitic Epipgraphy and Palaeography.* 2nd ed. Jerusalem: Magnes / Leiden: Brill
1996   Gleanings of Some Pottery Inscriptions. *IEJ* 46: 44–51.
2000   Hebrew and Aramaic Inscriptions. Pp. 1–4 in *Excavations at the City of David 1987–1985 Directed by Yigal Shiloh. VI: Inscriptions.* Qedem 41. Jerusalem: The Hebrew University of Jerusalem.

Naveh, Joseph, and Greenfield, Jonas C.
1984   Hebrew and Aramaic in the Persian period. Pp. 115–29 in vol. 1 of *The Cambridge History of Judaism*, ed. W. D. Davies and L. Finkelstein. Cambridge: Cambridge University Press.

Pakkala, Juha
2004   *Ezra the Scribe: The Development of Ezra 7–10 and Nehemia 8.* BZAW 347. Berlin: de Gruyter.

Pichon, Christophe
1997   La prohibition des marriages mixtes par Néhémie (XIII 23–31). *VT* 47: 168–99.

Polak, Frank H.
2006   Sociolinguistics and the Judean Speech Community in the Achaemenid Empire. Pp. 589–628 in *Judah and the Judeans in the Persian Period*, ed. Oded Lipschits and Manfred Oeming. Winona Lake, IN: Eisenbrauns.

Qimron, Elisha
1994   *Qumran Cave 4 V: Miqṣat Maʿaśe Ha-Torah.* DJD 4. Oxford: Clarendon.
2000   The Nature of DSS Hebrew and Its Relation to BH and MH. Pp. 232–44 in *Diggers at the Well: Proceedings of a Third International Symposium on the Hebrew of the Dead Sea Scrolls and Ben Sira*, ed. Takamitsu Muraoka and John F. Elwolde. STDJ 36. Leiden: Brill.

Rabin, Chaim
1958   The Historical Background of Qumran Hebrew. Pp. 144–61 in *Aspects of the Dead Sea Scrolls*, ed. Chaim Rabin and Yigael Yadin. ScrHier 4. Jerusalem: Magnes.

Reinmuth, Titus
2002   *Der Bericht Nehemias: Zur literarischen Eigenart, traditionsgeschichtlichen Prägung und innerbiblischen Rezeption des Ich-Berichts Nehemias.* OBO 183. Freiburg: Universitätsverlag / Göttingen: Vandenhoeck & Ruprecht.

Röllig, Wolfgang
2003   Siegel und Gewichte. Pp. 81–456 in vol. 2/2 of *Handbuch der althebräischen Epigraphik,* by Johannes Renz and Wolfgang Röllig. Darmstadt: Wissenschaftliche Buchgesellschaft.

Rössler, Otto
1952   Der semitische Charakter der libyschen Sprache. *ZA* 50: 121–50.

Rudolph, Wilhelm
1949   *Esra und Nehemia samt 3. Esra.* HAT 2. Tübingen: Mohr Siebeck.

Segal, Moses Hirsch
1909   Mishnaic Hebrew and Its Relation to Biblical Hebrew and to Aramaic. *JQR* 20: 647–737.
1927   *A Grammar of Mishnaic Hebrew.* Oxford: Clarendon.

Schniedewind, William M.
2000   Linguistic Ideology in Qumran Hebrew. Pp. 245–55 in *Diggers at the Well: Proceedings of a Third International Symposium on the Hebrew of the Dead Sea Scrolls and Ben Sira,* ed. Takamitsu Muraoka and John F. Elwolde. STDJ 36. Leiden: Brill.
2006   Aramaic, the Death of Written Hebrew, and Language Shift in the Persian Period. Pp. 137–47 in *Margins of Writing, Origins of Cultures,* ed. Seth L. Sanders. OIS 2. Chicago: The Oriental Institute of the University of Chicago.

Stern, Ephraim
1982   *Material Culture of the Land of the Bible in the Persian Period 538–332 B.C.* Warminster: Aris & Phillips / Jerusalem: Israel Exploration Society.

Sukenik, Elazar Lipa
1945   Three Ancient Seals. *Kedem* 2: 8–10.

Waltke, Bruce K., and O'Connor, M.
1990   *An Introduction to Biblical Hebrew Syntax.* Winona Lake, IN: Eisenbrauns.

Williamson, H. G. M.
1985   *Ezra, Nehemiah.* WBC 16. Waco, TX: Word.

Wright, Jacob L.
2005   *Rebuilding Identity: The Nehemiah-Memoir and Its Earliest Readers.* BZAW 348. Berlin: de Gruyter.

Yadin, Yigael, and Naveh, Joseph
1989   The Aramaic and Hebrew Ostraca and Jar Inscriptions. Pp. 1–68 + pls. 1–60 in *The Masada Reports, Masada I: The Yigael Yadin Excavations, 1963–*

1965. Final Reports, ed. Joseph Aviram, Foerster Gideon, and Ehud Netzer. Jerusalem: Yigael Yadin Memorial Funds, Hebrew University and Israel Exploration Society.

Yardeni, Ada
  2000   *Textbook of Aramaic, Hebrew and Nabataean Documentary Texts from the Judaean Desert and Related Material A/B.* Jerusalem: The Hebrew University.

Archaeology and Archaiologias: *Relating Excavations to History in Fourth-Century* B.C.E. *Palestine*

LESTER L. GRABBE
University of Hull

It is my firm belief that any new understanding of history in the fourth century B.C.E. is likely to come from archaeology. Barring a pleasant surprise, we are unlikely to increase our fund of classical texts describing this period of Persian history. Sadly, the classical texts we have now—especially Diodorus Siculus and the Alexander historians—are probably all we shall ever have. This makes the recent and future (one hopes) finds from archaeology most important.

A number of writings from antiquity have the title of *archaiologia*, the Greek word from which we derive "archaeology." A good example is Josephus's *Antiquities of the Jews* which in Greek is *Ioudaïkēs Archaiologias* (Ἰουδαϊκὴς Ἀρχαιολογίας), but there are a number of similar works, regardless of what they are called. The original title of some of the writings on this topic is unknown, but the aim is ostensibly to describe the antiquities or ancient history of a particular people or peoples. In most cases, the backbone of history is derived from works of this sort, however problematic they might be. But just as they can provide a context for the finds of material culture, the artifacts can serve to check their stories and suggest new interpretations, corrections, and even rejections. I make this point because a recent "biblical history of Israel" states the following about archaeology:

> in the modern period of histiography it has sometimes been assumed that archaeological remains offer us the prospect of grounding historical statements in something more solid than testimony. . . . This kind of view of the nature of archaeological evidence has been common among historians of Israel, even where they have sometimes recognized that it cannot be entirely correct and have found space in one part of their minds for the contrary idea . . . that archaeological data are no more "objective" or "neutral" than other sorts. . . . In fact, *all* archaeologists tell us

stories about the past that are just as ideologically loaded as any other historical narrative and are certainly not simply a neutral recounting of the facts. (Provan, Long, and Longman 2003: 63)

This is of course true up to a point: artifacts indeed have to be interpreted, just as do texts. But it misses the important fact that artifacts are *realia*—they exist; they are the product of actual ancient peoples. Texts, on the other hand, are products of the imagination. It is always possible that a text is entirely fantasy. I would suggest that sending an archaeological expedition in search of Hogwarts is not likely to be very productive.

In order to explore the issue of relating ancient texts and archaeology, I want to take three well-known examples from fifth- to fourth-century Phoenician history that have been commonly used to explain archaeology.[1] Specifically, I want to look at the question of the "Megabyzus rebellion," the "Tennes rebellion," and the "Revolt of the Satraps."

"The Revolt of Megabyzus"

Our first example is actually earlier than the fourth century, but it is useful because it has been widely used to relate events and archaeology (Bigwood 1976; Hoglund 1992: 97–164; Briant 2002: 573–79). Not long after Artaxerxes I took the throne, Egypt rebelled under Inarus about 463 B.C.E. (Diodorus 11.71.3–6; Thucydides 1.104.1). The Egyptians enlisted the help of Athens, which sent a fleet of ships. Artaxerxes dispatched a force under Achaemenes, but the Persians were defeated, Achaemenes was killed, and the remnants of the Persian army were besieged by the Greeks in a place called the "White Fortress" (Diodorus 11.74.1–6; Thucydides 1.104.2). Artaxerxes sent another army about 461 B.C.E. under Artabazus and Megabyzus (Diodorus 11.75.1–4; Thucydides 1.109.3), who defeated the Greeks and rescued the besieged Persians (Diodorus 11.77.1–5; Thucydides 1.109.4). The Greeks took a stand, and the Persian generals decided to come to terms with them

---

1. In their volume on Apollonius-Arsuf, Roll and Tal (1999: 211–14) include a chart of strata from a number of sites in the Phoenician area of the fourth century B.C.E. and the historical events that might be associated with them. This is a very useful summary in tabular form, and the written commentary that precedes it is both useful and interesting. It is, of course, a "maximal" correlation and in that sense forms a hypothesis that remains to be tested. Indeed, I take it not as a definitive statement but rather as a catalog of data and possibilities (for example, reference is often made to other interpretations). But it will serve as a useful list from which to pick some examples for the sake of my essay here.

and allow them to leave Egypt unmolested; however, Thucydides says that few made it home (1.110.1).

This is where the story ends as far as Diodorus and Thucydides are concerned, but according to Ctesias (Photius §§34–46 = *FGH* 688 frg. 14), the Greeks who surrendered were still in Persian custody some five years later and were surrendered to Achaemenes' mother, who took her revenge on them for the death of her son, despite Megabyzus's promise of safety. Megabyzus was appalled at this. Having been given permission to return to his satrapy of Syria, he then raised an army and revolted against the emperor about 455 B.C.E. After inflicting a number of defeats on the Persian army, he eventually came to terms with Artaxerxes.

There are several problems with the scenario. It is typical of Ctesias to see events in terms of personal motivations. Neither Thucydides nor Diodorus knows anything about the slaughter of Greek prisoners for whom the Persians had given personal guarantees of safety. They may not have had any reason to discuss Megabyzus further, but they would probably have recorded the event that supposedly made Megabyzus revolt (that is, the slaughter of Greek prisoners whose safety had been guaranteed). But perhaps he revolted for quite another reason? It is possible but, again, this period of time that led up to the Peace of Callias is reasonably well recorded by the Greek historians.

"The Revolt of the Satraps"

According to Diodorus Siculus (15.90–93), a great revolt of Ionic cities, along with an uprising of some of the Asia Minor satraps took place against Artaxerxes III shortly before 360 B.C.E. In addition to Ionians, those defecting included Lycians, Pisidians, Pamphylians, Carians, Syrians, Phoenicians, and "nearly all the coastal dwellers" (15.90.3). Diodorus states that the two most prominent of the rebels were Ariobarzanes, satrap of Phrygia, and Mausolus, satrap of Caria. Yet the one chosen to be general of the rebels was Orontes, satrap of Mysia, though he plotted to betray the insurgents to the king of Persian. But the actual description of fighting relates to Datames, satrap of Cappadocia, not mentioned heretofore. Datames fought against an invading Persian army, was betrayed by his own father-in-law, but nevertheless won a great victory. Artaxerxes arranged to have him assassinated. Orontes and the other rebels are not further mentioned.

At the same time as the events in Asia Minor, according to Diodorus, Tachos, the king of Egypt, took advantage by gathering ships and mercenaries to fight against the Persians. He gained the official aid of Sparta, and the Spartan general Agesilaus commanded the mercenary army. Against advice, Tachos accompanied his army. While it was en-camped "in the region of Phoenicia" (Diodorus 15.92.3), the person left in charge in Egypt revolted against Tachos and enlisted the king's own son, Nectanebo, against him. (Nectanebo had been sent by Tachos to besiege the cities of Syria when this happened.) Tachos made peace with Artaxerxes, who appointed him to take charge of the army and recapture Egypt. With Agesilaus's help, Tachos defeated the rebels and retook the throne of Egypt.

There are a number of problems with Diodorus's account, one of the main problems being the lack of any other continuous narrative of the revolt (Briant 2002: 656–75). Several different figures are mentioned, but their relationship is not always clear. There is also the fact that a number are said to have betrayed their cause and made deals with the emperor. Also, was there a connection between the supposed rebels in Asia Minor and the rebels in Egypt? There is credible evidence of some communication between the groups, but did any of them join together for concerted action? For example, with regard to Mausolus, Diodorus names him as a "prominent" member of the rebellion but does not make him a leader, as one might expect, nor does he give any detail of his activities. Everything else we have on Mausolus suggests that he was a loyal subject of the Persian king. Only one incident, mentioned by another writer (Xenophon, *Agesilaus* 2.26–27), shows some ques-tionable activity, but the exact significance of his actions is unclear—it is not an undisputed example of treason against the emperor.

The real issue for us, though, is whether Tachos or others from Egypt or any of the rebels named for Asia Minor carried out the de-struction of sites in Syria. Tachos was not that strong when he invaded Phoenicia in 362/361. Although according to Diodorus he dispatched Nectanebo to besiege "the cities in Syria," his own troops immediately revolted (Diodorus 15.92.4; Weiskopf 1989: 83). Briant (2002: 665) has this to say about this episode:

> It is possible that Tachos, then on the coast . . . , ordered Nectanebo to turn toward the interior . . . , the "cities" perhaps designating Achaeme-nid fortresses such as Arad or Beer-sheba; but archaeological excava-tions have not revealed any destructions at this date. The real problem is that it is very difficult to understand what Diodorus means by the term "Syria." . . . Nectanebo's mission would have been to subdue fortresses located on the coast in "Phoenician Syria"; but this is just a guess. All in all, however, it is clear that the little information available is flimsy and

incomplete, but there is nothing to prove that the campaign by Tachos and Nectanebo put Syro-Phoenicia to fire and the sword, Diodorus notwithstanding (XV.90.3: Syrians and Phoenicians).

Furthermore, there is evidence that the Sidonians remained loyal to the Persian king, even during this period (Briant 2002: 664). An Athenian inscription offers thanks to Straton of Sidon for facilitating the movment of ambassadors to the Persian court (Tod 1948: text 139). Moreover, when Tachos decided to come to terms with Artaxerxes, he took refuge in Sidon (Xenophon, *Agesilaus* 2.30).

Simon Hornblower recognizes the problems but also asserts that "Diodorus' source surely did not invent the basic fact" (*OCD* 1359). But we need to remember that Diodorus has associated two separate regions, and what happened in Anatolia may have had no effect on what happened in Egypt. Briant concludes a lengthy discussion as follows (2002: 674):

> While we cannot forget the persistent uncertainties that have been pointed out all along the way, we can at least state with certainty that Diodorus's thesis is not confirmed by the rest of the evidence. We are not dealing with a general, coordinated conflagration on the western front in 361 but rather with a series of limited local revolts over the course of a decade. . . . On one side, we stress once more that the Persians, despite the King's determination and great preparations, proved incapable of retaking the Nile Valley; moreover, at one point, the pharaoh even took the offensive. . . . On the other side, it seems difficult to assert that the satrapal revolts attested in Asia Minor illustrate a deep and irreversible degradation of the control that the central authority exercised over the governors. . . . there was in fact no alternative to Achaemenid dynastic continuity.

Thus, there was a revolt—or revolts—but probably less serious than Diodorus states. Accepting that some sort of revolt or revolts took place, which is reasonable, the main question remains: what effect did this/these revolt(s) have on Palestine? In spite of Diodorus (15.92.4), it seems unlikely that a general campaign of destroying the Syrian and Phoenician cities took place (Briant 2002: 664–65). Although some possible raids into the interior cannot be ruled out, an extensive or systematic campaign seems unlikely.

"The Tennes Rebellion"

The Tennes rebellion has become such a commonplace of Persian-period discussions that it is almost axiomatic. It is perhaps surprising that the unassuming article by Daniel Barag in the 1966 *BASOR* was so influential, but one reason no doubt is that it seemed to fill in a period in Judah's history, about which we otherwise knew almost nothing. But Barag's view is still a hypothesis and one must ask the question: how solid is it? This is a bit tricky to evaluate, because part of Barag's argument was already archaeological. But there are also other elements. At the core of the reconstruction is a passage in Diodorus (16.41–45): he describes a rebellion of Cyprus and Phoenicia about the year 350. Egypt had rebelled under Artaxerxes II, and it was left to Artaxerxes III to do something about it. About the same time, the Sidonians were upset by the high-handed manner in which the local Persian administrators treated them, and they revolted. They secured an alliance with Nectanebo, king of Egypt, and gathered a force of triremes and mercenaries. Their initial hostile acts consisted only of burning the king's *paradeisos* (park) and the fodder stored up for the Persian military horses and punishing the Persian officials who had acted badly toward them.

At some point, Belesys, satrap of Syria, and Mazaeus, governor of Cilicia, came against Phoenicia but were defeated by Tennes, king of Sidon, with the help of Greek mercenaries. In the meantime, Cyprus also revolted, encouraged by the actions of the Phoenicians, but Artaxerxes III sent Idreieus, ruler of Caria, against the rebels. It was at this point that Artaxerxes III brought his army to Phoenicia. Now threatened with defeat and worse, Tennes secretly sent a trusted associate to negotiate with Artaxerxes: Tennes would betray Sidon to him if the king would drop any charges. This was agreed, Tennes betrayed the city, and then, because he was of no further use to the Persians, Artaxerxes had him executed. Seeing that their city was recaptured by the Persians, the Sidonians burned their city down as an act of suicide, and all the other cities submitted.

Thus far, the Tennes rebellion is an account of one more revolt against Persian rule, but the prevalent theory goes beyond this to claim a significant place for the Tennes rebellion in the history of Palestine. It is argued that certain late accounts indicate that Judah was caught up in this revolt: (a) Eusebius (*Chron.* on the 105th Olympiad [Helm 1956: 121]); (b) Orosius (*Adver. pagan.* 3.7.6), who basically agrees with Eusebius; (c) Syncellus (1.486.10–14); and (d) Solinus (*Collect.* 35.4 = M. Stern 1974–84: 2.418–22). Finally, a number of archaeological sites in the Galilean region are examined with the argument advanced that they show layers of destruction for the mid-fourth century at the various sites.

In fact, a number of classical scholars have investigated the theory and have found significant problems with it. In what follows, I will present some of the main points (Widengren 1977: 501–2; Grainger 1991: 24–30; Briant 2002: 682–85, 1004–5). First, as noted above, our main source for the "Tennes rebellion" is Diodorus Siculus. A number of points about his account are problematic (Briant 2002: 683–85), and other issues are still opaque to the modern historian. The precise dates of the revolt are uncertain, but it appears to have been rather more short-lived than the dates 351–345 often given (Briant 2002: 683–84). The reasons for the revolt are unclear, and Diodorus's statement (16.41.2) that it was due to the overbearing manner of the Persians is not very credible. More likely is that the machinations of the Egyptian king Nectanebo II lay behind it (Grainger 1991: 24; Briant 2002: 684–85). Tennes' betrayal of the city of Sidon is also puzzling. On the one hand, he would hardly have been unaware of the resources that the Persian king would be able to bring to bear on him when he initiated the revolt. On the other hand, if he relied on help from Egypt but came to realize it would not be forthcoming, betrayal of his own city no doubt seemed the logical way of surviving. Thus, a number of questions about Diodorus's account remain unanswered.

Second, the sources seeming to associate the Jews with the rebellion are "suspect and contradictory," especially on the chronological level (Briant 2002: 685). The trustworthiness of Eusebius's tradition is called in question by his misdating of Artaxerxes' reign by 40 years. The statement assigned to Hecataeus of Abdera (Josephus, *Ag. Ap.* 1.22 §194; Josephus's alleged quotations of Hecataeus are problematic) about deportation of the Jews by the Persians probably involves a confusion of the Persian activities with the Babylonian captivity. While some Jews may indeed have been settled in Hyrcania by the Persians during the fourth century, there are a number of possible reasons other than participation in a rebellion. Furthermore, Diodorus does not say anything about the Jews, which one might expect. Similarly, Josephus is silent about a rebellion by the Jews, suggesting that he was either ignorant of any such episode or, inexplicably, suppressed it.

Third, Josephus's reference to a Persian official Bagoses, during whose time the temple was defiled is best identified with the governor known from the Elephantine papyri (Grabbe 1992). Fourth, most of the archaeological sites allegedly destroyed lie outside Judah proper, with the exception of Jericho. There appears to be little archaeology of Jericho remaining from the Persian period, so the question of habitation—

much less destruction—is difficult to answer (Holland 1997: 224). As for the Palestinian sites outside Judah, there is no evidence to associate the various destructions with any one particular date; on the contrary, according to the usual interpretation (E. Stern 1982: 253–55; Roll and Tal 1999: 210–14) the destructions of these sites are to be associated with a variety of campaigns and revolts over about 150 years during the fifth and fourth centuries. Furthermore, it is difficult to distinguish between pottery of 345 B.C.E. and pottery of a decade earlier or pottery of the later time of Alexander. In other words, some of the destruction layers that Barag associates with the Sidonian revolt may in fact have been caused either by the later Greek conquest or by events earlier in the century.

Indeed, there is a serious question whether any of the destructions in the coastal cities should be associated with the "Tennes rebellion," for only the city of Sidon seems to have been involved. Although Diodorus says that "the Phoenicians" revolted (16.40.5) and that Tennes persuaded "the other Phoenicians" to seek their freedom (16.41.3), no other Phoenician city is in fact named as having done anything, and only Sidon was punished. Judging from Diodorus's account, there does not seem to have been widespread destruction in Phoenica, except for Sidon itself. There is even a contradiction with regard to Sidon, because it was a flourishing city only a dozen years later, when Alexander invaded (Arrian, *Alexander* 2.20; Quintus Curtius 4.1.15; Grainger 1991: 30).

In sum, although the rebellion of Tennes was potentially serious, it seems to have collapsed suddenly without any major fighting (apart from a preliminary engagement in which the combined armies of the satraps Belesys and Mazaeus were defeated by the Phoenicians [Diodorus 16.42.1–2]). The only city destroyed was Sidon, and this is alleged to have been burned by the Sidonians themselves. There is little evidence that other areas of Phoenicia suffered from fighting, much less Samaria or Judah or other areas of the Palestinian interior. As John Grainger wrote (1991: 25):

> It has also been suggested that the revolt spread to Palestine. The evidence is entirely archaeological, and consists of locating any change of occupation or a destruction which can be dated to the fourth century BC. The theory is a misuse of archaeological evidence and betrays a complete misunderstanding of its nature, as well as displaying a complete disregard for the evidence of *several* Persian campaigns in Palestine during the century. The notion is bad archaeology and bad history, and can be ignored.

Implications for Writing History

These three examples illustrate the problem that historians quite frequently face when they start to put together the various sources. Sources often disagree, or seem to disagree. The danger is to ignore differences and focus on agreements, especially if it seems to lead to a conventional or desired interpretation. We have many examples of this in relation to archaeology and the biblical text. We are all aware of the dangers of looking for direct correlations between archaeological finds and events described in texts, such as specific strata that relate directly to specific historical events. A particular example is the Albright school's finding of Joshua's conquest in the strata of a variety of tells. In his recent reexamination of Samaria, Ron Tappy found that time and again the published report of Kenyon and the Crowfoots made correlations between the archaeology of the site and the biblical text that were not supported by the actual excavated finds. He noted,

> [I]n addressing the exclusion of important data from the final reports of the work at Samaria, and by considering anew the implications of those data, I have shown again that Kenyon's archaeological chronology seems tied too directly to generally accepted historical dates (Jehu's coup) and/or presumed historical events (Assyrian military destruction of Samaria). Trends and fashions in material culture are not divorced from such significant historical events or even from regnal lists, but they ultimately establish a life of their own and, in doing so, can run at cross currents with changes on the throne, specific military campaigns, internal *coups* and rebellion, attempted political and religious reforms, and the like. In short, a direct correspondence between archaeological history and political history does not always exist. (Tappy 2001: 441)

> Instead, we must evaluate excavated remains on their own merit and date them first and foremost by other remains from secure deposits at contemporaneous sites. Only then should we make historical connections. (Tappy 1992: 215)

Relating archaeology and texts is a complicated business. Archaeology often provides valuable parameters of what is possible, as well as providing data that no other source can provide, but archaeology can usually also be explained by a variety of scenarios. A destruction layer shows that the city was destroyed, an archaeological fact; but by whom, when, and why is usually a matter of interpretation. We always have to keep in mind that the interpretation of a text that is consistent with the archaeology is not necessarily the right one. In the examples we looked at, certain strata of Phoenician sites were consistent with the

Tennes rebellion and the Satraps' Revolt and other alleged events, as pointed out by Roll and Tal. The problem was not with the archaeology but with the historical reconstruction. Once the problems with the textual sources were considered, the correlations with specific archaeological data became problematic.

This illustrates why our historical sources need to be analyzed independently. For the final step, which is the historical reconstruction, they need to be brought together, but too often the independent criticism of the individual sources is bypassed. What does each source say in its own right? What are its biases and prejudices, its ideology, its particular perspective? What are its limitations? What are the different ways it could be interpreted? The destructions of sites in the fifth and fourth centuries seem to be clear. The question is what may have caused them. It is likely that armies moved through the area many times during the second half of the Persian period, especially considering the importance of Phoenicia as a staging post for naval and other expeditions. Egypt was a valuable but rebellious part of the Empire, and armies periodically marched down the coast or embarked on ships from Phoenician ports. They may have been associated with some of the revolts discussed above, but regardless, there were almost bound to be military campaigns that have not been recorded in our extant historical texts from antiquity. However, we should also be open to the possibility that some site destructions may have been due to causes other than military attacks.

References

Barag, Daniel
    1966   The Effects of the Tennes Rebellion on Palestine. *BASOR* 183: 6–12.
Bigwood, J. M.
    1976   Ctesias' Account of the Revolt of Inarus. *Phoenix* 30: 1–25.
Briant, Pierre
    2002   *From Cyrus to Alexander: A History of the Persian Empire*, trans. Peter T. Daniels. Winona Lake, IN: Eisenbrauns. [ET of *Histoire de l'Empire perse de Cyrus à Alexandre*. Paris: Fayard, 1996.]
FGH = Jacoby, F.
    1923–58   *Die Fragmente der griechischen Historiker*. Berlin: Weidmann.
Grabbe, Lester L.
    1992   Who Was the Bagoses of Josephus (*Ant.* 11.7.1 §§297–301)? *Transeu* 5: 49–55.
Grainger, J. D.
    1991   *Hellenistic Phoenicia*. Oxford: Clarendon.

Helm, R. (ed.)
  1956   *Die Chronik des Hieronymus.* Eusebius Werke 7. GCS. Berlin: Akademie.
Hoglund, Kenneth G.
  1992   *Achaemenid Imperial Administration in Syria–Palestine and the Missions of Ezra and Nehemiah.* SBLDS 125. Atlanta: Scholars Press.
Holland, Thomas A.
  1997   Jericho. *OEANE* 3: 220–24.
Hornblower, Simon
  1982   *Mausolus.* Oxford: Clarendon.
  1996   Satraps' Revolt. *OCD* 1359.
OCD = Hornblower, S., and Spawforth, A. (eds.)
  1996   *The Oxford Classical Dictionary.* 3rd ed. Oxford: Oxford University Press.
Provan, Iain; Long, V. Philips; and Longman, Tremper, III
  2003   *A Biblical History of Israel.* Louisville: Westminster John Knox.
Roll, Israel, and Tal, Oren
  1999   *Apollonia-Arsuf, Final Report of the Excavations, Volume 1: The Persian and Hellenistic Periods.* Institute of Archaeology Monograph 16. Tel Aviv: Institute of Archaeology.
Stern, Ephraim
  1982   *Material Culture of the Land of the Bible in the Persian Period 538–332 B.C.* Jerusalem: Israel Exploration Society / Warminster: Aris & Phillips.
Stern, Menahem
  1974–84   *Greek and Latin Authors on Jews and Judaism.* 3 vols. Jerusalem: Israel Academy of Arts and Sciences.
Tappy, Ron E.
  1992   *The Archaeology of Israelite Samaria, Volume 1: Early Iron Age through the Ninth Century B.C.E.* HSS 44. Atlanta: Scholars Press.
  2001   *The Archaeology of Israelite Samaria, Volume 2: The Eighth Century B.C.E.* HSS 50. Winona Lake, IN: Eisenbrauns.
Tod, M. N.
  1948   *A Selection of Greek Historical Inscriptions.* Oxford: Clarendon.
Weiskopf, Michael
  1989   *The So-Called "Great Satraps' Revolt," 366–360 B.C.: Concerning Local Instability in the Achaemenid Far West.* Historia-Einzelschriften 63. Stuttgart: Franz Steiner.
Widengren, Geo
  1977   The Persian Period. Pp. 489–538 in *Israelite and Judaean History,* ed. John H. Hayes and J. Maxwell Miller. Philadelphia: Fortress.

PART 3

*Edom and Samaria:
Judah's Neighbors in the Late Persian
and Early Hellenistic Periods*

Idumea in the Late Persian Period (Fourth Century B.C.E.)

AMOS KLONER and IAN STERN
Bar-Ilan University

Borders and Geographical Site Distribution

The borders of Idumea are difficult to define with precision, but were, generally speaking, Emek Ha-Elah in the north extending south toward Keilah and then southeast of Beth-zur. From Beth-zur, the line probably continued east through an area shown in the archaeological surveys to have been almost uninhabited until just south of En Gedi on the Dead Sea. The eastern border most likely ran along the Rift Valley south of En Gedi, although there, no settlements from this period were found that far east. It is conceivable that these desert areas were inhabited by nomads, perhaps connected to Arab or Nabatean or Qedarite tribes.

The western border may have been along the line of the existing settlements of Tel Zafit, Tel Erani, Tell el-Hesi, Tell Jemmeh, and Tell el-Farah, although this border is difficult to establish. It is not clear whether the last 2 sites—Tell Jemmeh and Tell el-Farah—are Idumean or belonged to the *ethnoi* of the settlements of the coastal plain, but the existence of Aramaic ostraca from the Persian period at these sites enable us tentatively to include them in the area of Idumea. Idumea's southern frontier extended as far south as the Beer-sheba valley and at times included the Negeb mountains. Both Tell el-Kheleifeh and Kadesh-barnea, along with a few other sites, revealed remains from the Persian period as well, although it is difficult to determine whether or not these areas were connected to the population centers farther to the north. In the Negeb mountains to the south, there were very few Persian-period settlements, and according to the latest publications these settlements were not inhabited during the fourth century B.C.E.

The settlement patterns discerned from the excavations and surveys provide us with a number of settlement clusters or blocks, made up primarily of small hamlets and farms, one located in the west, an area that included Mareshah, Kh. el Kom (Makkedah), and Idna (the only 3 identifiable sites mentioned in the epigraphic material). Another smaller cluster existed in the central highlands but did not include Hebron. The vast number of fourth-century B.C.E. Aramaic ostraca have provided, for the first time, a comprehensive picture of the ethnic makeup of the province and to some extent the interrelationships among these groups. In addition, the inclusion of so many tax dockets strongly points to administrative activity that cannot be connected definitively to any province. A glance at the excavations at Mareshah indicate that it was inhabited in the Iron Age, the Persian period, and the Hellenistic era, although not necessarily in a continuous settlement. Persian-period remains there, including diagnostic finds such as loom weights, figurines, and Aramaic ostraca, found in almost all areas around the site, as well as the distinct signs of a fortified city are strong indications that the city was an important center at this time.

The northern border and the area of Yehud are depicted in the biblical accounts and are reinforced by archaeological finds—the geographical distribution of Yehud seals almost completely coincides with the boundaries described in the various lists in the books of Ezra and Nehemiah. Large numbers of small seal impressions from the end of the fifth century B.C.E. have been discovered with the inscription *yhd*. At this time, stamps with Achaemenid motifs were replaced by seals with only the province's name and sometimes with schematic symbols. It is very important to note that not a single *yhd* stamp has been found in Idumea. The diagnostic finds used to determine the borders of the provinces of Yehud and Idumea include coins, seal impressions, figurines, and pottery. To some extent, the borders were defined according to an absence of evidence. That is to say, while no distinctly Idumean seals or coins have been found, seals and coins from Yehud have been found, and their provenance, in conjunction with the biblical material, allows us tentatively to define the Yehud-Idumean border. The inverse is true with relation to figurines: their absence in Yehud and their prevalence in Idumea help us to define the borders of the two provinces.

Persian-period artifacts were found in 159 sites and are identified on a map recently drawn by Ian Stern (2005). They consist of two main groups of sites that existed in Idumea. A line running north-northeast by south-southwest between Jerusalem and Beer-sheba divides these two groups: a group of sites in the east in the Hebron mountains (51 sites) and the larger group to the west of this line in the Shephelah (108 sites), including the upper and lower Shephelah.

It should be mentioned that the basic information for the data of the 159 sites of Persian Period Idumea comes from surveys and a very few excavations. The two surveys used here are Avi Ofer's survey (1993) in the Hebron mountains (the eastern group of sites) and Yehuda Dagan's survey (1992; forthcoming) in the Shephelah. Surveys conducted in the 1960s by Kochavi (1972) in the Hebron mountains and other works were also used. It should be mentioned, on the one hand, that surveys are very limited sources of information because of three factors: (1) the easily mistaken identification of pottery; (2) the very low number of sherds collected in many sites; and (3) the possible biases of the persons collecting them. On the other hand, this map and site list is the first produced for Idumea for the fourth century B.C.E. and, as such, is extremely valuable.

Of the 51 sites to the east of the line, 3 were sites that were settled both in the Iron Age and the Persian period, and 30 contained remains from all three periods: the Iron Age, the Persian era, and the Hellenistic era. These statistics suggest that 33 of the 51 sites (approximately 65%) were settled both in the Iron Age and again in the Persian period. Only 18 new sites (or 35% of the total) were newly established in this area in the Persian period. Yet, in lower Idumea in the Shephelah, 45 (42%) of the total 108 sites were established in areas that had previously been settled in the Iron Age, and 63 new sites (58%) were established in the Persian period. These figures show that during the Persian period there was clearly a more dramatic settlement increase in the Shephelah—this region more than doubling the number of settled sites. This was probably due to increased economic opportunities in conjunction with immigration from outlying areas, possibly including areas to the south and east. One should not forget that in the Shephelah most, if not all of the sites also contain hewn subterranean complexes that preserve very important archaeological data.

The Population in Idumea in the Fourth Century B.C.E.
Based on the Available Epigraphic Material

During the past two decades, over 1,600 Aramaic ostraca that were identified as having a provenance somewhere in Idumea have appeared on the antiquities market (Porten and Yardeni 2004: 161). Of these, 1,380 were considered legible, and of these approximately 800 have been published in the last decade. On the approximately 200 ostraca published by Eph'al and Naveh (1996), there are close to 150 personal names, all of which, according to the authors, have a West Semitic derivation. Names that were not given a more specific designation were designated simply "West Semitic." The same system was applied to other epigraphic collections.

The vast majority of the ostraca can be dated to the fourth century B.C.E. Eph'al and Naveh (1996) date their material in a range from 10 Sivan in Artaxerxes II's 42nd year (14 June 363 B.C.E.) to 20 Shevat of Alexander IV's 5th year (22 Febrary 311 B.C.E.). Lemaire's materials (1996; 2002) are within the same chronological range. The Mareshah corpus included two fifth-century B.C.E. ostraca; the remaining material is mainly from the fourth century B.C.E., with some from the third and even the beginning of the second century B.C.E.

The importance of ostraca from a known provenance, albeit a small percentage of the total number, cannot be overstated. The 1,300 names represented in this study are more than a representative sampling of the onomasticon of late-Persian-period Idumea. As Porten and Yardeni (2004: 168) correctly point out, the formats of these ostraca are varied, presenting quite a few patterns. They generally include a regnal date, the name of the individual(s) paying, the person(s) who received the payment, and the amount of payment in goods. Occasionally a toponym is included as well as a patronym and/or familial/clan/tribal associations.

A total of 15 different toponyms were found, occurring a total of 37 times, although only 3 (Makkedah 16 times, Mareshah 4 times, and Idna once) can be identified with any certainty. The 4th toponym, Aqab or 'qb, is identified by Ian Stern (2005) with Ḥorvat Aqeva. The 5th toponym mentioned is Beth Hepher.

The ethnic breakdown reflected by the ostraca reveals a very mixed population within late-Persian-period Idumea. The approximately 1,300 names recorded on the ostraca of the period published so far were used for a statistical analysis that yielded the following percentages: approximately 32% Arab names, 27% Idumean names, 25% West Semitic names, 10% Judahite names, and 5% Phoenician names (the remaining 1% were smaller ethnicities; see table 1). It is worth emphasizing the similarity between the percentages of Arab, Idumea, Judahite, West Semitic, and Phoenician names from Mareshah and the percentages from an unknown provenance.

We know that boundaries between ethnic groups exist despite the fact that there is interaction both socially and economically, and in fact ethnic distinctions can exist not due to a lack of interaction but in many cases as a result of interaction. Coexistence among various eth-

Table 1. Ethnicity of Names from Selected Idumean Sites

Ethnicity	Arad	Beer-sheba	Tell Jemmeh	Mareshah	Unknown Provenance	Average from All Sites
Arab	12.24%	42.62%	12.50%	29.67%	32.20%	31.51%
Aramean	0%	3.28%	0%	0%	0%	0.19%
Babylonian	0%	0%	0%	3.30%	0.35%	0.56%
Idumea	14.29%	24.59%	12.50%	26.37%	28.10%	26.72%
Iranian	0%	4.92%	0%	0%	0%	0.28%
Judahite	61.22%	19.67%	62.50%	8.79%	5.50%	9.60%
Phoenician	0%	1.64%	12.50%	4.40%	5.62%	5.08%
West Semitic	12.25%	3.28%	0%	27.47%	28.23%	25.12%
Grand Total	100%	100%	100%	100%	100%	100%

nic groups under the Persians and later under the Ptolemies did not provoke or generate a competitive atmosphere that resulted in ethnocentrism. This is manifest by the prosopography on various ostraca and inscriptions. If we look at the ethnic patterns, the picture becomes more understandable. The behavior of all of the ethnic groups was generally consistent. There was almost a complete integration of ethnicities in Persian Idumea. For example, among the 30 names in the database identified as Idumean, approximately 10% were connected to an Arab clan or father, 23% to Judahites, 20% to Western Semites, 23% to Phoenicians, and 23% to Idumeans. In fact, only a minority of each group showed ethnic continuity as expressed through their particular ethnic onomasticon. This suggests, on the one hand, that each ethnic group eventually ceased to be a majority within its own clan. On the other hand, it is quite clear that each ethnic group continued to maintain its own identity. We have evidence for this in the third and in the beginning of the second century B.C.E. at Mareshah as well.

References

Dagan, Y.
   1992   *Archaeological Survey of Israel: Map of Lachish (98).* Jerusalem: Israel Antiquities Authority and Archaeological Survey of Israel.
   forthcoming   *Archaeological Survey of the Maps of Amatzia, Bet Guvrin and Other Maps in the Shephela.*
Eph'al, I., and Naveh, J.
   1996   *Aramaic Ostraca of the Fourth Century BC from Idumaea.* Jerusalem: Magnes.

Kochavi, M.
   1972   *Survey of Judah, Samaria, Golan 1967–1968* [Hebrew]. Jerusalem: Archaeological Survey of Israel.
Lemaire, A.
   1996   *Nouvelles inscriptions araméennes d'Idumée du Musée d'Israël.* Transeu Supplement 3. Paris: Gabalda.
   2002   *Nouvelles inscriptions araméennes d'Idumée du Musée d'Israël.* Vol 2: *Collections Moussaïeff, Jeselsohn, Welch et divers.* Transeu Supplement 9. Paris: Gabalda.
Ofer, A.
   1993   *The Highland of Judah during the Biblical Period* [Hebrew]. Ph.D. dissertation, Tel Aviv University.
Porten, B., and Yardeni, A.
   2004   On Problems of Identity and Chronology in the Idumean Ostraca. Pp. 161–84 in *Teshurot Lavishur Studies in the Bible and the Ancient Near East*, ed. M. Heltzer and M. Malul. Tel Aviv.
Stern, I.
   2005   *Idumaea in the Persian Period: The Interaction between Ethnic Groups as Reflected in the Material Culture.* Ph.D. dissertation. Bar-Ilan University.

The Onomasticon of Mareshah in the Persian and Hellenistic Periods

ESTHER ESHEL

Bar-Ilan University

Before discussing the importance of the names from Mareshah, we must briefly review the history of the city and its importance. Mareshah is first mentioned in the Bible in Josh 15:44 among the cities of Judah, and in the genealogies of 1 Chr 2:42 it belongs to the Calebites. Mareshah is included in the list of Rehoboam's fortified cities defending the southwestern borders of Judah (2 Chr 11:8). According to the book of Chronicles, Zerah the Ethiopian, who invaded the land of Israel in the time of King Asa, reached Mareshah at the beginning of the ninth century B.C.E. but was repulsed in a battle fought north of Mareshah (2 Chr 14:8–9). From the seventh century B.C.E., two Hebrew inscriptions have been found at Mareshah (Kloner and Eshel 1999).

The city of Mareshah (Marisa) is mentioned by Josephus in the vicinity of towns in the Shephelah. The location was also corroborated by Eusebius (*Onom.* 130:10), who located it two miles from Beth-Guvrin (Freeman-Grenville, Chapman, and Taylor 2003: 72). The site was identified with Tell Ṣandaḥanna, located in the Shephelah, about 2 km south of Beth Guvrin and 30 km east of Ashkelon.

After the destruction of the First Temple, Mareshah, as part of southern Judah, became Edomite territory. In the Hellenistic period, it replaced Lachish as the main city in western Idumea, as mentioned in the Zenon Papyri (Tcherikover 1937: 40–42). In the Hellenistic period, a Sidonian community settled in Mareshah. During the Hasmonean Wars, Mareshah served as a base for attacks on Judea and therefore suffered acts of retaliation by the Maccabees (1 Macc 5:66; Rappaport 2004: 184–85). Hyrcanus I captured Mareshah together with Idumea in 112 B.C.E., and he destroyed the city in 108 B.C.E. (Barag 1993; Finkielsztejn 1998). Herod's family probably originated from Mareshah. The city ruins remained in Hasmonean hands until Pompey's conquest of Judea. The city was rebuilt by Gabinius, governor of Syria, in 57 B.C.E. Mareshah was probably handed over to Herod together with the rest of western

Idumea in 40 B.C.E. In the same year, the Parthians utterly destroyed the "strong city," which had only recently been rebuilt. Beth Guvrin replaced Mareshah as the capital of the district, and Mareshah never regained its importance (Avi-Yonah and Kloner 1993: 948). Three Hebrew inscriptions from the early Roman period were found in Mareshah.

The site of Mareshah was partially excavated in the summer of 1900, by Bliss and Macalister (1902: 52–61), as part of the four excavations carried out in the Shephelah between 1898 and 1900. Since 1998, new excavations at Mareshah have been carried out by Kloner (2003: 9–30). The finds from Mareshah constitute one of the richest repertoires from the Hellenistic period discovered in the country. More than 200 Greek inscriptions, mostly ostraca, were found at Mareshah and will be published in the future by Korzakova (Kloner, Eshel, and Korzakova forthcoming).

Of the 72 inscribed sherds and ostraca written in Semitic script discovered at Mareshah, 68 can be dated to the Persian and Hellenistic periods, between the fifth and the second centuries B.C.E. Sixty-four of these inscriptions are written in the Aramaic script and language, 2 are written in the Aramaic script but in the Edomite language, and 2 are written in Phoenician (Kloner, Eshel, and Korzakova forthcoming).

The following examination proceeds along several lines:

1. Types of names including theophoric and nontheophoric elements.
2. Ethnic origins, including the origins of the Edomites. Because the area was under Idumean rule, most of the names belong to this category as well as the category of Nabateans/Arabs. Minority groups include Egyptian and Babylonian names.
3. The generational divergence.

The inscriptions from Mareshah, dated to the Persian and Hellenistic periods, resemble three other major corpora of inscriptions dated to the same period: two found in excavations at Beer-sheba and Arad; and another corpus that came through the antiquities market, presumably partly originating in El-Kom, which is to be identified with Makkedah—another city in Idumea (Eph'al and Naveh 1996; Lemaire 1996; 2002).

In what follows, I will discuss the significance of the onomasticon of Mareshah to our understanding of the history of Mareshah and the composition of its population in the Persian and Hellenistic periods. Altogether, the Mareshah collection includes 103 complete names and 9 incomplete names. We have to distinguish between two types of inscriptions: one represented by two Phoenician inscriptions, and the other by the majority of Aramaic inscriptions. The Phoenician inscriptions are more homogenous in nature than the others.

In the Phoenician inscriptions, only three Phoenician names appear. These names are hitherto unknown: BLRM, ʿKBRM, and BTMṬRM. The first name, BLRM, includes (1) the element BL, which is probably an abbreviated form of the deity BʿL, as in BL ḤMN (= BʿL ḤMN); thus it should be read as BʿLRM; and (2) RM, which is found in various Phoenician names, such as RMKʿT, as well as in other West Semitic names. The name ʿKBRM is mentioned in two inscriptions from Carthage, which do not postdate the third century B.C.E. Finally, the woman's name BTMṬRM is a Punic name, and the element MṬR is a name in and of itself and is included in the name MṬRŠBDʿ. MṬR is a theophoric element in names from Mari. The meaning of the name BTMṬRM is 'a daughter of a noble family'. The element BT is known from other Phoenician names, such as BTNʿM, BTŠLM, BTBʿL, and BTNʿMT (Benz 1972: 293). Two more women are mentioned in the Mareshah onomasticon. The first was the bride Arsinoe, mentioned in a marriage contract dated to 176 B.C.E.; the other was named 'the daughter of YṢR'.

As noted above, the main corpus is composed of 64 Aramaic inscriptions from the Persian and Hellenistic periods. To these ostraca, 827 names found in Samaria and Idumea that date to the same period can be added to give us a fuller picture of this era (Zadok 1998).

Names Including Theophoric and Nontheophoric Elements

The Mareshah onomasticon includes various theophoric elements, among them: ʾL- in the names ḤNNʾL, ʾLḤNY; BʿL in BLRM = BʿLRM, BʿLDKR, BʿLNTN; MLK in ʿBDMLK; NBW in NBWPDY; and QWS in many Edomite names. In addition, one should add a large proportion of nontheophoric names of West Semitic origin, such as: ḤLPN, YṢR, MTN, and MTQ.

The Mareshah corpus includes 13 names with the theophoric element QWS; for example, QWSYTʿ, QWSYNQM, QWSYHB, QWSYD, QWSḤNN, QWSZBD, QWSRM, QWSʿYR, QWSNTN, and ʿBDQWS. Some of these occur more than once; for example, the name QWSRM appears in 5 different inscriptions. To these data, one should add the name ʿSW, who was probably an Edomite, based on Gen 36:1: "Esau, that is, Edom." It should be noted that some of the Edomite names already published were preserved in Greek inscriptions found in Mareshah, such as QWSNTN—in Greek κοσνατανός ('Kosnatanos'; Peters and Thiersch 1905: 44, 54).

The other main group of names documented in the Mareshah onomasticon is the Nabatean or Arabic group. Before listing them, I need to make some introductory remarks concerning the Arabs. With the destruction of the Kingdom of Judah and the collapse of the Edomite kingdom, which ruled over Transjordan and the Negeb until the first third of the sixth century B.C.E., the Arabs were among the nomads who penetrated the territory of Palestine during the sixth and fifth centuries B.C.E. From Nehemiah's Memoirs, we learn that the Arabs were listed among the enemies of Judah (Neh 4:1), and Geshem, their leader, was one of Nehemiah's adversaries (Neh 2:19; 6:1, 6). Based on the works of classical writers, such as Herodotus, Diodorus, and Polybius, we know some things about the Arabs in Palestine and Transjordan. The term *Arabs* designates the nomads between Egypt and the Arabian Peninsula, and it applies both to tribes and to tribal federations. According to these sources, during the fifth and the fourth centuries B.C.E., the Arabs lived in the Negeb, and their capital was Gaza, ruled (at one point) by Geshem (Eph'al 1982: 197).

The first reference to the Nabateans is found in the work of Diodorus (19.94–100), which describes events that occurred in 312 B.C.E. Some scholars suggest identifying their ancestors with *Nabaitaya*, mentioned in an Assyrian document dated to the seventh century B.C.E., and with נבי(ו)ת mentioned in the Bible. In this respect, the discovery of the name NBYT in the Jebel Ghunaym inscriptions is important, because we have for the first time the name of the people of Nabaioth rendered in the ancient Arab dialect of the sixth-century B.C.E. Tema' region. Thus, we must reject the identification of Nabaioth (and NBYT, with a *taw*) with the Nabateans (and NBṬW, with a *ṭet*; Eph'al 1982: 222–23).

As for the Arabic/Nabatean names included in the Mareshah corpus, one should note the largest group with the typical ending *-u*: 'GMW, 'SDW, WTRW, ḤYYW, 'BDW, and 'ZYZW; as well as the names BYN, BNṢL, GMRT, DḤL'LW, PḤRY, and SR'; in addition to some hitherto unknown names, such as PṢY'L and 'LYṢL.

Other minority names are documented in the Mareshah ostraca in small numbers, including Egyptian elements, such as SMRR', in which the Egyptian deity Re is referenced; as well as Babylonian names, such as NBWPDY. Nabu was a Babylonian deity who was also worshiped by the Arameans and is therefore included as an element of some Aramaic names, such as NBWʾLH. Another Babylonian name is MNKY 'Mannuki'. Finally, one should add a large group of West Semitic names, some of which are known from the Bible, such as ʿZRʾ, ZRDʾ, BNY, ʾYLWN, ṢḤR, and ʿNY.

Ethnic Origins

In addition to names, the ostraca from Mareshah mention some ethnic groups, among them the Qedarites (QDRYN) and the Arabs (ʾRBYN). The name QDRYN derives from the name *Qedar* (see Gen 25:13, Isa 21:17, and especially Jer 49:28–33). The earliest reference to the Qedarites appears in a stele of Tiglath-Pileser III from Iran dated to the eighth century B.C.E., in which leaders from the western part of Mesopotamia are listed. During the eighth and seventh centuries B.C.E., their territory stretched eastward from the western border of Babylon. During the seventh century, they invaded the regions of Transjordan and southern Syria and were among the nomadic groups who put pressure on the settled area from the Jebel Bishri region to the outskirts of Damascus (Ephʿal 1982: 223–27). The name Qedar also appears in an Aramaic inscription written on a silver vessel, dated to the late fifth century, found at Tell el-Maskhuṭeh, in lower Egypt, probably originating from the shrine there, which reads: "That-which Qainū son of Gashmu, king of Qedar, brought-in-offering to han-ʾIlāt" (Rabinowitz 1956: 5–9). This inscription testifies to a Qedarite presence in the eastern approaches to Egypt. From the work of Herodotus, we know that the Qedarites lived in northern Sinai and near the Egyptian eastern border and were "perhaps engaged in keeping that border secure for the Achaemenid authorities. Such breadth of Qedarite distribution suggests a federation of tribes with various sub-divisions" (Ephʿal 1982: 226).

In the ostraca from Mareshah, a group of people designated by their place of origin is mentioned: "the children of Zarda." Zered is the name of a wadi running to the Dead Sea on the Moab border (Deut 2:13–14, Num 21:12), which may be the origin of these people. Another group is designated by their clan: MṬH DʾYN 'the clan of DʾYN', a group of unknown origin.

Most of the names included in the Mareshah onomasticon are known from other parallel corpora dating to the same period, mainly from the Arad and the Beer-sheba ostraca, as well as ostraca from Kh. el-Kôm. Other names, found at Mareshah, such as MTQ and SMRRʿ, are hitherto unknown.

Thus, the study of the onomasticon of the Mareshah collection shows the variety of the city's inhabitants during the Persian and Hellenistic periods. As is evident from the onomasticon, the city of Mareshah in this period of prosperity included a variety of ethnic groups. The people's names originated from Babylon in the east, Egypt in the west, and the Transjordan. Nevertheless, the main ethnic groups were Edomites and Nabateans/Arabs. This sort of variety is also known in parallel corpora of names of the fourth century B.C.E. from Arad, Beer-sheba, and Kh. el-Kôm.

If we take a look at the broader picture of Idumea during the Persian and the early Hellenistic periods, we find that the Beer-sheba ostraca include more than 30 names, divided by Naveh into three groups: "A third are compounded with the Edomite theophoric element *Qaus*: another third are clearly Arabic, while most of the remaining names are common Semitic. There is only one Iranian name, BGN" (Naveh 1979: 194).

A different picture emerges from the Arad ostraca. The majority of the names included in the Arad Aramaic ostraca are Jewish names with the -YH theophoric element (for example, MTNYH, ʾQBYH). In Arad most of the soldiers were Jews. Only ʾBDʾNNY was defined as Babylonian (or Aramean); a military unit was named after him. There are also Arabic names (for example, MLKW, ʿYDW); some include Edomite names (for example, QWSYNQM); and others are "general Semitic names: Hebrew, Ammonite or Edomite" (Naveh 1981: 176).

Parts of the corpus of ostraca presumably found at Kh. el-Kôm were published in three monographs. The first part is the Israel Museum collection (Lemaire 1996) and the second is the Ephʿal-Naveh collection (1996). The Israel Museum collection has a little more than 200 names, all Semitic in nature. The only non-Semitic names are the king's name, אלכסנדר, as recorded in a date formula, and an Egyptian name, פמת. In this collection, there are 3 Aramaic names with the element NBW. The most popular theophoric names include QWS (25 different names). The element BʿL, which is of Phoenician-Philistine origin, is included in 8 names. And finally, the Israelite element (YHW/YW) is found in 4 names. In his study of the names, Lemaire divided the names into three main groups: north Arabic, Edomite, and Aramaic; in addition to two so-called minority groups, Hebrew and Phoenician-Philistine.

The Ephʿal-Naveh collection includes about 150 personal names. All have a West Semitic derivation. Out of 61 names with theophoric elements, 20 have QWS, 18 Baʿal, and 3 YHW. Some have Babylonian or Mesopotamian elements (NTNSYN, ŠMŠDN, ʿBDŠMŠ) or Egyptian elements (ʿBDYSY, ʿBDʾWSYRY); "the verbal or nominal elements accompanying the divine elements are, however, West Semitic, and this indicates that these names are West Semitic" (Ephʿal and Naveh 1996: 15). In addition, 24 names (nontheophoric) have a *waw* ending, which is typical in Arabic and Nabatean names. Twelve others have Arabic elements.

In 2002, another group of ostraca dated to the same period and included in various private collections were published by Lemaire. This corpus adds about 400 names. The majority of these names are West Semitic, with some exceptional Greek names from the Hellenistic period. Among them are PLPS MLKʾ, who is King Philip Arrhidaeus (323–317 B.C.E.), as well as 4 Iranian names, 3 Egyptian names, and 1 Akkadian name.

The problems with the Mareshah corpus are the disjointed nature of the inscriptions (most of which are dockets and lists of names or separate names probably used for tags) and the inability to establish a chronology. All we can say is that on some ostraca a variety of names exist side by side. This is the case, for example, in an eight-line list of names, entitled "The Dʾayan clan," which includes West Semitic names as well as Arabic, Nabatean, and Egyptian names.

The multicultural population of Marehsah may be compared with the situation at another site not far from Mareshah—Ashkelon. The city of Ashkelon was destroyed in 604 B.C.E. by the Assyrians but recovered in the fifth century B.C.E. under Persian rule. It is mentioned as a city of the Tyrians in the second half of the fourth century by Pseudo-Scylax (Müller 1882: 79). A fourth-century Phoenician scarab testifies to the Phoenician influence at Ashkelon (Rahmani 1976). A stele from Athens, dated probably to the fourth century, was erected by a Sidonite to the memory of an Ascalonian (Donner and Röllig 1971: 13 [no. 54]). This inscription can be compared with the Greek inscription of a Sidonian family found in Tomb I of the Mareshah necropolis, which speaks of a family member, Apollophanes, who was "thirty-three years chief of the Sidonians at Marisê" (Peters and Thiersch 1905: 38).

In the Persian remains of Ashkelon, a "considerable number of ostraca found have been inscribed in Phoenician and (in less degree) in Aramaic script" (Cross 1996). These Phoenician inscriptions include some ostraca bearing Phoenician personal names, dated between the end of the sixth century and the fourth century B.C.E., and an east Greek bowl incised in Phoenician script with the word 'cakes' (ʿGM;

Stager 1993: 108).[1] Thus, Ashkelon represents a site that was populated
in the Persian period by Phoenicians and that was highly influenced by
their cult. In contrast, Mareshah represents more of the Edomite-
Arabic population, with various other minorities, among them the
Phoenicians. In light of this, we might consider the identification of
"the language of Ashdod" mentioned in Neh 13:24 to be Phoenician.

The Generational Divergence

Another line of inquiry that one can take in the study of such a
colorful population as Mareshah is to check generational divergence:
whether people changed their children's names to a different type. This
is the case, for example, in the Edomite marriage contract, in which we
learn of a change in the name-giving practice in Mareshah. There, the
groom's name is "QWSRM, son of QWSYD," both the father and son
clearly having Edomite names. The same is true of the bride's father,
called "QWSYD, son of QWSYHB." Nevertheless, the bride's name is
Arsinoe, a typical Greek name—the only Greek name in the Semitic
corpus. This is a significant phenomenon.

Only in some cases do we have the name of a man's father, for example, "NHRY, son of 'ZYZW"; "SYB' and SR', his son," where SYB' is
a general West Semitic name, and SR' is an Arabic/Nabatean name.
We also have Arabic/Nabatean names of a father and a son: "Sab'u,
son of WTRW."

In comparison, we may look at the names of people who were buried
in the Necropolis of Mareshah, especially in the graves published by Peters and Thiersch in 1905. In this corpus, it is easier to trace the changes
that occurred in one family. The Sidonian community is mentioned in
the epitaph of Apollophanes, the son of Sesmaios, who was "thirty-
three years chief of the Sidonians at Marisê." The date of these tombs is
between 196 and 119 B.C.E. Another Sidonian is mentioned in the inscription: "the Sidonian woman Philotion." Of the 49 names of people
buried in these four tombs, there are 8 Phoenician names. In Tomb I, out
of 30 names, 4 are Phoenician: Sesmaios, the father of Apollophanes;
Meerbal, the father of Demetrius, his name being identified with the
Phoenician name Maharbal or Maherbal (MHRB'L), meaning 'gift of
Ba'al'; and 2 people named Straton, from 'STRT, with a Greek formative

---

    1. The same is true with the finds at Eliachin in the central Sharon Plain, in which
both Phoenician and Aramaic inscriptions from the fifth century B.C.E. were found
(Deutsch and Heltzer 1994: 69–89).

ending. In Tomb II, out of 11 names, 2 are Phoenician: Badon, from BD'
or BD'; and Balsalo—B'LṢLḤ. In Tomb IV there are 4 names, 2 of which
are possibly Phoenician: Sariah found in Palmyrene; and Patrobala,
which is a combination of the Greek πατρο- with the Semitic element
B'L, which is equivalent to 'BYB'L. In the same tombs, there are 3
Edomite names: QWSNTN, QWSBNH, and QWSYD. Two are of Aramaic origin: BB' and BBT'; and 2 are Egyptian names: Ammonios and
Pobeus (Peters and Thiersch 1905: 37–72).

Finally, I would like to address the issue of names phrased "son of X."
In the Mareshah ostraca, there is one example of this sort of name: "son
of ṢPWN." This name probably means 'inhabitant of the north' or 'son
of ṢPWN'. If we read 'inhabitant of the north', the name can be compared with Hananiah's epithet NWTWS (from Greek Νότος), which
occurs in a text from Qumran, similar to "Simʿon son of Notos," mentioned in Ostracon no. 462 from Masada, where Notos means 'inhabitant of the south' (Yadin and Naveh 1989: 40); and compared with the
epithet son of DRWM' 'inhabitant of the south', mentioned in *b. Giṭ* 57a.[2]

References to a man as "the son of X" were common in all periods.
For example, during the late Iron Age, we find the names "son of
ḤMD'" (Arad Ostracon no. 55) and "son of NTNYHW" (Arad Ostracon no. 56; Aharoni 1981: 86–87) and lists of family names, such as the
"sons of Koraḥ" Similarly, there are individual names, alongside numbers, written on a bowl. Two of the names are in the form "the son of
X": "son of GLGL," and "son of ṢMḤ" (Arad Ostracon no. 49; Aharoni
1981: 80–83).

To that one might add some people named by their epithet. This is
the case in the name KNBWN, and possibly the name ŠLḤ'. The name
KNBWN is found in Masada ostracon no. 430, "son of KNBWN" (Yadin
and Naveh 1989: 28, pl. 25). This epithet was understood by Naveh as
derived from the Syriac KBWN', meaning 'a round cake'. Thus,
KNBWN "was presumably the appellation of a fat person" (Naveh
1990: 122). The word ŠLḤ' is found in *y. Šabb.* 7a(12) (= *b. Šabb.* 49b),
where ŠLḤ' means 'a dealer of hides'. Thus, the name SLḤ' may be
based on the man's profession. This phenomenon was studied by
Naveh (1990), who included both literary and epigraphic sources, such
as the inscription on an ossuary lid from Bethphage. He came to the
conclusion that naming people by their nickname "is characteristic of
people who lived together in a familiar environment" (Naveh 1990:

---

2. For the reading 'son of ṢPWN', see Gen 46:16 and Num 26:15; see also Eshel 2000:
480–82.

111). These nicknames could designate a person's origin (such as son of
ṢPWN), occupation (perhaps ŠLḤ), characteristic, nature, or even
physical defect (such as "son of KNBWN").

Conclusions

We have looked at the onomasticon of Maresha, checking types of
names, ethnic origins, and changes over time. Regarding types of
names, we have seen that the majority of people bore general West
Semitic names with nontheophoric elements, while others had theophoric names of various deities from Edom, Phoenicia-Philistia, Babylonia, and Egypt. That the majority of names are Edomite makes sense,
because the area was under Idumean rule. Also prominent are Nabatean and Arab names. These combinations show the validity of Zadok's conclusion (1998: 821) that "Edomite presumably had a special
relationship to Nabateans."

Regarding the question of a chronological continuity of names, one
should accept the conclusion of Zadok (1998: 821), that "there is a certain onomastic continuity between the Edomite (pre-Achaemenid)/
early Idumean and the later names." Finally, from our corpus of inscriptions, there is some evidence of a certain amount of change over
time, such as an Edomite father giving his daughter a Greek name. But
it should be noted that this is an exception and that no other Greek
names were preserved within the Semitic corpus. This fact raises the
broader question of the interrelations among the various ethnic groups
in Mareshah. This question cannot be answered only on the basis of the
ostraca collection but deserves a wider and separate discussion.

We hope that future finds in Mareshah together with additional
publications of other corpora dating to the Persian and the Hellenistic
periods will further enrich our knowledge of the population of Palestine during these periods.

References

Aharoni, Y.
  1981   *Arad Inscriptions.* JDS. Jerusalem: Israel Exploration Society.
Avi-Yonah, M., and Kloner, A.
  1993   Mareshah (Marisa). Pp. 948–57 in *NEAEHL*
Barag, D.
  1993   New Evidence on the Foreign Policy of John Hyrcanus I. *Israel Numis-
         matic Journal* 12: 1–12.

Benz, F. L.
1972   Personal Names in the Phoenician and Punic Inscriptions: A Catalogue, Grammatical Study, and Glossary of Elements. Rome: Pontifical Biblical Institute.
Bliss, F. J., and Macalister, R. A. S.
1902   Excavations in Palestine during the Years 1898–1900. London: Committee of the Palestine Exploration Fund.
Cross, F. M.
1996   A Philistine Ostraca from Ashkelon. BAR 22: 64–65.
Deutsch, R., and Heltzer, M.
1994   Forty New Ancient West Semitic Inscriptions. Tel Aviv–Jaffa: Archaeological Center Publication.
Donner, H., and Röllig, W.
1971   Kanaanäische und aramäische Inschriften, Vol. 1. 3rd ed. Wiesbaden: Harrassowitz.
Ephʿal, I.
1982   The Ancient Arabs. Jerusalem: Magnes / Leiden: Brill.
Ephʿal, I., and Naveh, J.
1996   Aramaic Ostraca of the Fourth Century BC from Idumaea. Jerusalem: Magnes.
Eshel, E.
2000   477. 4QRebukes Reported by the Overseer. Pp. 474–83 in Qumran Cave 4: XXVI, Cryptic Texts and Miscellanea, Part 1. Edited by S. J. Pfann et al. DJD 36. Oxford: Clarendon.
Finkielsztejn, G.
1998   More Evidence on John Hyrcanus I's Conquests: Lead Weights and Rhodian Amphora Stamps. Bulletin of the Anglo-Israel Archaeological Society 16: 33–63.
Freeman-Grenville, G. S. P.; Chapman, R. L., III; and Taylor, J. E.
2003   The Onomasticon by Eusebius of Caesarea. Jerusalem: Carta.
Kloner, A.
2003   Maresha Excavations Finds, Report I, Subterranean Complexes 21, 44, 70. IAA Report 17. Jerusalem: Israel Antiquities Authority.
Kloner, A., and Eshel, E.
1999   A Seventh-Century BCE List of Names from Maresha. ErIsr 26 (Cross Volume): 147–50. [Hebrew]
Kloner, A.; Eshel, E.; and Korzakova, H.
Forthcoming   Maresha Excavations Finds, Report II: Epigraphy. IAA Report. Jerusalem: Israel Antiquities Authority.
Lemaire, A.
1996   Nouvelles inscriptions araméennes d'Idumée du Musée d'Israël. Transeu Supplement 3. Paris: Gabalda.
2002   Nouvelles inscriptions araméennes d'Idumée du Musée d'Israël. Vol. 2: Collections Moussaïeff, Jeselsohn, Welch et divers. Transeu Supplement 9. Paris: Gabalda.

Müller, C. O.
1882 *Geographi Graeci minores*. Vol. 1. Paris: Didot. [Repr., Hildesheim: Olms, 1965.]
Naveh, J.
1979 The Aramaic Ostraca from Tel Beer-Sheba (Seasons 1971–1976). *Tel Aviv* 6: 182–98.
1981 The Aramaic Ostraca from Tel Arad. Pp. 153–76 in *Arad Inscriptions*, ed. Y. Aharoni. Jerusalem: Israel Exploration Society.
1990 Nameless People. *IEJ* 40: 108–23.
Peters, J. P., and Thiersch, H.
1905 *Painted Tombs in the Necropolis of Marissa*. London: Palestine Exploration Fund.
Rabinowitz, I.
1956 Aramaic Inscriptions of the Fifth Century B.C.E. from a North-Arab Shrine in Egypt. *JNES* 15: 1–9.
Rahmani, L. Y.
1976 A Phoenician Scarab from Ashkelon. *'Atiqot* 11: 110–11.
Rappaport, U.
2004 *The First Book of Maccabees*. Jerusalem: Yad Ben-Zvi. [Hebrew]
Stager, L. E.
1993 Ashkelon. Pp. 103–12 in *NEAEHL*.
Tcherikover, V.
1937 Palestine under the Ptolemies (A Contribution to the Study of the Zenon Papyri). *Mizraim* 4–5: 9–90.
1959 *Hellenistic Civilization and the Jews*. Philadelphia: Jewish Publication Society.
Yadin, Y., and Naveh, J.
1989 The Aramaic and Hebrew Ostraca and Jar Inscriptions. Pp. 1–68 and pls. 1–60 in *Masada I: The Yigael Yadin Excavations 1963–1965: Final Reports*. The Masada Reports. Jerusalem: Israel Exploration Society.
Zadok, R.
1998 A Prosopography of Samaria and Edom/Idomea. *UF* 30: 781–828.

The Dating of the First Phase of the Samaritan Temple on Mount Gerizim in Light of the Archaeological Evidence

YITZHAK MAGEN

Staff Officer of Archaeology
Civil Administration of Judea and Samaria

Introduction

Mount Gerizim, known in Arabic as Jebl a-Tur, is situated south of the city of Shechem and rises to a height of 886 m above sea level. Mount Gerizim and Mt. Ebal, at an elevation of 930 m, are the two highest peaks in Samaria. Excavations at the site were initiated in the beginning of 1983 and continued uninterrupted until 2006. The excavations uncovered large parts of the Hellenistic city, which covers some 400 dunams, and of the Samaritan sacred precinct, as well as a Late-Roman-period citadel and a Byzantine church precinct.[1] The Roman Temple to Zeus Hypsistos north of the city, on the northern hill, was reexcavated.[2]

---

1. Y. A. Reifenberg, "Mount Gerizim," *ErIsr* 1 (Schwabe Volume; 1951) 74–76; Y. Magen, "A Fortified Town of the Hellenistic Period on Mount Gerizim," *Qadmoniot* 19/75–76 (1986) 91–101 [Hebrew]; idem, "The Samaritans in Shechem and the Blessed Mount Gerizim," in *Samaria and Benjamin: A Collection of Studies in Historical Geography* (ed. Z. Erlich; 2 vols.; Tel Aviv, 1987–91) 1:177–210 [Hebrew]; idem, "Mt. Gerizim—A Temple City [1]," *Qadmoniot* 23/91–92 (1990) 70–96 [Hebrew]; idem, "The Church of Mary Theotokos on Mount Gerizim," in *Christian Archaeology in the Holy Land: New Discoveries* (ed. G. C. Bottini, L. Di Segni, and E. Alliata; Studium Biblicum Franciscanum: Collectio Maior 36; Jerusalem, 1990) 333–42; L. Di Segni, "The Church of Mary Theotokos on Mount Gerizim," in ibid., 343–50; Y. Magen, "Mount Gerizim and the Samaritans," in *Early Christianity in Context* (ed. E. Testa and E. Alliata; Studium Biblicum Franciscanum: Collectio Maior 38; Jerusalem, 1993) 91–148; idem, "Mount Gerizim," *NEAEHL* 2:484–92; idem, "Mt. Gerizim—A Temple City [2]," *Qadmoniot* 33/120 (2000) 74–118 [Hebrew]; idem, "Mt. Gerizim during the Roman and Byzantine Period," *Qadmoniot* 33/120 (2000) 134–43 [Hebrew]; Y. Magen, H. Misgav, and L. Tsfania, *Mount Gerizim Excavations, 1: The Aramaic, Hebrew and Samaritan Inscriptions* (Judea and Samaria Publications 2; Jerusalem, 2004).
2. Y. Magen, *Flavia Neapolis: Shechem in the Roman Period* (Judea and Samaria Publications 5; Jerusalem, 2005) 226–37 [Hebrew]. There is no evidence for the claim that the

Fig. 1. Aerial photograph of Mt. Gerizim and the modern-day Samaritan village.

The Excavations

The archaeological discoveries on Mt. Gerizim may be divided into three groups: (1) the sacred precinct from the Persian period; (2) the sacred precinct from the Hellenistic period; and (3) the Hellenistic city (figs. 1–2). The Samaritan sacred precinct was the first structure to be built on Mt. Gerizim and occupies the highest spot on the mount. The Hellenistic period was when a city was first built around it, reaching its greatest dimensions in the second century B.C.E. Josephus relates that the temple on Mt. Gerizim resembled the temple in Jerusalem (*Ant.* 11.310, 12.255; *J.W.* 1.62). Two main phases of the temple have been revealed: the first phase featured the Persian-period sacred precinct, constructed in the mid-fifth century B.C.E.; and the second phase dates

Samaritan temple mentioned by Josephus is underneath the Roman temple in Tell er-Râs, north of Mt. Gerizim. Nevertheless, some scholars continue to ascribe to this erroneous theory; see, for example: R. J. Bull, "The Excavation of Tell er-Râs on Mt. Gerizim," *BASOR* 190 (1986) 4–20; idem, "Er-Râs, Tell (Mount Gerizim)," *NEAEHL* 4:1015–22. See also A. Kasher, "Samaritans in Hellenistic Egypt," in *The Samaritans* (ed. E. Stern and H. Eshel; Jerusalem, 2002) 154 n. 3 [Hebrew].

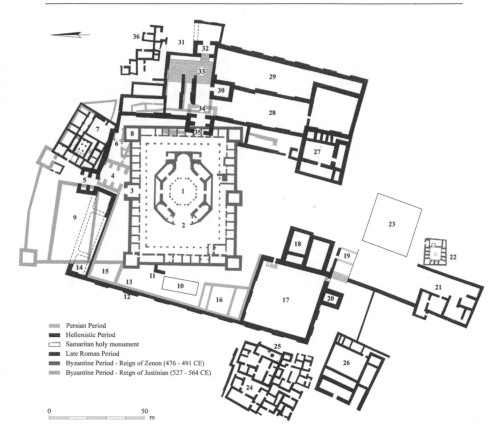

1. The Byzantine church of Mary Theotokos
2. Fortified Byzantine enclosure
3. Gate of the Byzantine enclosure
4. Northern chamber gate of the Persian sacred precinct
5. Northern chamber gate of the Hellenistic sacred precinct
6. Byzantine gate of the northern enclosure from the time of Justinian I
7. Late Roman fortress.
8. Northeastern tower of the Byzantine enclosure — tomb of Sheikh Ghanem
9. Byzantine plastered pool
10. "The Twelve Stones"
11. Foundations of the Samaritan temple
12–13. Walls of the sacred precinct
14. Northwestern tower of the Hellenistic sacred precinct
15–16. Courtyards in the corners of the Persian sacred precinct
17. Hellenistic fortified enclosure
18. Hellenistic public buildings
19. Western gate of the Hellenistic sacred precinct
20. Hellenistic tower protecting the western gate to sacred precinct
21. Hellenistic public building (Building J)
22. Byzantine winepress
23. "Everlasting Hill"
24. Hellenistic mansion, including olive press, dwelling, and shops (P-I)
25. Hellenistic olive press
26. Hellenistic public building (P-II)
27. Southwestern Hellenistic citadel
28–29. Courtyards for accommodating pilgrims within the walls of the Hellenistic sacred precinct
30. Hellenistic tower protecting the ascent to the sacred precinct.
31. Hellenistic paved street leading to the eastern city gate
32. Eastern gate of the Hellenistic sacred precinct
33. Monumental staircase leading to the eastern gate of the Hellenistic sacred precinct
34. Eastern gate of the Hellenistic sacred precinct
35. Remains of an ancient altar, apparently dating to the Persian period
36. Late Hellenistic residential quarter (Areas S)

Fig. 2. General plan of the sacred precinct in the Persian, Hellenistic, Late Roman, and Byzantine periods.

Fig. 3. Northern view of the sacred precinct.

to the early second century B.C.E., during the reign of Antiochus III, when a new temple and precinct were built. This temple was destroyed by John Hyrcanus I (figs. 3–4).

The Sacred Precinct

During the Persian period, the precinct measured, not including its gates, some 96 × 98 m (fig. 5). Its western wall, preserved in its entire length and to a height of 2 m, extends for some 84 m and is 1.3 m thick. It was built of large fieldstones wrested from the upper layers of the bedrock, in contrast to the Hellenistic precinct, which was constructed of smooth stones quarried from farther down. Unroofed courtyards were unearthed at the two corners of the western wall: the southern courtyard measured 12 × 21.5 m, and the northern one, the length of which has not been determined, is 12.5 m wide. Despite the easy access to the site from the west, no gates were discovered in the western wall. This lack of gates may be due to the location of the Holy of Holies, the extremely hallowed rear extremity of the temple. I believe that the current Samaritan sacred site known as "The Twelve Stones" is located in the area of the Holy of Holies. In the center of the northern wall, which is 73 m long, stood a gate with six (or eight) chambers, measuring 14 × 15 m in size. To its east is a large public building, 11 × 12 m,

Fig. 4. Eastern view of the sacred precinct. Note the monumental staircase and the courtyards flanking it on the north and south.

which contained thousands of burned bones from sacrifices, together with a great quantity of ashes, possibly the "House of Ashes" adjoining the altar in which the burning of the sacrifices was completed. Most of the eastern precinct wall was damaged by later construction, both Hellenistic and Byzantine. Because of the steep slope to the east, the wall and eastern gate of the Hellenistic precinct were constructed over the Persian-period wall, completely destroying it in the process. Numerous finds from the Persian and early Hellenistic periods were uncovered there. We presume the existence of a chamber gate in the east, similar to the gate on the northern side, with access provided by a staircase. The southern gate as well was almost entirely destroyed by Hellenistic construction and by the changes in the direction of the entrances to the sacred precinct. The Persian-period enclosure most likely featured three chamber gates: to the north, the east, and the south, reminiscent of the temple gates depicted in the book of Ezekiel (40:10–16), which was the basis for the temple built by the returning Babylonian exiles. The temple built by the returnees served, in turn, as the model for the temple erected by the Samaritans on Mt. Gerizim.

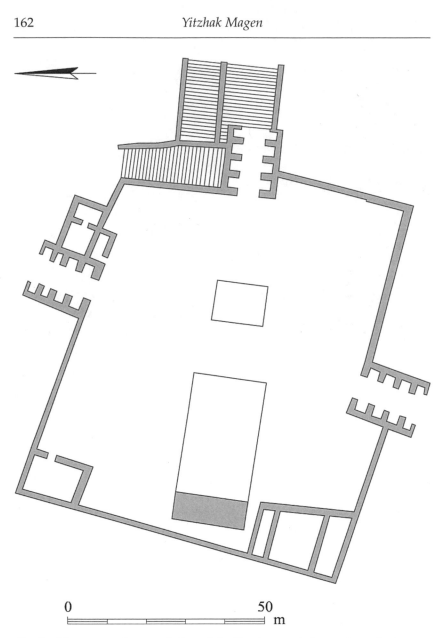

Fig. 5. The proposed general plan of the Persian-period sacred precinct.

The precinct yielded thousands of pottery vessels and burned bones of sacrifices—of sheep, goats, cattle, and doves. The coins from the Persian period, the pottery vessels, and Carbon 14 (C-14) testing at the site enable us to ascribe the first phase of the temple to the mid-fifth

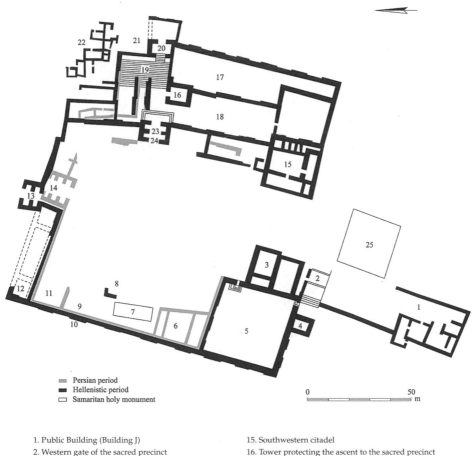

Fig. 6. General plan of the Persian- and Hellenistic-period sacred precinct.

Legend:
- Persian period
- Hellenistic period
- Samaritan holy monument

0   50 m

1. Public Building (Building J)
2. Western gate of the sacred precinct
3. Public building
4. Tower protecting the western gate
5. Fortified enclosure
6. Courtyards in the corner of the sacred precinct
7. "The Twelve Stones"
8. Foundations of the Samaritan temple
9–10. Walls of the sacred precinct
11. Courtyard in the corner of the sacred precinct
12. Northwestern tower of the sacred precinct
13–14. Northern gate of the sacred precinct

15. Southwestern citadel
16. Tower protecting the ascent to the sacred precinct
17–18. Courtyards for accommodating pilgrims within the walls of the sacred precinct
19. Monumental staircase leading to the eastern gate of the sacred precinct
20. Eastern gate of the sacred precinct
21. Paved street leading to the eastern gate
22. Residential quarter
23. Eastern gate of the sacred precinct
24. Remains of an altar beneath the eastern gate, apparently dating to the Persian period
25. "Everlasting Hill"

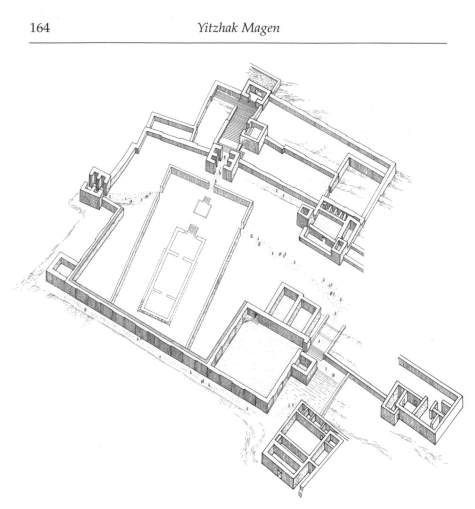

Fig. 7. Reconstruction of the Hellenistic-period sacred precinct.

century B.C.E. This temple was active for approximately 250 years, until the establishment of the new temple in the Hellenistic period.

The Hellenistic-Period Precinct

A large, magnificent precinct with 2.6-m-thick walls was built in the early second century B.C.E., with a white, ashlar-built temple standing in its center (figs. 6–7). This temple stood for some 90 years until its destruction at the end of that century. (The temple and the entire precinct were leveled when a Byzantine church was built in the same place together with its surrounding precinct.) Only the outer walls of the Hellenistic temple survived. The Hellenistic precinct, measuring 136 × 212 m, was not modeled after the Jerusalem temple but incorporated

Greek architectural elements not present in the first phase. Only the outer bounds of the precinct were expanded, while the early nucleus retained its original dimensions, with the addition of surrounding structures and citadels. The western wall remained as it was, with an additional external plastered wall built of headers and stretchers. The western wall of the second phase, like its predecessor, had no gate. The shape of the southern precinct wing differed greatly from the southern precinct of the first phase because large public buildings were added. The precinct entrance was moved to the west; entrance was by means of an impressive, 9-m-wide staircase, of which seven steps are preserved. The steps ascended to a paved plaza that faced north toward the temple. A square tower that measured 8.5 × 9 m and protected the gate was built opposite the staircase, and a fortified complex, 38 × 39 m with 3-m-thick plastered offsets-and-insets walls was erected near the gate, allowing control over the people entering the sacred precinct.

Farther to the south, large public structures were built that served the temple and the people entering the edifice. The northern wall of the complex, preserved along its entire length, contained the northern gate that was built near the Persian-period gate. The Hellenistic wall, which abutted the Persian-period wall on the outside, was also constructed of offsets and insets and featured a fortified tower built of large stones in its northwestern corner. The early six-chamber gate was replaced by a smaller though magnificent gate, with only four chambers, each of which measured 2.5 × 3.0 m, extending for a total length of 10 m, and paved with finely fitting stone slabs. The entrance was 3.6 m wide. The gate was built north of the early gate, apparently to allow entry to the precinct while construction was underway.

The southern precinct wall, constructed on a steep slope, was 93 m long. The large gate in its center, measuring 10 × 14 m, featured four chambers and an entrance approximately 4.7 m wide. The northeastern corner was constructed of especially large stones that extended deep into the ground. The large citadel in the southeastern corner, constructed around a central courtyard measuring 24 × 25 m, had especially thick walls and was two or possibly three stories high. In its center is an imposing reception room that is preserved in its entirety. The eastern wing of the precinct featured double fortifications with massive retaining walls; its construction of offsets and insets formed large courtyards, where the pilgrims stopped before entering the temple.

The eastern gate, which served the pilgrims arriving from Shechem, ascended to a broad staircase on the north, 34 m in length, while to the

Fig. 8. Proto-Ionic capitals unearthed in the debris from the Persian-period temple.

south it was bounded by thick retaining walls and a monumental guard tower. A total of approximately 57 stairs traversed the height differential of 15.5 m between the upper and lower levels. The staircase was 23 m wide at its lower end. The staircase descends to a magnificent two-chamber gate that was closed by means of two wooden doors with brass hinges, preserved in situ. The lower part of the street that led from the gate to the north expanded to a width of 16 m.

Excursus: The Finds Attesting the Existence of a
Temple to the LORD *on Mount Gerizim*

Numerous discoveries from the sacred precinct substantiate the existence of a Temple to the LORD. Dozens of finely dressed ashlars of similar size and fashioned with stone masons' marks had been removed from the temple's walls and were unearthed in the excavations. These stones, the only ashlars discovered on Mt. Gerizim in either private or public construction, were quarried away from Mt. Gerizim before being brought to the site. The debris yielded proto-Ionic or Aeolic capitals belonging to the early temple from the Persian period (fig. 8).[3]

The inscriptions discovered on Mt. Gerizim are the most striking indication of the existence of a temple. Some contain the titles of the priests who served as religious functionaries (fig. 9),[4] while others contain the formulas "before the God in this place," "before (the) God," or

---

3. E. Stern and Y. Magen, "The First Phase of the Samaritan Temple on Mt. Gerizim: New Archaeological Evidence," *Qadmoniot* 33/120 (2000) 119–24 [Hebrew]; eidem, "Archaeological Evidence for the First Stage of the Samaritan Temple on Mount Gerizim," *IEJ* 52 (2002) 49–57.

4. Magen, Misgav, and Tsfania, *Mount Gerizim Excavations,* 1: *The Aramaic, Hebrew and Samaritan Inscriptions,* 67, no. 24; 68, no. 25; 253–54, no. 382; 257–59, nos. 388–89.

Fig. 9. Aramaic inscription from the site mentioning "Pinhas the Priest" and "their brothers the priests."

Fig. 10. Aramaic inscription from the site containing the phrase "before God."

"before the LORD," which are always indicative of a temple (fig. 10).[5] An additional inscription in Hebrew notes "that which Joseph offered for his wife and his sons before the LORD in the temple" (fig. 11).[6] Yet

---

5. Ibid., 18–19, 142–48, nos. 151–56.
6. Ibid., 141–42, no. 150.

Fig. 11. Hebrew inscription from the site reading "that which Joseph offered for his wife and for his sons before the LORD in the temple."

another inscription mentions the "house of sacrifice," an expression that parallels an expression used to refer to the temple in Jerusalem (2 Chr 7:12).[7] An inscription in Paleo-Hebrew script contains the Tetragrammaton, apparently as part of the phrase "the house of the LORD" (fig. 12).[8] A Greek inscription on a sundial contains the phrase "Highest God," which is the name of the LORD in Greek.[9] Perhaps the most fascinating discovery is a small gold bell with a silver clapper from the fringes of the high priest's ephod (Exod 28:33–35; fig. 13).[10]

The Hellenistic City

The city was established on the southern ridge of the mountain, surrounding the sacred precinct from the Persian period that had been

---

7. Ibid., 171–72, no. 199.
8. Ibid., 254–55, no. 383.
9. Magen, "Mt. Gerizim—A Temple City [2]," pl. 4, upper right-hand corner.
10. Ibid., pl. 1, lower right-hand corner.

Fig. 12. Paleo-Hebrew inscription containing the Tetragrammaton.

built on the lofty site that oversees Shechem and the eastern valleys. Two central roads led to the city: one road that provided easy passage from Shechem in the west to the Roman temple and another road east of the longitudinal route that reaches Shechem from the south. The site of the city on Mt. Gerizim offered no natural advantages: it was built on a high, barren peak, without natural sources of water, and was far from the central crossroads of Samaria. This strengthens the hypothesis that the town was established for ritual-religious reasons around a sacred site and was a temple city inhabited by priests.

The city spanned an area of some 500 × 800 m (approximately 400 dunams; fig. 14). Most of the residential quarters were built to the south and the west, due to the gradual descent of the rock formation in these directions. There was sparse construction to the north, and the extremely steep side on the east required extensive quarrying for the construction of the very limited number of dwellings there. The city was not encompassed by a wall, and thus its boundaries were not delineated in advance by walls and towers. Its layout does not exhibit urban planning, and the city gradually expanded as additional buildings, streets, and quarters were constructed, without any apparent order. The lack of a wall hindered the defense of the city at the time of the Hasmonean conquest, and the city's defenders were forced to erect barricades and fortify each street and dwelling separately. The enclosure surrounding the temple was the only part of the city that had

Fig. 13. Reconstruction of a high priest's garments. Note the small bells hanging from the fringes of the ephod. The small golden bell (above) was found in the area of the sacred precinct.

been fortified during the second phase of the temple, in the Hellenistic period.

For the purposes of our description, we divided the city into the following residential quarters: the southern quarter (the largest) and the citadel to the south of the city; the southwestern quarter and the mansion; the southern slope; the northern quarter; and the northwestern quarter.

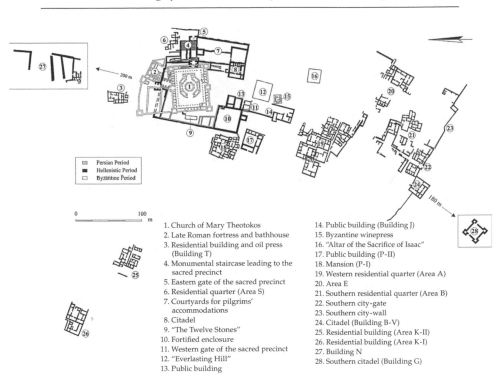

1. Church of Mary Theotokos
2. Late Roman fortress and bathhouse
3. Residential building and oil press (Building T)
4. Monumental staircase leading to the sacred precinct
5. Eastern gate of the sacred precinct
6. Residential quarter (Area S)
7. Courtyards for pilgrims' accommodations
8. Citadel
9. "The Twelve Stones"
10. Fortified enclosure
11. Western gate of the sacred precinct
12. "Everlasting Hill"
13. Public building
14. Public building (Building J)
15. Byzantine winepress
16. "Altar of the Sacrifice of Isaac"
17. Public building (P-II)
18. Mansion (P-I)
19. Western residential quarter (Area A)
20. Area E
21. Southern residential quarter (Area B)
22. Southern city-gate
23. Southern city-wall
24. Citadel (Building B-V)
25. Residential building (Area K-II)
26. Residential building (Area K-I)
27. Building N
28. Southern citadel (Building G)

Fig. 14. General plan of the archaeological remains at the site.

The southern quarter is situated at the southern extremity of the city and is bounded by an improvised wall formed from the walls of the outermost dwellings that adjoin one another. The quarter's length from east to west was approximately 300 m, and its width from north to south, some 120 m. This densely populated quarter was bisected by a central thoroughfare that began at the southern, two-chamber gate, ended in two large plazas (fig. 15), and was joined on the east and the west by alleys that led to the dwellings. The gate was flanked by two large public structures that were built around a central courtyard and were probably connected to the gate. The excavations close to the gate unearthed a citadel that extended from the southern wall that was formed by the outer walls of the city's dwellings. An additional group of structures comprising a central building and surrounding store-houses was discovered northeast of the city gate. The central structure, surrounding a large courtyard, contains an imposing reception room with two columns with Doric capitals that created a portico in its fa-cade. A citadel with four towers was unearthed some 180 m to the

Fig. 15. Southwestern view of Buildings B-III and B-IV, which flanked the southern city gate.

Fig. 16. Southern view of the western quarter (Area A).

Fig. 17. Western view of Complex P-I following restoration.

south of the city wall, at the end of the spur, along the route that ascended to Mt. Gerizim from the east.

Excavations at Mt. Gerizim began in 1982 in the western quarter and uncovered a large, densely populated residential quarter. This quarter is at ground level 5 m higher than the ground level of the southern quarter, from which it is separated by a raised stone precipice surrounded by a sort of wall and the walls of the outermost dwellings. The dwellings that were uncovered are built on both sides of an east–west street measuring some 2 × 75 m. Nine structures were exposed along the street, some large and impressive and others more modest (fig. 16).

A patrician dwelling (Complex P-I) was unearthed west of the sacred precinct—the likes of which has yet to be found elsewhere on the site. Built on a steep slope, the compound is composed of three different parts: an oil press (Building P-Ia), residential and commercial rooms (Buildings P-Ib, Ic, Ie), and a magnificent residential structure (Building P-Id; figs. 17–18).

The eastern section of the city is marked by forbidding slopes that prevented the establishment of a residential quarter. Due to the Seleucid authorities' ban on fortifying the city, the steep slopes were not

Fig. 18. The central courtyard of the oil press (Building P-Ia), with the crushing- and pressing-room on the left.

Fig. 19. Eastern view of Building E-I, located on the steep eastern slopes of the city in place of a defensive wall.

Fig. 20. Equipment for pressing oil in Building K-Ib, located in the northwest of the city.

used to erect a reinforced wall. In lieu of a defensive wall, particularly tall public structures were built. Two structures of this sort were excavated on the eastern slope, to the south of the sacred precinct: one, a small structure in the upper part of the eastern slope; and the other, a large building to which access was provided by a broad staircase descending from west to east (fig. 19).

A dwelling, preserved to the second story, was discovered in the quarter north of the sacred precinct. Identical in plan to the structures in the other areas, it reflects two building phases: the dwelling was constructed in the first phase, while in the second it was turned into an oil press, which was preserved in its entirety. Excavations also revealed a Crusader-period oven for Samaritan Passover sacrifices that was built of small, roughly-hewn stones and that contained burned sheep bones and olive branches.

A residential and workshop quarter established at the fringes of the Hellenistic city was uncovered in the northwest of the city, in the area of the modern Samaritan neighborhood. Two groups of buildings came to light: one is the continuation of the Hellenistic western quarter, and the other is about 70 m to the west, beyond the official bounds of the city. The latter was used for storage, dwellings, and workshops and contained an oil press (fig. 20).

Dating the First Phase of the Temple and the Surrounding Precinct

Excavations on Mt. Gerizim, conducted over the course of more than 23 years, yielded tens of thousands of finds, such as pottery, stone, metal, and glass vessels, and more than 14,000 coins. These rich finds enable us to reconstruct the history of the site with a great degree of certainty: when it was established and when it was destroyed. In this essay I will not describe in detail all the finds uncovered at the site, because most are still undergoing various stages of processing for final publication. Nonetheless, even at this stage of research a few chronological observations may already be made that will shed light on the general historical framework of the site's history, especially its first phase.

This section is devoted to the Persian period, with the goal of ending the long-standing debate concerning the beginnings of the Samaritan temple at the site. I anticipate that the presentation of the ceramic finds, the coins, and the C-14 examinations of the bones and ashes of the sacrifices will securely date the construction of the first phase of the temple to the mid-fifth century B.C.E. and not to the late fourth century B.C.E.—the time of Alexander the Great—as was claimed by Josephus (and subsequently by later scholars).

The Pottery

Almost all the ceramic finds from the Persian period were discovered in the sacred precinct.[11] The private and public construction outside the precinct yielded very few pottery vessels that could be dated to the late Persian or early Ptolemaic periods. A similar picture emerges from the distribution of the Persian-period coins: most were uncovered in the sacred precinct, and only a few were found in other parts of the city.

The precinct itself produced loci that contained only Persian-period pottery, along with mixed loci with pottery from both the Persian and early Hellenistic (Ptolemaic) periods, a picture that is also reflected in the numismatic finds from the precinct. This is not surprising, because the sacred precinct of the first phase continued in use unchanged until the late third century B.C.E., during the reign of Antiochus III.

---

11. The ceramic finds were processed by Irina Eisenstadt and Evgeny Aharanovich.

Mount Gerizim is one of the few sites in Samaria to contain a stratum clearly dated to the Persian period. In central sites in the region of Samaria, such as the city of Samaria, biblical Shechem (Tell Balâṭah), and Qedumim, most of the finds from this period were discovered in pits or in fill and not in orderly habitation levels. The explanation normally given by scholars for this phenomenon is the destruction of the Persian-period strata by the massive construction undertaken during the Hellenistic and Roman periods.[12] The few stratigraphic excavations and the paucity of finds dating to the Persian period in the region of Samaria do not enable us to present ceramic parallels from the region for the pottery discovered on Mt. Gerizim, thus compelling us to use pottery vessels uncovered in excavations in other parts of Israel as parallels.

The archaeological and historical picture of the Persian period in Samaria is complex and differs from the picture in Judea and Benjamin. The settlement upheaval and the destruction of the Northern Kingdom occurred in the late eighth century B.C.E., followed by the Assyrian resettlement of peoples brought from neighboring lands. Presumably, these peoples joined the remnant that was left in Samaria. These fateful historical events hardly left any traces in the material culture of Samaria.[13] There was no settlement break in this area between the Assyrian, Babylonian, and Persian periods, and consequently many vessels fashioned in the style current in the seventh and sixth centuries B.C.E. continued in use in the Persian period. This may explain the presence in Persian-period Samarian assemblages of a few fragments that are reminiscent of Iron Age vessel types. Nevertheless, extensive examination of the ceramic finds from Mt. Gerizim itself did not reveal any Iron Age finds. These vessel types were continuing the ceramic tradition of the seventh and sixth centuries and remained in use in the fifth century, but they themselves are not Iron Age vessels. As was noted above,

---

12. E. Stern, *Material Culture of the Land of the Bible in the Persian Period, 538–332 B.C.* (Jerusalem, 1982) 29–31.

13. A. Zertal, "The Wedge-Decorated Bowl and Origin of the Cuthaeans," *ErIsr* 20 (Yadin Volume; 1989) 181–87 [Hebrew]; idem, "The Province of Samaria (Assyrian *Samerina*) in the Late Iron Age (Iron Age III)," in *Judah and the Judeans in the Neo-Babylonian Period* (ed. O. Lipschits and J. Blenkinsopp; Winona Lake, IN, 2003) 377–412. Zertal's claim that the wedge decorations are evidence for the existence of peoples brought by the Assyrian king and settled in Samaria is unacceptable. Furthermore, I do not accept Zertal's use of the term "Cuthean" for these peoples. Cuth was one of several cities from which various peoples were brought to Samaria (2 Kgs 17:24). To spite the Samaritans, the Sages dubbed them "Cutheans," and therefore this pottery type should not be attributed to the latter.

a habitation level from the Iron Age was not unearthed on Mt. Gerizim, and there is no evidence of settlement from the time of the Assyrian conquest or from the time of Babylonian rule in the land of Israel.

The ceramic assemblage presented here was for the most part taken from the clean pre-Hellenistic loci of the sacred precinct that also yielded Persian-period coins. Most of the pottery vessels are characteristic of the Persian period and include juglets, flasks, cooking pots, kraters frequently ornamented with wedge decorations, bowls (some, not all, of the bowls were red-slipped and burnished), oil lamps with a flat base, and fragments of Attic vessels.

The ceramic parallels are mostly from the hill country, as well as from the Judean Shephelah and northern Sharon (figs. 21–26, pp. 195–205). Most date to the Persian period, mainly the fifth century B.C.E.: Tell Balâṭah (Level 5), the late sixth to early fifth centuries B.C.E.;[14] Qadum, the sixth to early fourth centuries B.C.E.;[15] the Holy Land Hotel, Jerusalem, the late sixth to fifth centuries B.C.E. (the upper stratum in Tomb 2);[16] the Armenian Garden, Jerusalem, the second half of the sixth to the fourth centuries B.C.E.;[17] Ramat Raḥel, the fifth to fourth centuries B.C.E.;[18] Bethel, the sixth century B.C.E.;[19] Tell el-Fûl (Period 3B), the sixth century B.C.E.;[20] Gezer (Levels 4–5A), the seventh to fourth centuries B.C.E.;[21] Tell el-Hesi (Level 5), the sixth to fifth centuries B.C.E.;[22] Tel Mevorakh (Levels 4–6), the sixth to fourth centuries B.C.E.;[23] and Samaria.[24] In addition to the pottery vessels, the sacred

---

14. N. L. Lapp, "The Stratum V Pottery from Balâṭah (Shechem)," *BASOR* 257 (1985) 19–44.

15. E. Stern and Y. Magen, "A Pottery Group of the Persian Period from Qadum in Samaria," *BASOR* 253 (1984) 9–27.

16. S. Ben-Arieh, "Salvage Excavations near the Holy Land Hotel, Jerusalem," *'Atiqot* 40 (2000) 1–24.

17. A. D. Tushingham, *Excavations in Jerusalem 1961–1967*, vol. 1 (Toronto, 1985).

18. Y. Aharoni, *Excavations at Ramat Rahel: Seasons 1959 and 1960* (Rome, 1962).

19. L. A. Sinclair, "Bethel Pottery of the 6th Century B.C.," in *The Excavation of Bethel (1934–1960)* (ed. J. L. Kelso; AASOR 39; Cambridge, 1968) 7–76.

20. N. L. Lapp, *The Third Campaign at Tell el-Ful: The Excavations of 1964* (AASOR 45; Cambridge, 1981).

21. S. Gitin, *Gezer III: A Ceramic Typology of the Late Iron II, Persian and Hellenistic Periods at Tell-Gezer* (Jerusalem, 1990).

22. W. J. Bennett and J. A. Blakely, *Tell el-Hesi: The Persian Period (Stratum V)* (Joint Archaeological Expedition to Tell el-Hesi 3; Winona Lake, IN, 1989).

23. E. Stern, *Excavations at Tel Mevorakh (1973–1976)* (Qedem 9; Jerusalem, 1978).

24. J. W. Crowfoot, G. M. Crowfoot, and K. M. Kenyon, *The Objects from Samaria* (London, 1957) 90–209.

precinct on Mt. Gerizim also yielded fragments of Attic ware that date to the fifth century B.C.E. (fig. 26:2–5).

After looking at the parallels, we can say that there are no early forms on Mt. Gerizim; all the pottery discovered at the site's sacred precinct is to be securely dated to the period between the fifth and the fourth centuries B.C.E., that is, before the conquest of Alexander the Great. This dating is further supported by the numismatic finds.

The Coins

Despite the abundance of coins at the site, the number of coins from the Persian period is relatively small. The reason for this is essentially technical: the fifth and the fourth centuries B.C.E. marked the first minting of coins in the land of Israel, and only a few coins were in everyday use at the time. Additionally, silver coins from the Persian period are extremely small, the detection of which requires the use of metal detectors, not the usual means (sifting and the like). Metal detectors came into use at Mt. Gerizim only in recent years, and many coins from the Persian period were probably overlooked in the years before this tool's introduction (figs. 27–29, pp. 207–11).

A total of 72 coins from the Persian period were discovered, of which 3 could not be identified.[25] The earliest coin is a drachma from Cyprus dated ca. 480 B.C.E. (fig. 27:1). A coin from Tyre dates to 450–400 B.C.E. (fig. 27:2). An additional coin from Tyre dates to ca. 400–332 B.C.E. (fig. 27:3), while a coin from Sidon dates to the late fifth century B.C.E. (fig. 27:4). The fifth century, which is at the center of the debate concerning the existence of a temple on Mt. Gerizim, is well represented; there is no doubt that the early coins faithfully attest the existence of the sacred precinct in the fifth century B.C.E.

The first half of the fourth century B.C.E. is also significantly represented in the discoveries at Mt. Gerizim. The following were found: an imitation of a Persian coin; a Phoenician standard dated to ca. 390–295; a Samaritan coin from ca. 375–332; 4 Persian coins of Straton I from Sidon dated to ca. 370–358; a Persian coin minted in Tyre dated to ca. 350–325; 6 Persian coins from Sidon of Euagoras II dated to ca. 345–342; a coin from Sidon dated to ca. 344–334; 4 Persian coins of Mazdi from

---

25. Preliminary identification of the coins was undertaken by Gabriela Bijovsky, based on the following sources: G. F. Hill, *Catalogue of the Greek Coins in the British Museum: Cyprus* (London, 1904); idem, *Catalogue of the Greek Coins in the British Museum: Phoenicia* (London, 1910); J. H. Kroll, *The Greek Coins* (Athenian Agora Series 26; Princeton, 1993); Y. Meshorer and S. Qedar, *The Coinage of Samaria in the 4th Century B.C.E.* (Jerusalem, 1991); eidem, *Samarian Coinage* (Israel Numismatic Society 9; Jerusalem, 1999).

Sidon dated to ca. 343–333; a Persian coin, an Attic standard, from Tyre dated to ca. 332–275; 18 Persian coins from Sidon dated to the first half of the fourth century; 5 Persian coins from Sidon assigned a general dating of the fourth century; a Phoenician coin from Byblos dated to the fourth century; and 18 Samaritan coins dated to the fourth century.

The Samaritan mint ceased when Alexander the Great conquered Israel and destroyed Samaria after the city's revolt. Some of the coins bear the name of the province and city of Samaria, and one features the word הרבעם, apparently the name Jeroboam, which also appears on other Samaritan coins.[26] This situation may be compared to that of Judea, where the minting of *yhd* coins continued into the Ptolemaic period.[27] I conclude, therefore, that all the Samaritan coins found on Mt. Gerizim, even if undated, preceded the time of the conquest of Alexander the Great (figs. 27–29).[28]

Carbon-14 Examination

Several C-14 samples were taken of charred wood and bones found at the site, all from the strata belonging to the early phase of the sacred precinct—the Persian–Ptolemaic period (450–200 B.C.E.), preceding the Seleucid conquest of the land of Israel in the time of Antiochus III. The results of the C-14 dating generally confirmed the dates we posited for the first phase of the precinct, based on the pottery and the coins discovered. The dates generated by the testing of samples are shown in table 1.[29]

To conclude this section on the dating of the first phase of the sacred precinct at the site, we may state, on the basis of the pottery, coins, and C-14 testing—and with a great degree of certainty—that the first phase of the precinct was built in the fifth century B.C.E. Relying solely on C-14 dating, the first phase of the precinct came to an end ca. 200 B.C.E., when the construction of the precinct's second phase began (during the reign of Antiochus III).

---

26. A. Spaer, "A Coin of Jeroboam?" *IEJ* 29 (1979) 13.

27. L. Mildenberg, "Yehud: A Preliminary Study of the Provincial Coinage of Judaea," in *Greek Numismatics and Archaeology: Essays in Honour of Margaret Thompson* (ed. O. Morkholm and N. M. Waggoner; Wetteren, 1979) 183–96; U. Rappaport, "The First Judean Coinage," *JJS* 33 (1981) 1–17; D. Barag, "A Silver Coin of Yohanan the High Priest and the Coinage of Judea in the 4th Century B.C.," *Israel Numismatic Journal* 9 (1986–87) 4–16 .

28. Meshorer and Qedar, *Samarian Coinage*, 78.

29. Testing was undertaken at the Weizmann Institute in Reḥovot, Israel, by Elesabeta Boaretto and Dror Segal of the Israel Antiquities Authority. I thank them for their assistance.

Table 1. Dates generated by C-14 testing

GREEK13C PBD %	Site	Calibrated age	C-14 age ± IGREEK year BP	Type	#	RT-RTA-RTP
–23.7	Area S, I.256 measured with the old system	760–710 B.C.E. (10.9%) 540–390 B.C.E. (57.3%)	2400 ± 50	charcoal	2171	RT
–26.7	Area S, L.256, B.1408–1409 measured with the old system	810–750 B.C.E. (26.1%) 690–660 B.C.E. (8.8%) 640–540 B.C.E. (57.3%)	2555 ± 50	charcoal	2172	.
–22.5	Area S, I.282 measured with the old system	380–200 B.C.E.	2235 ± 40	charcoal	2237	RT
–22.9	Area S, L.256	480–470 B.C.E. (2.4%) 280–260 B.C.E. (6.4%) 420–350 B.C.E. (59.0%)	2330 ± 40	charcoal	2239	RT
–22.9	Area S, L.256, B.3330	380–200 B.C.E.	2230 ± 40	charcoal		RT
–22.7	Area S, L.256, B.330	390–350 B.C.E. (22.7%) 300–200 B.C.E. (45.5%)	2250 ± 40	charcoal		RT
–22.9	Area S, L.622, B.7166	360–270 B.C.E. (34.2%) 260–170 B.C.E. (34%)	2185 ± 60	charcoal		RT
–22.6	Area S, L.297, B.22634/22318	390–200 B.C.E.	2245 ± 25	charcoal		RT
–22.3	Area S, L.619, B.7113	380–350 B.C.E. (19.4%) 300–210 B.C.E. (48.8%)	2240 ± 25	charcoal		RT
–21.98	Area P, L.4054, B.40427	370–200 B.C.E.	2225 ± 25	charcoal		RT
–22.14	Area P, L.4619, B.224	520–380 B.C.E.	2360 ± 40	bone (burned)		RT

Mount Gerizim in the Ptolemaic Period

The revolts against Alexander the Great by the city of Samaria led to the destruction of the province of Samaria and its capital city. The Samaritans lost their political and military freedom along with their

province's right to mint coins as they had done during the Persian period. However, the ceramic and numismatic evidence demonstrates the
continued existence of the sacred precinct, which was not abandoned in
the wake of the uprising. A wave of construction at Mt. Gerizim began
in the Ptolemaic period; the southern quarter was built and possibly
also other structures around the sacred precinct. In the Persian period,
the Samaritan religious leadership resided in the city of Samaria, together with the political leadership of the province of Samaria. There is
no evidence that the governor of Samaria also functioned as high priest
in the temple on Mt. Gerizim, except for the account in Josephus
(*Ant.* 11.310) of a promise by Sanballat the Horonite to his son-in-law
Ephraim, assuring him of secular power along with the office of high
priest. Sanballat's sons might have served as priests on Mt. Gerizim, as
I believe is indicated by the Elephantine papyri.[30] After the destruction
of the city of Samaria and the revocation of Samaritan self-rule, the
priests became the ruling class of the Samaritan people that was now
concentrated around the temple on Mt. Gerizim. The high priest was
the head of the theocratic state. In the wake of the destruction of the
city of Samaria by Alexander the Great, all the priestly religious functionaries left the city and moved to Mt. Gerizim.[31] Hence, Mt. Gerizim
became the religious, national, economic, and political center of the
Samaritans during the Ptolemaic period. Following its rebellion and
destruction, Samaria became a Macedonian city. At the same time, Mt.
Gerizim and its temple continued to exist and flourished as the center
of the Samaritans who believed in YHWH.

Coins from the early Ptolemaic period were also found outside the
sacred precinct—approximately 30 Ptolemaic coins out of a total of 430
discovered scattered throughout the site and the sacred precinct[32]
were found in the southern quarter, which was most likely the first
residential quarter to be built on Mt. Gerizim. The early Ptolemaic
coins lead us to assume the continuity of Samaritan settlement on Mt.
Gerizim. The conquest by Alexander the Great and the destruction of
the city of Samaria did not result in the abandonment of the Samaritan

---

30. A. E. Cowley, *Aramaic Papyri of the Fifth Century* B.C. (Oxford, 1923) 108–22, nos.
30–31; E. Kraeling, *The Brooklyn Museum Aramaic Papyri* (New Haven, CT, 1953) 83–99.

31. M. Stern, *Greek and Latin Authors on Jews and Judaism* (3 vols.; Jerusalem, 1974–84)
1:447; F. M. Cross, "The Papyri and Their Historical Implications," in *Discoveries in the
Wadi ed-Daliyeh* (ed. P. W. Lapp and N. L. Lapp; AASOR 41; Cambridge, MA, 1974) 17;
J. E. Atkinson, *A Commentary on Q. Curtius Rufus' Historiae Alexandri Magni: Books 3 and 4*
(Amsterdam, 1980) 19–57.

32. The coins were identified by G. Bijovsky.

settlement on Mt. Gerizim. Two tetradrachma of Alexander the Great dated to ca. 336–323 B.C.E. and minted in Macedonia (Amphipolis) along with two Sidonean didrachma dated to ca. 310–301 B.C.E. were discovered at the site. These coins attest to settlement continuity from the Persian to the Hellenistic periods, and this assertion is reinforced by the discovery of 103 coins of Ptolemy I Soter that can be dated to ca. 310–283 B.C.E. From the time of Ptolemy II Philadelphus (285–246 B.C.E.), the excavations uncovered 222 coins minted at Tyre, Alexandria, Sidon, and Berytus (Beirut), as well as 13 coins of Ptolemy III Euergetes dated to ca. 246–221 B.C.E. Two coins of Ptolemy IV Philopator date to ca. 221–205 B.C.E., and 1 coin of Ptolemy VI Philometor dates to ca. 175–174 B.C.E. Along with these Ptolemaic coins, a *yhd* coin minted in Judea and dated to ca. 285–270 B.C.E. came to light. The Jewish minting of coins continued after the conquest of the land by Alexander the Great. In addition to the bronze coins, silver and gold coins were discovered as well. The wealth of coins from this period alludes to extensive development and economic growth on Mt. Gerizim, which may be the basis of the error of the historical sources on which Josephus relied in dating the beginnings of the temple on Mt. Gerizim to the early Ptolemaic period. In sum, the temple on Mt. Gerizim was established in the mid-fifth century B.C.E., while the city was founded in the late fourth century and destroyed in the time of John Hyrcanus I (111–110 B.C.E.).

The History of Mount Gerizim

The name *Mt. Gerizim* is bound up in the Torah with the Israelite beginnings in the land of Canaan. The Torah commands the Israelites upon their entrance into the land of Israel to conduct the ceremony of blessings and curses on Mt. Gerizim and Mt. Ebal (Deut 11:29–30):

> When the LORD your God brings you into the land that you are about to invade and occupy, you shall pronounce the blessing on Mt. Gerizim and the curse on Mt. Ebal. Both are on the other side of the Jordan, beyond the west road that is in the land of the Canaanites who dwell in the Arabah—near Gilgal, by the terebinths of Moreh.

Deuteronomy later returns to the blessings and curses as well as the division of the tribes between the two mountains (27:11–26). The Israelites are commanded to build an altar on Mt. Ebal (MT Deut 27:7–8), although the Samaritan Torah mandates the erection of this altar on Mt. Gerizim, which, according to Samaritan tradition, is the site of the tabernacle—not Shiloh.[33] Mount Gerizim is also mentioned in the parable of Jotham (Judg 9:7): "he went and stood on top of Mt. Gerizim."

How should the expression "you shall pronounce the blessing" be understood? Does this mean a sacred site at which animals were slaughtered and sacrificed? If so, why is the place not then mentioned as a ritual site by the Torah or by biblical sources relating to the period of the monarchy? At this stage of research and following many years of intensive excavations, no archaeological evidence has been found pointing to the existence of a ritual site; nor, indeed, were any finds discovered from the period of the Israelite settlement or the Israelite monarchy.

The traditions of the books of Genesis, Deuteronomy, Joshua, and Judges hallow Shechem over all other cities in the land of Israel, and the main rite of the people of Israel was practiced there. Abraham built an altar at the terebinth of Moreh, at the place where the LORD "appeared to him" (Gen 12:6–7). Jacob erected an altar on the parcel of land that he had purchased and called it "God, the God of Israel" (Gen 33:19–20). The places named *'ēlâ* and *'ēlôn* ('oak' or 'terebinth') in the Bible are ritual sites, of which there are many at Shechem: "the terebinth that was near Shechem" (Gen 35:4); "at the terebinth of the pillar at Shechem" (Judg 9:6); "the oak in the sacred precinct of the LORD" (Josh 24:26). Joshua assembles the tribes of Israel at Shechem and they gather (Josh 24:1) "before God," a phrase that the Bible reserves for a ritual site where God is present. There was a temple to the LORD at Shechem (Josh 24:26). The book of Judges speaks of Baal-berith (9:4) and the temple of El-berith (9:46), most likely in reference to additional ritual sites. Shechem is, therefore, a sacred ritual city with two hallowed mounts: Mt. Ebal and Mt. Gerizim. The establishment of the temple on Mt. Gerizim by Sanballat the Horonite in the Persian period was not by chance or the result of a hasty decision. The sanctity of the mount and of Shechem was deeply rooted in the Northern Israelite

---

33. Samaritans do not believe in the existence of a temple on Mt. Gerizim; they maintain that the tabernacle stood on this spot from the days of Yehoshua/Joshua bin Nun on. At some point, the age of the *Fanūta* (God's concealing of the face) will begin, when the *Taheb*—the Messiah—will arrive and spread the presence of God on the mount, and the tabernacle will then disappear; the tent of meeting will be resurrected and the tabernacle will be rebuilt, ushering in the age of *Rḥwta* (God's revealing of the face). The Samaritan chronicle of Abu'l-Fath speaks of the construction of an altar and temple on Mt. Gerizim by the high priest Abdal that was destroyed by the Jews during the reign of Simon Maccabeus; see P. Stenhouse, *The Kitab al-Tarikh of Abu'l-Fath: Translated with Notes* (Sydney, 1985) 97. See also R. Pummer, "Samaritan Material Remains and Archaeology," in *The Samaritans* (ed. A. D. Crown; Tübingen, 1989) 172.

tradition, as expressed in the Torah and the books of Joshua and Judges. The holiness of these sites was probably accepted by the Israelite inhabitants of Samaria as well.

Many ritual sites in the land of Israel were built beyond the bounds of the major cities. The temple in Jerusalem was constructed on a high hill, distant from the City of David. The sacred site of Hebron was established at Elonei Mamre. It, too, was located quite far from Tell Rumeidah (biblical Hebron). The construction in the Persian period of the temple on Mt. Gerizim and not within the city of Shechem was thus not an unusual act. To some degree, this remoteness mimicked the location of the temple in Jerusalem. Mount Gerizim is the sacred mount of Shechem, just as Mt. Moriah is the holy mount of the city of Jerusalem (the City of David).

Before discussing the question of when and why the Samaritan temple was built at Mt. Gerizim, I will go into a little more detail on the history of Samaria from its destruction until the Persian period. In 722 B.C.E., Shalmaneser V besieged Samaria following the revolt by Hoshea, son of Elah (2 Kgs 17:3–6, 18:9–11). Shalmaneser died shortly after the conquest of the city and did not complete the conquest of the region and the exile of its inhabitants, which were completed by Sargon II. The latter records that he captured the city of Samaria in 720, took 27,290 captives, rebuilt the city, and resettled it with various exiles[34] who were brought to Samaria from other Mesopotamian cities in several waves. The first was during the time of Shalmaneser and Sargon II (2 Kgs 17:24); two additional waves were brought to Samaria during the time of Esarhaddon (Ezra 4:2) and in the time of Asnapper (= Ashurbanipal; Ezra 4:10).[35]

The biblical and apocryphal sources present quite a clear picture. Samaria was conquered by the Assyrians and its population exiled, to

---

34. A. G. Lie, *The Inscription of Sargon II, King of Assyia*, vol. 1: *The Annals* (Paris, 1929) 10–17, 23–26; H. Tadmor, "The Campaigns of Sargon II of Assur: A Chronological Historical Study," *JCS* 12 (1958) 20–40, 77–100; I. Eph'al, "The End of the Kingdom of Israel," in *The Age of the Monarchies: Political History* (ed. A. Malamat; WHJP 4; Jerusalem, 1979) 121–30 [Hebrew]; S. Talmon, "The Beginning of the Return to Zion," in *The Restoration: The Persian Period* (ed. H. Tadmor; WHJP 6; Jerusalem, 1980) 27–28 [Hebrew]; A. Demsky, "The Days of Ezra and Nehemia," in ibid., 40–65 [Hebrew]; N. Na'aman, "The Historical Background to the Conquest of Samaria (720 B.C.), *Bib* 71 (1990) 206–25; F. M. Cross, "Samaria and Jerusalem during the Persian Period," in *The Samaritans* (ed. E. Stern and H. Eshel; Jerusalem, 2002) 45–70 [Hebrew].

35. B. Oded, *Mass Deportations and Deportees in the Neo-Assyrian Empire* (Wiesbaden, 1979); N. Na'aman and R. Zadok, "Population Changes in Palestine following Assyrian Deportations," *TA* 20 (1993) 104–24.

be replaced by different peoples.[36] Their religion is portrayed in a certain way by the book of Kings. They did not acknowledge the law of the God of the land, so God sent lions among them, who killed them, until an Israelite priest from among the exiles was sent back to teach them "the rules of the God of the land" (2 Kgs 17:25–29). These peoples observed a syncretistic rite: "These nations worshiped the LORD, but they also served their idols" (2 Kgs 17:41). According to the book of Kings, Samaria was bereft of Israelites, and the population of that region after the destruction of Samaria consisted of the peoples brought by the Assyrian ruler. When Kings goes into detail concerning the reforms of Josiah (2 Kgs 23:15, 19), it makes no mention of the inhabitants of Samaria or of any Israelite remnant.

The view expressed by the book of Chronicles, composed in the late Return to Zion period, is diametrically opposed to the viewpoint of Kings. It tells of King Hezekiah's attempts to draw the Ephraimites and Manassites closer to Judah after the destruction of Samaria, including inviting them to come and celebrate Passover in Jerusalem (2 Chr 30:1, 10–11). It then relates that Israelites from the tribes of Issachar and Zebulon were in attendance in Jerusalem as well (2 Chr 30:18). According to Chronicles, the money for the temple repairs conducted in the time of Josiah came from Judah, Benjamin, Manasseh, and Ephraim, and from all "the remnant of Israel" (2 Chr 34:9). This detail is missing from the account in Kings, which does mention the renovations of Josiah. Jeremiah tells of people from Shechem, Shiloh, and Samaria who brought frankincense and a grain offering to the house of the LORD (Jer 41:5).

Chronicles relates that "the remnant of Israel" was left in Samaria and that the Judean kings sought to effect a rapprochement and to create for them a new religious framework centered in Jerusalem. Here, this remnant is regarded as an integral part of the Israelite people, which was composed of more than one group and of which the residents of Samaria were a legitimate element.[37] There is no hint of the peoples brought by the Assyrian monarch and resettled in Samaria but

---

36. S. Talmon, "Biblical Traditions on Samaritan History," in *The Samaritans* (ed. E. Stern and H. Eshel; Jerusalem, 2002) 7–27 [Hebrew]; M. Cogan, "The Early Biblical Polemic concerning the Residents of Samaria," in ibid., 28–33 [Hebrew].

37. S. Japhet, "The Supposed Common Authorship of Chronicles and Ezra-Nehemia Investigated Anew," *VT* 18 (1968) 330–71; idem, "The Historical Reliability of Chronicles," *JSOT* 33 (1985) 83–107 (both articles now repr. in idem, *From the Rivers of Babylon to the Highlands of Judah: Collected Studies on the Restoration Period* [Winona Lake, IN, 2006] 1–37 and 117–36, respectively).

only of the remnant of the Israelite tribes of Manasseh and Ephraim. The author of Chronicles conceals the information that is given prominence in Kings, and vice versa. The position of Chronicles is contrary not only to Kings but also to the books of Ezra and Nehemiah. In response to the derision of Sanballat, Tobiah the Ammonite, and Geshem the Arab, Nehemiah declares, "But you have no share or claim or record in Jerusalem" (Neh 2:20) with ṣĕdāḳâ here meaning 'inheritance' (see Isa 54:17). According to Nehemiah, the people of Samaria were not part of the holy stock and the exiled people. The books of Ezra and Nehemiah adopt a narrow sectarian approach that seeks to maintain the uniqueness and racial purity of the exiles in Babylonia, while Chronicles is more broad-minded and views the Israelite nation as a great people that includes all the tribes, both Judah and Israel.

The historical truth is most likely that the Assyrians were not successful in exiling all of the inhabitants of the Northern Kingdom, and Samaria retained a considerable population, some of which fled southward at the time of the conquest of Judah and the peripheral areas, while another part survived the Assyrian conquest. I maintain that the accelerated settling and development of the fringe areas and Jerusalem in the seventh century B.C.E. resulted from the flight of Israelite refugees and their resettling in Judah, and I therefore give greater credence to the version of Chronicles. A considerable Israelite population remained in Samaria, and the Judean kings Hezekiah and Josiah took steps to draw them closer.[38] However, years later, Judah also was exiled. During the Persian period, there were two provinces in these areas: Samaria and Judea. The former was composed of the Israelite remnant and the peoples brought by the Assyrians. The majority of Benjamin and Judah, on the other hand, were sent into exile in Babylonia, where they underwent an essential change and returned with a different outlook. The religious and national world view of the Jews who returned from Babylonia, especially the returnees in the later stages (during the time of Ezra and Nehemiah), no longer resembled the world view of the Israelite remnant in Samaria.

Two provinces were formed in the late sixth century B.C.E.: large, rich Samaria, and Judah, impoverished and limited in territory because its southern part had been seized by the Idumeans. We do not know for certain whether the people of Samaria maintained religious-ritual contact with Jerusalem or whether they actually came en masse to offer

---

38. J. Rosenbaum, "Hezekiah's Reform and the Deuteronomistic Tradition," *HTR* 72 (1979) 23–44; N. Naʾaman, "The Kingdom of Judah under Josiah," *TA* 18 (1991) 3–71.

sacrifices at the Temple of the LORD in Jerusalem, despite the testimony in Ezra concerning the "adversaries of Judah" (4:1–3). In either event, the archaeological finds from Mt. Gerizim attest that "Sanballat the Horonite" mentioned in the book of Nehemiah (Sanballat I) established a temple on Mt. Gerizim. He apparently was a scion of a veteran Samaritan family of the Israelite remnant, from the early Israelite stratum, which originated in Horon. It is possible that Horon can be identified with the village of Hawara at the foot of Mt. Gerizim, but this remains in the realm of conjecture.[39] Sanballat was in charge of the garrison force in Samaria and was appointed governor of the province prior to Nehemiah's arrival in Judea in 444 B.C.E., apparently the first to occupy this post from among the indigenous Israelite population.[40] He understood the connection between political and religious independence, similar to Jeroboam before him (who was a revered figure in Persian-period Samaria and whose name appears on Samaria coins): "Jeroboam said to himself, 'Now the kingdom may well revert to the House of David. If these people go up to offer sacrifices at the House of the LORD in Jerusalem, the heart of these people will turn back to their master'" (1 Kgs 12:26–27). Sanballat realized that a sacred site that would unite Samaria and the Samaritans was necessary in order to establish an independent Samaritan entity, along with an army and administration. He identified a sacred site with a lengthy tradition that was unblemished by idolatry in the area under his rule: Mt. Gerizim. He lacked religious functionaries, however, fit priests and Levites from the stock of Aaron. Significantly, Chronicles reports that in the time of Jeroboam the priests and Levites in the Northern Kingdom had left their homes and lands and migrated to Judah, and Jeroboam replaced them with the priests of the shrines (2 Chr 11:13–15). Sanballat did not desire the priests of Baal, who were almost certainly to be found in Samaria, but preferred to engage a high priest of the most distinguished lineage, the family of the high priest in Jerusalem: "One of the sons of

---

39. S. Feigin, "Etymological Notes," *AJSL* 43 (1926) 58. R. Zadok believes that Sanballat the Horonite came from Beth Horon in the Land of Benjamin, to which exiles and Assyrian clerks were sent (Zadok, "Samaritan Notes," *BO* 42 [1985] 569–70). See also: I. Press, "Where Did Sanballat the Honorite Live?" *Yediot* 9/4 (1942) 106–7 [Hebrew]; Y. Grintz, *Book of Judith* (Jerusalem, 1957) 100–102; idem, *Chapters in the History of the Second Temple Times* (Jerusalem, 1969) 37 n. 10.

40. F. M. Cross argues that, contrary to the policy of the Assyrians, Persian policy was to appoint members of the local population as governors of the provinces (Cross, "Samaria and Jerusalem during the Persian Period," 59 n. 59).

Jehoiada, son of the high priest Eliashib, was a son-in-law of Sanballat the Horonite; I [Nehemiah] drove him away from me" (Neh 13:28).

Sanballat went one step further; not only did he appoint a high priest at Mt. Gerizim, a grandson of Eliashib, the high priest in Jerusalem, who during his priesthood also maintained good relations with Tobiah, the Ammonite slave (Neh 13:4), he even gave him his daughter in marriage, thus turning his progeny into fit priests of the most impeccable lineage. This fulfilled the two central conditions for the validation and importance of the temple on Mt. Gerizim: a sacred site with a proven religious tradition from the Torah—the mount of blessing; and a high priest from the elite of the Jerusalem priesthood, from the descendants of Aaron. The many inscriptions discovered on Mt. Gerizim that contain clearly priestly names and the title "priest" confirm the historical veracity of the account in Nehemiah.

It cannot be precisely determined whether the marriage of Sanballat's daughter took place before Nehemiah returned to Israel or afterward, when he left the land and returned to serve the Babylonian king (Neh 13:6). After Nehemiah's return to the land of Israel, he paints a harsh picture of the temple in Jerusalem and the inferior and difficult economic and personal standing of the priests, who were compelled to leave the temple and return to their fields: "I censured the prefects, saying, 'How is it that the House of God has been neglected?' Then I recalled [the Levites] and installed them again in their posts" (Neh 13:10–11). We learn from this testimony and possibly also from the book of Malachi (which is to be attributed to this period) of the pressing circumstances of the priests and the temple in Jerusalem. It therefore was not challenging for Sanballat to persuade the grandson of Eliashib to marry his daughter or to summon additional Jewish priests to serve in the temple on Mt. Gerizim, as in the account by Josephus (*Ant.* 11.312, 346).

Sanballat thereby came full circle: he established a Temple to YHWH–God Almighty on Mt. Gerizim in which priests from Jerusalem served, and the members of his family became high priests at the mount. It should be stressed that priestly status in Judaism is patrimonial, and therefore the offspring of the Jewish priest who married Sanballat's daughter would be fit priests in all respects. This historical re-creation might be a bit far-reaching, but the archaeological discoveries on Mt. Gerizim, especially the inscriptions with the title "priest" and the numerous Hebrew names discovered there lend credence to this scenario.

The Establishment of the Samaritan Temple on Mount Gerizim according to Josephus

Josephus describes Sanballat's construction of the Samaritan temple on Mt. Gerizim as a copy of the Jerusalem temple (*Ant.* 11.302–12, 321–25) and relates that Sanballat the Cuthean was sent to Samaria as governor by the Persian king Darius III (336–331 B.C.E.). Sanballat's daughter Nikaso was married to a Jerusalem priest named Manasseh, the brother of Jehoiada the high priest. The elders of Jerusalem and Jehoiada reproached him for marrying a Samaritan woman whom they regarded as a Gentile, and gave him an ultimatum: either he would part from his Samaritan wife or he was not to approach the altar. Manasseh came to his father-in-law and informed him that, while he loved his wife, he was unwilling to forego the high priesthood that he had inherited from his father. His father-in-law, Sanballat, promised to build him a temple on Mt. Gerizim and to appoint him to rule all the land of Samaria, under him (Sanballat). Josephus then relates that many Israelites were joined by marital ties to Samaritans and moved to reside with them, which caused much bewilderment in Jerusalem.

Close to these events, Alexander the Great invaded the land of Israel, and Sanballat decided to cast his lot with the Greek king. He assembled his army and came to Tyre during the siege of the city. Sanballat submitted to Alexander and used this opportunity to request permission to build a temple on Mt. Gerizim. Alexander consented, and Sanballat devoted all his efforts to the construction of the temple, immediately after which he died.

The erection of the temple by Sanballat has drawn much scholarly attention, and most scholars question the historical accuracy of Josephus's account of the events leading up to the establishment of the Samaritan temple on Mt. Gerizim.[41] Their doubts were aroused by the

---

41. Numerous scholars have dealt with this topic and they have offered a wide array of theories. It should be stressed that most dismiss the evidence presented by Josephus for the construction of a temple in the days of Sanballat and the conquest of the land by Alexander the Great, and most also regard Josephus's tale of the meeting between Alexander and the Jewish high priest in Jerusalem as a legend; see: J. Gutman, "Alexander of Macedonia in the Land of Israel," *Tarbiz* 11 (1940) 271–94 [Hebrew]; A. Schalit, "A Chapter in the History of the Parties' Wars in Jerusalem at the End of the Fifth and Beginning of the Fourth Centuries BCE," in *Yohanan Levy Volume* (ed. M. Schwabe and I. Gutman; Jerusalem, 1949) 252–72 [Hebrew]; D. Golan, "Josephus, Alexander's Visit to Jerusalem, and Modern Historiography," in *Josephus Flavius: Historian of Eretz-Israel in the Hellenistic–Roman Period. Collected Papers* (ed. U. Rappaport; Jerusalem, 1982) 29–55 [Hebrew; English summary, pp. v–vii]. A. Kasher, however, maintains that the evidence given by Josephus

duplication in the narrative of the marriage of Sanballat's daughter to Manasseh, the brother of Jehoiada the high priest in Jerusalem, based on Neh 13:28. More than a century separates the two narratives of Josephus and Nehemiah. Another question is connected with the construction of the temple: the time of the final split between the Samaritans and the Jews, which, according to many scholars, reached its climax with the establishment of the temple on Mt. Gerizim. The discoveries on Mt. Gerizim reveal Josephus's error in attributing this to the time of Sanballat, governor of Samaria during the reign of Darius III, when the land of Israel was conquered by Alexander the Great. The temple on Mt. Gerizim was built during the time of Nehemiah and his contemporary, Sanballat the Horonite (mid-fifth century B.C.E.). The city surrounding Mt. Gerizim was established after the destruction of Samaria by Alexander the Great.

The temple on Mt. Gerizim had already stood for more than a century at the time of Alexander's conquest. The Roman historian Curtius Rufus relates that the city of Samaria rebelled and its inhabitants burned Andromachus, the governor of Coele–Syria, alive. Alexander lost no time in marching on Samaria and punishing the murderers, and he appointed Menon in place of the dead governor (Curtius Rufus,

---

for the construction of a temple by Sanballat should be accepted, as should the meeting between the high priest and Alexander (see A. Kasher, "The Campaign of Alexander the Great in the Land of Israel," *Beth Mikra* 20 [1975] 187–208 [Hebrew]; idem, "Samaritans in Hellenistic Egypt," in *The Samaritans* [ed. E. Stern and H. Eshel; Jerusalem, 2002] 154 n. 3 [Hebrew]). M. Mor also takes this view ("The Samaritan Temple at Mount Gerizim," *Beth Mikra* 38 (1993) 313–27 [Hebrew]). For more on Alexander, Sanballat, and the temple, see R. Marcus, *Josephus: Jewish Antiquities* VI (LCL; Cambridge, MA, 1937) 498–532, appendixes B, C. In light of the discoveries at Wâdi ed-Dâliyeh, G. E. Wright and F. M. Cross accepted the evidence given by Josephus regarding the construction of the temple; see: F. M. Cross, "The Discovery of the Samaria Papyri," *BA* 26 (1963) 110–21; idem, "Aspects of Samaritan and Jewish History in Late Persian and Hellenistic Times," *HTR* 59 (1966) 201–11; G. E. Wright, *Shechem: The Biography of a Biblical City* (New York, 1965) 170–84. See also: H. H. Rowley, "Sanballat and the Samaritan Temple," *BJRL* 38 (1955–56) 166–98; R. J. Coggins, *Samaritans and Jews: The Origins of Samaritanism Reconsidered* (Oxford, 1975); S. J. D. Cohen, "Alexander the Great and Jaddus the High Priest according to Josephus," *AJSR* 7–8 (1982–83) 41–68; L. L. Grabbe, "Josephus and the Reconstruction of the Judean Restoration," *JBL* 106 (1987) 231–46; M. Mor, "The Persian, Hellenistic and Hasmonean Period," in *The Samaritans* (ed. A. D. Crown; Tübingen, 1989) 1–18; D. R. Schwartz, "On Some Papyri and Josephus' Sources and Chronology for the Persian Period," *JSJ* 21 (1990) 175–99; idem, "On Some Papyri and Josephus' Sources and Chronology for the Persian Period," in *The Samaritans* (ed. E. Stern and H. Eshel; Jerusalem, 2002) 107–28 [Hebrew]; A. Momigliano, *Essays on Ancient and Modern Judaism* (Chicago, 1994) 79–87.

Historiae Alexandri Magni 4.8.9–11).[42] He also punished the city of Samaria and turned it into a Macedonian city. The Samaritans lost their capital and the limited independence that they had enjoyed in the Persian period.

The ceramic and numismatic finds from Mt. Gerizim lead us to conclude that the Samaritan sacred precinct remained active even following Alexander the Great's conquest of the land of Israel. The excavations revealed numerous coins of Alexander and his successors, the Ptolemies, dated from the late fourth to early third centuries B.C.E. During the Ptolemaic period, the Samaritans, following the loss of their independence and capital city, were now concentrated around the sacred site on Mt. Gerizim and rallied around their religious leadership, the high priests, who became the leaders of the people as a whole. Mt. Gerizim and the temple were the center not only of the Samaritans' ritual but also of their administration and economy. In the Ptolemaic period, Mt. Gerizim became the residence for the Samaritan priesthood and nobility. This period was also marked by division between the Samaritan pagans remaining from the Persian period, who were now joined by the idolatrous Greek population that entered Samaria after the Hellenistic conquest; and the god-fearing Samaritans, who worshiped YHWH on Mt. Gerizim and who were mainly of Israelite descent, from the Israelite remnant in Samaria. Paradoxically, the destruction of Samaria united the Samaritan people around Mt. Gerizim and transformed it into their capital and temple city.

Josephus's error in dating the construction of the temple might, therefore, be explained by the time difference between the construction of the temple on Mt. Gerizim in the Persian period and the founding of the city on Mt. Gerizim in the Hellenistic period following the destruction of Samaria. This was not the only mistake Josephus made regarding the events that befell Mt. Gerizim and the Samaritans in the Hellenistic period. He was silent regarding the destruction of Samaria by Alexander the Great and erroneously believed that Shechem, not Samaria, was the capital of the Samaritan people during the Persian period and immediately preceding the conquest by Alexander. He also

---

42. Curtius Rufus, *Historiae Alexandri Magni* 4.8.9–11; Stern, *Greek and Latin Authors on Jews and Judaism*, 1:447. See also: Georgius Syncellus, *Chronographia* (ed. G. Dindorf; Corpus Scriptorum Historiae Byzantinae 49; Bonn, 1829) 496; A. Schoene, *Die Weltchronik des Eusebius in ihrer Bearbeitung durch Hieronymus* (Berlin, 1900) 114; Hieronymus, *Die Chronik des Hieronymus* (Die Griechischen Christlichen Schriftsteller 34; ed. R. Helm; Leipzig, 1926) 123. See also E. Schürer, *The History of the Jewish People in the Age of Jesus Christ (175 B.C.–A.D. 135)* (3 vols.; Edinburgh, 1973–87) 2:160–61.

incorrectly dated the conquest and destruction of Mt. Gerizim by John Hyrcanus I to 128 B.C.E., immediately after the death of Antiochus VII (*Ant.* 13.254–58; *J.W.* 1.62). Based on the archaeological finds, Mt. Gerizim, Shechem, and Mareshah were all destroyed ca. 110 B.C.E.[43] We do not know on which historical sources Josephus relied when he wrote the history of the Samaritan people in the Persian and Hellenistic periods. The archaeological testimonies from Mt. Gerizim demonstrate that he erred in describing the historical facts.

---

43. Numerous scholars have questioned the early date that Josephus gives to the conquests of John Hyrcanus I. Josephus writes that Hyrcanus set out for war immediately after the death of Antiochus VII, in 128 B.C.E. However, excavations at Mt. Gerizim, Shechem, and Mareshah (sites conquered by Hyrcanus during the said campaign) indicate that the conquest, in fact, occurred many years after 128 B.C.E. Excavations at Tell Balâṭah have exposed coins of Antiochus VIII, dated ca. 121–120 B.C.E., and a coin dating to ca. 112–111 B.C.E.—meaning, several years after the death of Antiochus VII, which, according to Josephus, was the year in which Hyrcanus laid siege to Mt. Gerizim. See: G. E. Wright, "The Second Campaign at Tell Balâṭah (Shechem)," *BASOR* 148 (1957) 27–28; L. E. Toombs and G. E. Wright, "The Third Campaign at Balâṭah (Shechem)," *BASOR* 161 (1961) 46–47. For a discussion of coins found at Tell Balâṭah dated to 110 B.C.E., see D. Barag and S. Qedar, "The Beginning of Hasmonean Coinage," *Israel Numismatic Journal* 4 (1980) 8–21. Coins dated to ca. 115–114 B.C.E. and 112–111 B.C.E. were found at Maresha; see A. Kloner, "Maresha," *Qadmoniot* 95–96 (1992) 70–85 [Hebrew]; idem, "Maresha," *NEAEHL* 3:948–57. See also G. Finkielsztejn, "More Evidence on John Hyrcanus I's Conquests: Lead Weights and Rhodian Amphora Stamps," *Bulletin of the Anglo-Israel Archaeological Society* 16 (1998) 33–63.

No.	Locus/Basket	Vessel Type	Parallels
1	4165-41669/2	Jar	Tell Balâṭah (Shechem): Lapp 1985: Fig. 5:25; Tell el-Hesi: Bennett and Blakely 1989: Fig. 145:16
2	4176-41/1	Jar	Holyland Hotel, Jerusalem: Ben-Arieh 2000: Fig. 16:2
3	4133-41162/1	Jar	Tell el-Hesi: Bennett and Blakely 1989: Fig. 146:12
4	4293-61/1	Jar	
5	4165-41667	Jar	Holyland Hotel, Jerusalem: Ben-Arieh 2000: Fig. 16:20
6	4289-51/1	Flask	Holyland Hotel, Jerusalem: Ben-Arieh 2000: Fig. 13:1
7	4606-108/1	Jug	
8	4606-110/3	Dipper / Juglet base	Tell el-Hesi: Bennett and Blakely 1989: Fig. 156:21
9	4296/4292-70/1	Cooking pot	
10	4168-42669/1	Hole-mouth jar	Qadum: Stern and Magen 1984: Fig. 4
11	4292-58/1	Krater	Tell el-Hesi: Bennett and Blakely 1989: Fig. 141:1
12	4165-41669/1	Krater	Tell Mevorakh: Stern 1978, Fig. 5:7
13	4155-41509	Krater	Holyland Hotel, Jerusalem: Ben-Arieh 2000: Fig. 8:1-3
14	4165-41653	Krater	Qadum: Stern and Magen 1984: Fig. 6:3
15	4162-41603/3	Krater	Tell Balâṭah (Shechem): Lapp 1985: Fig. 6:1
16	4608-122	Bowl	Holyland Hotel, Jerusalem: Ben-Arieh 2000: Fig. 6:7; Gezer: Gitin 1990: Pl. 27:28
17	4162-41603/2	Bowl	Tell el-Hesi: Bennett and Blakely 1989: Fig. 139:7
18	4163-41634	Bowl	
19	4162-41627/2	Lamp	Tell el-Hesi: Bennett and Blakely 1989: Fig. 152:42

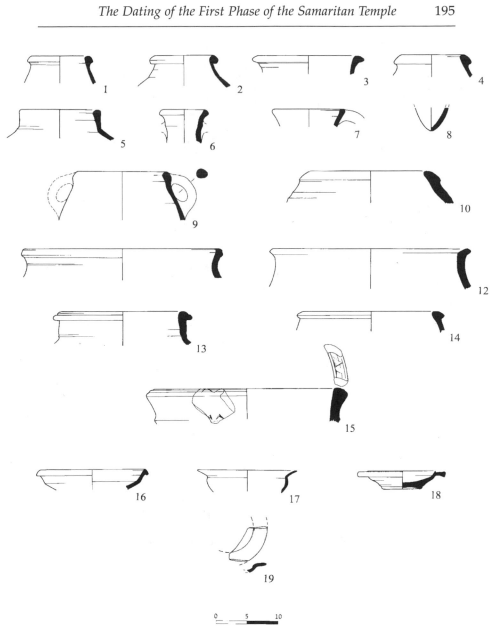

Fig. 21. Pottery from Area P, the "Twelve Stones" area.

No.	Locus/Basket	Vessel Type	Parallels
1	785-8964/5	Jar	Armenian Garden, Jerusalem: Tushingham 1985: Fig.15:15
2	7001-9509	Jar? / Jug?	Parallel for the decoration only, Tell Balâṭah (Shechem): Lapp 1985: Fig. 6:7
3	785-9127/6	Small jar	
4	785-9006/1	Jug	Tell Balâṭah (Shechem): Lapp 1985: Fig. 5:3
5	775-8445/1	Juglet	Tell el-Hesi: Bennett and Blakely 1989: Fig. 144:10; Holyland Hotel, Jerusalem: Ben-Arieh 2000: Fig. 11:3
6	756-8827	Krater	Holyland Hotel, Jerusalem: Ben-Arieh 2000: Fig. 8:1
7	777-8523/1	Krater	Armenian Garden, Jerusalem: Tushingham 1985: Fig. 15:10; Tell Balâṭah (Shechem): Lapp 1985: Fig. 4:14
8	7047-10665/4	Krater	Tell el-Fûl: Lapp 1981: Pl. 65:5
9	785-8768/2	Krater	Tell el-Fûl: Lapp 1981: Pl. 65:5
10	7012-9871	Krater	Tell Balâṭah (Shechem): Lapp 1985: Fig. 6:9-10
11	7012-9577	Krater	Qadum: Stern and Magen 1984: Fig. 6:5; Tell Mevorakh: Stern 1978: Fig. 5:5
12	785-9031/4	Krater	Qadum: Stern and Magen 1984: Fig. 6:5; Tell Mevorakh: Stern 1978: Fig. 5:5; Armenian Garden, Jerusalem: Tushingham 1985: Fig. 16:6
13	7012-9731	Basin	Qadum: Stern and Magen 1984: Fig. 5:11; Gezer: Gitin 1990: Pl. 30:7
14	785-8763/3	Basin	Qadum: Stern and Magen 1984: Fig. 5:13; Tell el-Hesi: Bennett and Blakely 1989: Fig. 137:1
15	788-8836/1	Bowl	Holyland Hotel, Jerusalem: Ben-Arieh 2000: Fig. 6:7; Armenian Garden, Jerusalem: Tushingham 1985: Fig. 14:8
16	785-8784/1	Deep bowl/Cup	Tell Mevorakh: Stern 1978: Fig. 5:3
17	791-9217	Bowl/Lid	
18	785-8799	Lamp	Tell el-Hesi: Bennett and Blakely 1989: Figs. 144:22–23, 163:7; Tell Balâṭah (Shechem): Lapp 1985: Fig. 7:20–22; Qadum: Stern and Magen 1984: Fig. 9:2–4

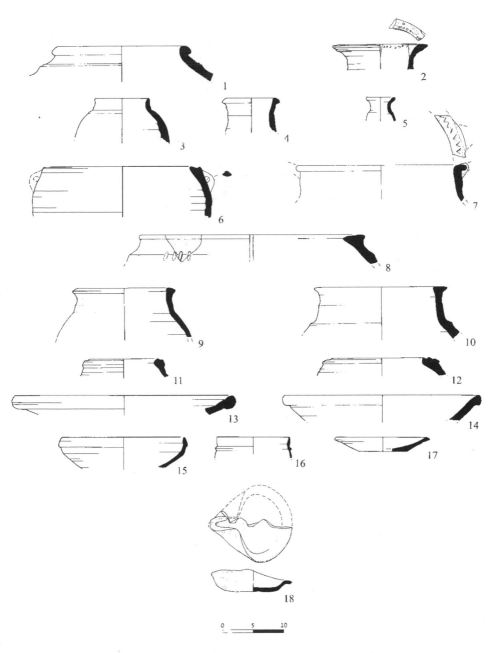

Fig. 22. Pottery from Area S (the Eastern Slope).

No.	Locus/Basket	Vessel Type	Parallels
1	617-7099/4	Jar	Tell el-Hesi: Bennett and Blakely 1989: Fig. 138:9
2	877-10936/2	Jar	Holyland Hotel, Jerusalem: Ben-Arieh 2000: Fig. 15:7; Bethel: Sinclair 1968: Pl. 67:11
3	635-7401	Jar handle	
4	870-10900/2	Jug	
5	878-10937/1	Juglet	
6	880-10948/1	Cooking pot	Samaria: Kenyon 1957: Fig. 30:24 (Period VI, Iron Age)
7	852-7434/3	Cooking pot	
8	852-7854/1	Krater	Tell Balâṭah (Shechem): Lapp 1985: Fig. 6:11
9	613-7116	Krater	Tell Balâṭah (Shechem): Lapp 1985: Fig. 6:7
10	870-10900/1	Impressed decoration from a krater	
11	904-11025/3	Krater	Tell Balâṭah (Shechem): Lapp 1985: Fig. 6:7–8
12	878-10937/3	Deep bowl	
13	617-7099/1	Basin	Gezer: Gitin 1990: Pl. 30:4
14	852-7434/1	Bowl	Holyland Hotel, Jerusalem: Ben-Arieh 2000: Fig. 6:10; Gezer: Gitin 1990: Pl. 27:24
15	878-10953/1	Bowl	
16	622-7612/3	Bowl	
17	905-11037/1	Bowl	Holyland Hotel, Jerusalem: Ben-Arieh 2000: Fig. 5:6 (middle layer, Persian period)
18	877-10943	Bowl	Holyland Hotel, Jerusalem: Ben-Arieh 2000: Fig. 6:13

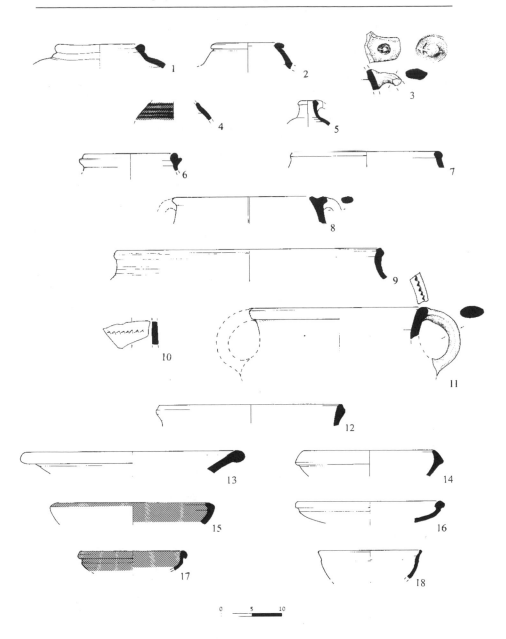

Fig. 23. Pottery from Area S (East).

No.	Locus/Basket	Vessel Type	Parallels
1	2245-22451/1	Jar	Holyland Hotel, Jerusalem: Ben-Arieh 2000: Fig. 16:6
2	2252-22559/1	Jar	
3	2253-22536	Jar	Tell el-Hesi: Bennett and Blakely 1989: Fig. 139:41
4	2243-22432/4	Jar	Holyland Hotel, Jerusalem: Ben-Arieh 2000: Fig. 16:2
5	2258-2255/1	Jar	Tell el-Hesi: Bennett and Blakely 1989: Fig. 150:9
6	2243-22432/2	Jar	
7	2253-22536/1	Jar/Jug	Tell el-Hesi: Bennett and Blakely 1989: Fig. 157:7
8	2232-22355/1	Basin	Armenian Garden, Jerusalem: Tushingham 1985: Fig. 14:3–4; Tell el-Hesi: Bennett and Blakely 1989: Fig. 155:17
9	2232-22399	Basin	Qadum: Stern and Magen 1984: Fig. 5:10
10	2245-22355/2	Bowl base	Gezer: Gitin 1990: Pl. 30:21
11	P4619-256	Bowl	Ramat Rachel: Aharoni 1962: Fig. 12:3
12	2249-22493/1	Bowl	
13	2232-223555/3	Bowl	Gezer: Gitin 1990: Pl. 24:4; Tell Mevorakh: Stern 1978: Fig. 4:9
14	2252-22559/2	Bowl	Holyland Hotel, Jerusalem: Ben-Arieh 2000: Fig. 6:15; Tell Mevorakh: Stern 1978: Fig. 5:2
15	2245-22451/3	Bowl	
16	2245-22494/1	Bowl	

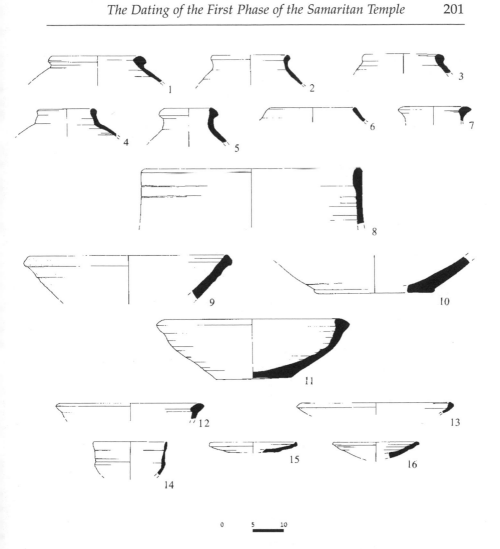

Fig. 24. Pottery from Area S (southern gate).

No.	Locus/Basket	Vessel Type	Parallels
1	442-4538C	Jar	
2	499-77/1	Jar	
3	499-60/2	Jar	Bethel: Sinclair 1968: Pl. 67:4
4	4999-40/2	Jar	
5	499-15/1	Jar	Tell Balâṭah (Shechem): Lapp 1985: Fig. 4:11
6	442-4538K/3	Jug	
7	497-2/1	Jug	
8	423-4198/2	Jug	
9	423-4198/3	Jug	Tell Balâṭah (Shechem): Lapp 1985: Fig. 5:10
10	499-75/5	Dipper / Juglet base	
11	442-4538K/1	Krater	Qadum: Stern and Magen 1984: Fig. 6:1–3; Tell Balâṭah (Shechem): Lapp 1985: Fig. 6:7-8
12	499-75/3	Krater	Tell Balâṭah (Shechem): Lapp 1985: Fig. 5:20
13	499-82/2	Krater	Qadum: Stern and Magen 1984: Fig. 5:2
14	499-40/1	Bowl	Armenian Garden, Jerusalem: Tushingham 1985: Fig. 14:11; Gezer: Gitin 1990: Pl. 27:24; Tell el-Fûl: Lapp 1981: Pl. 63:10
15	499-14/7	Bowl	Tell Balâṭah (Shechem): Lapp 1985: Fig. 5:16; Tell Mevorakh: Stern 1978: Fig. 4:12
16	498-65/1	Bowl	
17	498-57/1	Bowl	Holyland Hotel, Jerusalem: Ben-Arieh 2000: Fig. 6:5–6

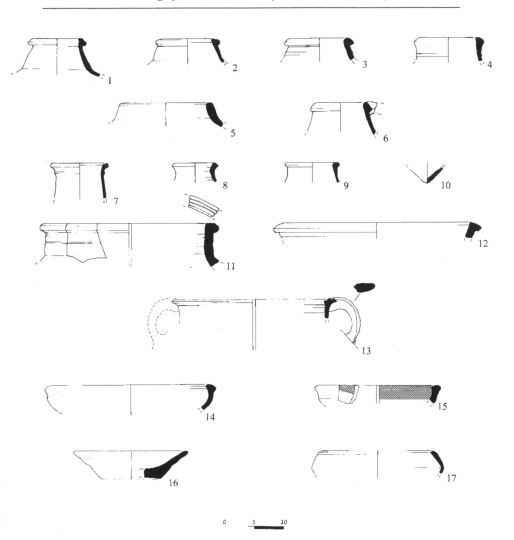

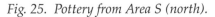

Fig. 25. Pottery from Area S (north).

No.	Locus/Basket	Vessel Type	Pottery Description
1	497-1	Krater	
2	770-8369	Lekythos rim and neck	Light·yellowish brown 10YR:6/4, black slip, glazed; very pale brown slip 10YR:7/4 on rim border
3	7006-9232	Lekythos, body	Light yellowish brown 10YR:6/4, concentric circles and net decoration: pale yellow 2.5YR:7/4 and black slip, glazed.
4	4186-41822	Lekythos, body	Light yellowish brown 10YR:6/4, pale yellow 2.5YR:7/4 and black slip, glazed. Traces of net decoration (?)
5	790-9068	Lekythos, base	Light reddish brown 5YR:6/4, white grits, black slip, glazed

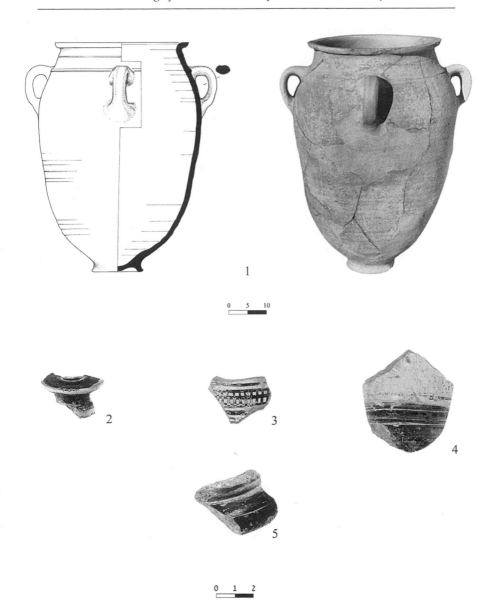

Fig. 26. Pottery from Area S (north) — no. 1; Attic pottery (Areas S and P)—nos. 2–5.

	K number	Coin type	Mint	Obverse	Reverse	Dating	Parallels
1	K-25277	Persian	Cyprus	Head of lion with jaws open	*Ankh* symbol in incuse square with spray of three leaves in each corner	ca. 480 B.C.E.	Hill 1904: 68, no. 2
2	K-19618	Persian standard	Tyre	Dolphin with murex shell below	Owl with crook and flail	ca. 450–400 B.C.E.	Hill 1910: 228, nos. 8-10
3	K-23305	Persian	Tyre	Winged hippocamp with dolphin below	Owl with crook and flail	ca. 400–332 B.C.E.	Hill 1910: 230, nos. 23-25
4	K-18615	Persian	Sidon	War-galley	King of Persia with bow and arrow	Late fifth century B.C.E.	Hill 1910: 140, no. 3

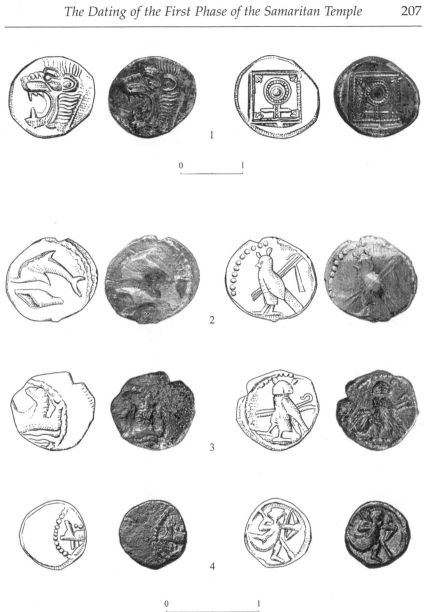

Fig. 27. Coins from Mt. Gerizim.

	K number	Coin type	Mint	Obverse	Reverse	Dating	Parallels
1	K-31423	Persian	Sidon	War-galley with zigzag line of waves below	King of Persia battling a lion	Euagoros II 354–342 B.C.E.	Hill 1910: 151, nos. 67-68
2	K-17007	Persian	Sidon	War-galley with two lines of waves below	King of Persia battling a lion, the letters מז in between	Mazdi 343–333 B.C.E.	Hill 1910: 154, no. 84
3	K-21110	Persian	Attic standard	Tyre	Melqarth riding on winged hippocamp, with dolphin and waves below	Owl with crook and flail	ca. 332-275 B.C.E.
4	K-27207	Persian imitation	Athens	Head of Athena	Owl, olive branches and crescent in upper left corner, the letters AOE on right	ca. 390-295 B.C.E.	Kroll 1993: 19, no. 16.

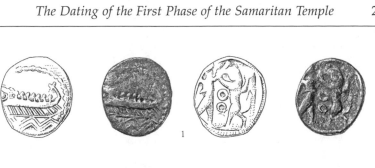

Fig. 28. Coins from Mt. Gerizim.

	K number	Coin type	Mint	Obverse	Reverse	Dating	Parallels
1	K-33355	Samarian	Samaria	Mask of a woman's face	Head of a lion	Fourth century until 332 B.C.E.	Meshorer and Qedar 1999: 113, no. 165
2	362000	Samarian	Samaria	Lion facing forward	Bearded man, Aramaic inscription reading (שמרי) נ	Fourth century until 332 B.C.E.	Meshorer 1999: 98, no. 83
3	32444	Samarian	Samaria	Man's head with helmet, Aramaic inscription reading (שמרי)נ	Winged horse	Fourth century until 332 B.C.E.	Meshorer and Qedar 1999: 83, nos. 1-2
4	21107	Samarian	Samaria	Head of a lion	Naked man battling a lion with dagger, Aramaic inscription reading (שמרי)נ	Fourth century until 332 B.C.E.	Meshorer and Qedar 1991: 53; Meshorer and Qedar 1999: 106, no. 127
5	185333	Samarian	Samaria	War-galley riding on waves	A king battling a lion	Fourth century until 332 B.C.E.	Meshorer and Qedar 1991: 47

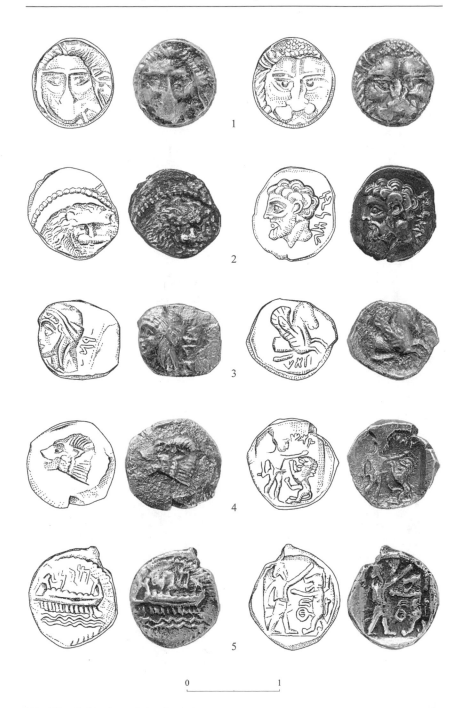

Fig. 29. Coins from Mt. Gerizim.

Do the Earliest Samaritan Inscriptions Already Indicate a Parting of the Ways?

BOB BECKING
Utrecht University

Introduction

The origins of Samaritanism are still hidden under the dust of the past. How, when, and where this religion (closely akin to Judaism and still alive in Israel and Palestine) emerged will remain a topic for scholarly debate for quite some time, I presume.[1] The well-known texts in the New Testament indicate that by the first century C.E. the parting of ways had taken place:[2] by the time of Jesus, Judaism and Samaritanism had developed into two separate religions. When this separation took place, however, is unclear. Earlier texts reflect antagonisms between North and South, between Samaria/Gerizim and Jerusalem. We should not, however, overinterpret the evidence. At best, some hints at proto-Samaritanism can be found (Bowman 1972; Zsengellér 1998).

The same methodological reserve holds for the problem of the origin of the Samaritan theology. The religious world view of the Samaritans is based on the Hebrew Bible or, to be more precise, on the Torah of Moses known to them in the form of the Samaritan Pentateuch.[3] The various differences between the Samaritan Pentateuch and the Masoretic traditions reveal glimpses of Samaritan concepts, such as the emphasis on Gerizim as the place that "YHWH your God has chosen."[4] The oldest-known manuscripts of the Samaritan Pentateuch are, however, to be dated to the ninth century C.E. Some scholars have drawn attention to the fact that a few of the so-called Samaritan readings in

---

1. Despite a flood of recent studies; for example: Mor 1989; Schur 1992; Albertz 1992: 576–89; Macchi 1994: 9–46; Nodet 1997: 122–201; Zsengellér 1998; Sacchi 2000: 152–59; Hjelm 2000; van der Horst 2004: 11–45; Anderson and Giles 2002: 1–50.

2. Luke 10:30–37; John 4; see, e.g., Bowman 1972: 57–90.

3. A modern critical edition of the Samaritan Pentateuch is still lacking.

4. See, e.g., SamP Exod 20:17, 21; Deut 12:5; 27:4.

the Pentateuch are also found in the Qumran scrolls.[5] Some of these readings have independently been transmitted in *Vetus Latina;* they also stand behind some statements in Josephus, *Antiquities* (e.g., *Ant.* 4.305). If it were true that these readings really reflected Samaritan ideas, then we would have traces of Samaritanism from the first century B.C.E. These ideas can also be found in the Samaritan Targum that probably emerged in the third century C.E.

Samaritan theology as a coherent system has never been fully developed (Macdonald 1964; Bowman 1972: 29–56; Macchi 1994: 15–18; Anderson and Giles 2002: 117–34; van der Horst 2004: 81–103). It is in the *Tibat Marqe* (formerly known as the *Memar Marqe*), which originated in the third–fourth centuries C.E., that we find the clearest clues about the Samaritan religion.[6] I will not delve into Samaritan theology here at length but only refer to some pivotal points. In the *Tibat Marqe,* various Samaritan creeds are transmitted. They vary among themselves, most likely due to different historical moments of emergence and to varying functions within the literary composition, but most of them share the following three tenets:

> We believe in you
> And in Moses your man
> And in your Scripture.[7]

Occasionally, a fourth element is added, as in the following example from the *Defter,*[8] the Samaritan liturgical prayer book stemming from the same period as the *Tibat Marqe:*

> We believe in you, O Lord,
> And in Moses the son of Amram your servant,
> And in your holy Law,
> And in Mount Gerizim, the chosen and sacred, the choicest
>   (mountain) in all earth.
> There is only one God.

In addition, the Samaritan "we-tradition" attests that the Samaritan high priest is a direct descendant of Moses. Samaritans believe in the *Šalšalet hak-kohanîm* 'Chain of Purity', which links the current high priest to Moses via Aaron, Eleazar, Ithamar, . . . Pinchas.[9] It is unclear

---

5. Especially in 4QpaleoExod[m]; see Tov 1989; Nodet 1997: 199–201; Zsengellér 1998: 35–42; Sacchi 2000: 155–57; Hjelm 2000: 87–94; Anderson and Giles 2002: 105–16.

6. See the edition by Ben-Hayyim 1988.

7. *Tibat Marqe* IV.9.

8. As edited by Cowley 1909.

9. The *Šalšelet;* see esp. Chronicle V; edited first by Gaster 1909, on the basis of two manuscripts.

how deeply these ideas are rooted in the Samaritan tradition (see Zsen-gellér 1998: 48–49; van der Horst 2004: 75, 97).

Inscriptions from Mount Gerizim

Archaeological excavations on Mount Gerizim have brought to light various structures that can only be interpreted as the remains of a Temple to YHWH. This temple apparently was built in the fifth century B.C.E. In the Hellenistic period, the temple was rebuilt after great damage had been done to the building. This damage was associated with the campaign of Alexander the Great. The complex was in use up to early medieval times. These archaeological data make clear that during the Second Temple period an alternative to the temple in Jerusalem was present and in use (Magen 2000; Hjelm 2005).[10]

In and around this temple, some 400 inscriptions were excavated. Due to the efforts of Yitzhak Magen, Haggai Misgav, and Levana Tsfa-nia (2004), they are now available for the scholarly world in a preliminary edition. It should be stressed that this is a preliminary edition. The edition suffers from the absence of a proper orthographic and paleographic discussion, which would have been helpful in dating the texts, albeit in the context of a relative chronology. The authors now differentiate between four kinds of scripts, the oldest of which, the "lapidary Aramaic script," is located quite broadly in the Persian and early Hellenistic eras. It should be observed that it is often unclear where the various inscriptions have been found. Their connection with the archaeological stratigraphy is more often vague than it is clear. What is more, the inscriptions are mainly written on stones that apparently were in use as building blocks. The editors do not inform their readers about the provenance of these building stones. Were the inscriptions made in situ or brought from home?

The Mount Gerizim inscriptions[11] cover the whole period in which the temple on Mount Gerizim was in use. The earliest inscriptions are written in a lapidary Aramaic script and stem from the fifth–fourth century B.C.E. At the other end of the temporal spectrum are inscriptions

---

10. The Gerizim temple is referred to in Josephus, *Ant.* 10.310–11. Its existence is implied in the Samaritan inscriptions from Delos dating to the third and second centuries B.C.E.; see Bruneau 1982; Pummer 1989; Anderson and Giles 2002: 29–30. Another counterpart to the Jerusalem temple in southern Maqqēdāh is known from an inscription edited by Lemaire 2002: 149–56 (text 283, pl. 48).

11. For convenience, I will use the acronym MGI to refer to the Mount Gerizim inscriptions.

written in medieval Samaritan script. The editors classify these inscriptions roughly in three categories:

1. dedicatory inscriptions containing the formula זי הקרב 'that which offered';
2. dedicatory inscriptions containing the formula לדכרן טב 'for good remembrance';
3. miscellaneous inscriptions.

The main body of the corpus consists of dedicatory inscriptions. They were written in Aramaic and Hebrew, using various scripts over the ages. The names of the dedicators are generally Israelite, with some Greek names appearing in the Hellenistic era (see also Hjelm 2005: 169–70). All of this indicates that the temple on Mount Gerizim was in use for worship of a Yahwistic character. I hesitate to be more precise at this point. The evidence available makes it impossible to decide among the three obvious options:

- continuation of Northern Israelite rituals (in line with the ideas of Zsengellér 1998);
- proto-Jewish rituals comparable to contemporary cults in Jerusalem or Elephantine;
- proto-Samaritan cult.

The fact that in later times the Samaritan script is dominant can be seen as an indication that, from a certain point on, the temple on Mount Gerizim was obviously used for Samaritan rituals.[12] Stating that from its earliest beginnings this temple was a Samaritan sanctuary (in the specifically religious connotation of the term *Samaritan*) would be premature, however.

Elements of Samaritanism?

That the inscriptions do not reveal a complete Samaritan theology is quite understandable in view of their *Gattung*. They nevertheless contain a few interesting clues that I would like to discuss. In what follows, I will concentrate on the earliest Samaritan inscriptions—that is, inscriptions that appear in lapidary Aramaic script.

1. The inscriptions contain various names that are known from the Chain of Purity, the succession of high priests to this day:

---

12. The absence of an orthographic discussion in MGI makes it impossible to establish a date for this transition.

- Eleazar is mentioned three times.[13]
- Pinchas is mentioned five times.[14]

I do not intend to imply that these names refer to priests from the pre-exilic period. The presence of these names only underscores their attractiveness. It is interesting to note that the names Moses and Joshua do not appear in these inscriptions.

2. As far as I can see, there is only one inscription that mentions the character of the offerings. MGI 199, a text written in lapidary Aramaic script, reads:

...] וֿפריׁן כל [...	...] and bulls in all [...
...] דב[ח בבית דבחא ...	... sacrific]ed in the "house of sacrifice" [...
...] אנה מהר דא [...	...] (incomprehensible)

The mention of the total number of bulls in combination with the expression "house of sacrifice" makes it clear that animals were offered at the sanctuary. The bringing of a פר 'young bull' as a sacrifice is quite common in the Hebrew Bible. In the cultic laws, the sacrifice of a פר 'young bull' is mentioned in a variety of cases.[15] The Aramaic expression בית דבחא 'house of sacrifice' is parallel to Hebrew בית זבח 'house of sacrifice', which occurs only once in the Hebrew Bible. In a theophany to Solomon (after the completion of the building of the temple), YHWH says to the king: "I have heard your prayer, and have chosen this place for myself as a house of sacrifice (בית זבח)" (2 Chr 7:12). In this text, the phrase בית זבח underscores the divine acceptance of the Jerusalem temple.[16] It should be noted that in the area of the Mount Gerizim temple, hundreds of thousands of animal bones—sheep, cattle, goats, pigeons—were found, the majority of which showed traces of burning (Naveh and Magen 1997; Magen, Misgav, and Tsfania 2004: 9). These remains of animal sacrifice concur with the stipulations in Leviticus 1–6. The findings are, however, not properly dated. This means that no conclusions can be drawn with respect to cult practice in the fifth–fourth century B.C.E.

3. The Aramaic expression בית דבחא 'house of sacrifice' is only one of a variety of expressions that indicate the sanctuary. Other synonyms are: אתרא 'the place'; מקדש 'the sanctuary'; אגר 'agorah'. As the editors

---

13. אלעזר: MGI 1, 32, 390.
14. פינחס: MGI 24, 25, 61, 384, 389.
15. So, for example, in a priestly cleansing sacrifice (Lev 4:3).
16. In 1 Kgs 9:3 the same idea is phrased in more Deuteronomistic language.

remark: "Such a proliferation of names teaches of the great importance ascribed to this temple by those who came to worship there" (Magen, Misgav, and Tsfania 2004: 181).

4. MGI 211 is a much later inscription, fairly damaged, that contains only two words in proto-Jewish script:

בית [. . .   . . .] house
ה]כלה . . .   . . . t]emple

Not much can be inferred from this inscription, although it seems to me that at some point in history the sanctuary on Mount Gerizim was construed to be a real temple, which implies that the precinct was considered as holy as the temple in Jerusalem.

5. Of great interest (albeit not for the fourth century B.C.E.) is a dedicatory inscription of the זי הקרב 'that-which-offered' type. MGI 11, an inscription in proto-Jewish script, reads in line 2: טורא ט[ב]א 'the good mountain'. Because the context is lost, it is unclear whether this morpheme is a place-name[17] or a reference to Mount Gerizim. It should be noted that Josephus mentions a Samaritan town by the name of Tura (or: Tira) Taba, where the Samaritans would gather before ascending Mount Gerizim in the time of Pontius Pilate (*Ant.* 18:86). In *Tibat Marqe* 94a, 224a, "the good mountain" is one of the 13 appellations for Mount Gerizim.[18] It is difficult to say whether the inscription under consideration is prior to Josephus or not.

6. Magen, Misgav, and Tsfania (2004: 70) propose an interesting reconstruction for a name in MGI 27, a document written in lapidary Aramaic. They propose reading והי[. . . in line 2 as the final three letters of the name Bagohi. A man named Bagohi is known as the Persian governor of Yehud to whom Yedoniah from Elephantine wrote a letter pleading for the rebuilding of the temple to Yahô in Elephantine after its destruction by the wicked Widranag.[19] Bagohi is the Aramaic form of the Persian name *Bagavahya* (Heb. בגוי, Ezra 2:2, 14; 8:14; Neh 7:7, 19; 10:16). The Greek form of the name, βαγωας, is well known because many eunuchs and other high officials bore this name.[20] It is obvious that והי[. . . could be the ending of a number of Hebrew and Aramaic

---

17. As suggested by Hjelm 2005: 169.
18. See also Magen, Misgav, and Tsfania 2004: 29, 57.
19. *TADAE* A.4.7; *TUAT* 1.254–58. The letter is also preserved in a second copy: *TADAE* A.4.8, next to a memorandum that summarizes the positive decision of Arshamesh (*TADAE* A.4.9). On this correspondence, see Kottsieper 2001.
20. Jdt 12:13, 13:1, 14:14; Diodorus Siculus, *Hist.* 31.19.2–3; 16.47.4 (an adviser to Artaxerxes III Ochus); Pliny, *Hist. Nat.* 13.41.

names. Bagohi is certainly not the only possible reconstruction here (Hjelm 2005: 170). Even if the reconstruction proposed is correct, it remains unproved that this Bagohi was the Persian governor of Yehud. Its reference only indicates that even persons with a Persian background could dedicate their offerings in the temple on Mount Gerizim. This feature distances the Gerizim sanctuary from the sanctuary in Jerusalem, which according to the traditions in Ezra and Nehemiah had a restrictive entrance policy; it was only open to Yehudites and certainly not to persons with connections to other nations.

7. In Samaritan theology, there is much attention given to the "Holy Law." In the dedicatory inscriptions from Mount Gerizim—of both types—no reference to the Law or its holiness can be found. It is only in a very late text that such a reference can be found. MGI 395 is a text that consists of verses from the book of Deuteronomy. In this text, the beginning of the Decalogue includes statements about the oneness of God. The stone probably was erected in the age of the Crusaders, when the Samaritan cult was renewed on Mount Gerizim. The inscription reads as follows:

1. I am the Lord your God.
2. You shall have no
3. other gods before me:
4. for the Lord is God;
5. besides Him there is no other.
6. For the Lord is God
7. in heaven above and on
8. the earth below; there is no other.
9. The Lord is our [G]od
10. the Lord [is one] for
11. the Lord [your God i]s
12. God of [God]s
13. and Lord of [Lord]s
14. and no fo[reign g]od is with him.

8. I would like to round off this section by referring to a medieval Samaritan *mezuzah* also found on Mount Gerizim, which contains this inscription (MGI 394):

The Lord is our G]od the Lo[rd is one . . .

These last two inscriptions, interesting as they may be, are by virtue of their late date no help in answering the question of the origin of the Samaritan religious world view.

Historical Conclusions

The archaeological excavations on Mount Gerizim and the written evidence unearthed there do not answer all questions about the origins of the Samaritans. A few conclusions can be drawn, nevertheless. The presence of a sanctuary on Mount Gerizim shows that from the Persian period onward an alternative temple to the Jerusalem temple was present within the boundaries of the land of Israel. Whether this temple was a continuation of a preexilic sanctuary cannot, or at least cannot yet be established. The existence of a great number of dedicatory inscriptions found in and around the temple area indicates that the sanctuary functioned as a holy spot, to which people journeyed in order to express their thanks to the Divine. The archaeological data, as published, give the impression that the temple on Mount Gerizim was a *Neuschöpfung*. Most likely the site was chosen, not because a sanctuary was on it, but because of the role that it had played in Northern Israelite traditions. Magen, Misgav, and Tsfania (2004: 10–12) even suggest that the building of the temple on Mount Gerizim was a deliberate political move taken by the governor Sanballat the Horonite. They infer that the temple on Mount Gerizim was constructed in an attempt to create a Samaritan corporate identity as early as the Persian period. In my opinion, this view is a nice example of interpreting a historical datum from its eventual outcome.

This implies that during the fifth and fourth centuries B.C.E., two competing Yahwistic identities arose: one in Yehud and one in the North. The written evidence excavated on Mount Gerizim does not allow the conclusion that, from its very beginning, the religion of the Samari(t)ans differed from the religion of the Yehudites. The only difference found is the probable acceptance of a foreigner as a dedicator on Mount Gerizim, in contrast to the concept of a restricted and circumscribed community, notions that we can infer from Ezra and Nehemiah (Becking 1999).

Until new evidence is found, we have to assume that the origins of Samaritanism as a specific religion are still buried under the dust of history and that the parting of the ways most likely was the result of a long process[21] of independent developments on both sides of the divide. The erection of an alternative temple on Mount Gerizim should, however, be seen as a first step in the process that eventually turned out to be decisive.

---

21. On the *longe durée*, see Braudel 1972.

Bibliography

Albertz, R.
1992   *Religionsgeschichte Israels in alttestamentlicher Zeit.* Grundrisse zum Alten Testament 8/1–2. Göttingen: Vandenhoeck & Ruprecht.

Anderson, R. T., and Giles, T.
2002   *The Keepers: An Introduction to the History and Culture of the Samaritans.* Peabody, MA: Hendrickson.

Becking, B.
1999   Continuity and Community: The Belief-System of the Book of Ezra. Pp. 256–75 in *The Crisis of Israelite Religion: Transformation of Religious Tradition in Exilic and Post-exilic Times,* ed. B. Becking and M. C. A. Korpel. OtSt 42. Leiden: Brill.

Ben-Hayyim, Z.
1988   *Tibat Marqe: A Collection of Samaritan Midrashim.* Jerusalem: Israel Academy of Science and Humanities.

Bowman, J.
1972   *The Samaritan Problem: Studies in the Relationship of Samaritanism, Judaism and Early Christianity.* PTMS 4. Pittsburgh: Pickwick.

Braudel, F.
1972   Geschichte und Sozialwissenschaften: La longe durée. Pp. 189–215 in *Geschichte und Soziologie,* ed. H.-U. Wehler. Neue wissenschaftliche Bibliothek 53. Cologne: Kiepenheuer und Witsch.

Bruneau, P.
1982   Les inscriptions de Délos et la juiverie délienne. *Bulletin de Correspondance Hellénique* 106: 465–504.

Cowley, A. E.
1909   *The Samaritan Liturgy.* 2 vols. Oxford: Oxford University Press.

Gaster, T.
1909   The Chain of Samaritan High Priests. *JRAS* 31: 393–420.

Hjelm, I.
2000   *The Samaritans and Early Judaism: A literary Analysis.* JSOTSup 303. Sheffield: Sheffield Academic Press.
2005   Changing Paradigms: Judaean and Samaritan Histories in Light of Recent Research. Pp. 161–79 in *Historie og Konstruktion: Festkrift til Niels Peter Lemche i anledning af 60 års fødselsdagen den 6. September 2005,* ed. M. Möller and T. L. Thompson. Forum for Bibelsk Eksegese 14. Copenhagen: Museum Tusculanums.

Horst, P. W. van der
2004   *De Samaritanen: Geschiedenis en godsdienst van een vergeten groepering.* Serie Wegwijs. Kampen: Kok.

Kottsieper, I.
2001   Die Religionspolitik der Achämeniden und die Juden von Elephantine. Pp. 150–78 in *Religion und Religionskontakte im Zeitalter der Achämeniden,* ed. R. G. Kratz. Veröffentlichungen der Wissenschaftlichen Gesellschaft für Theologie. Gütersloh: Mohn.

Lemaire, A.
2002   *Nouvelles Inscriptions araméennes d'Idumée Tome II.* Transeu Supplement 9. Paris: Gabalda.

Macchi, J.-D.
1994   *Les Samaritains: Histoire d'une légende.* Monde de la Bible 30. Geneva: Labor & Fides.

Macdonald, J.
1964   *The Theology of the Samaritans.* NTL. London: SCM.

Magen, Y.
2000   Mount Gerizim: A Temple City. *Qadmoniot* 33/2: 74–118.

Magen, Y.; Misgav, H.; and Tsfania, L.
2004   *Mount Gerizim Excavations, Volume 1: The Aramaic, Hebrew and Samaritan Inscriptions.* Judea and Samaria Publications 2. Jerusalem: Israel Exploration Society.

Mor, R.
1989   The Persian, Hellenistic, and Hasmonaean Period. Pp. 1–18 in *The Samaritans,* ed. A. D. Crown. Tübingen: Mohr Siebeck.

Naveh, J., and Magen, Y.
1997   Aramaic and Hebrew Inscriptions of the Second Century B.C.E. at Mount Gerizim. *'Atiqot* 32: 9–17.

Nodet, E.
1997   *A Search for the Origins of Judaism.* JSOTSup 248. Sheffield: Sheffield Academic Press.

Pummer, R.
1989   Samaritan Rituals and Customs. Pp. 650–90 in *The Samaritans,* ed. A. D. Crown. Tübingen: Mohr Siebeck.

Sacchi, P.
2000   *The History of the Second Temple Period.* JSOTSup 285. Sheffield: Sheffield Academic Press.

Schur, N.
1992   *History of the Samaritans.* 2nd ed. BEATAJ 18. Frankfurt: Peter Lang.

Tov, E.
1989   Proto-Samaritan Texts and the Samaritan Pentateuch. Pp. 397–407 in *The Samaritans,* ed. A. D. Crown. Tübingen: Mohr Siebeck.

Zsengellér, J.
1998   *Gerizim as Israel: Northern Tradition of the Old Testament and the Early History of the Samaritans.* Utrechtse Theologische Reeks 38. Utrecht: Faculteit der Godgeleerdheid.

The Governors of Samaria in the Fifth and Fourth Centuries B.C.E.

Hanan Eshel

Bar-Ilan University

Documents found in Wâdi ed-Dâliyeh and coins minted in the city of Samaria offer important evidence about the governors of Samaria who ruled during the fifth and fourth centuries B.C.E. In this essay, I would like to present all the data currently available in order to reconstruct the list of Samaria's governors during the Persian period.

In 1962, Beduoin of the Taʿâmireh tribe discovered a group of important finds in a cave in Wâdi ed-Dâliyeh, 14 km northwest of Jericho. The cave contained the skeletons of roughly 300 inhabitants of the city of Samaria who had taken flight to the desert upon the arrival of the armies of Alexander the Great and a group of finds and documents recording financial transactions that were brought to the cave by the refugees.[1] After most of the finds were purchased from the Bedouin, Paul Lapp of the American School of Oriental Research in Jerusalem conducted two seasons of excavations in the caves of Wâdi ed-Dâliyeh.[2] The documents purchased from the Bedouin and the papyri fragments unearthed in the two excavation seasons were handed over to Prof. Frank Cross for publication.[3] The cave yielded fragments of 18 legal documents, which were complete enough to be called papyri, and fragments of 20 other documents.[4] Also found in the cave were 128

---

1. F. M. Cross, "The Discovery of the Samaria Papyri," *BA* 26 (1963) 110–21.

2. P. W. Lapp and N. L. Lapp (eds.), *Discoveries in the Wadi ed-Daliyeh* (AASOR 41; Cambridge, MA: American School of Oriental Research, 1974).

3. F. M. Cross, "The Papyri and Their Historical Implications," in *Discoveries in the Wadi ed-Daliyeh* (ed. P. W. Lapp and N. L. Lapp; AASOR 41; Cambridge, MA: American School of Oriental Research, 1974) 17–29.

4. The photographs of all the documents revealed in Wâdi ed-Dâliyeh and the reading of the 11 more-complete documents are included in the official edition published by D. M. Gropp, "The Samaria Papyri from Wadi Daliyeh," in *Wadi Daliyeh II and Qumran Cave 4:XXVIII* (ed. D. M. Gropp et al.; DJD 28; Oxford: Clarendon, 2001) 3–116.

bullas that were used to seal the documents.[5] All of the Wâdi ed-Dâliyeh texts are legal documents written on papyri in Aramaic. Ten record the sale of slaves (Documents 1–9, 18),[6] and two record the use of a slave as a pledge for a loan (Documents 10, 12).[7] Another tells of a judicial decision related to a dispute on the question of the ownership of a certain slave (Document 11). One notes the release of a slave or the cessation of the slave's use as a pledge (Document 13). Three documents deal with the sale of real estate: Document 14 describes a transaction in which a *niskah* (a room in a sanctuary) was sold;[8] a second document is a deed from the sale of a house (Document 15);[9] a third records the sale of a vineyard or its use as a pledge for a loan (Document 16). Also found were a receipt for the return of money associated with a pledge (Document 17), a small fragment bearing a legal declaration taken under oath (Fragment 23), and a fragment of a deed of loan (Fragment 37).[10] Fragment 22, the earliest legal declaration from Wâdi ed-Dâliyeh, is dated to sometime between Year 30 and Year 39 of the reign of Artaxerxes II, that is, 375–365 B.C.E.[11] Document 1, which is probably the latest document of the cave, was written in 335 B.C.E., on the eve of the Macedonian invasion.[12]

Document 16 from Wâdi ed-Dâliyeh is the deed of sale of a vineyard or of its use as a pledge for a loan, the date of which is not preserved. This document was sealed with a bulla bearing the inscription:

---

5. The bullas from Wâdi ed-Dâliyeh were published by M. J. W. Leith, *Wadi Daliyeh I: The Wadi Daliyeh Seal Impressions* (DJD 24; Oxford: Clarendon, 1997).

6. The sale deeds for slaves were fully published by Gropp, "Samaria Papyri," 33–96, 113–16.

7. Only Document 10 has been fully published: ibid., 97–101.

8. A reading of the remains of this document was not included in Gropp's edition. For the photograph of this document, see ibid., pl. 16; on the importance of this document, see my "Wadi ed-Daliyeh Papyrus 14 and the Samaritan Temple," *Zion* 61 (1996) 359–65 [Hebrew].

9. Document 15 was published by Gropp, "Samaria Papyri," 103–12.

10. This fragment was unearthed in the excavations of P. Lapp in the Wâdi ed-Dâliyeh cave and read by Cross, "Papyri and Their Historical Implications," 25.

11. Idem, "Discovery," 115 n. 6.

12. Document 1 from Wâdi ed-Dâliyeh was first published by F. M. Cross, "Samaria Papyrus 1: An Aramaic Slave Conveyance of 335 B.C.E. Found in the Wâdi ed-Dâliyeh," *ErIsr* 18 (Avigad Volume; 1985) 7*–17*. Later Cross corrected a number of details in the reconstruction that he had suggested for this document, in an article in which he also published Document 2, "A Report on the Samaria Papyri," in *Congress Volume: Jerusalem, 1986* (ed. J. A. Emerton; VTSup 40; Leiden: Brill, 1988) 17–26. Document 1 is included in Gropp's edition, "Samaria Papyri," 33–34. Gropp mentions on p. 34 that he was not able to locate the document at the Rockefeller Museum in Jerusalem and that its location is unknown to him. Document 1 is exhibited at the Israel Museum.

"]YHW BN [SNʾ]BLṬ, governor of Samaria," in Hebrew script.[13] When Cross first examined the Wâdi ed-Dâliyeh documents during the negotiations with the Bedouin over the finds, the documents were rolled up, and this bulla provided the first hint at the date of the Wâdi ed-Dâliyeh finds. When Cross read the inscription on the bulla, he estimated that the Sanballat mentioned on the bulla should be identified with the Sanballat, governor of Samaria, who is mentioned in the book of Nehemiah.[14] This governor is also mentioned in an Aramaic document discovered in Elephantine in Upper Egypt (Cowley 30), published in 1905, which names "Delaiah and Shelemaih, sons of Sanballat, governor of Samaria" (line 29). The Sanballat mentioned in the Elephantine letter is the Sanballat of Nehemiah. The document on which he and his sons are mentioned was written in 407 B.C.E.[15]

After the Wâdi ed-Dâliyeh documents were bought and dispersed, it became clear that they should be dated to the fourth century B.C.E. and that more than one man by the name of Sanballat had ruled in the city of Samaria. The rulers of Samaria in the fourth century B.C.E. are mentioned in the Wâdi ed-Dâliyeh documents, because it was customary to sign deeds of slave sales in the presence of the Samarian governor and an official bearing the title *sgnʾ* ('prefect').[16] Unfortunately, many of the names of the governors and officials mentioned in the slave documents from Wâdi ed-Dâliyeh are not preserved.[17] Document 7, written on 5 Adar, Year 4 of the reign of Artaxerxes III (i.e., March of 354 B.C.E.), states (line 17): "before [Ha]naniah, governor of

---

13. A photograph of Document 16, still rolled up and sealed by the bulla, appears in Gropp's "Samaria Papyri," pl. 17; for an enlarged photograph of the bulla, see Cross, "Papyri and Their Historical Implications," 18 and pl. 61.

14. Idem, "Discovery," 111.

15. A. E. Cowley, *Aramaic Papyri of the Fifth Century* B.C. (Oxford: Clarendon, 1923) 108–19.

16. The title *sgnʾ* (prefect) originates from Assyrian *saknu*. On this title, see R. A. Henshaw, "The Office of *Saknu* in Neo-Assyrian Times, I," *JAOS* 87 (1967) 517–25; idem, "The Office of *Saknu* in Neo-Assyrian Times, II," *JAOS* 88 (1968) 461–83. It seems that there is no relation between the terms *sgnʾ* and *sgnym*, which originated in Akkadian, and the title *skn*, documented in Ugaritic and Phoenician (as in Ahiram's coffin; cf. Isa 22:15). The title *sgn* is mentioned in the Hebrew Bible, beginning with the Babylonian period (see Jer 51:23 and Ezek 23:6) and continuing in use in the Persian period (Isa 41:25). In Jerusalem, *sgnym* served in the Persian period (Neh 2:16, Ezra 9:2). From the usual phrase "governors and prefects (*sgnym*)" in the biblical sources, one can learn that *sgnym* were lower-ranking officials than governors; H. G. M. Williamson, *Ezra, Nehemiah* (WBC 16; Waco, TX: Word, 1985) 132.

17. All the formulas attesting that the slave sale documents were signed in the presence of the governor and the prefect (*sgnʾ*) have been gathered by Gropp, "Samaria Papyri," 18.

Samaria, Siyat[on, the prefect]."[18] Document 8 mentions (line 12):
"ʾIsiyaton, the prefect"; this is apparently the same official who was active during the reign of Hananiah and is mentioned in Document 7.[19]
Document 9 (line 14) notes that the papyrus was sealed "before Han
[. . .]"; Gropp proposed the reconstruction 'Han[aniah, governor of Sa-
maria]'. The date of this document did not survive.[20] On Document 5,
line 14, the name ʿAqabiah is mentioned, and Gropp reconstructs:
'ʿAqabiah[the prefect'.[21] Document 11 mentions "[Yesh]ua, son of Sanballat, (and) Hanan, the prefect."[22]

At first Cross suggested that the bulla that sealed Document 16
should read: "[Hanan]iah, son of Sanballat, governor of Samaria,"[23]
but later he noted that, because the bottoms of the letter *nun* are not
preserved on the bulla, the reconstruction '[Yesha]iah, son of Sanballat,
governor of Samaria' is preferable.[24] Cross founded this revision on
Document 11: "[Yesh]ua, son of Sanballat, (and) Hanan, the prefect."
He reasoned that the prefect mentioned in Document 11 is Hananiah,
the governor, mentioned in Documents 7 and 9. Therefore, claimed
Cross, Yeshaiah governed Samaria before 354 B.C.E. He assumed that
Hanan/Hananiah was the younger brother of Yeshua/Yeshaiah and
that both of them were the sons of Sanballat II. Cross suggested that
Yeshaiah was initially the governor, with Hananiah as his prefect, and
that later Hananiah became the governor in place of his brother.[25]
Cross assumed that at the end of Persian rule, after the governorship of
the sons of Sanballat II, Yeshaiah and Hananiah, an additional governor, Sanballat III, came to power in Samaria; this is the governor mentioned by Josephus in *Ant.* 11.302–45. In light of these data, Cross
proposed the reconstruction of the succession of Samarian governors
in the Persian period shown on p. 227.[26]

---

18. Ibid., 80–83.

19. Ibid., 88–89. The name Isiyaton is Phoenician. Cowley 30–31 mentions a man with
a similar name, Ostanes, who was one of Jerusalem's leaders in the fifth century B.C.E. On
this name, see my "Israelite Names from Samaria in the Persian Period," in *These Are the
Names* (ed. A. Demsky, J. A. Reif, and J. Tabory; Ramat-Gan: Bar-Ilan University, 1992) 21
n. 14 [Hebrew].

20. Gropp, "Samaria Papyri," 94–95.

21. Ibid., 70–71.

22. On this reading, see Cross, "Discovery," 111 n. 2.

23. Ibid., 111.

24. See idem, "Aspects of Samaritan and Jewish History in Late Persian and Hellenistic Times," *HTR* 59 (1966) 204 n. 12.

25. Ibid., 204.

26. In 1963, Cross proposed a slightly different list: Sanballat I, Delaiah son of
Sanballat I, Sanballat II, Hananiah son of Sanballat II, Sanballat III, in "Discovery," 120. In

Governor	Date	Source
Sanballat I	mid-5th c. B.C.E.	Nehemiah, Cowley 30
Delaiah	end of 5th c., beg. of 4th c. B.C.E.	Cowley 30–32
Shelemiah	beg. of 4th c. B.C.E.	Cowley 30
Sanballat II	first half of 4th c. B.C.E.	Wâdi ed-Dâliyeh bulla, Documents 5 (?), 11
Yeshua/Yeshaiah	first half of 4th c. B.C.E.	Wâdi ed-Dâliyeh bulla, Documents 1, 11
Hananiah	mid-4th c. B.C.E.	Wâdi ed-Dâliyeh Document 7
Sanballat III	second half of 4th c. B.C.E.	Josephus, *Ant.* 302–45

When Cross reconstructed the list of Samarian governors from the fifth–fourth century B.C.E., the coins minted in Samaria in the Persian period had not yet been published.[27] Two volumes on these coins have since been released.[28] The discussion below is based on the second volume, in which 224 types of coins minted in Samaria are discussed. A large portion of the Samarian coins were included in two hoards. One was purchased in Nablus in 1968 and has been referred to as the "Nablus hoard" by scholars, even though some note that this hoard was discovered by Bedouin in the Wâdi ed-Dâliyeh cave.[29] It includes 965 silver coins found together with jewelry. Among the coins of the Nablus

---

1966, after Cross reconstructed the bulla [YŠ']YHW BN [SN']BLT in place of [HNN]YHW BN [SN']BLṬ, he changed his theory.

27. Cross himself noted this and wrote that once the coins are published the list of Samarian governors will need to be updated ("Report," 20).

28. Y. Meshorer and S. Qedar, *The Coinage of Samaria in the Fourth Century* BCE (Jerusalem: Numismatic Fine Arts International, 1991); idem, *Samarian Coinage* (Jerusalem: Israel Numismatic Society, 1999).

29. Cross, "Report," 20 n. 4; Leith, *Wadi Daliyeh Seal Impressions*, 4–5 n. 12. One must reject Cross's claim, quoted by Leith, that the "Samaria hoard" was discovered in Wâdi ed-Dâliyeh, because this hoard was buried in 354 B.C.E. There is a rumor among antiquities dealers in Nablus that the Nablus hoard was not found in Wâdi ed-Dâliyeh but near the village of Jinsafut, located along the Qalqilyah-Nablus road. I am grateful to Dan Barag for informing me of this. If this rumor is indeed true, it is possible that the Nablus hoard was discovered at the fourth-century B.C.E. fortress excavated by Arie Bornstein on the southern summit of the saddle west of Jinsafut. According to A. Spear (personal communication), the Nablus hoard was found at Kutsra, a village north of Shiloh at the Toparchie of Akrabeh.

hoard are: 131 Tyrian coins, 206 imitations of Athenian coins, 625 coins minted in Samaria, and 3 coins from northern Anatolia—2 from Sinope and 1 from Amisus on the Black Sea coast.[30] Based on the Tyrian coins, not one of which dates later than 338/7 B.C.E., and on the appearance of the letters MZ on some of the Tyrian coins and some of the Samarian coins included in this hoard, it has been established that the coins of the Nablus hoard were buried in 338/7 B.C.E., before the time of the Macedonian invasion.[31] The letters MZ refer to coins issued by Mazday, who ruled the satrapy of Transeuphratesia from 345 B.C.E. to the defeat of Babylon by the Macedonians in 334 B.C.E.[32]

The second hoard is claimed by antiquities dealers to have been uncovered in the city of Samaria, and accordingly has been labeled the "Samaria hoard." Purchased together with the hoard was the pyxis (a ceramic juglet) in which the jewelry and the 334 coins of this hoard were found. The "Samaria hoard" includes: 32 coins from the Tyre mint, 43 from Sidon, 11 from Aradus, 66 imitations of Athenian prototypes, and 182 coins from the Samaria mint.[33] Based on the absence of coins bearing the letters MZ and on the fact that all of the Phoenician coins of the Samaria hoard date to between Year 1 and Year 14 of Artaxerxes III (who assumed the throne in 358 B.C.E., so that the latest coins of this hoard are from 345 B.C.E.), it was established that the Samaria hoard was buried in 345 B.C.E. In this year, the Persians returned to rule in Palestine after they defeated Tennes, king of Sidon, and conquered his city. Following these events, Mazday was appointed satrap of Transeuphratia.[34]

On one of the coins struck in Samaria there is a galley of a battleship sailing on waves (a motif taken from the coins of Sidon) with the letters DL (Samaria Coin 22).[35] Meshorer and Qedar propose reconstructing

---

30. A. Spaer and S. Hurter, "Nablus (anc. Neopolis)," in *An Inventory of Greek Coin Hoards* (ed. M. Thompson, O. Mørkholm and C. M. Kraay; New York: American Numismatic Society, 1973) 205–6.

31. Meshorer and Qedar, *Coinage of Samaria,* 66–67. I would like to thank A. Spear for discussing with me details concerning the date and findspot of the Nablus hoard.

32. L. Mildenberg, "Notes on the Coin Issues of Mazday," *Israel Numismatic Journal* 11 (1990–1) 9–23. Of the Samaria coins, three issues bear the name MZ[DY] (Samaria Coins 74, 84, and 100); Meshorer and Qedar, *Samarian Coinage,* 97, 99, 102.

33. The Samaria hoard was fully published in the first volume by Meshorer and Qedar, *Coinage of Samaria,* 65–80.

34. On these events, see D. Barag, "The Effects of the Tennes Rebellion on Palestine," *BASOR* 183 (1966) 6–12; I. Eph'al, "Syria–Palestine under Achaemenid Rule," in *The Cambridge Ancient History, IV: Persia, Greece and the Western Mediterranean c. 525 to 479 B.C.* (Cambridge: Cambridge University Press, 1988) 145–46.

35. Meshorer and Qedar, *Samarian Coinage,* 87, no. 22.

the name on the coin as DL[YH] and identifying the governor who struck the coin with Delaiah, son of Sanballat I, who is mentioned in the petition of the Jews of Elephantine to Bigvai, the governor of Judea, and in the reply to this petition (Cowley 30–32).[36] If we accept this suggestion, then it appears that this coin was minted at the end of the fifth or the beginning of the fourth century B.C.E.[37] Likewise, ten types of coins from the Samaria hoard bear the name ŠL[MYH] (Samaria Coins 61–70).[38] This ruler can be identified with Sanballat I's second son, Shelemiah, also mentioned in the petition of the Elephantine Jews.[39] The coins of Delaiah and Shelemiah are not included in the Samaria hoard or in the Nablus hoard; they were found in the area of Samaria but not as part of the two hoards.

One of the coins of the Samarian mint bears the inscription SN'BL (Samarian Coin 55), and others bear the letters SN (Samaria Coins 49–54 and 56), which Meshorer and Qedar have reconstructed as SN['BLT].[40] Meshorer and Qedar identified the SN'BL[Ṭ] who struck these Samarian coins as Sanballat II, for they reason that there is no doubt that these coins were issued in the fourth century B.C.E.[41] Not a single coin with SN'BL[Ṭ] is included either in the Samaria hoard or in the Nablus hoard.

A comparison between the Samaria hoard and the Nablus hoard is enlightening. The Samaria hoard, buried in 345 B.C.E., appears to include only one coin on which the name BOD appears. Meshorer and Qedar suggested that it is an abbreviation of the name BDYḤBL (Samaria Coin 21).[42] Nevertheless, in the Nablus hoard, left in 338/7 B.C.E., coins bearing the following names appear: B[GB]T (Coins 4–6), BDYH (Coin 11), BDYḤBL (Coins 13–17), and YHW'NH (Coin 40).[43]

The name-bearing coins of the Samarian mint are undated, except for the coins of BGBT, which include the date Year 14—apparently of Artaxerxes III (Samaria Coins 4–5).[44] This king assumed the throne in

---

36. Cowley, *Aramaic Papyri*, 108–24.

37. Meshorer and Qedar, *Samarian Coinage*, 22; Meshorer and Qedar reason that minting began in the city of Samaria in 372 B.C.E. (see p. 71 there). If we accept this, as well as the identification of the DL[YH] appearing on the coins with the governor Delaiah mentioned in the Elephantine letters, it follows that Delaiah ruled in Samaria from 407 to at least 372 B.C.E.

38. Meshorer and Qedar, ibid., 94–96, nos. 61–70.

39. Ibid., 28.

40. Ibid., 92–93, nos. 49–56.

41. Ibid., 26–27.

42. Ibid., 87.

43. Ibid., 83–86, 90.

44. Ibid., 83–84, nos. 4–5.

358 B.C.E., so Year 14 refers to 346/5 B.C.E.[45] Yet it appears that, even though BGBT struck coins dated to one year prior to when the Samaria hoard was buried, not one coin bearing his name was included in that hoard.

Ya'akov Meshorer and Shraga Qedar reasoned that the 2 individuals (BDYH and YHW'NH) whose names appear on the coins of the Nablus hoard but not on the coins of the Samaria hoard issued coins between 346 and 333/2 B.C.E., which is to say, in the last 13 years of Persian rule in Samaria.[46]

A common name on Samarian coinage that does not appear in the two hoards is YRB'M ('Jeroboam'; Coins 41–46).[47] No one can know whether the name Jeroboam was given to this resident of Samaria at birth or whether he adopted it once he gained prominence. Hayim Tadmor established, without resolving this question, that the use of the archaic name Jeroboam is instructive with regard to "the expression of autonomy of the Samaritans, who in this way sought to mark the beginning of a new era, similar to the one commenced when Jeroboam son of Nebat left Jerusalem and the House of David."[48] It seems that Samaria Coin 45, on which the name Jeroboam appears together with the depiction of a shrine, strengthens the supposition that this Jeroboam saw himself as the successor of Jeroboam, son of Nebat, and Jeroboam, son of Jehoash, the great kings of Israel.[49] The Jeroboam coins are evidence that the Samaritans of the fourth century B.C.E. considered themselves to be perpetuators of a tradition crystallized in the city of Samaria in the Iron Age.

When coins with the name YDW' (Jaddua) were published, Arnold Spaer claimed that these coins were from Jerusalem and that Jaddua is the high priest mentioned in Neh 12:22.[50] However, it has since become clear that these coins were issued in Samaria (Samaria Coin 39) and that Jaddua should not be identified with the high priest cited in the book of Nehemiah.[51]

45. Ibid., 71.

46. Ibid. Meshorer and Qedar reason there that all of the coins included in the Nablus hoard were minted in the last 13 years of Persian rule in Palestine—that is, between 346 and 333/2 B.C.E.

47. A. Spaer, "A Coin of Jeroboam?" *IEJ* 29 (1979) 218; idem, "More about Jeroboam," *Israel Numismatic Journal* 4 (1980) 2–3; Meshorer and Qedar, *Samarian Coinage*, 24–25, 91–92, nos. 41–46.

48. H. Tadmor, "The Restoration Period," in *The History of Eretz Israel, II: Israel and Judah in the Biblical Period* (ed. I. Eph'al; Jerusalem: Keter, 1984) 283 [Hebrew].

49. Meshorer and Qedar, *Samarian Coinage*, 47–48.

50. A. Spaer, "Jaddua the High Priest?" *Israel Numismatic Journal* 9 (1987) 1–3.

51. Meshorer and Qedar, *Samarian Coinage*, 23–24.

Of the Samarian coins not appearing in the two hoards, there are 2 that bear the name ḤNNYH (Coins 37–38).[52] We can assume that these coins were minted by Hananiah, the governor of Samaria mentioned in Wâdi ed-Dâliyeh Documents 7 and 9, who governed Samaria in 345 B.C.E.[53] Also absent from the two hoards are 5 additional names of individuals who were apparently active in the city of Samaria in the fourth century B.C.E.: WNY (Samaria Coin 71), ḤYM (Coin 36), MNPT (Coin 48), ʿBDYʾL (Coins 57–59), and ŠHRW (Coin 60).[54]

In summary, the Samarian coins of the Persian period bear 4 names of individuals who governed Samaria: Del[aliah], Shel[emiah], Sanball[at], and Hananiah. Likewise, appearing on the coins of the Samaria mint are 11 names of other officials not known from historical sources. We suppose that these individuals were active in the city in the fourth century B.C.E.[55] Given Meshorer and Qedar's supposition that all of the Samaria issues were struck within a period of 40 years, between 372 and 333/2 B.C.E., one might assume that these individuals served contemporaneously in various positions.[56] In order to establish who BGBT, BDYḤBL, BDYH, WNY, ḤYM, YDWʿ, YHWʿNH, YRBʿM, MNPT, ʿBDYʾL, and ŠRW were, we should turn to the Yehud coins, struck contemporaneously in a province adjacent to Samaria. The Yehud coins include private names appearing together with titles. Some bear the title "Yehizqiyah, the governor," and one coin has "Yohanan, the priest."[57] Because the Yehud coins mention the name of a governor and a high priest, we may assume that the same was true on the coins of Samaria. Thus it seems that some of the 11 individuals listed above served as governors, while others were high priests.[58] Some scholars

---

52. Ibid., 90, nos. 37–38.

53. Ibid., 23.

54. Ibid., 90, 92, 94, 96. For previously unrecorded issues of Samaria coins bearing the name SHRW, see H. Gitler and O. Tal, "Coins with the Aramaic Legend *ŠHRW* and other Unrecorded Samarian Issues," *Swiss Numismatic Review* 85 (2006) 47–60.

55. Aside from these names, the Samaria coins (nos. 1 and 2) also display the Greek name Pharnabazos, the satrap of Cilicia (413–373 B.C.E.), who lived in Dascylium, located to the east of the Dardanelles. On the basis of these 2 coins, Meshorer and Qedar established that the Samaria coins began being struck before 372 B.C.E. (*Samarian Coinage*, 28–29, 83).

56. Ibid., 71.

57. Y. Meshorer, *A Treasury of Jewish Coins* (Jerusalem: Yad Ben-Zvi, 2001) 199, pl. 3, nos. 20, 22–26; D. Barag, "A Silver Coin of Yohanan the High Priest and the Coinage of Judea in the Fourth Century B.C.," *Israel Numismatic Journal* 9 (1987) 4–21; L. S. Fried, "A Silver Coin of Yohanan Hakkohen," *Transeu* 24 (2003) 47–67.

58. On the assumption that there was an important sanctuary in Samaria in the fourth century B.C.E., see my "Prayer of Joseph from Qumran, a Papyrus from Masada and the Samaritan Temple on *APAPIZIN*," *Zion* 56 (1991) 125–36 [Hebrew]; idem, "The

have suggested that some functioned as officials in charge of the treasury or the mint of Samaria.[59]

In light of the evidence from the Wâdi ed-Dâliyeh documents and the coins of Samaria, there is no proof that the Hananiah who ruled Samaria in 354 B.C.E. was the son of Sanballat II.[60] Similarly, we cannot assume that ḤNN, the official during the reign of Yeshua, son of Sanballat II, is Hananiah, the governor, because it is clear that no other prefect (*sgnʾ*) was later appointed to be governor (as holds true for Isiyaton and ʿAqabiah).[61] Furthermore, the Wâdi ed-Dâliyeh documents offer no evidence of a Sanballat III in the city of Samaria on the eve of Alexander the Great's conquest.[62] The absence of evidence of a third governor by the name of Sanballat accords well with the difficulties in Josephus's description in *Ant.* 11.306–25. The description is full of contradictions and raises many difficulties. Several scholars have discussed the problems in this description, and today most agree that it should not be taken as a historical description.[63] It appears as though Josephus

---

Samaritan Temple on Mt. Gerizim and the Historical Research," *Beit Mikra* 39 (1994) 141–55 [Hebrew]; idem, "Wadi ed-Daliyeh 14."

59. The suggestion that some of the individuals whose names are documented on the Samaria coins were officials over the Samaria mint was first made by E. Stern, "A Hoard of Persian Period Bullae from the Vicinity of Samaria," *Michmanim* 6 (1992) 30 [Hebrew]; idem, "A Hoard of Persian Period Bullae from the Vicinity of Samaria," in *The Samaritans* (ed. E. Stern and H. Eshel; Jerusalem: Yad Ben-Zvi, 2002) 103 [Hebrew]. This suggestion was accepted by Cross, "Report," 20. A. Lemaire sees Samaria Coin 25, on which the name MBGY appears, as offering support of this. This name also appears on coins minted in other cities in the Transeuphratesia satrapy, and Lemaire reasons that MBGY was in charge of minting coins throughout the province. I would like to thank A. Lemaire for this suggestion (private communication).

60. The only evidence for this was the first reading of the bullas as: "[HNN]YHW BN [SNʾ]BLṬ, governor of Samaria." However, this reading was later changed to [YŠʿ]YHW BN [SNʾ]BLṬ, governor of Samaria."

61. These names do not appear on the Samaria coins. If coins are found bearing these names, then there will be reason to discuss whether names of prefects appear on the Samaria coins or whether these officials were indeed appointed to be governors.

62. Cross was of the opinion that, in the Persian period, noble families in Jerusalem and Samaria practiced papponymy, that is, the naming of a grandson after his grandfather. In accord with this view, he reconstructed the list of high priests in Jerusalem and the governors of Samaria. Regarding the list of high priests, his claim is no longer accepted; see J. C. VanderKam, "Jewish High Priests of the Persian Period: Is the List Complete?" in *Priesthood and Cult in Ancient Israel* (ed. G. A. Anderson and S. M. Olyan; JSOTSup 125; Sheffield: JSOT Press, 1991) 67–91. In my opinion, the list of the Samaria governors should also be revised.

63. See, for example, A. Momigliano, "Flavius Josephus and Alexander's Visit to Jerusalem," *Athenaeum* 57 (1979) 442–48; S. J. D. Cohen, "Alexander the Great and Jaddus the High Priest according to Josephus," *AJSR* 7–8 (1983) 41–68; B. Bar-Kochva, *Judas*

did not know that more than one leader by the name of Sanballat had been in power in Samaria, and thus he did not mention Sanballat at all in his portrayal of the period of Nehemiah (*Ant.* 11.159–83). This fact, compounded with the evidence from the Wâdi ed-Dâliyeh documents, in which there is no evidence for the existence of a Sanballat III, indicates that we cannot assume that a Sanballat III was appointed to be governor of Samaria on the eve of the Macedonian invasion.[64]

Given the present numismatic evidence, I suggest an alternative reconstruction of the list of governors of Samaria from the mid-fifth century B.C.E. to the Macedonian invasion. Because the positions of BDYH, BDYḤBL, WNY, ḤYM, YDWʿ, YHWʿNH, YRBʿM, MNPT, ʿBDYʾL, and ŠHRW cannot be established and neither can their exact dates of service, they are not mentioned on the table. BGBT struck coins in 346/5 B.C.E., but we do not know whether he was a governor, a high priest, or an official. Because there is evidence that Hananiah ruled in Samaria in 354 B.C.E., it seems that BGBT was a high priest or an official 9 years later (in 346 B.C.E.), but we also know that the governors of Samaria in the fourth century replaced one another frequently. We may suppose that some of the individuals mentioned on the Samarian coins but not known from historical sources—BGBT, BDYḤBL, BDYH, WNY, ḤYM, YDWʿ, YHWʿNH, YRBʿM, MNPT, ʿBDYʾL, and ŠHRW—served as governors in Samaria, some certainly were high priests, while others were important officials in the city of Samaria in the fourth century. We may hope that in the future more details will come to light on these figures so that we can establish their titles and years of service.[65] For now, until

---

Maccabaeus (Cambridge: Cambridge University Press, 1989) 131 n. 3; D. R. Schwartz, "On Some Papyri and Josephus' Sources and Chronology for the Persian Period," *JSJ* 21 (1990) 175–99; J. C. VanderKam, *From Joshua to Caiaphas: High Priests after the Exile* (Minneapolis: Fortress, 2004) 64–85.

64. D. Gropp was of the opinion that in all likelihood there was not a third governor by the name of Sanballat. Accordingly, in his doctoral dissertation, Gropp reconstructed line 11 of Wâdi ed-Dâliyeh Document 1, dated to 335 B.C.E.: 'be[fore Yeshua son of Sanballat, governor of Samaria, Hanan the prefect]', in *The Samaria Papyri from Wadi ed-Daliyeh: The Slave Sales* (Ph.D. Diss., Harvard University, 1986) 1–3. This indicates that Gropp reasoned that Yeshua governed over Samaria on the eve of the Macedonian invasion. However, he did not include this reconstruction in the official published volume; see his "Samaria Papyri," 34. Meshorer and Qedar were also of the opinion that there was no governor by the name of Sanballat III, *Samarian Coinage*, 26–27.

65. My hope is that in the future Samaria coins will be discovered with private names appearing alongside titles, as we have on the Yehud coins, so that we may know the positions of some of the individuals whose names appear on the coins struck in the city of Samaria. Likewise, I hope that additional hoards (similar to the Samaria hoard) will be found, dated to 345 B.C.E., when the Persians returned to rule Palestine after crushing the

the positions of these 11 individuals mentioned on the Samarian coins are illuminated, the following list of governors for Samaria can be reconstructed:[66]

Governor	Officials	Date	Source
Sanballat I	Rehum and Shimshai	mid-5th c. B.C.E.	Nehemiah, Ezra 4, Cowley 30
Delaiah	?	end of 5th c., beg. of 4th c. B.C.E.	Cowley 30–32, Samaria Coin 22
Shelemiah	?	beg. of 4th c. B.C.E.	Cowley 30, Samaria Coins 61–70
Hananiah	Isiyaton/Siyaton, Bagabatas	mid-4th c. B.C.E.	Wâdī ed-Dâliyeh Documents 7, 9; Samaria Coins 37–38
Sanballat II	Aqavia (?)	second half of 4th c. B.C.E.	Wâdī ed-Dâliyeh bulla and Document 14, Samaria Coins 49–56
Yeshua/ Yeshaiah	Hanan	second half of 4th c. B.C.E.	Wâdi ed-Dâliyeh bulla, Documents 1, 14

Tennes revolt. If these hoards are sufficiently large and include Samaria coins bearing the names of Delaiah, Shelemiah, and Hananiah, without coins of Sanballat, we will have proof that the new reconstruction is correct.

66. In 2005, M. Mor published an essay that defends Cross's reconstruction: "The Samaritan Shrine: A Solvable Enigma!" in *Samaritan, Hebrew and Aramaic Studies* (ed. M. Bar-Asher and M. Florentin; Jerusalem: Bialik Institute, 2005) 41–58 [Hebrew]. This essay was written before the official publication of the Wâdi ed-Dâliyeh documents (Gropp, "Samaria Papyri") and before the second volume of Meshorer and Qedar (*Samarian Coinage*) was released. Thus a retort here to Mor's claims seems unnecessary.

PART 4

Biblical Literature in the Late Persian and Hellenistic Periods

The Late Persian Formation of the Torah: Observations on Deuteronomy 34

KONRAD SCHMID
University of Zurich

Introduction

One of the most important literary developments in the formation of the Hebrew Bible that probably took place in the fourth century is the formation of the Torah.[1] This dating is based on quite a broad

Author's note: I wish to thank Bernard M. Levinson and Gary N. Knoppers for their helpful comments and for improving my English.

1. Its basic completion during the late Persian era is indicated by several facts. For one, Chronicles and Ezra-Nehemiah assume a fixed written Torah. However, the traditional date in the Persian era for these passages in Chronicles and Ezra-Nehemiah is increasingly questioned and is now considered to have been a longer history of literary growth that extends to remarkably later times (see most recently Juha Pakkala, *Ezra the Scribe: The Development of Ezra 7–10 and Nehemia 8* [BZAW 347; Berlin: de Gruyter, 2004]; Reinhard G. Kratz, *The Composition of the Narrative Books of the Old Testament* [trans. John Bowden; London: T. & T. Clark, 2005]). Nevertheless, the older sections of Ezra, in Ezra 10, seem to refer back to fully developed literary Torah texts, such as Deut 7:1–6, and this would support the traditional argument. Furthermore, the LXX translation of the Torah marks a *terminus ante quem*, which can be dated to the middle of the third century B.C.E. (see, e.g., Folker Siegert, *Zwischen Hebräischer Bibel und Altem Testament: Eine Einführung in die Septuaginta* [Münsteraner judaistische Studien 9; Münster: LIT-Verlag, 2001] 42). Finally, there is a remarkable argument from silence: we find no clear literary reflection of the collapse of the Persian Empire in the Torah, as there is in the prophetic books in texts that speak distinctly of world judgment (Isa 34:2–4; Jer 25:27–31, 45:4–5; Joel 4:12–16; Mic 7:12–13; Zeph 3:8; see my *Buchgestalten des Jeremiabuches: Untersuchungen zur Redaktion und Rezeption von Jer 30–33 im Kontext des Buches* [WMANT 72; Neukirchen-Vluyn: Neukirchener Verlag, 1996] 305–9) and that can best be explained as a literary reaction to the breakdown of the Persian Empire. The literary substance of the Torah thus seems to be pre-Hellenistic. To be sure, this late Persian date for the Torah does not exclude minor changes to the text, such as the chronological system in Genesis 5 or 11 or in Numbers 22–24, which might stem even from the Maccabean period. On this point, see my *Erzväter und Exodus: Untersuchungen zur doppelten Begründung der Ursprünge Israels innerhalb der Geschichtsbücher des Alten Testaments* (WMANT 81; Neukirchen-Vluyn: Neukirchener Verlag, 1999) 19–22. These later changes are, however, quite limited in quantity and of minor importance. They do not challenge the general notion of a Torah formation in the fourth century.

consensus, and I will refrain from discussing the reasons here. But how did the Torah as a literary entity come into being? Was there a specific Torah redaction that has shaped the Pentateuch *as Torah*?

Within the classic documentary hypothesis, the explanation for the formation of the Torah was not a much-debated problem. According to the documentary hypothesis, it was R^P, the redactor of the Pentateuch, who established the Torah by merging P and JED into one another, and the extension of the Torah was taken over from P. It ends with the death of Moses. This traditional view, however, was challenged in an important study by Lothar Perlitt in 1988.[2] He questioned whether there were any P texts in Deuteronomy at all. In Deuteronomy 34, according to Perlitt, the language of the verses traditionally ascribed to P (vv. 1 and 7–9) is not clearly Priestly, and the narrative of these verses does not flow well enough to constitute a source text. Deuteronomy 34, he concluded, is not from P, just as there are no traces of P elsewhere in Deuteronomy. In the context of European scholarship, Perlitt's arguments have gained wide acceptance.[3] If Perlitt is right, and it seems that he is,[4] then the formation of the Torah with the death of Moses as the conclusion can no longer be explained just as a consequence of the redactional insertion of P into JED.

Is there an alternative solution? Some recent trends in European scholarship on Deuteronomy 34 seem to follow the theory that the Torah as a literary entity reaching from Genesis to Deuteronomy was not closed and shaped *for a specific purpose at all*. Christian Frevel in his monograph on P in 1999, for example, states: "Deuteronomy 34 grew into its role as the ending of the Pentateuch; it was not composed as the ending. . . . The entity 'Pentateuch' was most likely completed successively in redaction history without redactional insertions into Deuteronomy 34."[5] To my mind, this assumption must be questioned.

---

2. Perlitt, "Priesterschrift im Deuteronomium?" *ZAW* 100 Supplement. (1988) 65–87.

3. See the overview by Eckart Otto, *Das Deuteronomium im Pentateuch und Hexateuch: Studien zur Literaturgeschichte von Pentateuch und Hexateuch im Lichte des Deuteronomiumrahmens* (FAT 30; Tübingen: Mohr Siebeck, 2000) 212–13 n. 248.

4. Despite the monograph by Christian Frevel, *Mit Blick auf das Land die Schöpfung erinnern: Zum Ende der Priestergrundschrift* (Herders biblische Studien 23; Freiburg im Breisgau: Herder, 1999).

5. Idem, "Ein vielsagender Abschied: Exegetische Blicke auf den Tod des Mose in Deut 34,1–12," *BZ* 45 (2001) 209–34 (p. 232: "Dtn 34 ist als Pentateuchschluß gewachsen, nicht gesetzt. . . . Die Größe Pentateuch wurde wahrscheinlich ohne einen redaktionellen Eintrag in Dtn 34 eher sukzessive abgeschlossen und in der Rezeptionsgeschichte geschaffen"; translation mine). In a similar vein, see also Reinhard G. Kratz, "Der vor- und der nachpriesterschriftliche Hexateuch," in *Abschied vom Jahwisten: Die Komposition*

In the following discussion, I want to argue for the opposite position. The Torah was deliberately shaped as Torah by several textual insertions in Deuteronomy 34 with a distinct theological profile. In other words, it is possible to detect elements of a clear "Torah" redaction or a "Pentateuchal redaction" in Deuteronomy 34. I will structure my arguments in three steps. First, some considerations about terminology are in order. Second, I will present three textual elements in Deuteronomy 34 that can be explained as "Torah-conscious" sayings. Third, I will draw some conclusions.

The Terminological Problem of a "Torah Redaction" or a "Pentateuchal Redaction"

Terminology in Hebrew Bible scholarship has often been a source of confusion. One of the most recent examples is the concept of a "Pentateuchal redaction" or of a "final redaction of the Pentateuch." This concept is used to describe either the redactional layer that combined the Yahwist and the Priestly Code (Christoph Levin) or the hand that first brought together the Priestly Code and Deuteronomy and continued to play a subsequent formative role (Eckart Otto) or, in even more general terms, the basic merging of Priestly and non-Priestly material in the Pentateuch (Jan Christian Gertz, Markus Witte).[6] All of these approaches to "Pentateuchal redaction" or the "final redaction of the

---

des Hexateuch in der jüngsten Diskussion (ed. Jan Christian Gertz et al.; BZAW 315; Berlin: de Gruyter, 2002) 295–323 (see esp. pp. 319 n. 110, 320: "Relegating Deut 34:7–8, 9, 10–12 to a certain 'source' or redaction is only possible by forcing it"; translation mine). He is most concerned with finding a literary element of his "old" Hexateuch, *Exodus 2– Joshua 12, in Deut 34:*5–6. This may or may not be correct. However, not much is dependent on an exact literary identification of the report of Moses' death that may have been part of the pre-Deuteronomistic Hexateuch. Even if one prefers Kratz's methodological option of relying on existing texts for the reconstruction of possible earlier stages, rather than assuming missing or repressed material, then it still is a question whether Deut 34:*5–6 is really determined by the method of subtraction proposed by Kratz (in his "Noch einmal: Theologie im Alten Testament," in *Vergegenwärtigung des Alten Testaments: Festschrift Rudolf Smend* [ed. Christoph Bultmann et al.; Göttingen: Vandenhoeck & Ruprecht, 2002] 310–26, esp. p. 322) and not by the traditional logic of source criticism: the death of Moses must have been reported between Numbers 25 and Joshua 2; thus, we must find old textual material in Deut 34:*5–6.

6. Christoph Levin, *Der Jahwist* (FRLANT 157; Göttingen: Vandenhoeck & Ruprecht, 1993); Otto, *Das Deuteronomium im Pentateuch und Hexateuch*; Jan Christian Gertz, *Tradition und Redaktion in der Exoduserzählung: Untersuchungen zur Endredaktion des Pentateuch* (FRLANT 186; Göttingen: Vandenhoeck & Ruprecht, 2000); Markus Witte, *Die biblische Urgeschichte: Redaktions- und theologiegeschichtliche Beobachtungen zu Genesis 1,1–11,26* (BZAW 265; Berlin: de Gruyter, 1998).

Pentateuch" are alike in that they actually speak to a *proto*-Pentateuchal redaction. The focus in all cases is on a process leading to the formation *of an important preliminary stage* but not leading to the *final* formation of the Pentateuch—if I may use this problematic term "final formation" for a moment. This is seen most clearly in Levin's terminology, when he speaks of "post-final redaction" (*endredaktionell*) in regard to several texts in the Torah. The inner semantics of this terminology is a contradiction in terms: a final redaction that does not complete the literary growth of a textual corpus is not a final redaction.

Levin's terminology can only be understood against the background of the classic documentary hypothesis. This hypothesis saw the "final" redaction of the Pentateuch in the mere combination of JED and P, while the redaction itself hardly *produced* any texts. As soon as the final Pentateuch is no longer seen as just the combination of JED and P (as is widely agreed upon today, at least in European research), then one can speak of post-final redaction texts when referring to post-priestly additions to the Pentateuch. Without the background of this history of Hebrew Bible scholarship, it is impossible to understand the use of this terminology.

For the sake of clear terminology, I opt for a restricted use of the term "Pentateuchal redaction" or the "Pentateuchal redactor" (whether he was a single author or a collective set of authors). With this term, I refer only to redactional texts that have to do with the formation of the Pentateuch—in canonical terms, the Torah—and that show an awareness of a literary horizon that comprises the entire Pentateuch. We should not speak of a *"final* redaction" of the Pentateuch in the singular. The absence of a uniform text of Genesis to Deuteronomy without variants suggests that a final redaction never took place: there were as many "final redactions" of the Pentateuch as we now have textual witnesses.[7]

In addition, we should not assume from the outset that a Pentateuchal redactor can be identified in the text, that we can search for him, and in consequence also find him. We could just as easily assume that the formation of the Torah was a process that was unproductive on a literary level. We must show, on the contrary, that there are textual passages in the Pentateuch that can be connected to the final composition of the Torah in terms of binding together the Torah complex from Genesis to Deuteronomy in a way that can be conceived literarily and theologically.

---

7. Erhard Blum, "Gibt es die Endgestalt des Pentateuch?" in *Congress Volume: Leuven 1989* (ed. John Adney Emerton; VTSup 43; Leiden: Brill, 1991) 46–57.

These texts exist. How many there are we may not be able to determine with final certainty. At the least, we can determine three motifs in the final chapter of the Torah, Deuteronomy 34, that fulfill the above-mentioned criteria.[8] I will first mention them briefly and then I will examine them more extensively in the second stage of my discussion.

First among these is the promise of the land to Abraham, Isaac, and Jacob as an oath in Deut 34:4, a "Leitmotiv," that is woven through all the books of the Torah but is subsequently missing in Joshua–2 Kings: "YHWH said to him: This is the land of which I swore to Abraham, to Isaac, and to Jacob, saying, 'To your descendants I will give it.'"[9] Second, we can mention the famous passage in Deut 34:10 on Moses as a prophet unlike all other prophets, "Never since has there arisen a prophet in Israel like Moses, whom YHWH knew face to face." This text separates the Torah in a qualitative way from the subsequent reading of the "Former Prophets" and thus establishes the Torah as a textual authority of "archtypal-prophecy" over against the books of the regular "prophets." Third and finally, there is the description of the death of Moses in Deut 34:7, in which Moses dies in the best of health at the age of 120, a text that refers back to the corresponding restriction of human life in Gen 6:3 and thus creates a literary frame for the Torah as a whole.

To my mind, these three motifs have not yet been recognized sufficiently *as Pentateuchal-redactional texts*. My discussion in the following sections must ignore many questions concerning Deuteronomy 34 and try to focus especially on this point.

---

8. For a different position, see Hans-Christoph Schmitt, "Dtn 34 als Verbindungs-stück zwischen Tetrateuch und Dtr. Geschichtswerk," in *Das Deuteronomium zwischen Pentateuch und Deuteronomistischem Geschichtswerk* (ed. Eckart Otto and Reinhard Achenbach; FRLANT 206; Göttingen: Vandenhoeck & Ruprecht, 2004) 181–92, esp. pp. 181–82. Schmitt denies the presence of redactional text(s) in Deuteronomy 34 that are "only" determined by the horizon established by the Pentateuch or the Hexateuch. He claims that Deuteronomy 34 also has connections to the Former Prophets. This claim by itself has little significance: not the connection itself is of importance but its thematic profile when determining the literary horizon of a text (because one also has to reckon with literary connections between materially separated corpora of texts). Therefore, it is not impossible that Deuteronomy 34, as a Torah-redaction text, shows literary connections not only with other texts within the Torah itself but also with the texts in the corpus of the Former Prophets. Schmitt also has to distance himself from the portrayal of Moses as a prophet above all prophets and is thus not able to interpret this portrayal in thematic detail.

9. David J. A. Clines, *The Theme of the Pentateuch* (JSOTSup 10; Sheffield: Sheffield Academic Press, 1978 [2nd ed. 1997]).

Three "Torah-Conscious" Motifs in Deuteronomy 34

The Promise of the Land to Abraham, Isaac,
and Jacob as an Oath (34:4)

The promise of the land is a very common theme in the Torah.[10] But there is a specific type of this promise that can be found only five times in the Torah: The notion of *the promise of the land to Abraham, Isaac, and Jacob as an oath*—without the apposition *'bwt* 'fathers'—is limited to Gen 50:24; Exod 32:12, 33:1; Num 32:11; and Deut 34:4.[11] If one adds the thematically related passage in Lev 26:42, this theologoumenon turns out to be the only one present in *all* five books of the Torah.

By the same token, it is especially noteworthy that the land promise as an oath to Abraham, Isaac, and Jacob can no longer be found in Joshua–2 Kings. The land promise as an oath to Abraham, Isaac, and Jacob is clearly and strictly a pentateuchal theme. It is even *the* theme of the Pentateuch, both from a synchronic point of view *and* from a redaction-historical point of view, as especially David Clines and Thomas Römer have pointed out.[12] Already these general observations suggest that Deut 34:4 could be one element of a pentateuchal redaction.

This point can be buttressed, if one sees that the five texts putting forward the notion of the land promise to Abraham, Isaac, and Jacob as an oath already seem to presuppose P and D. Thus, they belong to the latest literary developments of the Torah. It seems that they have combined the motif of the land promise as an oath that is prominent in the Deuteronomistic sections of Deuteronomy (see Deut 1:8, 35; 6:10, 18, 23; 7:13; 8:1; 9:5; 10:11; 11:9, 21; 19:8; 26:3, 15; 28:11; 30:20; 31:7, 20–21; 34:4) with the Priestly conviction that God's acting toward Israel is rooted in the covenant with the ancestors (see Genesis 17). The result is the notion of the promise of the land to Abraham, Isaac, and Jacob as an oath. Of course, one would need to demonstrate this by detailed redaction-critical investigations into the five relevant texts, but here I refer the reader to a detailed book by Thomas Römer.[13]

---

10. See, for instance, Gen 12:7; 13:15, 17; 15:7, 18; 17:8; 24:7; 28:4, 13; 35:12; 48:4; 50:24; Exod 13:5, 11; 32:13; 33:1; Lev 18:3; 19:23; 20:24; 23:10; 25:2, 38; Num 11:12; 14:16, 23; 32:11; Deut 1:8, 35; 6:10, 18, 23; 7:13; 8:1; 10:11; 11:9, 21; 19:8; 26:3, 15; 28:11; 30:20; 31:7, 20–21; 34:4.

11. Schmid, *Erzväter*, 296–99.

12. Clines, *The Theme of the Pentateuch*; Thomas Römer, *Israels Väter: Untersuchungen zur Väterthematik im Deuteronomium und in der deuteronomistischen Tradition* (OBO 99; Fribourg: Editions Universitaires / Göttingen: Vandenhoeck & Ruprecht, 1990) 566.

13. Römer, *Israels Väter.*

There is another argument that supports the interpretation of Deut 34:4 as a pentateuchal redaction passage. Deut 34:4 clearly refers back to the beginning of the Pentateuch in Gen 12:7 and 13:15 and thus forms an *inclusio*. First, Deut 34:4 quotes the promise of the land given in Gen 12:7:

And Y<small>HWH</small> said to him: "This is the land of which I swore to Abraham, to Isaac, and to Jacob, saying, '*To your descendants I will give* it (*lzrʿkʾ tnnh*).'" (Deut 34:4)	Then Y<small>HWH</small> appeared to Abram, and said, "*To your descendants I will give* this land (*lzrʿk ʾtn ʾt hʾrṣ hzʾt*)." (Gen 12:7)

Second, there are clear connections between Deut 34:1–4 and Gen 13:10–15:

Then Moses went up from the plains of Moab to Mount Nebo, to the top of Pisgah, which is opposite Jericho, and Y<small>HWH</small> made him *see all the land*: Gilead as far as Dan, all Naphtali, the land of Ephraim and Manasseh, all the land of Judah as far as the Western Sea, the Negeb, and *the plain (kkr)* of the valley of Jericho, the city of palm trees—as far as *Zoar*. And Y<small>HWH</small> said to him: "This is the land of which I swore to Abraham, to Isaac, and to Jacob, saying, '*To your descendants I will give* it.'" (Deut 34:1–4)	Lot looked about him, and *saw* that *the plain (kkr)* of the Jordan was well watered everywhere like the garden of Y<small>HWH</small>, like the land of Egypt, in the direction of *Zoar; . . .* And Y<small>HWH</small> said to Abram, after Lot had separated from him, "Raise your eyes now, and *see* from the place where you are, northward and southward and eastward and westward; for *all the land* that you *see I will give* to you and *to your descendants* forever." (Gen 13:10–15)

The parallels between Deut 34:1–4 and Gen 12:7 on the one hand and Gen 13:10–15 on the other hand are especially remarkable, because Gen 12:1–3, 7 and 13:10–17 belong closely together and may be part of one and the same narrative arc, as Matthias Köckert has suggested.[14]

And Y<small>HWH</small> said to Abram, "Go from your country and your kindred and your father's house to *the land* that *I will make you see*. I will make of you a great nation, and I will bless you, and	And Y<small>HWH</small> *said to Abram*, after Lot had separated from him, "Raise your eyes now, and *see* from the place where you are, northward and southward and eastward and

---

14. See Matthias Köckert, *Väergott und Väterverheißungen: Eine Auseinandersetzung mit Albrecht Alt und seinen Erben* (FRLANT 142; Göttingen: Vandenhoeck & Ruprecht, 1988) 250–55; Erhard Blum, *Studien zur Komposition des Pentateuch* (BZAW 189; Berlin: de Gruyter, 1990) 214 n. 35.

make your name great, so that you will be a blessing. I will bless those who bless you, and the one who curses you I will curse; and in you all the families of the earth shall be blessed." (Gen 12:1–3) Then YHWH appeared to Abram, and said, *"To your descendants I will give this land."* (Gen 12:7)

westward; for *all the land* that you *see I will give* to you and *to your descendants* forever." (Gen 13:15)

Deut 34:1–4 seems to take up the network of promises in Genesis 12–13 and stresses the fact that the land promised to Abraham is still being promised to Israel. Deut 34:4 and Gen 12:7 both highlight the *descendants* as the recipients of the land. Like Abraham, Moses can see the land, but Moses is denied entrance to it.

If it is correct that the *promise of the land to Abraham, Isaac, and Jacob as an oath* (34:4) is *the* "theme of the Pentateuch" (Clines), then the Torah has a prophetic flavor. It ends prior to the entering of the land, but the land is promised to Israel. Israel thus receives a basic prophetic promise in the Torah. And this brings us to the next, obviously corresponding point: the depiction of Moses as incomparable prophet in Deut 34:10. To my mind, this motif is clearly "Torah-conscious" as well.

Moses as a Prophet above All Prophets (34:10)

Scholars have long recognized the thematic importance of the statement in Deut 34:10.[15] In this text, Moses is fundamentally separated from all other prophets and established as an arch-prophet, unmatched by any of the subsequent prophets. In terms of redaction history, one especially noteworthy aspect of this statement is that it allows a contradiction to previous statements in Deuteronomy in order to establish the incomparable status of Moses. The contradiction of Deut 18:15 is especially clear: "YHWH your God will raise up (*yqym*) for you a prophet like me from among your own people; you shall heed such a prophet" (Deut 18:15).

The promise in Deut 18:15, centered on *qwm* (impf.), is essentially abrogated in Deut 34:10 (*qwm* pf.): "Never since has there arisen (*qm*) a prophet in Israel like Moses, whom YHWH knew face to face" (Deut

---

15. Joseph Blenkinsopp, *Prophecy and Canon* (London: SCM, 1977) 80–95; Antonius H. J. Gunneweg, "Das Gesetz und die Propheten: Eine Auslegung von Ex 33,7–11; Num 11,4–12,8; Dtn 31,14f; 34,10," *ZAW* 102 (1990) 169–80. Gerhard von Rad (*Das fünfte Buch Mose Deuteronomium* [ATD 8; Göttingen: Vandenhoeck & Ruprecht, 1964] 150) limits his observations to this short notice: "The evaluation of Moses as a prophet, even as a prophet without equal, is of course deuteronomistic" (translation mine).

34:10). Why does Deut 34:10 stand out against Deut 18:15? The reason is most likely the need to break up the chain of prophetic succession beginning with Moses. Whereas Deut 18:15 *envisions* Moses as arch-prophet and envisions *a succession* of prophets, Deut 34:10 wants to *separate* Moses from all other prophets. The reason for this separation of "Moses" and the "prophets" is most easily found in the formation of Torah. Moses must be separated from the prophets as soon as the Torah is seen as superior to the Prophets (that is, Joshua–Malachi as a section of the canon referred to as the "Prophets").

Crüsemann concluded from Deut 34:10 that the primary thrust of the Pentateuch "must be seen as deeply un-prophetic and non-eschatological, in a certain sense even anti-eschatological,"[16] a conclusion that has been (to my mind rightly) criticized in other contexts.[17] The simple fact that Moses is referred to as a *prophet*, moreover as *the* prophet, stands against Crüsemann's conclusion. There are other observations pointing us to the fact that the Torah *also* has *prophetic* characteristics, such as its open ending (from a literary point of view), before the entrance into the land solemnly promised to the patriarchs. It should thus be clear that Moses is placed *above* the prophets for the sake of the prevalence of the Torah. He is not established as an anti-prophet, *against* the prophets.

The immediately following passage, Deut 34:11–12, fits well with the statement in Deut 34:10 regarding its theological profile:[18]

> Never since has there arisen a prophet in Israel like Moses, whom YHWH knew face to face, regarding [*l*] all the *signs and wonders* [cf. Deut 6:22, 28:6, etc.] that YHWH sent him to perform *in the land of Egypt, against Pharaoh and all his servants and his entire land*, and regarding *the strong hand* and all the *great terrors* [cf. Deut 4:34, 26:8; Jer 32:21] that Moses performed *in the sight of all Israel*. (Deut 34:10–12)

---

16. Frank Crüsemann, *Die Tora: Theologie und Sozialgeschichte des alttestamentlichen Gesetzes* (Munich: Chr. Kaiser, 1992) 402 (translation mine). See idem, "Israel in der Perserzeit," in *Max Webers Sicht des antiken Christentums* (ed. Wolfgang Schluchter; Suhrkamp Taschenbuch Wissenschaft 548; Frankfurt a.M.: Suhrkamp, 1985) 205–32, esp. p. 214 with recourse to Blenkinsopp. This thesis has been recently taken up by Otto, *Das Deuteronomium im Pentateuch und Hexateuch*, 230, 232.

17. Blum, *Pentateuch*, 359; see also Stephen B. Chapman, *The Law and the Prophets: A Study in Hebrew Bible Canon Formation* (FAT 27; Tübingen: Mohr Siebeck, 2000) 127–31.

18. Chapman, *The Law and the Prophets*, 113–31; idem, "A Canonical Approach to Hebrew Bible Theology? Deuteronomy 34:10–12 and Malachi 3:22–24 as Programmatic Conclusions," *HBT* 25 (2003) 121–45.

This text has always aroused pronounced scholarly interest because divine predicates are very boldly transferred to Moses himself.[19] Moses performs *"signs and wonders"*; his attributes are *"the strong hand"* and the *"great terror."* Conventionally, biblical texts assign these attributes to God and *to God alone*. In addition to the passages in Deut 4:34, 6:22, 26:8, 28:6; Jer 32:21, and others mentioned above in the context of the translation of Deut 34:11–12, we should also quote Deut 29:1–2, because Deut 34:11 seems to point back especially to this text (the phrase "in the land of Egypt, against Pharaoh and all his servants and his entire land" appears only in Deut 29:1 and 34:11):[20] "Moses summoned *all Israel* and said to them: You have seen all that YHWH did before your eyes *in the land of Egypt, to Pharaoh and to all his servants and to all his land*, the *great* trials that *your eyes* saw, and those *great signs and wonders*" (Deut 29:1–2). Deut 29:1, however, also refers to the great signs and wonders of YHWH. Deut 34:11–12 obviously reinterprets this text and places Moses in the closest possible proximity to God—most likely in order to justify his status as the incomparable prophet who is closer to God than to human beings.

Deut 34:10 also states that God interacted with Moses face to face, a notion that can be found in Exod 33:11; Num 12:8, 14:14 as well (see also Exod 24:10).[21] However similar to the relationship between Deut 34:10 and 18:15, this statement contradicts the former pentateuchal tradition, which in Exod 33:20[22] explicitly negated this fact, "He [Moses] said, 'Show me your glory, I pray.' . . . And YHWH continued, 'See, there is a place by me where you shall stand on the rock; . . . you shall see my back; but my face shall not be seen'" (Exod 33:18–23).

The statement that God interacted with Moses "face to face" in Deut 34:10 fits well with the distance established between Moses and

---

19. Andrew D. H. Mayes, *Deuteronomy* (NCB; London: Oliphants, 1979) 414; Dennis T. Olson, *Deuteronomy and the Death of Moses: A Theological Reading* (OBT; Minneapolis: Fortress, 1994) 169–70; with differentiations, Chapman, *Law*, 126–27.

20. Otto, *Deuteronomium*, 228–29.

21. On Num 12:8, see Christoph Uehlinger, "'Hat YHWH denn wirklich nur mit Mose geredet?' Biblische Exegese zwischen Religionsgeschichte und Theologie, am Beispiel von Num 12," *BZ* 47 (2003) 230–59.

22. Christoph Dohmen, "'Nicht sieht mich der Mensch und lebt' (Ex 33,20): Aspekte der Gottesschau im Alten Testament," *Jahrbuch für Biblische Theologie* 13 (1998) 31–51; Friedhelm Hartenstein, "Das 'Angesicht Gottes' in Exodus 32–34," in *Gottes Volk am Sinai: Untersuchungen zu Ex 32–34 und Deut 9–10* (ed. Matthias Köckert and Erhard Blum; Veröffentlichungen der Wissenschaftlichen Gesellschaft für Theologie 18; Gütersloh: Gütersloher, 2001) 157–83.

other human beings for the sake of his closeness to God. We can thus assume the same thematic intention here as with the statements in Deut 34:11. The similar concept in Exod 33:11; Num 12:8, and 14:14 may be a trace of the same pentateuchal redaction in previous books.

It is further possible that the motive behind Moses' burial *by* Y\HWH *himself* (34:6), unique in the entire Hebrew Bible and corrected by the Samaritan Pentateuch (*wyqbrw* 'they buried' instead of *wyqbr* 'He buried'), is also to place Moses in an intimate proximity to God that is without analogy. The process of "theologizing" Moses is best explained by the desire to confer authoritative status on the Torah (for which "Moses" stands). "Moses" is placed in close connection to God so that the Torah can lay claim to equivalent authority.[23]

In addition to the motifs in vv. 4 and 10–12, there is a third motif in Deuteronomy 34 that must be connected with the formation of the Torah: the notion of Moses' death following a life-span of 120 years (34:7).

The Death of Moses Following a Life-Span of 120 Years (34:7)

The formulation in Deut 34:7 that Moses died at the age of 120 years ("Moses was one hundred twenty years old when he died") is followed by an amazing statement that he did so in the best of health: "His sight was unimpaired and his vigor had not abated."[24] This statement is especially striking, because it also contradicts Deut 31:1–2: "When Moses had finished speaking all these words to all Israel, he said to them: 'I am now one hundred twenty years old. I am no longer able to set forth and come home'" (Deut 31:1–2). Here, too, Moses is 120 years old, yet he is obviously no longer in his prime; he is no longer able to set forth and come home (*lz't wlbw'*)—that is, most likely, he is no longer capable of military leadership.

This contradiction might be smoothed over by a harmonizing reader, because Deut 31:2 is a *personal* statement *by Moses himself*, whereas Deut 34:7 is a narrative statement *about* Moses. Thus, it may become clear that Moses' personal assessment of his health does not accord

---

23. Similar processes are present in the final passages of the *Nebi'im* in Mal 3:22–24: on the one hand, the *Nebi'im* are connected back to the Torah of Moses ("remember the Torah of Moses," 3:22); on the other hand, the text emphasizes "the prophet" Elijah (3:23) and his coming (probably none other than Malachi "my messenger" himself)—Elijah is the only post-Mosaic prophet who had immediate contact with God following his ascension to heaven. The introduction of Elijah emphasizes that the *Nebi'im* can lay claim to the same direct relationship with God that the Torah does.

24. Otto (*Deuteronomium im Pentateuch*, 226) points to the antithetic composition of Isaac (Gen 27:1) and Moses (Deut 34:7), both connected by the term *khh*, used only here.

with the actual status of his health (which, in truth, was better).[25] Still, Deut 34:7 remains striking: why does the narrative emphasize Moses' good health in the face of the previous context? Deut 34:7, as Josephus (*Ant.* 1.152, 3.95, 4.176–93) noted, is motivated by the life-span of 120 years mentioned in Gen 6:3, "Then YHWH said: My spirit shall not abide in mortals forever, for they are flesh; their days shall be one hundred twenty years."[26] In the light of Gen 6:3, the emphasis on Moses' health in Deut 34:7 can (and must) be understood as follows: Moses dies in Deuteronomy 34 for no other reason than that *his life-span has reached the limit set by God in Gen 6:3.*[27]

The connection between Deut 34:7 and Gen 6:3 has been recognized by previous writers,[28] but this connection has not been evaluated appropriately. As far as I know, this thematic connection is the only literary inclusio that draws a line from the ending of the Torah not only to the beginning of the patriarchal narratives in Genesis 12–13 but also to the primeval narrative.[29] Regarding the theological intent of this inclusio, one can detect a distinctive theological profile. The statement in Deut 34:7 that Moses is not allowed to enter the promised land simply because his life-span has run out—and not because of any sort of wrongdoing—offers, in contrast to the "D" tradition (cf. Deut 1:34–37,

---

25. Ibid.; see also Jeffrey H. Tigay, "The Significance of the End of Deuteronomy (Deuteronomy 34:10–12)," in *Texts, Temples, and Traditions: A Tribute to Menahem Haran* (ed. Michael V. Fox et al.; Winona Lake, IN: Eisenbrauns, 1996) 137–43.

26. See Klaus Haacker and Peter Schäfer, "Nachbiblische Traditionen vom Tod des Mose," in *Josephus-Studien: Otto Michel zum 70. Geburtstag* (ed. O. Betz, K. Haacker, and M. Hengel; Göttingen: Vandenhoeck & Ruprecht, 1974) 147–74, esp. p. 148.

27. In regard to the specific number 120, see the observations of Helge S. Kvanvig, "Gen 6,1–4 as an Antediluvian Event," *SJOT* 16 (2002) 79–112, esp. p. 99. Hermann Gunkel (*Genesis* [6th ed.; HKAT 1/1; Göttingen: Vandenhoeck & Ruprecht, 1964] 58) points to Herodotus, *Histories* 3.23 as a parallel to the life-span of "120 years" (in this case of Ethiopians). The issue at hand in Deut 34:7 seems similar to Psalm 90, which laments enduring collective misery in the face of the limited human life-span. Contrary to Psalm 90, Deut 34:7 does not lament this limitation; instead, it simply states it and accepts it as a divine ordinance; Thomas Krüger, "Psalm 90 und die 'Vergänglichkeit des Mensche,'" *Bib* 75 (1994) 191–219 (= idem, *Kritische Weisheit: Studien zur weisheitlichen Traditionskritik im Alten Testament* [Zurich: Pano, 1997] 67–89).

28. See, early on, Benno Jacob, *Das erste Buch der Tora: Genesis* (New York: Schocken, 1934) 176–77.

29. But note also the connection between Gen 6:5–8, 8:20–22 ("evil heart"); and Deut 30:6 ("circumcision of the heart"); see Thomas Krüger, "Das menschliche Herz und die Weisung Gottes: Elemente einer Diskussion über Möglichkeiten und Grenzen der Tora-Rezeption im Alten Testament," in *Rezeption und Auslegung im Alten Testament und in seinem Umfeld: Ein Symposium aus Anlass des 60. Geburtstags von Odil Hannes Steck* (ed. Thomas Krüger and Reinhard G. Kratz; OBO 153; Fribourg: Editions Universitaires / Göttingen: Vandenhoeck & Ruprecht, 1997) 65–92.

3:25–27) on the one hand and the "P" tradition (cf. Num 20:12) on the other hand, a *third* reason why Moses may not enter the promised land.[30]

The "Priestly" tradition—probably not "P^g" (that is, the *Grundschrift* or basic layer of the Priestly Code) but "P^s" (one of the secondary expansions of the Priestly Code)—in Num 20:12 assumes that Moses went against God by *striking* the rock, whereas God had ordered a *verbal* miracle ("command the rock," Num 20:8), and possibly even doubted that striking the rock would bring forth water; thus Moses was guilty of faithlessness.[31] The "Deuteronomistic" tradition, on the other hand, includes Moses in the collective guilt of the people: "YHWH was even angry with me *on your account*."[32] Both "explanations" reckon with Moses' guilt, whether on a personal level (as in accordance with Priestly thought) or on a collective level (following Deutoronomistic thinking).

In contrast, Deut 34:7 agrees with *neither* of these two positions.[33] It mentions *none* of these explanations for Moses' death. Instead, it offers its own interpretation: Moses is not allowed to enter the promised land, because his life-span of 120 years has just now run out. Moses' death east of the Jordan *is not caused by personal or collective guilt but by fate*— that is, by the divinely ordained limitation of the human life-span.

The interesting fact that now needs to be highlighted is this: the theological profile of Deut 34:7 (Moses' death has nothing to do with personal guilt but, rather, with fate) matches the thematic thrust of Gen 6:3 within the framework of Gen 6:1–4, as Manfred Oeming has shown.[34] Even if the redactional inclusion of the narrative of the "angel marriages" in Gen 6:1–4 (and thus also Gen 6:3) is a matter of debate (it has even been suggested that there is a link to the Book of Watchers in *1 Enoch* [6–11]),[35] we can at least state that the heavenly interference of

---

30. For a placement of the D material within redaction history, see Otto, *Deuteronomium im Pentateuch*, 22–23; and Frevel, *Abschied*, 220–2 n. 37.

31. The statement—kept vague probably out of respect for Moses—in Num 20:10 (המן־הסלע הזה נוציא לכם מים) would then be interpreted as follows: "Should we really be able to produce water from this rock?"

32. Compare Deut 1:36 and 3:26 (גם־בי התאנף יהוה בגללכם).

33. Thomas Römer, "Deuteronomium 34 zwischen Pentateuch, Hexateuch und deuteronomistischem Geschichtswerk," *ZABR* 5 (1999) 167–78; Thomas Römer and Mark Z. Brettler, "Deuteronomy 34 and the Case for a Persian Hexateuch," *JBL* 119 (2000) 401–19, esp. p. 408.

34. M. Oeming, "Sünde als Verhägnis: Gen 6,1–4 im Rahmen der Urgeschichte des Jahwisten," *TTZ* 102 (1993) 34–50.

35. Mirjam and Ruben Zimmermann, "'Heilige Hochzeit' der Göttersöhne und Menschentöchter," *ZAW* 111 (1999) 327–52; Kvanvig, "Antediluvian Event," 79–112; idem, "The Watcher Story and Genesis: An Intertextual Reading," *SJOT* 18 (2004) 163–83.

divine sons with human daughters in its current literary position offers an (additional) reason for the Flood: the Flood solves the problem created by the mixing of the divine and human sphere, which was not caused by human guilt but by transcendent fate.[36]

If we combine this theological connection with the fact that Gen 6:3/Deut 34:7 is the only literary bracket around the Pentateuch as a whole, including the primeval narrative,[37] then we may reach the conclusion that we are looking at an "empirical" element of pentateuchal theology: the Pentateuch contains, from the point of view of the pentateuchal redactor, a legal theology explaining that punishment results not only from human misdeed, say sin, but also from fateful ordinances.

Deut 34:7 thus promotes a different perspective on the theology of the Torah. As a textual corpus containing much legal material, the Torah in its canonical shape promotes neither a simple idea of retribution nor a dominant theology of divine grace, as introduced by the Priestly Code. The redaction that created the Torah added a third perspective (probably influenced by a sapiential point of view) to punishment and grace as the divine regulators of world order: there are realities in the world that are the way they are because they were ordained to be that way. *Nota bene*: the limitation of human life to 120 years is not just seen negatively. It contrasts with the exceptionally long life-spans of the patriarchs before the Flood in P that were primarily used to accumulate *hms* 'violence'. If a human being lives for only 120 years, then the time in which he can multiply violence is also limited.

Concluding Remarks

With Deut 34:4, 7, and 10–12, we have three passages that can be connected with the formation of the Pentateuch as Torah, and thus seem to belong together. Deut 34:7 refers back to the primeval narratives, Deut 34:4 to the patriarchal narratives, and Deut 34:10–12 to the Moses narratives; thus, allusions to the three main thematic sections of the Torah are combined in Deuteronomy 34.

---

36. David J. A. Clines, "The Significance of the 'Son of God' Episode (Genesis 6:1–4) in the Context of the 'Primeval History' (Genesis 1–11)," *JSOT* 13 (1979) 33–46; Ronald S. Hendel, "Of Demigods and the Deluge: Towards an Interpretation of Genesis 6:1–4," *JBL* 106 (1987) 13–26.

37. Frevel (*Abschied*, 230) paradoxically states, "daß Dtn 34 nicht auf den Beginn des Pentateuch, weder auf die Schöpfung noch auf die Urgeschichte zurückverweist" (although according to his opinion as well, Deut 34:7 looks back to Gen 6:3; *Abschied*, 223).

Deut 34:7   Primeval story (Genesis 1–11)
Deut 34:4   Patriarchal story (Genesis 12–50)
Deut 34:10–12   Moses story (Exodus–Deuteronomy)

In this perspective, Deuteronomy 34 clearly exhibits characteristics of
a pentateuchal redaction. I will have to refrain here from a detailed
redaction-historical discussion of this chapter, which seems to have
been written in several stages.[38] But we may maintain that at least in
vv. 4, 7, and 10–12 a redactional reworking can be detected that has to
be connected with the formation of the Torah, which can be dated to
the late Persian period.[39] It focuses on the promise of the land, the status of the Torah as arch-prophecy superior to regular prophecy, and on
a theology of fate that completes traditional notions such as grace and
the interrelationship between sin and sanction.

---

38. Florentino García López, "Deut 34, Dtr History and the Pentateuch," in *Studies
in Deuteronomy: Festschrift Casper J. Labuschagne* (ed. Florentino García Martínez et al.;
VTSup 53; Leiden: Brill, 1994) 47–61; Römer, "Deuteronomium 34"; Otto, *Deuteronomium
im Pentateuch*, 211–33; Kratz, "Hexateuch," 316–22.

39. See n. 1.

The Pentateuch, the Prophets, and the Torah in the Fifth and Fourth Centuries B.C.E.

REINHARD ACHENBACH

Westfälische Wilhelms-Universität, Münster

The question of the redaction history of the Pentateuch has been the subject of much debate over the past decades. The problem is intrinsically intertwined with the process of canonization in general. On the basis of my studies on the Pentateuch, I would like to add some preliminary thoughts on the problem of how the redaction history of the prophetic books and the redaction of the Pentateuch in the Persian period could be correlated.[1] According to the study of Schams (1998; see also Otto 2004), we can assume that the official scribes who produced the scriptures prior to the Hellenistic era did their work alongside other priestly (or Levitical) tasks. Although the biblical text may have a very complex history of transmission, influenced by several stages of composition, redaction, rewriting, and reediting,[2] and knowing that every text has its own complex history of development,[3] we may consider the redaction history of the Pentateuch and the Prophets to be complementary, to a certain extent, in that the priests took over the transmission of prophetic literature.[4]

Redaction History of the Pentateuch

We have received the preexilic materials in the Pentateuch in a fragmented state, either because a consistent source did not exist after the

---

1. This question has previously been discussed in the debate about canonization; see Blenkinsopp 1977; Steck 1991a: 11–24. For further literature, see Chapman, 2000: 1–70.

2. For an evaluation of the complex development of prophetic literature, including the difficult issue of correlating diachronic and synchronic aspects, see, for example, Kratz 1997: 9–28; and Jeremias 1997: 29–44.

3. See, for instance, the book of Jeremiah as an example of the problem of correlating text-history and the development of a prophetic book (Schmid 1996).

4. We may conclude from Sirach 24 that in Hellenistic times scribal teaching included the study of the Torah and of prophecy (Blenkinsopp 1977: 128–32). That the transmission of prophetic Scripture had come under Priestly and Levitical influence we can see from Chronicles (Blenkinsopp 1977: 132–38; Steck 1991a: 112–44).

Babylonian Exile or because the sources became fragmented through several overlapping redactional reworkings.[5] We presume that we have a preexilic Covenant Code, an "Ur"–Deuteronomy, some wisdom material (the primeval history, Genesis 2–8*; the Joseph story?), the narrative cycles of the ancestral stories, an Exodus–Mountain of God, desert wandering, and Conquest story, and beyond that the chronicles and legends of the kingdoms of Israel and Judah.

During exilic times, the Deuteronomistic reinterpretation of the chronicle material led to the Deuteronomistic edition of Samuel–Kings and to other Deuteronomistic reworkings of the preexilic materials, including a Deuteronomistic Deuteronomy. Priestly traditions and *toroth* were collected in several places, one in which the Priestly Code originated and another in the circle associated with Ezekiel. We can also observe a tradition of Jeremianic prophecy and legends (connected to Egypt?) and a Babylonian collection of oracles that is known by the anonymous label of Deutero-Isaiah.

When it became possible to rebuild the Second Temple during the reign of Darius, the attempt to establish a new Davidic dynasty in Yehud was hindered. The Deutero-Isaianic texts were used instead to proclaim the founder of the new Achaemenid dynasty, Cyrus, to be the messiah of Israel (Isa 44:24–45:7). Consequently, the traditional plea for kingship in Israel was delegitimized by theocratic and *torah*-oriented ("nomistic") pupils of the Deuteronomists (see 1 Sam 8:12, 10:19, 12:12b–13a). The legitimation of Israel within the limitations of early Persian rule could only be achieved by referring back to the ancient history of Israel and the covenant, on the one hand, and by believing in prophetic visions of restoration and a new covenant theology, on the other. This led to the unification of preexilic, exilic Priestly, and Deuteronomistic materials in the Hexateuch during the first half of the fifth century B.C.E. The redactor of the Hexateuch used the Priestly Code to unite the ancestral history with the Exodus story (Schmid 1999: 56–78).[6] On the other hand, he used the Conquest story in its Deuteronomistic version, including Deuteronomy–Joshua (ending with Joshua 24), and supplemented his story with the pre-Deuteronomistic materials in Exodus and Numbers, including the Covenant Code, which he

---

5. In what follows, please refer to my earlier analyses (Achenbach 2003; 2004: 56–80).

6. For description of the Hexateuch redactor's work, see Otto 2000a: 1–109, 156–233. The terms *redactor* and *redaction* refer to biblical writers as compilers and composers in a living process of transmission, rewriting, and reediting of diverse ancient materials into consistent fables, sagas, or other genres of composite texts in the Hebrew Bible. For a discussion of the term, see Ska 2005.

correlated with Deuteronomy on the basis of the Deuteronomistic Decalogue. He harmonized the story of the Mountain of God (Exodus 18–19*) with the Horeb interpretation of the Deuteronomists (Deuteronomy 5) and the Sinaitic tabernacle story (Exodus 25–29–Leviticus 9*) of the Priestly code.[7] In a critical reflection upon the devastating role of ancient Israel's priesthood, he described Aaron's disaster at the Mountain of God (Exodus 32*) and developed the idea of a Levitical priesthood, to whom the Mosaic *torah* and Covenant–Law were entrusted together with the ark (from P, Exod 25:10–22*) in the reworked Deuteronomistic text of Deut 10:1–5, 8–9*. In this way, the Levitical priests were established (Exod 32:25–29 → Deut 10:8–9 → Josh 8:30–35); thus, the concept of the *Levitical priesthood* is not older than the redactional link between P and D that was created by the Hexateuchal redactor (Achenbach 1999; 2004: 76–78).[8]

The period before the judges was now considered to be the time when Israel still remembered Moses and the covenant and when Joshua passed the *torah* of Moses and the Law on to Israel and renewed the covenant (Joshua 24). Consequently, the election of a king was considered blasphemous, and there are some antimonarchical additions in Judg 6:8–10; 8:22–23; 10:14, 16; 1 Sam 7:3–4, 8:6–20*, 10:18–19a, and 12:12b–13a that pick up themes from Josh 24:1–28 (Müller 2004; Achenbach 2005b: 143–44, 148–52). According to this view, only the prophets remained to remind Israel to keep the *torah* after Joshua's time. As a result of the Deuteronomistic reediting of the history of the kingdoms in Samuel–Kings, hope rested not on the renewal of the Davidic kingdom but on the promise of Moses that YHWH would raise a prophet like himself who "will tell them everything I command him" (Deut 18:18). The Hexateuch, accordingly, reflects the conditions of the traditions associated with the Second Temple around the time of Nehemiah. Several regulations concerning the cult did not yet exist (see Nehemiah 10*), several social regulations did not work (Nehemiah 5*), the relations between the people in Yehud/Israel and their "brothers" in the North and in Edom, and so on, were problematic. The *peḥah* was still the most decisive man in political and religious affairs. It could be that he described himself as the Servant of YHWH in the tradition of a dynastic religion.

---

7. For further discussion of the issue of the existence of an Enneateuch and of the central function of Joshua 24 in that context, see Achenbach 2005.

8. Please note that, in my essay, the use of an arrow indicates a line of dependence. Hence, when I write "Exod 32:25–29 → Deut 10:8–9 → Josh 8:30–35," it means that Exod 32:25–29 is reused in Deut 10:8–9 and the latter, in turn, is reused in Josh 8:30–35.

A new kind of tradition emerged when increasing cultic activities during the second half of the fifth century demanded new regulations. The elaboration of legislation concerning the personal ritual for purification and atonement of sin (Leviticus 4–7, 11–15) very likely reflects the increasing role played by priestly circles in the administration of justice in Jerusalem (Nihan 2005: 216–18). The Mosaic Law changed its character when the Holiness Code was introduced. As a result of a redactional reworking of the Dathan-Abiram story in Numbers 16, involving the introduction of the story of the 250 laymen challenging Aaron, every non-priestly activity in the center of the cultic temple ritual was prohibited.[9] This was especially true of individual incense rituals, which were popular during the Persian period (Nihan 2005: 218). Laymen were not allowed to come near the sanctuary (Num 16:2–4*, 16–18*, 24a*, 27a*, 35). As we can observe in the redacted Pentateuch, Moses was now considered to stand above all post-Mosaic prophetic tradition. The pentateuchal redactor reworked Genesis–Deuteronomy, for example, in the introduction to the Sinai pericope (Exod 19:3b–8*), at the end of the Holiness Code in Leviticus 26*, and in Numbers 10–25*. His work ends with the programmatic sentence in Deut 34:10: "Since then no prophet has risen in Israel like Moses, whom Yhwh knew face to face!"[10]

The canonical shape of the Law codes is traced back to the revelation delivered on the mount itself, when in Exod 24:12b YHWH states that he will not only give the stone tablets of the Decalogue to Moses but also "the *torah* and the *miṣwah* I have written for their instruction." This *torah* also includes Deuteronomy as canonical Law.[11] Aaron as the later high priest is now the "mouth," receiving the word of YHWH from Moses as ʾĕlōhîm (Exod 4:15–16)! Miriam the prophetess stands beneath Moses (Num 12:6–8). The prophetic character of the seer Balaam is diminished by introducing the donkey legend (Num 22:21–35*). Mixed marriages are totally rejected (Num 25:1–5). *Torah* teaching is the task of priests in the Aaronide (= ancient Israelite) and Levitic lineage (Deut 33:8–11). The covenant is interpreted as the document of a

---

9. For a close analysis of Numbers 16–18, see Achenbach 2003: 37–172. The story was reworked again sometime later into the narrative of the rebellion of Korah and the Levites in a theocratic reediting of Numbers.

10. That there is an intrinsic connection between the texts referring to the "face-to-face" tradition in Deut 34:10–12, Num 12:6–8, Exod 33:11, and Num 11:16–30* and the canonization of the Law in relation to prophecy has already been observed by Blenkinsopp (1977: 80–95).

11. There is an important debate on this text between Braulik (2004) and Otto (2005).

mamleket kōhănîm (Exod 19:6).[12] During the fourth century B.C.E., the Pentateuch becomes the *torah*-document in general and is expanded by substantial hierocratic and theocratic editings (Numbers 1–10, 15–19, 25–36*). The system of the post-Ezra period is established. The term *torah* now refers to the entire teaching of Moses, which he received from God according to Exodus 12–18 and Exodus 19–Deuteronomy 33.

Torah in the Pentateuch

The word *torah* is mentioned several times in the Pentateuch. It is generally assumed that the Deuteronomistic use of the term is a prerequisite for the pentateuchal understanding of Mosaic *torah*. In Deuteronomy, *torah* is mentioned in the Deuteronomistic frame (Deut 28:58, 61) in the context of the final admonition "if you do not diligently observe all the words of this *torah* that are written in this scripture . . ." (*kol-dibrê hattôrâ hazzō't hakkĕtûbîm bassēper hazzeh*; compare with 28:61: *sēper hattôrâ hazzō't*). It refers to the written document of the covenant, which is considered a treaty between YHWH and Israel that took place at Mount Horeb (Deut 5:3). The character of a binding treaty document is expressed by the word *sēper*, which we know already from the treaties from Sefire (see *spr'*, Sefire I B 33; II B 9, 10; II C 13; III 4, 14, 17, 23).[13] The late Deuteronomistic editors of 2 Kings 22–23 had the idea that it was this *sēper* that was found in the temple by the priest Hilkiah (2 Kgs 22:8, 11; 23:24). The historical frame that combines the Deuteronomistic Deuteronomy (DtrD = Deuteronomy 5–28*) with the Conquest story in Joshua (DtrC = Deuteronomy 1–3 [5–28], 29–30*, 34:5–6* + Joshua 1–12*, 23*; Judg 2:6–9) refers to this Deuteronomistic scripture as a document of the covenant in the lands of Moab (28:69; 29:19-20, 26—*sēper hattôrâ hazzeh*; 29:20, 30:10; cf. Josh 23:6; Lemaire and Durand 1984; Otto 2000a). The author of the additional remark in 2 Kgs 23:25 indicates accordingly that the *sēper* was of Mosaic origin.[14] For the continuation of teaching according to the revelation from Mount Horeb, the Deuteronomists seem to put all their hopes on continual prophetic revelation in accordance with the teaching of Moses, when they write in the words of Moses himself: "YHWH your God will

---

12. On this text's being part of a pentateuchal redaction, see Otto 1996: esp. pp. 76–78; Ska 1996; Achenbach 2003: 55–58.

13. Lemaire and Durand 1984: 113–31. For further treatment of the Deuteronomistic context, see Otto 2000a: 181 n. 125.

14. For the secondary character of 2 Kgs 23:25, see Knoppers 1994: 218–19.

raise up for you a prophet like me from among your own brothers" (Deut 18:15).[15]

Inside Deuteronomy there is another layer in which the word *torah* refers to the oral *torah* that the Levitical priests were obliged to give those who asked for instruction at the central sanctuary (Deut 17:8–13*, secondary v. 9a + *hakkōhănîm hallěwîyim wě-*, 10, 11a). The basic Deuteronomic layer of this text mentioned only the local judge, *šōpēṭ*. Additionally, for ordeals involving more-complex issues, it mentioned "the priest in service" (v. 12; Gertz 1994: 59–72). The construct of Levitical priesthood is post-Deuteronomistic and belongs to a Hexateuchal layer of the narrative in Exod 32:25–29, Deut 10:8–9. So in Deut 31:9–12, the post-Deuteronomistic redactor of the Hexateuch consequently seems to stand in one line with the secondary layer in Deut 17:8–13*, where it says that Moses wrote down "this law," that is, Deuteronomy, and gave it to the priests from the "sons of Levi" who carried the ark of the covenant of YHWH and to the elders of Israel. If there ever is a king elected in Israel, this book should be given to him for his permanent study (Deut 17:18–19). Joshua has to write it on stones after Israel has entered the Promised Land (Deut 27:3, 8, 26), and he does so in the presence of the Levitical priests (Josh 8:31, 32, 34). The admonitions of Moses in the late Deuteronomistic layers to observe the words of this *torah* (Deut 28:58, 61; 29:21, 29; and 30:10), which have an echo in the farewell speech of Joshua (Josh 23:6), are included in the picture of the written Law, which later is transmitted in the frame of the Hexateuchal redaction.

The redactor of the Hexateuch seems to have the idea that the law code in the version owned by Joshua was the one in which he included even the story of the last covenantal act in Josh 24:26. The narrative concept of this redactional layer finds no continuation in the books of Judges, Samuel, and Kings; nowhere do we find any indication that there was any continuation of the Levitical priestly tradition of the *torah*. After Joshua's death according to Judg 2:10–12, and 3:7, the Israelites forgot everything. The redactor of the Hexateuch simply accepted this view, so there was no need for him to continue the story of the Levitical law code in the following books. The story of the Hexateuch was a salvation story at last, which included everything necessary for Israel's existence in the Promised Land. What followed in the times of Judges and Kings was almost entirely a history of disobedience and decline.

---

15. For the late Deuteronomistic origin of this concept, see Preuss 1982: 138.

The pentateuchal redactor seems to have believed that there was an exemplar of the *torah* of Moses put beside the ark (Deut 31:24–27), which later could be "be found again" by chance in the temple (2 Kings 22). He already has a different view of the priestly institutions, differentiating between the priests as *clerus maior* and the Levites as *clerus minor* (Deut 32:25). Principally, it is in the blessing of Moses that he stresses that it will be the task of the priests to teach Israel the *torah* (Deut 33:4, 10). Additionally, he now also understands the teaching of Moses, including his prophetic poetry in Deuteronomy 32, to be included in the *torah* (Deut 32:44–47), and a later revision of the book of Joshua says that Joshua carefully acted in accordance with this *torah* (Josh 1:7–8, 22:5).

If we look for further evidence of the use of the term *torah* in the Pentateuch, the first samples in Genesis are, in some sense, anachronistic. In Gen 26:5, YHWH states that "Abraham obeyed my voice and kept my requirements, my commandments, my statutes, and my instructions" (*mišmartay miṣwôtay ḥuqqôtay wĕtôrōtay*). The text implies an unmediated instruction of Abraham and thus draws a parallel between the forefather and Moses. Abraham himself is called a "prophet" by YHWH (Gen 20:7). Gen 26:5 is part of a pentateuchal redaction. The next person who receives instructions from YHWH called *torah* is Moses himself, in Exod 12:49. There, in accordance with stipulations in the Holiness Code (Lev 19:34, 24:22), it states that there can only be one *torah* concerning Passover for the native and for the alien. According to Exod 16:4b, it is assumed that Israel already knows YHWH's *torah* concerning the Sabbath (see 16:28). The author obviously refers back to Exod 15:24b, 25, which states that Moses already gave instructions to Israel during their wandering through the desert. In an additional note or *Fortschreibung* to Exod 18:16b, 19–20, which (together with v. 15b) interrupts the original narrative (18:15a . . . 16a, 17–18, 21–26) and is not even considered in the parallel (Deut 1:9–18*), there is a description that gives us an impression of the concept of the redactors: before Moses received the written *torah* from YHWH, he had to ask for heavenly oracles and instruction, which he then made known to the people.

This issue is resolved in Exod 24:12b: YHWH gives Moses written instruction containing the *torah* and the *miṣwah* in order to teach the people. At the end of the Holiness Code in Lev 26:46, it becomes obvious that the revelation from Sinai contained in Exodus 25–Leviticus 26 is considered by the author to be the content of the *torah*, which Moses received on the mountain according to Exod 24:12b. Inside this corpus, the word only refers to priestly instruction in the latest Priestly layers (Lev 6:14, 25; 7:1, 7, 11, 37; 11:46; 12:7; 13:59; 14:2, 32, 54, 57; 15:32; Nihan 2005: 249–83). They may come from Priestly collections from the early Second Temple period, which existed beside the Hexateuch and which now are incorporated in the wider frame of the Mosaic *torah*. They are supplied in even later instructions, which are thought to come from later revelations in the *'ōhel mô'ēd* (Num 1:1 → Num 5:29, 30; 6:13, 21; 15:16, 29; 19:2, 14). They can later on be transmitted by the high priest (Num 31:21). From Deut 1:5 it becomes evident that the redactor, who wanted to clarify where in the Pentateuch the *torah* of Moses is included, understood the book of Deuteronomy as a Mosaic explanation of the meaning and impact of the older revelation (cf. Deut 4:8, 44).

To conclude, we do not have the same horizon of understanding in all cases in which *torah* is mentioned in Deuteronomy. First, there is a Deuteronomistic layer in Deuteronomy 28 in which *torah* is connected to the idea of the written document of a treaty, Deut 28:58: *kol-dibrê hattôrâ hazzō't hakkĕtûbîm bassēper hazzeh* (cf. 28:61: *sēper hattôrâ hazzō't*). This document makes sure that the regulations and commandments of the ancient law code are accepted as part of a covenant from ancient times at Mount Horeb and that Moses was a prophetic mediator (Deut 18:15–18). The concept of the *sēper hattôrâ* was accepted by later Deuteronomists (Deuteronomy 29–30; Joshua 23). Second, there is a layer belonging to a Hexateuchal redaction in Deut 17:8–13*, 18–19; 27:3, 8, 26; 31:9–12; Josh 8:31, 32, 34; 24:26*. This layer includes the late Deuteronomistic idea of the prophetic character of Moses in Deut 18:15–18. Third, there is a layer belonging to the pentateuchal redaction that combines the concept of *torah* with the Priestly sacral regulations and the Holiness Code. Following Exod 24:12b, the Holiness Code and Deuteronomy are both related to Yhwh's revelation to Moses and, with that, the Mosaic *torah* resumes in Exodus 25–Deuteronomy 33 (cf. Lev 26:46; Deut 1:5; 4:8, 44; 31:24ff.; 33:4, 10). By introducing the book of Deuteronomy as teachings in order to explain the *torah* of Yhwh, its *torah* and *miṣwah* are connected to the revelation from Sinai in Exod 24:12b (cf. Deut 4:44, 6:1, 33:2). This redaction led to some revision in the form of later theocratizing additions in Josh 1:7–8 and 22:5. The authors wanted to confirm that Joshua acted under the guidance of Eleazar, the high priest (cf. Num 27:18–23; Deut 34:9; Josh 14:1, 19:51, 24:33).

All other texts in which the *torah* is mentioned can be harmonized with these explanations by means of complementary readings of the different layers: the *torah* found during the reign of Josiah can be identified with the *torah* of Moses, and the *torah* at the time of Ezra (Neh 8:8) can be connected to the tradition of the exemplar that Joshua wrote for the use far from the sanctuary (Josh 24:26, looking back to Josh 8:30–35). So the later redactors were acutely aware of the existence of different written versions of the *torah*. At any rate, for the redactor of the Pentateuch there seemed to be a certain responsibility for the high priests as the successors of Aaron to teach the Mosaic *torah* and to enact control over all further revelation. Obviously, the redactional ending of Deut 34:10–12 has a programmatic impact on the transmission of prophetic texts. So Otto (2000a: 232) rightly states: "Mit Moses Tod ist eine Epoche der Offenbarung zu Ende gegangen, die so keine Fortsetzung finden wird. . . . Wenn nach Moses Tod kein Prophet mehr sein wird wie er, so wird der Pentateuch von dem sich formierenden Propheten-kanon unter Einschluß der Vorderen Propheten als mit besonderer Dignität und Präferenz ausgestattet abgehoben." For the pentateuchal redactor, the immediate vision of YHWH gives Moses a legitimation above every other prophetic (or Priestly) revelation (Num 12:6–8).

According to the pentateuchal redactor, the privilege of the transmission and interpretation of *torah* is handed over to Aaron and the institution of the high priest. All rewritings of the Pentateuch that followed this redaction during several phases of theocratic editions, especially in the book of Numbers, accepted this hierocratic concept. They stated that those who had the task of implementing the requirements of the *torah* were obliged to act in accordance with the spiritual authorization of Moses (cf. Num 27:15–23, Deut 34:9). The story of the 70 elders in Num 11:24–30 has a double function in that context. First, the "prophetic spirit" is connected with an ideal institution. Second, the prophetic spirit, as marked by Moses, may come over all the people of Israel (Num 11:29)! There remains no place for a prophecy that is independent of the control of hierocratically and theocratically minded institutions. The redactional inclusio formed by Mal 3:22–24 and Josh 1:7 (Steck 1991a: 134–35; Nogalski 1993: 241–43; Hengel 1994: 19) is a milestone of canonical formation at the end of a process of rewriting that begins with the pentateuchal redaction (around 400 B.C.E.) and sets a frame that is not only formative for the theocratic rewritings in the Pentateuch but is also a prerequisite for the late eschatological rewritings in the Prophets during the fourth century B.C.E. and, possibly, even somewhat later, during Ptolemaic times.[16]

---

16. See Steck 1991a: 26–55, esp. on Zechariah 9–14.

The Prophets and the Pentateuch as Torah

Former Prophets

If we look at the references to *torah* in the Former Prophets, we find a complementary picture. The Mosaic *torah* is not mentioned in the books of Judges and Samuel![17] The narration of the Hexateuch redaction has not been continued throughout the books of the "Enneateuch"! Instead, we find some references to *torah* in Kings in which it is not easy to distinguish between late Deuteronomistic and post-Deuteronomistic references. It seems that there is no clear system behind these references to the *torah* in Kings. David's testament in 1 Kgs 2:3 must be considered post-Deuteronomistic, because it is not at all clear how David would have known the *torah*, which he refers to as "His statutes, His commandments, His ordinances, and His testimonies, as it is written in the *torah* of Moses." The same may also be said about 2 Kgs 10:30–31 and 2 Kgs 14:6. 2 Kgs 10:30 mentions a prophetic word of YHWH for Jehu with the promise of the throne of Israel, but v. 31 explains why it was not fulfilled: "Jehu was not careful to follow the *torah* of YHWH, the God of Israel, with all his heart." 2 Kgs 14:6 says that Amaziah did not kill the sons of the assassins, according to the *sēper tôrat-Mōšeh*, in which YHWH commanded that the parents shall not be put to death for the children and vice versa. (Deut 24:16). According to 2 Kgs 21:7–8, Manasseh took the carved Asherah pole that he had made and put it in the temple, of which YHWH had said to David and to his son Solomon: "In this temple and in Jerusalem, which I have chosen . . . I will not again make the feet of the Israelites wander from the land I gave to their forefathers, if only they will be careful to do everything I commanded them and keep the whole *torah*, which my servant Moses commanded them." All the passages that are consistent with Judg 2:6–12 should be understood as referring to a forgotten *torah* from the time of Moses and Joshua, or—eventually, in 2 Kgs 10:31—to a prophetic *torah*. They seem to be secondary additions, not by means of a systematic reworking or editing of the Deuteronomistic texts, but by means of occasional interpolations by later editors. That the *torah* found in the temple was identical with a *torah* of Moses is not mentioned in the basic layers of the story (2 Kgs 22:8, 11, 24) but only in an addition at the end (2 Kgs 23:25)!

---

17. That YHWH even gave *torah* through the prophet Nathan is stated in 2 Sam 7:19. But this *torah* is explicitly called *tôrat hāʾādām* 'torah of man'!

Compared with this late Deuteronomistic layer, there is a secondary layer in 2 Kgs 17:13–17*.[18] Developing lines of research from the works of Steck and Smend, Maier has argued that the concept of prophetic warnings in 2 Kgs 17:13–17, and 20 is secondary within the Deuteronomistic context of the chapter and might even be dated to postexilic times,[19] because it already presupposes the connection between a written form of *torah* and covenant theology.[20] The prophets are described as those who persistently held the people accountable for remembering the *torah* and the commandments. 2 Kgs 17:13 reads, "YHWH warned Israel and Judah by every prophet and every seer, saying: 'Turn from your evil ways and keep my commandments and my statutes, in accordance with all the *torah* that I commanded your ancestors and that I sent to you by my servants the prophets.'" The passage ends with the statement (v. 23) "until YHWH removed them from his presence, as he had warned through all his servants, the prophets. So the people of Israel were taken from their homeland into exile in Assyria, and they are still there." This accords with the expectations as laid out in Deut 18:15, 18—that, after the time of Moses, God would send prophets to teach the word of YHWH. The redactor of the Hexateuch shared this view. Evidence for this idea is mainly found outside the Deuteronomistic History, especially in the book of Jeremiah (Chiesa 1973: 17–26).

But there is even a third layer of 2 Kgs 17:34–39*, in which the people in the province of Samaria are blamed for not observing the *torah* that YHWH wrote (v. 37). This refers back to Exod 24:12b and clearly is connected with the view of the pentateuchal redactor, who by this addition legitimizes the canonical shape of the law codes (that is, the Holiness Code and Deuteronomistic Deuteronomy; Achenbach 2005a). Braulik (2004) has shown that Exod 24:12b is reflected in Josh 22:5 and in 2 Kgs 17:34, 37, and that the same verbiage is continued only in Chronicles (2 Chr 14:3, 31:21). According to this layer, there exists only one *torah*, the *torah* of Moses, and this *torah* comes from YHWH himself.

---

18. The literary history of 2 Kings 17 is complex; for the possibility that 2 Kgs 17:7aβ–17 is an addition, see McKenzie 1991: 140–42, 152; Knoppers 1994: 64 n. 36.

19. Maier (2002: 135, 149–57, 361) shows that 2 Kgs 17:13ff. do not represent *the* Deuteronomistic concept of prophets as surmised by Steck (1967) but a very late, Deuteronomistic-influenced addition, which to her mind could be even later than the redactional reworking of Jer 25:5, 35:15, 44:5.

20. See Maier 2002: 149–50. Once this view was established as an interpretation of the function of the prophets in general, it could also be applied in the composition of later texts. In this context, see Zech 1:4–6; 7:7, 12; 2 Chr 36:14–26; Neh 9:26, 30 (see Steck 1967: 60–64, 70–72).

The Samarian people are blamed for syncretism (2 Kgs 17:34): "To this day they continue to practice their former customs. They do not worship YHWH and they do not follow the statutes and the ordinances and the *torah* and the commandment that YHWH commanded the children of Jacob, whom he named Israel" (cf. Gen 32:29). 2 Kgs 17:35–39 hints at the first covenant, and the parenesis in v. 37 speaks about "the statutes and the ordinances and the *torah* and the commandment that he (!) wrote for you, you shall always be careful to observe."[21] *Torah* here is part of the divine teachings of commandments, which YHWH himself wrote for Israel (v. 37)! So it is obvious that in 2 Kgs 17:34–40 we have a different layer from the layer in vv. 13–23. The text states that only those who behave according to YHWH's laws and commandments have the right to refer to Jacob-Israel's heritage. The people from Samaria are not considered to be part of this group. The text reflects a stage in the tradition that lies after the time of Nehemiah. There is only one place in the Pentateuch in which YHWH himself writes the *torah*; that is Exod 24:12b (Pentateuch redaction). The addition here seems to date to an even later time and belongs, therefore, to the theocratic revisions of the book of Kings in the fourth century B.C.E.

In conclusion, several layers can be distinguished concerning the mention of *torah* in the Former Prophets in relation to the layers in the Pentateuch: (1) a late Deuteronomistic phase in the second half of the sixth century B.C.E., which interprets the Deuteronomistic Deuteronomy as a document of a covenant saying that the *torah* was derived from Moses; (2) a post-Deuteronomistic phase in the first half of the fifth century B.C.E. in which the concept of 2 Kgs 17:13 that YHWH had sent the prophets to warn the people and to demand that they follow the *torah* of YHWH is connected with the expectation that there would come a prophet like Moses (according to Deut 18:15), who could teach the people the *torah*. This phase is completed by the Hexateuch redaction, saying that *torah* was passed on to Levitical priests and to Joshua; (3) a phase of the development of Priestly regulations and the Pentateuch (second half of the fifth century B.C.E.) and, around the time of Ezra, the pentateuchal redaction, saying that the Mosaic *torah* went back to the scripture of YHWH from Sinai (Exod 24:12b). It contained Exodus 25–Leviticus 26. There was an increasing influence by hierocratic priests on the transmission of scripture during the post-Ezra period (fourth century B.C.E.). The more the pentateuchal text was can-

---

21. The story in Exod 18:12–26 has been reworked according to the example of Deut 17:8–13 in Exod 18:15b, 16b, 19–20.

onized, the more the text of Samuel and Kings became fluent. Theocratic revisions introduced an anti-Samarian critique in 2 Kgs 17:34, 37, and their authors were also interested in the reworking of 1 Kings 6–8, the section dealing with the temple construction.

The Book of Jeremiah

It seems that in the redactional layers of the prophetic writings, once the prophetic oracles had been collected and had undergone written transmission,[22] a corresponding development in the redaction history of the Pentateuch and the Former Prophets transpired. One indication of this is the use of the term *torah*—a correlation with the late Deuteronomistic and post-Deuteronomistic layers in the prophetic books. For the fourth century B.C.E., we should look at the instances in which the concept of pentateuchal redaction may have already influenced the formation of prophetic literature.

The book of Jeremiah went through several stages of growth.[23] When there was still a Deuteronomistic influence on the editors of the book, the prophet appears as one of the prophets who, according to 2 Kgs 17:13, had warned Judah (Jer 7:13, 11:7, 25:3). The phrase "his/my servants the prophets" appears with some regularity in the Deuteronomistic layers of Kings and Jeremiah.[24] In the next phase of redaction, Jeremiah himself appears as a teacher of *torah* in succession to Moses.[25] In her study of Jeremiah, Maier finds several layers of references to *torah* in the book.[26] There is no reference in the original Jeremiah to any

---

22. Jeremias (1981: specifically, p. 93) argues: "es geht im Prozeß der Überlieferung und auch der schriftlichen Niederlegung . . . die geschichtliche Stunde der Ursprungssituation (scil. des Prophetenwortes) . . . nicht verloren; sie wird vielmehr beharrlich festgehalten als ein unverlierbares Wesensmerkmal des prophetischen Wortes. Aber sie enthält eine neue Funktion. Sie bleibt nicht länger alleiniger Zielpunkt des Wortes, sondern erhält Modellcharakter, wird zur Trägerin von grundsätzlichen Erkenntnissen über das Verhältnis Gott—Mensch, die auf andere geschichtliche Situationen übertragbar sind."

23. There are a lot of different suggestions for explaining the final shape of the book; see the discussion of Albertz (2001: 231–59), who surmises three stages of Deuteronomistic redaction by the end of the sixth century, a small layer of later additions during the fifth century, and many late additions during the fourth century B.C.E.

24. See 2 Kgs 17:13, 23; 21:10; 24:2b (cf. 1 Kgs 14:18; 2 Kgs 9:7, 14:25) and Jer 7:25, 25:4, 26:5, 29:19, 35:15, 44:4. Blenkinsopp (1977: 101) states: "The phrase, 'his servants the prophets,' which occurs with some regularity in Deuteronomic material of the exilic age and expecially in the Jeremian C source, suggests that for the first time the prophets were being viewed as a series, and that therefore, by implication, prophecy was beginning to be seen as essentially a past phenomenon."

25. According to Albertz (2001: 250–52) this is a secondary Deuteronomistic phase.

26. See Maier 2002: 282–352. The main problem with her analysis is the rather vague concept of what should be called "Deuteronomistic." But if there are not only

torah. But already in the beginning of the book in Jer 1:9b the prophet is depicted as a person according to the promise of Deut 18:18 (*nābî' 'āqîm lāhem miqqereb 'ăḥêhem kāmôkā wĕnātattî dĕbāray bĕpîw wĕdibber 'ălêhem 'ēt kol-'ăšer 'ăṣannenû*) → Jer 1:9, *wayyišlaḥ Yhwh 'et-yādô wayyagaʿ ʿal-pî wayyōmer Yhwh 'elay hinnēh nātattî dĕbāray bĕpîkā*.[27] The text refers to Yʜᴡʜ's *torah* as it was given by Moses. Correspondingly, we read in Jer 26:4: "You shall say to them: 'Thus says Yʜᴡʜ: If you will not listen to me, to walk in my *torah* which I have set before you'" (*bĕtôrātî 'ăšer nātattî lipnêkem*). In Jer 26:5, 7, 10–16, the prophet is described as a teacher of the *torah* and mediator according to the expectations of Deut 18:15, 18. Hossfeld has noted that in Jeremiah 26 there is also a connection with Deut 18:20. The account of Jeremiah 26 was on "ein 'Lehrzuchtverfahren,' bei dem sich im Sinne von Deut 18:20 ein Prophet vor einem Gericht gegen den Verdacht der Vermessenheit zu verteidigen hatte und bei dem damit die Echtheit seiner Botschaft festgestellt werden sollte" (Hossfeldt and Meyer 1974: 8; cf. Rüterswörden 1991: 329–30). The prophet is portrayed in accordance with the measures found in Deut 18:22.

All other references to *torah* in Jeremiah seem to be no older than this concept—that is, Jer 2:8; 6:19; 8:8; 9:12; 16:11; 18:18; 31:33; 32:23; 44:10, 23—although it is not easy to say, in all cases, whether the texts refer to a complete edition of the Pentateuch or to an earlier stage of that work.[28] Jer 2:8 ("The priests did not say, 'Where is Yʜᴡʜ?' Those who handle the *torah* did not know me; the rulers transgressed against me, the prophets prophesied by Baal") can be connected to a layer, which Maier (2002: 354) assumes is "late exilic," but it may be even later. This text considers the teaching of *torah* to be the task of priests, who rely upon a written collection of texts (Maier 2002: 282–98, 310–11; G. Fischer 2005: 159). The opposition is said to have stated the opposite position: "Then they said, Come, let us make plots against Jeremiah,

---

Deuteronomistic but also post-Deuteronomistic stages of redaction in the Hexateuch and the Pentateuch, these stages must also be considered in relating terms and concepts in the prophets to Hexateuchal and pentateuchal or Enneateuchal texts. So, even after the publication of Maier's detailed analysis, there remains the need for further investigation.

27. See Thiel 1973: 67; Herrmann 1986: 65ff.; Rüterswörden 1991 (esp. p. 330); Otto 2000a: 208. For further literature and discussion, see G. Fischer (2005: 135-36), who even reads the text in congruity with Deut 34:10–12, a text that must be interpreted as a reaction against the tendency to put Jeremiah over the Torah of Moses! It is not clear why Jer 1:9 is not discussed extensively by Maier.

28. G. Fischer (2005: 275, 335) leaves the question open for Jer 6:19 but surmises that already in Jer 8:8 *torah* means the books of Genesis through Deuteronomy.

for *torah* shall not perish from the priest, nor counsel from the wise, nor the word from the prophet. Come, let us bring charges against him, and let us not heed any of his words" (Jer 18:18). Jeremiah seems to be interpreted by the redactors according to the views of the Hexateuch redaction. From their perspective, the teaching of *torah* was a priestly task (Deut 17:9–11) supported by the prophetic mediator Moses. According to Deut 18:15–18 the prophet himself exhibits the features of a teacher of *torah* (for example, the sermon on keeping the Sabbath holy in Jer 17:19–27; cf. Neh 13:15–22).[29] The *torah* the prophet teaches is, according to Jeremiah 7, an explanation of Hexateuchal Law (Covenant Code and Deuteronomy). Although Jeremiah is not a lawgiver, he is teaching the *torah* according to YHWH's *torah*.

After the redactor of the Pentateuch had promoted the priority of the Mosaic *torah*, Jeremiah was understood as someone who demanded that the people keep YHWH's *torah* in the form of the Pentateuch (Jer 9:12; 16:11; 32:23; 44:10, 23) and who blamed the priests and scribes for not handling the *torah* correctly—or even for turning it into lies (Jer 8:8; cf. 2:8, 18:18). The interpretation of the disaster that fell on Israel is now related to YHWH's *torah*: "Because they have rejected my *torah*" (Jer 6:19). In Jer 9:12 this interpretation refers to Deut 4:8–10. This text already recognizes the *torah* as part of the entire Pentateuch and criticizes the misguided instruction of Israel.[30] The renewal of the covenant accordingly cannot follow a traditional Deuteronomistic ritual of covenant renewal. The only chance is if God himself changes the hearts of the people to act according to the (entire) *torah* (Jer 31:31–34). Jer 31:33 takes up a line of covenant theology that had its origins in Deuteronomistic texts (Deut 29:3, 30:6) and that then was continued by the Pentateuch redactor in Lev 26:41 (cf. Jer 9:25) and Deut 31:21. Traces of this idea are to be found in Jer 24:7, 31:33, 32:39–40, and in Ezek 11:19, 36:26–27. The renewal of Israelite hearts to enable the people to fulfill the *torah* seems to be a theme of the prophetic styling of texts in the latest phase of redaction. This is the reason why in certain expansions in Jeremiah we find the concept of a "New Covenant" for the postexilic

---

29. Maier (2002: 356–59) adds Jer 7:1–8:3, 11:1–14, 22:1–5, 34:8–22; cf. Neh 5:1–13. The texts cannot be discussed here. According to the divergent analyses of Levin (1985), Albertz (2001: 231–60), Stipp (1995: 225–62), and others, they may belong to different layers of the book.

30. See G. Fischer, 2005: 357. There are passages in Jeremiah in which, according to Fishbane (1989: 12–14), there are exegetical transformations of texts from different layers of the Pentateuch. These are post-Pentateuch redactional in nature. See Jer 2:3 in connection with Exod 19:5–6, Deut 7:6, Lev 22:14–16.

Jewish community (Jer 31:31–34, 34:12–17).[31] The prophecy of Moses, according to the pentateuchal redaction, already knows everything about the coming violation of the covenant (cf. Lev 26:15–45, Deut 4:25–31). The redactor who reworked the message of Jeremiah may have protested against this fixation on covenant theology from a spiritual point of view (Jer 31:31–34; Otto 2000a: 232 n. 316), but even according to this prophecy the only proper contents of the law can be the law as it was defined by the authors of the Mosaic *torah*. The conversion of former *torah* teaching into "prophetic" teaching must come from God's own inspiration (Krüger 1997).

When, during the last phase of transmission, hierocratic and theocratic thought and the Priestly interpretation of Mosaic *torah* prevailed over the prophetic tradition, the editing of prophetic texts turned to eschatological issues. Therefore, the latest texts in the editing of Jeremiah from the fourth and third century B.C.E. treat matters that can be read as an addition to the prophetic visions of the Pentateuch but not as the continuation of a revelation of *torah* to the prophets. The universal perspective of the Pentateuch is brought into the sphere of the conversion of the peoples and of prophetic wisdom teachings.[32]

The Book of Isaiah

There is no trace of a connection between Isaiah and the *torah* in the oldest layers of the book. Where the term first appears, it seems to be influenced by Deuteronomistic teaching. Isaiah is also depicted as one who warns the rebellious people (Isa 30:9; cf. Isa 5:24).[33] These texts are

---

31. Otto (2002: esp. pp. 76–77) states with respect to Jer 31:31–34: "Jer 31,31–34 ist der schärfste Gegentext in der Hebräischen Bibel zu dem postdtr Kapitel Dtn 31, das in der Hexateuchredaktion Gelenkfunktion und in der Überarbeitung durch die Pentateuchredaktion Abschlußfunktion hat. Jer 31,31–34 wendet sich nicht nur gegen die mosaische Verschriftung der Tora (Dtn 31,9), sondern auch gegen die Belehrung 'der Kleinen durch die Großen' (Dtn 31,12). Damit abrogiert Jer 31,31–34 ... nicht nur die Verschriftungs- und Belehrungstheorie der Pentateuchredaktion der Tora, sondern vor allem ihre an Mose gebundene Offenbarungstheorie."

32. For the latest layers in Jeremiah, see for example, Jer 3:16–18; 9:22–23, 24–25; 10:1–16; 12:12*; 15:21; 16:14–15, 19–21; 17:5–13; 25:9–34*; chap. 33.

33. For the late dating of these words, see Becker 1997: 142–43, 251–57. In Isa 30:8–9 the prophet is asked to write down the words of judgment on a tablet or on a *sēper ḥuqqâ* so that they can be read in later times. The ancient generation is criticized in Isa 30:9: "For they are a rebellious people, faithless children, children who will not hear the *torah* of YHWH." Here, it seems, the prophet is considered not the immediate mediator of prophetic *torah* but someone whose words are meant to lead the people to follow the ways of the written *torah*, which was the *torah* of YHWH and which was given by the mediation of Moses. For a similar case, see Isa 5:24b.

partly influenced by the redactional combination of Isaianic oracles with the Deuteronomistic History in Isaiah 36–39* and clearly represent a post-Deuteronomistic layer of redaction by redactors close to the ideas of the Hexateuch redaction and the post-Deuteronomistic redactions in Jeremiah.

In Deutero-Isaiah, the task of teaching *torah* is handed over to the Servant of YHWH. Note, for example, Isa 42:4: "He will not grow faint or be crushed until he has established justice on earth and the coastlands wait for his *torah*!" (see also Isa 42:19, 21, 24; 51:4, 7). After kingship was not reestablished under Zerubbabel and the title of YHWH's Messiah was handed to the Persian Great King Cyrus, the idea that Moses (and also his successor, Joshua) was an *'ebed* YHWH was established in the Hexateuch. This means that the head or leader of Jacob/Israel, who was going to lead the people in the Mosaic succession, was obliged to fit the image of the Servant of YHWH in continuation of a prophetic and Mosaic spirit. This Servant was said to be elected as the latest of the Davidic dynasty, installed by the spirit of YHWH, and expected to teach the law of YHWH to the peoples of the earth (Isa 42:1). At the same time, this servant represents Israel; thus, Israel itself can be seen in the tradition of being the Servant of YHWH—although disobedient to the *torah*. Thus, in Isa 42:21, 24, we read: "YHWH is pleased for the sake of his righteousness to make the *torah* great and glorious. . . . Is it not YHWH, against whom we have sinned? For they would not follow his ways, they did not obey his *torah*." YHWH himself, after he has established the idea of the *'ebed* YHWH, lets the prophet issue the self-proclamation of the Servant in Isa 51:4, 7: "Listen to me, my people . . . for *torah* will go out from me, and my justice for a light to the peoples. . . . Listen to me, you who know righteousness, you people who have my teaching in your hearts; do not fear the reproach of others, and do not be dismayed when they revile you!" The idea of the universal validity and meaning of *torah* is now established, even among the people of the *gôlâ*.

This layer seems to pick up late Deuteronomistic concepts of the prophets and their followers as servants of YHWH (cf. 2 Kgs 9:7, 10:23; cf. Isa 54:17). In the Hexateuchal layers, it is Moses who represents "the Servant of YHWH" (cf. Deut 34:5; Josh 1:1, 13, 15; 8:31, 33; 11:12; 13:8; 14:7; 24:29; secondary in Judg 2:8, 2 Kgs 18:12). Once this Hexateuchal view of Moses as the Servant of YHWH was established, he was considered to be the main, the outstanding prophet. All other prophets could only be successors, and all Israelites believing in YHWH's *torah* and the prophets could be called "Servants of YHWH" (2 Kgs 9:7, Isa 54:17).[34]

In the late redactional layers of the book of Isaiah, the prophet is generally described as a teacher of YHWH's *torah* (cf. Isa 1:10, "Hear the Word of YHWH, you rulers of Sodom! Listen to the *torah* of our God, you people of Gomorrah!"). The oracles of the prophet himself are interpreted as containing *torah* or as a "seal" of the *torah*, as it says in Isa 8:16, 20. Isa 1:10–17 belongs to the latest, postexilic and post-Deuteronomistic layers in the frame of the book and is part of its redactional introduction, which according to the analysis of Becker (1997: 176–99) and others treats a "theology of disobedience."[35] The prophet in a liturgically styled lawsuit before God passes the *torah* of God to the rulers and the people of Jerusalem, showing their disobedience. There are several indications that the text of Isa 1:2–20 refers back to the text of blessings and curses at the end of the law codes in the Mosaic *torah* (cf. Isa 1:2a; Deut 32:1, 30:19; Isa 1:7 // Lev 26:33; Deut 28:51, 29:22). Israel is compared with the disobedient son (cf. Isa 1:2–3; Deut 21:18–21; 32:1, 5–6; cf. Isa 1:4–6; Deut 28:35, 29:21; cf. Jer 5:3, 8:18) and Jerusalem is addressed as "Sodom and Gomorrah" (cf. Isa 1:7b, 9; Deut 29:22; Isa 1:5b//Deut 29:21; Berges 1998: 56–68). The authors present Isaiah as a man actualizing the Mosaic *torah* (Lohfink 1994: esp. p. 46). They want to address their audience by using the 1st-plural "we" in connection with the idea of the group of the holy remnant (Isa 1:8–9) that is living in the ruins of Jerusalem and in the surroundings of Mount Zion (Berges 1998: 64–65).

The *torah* is dealing with two questions. First, is there any meaning in the multitude of offerings (Isa 1:11)? Second, is there any meaning in visiting the temple so often (v. 12)? The answer to both is that there is not. This is explained in a negative way in vv. 13–15, and positively with nine imperatives in vv. 16–17: "Wash yourselves! Make your-

---

34. The context could be extended to include David and the Davidic kings (Ps 18:1, 36:1, 89:21). For later use, see Ps 113:1, 134:1, 135:1. In this context, for Moses as Servant, see 2 Chr 1:3, 24:6. There are interdependent relations between the text of the Hexateuch redactor (who reacts to prophetic kerygma and prophetic texts) and later texts (which react to the concept of the Hexateuch's redactor). See Isa 50:2* → Num 11:23 → Isa 59:1; and see Achenbach 2003: 229–30, 261–62.

35. For more analyses that show the redactional character of the chapter, see Vermeylen (1977: 42–70, 108ff.), who considers the text to be a "résumé-programme de la doctrine du prophète" within a Deuteronomistic edition. See also Barth (1977: 217–20), who looks at the text as a redactional work from exilic times and Werner (1986: 126–33), who surmises a composition of a postexilic redactor. Beuken (2003: 66–87, esp. 69) assumes a redaction dating approximately to the time of Nehemiah.

selves clean! Take your evil deeds out of my sight! Stop doing wrong! Learn to do right! Seek justice! Encourage the oppressed! Defend the cause of the fatherless! Plead the case of the widow!" This *torah* does not question the existence of a Mosaic *torah* at all; it is demanding cleanliness and purification in a ritual and judicial sense by demanding justice within social contexts. In its conclusion, the text presents two ways: the way of repentance and forgiveness and the way of rebellion and punishment. The late redactors of the Pentateuch also ascribed these motifs to the teaching of the "prophet" Moses (cf. Deut 11:26ff., 30:11–20; Lev 26:14–33). It was shown by Steck and others that there are many thematic links between Isa 1:2–20 and Isa 56:1–8, 58:1–14, and 66:1–6 that show a connection to a certain context of tradition (Steck 1991b: esp. p. 265; Vermeylen 1978: 464–65; Loretz 1984: 120; Tomasin 1993: esp. pp. 86–88). The redactors are concerned with the theme of conversion and return to Zion, and Steck called the layers that are connected with this issue an *Umkehr-Redaktion* (see also 1:27–28, 56:9–59:21).[36] We cannot discuss extensively the complicated matters of redaction here. It must be sufficient to note that there are certain redactional features in the book of Isaiah from postexilic times around the era of Nehemiah and later that refer to the prophet as a teacher of *torah* in line with the Mosaic teaching.[37]

The more the texts of the Pentateuch became canonical, the more the discussions on *torah* matters were introduced into prophetic scriptures. In Isa 8:16 ("Bind up the testimony, seal [it] up *as torah* among my disciples") the teaching of Isaiah is understood as containing *torah* of YHWH, which must be sealed to remain unchanged until it is fulfilled. The text is at a later time connected to the admonition in vv. 19–20: "When men tell you to consult mediums and spiritists, . . . to the *torah* and to the testimony! If they do not speak according to this word, they have no light of dawn!" On the one hand, the text first seems to understand prophetic teaching as *torah*. On the other hand, it seems to use the prophetic *torah* as a measure for the inspiration of all other divination in general. In the latter case, the words of the prophet serve as a source of really inspired prophecy, to which all other divination must

---

36. See Steck 1991b: 192. Berges (1998: 71–72) wants to connect Isa 2:2–4 with the same redactional layer. Becker (1997: 195) does not share this view: vv. 27–28 seem to interrupt the linkage between 1:21–26 and 2:2–4.

37. Sweeney (1996: esp. p. 63) shows that, although the places in which *torah* is mentioned in Isaiah belong to different literary layers, it seems possible with a complementary hermeneutical reading to integrate these texts into one teaching, identifying *torah* as "the teaching of YHWH, expressed by the prophet."

adjust. The line in v. 16: (*ṣôr tĕʿûdâ ḥătôm tôrâ*) is inverted in v. 20 (*lĕtôrâ wĕlitʿûdâ*) and in this way the prophetic testimony serves as *torah*.[38] It seems that, from the time of this text on, the message of the book was understood as part of prophetic teaching to a certain circle of scribes and "disciples," so that here we have one of the oldest pieces of evidence for the concept of a prophetic *torah*-teaching.

However, Trito-Isaiah (Isaiah 56–66), who is in dialogue with matters of *torah*, does not even mention the word *torah*. But scholars have observed in these chapters further prophetic performances of *torah* teaching, which to some extent contradict the teachings of the Mosaic *torah*.[39] Isa 56:1–8 and 63:1–66:24* seem to be in conflict with the priestly authors of the Pentateuch.[40] There was, for example, a serious discussion on the status of foreigners following the interpretation of Deut 23:2–9 in Trito-Isaiah (see Isa 56:6–7). The conflict between "eschatological" and "theocratic" views among different priestly and scribal schools may have been the reason why the interpretation of the Mosaic *torah* as the only measure for true and false prophecy and revelation became increasingly strict in the redacted Pentateuch (cf. Num 11:24–30, 12:6–8; Deut 34:10–12). On the other hand, there are indications of a redactional framing of Trito-Isaiah in connection with late layers of Isaiah 1. According to observations made by U. Berges, the critical passages of Isa 1:10–17 and 1:18–20 are reflected in a redaction demanding conversion (*Umkehr-Redaktion*) in Isa 1:27–28 and 56:9–59:21 (Berges 1998: 65.463–80).

Isa 1:10–17 is followed by an even later addition in Isa 1:21–26, 2:2–5, which is part of an eschatologically oriented editorial rewriting. Here the *torah* has gained a universal status among all peoples of the world. In this last phase of redaction, the *torah* is expected to come from Zion, and now it is merely connected with priestly teaching, which integrates the prophetic impulses. *Torah* teaching has a univer-

---

38. This may be the reason why Berges (1998: 110) and Beuken (2003: 230–31) consider the text to be part of Isaiah's own text, whereas Becker (1997: 114–20) considers the verses to be redactional. The concept of combining prophetic teaching and *torah* teaching here presupposes the ideas of Deut 18:15–18 but not Deut 34:10–12.

39. See Isa 56:3, 66:21. For the special literary character of Isaiah 56–66, see Blenkinsopp 2003: 37–41 (esp. p. 37): "It is apparent that the classical prophetic genres . . . are breaking up and giving way to longer, less structured discourses." See also Wells 1996.

40. Berges (1998: 481ff.) speaks about "Die Redaktion der Knechtsgemeinde" (Isa 56:1–8, 63:1–66:24). After the Pentateuch was canonized to a certain extent by the Pentateuch redactor, a part of the discussions among scribes switched to the scriptures of the *corpus propheticum* (Otto 2002: esp. pp. 76–83, "Die postdeuteronomistische Schriftauslegung des Deuteronomiums in Nebiim und Ketubim!").

sal impact (cf. Isa 2:3, 24:5). In Isaiah, Moses is mentioned only in Isa 63:11–14, in the context of a liturgy with a community lament, recalling the remembrance of Moses' leadership and holy spirit.[41] The authors connect themselves to this idea of Mosaic spirituality, which can be traced in the layers of the theocratic reworkings of the Pentateuch (cf. Deut 34:9; Achenbach 2003: 557–67; Berges 1998: 487–88). It is obvious that these layers belong to the last phase of redaction of the book, in which the theocratic impulses of the scribes who canonized the Pentateuch heavily influenced the editors of prophetic texts. In the latest redactional layers of the book, we find the idea of *torah* teaching on Mount Zion, where it must be a Priestly teaching that is even open to foreign people. Yet, the people of the earth will be judged for having transgressed the *torah* (Isa 24:5) and for having broken the "everlasting covenant," which can only refer to Gen 9:6, 16. However, at the end there is the concept of a universal assembly of the nations on Mount Zion again (Isa 66:18–24*). Isaiah 66 binds the messages of Isaiah 1 and Isa 2:2–4 together in one text (I. Fischer 1995: 23–24). In the latest layers of the book of Isaiah, the authors have accepted the priority of the Mosaic *torah*. According to the analyses of Steck, there is still an ongoing continual process of *Fortschreibung* from the time of Alexander through the Ptolemaic period in the book of Isaiah and in the book of the Twelve Prophets (Steck 1991a: 26–60).

To conclude, it seems that in the redaction history of the book of Isaiah there is a stage in which redactors try to correlate Isaiah with the Deuteronomistic historical traditions, and they understand Isaiah as the prophetic reminder of the *torah*. The authors of Deutero-Isaiah favored the concept of a *torah* teaching by the Servant of YHWH. This concept is to some extent close to the concept of the redactor of the Hexateuch, who looks at Moses as the servant of YHWH. During the post-Nehemiah phase of history in the fifth century, the prophet could be understood as the *torah* teacher for Israel.[42] Discussions on matters of *torah* are introduced into the prophetic literature. But after Ezra, during the fourth century B.C.E., the development of an antiprophetic hierocratic redaction of the Pentateuch took control over the teaching, so that the latest layers of the book refer to the *torah* teaching from Zion only. There cannot be a *torah* beyond the teachings of Moses, but

---

41. Isa 63:7–14 can be viewed as an interpretation of Exod 14:29, Exodus 33, and Numbers 11 (Achenbach 2003: 261–62).

42. For a synchronic study of this theme in Isaiah, Jeremiah, and Deuteronomy, see Finsterbusch 2004.

according to the spiritual and eschatological hopes of the late authors there must be one *torah* for all nations in the end (cf. 1:13; 2:2-3; 66:18, 23; Deut 4:6ff.; 26:19; 33:3ff., 29).

The Book of Ezekiel

Although throughout the whole book of Ezekiel (as in Jeremiah) the prophet is depicted as an authoritative prophetic teacher of priestly origin,[43] in Ezekiel 1–40 we find only two references to *torah*—and only as Priestly *torah* (Ezek 7:26, 22:26; cf. Lev 10:10, Zeph 3:4). With respect to Ezek 7:26, scholars assume that this text was formed by disciples who were rather close to Ezekiel (Albertz 2001: 264).[44] The concept is close to the ideas of Jer 18:18.

Ezek 7:26	Jer 18:18
hōwâ ʿal-hōwâ tābôʾ	*wayyōʾmrû lĕkû wĕnaḥšĕbâ ʿal-yirmeyāhû maḥăšābôt*
ûšmuʿâ ʾel-šmûʿâ tihyeh	
ûbiqšû ḥāzôn minnābîʾ	*tôrâ mikkōhēn*
wĕtôrâ tōʾbad mikkōhēn	*wĕʿēṣâ mēḥākām*
wĕʿēṣâ mizzĕqēnîm	*wĕdābār minnābîʾ*

The singular expression *hōwâ* appears only in Isa 47:11, an oracle of disaster against Babel. It could be that the text reflects language and concepts from preexilic times (Greenberg 2001: 191). It is plausible to assume that the quest for ritual instruction had to be answered by priests, while the quest for oracles had to be answered by prophets, and the quest for solutions in difficult situations of conflict had to be answered by elders or judges. Both circles, the circle who transmitted the Jeremianic tradition as well as the circle who transmitted the Ezekielian tradition, still had these functions in mind. In Ezek 22:26, a text that according to the analyses of Pohlmann (2002: 331) belongs to a similar layer, it becomes clearer where the core of Priestly *torah* was expected:

---

43. The reconstruction of the genesis of the book is much more complicated than a holistic interpretation (e.g., Greenberg 2001) can show; see Pohlmann 1996: 33–42. Schöpflin (2002: 343–58), who considers the whole book to be pseudepigraphic, still finds traces of an inner development of editions according to the picture given in this essay. First, the prophet seems to be a prophet in accordance with 2 Kgs 17:13; then he becomes a teacher according to Deut 18:18. At the end, the Priestly circles of Zadokites, who influenced the transmission of the book, tried to establish the book as a document of revelation almost equal to Moses. Although the editors of the Holiness Code took over a lot of Priestly material that accorded with the traditions of the Ezekielian circle, in the end they followed the line of the priests who combined P and D in the Pentateuch.

44. Even for Pohlmann (1996: 121), Ezek 7:26 belongs to a basic layer of the chapter.

kōhănêhā hāmĕsû tôrātî wayhallĕlû qŏdāšay bên-qōdĕš lĕḥōl lō᾽ hibdîlû ûbên-haṭṭāmē᾽ lĕṭāhôr lō᾽ hôdî῾û! In this way, the authors apply a specific Priestly view to what they consider to be the main task of priests: to distinguish between the holy and profane, the pure and impure. The Priestly measure later appeared in Ezek 44:23 and was also introduced into the Pentateuch in Lev 10:10. The context of Ezek 22:26 is comparable to the context of 7:26: a fundamental criticism against the leaders (v. 25: *nĕśî᾽êhā** [conj.; see BHS]), the priests (v. 26: *kōhănêhā*), the officials (v. 27: *śārêhā*), the prophets (v. 28: *nĕbî᾽êhā*), and the "people of the land," the landowners (v. 29: *῾am-hā᾽āreṣ*).

But in Ezekiel 40–48, it is "Ezekiel" who is described as a priestly prophet, revealing the hitherto unknown *torah* of YHWH concerning the Second Temple. After the punishment of the defilement of the holy name by idols ("prostitution") through the priests and the punishment of all the kings, the "prophet" is called to give new instructions on the rebuilding of the temple (Ezek 43:10–12) and the ordinances concerning the people "who may be admitted to the sanctuary and the task of giving *torah* in legal and in sacral cases" (Ezek 44:5.24). So the idea of the Zadokite authors of Ezekiel 40–48 is that the prophetic teaching during the exilic time ends in the revelation of the statutes of the Second Temple and in passing on the instructions for the Second Temple to the priests, whose responsibility will be renewed after the Exile.[45] It was mainly the texts from the Ezekielian tradition that had the strongest impact on the hierocratic Priestly expansions of the Pentateuch, especially the Holiness Code, which were part of the Pentateuch redaction. The Hexateuch redactor's idea of the Levitical priesthood, in particular, was changed by the idea of one leading Zadokite priesthood and the rejection of Levites from other genealogical roots (cf. Num 16:1–17:18).[46]

But the influence of the Ezekiel tradition was integrated with other concurrent traditions, especially in the Deuteronomistic and Priestly streams, and its influence was restricted by stating that it was only Moses and the Mosaic revelation that had the right to claim canonical authority concerning the *torah*. It could be that to deal with the problem of finding a way to produce complementary readings, the function of which was to combine the text of the Hexateuch redactor (including P, Deuteronomistic, and pre-Priestly/Deuteronomistic materials) with

---

45. For a detailed analysis of these chapters, see Rudnig 2000; 2002.

46. For the Zadokite adaption of the Aaron legend in the theocratic reworking of the Pentateuch, see Achenbach 2003: 91–123.

materials and traditions from the Zadokite-influenced Priestly school in the Holiness Code, led to the decision not to leave everything to the Zadokites from the Ezekielian circle but basically to look for compatibility with the other "Mosaic" tradition. The Holiness Code became the hermeneutical key for the interpretation of P and Deuteronomy for the Pentateuch redactor. At the same time, the Pentateuch redactor seems to have rejected all prophetic tradition as secondary compared with the "Mosaic" tradition (Deut 34:10, 12).

Nevertheless, many features, especially the idea of the wandering *kabôd* (cf. Ezek 11:22–23, 43:4), are accepted by the redactor of the Pentateuch as constitutive elements in his redactional work. So the Pentateuch redaction is not based on prophetic *torah* but on stating that the Priestly and other *torah* had come from the prophet Moses, who was considered to stand above all prophecy ever to come (Deut 34:10–12). Consequently, the *toroth* from the Second Temple could only be introduced into the *torah* in late Priestly expansions by theocratic editings. They can be called "pre-chronistic," and they prepare for the genealogical integration of the Zadokites and their tradition (Exod 6:14–27, 1 Chr 5:27–34). They add ordinances and statutes concerning the Levites, who are given a strictly subordinate status in the priestly hierarchy (Numbers 3–4, 18). The real prophetic "spirit" can only be a Mosaic spirit, which must not affect special prophets but the leaders of Israel such as Joshua (cf. Num 27:18, Deut 34:9) and the 70 elders (Num 11:16–17, 24–25) and hopefully all Israel (Num 11:26–30; cf. Joel 3) in order to inspire them to keep the *torah*. Under these conditions, *torah* can only be derived from Priestly teaching that has Mosaic and divine legitimation. Prophetic *torah* is not needed any longer, except from the prophet Moses. The prophets can only be understood as explaining the meaning of the *torah*.

The Dodekapropheton

The *Dodekapropheton* mirrors the view of the prophets in this late development. Most references to the *torah* are secondary here, and most of them seem to be later than the Pentateuch redaction, so they are post-Pentateuch-redactional in nature. The oldest reference to *torah* may be Hos 4:6. Here, the term is confined to meaning a priestly *torah* that must be delivered to people who ask for correct sacrificial instruction.[47] We

---

47. Jeremias (1983: 63), still thinks the text belongs to the ancient prophetic tradition; but in her recent dissertation, Rudnig-Zelt (2003: 170–81) surmises that the general way of arguing in the text may be a hint of a much later use of the term than is traditionally assumed by scholars.

may also observe older layers in Hag 2:11–12, where the text takes up the tradition of Priestly *toroth*.[48] Zech 7:1–6 is the only postexilic text to add prophetic teaching concerning the *toroth* for fasting (vv. 9–10; cf. Exod 22:10, 21; Mic 6:8). Zech 7:7–14 takes up the idea of the prophetic warnings according to the late layers in 2 Kgs 17:13–23 and still stands in the tradition of the theology of the early postexilic era.

When in Hos 8:1 Israel is blamed for having rebelled against the *torah*, the term is connected with covenantal theology in post-Deuteronomistic language (Jeremias 1983: 104; Rudnig-Zelt 2003: 167–68). Additionally, Hos 8:12 says that Ephraim, although he makes many offerings (vv. 11, 13; cf. Isa 1:11), rejects the *torah* written by the LORD. This text clearly refers to Exod 24:12b. The rationale in Hos 8:13 is close to the late redactional text in Isa 1:11. So in both cases it can be assumed that the references to *torah* in Hos 8:1, 12 are later than the redaction of the Pentateuch.

Whereas in Hosea the Northern Kingdom is criticized, in Amos 2:4–5 the criticism is extended to Judah. The text states that Judah has received punishment, for the people have rejected the *torah* of YHWH (*m's*, as in Isa 5:24, Jer 6:19; cf. Hos 4:6, *wattiškaḥ tôrat 'ĕlōhêkā*, parallel to *kî-'attâ haddaʿat māʾastā*). Hab 1:4–6 states that the Babylonian Exile occurred due to the negligence of *torah* observances. Zeph 3:4 blames the priests in the same way that Ezek 22:26 does (priests have profaned what is sacred; cf. Lev 10:10). Finally, parallel to the redaction of the book of Isaiah, the vision of Isa 2:3 can be found also in Mic 4:2. Whereas the references in Hos 4:6, Amos 2:4–5, Hab 1:4–6, and Zeph 3:4 may belong to layers that are parallel to the Hexateuch redaction or Priestly language of the late sixth and early fifth century, Hos 8:1, 12 and Mic 4:2 already are post-Pentateuch-redactional.

After the redactional closure of the Pentateuch, discussions among scribes shifted to prophetic texts.[49] We may observe already a serious discussion of the status of foreigners (following the interpretation of

---

48. Hag 2:11–12 reads, "Thus says YHWH Sabaoth: Ask the priests for a *torah*: If a person carries consecrated meat in the fold of his garment. . . ."

49. For examples, see Otto 2002: 76–83. He writes (p. 83), "Erst mit der Schließung des Pentateuch als *norma normans* (Neh 13,1–3) im 3. Jh. v. Chr. verlagern sich die schriftgelehrten Dispute um die Toraauslegung aus der Tora heraus in das corpus propheticum. So werden nicht zuletzt in Jes 56; 66; Joel 4; Sach 9 und Obadja Diskussionen um die Applikation des Gemeindegesetzes in Dtn 23,2–9 geführt, die in der Tora nach deren Abschluß keinen Ort mehr fanden, so daß die Schriftgelehrten des 3. Jh. v. Chr. sich einen Prophetenmantel umhängen mußten, um die Tora kritisch fortschreiben und revidieren zu können. Schließlich wurde in Sach 13 mit Argumenten der Schriftexegese von Num 11 auch diese Toradiskussion im *corpus propheticum* beendet."

Deut 23:2–9) in Trito-Isaiah. There is another fundamental discussion on inspiration (in connection with Num 11:29) in Joel 3:1–5 and 4. Controversial positions could be formulated in other contexts. In the end, the normative impact of the Priestly theocratic traditors of the Pentateuch gained acceptance. The prophets could only be read as exegetes of the *torah*. The Chronicler considered the prophets scribes (1 Chr 29:29; cf. Isa 1:1 and 2 Chr 32:32). During Ptolemaic times, the theocratically educated scribes proclaimed the end of prophecy itself (Zech 13:2–6).

The pseudepigraphic book of Malachi is a unique appendix to the *Dodekapropheton*;[50] Malachi criticizes developments in the cult in late Persian times. The criticism of the priestly defilement of the altar is founded on measures that are partly formulated outside the *torah* (Mal 1:6, 11–12; Ezek 44:6–7, 36:20–22; Neh 9:32) or even beyond it (Mal 1:8, Deut 15:21). When Mal 2:4–6 refers to an eternal covenant for Levi, the text treats a concept that is even later than the latest hierocratic layer in Num 25:10–13. Here, the theocratic scribes speak about the eternal covenant of priesthood for Phineas the high priest. The Blessing of Moses in Deut 33:10 at the end of the Pentateuch says about priests of Levitical origin: "Let them (pl.!) teach Jacob your laws and your *torah* to Israel." The author of Malachi 2 believes that the *torah* was already in the mouth of the ancestor of all the priests, Levi himself. The concept of a covenant with Levi has been developed in continuation with Num 25:10–13 and Deut 33:8–10 by the interpretation of the events in Shechem (Genesis 34), for which we do not have written testimony before *Jub.* 30:18 and *T. Lev.* 5.[51] According to the redacted Pentateuch, the forefathers Abraham and Jacob must have been considered prophets (Gen 20:7, chap. 49), because they were known already to act according to the Mosaic Law, which later on was revealed to Moses. This legend was expanded to include the ancestor of the priests, Levi, whose sons took over the *torah* from Moses. This is the reason why the *torah* of

---

50. The entire book of Malachi must be considered pseudepigraphic literature, representing the latest state of the biblical prophetic movement, when oppositional priestly groups had already taken the cloak of the prophets. The secondary appendix already had a function in the process of the canonization of the prophets in addition to the Pentateuch and the Mosaic Torah. On this matter, see Chapman (2000: 131–49), although it seems inappropriate to call the "theological grammar" of that canon formation "Deuteronomistic," because it does not belong to the immediate circle of sixth-century Deuteronomism but to the context of the fourth- to third-century tradition of Priestly scribes. For the suggestion to correlate three phases of the development of the book with the latest layers of the redaction of the *Dodekapropheten*, see Bosshard and Kratz 1990: 27–46.

51. On the special "cotextuality" of Malachi, see Utzschneider 1989: 64–70.

Moses, that is, the Pentateuch, is mentioned for the first and the last time in the later prophets only in Mal 3:22! The concept of a covenant with the priesthood and the Levites seems to be part of the Chronistic editing of Neh 13:29.[52] At this time (that is, the end of the fourth century B.C.E.), the Pentateuch had a canonical shape, which made it resistant to changes through prophetic influence. Only an "angel" or messenger (= Malachi) could come, sent from heaven with prophetic messages for the priests. Further *Fortschreibung* could only be connected to existing prophetic scripture to secure further transmission, as we can see for Deutero-Zechariah (end of the fourth century B.C.E.) and Trito-Zechariah (third century B.C.E.).[53] All measures concerning the Second Temple that came after Ezekiel 40–48 and Zechariah could only be referred to by legends in connection with the measures taken by David, Solomon, and the kings in Chronicles. For the Chronicler, prophecy was an instrument of historical midrashic legends, and prophets were thought to be authors of historical narratives (1 Chr 29:29–30; Schniedewind 1997). The only "prophet" to be expected was the "father of Israel" returning from heaven, Elijah (Mal 3:23–24)—not to teach the *torah* but to convert Israel and restore religious peace. The job of criticizing the priests was transferred to scribes and inner-priestly critics taking the cloak of the prophets in order to discuss the correct exegesis of the *torah* in the light of the prophetic *tĕʿûdâ* (Isa 8:16; Rüterswörden 1991).

Conclusion

This essay suggests some categories for reconstructing the redaction history of the canon, beginning with the redaction history of the Pentateuch. In the late Deuteronomistic phase, there was a tendency to depict the prophets as men who provided warnings in the sense of 2 Kgs 17:13. After the restoration of the temple it became obvious that the

---

52. Albertz (2004: 13–32) assumes that the literary kernel of the so-called Nehemiah Memoirs in Neh 1:1–7:5a; 12:31–32, 37–40; 13:4–31 (vv. 7:1b; 13:6, 7a, 22, 30a are secondary) already reflects the social impact of the the binary cultic concept of holy and profane, clean and unclean, we and the *goyyîm*, and so on. He surmises that it was established by Nehemiah, who already referred to a *torah* containing Numbers 18. It could be that the measures of Nehemiah prepared the way for the adoption of these concepts by a certain Priestly party in the temple. Yet, we have to consider that Nehemiah 7–8* was placed before Nehemiah 10 and 12–13 by later, Chronistic editors, who reworked the text especially in these chapters. Neh 13:29 already reflects a postcanonical interpretation of Deut 33:8–11!

53. For the dating, see Bosshard and Kratz 1990; Steck 1991a: 30–60.

Davidic kingdom would not be reinstated. In order to give the "servants of Yhwh" an orientation, the Hexateuch redactor combined P, pre-Deuteronomistic, pre-P, and D traditions and strengthened the idea of a Mosaic (Levitic) priesthood that was obligated to teach the Mosaic *torah*. The prophets were read as teachers of the *torah*, and prophetic teaching was used to influence developments in the first half of the fifth century B.C.E. Jeremiah, Isaiah, and even Ezekiel appeared as teachers of God's will, partly in succession to Moses (Jeremiah). In the second half of the fifth century, the influence of priestly sacral regulations and the discussions about the basic orders for the cult and the sabbath increased. As a result, an enlarged Priestly Code, including the Holiness Code, became part of the Pentateuch.

Ezra may have been the initiator of a new development at the beginning of the fourth century. Mosaic *torah* was even assumed to stand over all prophetic *torah* (Deut 34:10–12). Under the influence of a hierocratic movement, the books of the prophets became collections that were read as interpretations and additional teachings alongside the *torah*. The prophets could only take up themes in accordance with the Mosaic *torah*. It was seen as their task to call the people to follow Yhwh's *torah* alone. Many of the references to *torah* in the prophetic books belong to this latest phase of redaction, during the fourth century B.C.E.

Bibliography

Achenbach, R.
  1999   Levitische Priester und Leviten im Deuteronomium: Überlegungen zur sog. "Levitisierung" des Priestertums. *ZABR* 5: 285–309.
  2003   *Die Vollendung der Tora: Studien zur Redaktionsgeschichte des Numeribuches im Kontext von Hexateuch und Pentateuch.* Beihefte zur Zeitschrift für altorientalische und biblische Rechtsgeschichte 3. Wiesbaden: Harrassowitz.
  2004   Grundlinien redaktioneller Arbeit in der Sinai-Perikope. Pp. 56–80 in *Das Deuteronomium zwischen Pentateuch und Deuteronomistischen Geschichtswerk,* ed. by E. Otto. FRLANT 206. Göttingen: Vandenhoeck & Ruprecht.
  2005a   Tora I: Altes Testament. Pp. 476–77 in vol. 8 of RGG. 4th ed. Tübingen: Mohr-Siebeck.
  2005b   Pentateuch, Hexateuch, Enneateuch: Eine Verhältnisbestimmung. *ZABR* 11: 122–54.
Albertz, R.
  2001   *Die Exilszeit: 6. Jahrhundert v. Chr.* Biblische Enzyklopädie 7. Stuttgart: Kohlhammer.

2004   Ethnische und kultische Konzepte in der Politik Nehemias. Pp. 13–32 in *"Das Manna fällt auch heute noch": Beiträge zur Geschichte und Theologie des Alten, Ersten Testaments (Festschrift E. Zenger)*, ed. by F.-L. Hossfeld and L. Schwienhorst-Schönberger. HBS 44. Freiburg: Herder.

Barth, H.

1977   *Die Jesaja-Worte in der Josiazeit: Israel und Assur als Thema einer produktiven Neuinterpretation der Jesajaüberlieferung.* WMANT 48. Neukirchen-Vluyn: Neukirchener Verlag.

Becker, U.

1997   *Jesaja: Von der Botschaft zum Buch.* FRLANT 178. Göttingen: Vandenhoeck & Ruprecht.

Berges, U.

1998   *Das Buch Jesaja: Komposition und Endgestalt.* Herders biblische Studien 16. Freiburg: Herder.

Beuken, W. A. M.

2003   *Jesaja 1–12.* HTKAT. Freiburg: Herder.

Blenkinsopp, J.

1977   *Prophecy and Canon: A Contribution to the Study of Jewish Origins.* University of Notre Dame Center for the Study of Judaism and Christianity in Antiquity 3. Notre Dame, IN: University of Notre Dame Press.

2003   *Isaiah 56–66: A New Translation with Introduction and Commentary.* AB 19b. New York: Doubleday.

Bosshard, E., and Kratz, R. G.

1990   Maleachi im Zwölfprophetenbuch. *BN* 52: 27–46.

Braulik, G.

2004   "Die Weisung und das Gebot" im Enneateuch. Pp. 115–40 in *"Das Manna fällt auch heute noch": Beiträge zur Geschichte und Theologie des Alten, Ersten Testaments (Festschrift E. Zenger)*, ed. F.-L. Hossfeld and L. Schwienhorst-Schönberger. Herders biblische Studien 44. Freiburg: Herder.

Chapman, S. B.

2000   *The Law and the Prophets: A Study in Old Testament Canon Formation.* FAT 27. Tübingen: Mohr-Siebeck.

Chiesa, B.

1973   La Promessa di un Profeta (Deut. 18,15–22). *BeO* 15 (Gruppo Biblico Milanese): 17–26.

Finsterbusch, K.

2004   *Weisung für Israel: Studien zum religiösen Lehren und Lernen im Deuteronomium und in seinem Umfeld.* FAT 44. Tübingen: Mohr-Siebeck.

Fischer, G.

2005   *Jeremia 1–25.* HTKAT. Freiburg: Herder.

Fischer, I.

1995   *Tora für Israel—Tora für die Völker: Das Konzept des Jesajabuches.* SBS 164. Stuttgart: Katholisches Bibelwerk.

Fishbane, M.
1989   *The Garments of Torah: Essays in Biblical Hermeneutics.* Indiana Studies in Biblical Literature. Bloomington: Indiana University Press.

Gertz, J. C.
1994   *Die Gerichtsorganisation Israels im deuteronomischen Gesetz.* FRLANT 165. Göttingen: Vandenhoeck & Ruprecht.

Greenberg, M.
2001   *Ezechiel 1–20.* HTKAT. Freiburg: Herder.

Hengel, M.
1994   "Schriftauslegung" und "Schriftwerdung" in der Zeit des Zweiten Tempels. Pp. 1–71 in *Schriftauslegung im antiken Judentum und im Urchristentum,* ed. M. Hengel. WUNT 73. Tübingen: Mohr-Siebeck.

Herrmann, S.
1986   *Jeremia.* BKAT 12/1. Neukirchen-Vluyn: Neukirchener Verlag.

Hossfeldt, F.-L., and Meyer, I.
1974   Der Prophet vor dem Tribunal. *ZAW* 86: 30–50.

Jeremias, J.
1981   "Ich bin wie ein Löwe für Efraim . . .": Aktualität und Allgemeingültigkeit im prophetischen Reden von Gott—Am Beispiel von Hos 5,8–14. Pp. 75–95 in *"Ich will euer Gott werden": Beispiele biblischen Redens von Gott.* SBS 100. Stuttgart: Katholisches Bibelwerk.
1983   *Der Prophet Hosea.* ATD 24/1. Göttingen: Vandenhoeck & Ruprecht.
1997   Rezeptionsprozesse in der prophetischen Überlieferung: Am Beispiel der Visionsberichte des Amos. Pp. 29–44 in *Rezeption und Auslegung im Alten Testament und in seinem Umfeld (Festschrift O. H. Steck),* ed. R. G. Kratz and T. Krüger. OBO 153. Freiburg: Universitätsverlag / Göttingen: Vandenhoeck & Ruprecht.

Knoppers, G. N.
1994   *Two Nations under God: The Deuteronomistic History of Solomon and the Dual Monarchies. Volume 2: The Reigns of Jeroboam, the Fall of Israel, and the Reign of Josiah.* HSM 53. Atlanta: Scholars Press.

Kratz, R. G.
1997   Die Redaktion der Prophetenbücher. Pp. 9–28 in *Rezeption und Auslegung im Alten Testament und in seinem Umfeld (Festschrift O. H. Steck),* ed. R. G. Kratz and T. Krüger. OBO 153. Freiburg: Universitätsverlag / Göttingen: Vandenhoeck & Ruprecht.

Krüger, T.
1997   Das menschliche Herz und die Weisung Gottes: Elemente einer Diskussion über die Möglichkeiten und Grenzen der Tora-Rezeption im Alten Testament. Pp. 65–92 in *Rezeption und Auslegung im Alten Testament und in seinem Umfeld (Festschrift O. H. Steck),* ed. R. G. Kratz and T. Krüger. OBO 153. Freiburg: Universitätsverlag / Göttingen: Vandenhoeck & Ruprecht.

Lemaire, A., and Durand, J.-M.
1984   *Les inscriptions araméennes de Sfiré et l'Assyrie de Shamshi-Ilu.* Hautes Études Orientales 20. Geneva: Droz.

Levin, C.
1985   *Die Verheißung des neuen Bundes in ihrem theologiegeschichtlichen Zusam-
       menhang ausgelegt.* FRLANT 137. Göttingen: Vandenhoeck & Ruprecht.
Lohfink, N.
1994   Bund und Tora bei der Völkerwallfahrt: Jesajabuch und Psalm 25.
       Pp. 37–83 in *Der Gott Israels und die Völker: Untersuchungen zum Jesaja-
       buch und zu den Psalmen,* ed. E. Zenger. SBS 154. Stuttgart: Katholisches
       Bibelwerk.
Loretz, O.
1984   *Der Prolog des Jesajabuches (1:1–2:5): Ugaritologische und kolometrische
       Studien zum Jesajabuch.* Altenberge: CIS.
Maier, C.
2002   *Jeremia als Lehrer der Tora: Soziale Gebote des Deuteronomiums in Fort-
       schreibungen des Jeremiabuches.* FRLANT 196. Göttingen: Vandenhoeck
       & Ruprecht.
McKenzie, S. L.
1991   *The Trouble with Kings: The Composition of the Book of Kings in the Deu-
       teronomistic History.* VTSup 42. Leiden: Brill.
Müller, R.
2004   *Königtum und Gottesherrschaft: Untersuchungen zur alttestamentlichen
       Monarchiekritik.* FAT n.s. 3. Tübingen: Mohr-Siebeck.
Nihan, C.
2004   *From Priestly Torah to Pentateuch: A Study in the Composition of the Book
       of Leviticus.* Ph.D. Dissertation, University of Lausanne.
Nogalski, J. D.
1993   *Literary Precursors to the Book of the Twelve.* BZAW 217. Berlin: de Gruyter.
Otto, E.
1996   Die nachpriesterschriftliche Pentateuchredaktion im Buch Exodus.
       Pp. 61–111 in *Studies in the Book of Exodus: Redaction–Reception–Inter-
       pretation,* ed. M. Vervenne. BETL 126. Leuven: Peeters.
2000a *Das Deuteronomium im Pentateuch und Hexateuch: Studien zur Literatur-
       geschichte von Pentateuch und Hexateuch im Lichte des Deuteronomium-
       rahmens.* FAT 30. Tübingen: Mohr-Siebeck.
2000b Deuteronomium und Pentateuch: Aspekte der gegenwärtigen De-
       batte. *ZABR* 6: 222–84.
2002   Die Literaturgeschichte des Deuteronomiums im Horizont der jüng-
       sten Deuteronomiums- und Pentateuchforschung. Pp. 1–91 in his
       *Gottes Recht als Menschenrecht. Rechts- und literaturhistorische Studien
       zum Deuteronomium.* Beihefte zur Zeitschrift für altorientalische und
       biblische Rechtsgeschichte 2. Wiesbaden: Harrassowitz. [Reprint of
       2000b]
2004   Vom biblischen Hebraismus der persischen Zeit zum rabbinischen Ju-
       daismus in römischer Zeit: Zur Geschichte der spätbiblischen und
       frühjüdischen Schriftgelehrsamkeit. *ZABR* 10: 1–49.
2005   Mose, der erste Schriftgelehrte: Deuteronomium 1,5 in der Fabel des
       Pentateuch. Pp. 273–84 in *L'Ecrit et l'Esprit: Etudes d'histoire du texte et*

de théologie biblique en hommage à Adrian Schenker, ed. D. Böhler, I. Himbaza, and P. Hugo. OBO 214. Freiburg: Universitätsverlag / Göttingen: Vandenhoeck & Ruprecht.

Pohlmann, K.-F.

1994 *Der Prophet Hesekiel/Ezechiel: Kapitel 1–19*. ATD 22/1. Göttingen: Vandenhoeck & Ruprecht.

2002 *Der Prophet Hesekiel/Ezechiel: Kapitel 20–48*. ATD 22/2. Göttingen: Vandenhoeck & Ruprecht.

Preuss, H. D.

1982 *Deuteronomium*. EdF 164. Darmstadt: Wissenschaftliche Buchgesellschaft.

Rudnig, T. A.

2000 *Heilig und Profan: Redaktionsgeschichtliche Studien zu Ez 40–48*. BZAW 287. Berlin: de Gruyter.

2002 *Ez 40–48: Die Vision vom neuen Tempel und der neuen Ordnung im Land*. Pp. 527–631 in K.-F. Pohlmann, *Das Buch des Propheten Hesekiel/Ezechiel: Kapitel 20–48*. ATD 22/2. Göttingen: Vandenhoeck & Ruprecht.

Rudnig-Zelt, S.

2003 *Hosea-Studien: Redaktionskritische Untersuchungen zur Genese des Hoseabuches*. Ph.D. Dissertation, University of Münster.

Rüterswörden, U.

1991 Es gibt keinen Exegeten in einem gesetzlosen Land (Prov 29,18 LXX): Erwägungen zum Thema: Der Prophet und die Thora. Pp. 326–47 in *Prophetie und geschichtliche Wirklichkeit im alten Israel (Festschrift S. Herrmann)*, ed. R. Liwak and S. Wagner. Stuttgart: Kohlhammer.

Schams, C.

1998 *Jewish Scribes in the Second-Temple Period*. JSOTSup 291. Sheffield: Sheffield Academic Press.

Schmid, K.

1996 *Buchgestalten des Jeremiabuches. Untersuchungen zur Redaktions- und Rezeptionsgeschichte von Jer 30–33 im Kontext des Buches*. WMANT 72. Neukirchen-Vluyn: Neukirchener Verlag.

1999 *Erzväter und Exodus: Untersuchungen zur doppelten Begründung der Ursprünge Israels innerhalb der Geschichtsbücher des Alten Testaments*. WMANT 81. Neukirchen-Vluyn: Neukirchener Verlag.

Schniedewind, W. M.

1996 Prophets and Prophecy in the Books of Chronicles. Pp. 204–24 in *The Chronicler as Historian*, ed. M. P. Graham, K. Hoglund, and S. L. McKenzie. JSOTSup 238. Sheffield: Sheffield Academic Press.

Schöpflin, K.

2002 *Theologie als Biographie im Ezechielbuch*. FAT 36. Tübingen: Mohr-Siebeck.

Ska, J.-L.

1996 Exode 19,3b–6 et l'identité de l'Israël postexilique. Pp. 289–317 in *Studies in the Book of Exodus: Redaction–Reception–Interpretation*, ed. M. Vervenne. BETL 126. Leuven: Peeters.

2005   A Plea on Behalf of the Biblical Redactors. *Studia Theologica (Nordic Journal of Theology)* 59/1: 4–18.

Steck, O. H.

1967   *Israel und das gewaltsame Geschick der Propheten: Untersuchungen zur Überlieferung des deuteronomistischen Geschichtsbildes im Alten Testament, Spätjudentum und Urchristentum.* WMANT 23. Neukirchen–Vluyn: Neukirchener Verlag.

1991a   *Der Abschluß der Prophetie im Alten Testament: Ein Versuch zur Frage der Vorgeschichte des Kanons.* Biblisch-theologische Studien 17. Neukirchen-Vluyn: Neukirchener Verlag.

1991b   Zu jüngsten Untersuchungen von Jes 56:9–59:21; 63:1–6. Pp. 192–213 in his *Studien zu Tritojesaja.* BZAW 203. Berlin: de Gruyter.

Stipp, H.-J.

1995   Probleme des redaktionsgeschichtlichen Modells der Entstehung des Jeremiabuches. Pp. 225–62 in *Jeremia und die "deuteronomistische Bewegung,"* ed. W. Groß. BBB 98. Weinheim: Athenäum.

Sweeney, M. A.

1996   The Book of Isaiah as Prophetic Torah. Pp. 50–67 in *New Visions of Isaiah,* ed. R. F. Melugin and M. A. Sweeney. JSOTSup 214. Sheffield: Sheffield Academic Press.

Thiel, W.

1973   *Die deuteronomistische Redaktion von Jeremia 1–25.* WMANT 41. Neukirchen-Vluyn: Neukirchener Verlag.

Tomasin, A. J.

1993   Isaiah 1.1–2,4 and 64–66, and the Composition of the Isaianic Corpus. *JSOT* 57: 81–98.

Utzschneider, H.

1989   *Künder oder Schreiber? Eine These zum Problem der "Schriftprophetie" auf Grund von Maleachi 1,6–2,9.* BEATAJ 19. Frankfurt a.M.: Peter Lang.

Vermeylen, J.

1977   *Du prophète Isaïe á l'apocalyptique: Isaïe, I–XXXV, miroir d'un demi-millénaire d'expérience religieuse en Israël.* Vol. 1. Paris: Gabalda.

1978   *Du prophète Isaïe á l'apocalyptique. Isaïe, I–XXXV, miroir d'un demi-millénaire d'expérience religieuse en Israël.* Vol. 2. Paris: Gabalda.

Wells, R. D.

1996   'Isaiah' as an Exponent of Torah: Isaiah 56.1–8. Pp. 140–55 in *New Visions of Isaiah.* JSOTSup 214. Sheffield: Sheffield Academic Press.

Werner, W.

1986   *Eschatologische Texte in Jesaja 1–39: Messias, Heiliger Rest, Völker.* FB 46. 2nd ed. Würzburg: Echter Verlag.

The Canonical Alignment of the
Book of Joshua

RAINER ALBERTZ

Westfälische Wilhelms-Universität, Münster

The question of when the canonization or promulgation of the Pentateuch should be dated is still a matter of dispute. Some scholars, such as Erhard Blum (1990: 351–55), assume the middle of the fifth century B.C.E. Others, such as myself (Albertz 1994: 2.470)—with the late dating of Ezra (398 B.C.E.) in mind—prefer the end of the fifth or the beginning of the fourth century, while Eckart Otto (2000: 261–63) and Reinhard Achenbach (2003: 629–33) reckon with a number of later editions during the fourth century B.C.E. and a series of later additions during the Hellenistic period. Because the Samarians accepted the same Pentateuch with only a few modifications, the exact date that the cultic split between the religious communities in Jerusalem and Gerizim took place is of crucial importance. Unfortunately, the answer cannot yet be given. The excavations on Mt. Gerizim performed by Yitzhaq Magen verified a Persian-period cult place that was certainly in use during the fourth century B.C.E. but may even have been founded during the fifth century (2000: 114–16).[1] Although the exact date is not yet established, it seems that the cultic split between the Judeans and Samarians occurred about 70 to 100 years earlier than Josephus reported that it did (*Ant.* 11.302–47). Josephus connected the split with Alexander's siege of Tyre (332 B.C.E.). Thus the archaeological evidence seems to support a relatively early or moderate date of the canonization of the Pentateuch rather than a late date.

The new debate on the Pentateuch has thus far not reached a consensus about the significance and date of its final edition. On the contrary, the recent proposals for late Priestly and post-Priestly redactions of the Pentateuch present us with a greater divergence of opinion than we had before.[2] Thus, I would like to focus on passages outside the

---

1. See also Magen's essay in this volume, pp. 157–193.
2. See the survey of Zenger in the 5th edition of his *Einleitung* (2004: 99–123).

Pentateuch that may reflect some of the results of its canonization: the so-called Priestly passages in the book of Joshua.

The Problem of the "Priestly" Passages in the Book of Joshua

The so-called Priestly passages in Joshua belong to the category of unsolved problems in Old Testament scholarship. Most scholars of the nineteenth and the first part of the twentieth century ascribed them to the Priestly source (P) and interpreted them as an indication that all the pentateuchal sources are continued in the book of Joshua. Consequently, they regarded Joshua as part of a Hexateuch, although Theodor Nöldeke, to whom we owe the reconstruction of the Priestly source, had already pointed out correctly: "Wir können . . . hier [that means in the book of Joshua] keinen zusammenhängenden Bericht der Grundschrift mehr zusammenbringen" (1869: 94–95). Thus, the source that constitutes the basic framework of the Pentateuch would exist in the book of Joshua only fragmentarily. In his commentary on Joshua, Martin Noth pointed out in 1938 that neither the Priestly passages nor the other pentateuchal sources established a connection between the book of Joshua and the Pentateuch (1938: viii). But, from his perspective, the Deuteronomistic redaction of the books of Deuteronomy and Joshua (Deut 3:23–29, 31:1–8; Joshua 1) did establish a connection between these two books. From this he concluded in 1943 that Joshua belonged to a Deuteronomistic History running from Deuteronomy 1 to 2 Kings 25 and that a Hexateuch never existed (Noth 1957: 211). In consequence of his hypothesis about the Deuteronomistic History, Noth was forced to minimize the significance of the Priestly passages in the book of Joshua. He reduced the texts in question (Josh 4:15–17, 19; 5:10–12; 9:14, 15b, 17–21; 14:1b; 18:1; 19:51a; 21:1–42), disputed their Priestly origin (1957: 182–90), and regarded the whole passage on the distribution of the land (Joshua 13–22) as secondary (1957: 45–47). But Noth could not explain why the Deuteronomistic book of Joshua, especially the second part, was heavily reworked and why it was expanded in many cases by passages that clearly speak a kind of Priestly language.

Admittedly, with respect to the so-called Priestly passages of the book of Joshua, Noth's hypothesis reveals a considerable weakness. Should we take this as an argument against the existence of the Deuteronomistic History in addition to all the other objections that Ernst Würthwein, Ernst Axel Knauf, Reinhard Kratz, Eckart Otto, and others have raised?[3] As far as I can see, none of the recent supporters of the Hexateuch hypothesis have taken into account the Priestly passages of the book of Joshua to any substantial degree. Thomas Römer only hinted that Priestly texts in a Deuteronomistic context (especially in Joshua 3–6 and 18) might have something to do with the Hexateuch redaction, which he thinks typically evidences a mixed Priestly-Deuteronomistic style (Römer 2001: 279). Should we return to the Hexateuch hypothesis of the nineteenth century somehow and give up the thesis of the Deuteronomistic History?[4] I would like to present a new proposal that, on the one hand, can defend the hypothesis of the Deuteronomistic History and, on the other hand, can demonstrate the significance of the canonization of the Pentateuch.

The Origin of the Priestly Passages in the Book of Joshua

The passages that can be clearly isolated as Priestly additions on the basis of literary-critical and linguistic criteria are the following: Josh 4:12–13, 15–17; 4:19* + 5:10–12; 8:33*; 9:15b, 18–21, 27*; 14:1–5; 17:2aβb–6; 18:1, (2–7); 19:51; 20:1 9; 21:1–42; 22:7–34; 24:33. I admit to one uncertainty in this list: I am not yet sure whether a pre-Priestly report on the distribution of the land actually existed (although I think it did) or whether chaps. 13–19 of Joshua were late Priestly products entirely (as argued by de Vos 2003: 301–7). It seems to me that these post-Deuteronomistic reports use geographical material that is similar to what was employed by the late Priestly authors of Numbers 26–36, but the order of tribes in Joshua 14–19 differs widely from the (ideal or accommodated) Priestly order that we find in Numbers 1–2, 26, and 34:14–29, and the distribution by lot is much more prominent. Furthermore, the language of the reports is not necessarily significantly Priestly. Hence, I will restrict myself temporarily to the passages that are significantly Priestly in language and concept.

Nearly all of these Priestly passages in Joshua have close references to passages in the Pentateuch, especially to the last 11 chapters of Numbers (26–36), which have generally been accepted as of late Priestly origin. Recently, Reinhard Achenbach tried to show that these chapters

---

3. See the critique of Würthwein 1994; Knauf 1996; Kratz 2000: 220–21; Otto 2002: 155. Kratz even calls the thesis of the Deuteronomistic History an "Irrweg der Forschung" (2000: 221).

4. This is what Kratz (2000: 218–25; 2002: 295–96) and Otto (2002: 154–55) suggest. The Deuteronomistic History hypothesis was recently defended by Römer (2001: 274).

belong to three theocratic editions, which he regards as later than the
redaction of the Pentateuch. Achenbach dates them to the fourth century (2003: 629). But I think that it is likewise possible to connect Numbers 26–36 to the final redaction of the Pentateuch, after the decision
against a Hexateuch (which had been a possibililty for a certain period) was made (around 400 B.C.E.).[5]

Because of this textual proximity, the old literary-critical scholars
as well as some modern redaction-critical scholars believe that the
Priestly passages in Joshua and the Priestly chapters at the end of
Numbers were written by the same author(s). But I have serious res-
ervations about this suggestion. There are many close parallels, and
there are also conspicuous differences in terminology. To take one example: Josh 22:12, 33 uses the Hebrew expression עלה . . . לצבא for the
military campaign, but the report of Moses' campaign against Midian
in Numbers 31 uses several expressions, such as צבא (Qal; v. 7), יצא לצבא
(vv. 27, 28), and יצא בצבא (v. 26)— and all differently.

There are also conceptual differences. The main idea of Num 26:52–
56 and 33:50–55, that the land should be fairly distributed among the
tribes based on their population, is only hinted at (see 17:14–18, 18:4)
but not really carried through. The supervisory commission for a fair
distribution, consisting of Joshua, Eleazar, and the leaders of the tribes,
is just mentioned at the beginning and the end (Josh 14:1, 19:51) but
not really shown in action. Moreover, Josh 20:1–9, at least in the Masoretic version, refers not only to the Priestly law of asylum in Numbers
35 but also to the Deuteronomic parallel in Deut 19:1–13. On the one
hand, in the Priestly passages of Joshua, the Priestly concept of the
Pentateuch is not fully worked out; on the other hand, these passages
also refer to non-Priestly laws of the Pentateuch. Thus it is reasonable
to conclude that the Priestly passages of Joshua do not belong to the
same edition as Numbers 26–36 but presuppose those texts and are
shaped by them in some way. But why did some late Priestly groups
add them to the book of Joshua? To answer this question, I would like
to look at these passages in more detail.

---

5. For the thesis of a late edition of a Hexateuch that tried to promote a concept of Israel that included the Samarians in the North, see Blum 1997: 194–206 and Römer 2001:
279. That this edition was not successful but was revised by a final Pentateuch redaction
is a matter of fact.

An Examination of the Passages

Joshua 4:12–13

Josh 4:12–13 interrupts the report about the crossing of the ark (vv. 11, 18) by informing readers that the Reubenites, the Gadites, and the half-tribe of Manasseh crossed the Jordan. Verse 12 refers back to Josh 1:14 and Deut 3:18 (cf. חמשים), where the two and a half tribes, whom Moses allowed to reside in the Transjordan, assured Joshua that they would assist their brothers in conquering the Cisjordan (Josh 1:12–18). In this way, the Deuteronomistic context is presupposed. However, v. 13 refers back to Numbers 32, citing v. 27 nearly verbatim. There, the Reubenites and the Gadites had promised to cross the Jordan "armed for war in front of YHWH." With this in view, the verses were inserted directly before the crossing of the ark was completed.

Why was it so important to mention the crossing of the Transjordanian tribes explicitly? In Numbers 32 their wish to settle in the Transjordan is taken by Moses as a dangerous sin, a possible rejection of God's promised land, which is—according to the Priestly concept—mostly restricted to the Cisjordan (vv. 6–15; cf. Numbers 34). Therefore, the crossing of the Jordan became an act of faith. Recall that Moses formulated a strict criterion: only if the Transjordanian tribes crossed the Jordan and helped their kin conquer the promised land would they inherit Gilead. Otherwise, they would get their landholding in the Cisjordan (Num 32:28–30). In the Deuteronomistic book of Joshua, following the conquest, the Transjordanian tribes were sent back to take over their eastern settlements (Josh 22:1–6), and thus the Priestly editors concluded that they must have complied with the demand given in Numbers 32. For this reason, the material dealing with the actual crossing of these tribes was inserted. Thus, in the Priestly addition of Josh 4:12–13, the book of Joshua was aligned with the criterion of Num 32:29–30.

Joshua 4:15–17

The explicit order to finish the crossing by carrying 'the ark of the testimony' (ארון העדות) out of the Jordan, which is superfluous in the narrative, serves to strengthen the parallels between Joshua 4 and Exodus 14, the crossing of the Sea of Reeds (cf. Exod 14:26, 27b). There is no alignment with a pentateuchal command in this case.

Joshua 4:19*, 5:10–12

The report on the first Passover-Mazzot in the promised land (Josh 5:10–12), taken together with the date given in 4:19a, clearly shows

Priestly features.[6] However, it interprets the various regulations made in the Pentateuch (Exod 12:1–20, Lev 23:4–14, Deut 16:1–8) in its own way.[7] Four days after the crossing of the Jordan, the Israelites were not yet able to harvest the first grain and bring their firstlings; they could only eat their unleavened cakes and parched grain from what had grown in the land (v. 11). Thus, the Mazzot was integrated into the Passover. The remark that, with the first Passover in the land, the manna ended refers readers back to Exod 16:35. In this manner, the Priestly editor confirmed that what was announced in the Pentateuch pertaining to a future time actually took place. By synchronizing the ceasing of manna with the arrival in Cisjordan, he also underlined his concept of the promised land: the wilderness period did not end until the crossing of the Jordan was completed. By adding a Passover festival at this point, he furnished the arrival in the promised land with the same dignity as the Exodus from Egypt (cf. Exodus 12). In this manner, the book of Joshua was aligned with the pentateuchal standard.

Joshua 8:33*

In the late Deuteronomistic addition of Josh 8:30–35, which is located at different places in the textual tradition (in 4QJosh^a before 5:2; in the LXX after 9:2), the parenthetic phrase כגר כאזרח 'resident alien and full citizen alike' is clearly a Priestly insertion (Lev 24:16, 22; cf. Exod 12:19; Num 9:14, etc.). By combining Moses' orders in Deut 27:2–8 and 31:12–13, a late Deuteronomistic editor created a ceremony of commitment between Mt. Ebal and Mt. Gerizim.[8] Joshua built an altar and sacrificed on it, a copy of the Law of Moses was written on its stones, and the book of the Law was read aloud to all the people standing on both sides of the altar. This scene can be regarded as a pre-

---

6. Noth (1957: 183, especially n. 2) takes the terms קלוי 'roasted' in Josh 5:11, which appears only in a different context in Lev 2:14, and עבור 'yield', which appears only here (Josh 5:11, 12) in the Hebrew Bible, as an argument that the passage cannot belong to P. However, because there are clear material and terminological links to Priestly passages in the Pentateuch (see also קלי in Lev 23:14), Noth's statement makes clear that the author of Josh 5:10–12, although of Priestly origin, cannot be identified with one of the Priestly authors and editors of the Pentateuch.

7. For the "midrashic" character of this Priestly passage, see Blum 2003: 300–302. He dates it to the late Persian or Hellenistic period (2003: 312–13).

8. Although Noth initially characterized Josh 8:30–35 as completely Deuteronomistic ([1943] 1957: 43), he later proposed an earlier tradition (1953: 51–53). He overlooked the Priestly intrusion in v. 33 (similarly Fritz 1994: 94). In his view, only the phrase כגר could be a gloss (p. 98). The possibility that the passage already belonged to the Deuteronomistic History is invalidated, however, because of its varying positions in the textual tradition.

Priestly alignment with the Pentateuch; in some way, it carries out what Moses had ordered to be done there in the future. So its position in Joshua 5, immediately after Israel had entered into the promised land, may be original.

In accord with the instructions of Deut 31:12, in Josh 8:35 alien peoples are mentioned as part of the audience to which the Torah was read. But, according to Deut 29:10, resident aliens were also included in the covenant ceremony in Moab. Under the influence of the book of Joshua, even "those who chop the wood and those who draw the water" were inserted in Deut 29:10 as examples of aliens. In Joshua 9, these functions were taken over by the Gibeonites after they had cleverly escaped annihilation. Thus the position of the text in the LXX is understandable.

Finally, the Priestly editor wanted to see the provision of Deut 29:10 carried out exactly and included the aliens even in the inner ceremony of commitment (Josh 8:33). Again, the book of Joshua—in contradiction to its original annihilation theology—was aligned with the standards of the Pentateuch. Because the passage now underlines the possible affiliation of aliens with Israel, it is located next to Joshua 9, where this problem is dealt with in the older material.

Joshua 9:15b, 18–21, 27*

The Priestly edition of the story of the Gibeonites is widely acknowledged; only its limits are disputed.[9] The editor wanted to offer a better explanation for the problem that the law of annihilation (Deut 20:16) was not executed in the case of the Gibeonites. The Israelites were not simply cheated by the tricky Gibeonites, who professed that they had come from a distant area; the Israelite leaders swore by YHWH (Josh 9:15b, 18) that they would let them live. Because Lev 19:12 prohibits Israelites from swearing by YHWH's name falsely, the oath could not be broken even when the deceit of the Gibeonites came to light. In this way, the offensive narrative was aligned with the moral standards of the pentateuchal law.

Joshua 14:1–5, 18:1, 19:51, 24:33

According to the Deuteronomistic concept, it is Joshua, the successor to Moses, who is supposed to distribute the Cisjordanian land among the Israelites (Deut 1:38, 3:28, 31:7; Josh 1:6 always with נחל in

---

9. Already Nöldeke (1869: 97) regarded Josh 9:15b, 17–22 as Priestly (similarly Noth 1957: 183: vv. 15b, 17–21). I agree with Fritz (1994: 106–7), who assigned vv. 15b, 18–21, 27 to RedP. Verse 17 does not show any Priestly language and is linked with vv. 16 and 22. In v. 27, only the clause לעדה ו is a Priestly insertion.

the *Hiphil*). In the Deuteronomistic version of the book, Joshua seems to carry out this order only very generally in Josh 11:23 (with נתן לנחלה as in Deut 29:7).[10] But also in the later explications, it is still in most cases Joshua who makes the decisions on the distribution of the land: he receives the order from God (Josh 13:7), acknowledges Caleb's claim (14:13–14), casts the lot (18:6, 8, 10), and allows the Josephites to expand their portion (17:14–18). Be that as it may, the late Priestly editors of the Pentateuch opposed the monarchic principle of the Deuteronomistic tradition and developed a different concept of the distribution of the land. According to these writers, the land should be distributed by a small commission headed by the high priest Eleazar and Joshua, who, in turn, were supported by the leaders (נשיא) of the nine and one-half affected tribes (Num 34:16–29). In this manner, all Israelites would participate in the distribution of the land, and the priests would inherit a leading position.

In the Pentateuch, the concept of apportionment by the high priest, Joshua, and leaders was vested with the authority of a divine order (Num 34:16–18); consequently, the Priestly editors of Joshua felt obliged to introduce it into Joshua and correct its monarchic view. The report about the distribution of the land of Cisjordan was framed by passages presenting the commission of Eleazar, Joshua, and the tribal leaders as the true distributors of the land (Josh 14:1–5, 19:51). All that is reported in between these texts is enclosed within the context of their higher authority. Moreover, the story of the second round of distribution is located within the passage about the assembly of all Israel next to the tabernacle put up in Shiloh (18:1, 19:51). When the editor calls the leaders of the tribes in Josh 14:1 and 19:51 (cf. 21:1), not נשיאים but ראשי האבות 'heads of the families', he wants to reveal the constitutional model behind his concept. The term is used for the members of the assembly of the elders in the postexilic Judean community who ruled together with the congregation of the priests under the auspices of the provincial government (Albertz 1994: 446–47). Thus the land commission, introduced in the book of Joshua, represents the postexilic self-government in some way. In this manner, the distribution of the land had to be brought into conformity with the "democratic standards" of the postexilic period that were conceptualized in the Pentateuch.

In the view of the late Priestly editors of the Pentateuch, the land commission had the task of ensuring a fair distribution of the land. The

---

10. See earlier, Noth 1957: 44–45 and later, de Vos 2003: 300.

larger tribes were to receive a larger portion, the smaller tribes a smaller one (Num 26:52–54, 33:54). The second census of the people in Numbers 26 takes aim at this important target. However, this principle of fair distribution under the control of the authorities is somehow countermined by another principle: the distribution by lot (see אך in Num 26:55–56). One could theoretically agree with Jacob Milgrom (1989: 480–82) that the size of the portion was determined by the number of people, and its location was determined by lot, but nowhere is this clearly stated.

There is some kind of competition at work between the two principles. If God guaranteed a fair distribution by lot, then the commission would have nothing to do. If the commission had full control, then the lot would be superfluous. In my view, the distribution by lot in the Priestly concept of Numbers is a concession to the received tradition in the book of Joshua in which the distribution by lot is anchored (Josh 18:2–10).[11] The topic of a fair distribution was only hinted at in the older material, when the Josephites asked for a larger portion, because they were a numerous people (17:14–18). But it did not become a problem, because (thanks to the wisdom of God) all other tribes received the portions they needed by lot. Hence, the Priestly editors of the book of Joshua did not feel obliged to deal with the topic of a fair distribution explicitly. There may have been some smaller adjustments to the text in that direction, but they remain uncertain (לפי נחלתם 18:4; למשפחותם 19:1, 10, etc.). Thus, in the case of the distribution of the land, the alignment with the Pentateuch remains incomplete. However, because of the introduction of the high priest Eleazar as the leader of the people along with Joshua, his death is reported in Josh 24:33.

---

11. See the restricting particle אך 'only, though', by which the distribution by lot is introduced as a second principle in Num 26:55, after the distribution according to the number of men (vv. 53–54) has been ordered. This looks like a compromise between different concepts. Anyhow, Achenbach (2003: 448–60) suspects that the entire motif of a distribution by lot in Joshua 13–19 depends on Num 26:55, 33:54, because it does not appear in Deuteronomy or elsewhere in the Deuteronomistic History. I think he is right in pointing out that the distribution by lot presupposed a land register and is not attested before the Babylonian and Persian period (Ezek 24:6, Mic 2:5, Neh 11:1). But this does not necessarily mean that it was of Priestly origin. In my view Joshua 13–19 was mostly postexilic and was dependent upon similar geographical material as that used by the Priestly editors of Numbers 26–36; nevertheless, it preceded these late Priestly chapters and therefore also the Priestly redaction of the book of Joshua.

Joshua 17:2aβb–6

In the report on the distribution of the land to the tribe of Manasseh, a special regulation has been inserted dealing with inheritance in a situation in which no male heir is available. This interpolation functions to carry out what was ordered by Moses in Num 27:1–11 and 36. This is the first of two instances in Joshua in which the land commission is summoned to make a concrete decision (the other instance is Josh 21:1). The daughters of Zelophehad refer to YHWH's command explicitly (Josh 17:4; cf. Num 27:4), and it becomes clear that the commission can do nothing other than to translate the Torah into action.

Joshua 20:1–9

In contrast to Volkmar Fritz (1994: 202–3), who found an older Deuteronomistic layer in Josh 20:1–5, 7, 8, I see the basic report on the establishment of cities of refuge (vv. 1–3*, 6–9*) as showing clear characteristics of Priestly style and content. This is especially true in the Septuagint (*Codex Vaticanus*), which is shorter than the Masoretic Text and refers only to the Priestly law of asylum in Num 35:9–34, while the MT also refers to the Deuteronomic law in Deut 19:1–13 and offers a compromise between the two (Rofé 1985: 140). Be that as it may, the fact that the Priestly author of Joshua 20 uses not only the normal term for the cities of refuge (ערי מקלט, v. 2; cf. Num 35:4, etc.) but also the unique expression ערי המועדה 'towns of appointment' (Josh 20:9) shows once more that he cannot be identified with the late Priestly editors of the Pentateuch but that he probably worked later.

The thesis of Martin Noth (1953: 127), used by Volkmar Fritz (1994: 203) and Richard D. Nelson (1997: 229), that Numbers 35 depends on Joshua 20–21, is not convincing, because Josh 20:2b refers back to Num 35:11, 13 explicitly (see, already, N. M. Nicolsky 1930: 152). On the contrary, the reason for adding Joshua 20 to Joshua 13–19 can only be understood when we realize that in Numbers 26–36 the establishment of cities of refuge belongs to the ideal program of land distribution. The divine order to establish those towns after the crossing of the Jordan in Num 35:9–15 is taken literally by the Priestly editor of the book of Joshua and carried out. And the same is true for the similar divine order in Deut 19:1–13 to select these towns after the conquest and colonization of the land. Thus in the case of Joshua 20, the Pentateuch was regarded as normative in a very strict sense.

It is not completely certain that Alexander Rofé (1986: 233) and Richard D. Nelson (1997: 228) are right when they think that the text transmitted by the Septuagint represents the older version of the chapter, because the syntax and content of v. 3 are a little bit idiosyncratic.[12] But if the Septuagint reading is older, we have two stages of alignment with the Pentateuch: the first is where the Priestly law of asylum (Num 35:15) was carried out, and the second is where the Deuteronomic law was integrated (Deut 19:1–13), and both laws were harmonized in a creative manner.[13] In the latter, both laws of asylum in the Pentateuch were obviously regarded as normative.

Joshua 21:1–42

Joshua 21 is linked to the report on the distribution in Josh 14:4 and 18:7 and therefore probably belongs to the same Priestly edition of the book of Joshua as the texts we have been discussing. The establishment of the Levitical cities is explicitly refering back to Num 35:1–8[14] and therefore clearly depends on this late Priestly law (against Noth 1953: 127; Fritz 1994: 210; Nelson 1997: 238). The heads of the Levitical families reminded the land commission of the divine order (Josh 21:2) and, without hesitating, the Israelites were ready to hand over the requested cities (v. 3). Hence, the commission did not have much to do; it only had to ensure that the pentateuchal law was properly translated into action.

First, the 48 cities required by the law (Num 35:7) were distributed by lot among the three Levite clans. In the first place, the Aaronide family of the Kohathites received a greater number than all the rest of the members of its clan (Josh 21:4–8). Second, the rest of the tribes gave a number of their towns to the Levites so that their 48 towns grew (vv. 9–10, 13–42). The cities of refuge were included in this number, as was the case in Num 35:6. Conspicuously, the Aaronide priests received only Judahite towns (Josh 21:13–19). Thus, the Priestly editor of the book of Joshua agreed with the Deuteronomic concept that all priests are Levites (Deut 18:1, 5–8; cf. Exod 6:16–25), but likewise he stressed the Priestly view in the Pentateuch that the Aaronides are the

---

12. Josh 20:3a marks a syntactical break in relation to v. 2 in the Septuagint. The object φυγαδευτήριον 'place of refuge', which is used in v. 2 in the pl. ("cities of refuge"), is repeated in the sing. to explain its purpose ("a place of refuge far a manslayer who kills a person unintentionally"). The sentence of v. 3a digresses from the form of address found in v. 2, while the sentence in v. 3b, "and the cities will be to you a place of refuge," harks back to v. 2 but tells us less than v. 3a does. In comparison, the syntax of v. 3 in the MT is much smoother. In sum, it cannot be totally ruled out that some parts of the Greek text were lost and were restored awkwardly later (e.g., v. 3a). It is conspicuous that in the second part (vv. 7–9) the Greek text follows the Hebrew nearly word for word.

13. Note the function of the elders as judges instead of the Levites in Josh 20:4.

14. See the clear reference of Josh 21:2 to Num 35:2–3.

privileged group separated from all other Levites (Numbers 3–4, 16–18). In any case, the prohibition on landholding for Levites and priests in the Pentateuch (see Deut 18:1–2, Num 18:20) was weakened a little bit by the Priestly editor of Joshua. Not just the Levites (Num 35:1–8) but also the Aaronides are explicitly allowed to own houses and cattle, as was envisioned in Ezek 45:1–8, 48:8–14.[15] Thus Joshua 21 should mainly be seen as an alignment with the Pentateuch; the divine law of Num 35:1–8 is carried out in a detailed and highly sophisticated manner. But in small ways it also accommodates the high standards of the Torah to the needs of the late postexilic Priesthood.

Joshua 22:7–34

The Deuteronomistic report on the dismissal of the Transjordanian tribes (Josh 22:1–6; see Noth 1953: 133) is amplified by the story about how these tribes built an altar east of the Jordan in Gilead and thus provoked a military conflict with the Cisjordanian congregation of Israel (vv. 9–34). Although Martin Noth theorized an older tradition (1953: 133), the Priestly origin of this story is now widely accepted (Fritz 1994: 221; Nelson 1997: 247). There is no consensus on the assignment of vv. 7–8.[16] But once we become aware that the altar story originally dealt only with the Reubenites and Gadites, who actually settled in Gilead,[17] it is reasonable to suppose that the Transjordanian part of Manasseh, mentioned in the Deuteronomistic passage before (22:1), was dispatched to Bashan separately. Thus, a Priestly origin of vv. 7–8 is likewise probable.

The meaning of this strange story only becomes clear if we realize that it reflects the difference between the Deuteronomistic and the Priestly concepts of land that are found in the Pentateuch (in a theological manner). For the Deuteronomistic editor, the conquest of the land began with the crossing of the river Arnon (Deut 2:24–37), so in his view Gilead (and Bashan) in Transjordan belonged to the promised land. For the late Priestly editors of the Pentateuch, who were aligned with the borders of the Egyptian province of Canaan in the second millennium B.C.E. (cf. Num 34:1–12), the promised land was mostly restricted to the land of Cisjordan; only the regions in northeastern Transjordan, such as Bashan and Aram–Damascus were included, but

---

15. See Albertz 1994: 432–36; 2003: 372–76).

16. Noth (1953: 133) takes Josh 22:7–8 as a redactional link. Fritz (1994: 226–27) and Nelson (1997: 251) regard the verses as a later addition.

17. So Josh 22:32–34 MT. The expressions "half-tribe of Manasseh" in vv. 7, 9–11, 13, 15, 21 and the "Manassites" in vv. 30, 31 are best explained as glosses (see Noth 1953: 133).

Gilead was definitely excluded.[18] Thus the Priestly editor of the book of Joshua had no problem with the eastern Manassites: they could just go back to their dwellings in Bashan (Josh 22:7–8). But he faced a serious problem with the return of the Reubenites and Gadites to Gilead. Why would they live outside the promised land in a possibly unclean country (v. 19)? All things considered, they should probably come back to Israel again (v. 19). How could they stay connected with YHWH and the congregation of Israel if YHWH had set a border in between (v. 25)? The solution to this problem was a huge altar erected in the foreign country that was not made for sacrifices but for witnessing the religious and ethnic solidarity of the Israelites abroad in spite of their territorial separation (vv. 26–29). At the same time, the Priestly editor made it clear that sacrificial cult outside the promised land (in Gilead or anywhere in the Diaspora) would be a sacrilege against YHWH and was therefore strictly forbidden (vv. 16–20).

Thus the Priestly editor of the book of Joshua was obligated to both traditions: to the Deuteronomic command of centralization and to the Priestly concept of the promised land of the Pentateuch. He corrected the wider land concept found in the books of Deuteronomy and Joshua, but he did not deny it totally. In contrast, according to him, Israelite existence was possible outside the promised country from early times on, as long as specific cultic restrictions were observed. Moreover, the Priestly editor used the Deuteronomistic concept of land for relating the affiliation of Diaspora Jews to the congregation of Israel. Thus Josh 22:7–34 can be seen as a creative alignment of the book of Joshua with the two contrasting but nevertheless prescriptive concepts of the promised land found in the Pentateuch.

Conclusion

Apart from Josh 4:15–17, all Priestly passages of the book of Joshua clearly refer to specific verses or concepts of the Pentateuch. Criteria and standards named in the Pentateuch (Num 32:29–30, Deut 29:10, Lev 19:12) are taken into account (Josh 4:12–13; 8:33*; 9:15, 18–21); announcements given in the Pentateuch (Exod 16:35) are confirmed (Josh 5:10–12); divine commandments and laws proclaimed in the Pentateuch (Num 34:16–18, 27:1–11, 35:9–34, 35:1–8) are carried out (Josh 14:1–5, 18:1, 19:51, 20:1–9, 21:1–42); and laws and concepts that compete with each other in the Pentateuch in some way (Num 35:9–34

---

18. See Keel and Küchler 1984: 244–50.

versus Deut 19:1–13; Num 34:1–12 versus Deuteronomy 2–3) are harmonized and interpreted in a creative manner. Apart from a few earlier influences of the book of Joshua on the Pentateuch,[19] all Priestly passages in the book of Joshua clearly show a material and literary dependency on passages in the Pentateuch. Because they often depend on Priestly texts, which are to be seen as a very late stage in the development of the Priestly tradition (Numbers 26–36), they can only be of very late origin.

Moreover, as shown above, the Pentateuchal criteria, standards, laws, and concepts are always regarded as normative in a rather strict way, even where competing laws and concepts in the Pentateuch exist. In our case, the contradictions are interpreted in a creative manner (Joshua 20 MT; 22:7–34). Hence, the Priestly passages can best be explained as aligning the book of Joshua with the book of Torah, which had become canonical in the meantime. With the canonization of the Pentateuch, the ideal Priestly concept of the seizure and the distribution of the promised land developed in Numbers 26–36 became authoritative. Because the Deuteronomistic book of Joshua, even after it was amplified by several additions (at least as part of the Hexateuch), differed widely from the canonical concept in many respects, some Priestly scribes felt obliged to bring it into line with the new foundational document of the Jewish community. By doing so, they were *Schriftgelehrte* in a strict sense.

Because the Levitical town list in 1 Chronicles 6 presupposes Joshua 21, the editing must have happened before the emergence of the Chronicler, whose work is mostly dated between the middle of the fourth and the beginning of the third century B.C.E.[20] Furthermore, the Chronicler regarded the Pentateuch as authoritative.[21] Thus the Priestly alignment of the book of Joshua is an early piece of evidence for the canonization of the Pentateuch. Consequently, the Pentateuch had probably become authoritative for the Jewish community and its *literati* at the end of the fifth or the beginning of the fourth century, at the latest. This date accords with the evidence given by Hecateus of Abdera, who clearly described a Torah-based Judaism in his short report about the Jews, written in the early Hellenistic period.[22] The process following the pro-

---

19. So Joshua 9 on Deut 29:10 and probably the lot concept in Joshua 13–19 on Num 26:55–56.

20. See the discussions in Japhet (2002: 50–54) and Knoppers (2003–4: 1.101–17).

21. See Albertz 1994: 547–50; and Bae 2005: 149–61.

22. For this interpretation, see Albertz 2001: 40–46.

mulgation of the Pentateuch, which led to the shaping of such a new Jewish way of life and world view, probably took several decades to complete.

Apart from the book of Joshua, the rest of the Deuteronomistic History shows only a few insertions of a Priestly nature (e.g., 1 Sam 2:22b, 1 Kgs 8:1–11*). Moreover, they are alignments that are not as prescriptive; actually, they are redactional links that try to demonstrate that there was an unbroken continuity between the Mosaic tabernacle and the Solomonic temple. Thus, the book of Joshua, which still deals with Israel's foundation history and belonged to the Hexateuch for a short period, obviously was of much more importance. Without such a far-reaching alignment with the demands and the concepts of the canonized Pentateuch, it would have been impossible to canonize the book of Joshua itself in later times. The canonical alignment of the books of Samuel and Kings was no longer done by editing but was a complete rewriting of Israel's preexilic history in the books of Chronicles. This finally paved the way for the canonization of the Former Prophets in the late third century.

References

Achenbach, R.
2003 *Die Vollendung der Tora: Studien zur Redaktionsgeschichte des Numeribuches im Kontext von Hexateuch und Pentateuch.* Beihefte zur Zeitschrift für altorientalische Rechtsgeschichte 3. Wiesbaden: Harrassowitz.

Albertz, R.
1994 *A History of Israelite Religion in the Old Testament Period.* 2 vols. Louisville: Westminster John Knox.
2001 An End of the Confusion? Why the Old Testament Cannot Be a Hellenistic Book. Pp. 30–46 in *Did Moses Speak Attic? Jewish Historiography and Scripture in the Hellenistic Period*, ed. L. L. Grabbe. JSOTSup 317. European Seminar in Historical Methodology 3. Sheffield: Sheffield Academic Press.
2003 *Israel in Exile: The History and Literature of the Sixth Century* B.C.E. Studies in Biblical Literature 3. Atlanta: Society of Biblical Literature.

Bae, H.-S.
2005 *Vereinte Suche nach JHWH: Die Hiskianische und Josianische Reform in der Chronik.* BZAW 355. Berlin: de Gruyter.

Blum, E.
1990 *Studien zur Komposition des Pentateuch.* BZAW 189. Berlin: de Gruyter.
1997 Der kompositionelle Knoten am Übergang von Josua zu Richter: Ein Entflechtungsvorschlag. Pp. 181–212 in *Deuteronomy and Deuteronomic Literature*, ed. M. Vervenne and J. Lust. BETL 54. Leuven: Peeters.

2003 Beschneidung und Passa in Kanaan: Beobachtungen und Mutmaßungen zu Jos 5. Pp. 292–322 in *Freiheit und Recht: Festschrift für Frank Crüsemann zum 65. Geburtstag*, ed. C. Hardmeier, R. Kessler, and A. Ruwe. Gütersloh: Chr. Kaiser/Gütersloher Verlagshaus.

Fritz, V.
1994 *Das Buch Josua*. HAT 1/7. Tübingen: Mohr Siebeck.

Japhet, S.
2002 *1 Chronik*. HTKAT. Freiburg: Herder.

Keel, O., and Küchler, M.
1984 *Orte und Landschaften der Bibel: Handbuch und Studienreiseführer zum Heiligen Land*. Vol. 1: *Geographisch-geschichtliche Landeskunde*. Zurich: Benzinger / Göttingen: Vandenhoeck & Ruprecht.

Knauf, E. A.
1996 L'"historiographie deutéronomiste" (DtrG) existe-t-elle? Pp. 409–18 in *Israël construit son histoire: L'historiographie deutéronomiste à la lumière récentes*. Le monde de la Bible 34. Geneva: Labor & Fides.

Knoppers, G. N.
2003-4 *I Chronicles: A New Translation with Introduction and Commentary.* 2 vols. AB 12–12A. New York: Doubleday.

Kratz, R. G.
2000 *Die Komposition der erzählenden Bücher des Alten Testaments*. Uni-Taschenbücher 2157. Göttingen: Vandenhoeck & Ruprecht.
2002 Der vor- und nachpriesterliche Hexateuch. Pp. 295–323 in *Abschied vom Jahwisten: Die Komposition des Hexateuch in der jüngsten Diskussion*, ed. J. C. Gertz, K. Schmid, and M. Witte. BZAW 315. Berlin: de Gruyter.

Magen, Y.
2000 Mt. Gerizim: A Temple City. *Qadmoniot* 120: 74–118.

Milgrom, J.
1989 *Numbers*. JPS Torah Commentary. Philadelphia: Jewish Publication Society.

Nelson, R. D.
1997 *Joshua: A Commentary.* OTL. Louisville: Westminster John Knox.

Nicolsky, N. M.
1930 Das Asylrecht in Israel. *ZAW* 48: 146–79.

Nöldeke, T.
1869 *Untersuchungen zur Kritik des Alten Testaments*. Kiel: Schwers.

Noth, M.
1938 *Das Buch Josua*. HAT 1/7. Tübingen: Mohr Siebeck.
1953 *Das Buch Josua*. HAT 1/7. 2nd, rev. edition. Tübingen: Mohr Siebeck.
1957 *Überlieferungsgeschichtliche Studien: Die sammelnden und bearbeiten Geschichtswerke im Alten Testament*. 2nd ed. (= 3rd ed., 1967). Tübingen: Niemeyer. [1st ed., *Überlieferungsgeschichchtliche Studien*. Schriften der Königsberger Gelehrten Gesellschaft: Geisteswissenschaftliche Klasse 18. Halle: Niemeyer, 1943]

Otto, E.
2000 *Das Deuteronomium im Pentateuch und Hexateuch: Studien zur Literatur-geschichte von Pentateuch und Hexateuch im Lichte des Deuteronomium-rahmens.* FAT 30. Tübingen: Mohr Siebeck.
2002 Forschungen zum nachpriesterlichen Pentateuch. *TRu* 67: 125–55.
Rofé, A.
1985 Joshua 20: Historico-Literary Criticism Illustrated. Pp. 131–47 in *Empirical Models for Biblical Criticism,* ed. J. H. Tigay. Philadelphia: University of Pennsylvania Press.
1986 The History of the Cities of Refuge in Biblical Law. Pp. 205–39 in *Studies in Bible,* ed. S. Japhet. ScrHier 31. Jerusalem: Magnes.
Römer, T. C.
2001 La fin de l'historiographie deutéronomiste et le retour de l'Hexateuque. *TZ* 57: 269–80.
Vos, J. C. de
2003 *Das Los Judas: Über Entstehung und Ziele der Landbeschreibung in Josua 15.* VTSup 95. Leiden: Brill.
Würthwein, E.
1994 Erwägungen zum sog. deuteronomistischen Geschichtswerk: Eine Skizze. Pp. 1–11 in *Studien zum deuteronomistischen Geschichtswerk.* BZAW 227. Berlin: de Gruyter.
Zenger, E., et al.
2004 *Einleitung in das Alte Testament.* 5th ed. Kohlhammer Studienbücher Theologie 1/1. Stuttgart: Kohlhammer.

Nehemiah and Sanballat:
The Enemy Without or Within?

GARY N. KNOPPERS

The Pennsylvania State University

In a famous episode in the work of Herodotus, the Athenian delegation addresses the Spartan delegation, reassuring them that the Athenians will not enter into a pact with Xerxes. In so doing, the Athenians speak of the need to avenge the destruction of their temples and images by the Persians (*Hist.* 8.144.1–2; cf. 5.102) and appeal to a larger sense of pan-Hellenic solidarity (*to Hellēnikon*): "the kinship of Greeks, one in blood and one in language. The shrines of the gods and the sacrifices belong to us in common and there is our common way of life. It would be indecent if the Athenians should prove false to all of these" (*Hist.* 8.144.2–3).[1] On the basis of this declaration that Herodotus attributes to the Athenian emissaries, one might think that the *Hellēnikon* was relatively straightforward and obvious.[2] Greeks are defined by the same blood (*homaimon*), the same language (*homomglōsson*), shared sanctuaries and sacrifices (*theōn hidrymata te koina kai thysiai*), and similar social customs (*ēthea te homotropa*).[3] But readers of Herodotus know

---

1. Whether the sequence of shared attributes is placed in a hierarchical order of importance is debated. Some think that blood is the most critical of all the common qualities listed by Herodotus: I. Malkin, "Introduction," in *Ancient Perceptions of Greek Ethnicity* (ed. I. Malkin; Cambridge: Harvard University Press, 2001) 1–28; D. Konstan, "*To Hellēnikon ethnos*: Ethnicity and the Construction of Ancient Greek Identity," in *Ancient Perceptions of Greek Ethnicity*, 29–50. Striking by their absence in this list of shared attributes are any references to political association or to ancestral territory. This may be part of Herodotus's achievement: J. Hall, *Ethnic Identity in Greek Antiquity* (Cambridge: Cambridge University Press, 1997) 44–45.

2. The discussion of attributes may be compared with the oft-quoted list of components assembled by the modern anthropologist A. D. Smith: a collective name, a common myth of descent, a shared history, a sense of a distinctive shared culture, an association with a specific territory, and a collective sense of solidarity: *The Ethnic Origins of Nations* (Oxford: Blackwell, 1986) 22–31.

3. In this context, the later comments of the Apostle Paul on the traits of what (from his perspective) constitutes Jewish identity are also relevant (Rom 2:17–3:8, 11:1–2).

305

that the Athenian answer delivered to the Spartans may be compared and contrasted with the earlier answer that the Athenian emissaries had just given to King Alexander II of Macedon (*Hist.* 8.139, 143). Readers of Herodotus would also know that only a few of the Greek city-states did, in fact, band together and resist the Persian invasion.

The degree to which a Spartan delegation would agree with the claims made by the Athenians is the subject of some debate. Relations between the two groups were hardly uncomplicated (e.g., *Hist.* 1.56–68, 152–53; 5.97; 7.133; 9.102). After all, the Spartan emissaries had just accused the Athenians of starting the war for their own ends and without consulting their neighboring city-states (*Hist.* 8.142). It seems that clearly defining one's larger collective identity is not always such a simple matter.

Modern discussions of the highly complex issue of ethnicity differ greatly in their approaches to and understanding of the topic.[4] Some scholars conceive of ethnicity as a tangible and inherently stable trait, a social and historical reality reflecting the existence of different groups, while others conceive of ethnicity as a much more malleable, mutable, and contested category, one that is very much shaped by perceptions, subjective claims, and changing social circumstances.[5]

In the first instance, scholars emphasize primordial origins, ties of blood, ties of birth, common myths, common religious institutions, and shared social structures as givens. Assumed cultural, national, or somatic traits bind the society together.[6] Founding myths, ancestral bonds to a common land, and shared genealogies may function as primordial charters to validate collective membership and to lend internal cohesiveness to the people in question. Given their emphasis on deeply-rooted kinship ties, the scholars in this camp think that ethnic groups are generally conservative in nature, persisting for many generations and, to a greater or lesser extent, resistant to change.

---

4. Malkin, "Introduction," 4–19; R. Thomas, "Ethnicity, Genealogy, and Hellenism in Herodotus," in *Ancient Perceptions of Greek Ethnicity* (ed. I. Malkin; Cambridge: Harvard University Press, 2001) 213–33.

5. F. Barth, *Ethnic Groups and Boundaries* (Boston: Little, Brown, 1969); R. H. Thompson, *Theories of Ethnicity: A Critical Appraisal* (New York: Greenwood, 1989); K. L. Sparks, *Ethnicity and Identity in Ancient Israel: Prolegomena to the Study of Ethnic Sentiments and Their Expression in the Hebrew Bible* (Winona Lake, IN: Eisenbrauns, 1998).

6. O. Patterson, "Context and Choice in Ethnic Allegiance: A Theoretical Framework and Caribbean Case Study," in *Ethnicity: Theory and Experience* (ed. N. Glazer and D. P. Moynihan; Cambridge: Harvard University Press, 1975) 308.

In the second instance, scholars view ethnicity as being much more situational, circumstantial, and fluid in character. The scholars in this camp do not deny the factors of blood, social customs, and religious structures, but they view the boundaries that separate groups as malleable and continually shifting. In this view, shared descent, ties to land, social customs, and cultic practices may serve as indexes of ethnic identity but are not necessarily criteria of ethnic identity. So, for example, the Attic orator Isocrates (*Paneg.* 50) in the fourth century B.C.E. moves beyond the definition of what constitutes Greek identity that one sees in Herodotus roughly a century earlier, shifting the emphasis away from blood (*homaimon*), descent (*genos*), and birth (*physis*) to a frame of mind (*dianoia*), a type of education or culture (*paideia*), and a certain temper (*ethos*).[7]

Seen from the perspective of this second approach, ethnic allegiances may result more from political, social, and economic interests than from strict genetic or kinship ties.[8] Members of a given ethnicity may realign their allegiance as a response to changing political, economic, or social circumstances. If a shift of this sort takes place, the boundaries of affected groups will change. Moreover, collective identities need not be entirely exclusionary or hierarchical in classification. Collective identities may be multiple and overlapping. One might be a member of a particular city state and a member of a larger pan-Hellenic people. The identity of the citizens of ancient Syracuse, for instance, could be articulated as Syracusans, Corinthian colonists, Siceliots, Dorians, or Greeks, according to different civic, political, cultic, and international contexts.[9]

Distinguishing between emic and etic categories of study, scholars contrast the views of what outsiders may say about the character of a group from what the members of the group say about themselves—their genesis, religious practices, civic identity, and way of life. Some groups, especially in complex societies, may display a clear sense of the

---

7. S. Saïd, "The Discourse of Identity in Greek Rhetoric from Isocrates to Aristides," in *Ancient Perceptions of Greek Ethnicity* (ed. I. Malkin; Cambridge: Harvard University Press, 2001) 275–99.

8. There is a subset of scholars within this second group of scholars who view the citation of primordial and kinship ties as simply serving the instrumental or situational needs of the groups that invent them, but this purely instrumental view of ethnicity may be regarded as too reductive and ahistorical to be helpful in understanding the long-term development of complex societies.

9. Malkin, "Introduction," 3.

self and "the other," actively defining their own identities by articulating both their own _ethnos_ and what they are not, the _ethnē_ that are their opposites.[10] Indeed, members within a group may disagree among themselves about the constitution, limits, and boundaries of their group or represent their collective identity differently in different historical contexts. One recalls the later complaint of Josephus (_Ant._ 9.290–91; 11.114–115, 340–44) about the Samaritans that when speaking to one audience in prosperous times they declared themselves to be Jews, or at least kin to the Jews, but when presenting themselves to another audience in difficult times (for the Jews) they declared themselves to be unrelated to the Jews.

The implications of this sort of flexibility in group identity are many, but one of them is that the typical behaviors of an ethnic group at any given time should not be accepted as fixed and immutable signs of permanent identity. Seen from this perspective, both the definition of the group and the definition of the other are related, evolving, and never-ending ventures that are always subject to revision.

When one comes to the book of Ezra-Nehemiah, one might initially think that the first approach, stressing the conservative nature of genealogies, kinship ties, religious rites, and common social mores, is the more appropriate approach. The book exhibits a distinctively bipolar view of identity; there are people who belong to the Judean community and people who do not. The people of Judah are to be contrasted with and set apart from their neighbors. The point bears investigation, because it very much affects how one might view the work of Nehemiah, his relations to his own constituents in Judah, and his relations to his declared adversaries, such as Sanballat and Tobiah. In what follows, I will first explore the stable, conservative approach as applied to Nehemiah's relations with his people and his contemporary critics. I will then complicate this approach by recourse to the insights provided by the second approach. These approaches to the subject of ethnicity may illumine both the program of the Judean governor and the program of the people who disagreed with him.

Methodologically, my focus will be on the first-person accounts in Nehemiah, the so-called Nehemiah memoir or Nehemiah memorial.

---

10. M. W. Hamilton, "Who Was a Jew? Jewish Ethnicity during the Achaemenid Period," _ResQ_ 37 (1995) 102–17; M. G. Brett, "Interpreting Ethnicity," in _Ethnicity and the Bible_ (ed. M. G. Brett; Leiden: Brill, 1996) 3–22; S. J. D. Cohen, _The Beginnings of Jewishness: Boundaries, Varieties, Uncertainties_ (Berkeley: University of California Press, 1999); B. Isaac, _The Invention of Racism in Classical Antiquity_ (Princeton: Princeton University Press, 2004).

Both what Nehemiah confesses and what he concedes may be revealing.[11] In my discussion, I will also pay some attention to other biblical evidence (for example, the lists and genealogies that appear in the book) and to some relevant extrabiblical evidence.

The Members Within and the Others Without

Already within the first verses of the first chapter of Nehemiah, one sees a strong sense of ethnicity expressed by the character of Nehemiah, an ethnicity that is keyed to a certain but limited ancestral territory. The king's cupbearer in the Persian court exhibits a keen sense of solidarity with the people of Judah and Jerusalem, in spite of the great geographic distance that separates them (Neh 1:1–2). His concern is with the Judeans (*ha-yĕhûdîm*), the remnant who survived the captivity, and with Jerusalem (Neh 1:2). The Judeans may be tied to the land; but, like Nehemiah, they may not all live there. Nehemiah considers himself to be a member of this society, even though he occupies a high position in the Achaemenid administration and resides in the fortress of Susa. Jerusalem is the city that houses the graves of his ancestors (2:3). In addition to the implied reference here, there are a couple of

---

11. J. Blenkinsopp takes the memoirs as basically comprising the first-person accounts in Neh 1:2–2:20; 3:33–7:5; 12:31–43; 13:4–31: *Ezra-Nehemiah* (OTL; Philadelphia: Westminster, 1988) 46–47. To this were added third-person accounts dealing with several of the same incidents (Neh 3:1–32; 11:1–2; 12:27–30, 44–47; 13:1–3), several lists and genealogies (7:6–72, 11:3–12:26), and editorial comments (e.g., 1:1; 12:27–29, 33–36, 41–42, 43). Some scholars, including Blenkinsopp, also see some of the first-person material in Nehemiah (for example, the prayer in 1:5–11a) as editorial. In his reconstruction, H. G. M. Williamson posits two stages in the composition of the memoir itself (the second stage containing 1:4–11; 3:36–37; 5:14–19; 6:14; 13:4–14, 15–22, 23–31): *Ezra, Nehemiah* (WBC 16; Waco, TX: Word, 1985) xxiv–xxviii. Like Blenkinsopp, Williamson thinks that a series of editorial additions were made to the work (e.g., Nehemiah 10; 11:1–2, 3–20, 21–36; 12:1–26, 27–43; 13:1–3). Developing and extending the view of Williamson, T. Rheinmuth distinguishes between a wall-building narrative and a memorial composition: *Der Bericht Nehemias: Zue literarischen Eigenart, traditionsgeschichtlichen Prägung und innerbiblischen Rezeption des Ich-Berichts Nehemias* (OBO 183; Göttingen: Vandenhoeck & Ruprecht, 2002). Some recent analyses have contended for a longer process of composition and for more editorial interventions in the first-person materials. See, for example, R. Kratz, *Composition of the Books of the Old Testament* (London: T. &. T. Clark, Continuum, 2005) 62–68. In his recent monograph, J. L. Wright argues that the original Nehemiah memorial was actually quite short: *Rebuilding Identity: The Nehemiah Memoir and Its Earliest Readers* (BZAW 348; Berlin: de Gruyter, 2004). Wright provides a convenient summary of his research elsewhere in this volume (pp. 333–348). A complete overview of the issues and an analysis of the relevant scholarship are impossible in this context.

other occasions in the Nehemiah memoir in which the term (*yĕhûdîm*) seems to carry a predominantly ethnic sense (e.g., Neh 4:6, 5:8).[12]

When he hears that "the survivors who remained from the captivity (*ha-pĕlêṭâ ʾăser-niš²ărû min-ha-šĕbî*) there in the province are in great trouble and disgrace," Nehemiah weeps, fasts, mourns, and utters a prayer that creatively alludes both to King Solomon's temple dedication prayer (1 Kgs 8:22–53) and to the promises of Deuteronomy (30:1–10).[13] His confession and petitions, spoken on behalf of himself, his ancestral house (*bêt-ʾābî*), and the children of Israel (*bĕnê yiśrāʾēl*), acknowledge the sins that "we have committed against you" (Neh 1:6). Hence, in the opening verses of Nehemiah one finds a clear understanding of the group with which Nehemiah identifies, the *yĕhûdîm*, as well as his assertion that this group may be identified with the people of Israel. The crucial correlation found here between the Judeans and Israel is not unique to this text. It recurs elsewhere in the Nehemiah memoir (1:6, 2:10, 13:18).[14]

Within the first-person narratives of Nehemiah, one finds a basic consistency in the terminology employed to describe the people with whom Nehemiah identifies. Most common are references to *ha-yĕhûdîm* 'the Judeans' (Neh 2:16; 3:33, 34; 4:6; 5:1, 17; 6:6; 13:23) and to *hāʿām, kol-hāʿām, hāʿām hazzeh* '(all) the/this (Judean) people' (e.g., Neh 3:38; 4:7,

---

12. In many cases, the term simply refers to the inhabitants of the province (cf. Josephus, *Ant.* 11.173). The shift from a purely territorial sense to an ethnic sense with religious overtones is attested elsewhere in the Hebrew Scriptures (e.g., Esth 2:5 and passim; Blenkinsopp, *Ezra-Nehemiah*, 223–25). Among the relevant pieces of extrabiblical evidence, the Elephantine papyri use of the term *yĕhûdîn* to refer to the members of the Elephantine colony (e.g., AP 6.3–10, 8.2, 10.3) and the recently-discovered cuneiform texts refer to *āl-Yāhūdu* 'the town of Judah', which is probably in the Babylon-Borsippa region. See further, F. Joannès and A. Lemaire, "Trois tablettes cunéiformes à l'onomastique ouest-sémitique," *Transeu* 17 (1999) 17–34; D. S. Vanderhooft, "New Evidence Pertaining to the Transition from Neo-Babylonian to Achaemenid Administration in Palestine," in *Yahwism after the Exile: Perspectives on Israelite Religion in the Persian Era* (ed. R. Albertz and B. Becking; Assen: Van Gorcum, 2003) 219–25; L. E. Pearce, "New Evidence for Judeans in Babylonia," in *Judah and the Judeans in the Persian Period* (ed. O. Lipschits and M. Oeming; Winona Lake, IN: Eisenbrauns, 2006) 399–411.

13. Both texts deal with exile, but one promises an actual return (Deut 30:3–5, 8–10), while the other promises divine compassion (1 Kgs 8:50). Deuteronomy 30 makes no mention of a central sanctuary, but 1 Kings 8 repeatedly does. Like the Passover invitation of Hezekiah (2 Chr 30:6–9), the Nehemiah prayer ingeniously selects features from both source texts to formulate its own distinctive appeal. On the Chronicler's text, see my "What Has Mt. Zion to Do with Mt. Gerizim? A Study in the Early Relations between the Jews and the Samaritans in the Persian Period," *Bulletin of the Canadian Society of Biblical Studies/Le société canadienne des études bibliques* 64 (2004–5) 22–28.

14. The same association with or identification of Judah, the people of Judah, and the Judahites with Israel is found elsewhere in Nehemiah (8:1; 9:1, 2; 10:34; 12:47).

16; 5:1, 13, 15, 18, 19; 7:4; cf. 13:1).[15] As might be expected, references to *yĕhûdâ* 'Judah' (Neh 4:4, 13:12), the house of Judah (Neh 4:10), and the children of Judah (Neh 13:16) also appear.[16] Apart from the allusions in the opening verses of Nehemiah (1:2, 3) to people who remained from the captivity (*šĕbî*), references to the Judean captivity do not elsewhere appear in the Nehemiah memoir.[17] In this context, the first-person Nehemiah narratives may be contrasted with the material in Ezra 1–6 (Ezra 3:8), the parallel lists of returnees in Ezra 2 and Nehemiah 7 (Ezra 2:1//Neh 7:6), and the Ezra materials (e.g., Ezra 8:35, 9:7; Neh 8:17; cf. Deut 21:10, 13; 28:41; 2 Chr 29:6) in which references of this sort do appear. One also thinks of the frequent references to the *bĕnê ha-gôlâ* 'the children of the Exile' (Ezra 4:1; 6:19–20; 8:35; 10:7, 16; compare *bĕnê gālûtâ* in Ezra 6:16), *hā'ōlîm miššĕbî ha-gôlâ* 'the ones who came up from the captivity of the Exile'; Ezra 2:1//Neh 7:6), and *ha-gôlâ* 'the Exile(s)" (Ezra 1:11, 9:4, 10:6; Neh 7:6) elsewhere in Ezra-Nehemiah.[18] These expressions are not found in the Nehemiah memoir.[19]

In the narratives and lists found elsewhere within the book of Ezra-Nehemiah, one occasionally finds references to Judah and Benjamin[20] as tribal entities with territorial associations (Ezra 1:5; 4:1; 10:9; Neh 11:1, 4, 7, 20, 25, 31, 36), but references of this sort are not to be found in the Nehemiah memoir. This evidence suggests that, when Nehemiah refers to the *yĕhûdîm*, he is almost always referring to the residents of the province of Judah.

If the Nehemiah materials present a clear sense of the protagonists in his story, consisting of Nehemiah himself and the Judeans, they also present clear notions of the antagonists who resist Nehemiah's mission on behalf of the Judeans. The major opposition to Nehemiah's initiatives does not stem from the Achaemenid king of his time. Quite the

---

15. The usage is also common elsewhere in Ezra-Nehemiah (Ezra 2:2, 70; 3:1, 11, 13; 8:15, 36; 10:1, 9, 11, 13; Neh 7:4, 5, 7, 72; 8:1, 3, 5, 6, 7, 9, 11, 12, 13, 16; 9:10; 10:15, 29, 35; 11:1, 24; 12:30, 38). The concentration on the territory of Judah, as opposed to a larger land of Israel, is telling.

16. In some cases, Judah appears as a personal name (e.g., Neh 11:9; 12:8, 34, 36).

17. There is a reference by Nehemiah to the *sibyâ* (Neh 3:36), but this is not a direct allusion to the Judean captivity. Rather, it is what Nehemiah wishes for Sanballat, Tobiah, and their followers.

18. Note also the 'assembly of the exile' (*qĕhal hā-gôlâ*) in Ezra 10:8, 12–16 and the 'assembly of God' (*qĕhāl hā'ĕlōhîm*) in Neh 13:1. In the latter case, the writers are quoting from the "Book of Moses," that is, from Deut 23:4–7.

19. The two concepts are linked, however, in the present text of Neh 7:1–5. The desire to increase the Judean population of Jerusalem leads Nehemiah to examine an old list (7:6–72) of returnees (//Ezra 2:1–70).

20. Occasionally, Benjamin appears as a personal name (e.g., Neh 3:23, 10:32).

contrary, this ruler plays the critical role of a powerful patron, sanctioning Nehemiah's return, supporting his rebuilding of the city walls, and enabling his return to Judah some years later. Artaxerxes is thus portrayed quite positively. The main opposition stems from locals—that is, the neighboring nations and their leaders.

One set of regular expressions found in the Nehemiah memoir involves the term *ha-gôyîm* 'the nations' (Neh 5:8, 9, 17; 6:6, 16; 13:26). What Nehemiah usually means by this term is the peoples surrounding the province of Yehud, *ha-gôyîm ʾăšer-sĕbîbōtênû* 'the nations roundabout us' (Neh 5:17; 6:6, 16), that is, the neighboring Samarians, Ashdodites, Arabs, Moabites, and Ammonites.[21] On one occasion, Nehemiah speaks of the *ʿammîm* 'peoples' with similar connotations (Neh 13:24), but the expression 'the people(s) of the land(s)' (*ʿam-hāʾāreṣ*; *ʿammê hāʾāreṣ*; *ʿammê hāʾărāṣôt*), which recurs frequently elsewhere in Ezra-Nehemiah (Ezra 3:3, 4:4; 9:1, 2, 11, 14; 10:2, 11; Neh 9:24, 30; 10:29, 31, 32), does not appear in the Nehemiah memoir.[22]

Closely related to Nehemiah's use of the nations is his use of *ʾō/ôyēb* 'enemy' (Neh 4:9; 5:9; 6:1, 16; cf. 9:28) and *ṣar* 'adversary' (Neh 4:5; cf. Ezra 4:1, Neh 9:27), because he equates the nations with his foes. So, for example, during his campaign to implement social reforms among his fellow Judeans, he upbraids the nobles and prefects, saying, "The thing that you're doing is not right. Is it not better that you walk in the fear of our God than (elicit) the reproach of the nations (*ha-gôyîm*), our enemies (*ʾôyĕbênû*; Neh 5:9)?" Later, when Nehemiah comments on the success of the wall rebuilding, he observes that "when all our enemies (*kol-ʾôyĕbênû*) heard (of it), all the nations (*kol-ha-gôyîm*) round about us were afraid and fell very low in their own estimation" (Neh 6:16). From Nehemiah's vantage point, Judah is surrounded by adversaries.

Just as Nehemiah attempts to align himself closely with the cause of his people, so the Nehemiah memoir closely links the opposition, "the nations roundabout," with their leaders.[23] So, for example, Nehemiah remarks that: "When word reached Sanballat, Tobiah, Geshem, the

---

21. Elsewhere in the book, see the reference to the 'nations of the lands' (*gôyē-hāʾāreṣ*) in Ezra 6:21. On one occasion in Nehemiah (13:26), the phrase "among the many nations" clearly has broader implications, because it is depicting the international situation in the era of Solomon.

22. The reference to the peoples in Neh 1:8 occurs in the context of an allusion to earlier tradition (Deut 30:1–3). Other references in the book to the (foreign) people(s) appear in Ezra 9:14; Neh 9:10, 22.

23. A notable exception is the ruler of Ashdod, who is never mentioned. The Ashdodites make a couple of appearances in the Nehemiah memoir, in each case in a negative context (Neh 4:1, 13:23–24).

Arab, and the rest of our enemies (*yeter 'ôyĕbênû*) that I had rebuilt the wall and not a breach remained in it . . . , they came to realize that this work had been accomplished with the help of our God" (Neh 6:1; cf. 4:9). Hence, although the Nehemiah memoir presents clear protagonists, it also presents clear antagonists, who oppose each of the new initiatives that Nehemiah pushes on behalf of his people.

The work justifies this blanket and unambiguously negative characterization of "the other" by pursuing a number of complementary literary strategies. One such strategy involves depicting the actions of Nehemiah's opponents as diametrically opposed to the well-being of the Jerusalem community. In fact, the Nehemiah narrative portrays an intensification of the threat that Nehemiah and the people encounter as the campaign to rebuild Jerusalem's walls proceeds.

The first introduction to Sanballat and to Tobiah in Nehemiah is negative. "When Sanballat, the Horonite, and Tobiah, the Ammonite servant, heard [of Nehemiah's arrival], it displeased them greatly that someone had come to seek the good of the children of Israel" (*bā' lĕbaqqēš ṭôbâ libnê yiśra'ēl*; Neh 2:10). As Blenkinsopp points out, the comment puns on Tobiah's name.[24] Nehemiah had come to Judah to advance the *ṭôbâ* of Israel, an Israel to whom *ṭôbîyāh*, as an Ammonite, could never belong (Deut 23:4–7; cf. Neh 13:1). Nehemiah's first direct address to Sanballat, Tobiah, and Geshem unambiguously responds to the scorn directed toward him:

> As for the God of heaven, he will make us prosper.
> As for us, his servants, we shall rise and rebuild.
> And as for you, you have no share (*ḥēleq*), claim (*ṣĕdāqâ*), or memorial (*zikkārôn*) in Jerusalem. (Neh 2:20)[25]

When Sanballat heard that the wall reconstruction had begun, he became very irritated (*wayyik'as harbēh*) and heaped scorn upon the Judeans (*wayyal'ēg 'al-ha-yĕhûdîm*; 3:33–34). When the campaign of intimidation fails, it gives way to a campaign of obstruction: "When Sanballat and Tobiah, and the Arabs, the Ammonites, and the Ashdodites heard that the breached parts of the walls had begun to be filled, it

---

24. Blenkinsopp, *Ezra-Nehemiah*, 219.

25. The comment would be especially stinging if Tobiah's family had a traditional memorial (*zikkarôn*) in Jerusalem. The text of Zech 6:14 suggests that a person by the name of Tobiah did have a *zikkārôn* in the temple, but it is unclear whether the Tobiah in Zechariah is an ancestor of or a relation to the Tobiah of Nehemiah's time. The case for a connection is proposed by B. Mazar, "The Tobiads," *IEJ* 7 (1957) 137–45, 229–38; and more recently by C. L. Meyers and E. M. Meyers, *Zechariah 1–8* (AB 25B; Garden City, NY: Doubleday, 1987) 340–43. On *zikkārôn*, see Num 10:10; 31:54; Qoh 1:11; 2:16; Sir 45:9, 11.

angered them greatly, and all of them conspired together to come to fight against Jerusalem and to throw it into confusion" (Neh 4:1–2). When the campaign of obstruction fails, it in turn gives way to conspiracies against Nehemiah—his person and his rule. One involves a possible summit in the Ono Valley proposed by Sanballat and Geshem, by which "they were reckoning to do me wrong" (Neh 6:1–2). Another involves Shemaiah b. Delaiah b. Mehetabᵓel (*mĕhêṭabᵓēl*), who attempts to humiliate Nehemiah by luring him into the sanctuary (*ha-hêkāl*; Neh 6:10–11).[26] A third involves "Noadiah, the prophetess, and the rest of the prophets," whom Nehemiah claims "were attempting to frighten me" (Neh 6:14).[27]

A related strategy that the Nehemiah memoir pursues to distance the Judean people from their neighbors is to associate the alienage of other peoples with undesirable and dangerous characteristics. One example is Nehemiah's treatment of *nāšîm nokrîyôt* 'foreign women' (Neh 13:26–27; cf. Ezra 10:2, 10, 11, 14, 17, 18, 44). Inveighing against the mixed marriages entered into by Judean men, Nehemiah cites the Deuteronomic prohibition of mixed marriages with indigenous peoples, laments the negative influence of King Solomon's foreign wives (Neh 13:26; cf. 1 Kgs 11:1–11), and invokes the language factor: "Also, in those days (*gām bayyāmîm hāhēm*), I saw Judeans marrying (lit., 'settling', *hôšîbîm*) Ashdodite, Ammonite, and Moabite women" (Neh 13:23).[28] Alluding to the injunction of Deut 7:3, Nehemiah adjures the Judean men to halt practices of this sort (Neh 13:25). In 1 Kings 11, Solomon's foreign marriages are associated with his construction of sanctuaries on their

---

26. Likely a member of the priestly class in Jerusalem, although some have argued for Shemaiah's prophetic status, for example, L. Grabbe, "Triumph of the Pious or Failure of the Xenophobes: The Ezra-Nehemiah Reforms and their *Nachgeschichte*," in *Jewish Local Patriotism and Self-Identification in the Graeco-Roman Period* (ed. S. Jones and S. Pearce; JSPSup 31; Sheffield: Sheffield Academic Press, 1998) 55. Shemaiah is a fairly common name in late texts (1 Chr 3:22; 4:37; 5:4; 2 Chr 11:2; 12:5, 7, 15; Ezra 8:13; 10:31), but it is particularly prevalent in Levitical (1 Chr 9:14, 16; 15:8; 26:4, 6, 7; 2 Chr 17:8; 29:14; 31:15; 35:9; Ezra 8:16; Neh 11:15) and priestly contexts (1 Chr 15:11; 24:6; Ezra 10:21; Neh 3:29; 10:9; 12:6, 18, 34, 35, 36). Moreover, one has to ask what sort of person could meet Nehemiah in the sanctuary with impunity.

27. The fear factor (cf. Deut 18:22) is stressed in the recent study of D. Shepherd, "Prophetaphobia: Fear and False Prophecy in Nehemiah vi," *VT* 55 (2005) 232–50.

28. The *Hiphil* of the root *yšb* is usually translated 'to marry' (cf. *HALOT* 445a; Eth. *ᵓawsaba* 'to marry'), but T. Eskenazi ("The Missions of Ezra and Nehemiah," in *Judah and the Judaeans in the Persian Period* [ed. O. Lipschits and M. Oeming; Winona Lake, IN: Eisenbrauns, 2006] 509–29) argues that it specifically refers to Judean men establishing their new wives in the community through the gift of land (Ezra 10:2, 10, 14, 17; Neh 13:23, 27; cf. Ps 68:7; 113:9).

behalf. But the issue foremost in Nehemiah's mind in this particular context is language, not cult: half of their sons "were speaking Ashdodite and did not know how to speak Judean, and likewise for the language of each people" (Neh 13:24).[29] Intermarriage is thus connected to the violation of an authoritative injunction, the incitation to sin, and the loss of the people's own distinctive tongue.

The attack against exogamy is buttressed through the exegesis and reapplication of older texts. Drawing upon and innovating beyond earlier moral and ritual traditions, the Judean governor associates marriage to alien women with pollution. As Olyan observes, Nehemiah presents the marriage of the son of Joiada (the son of the high priest Eliashib) with the daughter of Sanballat as a defilement of the priestly bloodline, an act that, if not punished and atoned for, would contaminate future generations of the priestly lineage (Neh 13:28–30).[30]

The short tale of how Nehemiah expels Tobiah and his furnishings from one of the temple chambers (Neh 13:4–9) presents another example of how the Nehemiah writing casts foreign status in an inherently negative light. The forced removal of Tobiah is necessary, because his presence in the temple area is viewed as ritually defiling the chamber he occupies. Indeed, Albertz argues that Nehemiah's very command that the room be purified presupposes the view that alienage was in and of itself ritually defiling.[31] Certainly, there are no other factors mentioned in Nehemiah's narration, such as a possible failure of Tobiah to observe purity rules that would justify his eviction and the consequent purification of the vacant temple chamber.

In short, the highly negative characterization of Sanballat, Tobiah, and Geshem near the very beginning of the Nehemiah memoir is justified by (what are presented as) the later actions undertaken by these leaders to thwart the wall rebuilding, to compromise and undermine Nehemiah's authority, to foment dissent with Nehemiah's leadership among the Judean people, and to bring harm to, if not eliminate, Nehemiah himself. Consistent with a binary view of ethnic identity, the contours of the people being defined are sharply set against those who are presented as the other. The first-person accounts thus present

---

29. Compare with 2 Kgs 18:26, 28; 2 Chr 32:8; Isa 36:11, 13.

30. S. M. Olyan, "Purity Ideology in Ezra-Nehemiah as a Tool to Reconstitute the Community," *JSJ* 35 (2004) 4–10.

31. R. Albertz, "Purity Strategies and Political Interests in the Policy of Nehemiah," in *Confronting the Past: Archaeological and Historical Essays on Ancient Israel in Honor of William G. Dever* (ed. S. Gitin, J. E. Wright, and J. P. Dessel; Winona Lake, IN: Eisenbrauns, 2006) 199-206.

matters in a clear-cut fashion. The proponent, Nehemiah, drives the action and seeks to implement positive change on behalf of Yhwh for the Judeans, while his adversaries, the neighboring nations and their leaders, try to frustrate, if not undo, these good reforms at every step.

In this context, the application of the dictum spoken by Herodotus's Athenian emissaries would seem to have some merit. The Judeans are not so different from the Greeks, being defined by blood, language, religious institutions, and a shared way of life. The cooperation and commingling with the nations threatens the distinctiveness of the Judean collective identity. Given the dangers that these peoples pose, it is no wonder that the words and actions of their leaders are treated with a hermeneutic of suspicion. The very dialectic between protagonists and antagonists defines the ideological, ethnic, and religious boundaries of the community and promotes a particular view of Judean life in the international context of foreign occupation.

The Others Within

Occasionally, signs of internal resistance to and subversion of initiatives taken by the Judean leader appear.[32] These indications of opposition within the community and their relationships to the opposition external to the community are particularly interesting, because they suggest that the issues of community solidarity and group boundaries were not as firm and fixed as Nehemiah would have liked them to be. The very struggle of Artaxerxes' cupbearer to enforce his view of Judean identity in the community suggests that this identity was itself a contested issue.

In what follows, I would like to look more closely at the portrayals of Sanballat and Tobiah and the way these leaders relate to members of Nehemiah's own community. In this context, what Nehemiah concedes in his denunciations of the Judeans who cooperated with his enemies is itself telling. Nehemiah's own actions warrant closer scrutiny. In some respects, his treatment of Sanballat and Tobiah seems to be consistent with the manner in which he treats his other adversaries, but in other respects, his treatment of these contemporaries seems to depart from the way he treats his other adversaries. At this point, the attempt to maintain (or create) clear boundaries between the members of the Judean community and the members of other communities begins to break down.

---

32. So, for instance, Neh 5:1–19; 6:10–14, 17–19; 13:4–5, 7, 17–18, 20–21, 23–28. Apart from the first-person narratives, see Neh 3:5.

Tobiah

I shall begin with the figure of Tobiah, whose very name, 'my good is Yhwh', suggests that this man had a Yahwistic connection. The point is not in doubt, but scholars disagree about his position and ethnic affiliation. I hold to the view that he was the governor of Ammon, rather than his being an assistant or subordinate to Sanballat in Samaria, although I do not wish to belabor this point.[33] Instead, for the purposes of this discussion, I would like to focus on the question of Tobiah's identity and his connections to a variety of Judeans in Jerusalem (Neh 2:10, 19; 3:35; 4:1; 6:1, 12, 14; 13:4–9). Some think that Tobiah belonged to an unidentified Yahwistic faction in Ammon,[34] while others think that he was a Judean, more specifically a Jerusalemite, whose family held an estate in Ammon.[35] This would explain both his keen interest in Jerusalemite affairs and his residency in Ammon. Some would go a step further and contend that Tobiah belonged to the *bĕnê gôlâ*, those who returned (or whose parents or grandparents returned) from

---

33. For the latter view, understanding Tobiah as a Samarian official working for Sanballat, see D. J. Clines, *Ezra, Nehemiah, Esther* (NCB; Grand Rapids: Eerdmans, 1984) 145; and Williamson, *Ezra, Nehemiah*, 183–84. In this interpretation, the epithet "Ammonite" refers to Tobiah's ethnic origins. Recent archaeological work in the area suggests that the late Iron II period marked the height of Ammonite prosperity and expansion. The region does not evince the destruction that is associated with the Babylonian campaigns to Judah. Instead, one finds continuity of occupation until some time in the fourth century B.C.E. Even at ʿIraq al-Amir (where some had posited an occupation gap from the Iron I era to the Hellenistic era), pottery from both the Iron II era and the Persian era is attested: C. C. Ji, "A New Look at the Tobiads in ʿIraq al-Amir," *LASBF* 48 (1998) 417–40. Aside from the material remains, there are some epigraphic materials, such as the Persian-period seal impression found at Tell ʿUmayri in Aramaic script, *šbʾ ʿmn* 'Shuba of Ammon', suggesting that Ammon may have been a small Persian province at this time: L. Herr, "The Ammonites in the Late Iron Age and Persian Period," in *Ancient Ammon* (ed. B. MacDonald and R. W. Younker; Leiden: Brill, 1999) 219–37. Of course, the text of Nehemiah indicates that Tobiah worked closely with Sanballat, but this does not seem to constitute adequate grounds to deny the possibility that Tobiah was a governor himself. On the contrary, the fact that Sanballat and Geshem held official positions would seem to increase the likelihood that Tobiah did as well: S. Mittmann, "Tobia, Sanballat und die persische Provinz Juda," *JNSL* 26 (2000) 2–13. On Geshem's (that is, Gashmu's) status as king of Qedar, see the discussion of the inscription on one of the Tell el-Maskūṭah bowls, dating to ca. 400 B.C.E. and mentioning Qaynu, the son of Gashmu: W. J. Dumbrell, "The Tell el-Maskhuṭa Bowls and the 'Kingdom' of Qedar in the Persian Period," *BASOR* 203 (1971) 33–44.

34. C. L. and E. M. Meyers, *Haggai, Zechariah 1–8* (AB 25B; Garden City, NY: Doubleday, 1987) 340–43.

35. In later centuries, the house of Tobiah (Tobias) would rival (and become connected by marriage to) the house of Onias for control of the Jerusalem high priesthood (2 Macc 3:1–12; Jos., *Ant.* 12.4): L. L. Grabbe, *Judaism from Cyrus to Hadrian* (2 vols.; Minneapolis: Fortress, 1992) 1.192–98.

Exile.[36] Still other scholars think that Tobiah was of mixed ancestry or was an Ammonite who had married a Judean.[37]

These are all valid possibilities, but I am suggesting yet another possibility—namely, that Tobiah viewed himself as a member of one of Israel's other sodalities, perhaps one of the Transjordanian tribes. I raise this northern tribe thesis as an option for two reasons. The first involves Tobiah's place of residence, which in traditional Israelite lore was a geographic area associated with the Transjordanian tribes. The second reason involves Nehemiah's complete dismissal of Tobiah and his derisive references to him as "the Ammonite" or "the Ammonite slave" (Neh 2:10, 19; 3:35). If Tobiah was a Judean and widely recognized as Judean in the Jerusalem community, it would be hard to see how the Judean governor could summarily reject him as a foreigner.[38] The fact that Tobiah normally resided in another territory, namely Ammon, would seem to be no counterargument to such a proposition, because Nehemiah normally also resided in another realm, the Achaemenid court in Susa (Neh 1:1, 5:14–16, 13:6–7). That Tobiah served as a state-appointed official in another geopolitical setting and in a *double entendre* is referred to by Nehemiah as 'the Ammonite servant' (*hā'ebed hā'ammōnî*; Neh 2:10, 19) should be no objection to Tobiah's Israelite status.[39] After all, Nehemiah also served as a state-appointed official in another geopolitical setting. Indeed, he ultimately worked for the same employer as Tobiah evidently did. But Tobiah's possible affiliation with

---

36. See, for instance, Mazar, "Tobiads," 230–38; Blenkinsopp, *Ezra-Nehemiah*, 92, 218–19; Mittmann, "Tobia," 4–13. Cf. Josephus, *Ant.* 12.160–236.

37. This last position comes closest to Nehemiah's own point of view, except that it explicitly acknowledges that Tobiah was a Yahwist.

38. Unless Tobiah was himself the product of a mixed marriage (so Clines, *Ezra, Nehemiah, Esther*, 145), "a half-Jew who had insinuated himself into the confidence of the upper classes of Jerusalem." But see Mittmann, "Tobia," 4–13.

39. Thus playing on what was probably one of his official titles, such as "servant of Ammon" or "servant of the king of Persia": A. Alt, "Judas Nachbarn zur Zeit Nehemias," *Kleine Schriften zur Geschichte des Volkes Israels* (3 vols.; Munich: Beck, 1953) 2.341–42; C. C. McCown, "The 'Araq el-Amir and the Tobiads," *BA* 20 (1957) 72; Mazar, "Tobiads," 144–45; Blenkinsopp, *Ezra-Nehemiah*, 218. Hence, the term *hā'ebed* is used with an adjective (*hā'ammōnî*), rather than in a construct state (cf. U. Kellerman, *Nehemia: Quellen, Überlieferung und Geschichte* [BZAW 102; Berlin: Alfred Töpelmann, 1967] 167–70; W. Rudolph, *Esra und Nehemia* [HAT 20; Tübingen: Mohr, 1949] 109), deliberately. By referring to Tobiah as the Ammonite servant (*hā'ebed hā'ammōnî*), Nehemiah disparages his opponent and draws attention to what he sees as Tobiah's divided loyalties. As the governor of Ammon, Tobiah was obliged to pursue the best interests of his body politic within the larger context of his duties in the Achaemenid Empire, but Tobiah also claimed to have had interests in Judah and Jerusalem.

(northern) Israel would not be enough for Nehemiah and his supporters. If Tobiah regarded himself as a member of one of the northern
tribes, Nehemiah could nevertheless dismiss him as a foreigner because Nehemiah basically equated Judah with Israel.[40]

Such an exclusive Judah-Israel correlation would have proved problematic, however, for many among Jerusalem's elite. It was one thing to
extend the list of autochthonous peoples with whom the Israelites
could not intermarry to include other nations such as the Moabites,
Egyptians, and Ammonites, who never appeared in any of the older
Pentateuchal lists.[41] An expansion of this sort is attested not only in
Nehemiah's own fulminations against Judean intermarriages with
the Moabites, Ashdodites, and Ammonites (13:23–27) but also in the
story of Ezra's marriage reforms, which included Canaanites, Hittites,
Perizzites, Jebusites, Ammonites, Moabites, Egyptians, and Amorites
(Ezra 9:1).[42] Moreover, the precedent for an expansion may be found in
parts of the Deuteronomistic History. One of Joshua's closing speeches
(23:3–5, 7, 11–13) and the story of Solomon's fall (1 Kgs 11:1–13) each
implicitly or explicitly extends the older interdiction against exogamy

---

40. Similar restricted usage can be found in some of the books of the Apocrypha or
Deutero-Canon (e.g., Jdt 4:1; 1 Macc 1:11, 20, 25, 30, 36, 43; 2 Macc 1:26; 11:6; Sus 48, 57 =
LXX Dan 13:48, 57).

41. The authors of Exod 34:11–16 and Deut 7:1–4 prohibit exogamy but solely with
the autochthonous Canaanite nations. The composition of these national lists in the Pentateuch admits to some variation: T. Ishida, "The Structure and Implications of the Lists
of Pre-Israelite Nations," *Bib* 60 (1979) 461–90. The standard list in Exodus comprises six
peoples: the Hittites, Amorites, Canaanites, Perizzites, Hivites, and Jebusites (Exod 3:8,
17; 33:2; 34:11). In Deuteronomy and the Deuteronomistic History, the list sometimes includes a seventh nation: the Girgashites (Deut 7:1; Josh 3:10, 24:11; Judg 3:5; cf. Deut
20:17). A more expansive list appears in Gen 15:19–21. Some of the variations in and
omissions of names in the MT, SamP, and LXX pentateuchal lists can be explained text-
critically (for example, haplography).

42. So the MT. LXX Ezra 9:1 and 1 Esd 8:68 read Edomites (הָאֲדֹמִי) instead of Amorites (הָאֱמֹרִי). Given the possibility of metathesis and the frequency of the confusion between *rêš* and *dālet*, it is not easy to tell which lemma represents the earlier reading. With
respect to Ezra 9:1, M. A. Fishbane defends the LXX reading of Edomites in keeping with
his view that the text of Ezra 9:1–2, 12 draws on both Deut 7:1–4 and 23:4–9 (the latter
mentions the Ammonites, Moabites, Egyptians, and Edomites in the context of admission or nonadmission into the assembly): *Biblical Interpretation in Ancient Israel* (Oxford:
Clarendon, 1985) 116. Williamson (*Ezra, Nehemiah,* 131) prefers, however, the MT's reading of Amorites and attributes the appearance of the Egyptians in Ezra 9:1–2 to the author's interpretation of Lev 18:3 (cf. Ezra 9:1–2, 10:1–44). Note that the list in the LXX of
1 Kgs 11:1 (but not the MT) also mentions the Amorites. Because the Amorites appear in
the prohibitions of Deut 7:1 and Exod 34:11, whereas the Edomites do not, the LXX
lemma of Ezra 9:1 appears to be the *lectio difficilior.*

to include populations that were never included in the original regis-
ters of aboriginal peoples.[43]

It is one thing to expand the list of indigenous nations; it is another
thing altogether to include other Israelites in the extended list. It is entirely conceivable that a good many of Nehemiah's own supporters
balked at including self-professed Israelites in the register of peoples
whom Judeans could not marry. These residents of the province of Judah could not take the step Nehemiah was quite willing to take and
label self-professed Israelites as aliens. In other words, I am arguing
that what was going on in Nehemiah's Judah was not simply a debate
about Judean identity but also a debate about Israelite identity. The
two were distinct but very much related projects.

The importance and timeliness of the Israel/Judah issue can be seen
from another historical writing that dates to the same general era as
Ezra-Nehemiah: the book of Chronicles.[44] There, one finds Israelites
living in the north, Israelites living in the south, Israelites living in exile, sojourners or resident aliens (*gērîm*), and foreigners who are sometimes described as "peoples of the land(s)."[45] Jacob's descendants are
composed of many tribes, each of which has its own particular genealogical profile, but they are nevertheless all Israelites. Some sodalities
prove to be less faithful than others during particular historical periods, such as the divided monarchy, but the misbehaviors do not render
these sodalities non-Israelite. In the Chronicler's work, including the
genealogies, one finds an expansive notion of the people of Israel, even
though the author insists that certain tribes—Judah, Benjamin, and
Levi—played more pivotal roles in the course of Israelite history than
the other tribes.[46]

---

43. One of the introductions to the period of the Judges (3:5–7) is also relevant in this
context, because it also links mixed marriages to Israelite decline. But MT Judg 3:5 maintains the older, six-nation pentateuchal list: G. N. Knoppers, "Sex, Religion, and Politics:
The Deuteronomist on Intermarriage," *HAR* 14 (1994) 121–41.

44. S. Japhet, *The Ideology of the Book of Chronicles and Its Place in Biblical Thought*
(BEATAJ 9; Frankfurt am Main: Peter Lang, 1989) 267–351; H. G. M. Williamson, *Israel in
the Books of Chronicles* (Cambridge: Cambridge University Press, 1977) 87–140; T. Willi,
Juda–Jehud–Israel: Studien zum Selbstverständnis des Judentums in persischer Zeit (FAT 12;
Tübingen: Mohr, 1995); G. N. Knoppers, *I Chronicles 1–9* (AB 12; New York: Doubleday,
2004) 83–85.

45. So, for instance, 1 Chr 5:25; 2 Chr 6:33; 13:9; 32:13, 19. For the *gērîm*, see 1 Chr 22:2;
2 Chr 2:16, 30:25). In 1 Chr 29:15, the term is used figuratively to apply to Israelites. By
contrast, the writers of Ezra-Nehemiah make no references to the *gērîm*.

46. Knoppers, *I Chronicles 1–9*, 245–65.

Over against the dominant picture presented in Kings (2 Kgs 17:1–34a), Chronicles depicts a sizable Israelite remnant remaining in the land following the Assyrian invasions and deportations (2 Chr 30:6–9). This Israelite remnant does not represent simply a token presence in the land. Quite the contrary, the surviving Israelites retain their tribal structure and respond (whether positively or negatively) to overtures from Judean kings. Some participate in the national Passover led by King Hezekiah (2 Chr 30:10–11) and contribute to his national reforms (2 Chr 31:1). Others contribute to Josiah's temple reforms (2 Chr 34:9) and participate in his national Passover (35:18).

The contrast between the presuppositions, methods, and perspectives inherent within the two works can be seen from another angle. In Chronicles, the northern tribes make appearances throughout the work, from the introductory section covering the tribal genealogies to the active involvement of Manasseh and Ephraim in Josiah's reforms near the end of the work (2 Chr 34:6–7, 9). In neither the Nehemiah first-person materials nor elsewhere in Ezra-Nehemiah does there seem to be a single reference to any of the northern tribes.[47] This evidence seems to confirm that Chronicles and Ezra-Nehemiah, two literary works that both stem from Jerusalemite scribes and that both date to the same general period, take very different approaches to the residents of the former Northern Kingdom.

To this line of argumentation, it could be objected that Chronicles deals with the preexilic period and Ezra-Nehemiah with the postexilic period. The differences might be explained by recourse to the different times upon which each work focuses. But this objection does not hold, as a brief comparison of the somewhat parallel lists of postexilic residents found in 1 Chr 9:2–18 and Neh 11:3–19 shows.[48] The writer of 1 Chr 9:3 declares that "in Jerusalem resided some of the descendants of Judah, some of the descendants of Benjamin, and some of the descendants of Ephraim and Manasseh." In the context of Chronicles, this is an important statement, because it asserts that some of the tribal diversity evident within the genealogies pertaining to Israel's past was

---

47. Simeon (Ezra 10:31) and Manasseh (Ezra 10:30, 33), and Joseph (Ezra 10:42, Neh 12:14) occasionally appear as personal names in some of the lists and lineages, but these same names do not appear as tribal eponyms in the work. The traditional names of the other northern tribes (Reuben, Issachar, Zebulun, Dan, Ephraim, Naphtali, Gad, Asher) evidently do not appear even as personal names in the book.

48. On the complex relationship between these texts, see my "Sources, Revisions, and Editions: The Lists of Jerusalem's Residents in MT and LXX Nehemiah 11 and 1 Chronicles 9," *Text* 20 (2000) 141–68.

also evident in Persian-period Jerusalem. In this context, the town appears as a mixed community, housing both northern and southern residents. But the parallel text in Neh 11:4 simply states: "in Jerusalem resided some of the descendants of Judah and some of the descendants of Benjamin." The Chronistic reference to "some of the descendants of Ephraim and Manasseh" inhabiting Jerusalem is lacking in MT and LXX Neh 11:4. One normally hesitates to read too much into the absence of certain names in a text, because an absence could be explained in many different ways. But in this case, the absence of Manasseh and Ephraim from the lemma of Nehemiah is significant. Both texts are true to their larger literary contexts. The mention of northerners residing in Jerusalem is in keeping with the Chronicler's comprehensive notion of Israelite identity.[49] The absence of the same tribal eponyms in Ezra-Nehemiah is in keeping with the restricted notion of Israelite identity espoused by the writers of this work.

Recognizing that the ethnic debates in Nehemiah's time did not simply center on the definition of the Judeans as opposed to the nations or the safekeeping of the children of the Exile as opposed to the peoples of the land but also involved the issue of Judah's relationship to Israel (and the definition of Israel itself) may help to explain some oddities in Nehemiah's policies. First, as Nehemiah himself concedes, his opponents enjoyed considerable support within the Judean community.[50] Nehemiah observes that the nobles of Judah (*ḥōrê yĕhûdâ*) were keeping up a brisk correspondence with Tobiah and that "there were many in Judah who were his sworn allies" (*ba'ălê šĕbû'â lô*; Neh 6:17–18). These associates would speak well of Tobiah to Nehemiah and relay Nehemiah's own words back to Tobiah (Neh 6:19).[51]

---

49. Japhet, *The Ideology of the Book of Chronicles*, 299–300; J. E. Dyck, "The Ideology of Identity in Chronicles," in *Ethnicity and the Bible* (ed. M. G. Brett; Leiden: Brill, 1996) 89–116.

50. This point is forcefully argued in the recent book of L. S. Fried, *The Priest and the Great King: Temple-Palace Relations in the Persian Empire* (Winona Lake, IN: Eisenbrauns, 2004) 156–212. She points to a variety of groups within Yehud who seem to have been at odds with Nehemiah. Whatever one thinks about the compositional history of Ezra-Nehemiah, one element in the narrative that must be borne in mind is the complicated relationship between Nehemiah and the people he ruled in Judah. I do not believe, however, that Nehemiah was as completely isolated as Fried would have it. For a general overview, see L. L. Grabbe, *A History of the Jews and Judaism in the Second Temple Period* (London: T. & T. Clark, 2004) 294–313.

51. Yet, all the time this was going on, as Nehemiah relates it, Tobiah was sending letters to intimidate him (Neh 6:19). From Nehemiah's perspective, this showed that Tobiah was behaving in a duplicitous manner.

The Judean governor also found himself at odds with "Noadiah, the prophetess, and the rest of the prophets," who Nehemiah claims "were attempting to frighten me" (Neh 6:14). This is a striking admission on Nehemiah's part. Given that the prophets Haggai and Zechariah staunchly supported the temple rebuilding in an earlier time (Ezra 5:1–2), what made all the prophets of the mid-fifth century sour on their political leader? Perhaps Nehemiah's headstrong character and prickly personality were factors, but one would think that more was going on than this to turn Judah's prophets *en masse* against their reformer ruler. Perhaps these prophets and this prophetess took issue with some elements of Nehemiah's reform program. Like earlier prophets in the tradition, such as Jeremiah and Ezekiel, these prophets may have held to and promoted a comprehensive understanding of Israel. These prophets inveighed against what they deemed to be infractions against God by individuals, groups, and peoples, but they maintained an integral view of the people they served. If this remained the case in the time of Nehemiah, the prophetic figures of his time would have been uneasy with the aspects of Nehemiah's separatist program that seemed to pit Judeans against all others.

Second, in an aside to the reader designed to explain the opposition within the community to his policies, Nehemiah informs his audience that Tobiah was the son-in-law of Shecaniah, the son of Arah.[52] Because Nehemiah repeatedly pronounces Tobiah to be an Ammonite, one might expect Nehemiah to construe this marriage as a case of intermarriage. Yet, Nehemiah takes no action against Tobiah, against his spouse, or against Shecaniah (Neh 6:18). By the standards presented in the lists of Ezra-Nehemiah, Tobiah's wife had an impeccable pedigree. The Arah family is mentioned as one of the more populous clans in the register of returned exiles in Ezra 2 and Nehemiah 7 (Ezra 2:5//Neh 7:10).

In his aside to the reader, Nehemiah also reveals that Jehohanan, Tobiah's son, had married the daughter of Meshullam, the son of Berechiah. In this manner, the family of Tobiah was linked to another of the major families in Judah. Meshullam, the son of Berechiah, the son of Meshezabel (*mĕšêzab'ēl*), appears in the list of wall-builders (Neh 3:4, 30).[53] Elsewhere, the names of both Meshullam and Meshezabel appear

---

52. A few Hebrew MSS of Neh 6:18 read Shebaniah. The list of wall-builders mentions a Shemaiah, son of Shecaniah (Neh 3:29). Was he also part of this same family?

53. Berechiah is a fairly common personal name in Chronicles (1 Chr 3:20; 6:39; 9:16; 15:17, 23; 2 Chr 28:12) but one that appears only twice in Ezra-Nehemiah, in each case referring to the same individual (Neh 3:4, 30).

as among the heads of the people who signed the covenant pledge (*ʾămānâ*; Neh 10:21–22). A later list in Nehemiah, pertaining to the repopulation of Jerusalem, mentions a Petaḥiah, son of Meshezabel, whose responsibility is no less than to serve "at the side of the king with respect to everything concerning the people" (Neh 11:24). This list traces the genealogical roots of Petaḥiah, the son of Meshezabel, back to Zeraḥ, the son of the patriarch Judah.[54]

The fact that Tobiah and Jehoḥanan, his son, married into such prominent Judean families suggests that not all Judeans who supported and participated in Nehemiah's building program also agreed with Nehemiah's views on other issues.[55] Even within the limited confines of the Judean community, one could be an ally of Nehemiah on one issue and an opponent of his on another issue.

Nehemiah's failure to move against either Tobiah or the affected Judean families may be subject to a number of explanations. He may have been biding his time, recognizing that the enemy without enjoyed close ties to the kin within. Or perhaps he did not act because he realized that he was dealing with what others (although not he) would call an inner-Israelite dispute. If these Judean families, unlike Nehemiah, viewed Tobiah and his family as Israelite in character, whatever Tobiah's precise ancestry, they would not have seen any problem in arranging nuptials between members of their families. On the contrary, they might well have viewed these marital agreements as strengthening the ties among the components of Israel's various tribes. Rather than viewing the matrimony as an act of impiety, they would have viewed it as an act of piety, an attempt to build a larger sense of pan-Israelite solidarity in spite of the tribal affiliations of each community.[56]

---

54. Aside from these references (Neh 3:4, 10:22, 11:24), no other *Měšêzabʾēl* appears in the Hebrew Bible. On the Akkadian element in this personal name, see R. Zadok, "Die nichthebräischischen Namen der Israeliten vor dem hellenistischer Zeitalter," *UF* 17 (1985) 389.

55. So also Williamson, *Ezra, Nehemiah*, 261.

56. If this was the case, or something close to it, the appointment of Tobiah to a temple chamber under the authority of the priest Eliashib (perhaps not to be equated with the high priest of the same name), while Nehemiah was away (Neh 13:4–9), would have represented an unacceptable escalation of an already problematic situation to Nehemiah. The presence of a person whom Nehemiah considered to be a foreigner in one of the temple rooms would be intolerable, given Nehemiah's views of the temple's holiness and ethnic alienage. In a play on house/temple furnishings (*kělê bêt-*), Nehemiah recounts how he evicted Tobiah and 'all of the furnishings of the house of Tobiah' (*kol-kělê bêt-ṭôbîyāh*) to restore purity to this part of the sanctuary complex and reinstall there 'the furnishings of the house of God' (*kělê bêt hāʾělōhîm*; Neh 13:8–9). Yet, even after this confrontation, Nehemiah does not act against Tobiah's marriage.

Sanballat

If the precise identity of Tobiah is disputed, virtually the same can be said for Sanballat. The situation may be, however, a little clearer in this case. The Horonite epithet given to Sanballat is revealing in more ways than one. Its use by Nehemiah was undoubtedly meant to be derisive, intended to belittle Sanballat as someone who hailed from a small town, one of the Beth Horons in the Shephelah northwest of Jerusalem.[57] Nehemiah never refers to Sanballat as the governor of Samaria.[58] By consistently referring to his contemporaries with irreverent epithets—Geshem the Arab, Tobiah the Ammonite, and Sanballat the Horonite—Nehemiah avoids granting them explicit legitimacy as his true peers, local leaders who had understandable interests, whether altruistic or not, in the standing, conduct, and fate of one of their neighbor(s).

The Horonite epithet is revealing in another way, because it signifies that Sanballat likely viewed himself as an Ephraimite.[59] This is not to deny the possibility that his family may have originally stemmed from Assyrian officials who governed Samaria from the late eighth century to the late seventh century, as some have claimed.[60] Rather, one has to

---

57. On the other less likely options, such as Haran in northern Mesopotamia (e.g., K. Galling, *Die Bücher der Chronik, Esra, Nehemia* [ATD 12; Göttingen: Vandenhoeck & Ruprecht, 1954] 219), Hauran, a one-time Assyrian province in the northern Transjordan (e.g., E. G. Kraeling, *The Brooklyn Museum Aramaic Papyri* [New Haven: Yale University Press, 1953] 107–8; Mittmann, "Tobia," 15–17), and Horonaim in Moab (e.g., Kellerman, *Nehemia*, 167; cf. Isa 15:5, Jer 48:3), see R. Zadok, "Samarian Notes," *BibOr* 42 (1985) 657–72; and Rudolph, *Esra und Nehemia*, 108. If Sanballat hailed from Horonaim, one would expect the epithet to read החרנימי, rather than החרני (Zadok, ibid., 570).

58. In the first-person texts of Nehemiah, Samaria is mentioned only in the context of its armed force (*ḥêl šōměrôn*; Neh 3:34). Elsewhere in Ezra-Nehemiah, see Ezra 4:10, 17; Alt, "Die Rolle Samarias bei der Enstehung des Judentums," *Kleine Schriften*, 2.323; Mittmann, "Tobia," 14.

59. The area to which he tries to lure Nehemiah (Kephirim) in the Plain of Ono was therefore closer to his own hometown than Nehemiah was to his (Neh 6:2; cf. Ezra 2:33//Neh 7:33, 11:34).

60. Along these same lines, some think that Sanballat was a descendant of Assyrian-sponsored immigrants, who came to the region following the fall of the Northern Kingdom (2 Kgs 17:24–34a). A. Lemaire believes that Sanballat was a descendant of one of the Israelites deported to Assyria: "Épigraphie et religion en Palestine à l'époque achéménide," *Transeu* 22 (2001) 104. Mittmann presents yet another view ("Tobia," 17–28), arguing that Sanballat belonged to the repatriated *běnê gôlâ*. Other possibilities are that Sanballat's parents gave him a Babylonian name (or that he himself took on the name) in much the same fashion as one sees Akkadian names appear for Judeans during this period (for example, Zerubbabel, Mordecai, Shenazzar, Sheshbazzar): Zadok, "Die nicht-hebräischischen Namen," 391–92; H. G. M. Williamson, "Sanballat," *ABD* 5:973. M. Dandamaev discusses the phenomenon of Babylonian names and second names among the

come to grips with the status and identity of Sanballat in the fifth century—centuries after the Assyrian conquests. Whether one construes his hometown as Lower Beth Horon or Upper Beth Horon, both sites are listed in biblical texts as Ephraimite holdings (Josh 16:3, 5; 18:13; 21:22 [// 1 Chr 6:53]; 1 Chr 7:24; 2 Chr 25:13).[61] Hence, whatever one makes of Tobiah's identity–Judean, half-Judean, Judean repatriate, northern Israelite, or Ammonite—Sanballat is implicitly associated with one of the major northern tribes. As an Ephraimite, he could and probably did claim the same Israelite nomenclature as Nehemiah claimed for himself. In the Elephantine papyri, the names attested for Sanballat's sons—'Delaiah' (דליהי) and 'Shelemiah' (שלמיה)—are Yahwistic in nature.[62] From the material remains of the Mt. Gerizim temple and the later textual remains found there, discussed elsewhere in these proceedings by Yitzhaq Magen and Bob Becking, it is clear that the Samarian worshipers at this sanctuary considered themselves to be Israelites.[63]

---

ethnic minorities in Neo-Babylonian and Achaemenid times: "Twin Towns and Ethnic Minorities in First-Millennium Babylonia," in *Commerce and Monetary Systems in the Ancient World: Means of Transmission and Cultural Interaction* (ed. R. Rollinger and C. Ulf; Melammu Symposia 5; Stuttgart: Franz Steiner, 2004) 137–49.

61. The evidence suggests that his family ruled Samaria for some one hundred years (AP 30:29 = 31:28; 32; Josephus, *Ant.* 11.302–25) and maintained close connections to the high priestly family in Jerusalem for generations: F. M. Cross, *From Epic to Canon: History and Literature in Ancient Israel* (Baltimore: Johns Hopkins University Press, 1998) 151–202. The Chronicler seems to have understood Beth Horon as abutting the Northern–Southern border of Judah during the dual monarchies (2 Chr 25:13). If this was still the case in postexilic times, it may partially explain why Sanballat, who stemmed from this border town, took such an interest in Judean affairs.

62. See, for example, TAD 1 A4.7:29; 1 A4.8:28; 1 A4.9; Josephus, *Ant.* 11.302–3, 310–11, 315, 321–24, 342; and the discussion of D. M. Gropp, "Sanballat," *Encyclopaedia of the Dead Sea Scrolls* (ed. L. S. Schiffman and J. C. VanderKam; Oxford: Oxford University Press, 2000) 823–25. In this context, the proper name "[Yešaʿ]yahu" (or "[Yadaʿ]yahu") appearing in the Wâdi ed-Dâliyeh bullas and papyri is pertinent. According to H. Eshel, Yešaʿyahu is the son of Sanballat II (second half of the fourth century B.C.E.): "The Rulers of Samaria during the Fifth and Fourth Centuries B.C.E.," *ErIsr* 26 (*Frank Moore Cross Volume*; 1999) 8–12 [Hebrew]. See also his essay elsewhere in this volume (pp. 223–234). Remember that the name of (apparently) another Samarian official or governor, Hananiah, was also Yahwistic in nature.

63. The late-third/early-second-century B.C.E. Samaritan inscription discovered on the Agean island of Delos mentions Mt. Gerizim and employs the term "Israelites" to refer to the Samaritans: P. Bruneau, "Les Israélites de Délos et la juiviere délienne," *Bulletin de Correspondance Hellénique* 106 (1982) 465–504; L. M. White, "The Delos Synagogue Revisited: Recent Fieldwork in the Graeco-Roman Diaspora," *HTR* 80 (1987)133–60. The Delos inscription confirms independently what we know from the archaeological and epigraphic finds from Mt. Gerizim, that during the Persian and Hellenistic periods, more than one community claimed to carry on the legacy of Israel's past.

This sort of evidence complicates ethnic identification, because according to the primordial school of ethnic thought ethnic identity has to do with blood, language, ancestral ties to land, cultic institutions, and social customs. Nehemiah and Sanballat represented distinct geopolitical entities but shared some common religious traits and institutions. The two men belonged to different tribes, but each of these tribes claimed a common progenitor (Jacob). From this vantage point, it may be reasonable to assert that the two ultimately shared common bloodlines. If, as seems likely, Sanballat considered himself to be an Israelite, he probably would have seen no religious issue in arranging for one of his daughters to marry one of the sons of Joiada, the son of Eliashib, the high priest (Neh 13:28). Indeed, in Sanballat's mind, he may have seen himself as recreating in a small and limited way the kind of northern-southern alliance that punctuated the earlier history of the Northern and Southern Kingdoms.[64]

To Nehemiah, the nuptials were an unbearable case of intermarriage at the highest religious level of his society, and hence he declares that "I drove him [the son of Joiada] away from me" (*wā'abrîḥhû mē-'ālāy*).[65] But there were obviously others within Nehemiah's own community, including its priestly establishment, who avidly disagreed with Nehemiah's position.[66] Given the historical ties between the Northern and Southern tribes, the members of Jerusalem's priestly families, along with Sanballat and his family, may well have viewed Nehemiah as the innovator, someone who was calling for a radical break from past tradition.

---

64. Nuptials arranged between elite members of the Northern and Southern tribes seem to have continued even after the fall of the Northern Kingdom (2 Kgs 21:19, 23:36). I want to thank Patricia Dutcher-Walls for these references.

65. The lemma of LXX Neh 13:38, *kai axebrasa autous* 'I drove them', clarifies the puzzle inherent in the Hebrew as to what happened to the Samarian wife. The strong rhetoric employed by the Judean governor is tantalizingly ambiguous. It is unclear what chasing him (and not her?) away entailed physically and legally. Did Nehemiah banish the culprit from the temple precincts, from Jerusalem, or from Judah altogether? If Nehemiah expelled Joiada's son from the province, as some assume, his actions went further than Ezra's procedures of divorce and dispossession (Williamson, *Ezra, Nehemiah*, 398–99; Blenkinsopp, *Ezra-Nehemiah*, 365). This incident may be the basis of the later claim, however garbled, by Josephus of how an independent Samaritan temple and priesthood were begun on Mt. Gerizim (*Ant.* 11.302–12). In the account of Josephus, an incident of this sort occurred in the fourth century B.C.E., not in the fifth century B.C.E., but Josephus does not deal directly in his *Antiquities* with the events narrated in Neh 13:4–29.

66. The Elephantine papyri (AP 30; 32) attest to later cooperation between the governors of Samaria and Judah: G. N. Knoppers, "Revisiting the Samarian Question in the Persian Period," in *Judah and the Judeans in the Persian Period* (ed. O. Lipschits and M. Oeming; Winona Lake, IN: Eisenbrauns, 2006) 278.

In this context, it bears pointing out that one of Sanballat's messages to Nehemiah hints at a common ethnicity. After Sanballat, Tobiah, and Geshem discovered that Nehemiah's wall reconstruction was complete, Sanballat repeatedly sent the same message to Nehemiah, the fifth time by his agent (*na'ărô*), who had an open letter with him (Neh 6:5). Written in this missive (*kātûb bâ*), according to Nehemiah, was: "Among the nations it is heard (*ba-gôyîm nišmā'*), and Gashmu also says that you and the Judeans are planning to rebel. Therefore, you are rebuilding the wall and you are becoming their king, according to these reports" (Neh 6:6). In this short message, Sanballat openly conveys what he has heard from unnamed sources. He presents himself as a confederate reporting allegations made by others about his counterpart in the south. The *gôyîm* appear as a collective third party exterior to Sanballat himself. In other words, Sanballat refers to the *gôyîm* in much the same way that Nehemiah does—as denoting other peoples. The implication seems to be that, whatever differences separate the two leaders, they nevertheless stand within the same larger circle of Israelites. What Sanballat has heard from others is then confirmed by Geshem, who is willing to make the accusation directly. It is true that *gôy* can sometimes refer to Israel itself in some texts within the Hebrew Bible.[67] But this is never the case in Ezra-Nehemiah. Of course, Nehemiah does not allow the message from Sanballat to divert him from pursuing his own agenda, but the message is itself revealing.

Turning to the factor of language, another common ethnic identity marker, this was something that united the two governors, rather than something that divided them. In the context of a book that calls attention to diplomatic correspondence written in Aramaic (Ezra 4:8–16, 17–22; 5:7–17; 6:2–5, 6–12), especially with respect to the regional Achaemenid authorities, one cannot help but observe that all of Sanballat's messages to Nehemiah are recorded and cited in Hebrew (Neh 2:19; 3:34; 4:5; 6:2, 4, 5–7) and that the converse also holds—all of Nehemiah's messages to Sanballat are recorded or cited in Hebrew (Neh 2:20; 6:3, 4, 8–9). To be sure, Nehemiah does not overtly raise the language issue with respect to any of his conversations with others. But he does complain about the children of Judean mixed marriages speaking other tongues, such as Ashdodite, and not knowing how to speak

---

67. A. Cody, "When Is the Chosen People Called a *gôy*?" *VT* 14 (1964) 1–6; R. E. Clements and G. J. Botterweck, "*gôy*," *TDOT* 2:429–31.

Judahite (*yĕhûdît*; Neh 13:23).[68] From his perspective, sharing a common language was a priority in maintaining a distinct community. Having a common language was evidently a problem for the offspring of the connubials with the Moabites, Ammonites, and Ashdodites, but it was ironically not a problem for the governors of Samaria and Judah. Nehemiah had more than his share of problems in dealing with his counterparts Sanballat and Tobiah, but none of these self-confessed problems involved a failure to understand what his contemporaries were saying to him.

Even from a religious standpoint, there is one occasion on which Nehemiah's own words hint at recognition that he, along with Sanballat and Tobiah, worship the same deity. When Nehemiah utters an imprecatory prayer in the context of the struggle to rebuild Jerusalem's walls, he appeals to God's own sense of honor and requests that God take a number of actions against his enemies, Sanballat and Tobiah (Neh 3:36–37). These implored actions include returning Sanballat and Tobiah's taunts upon their heads, sending them as plunder into a land of captivity (*bĕ'ereṣ šibyâ*),[69] and neither covering up their iniquity (*wĕ'al-tĕkas 'al-'ănônām*)[70] nor letting their sin be blotted out before God (*wĕḥaṭṭātām millĕpānêka 'al-timmāḥeh*).[71] As commentators have pointed out, there are parallels between Nehemiah's prayer and the structure of some imprecatory psalms, including the address, the complaint, the petitions, and so forth, but this appeal has a very limited and specific set of enemies in view.[72] There are also parallels between the terms Nehemiah employs and the terms employed both in the imprecatory psalms and in the lament psalms. But the imprecatory psalms, along with some of Jeremiah's laments, normally speak of the enemy or enemies in vague, general terms. Why would Nehemiah worry about God's forgiving Sanballat and Tobiah and allowing their sins to be blotted out unless Nehemiah implicitly recognized that his foes worshiped

---

68. Compare with 2 Kgs 18:26, 28; 2 Chr 32:8; Isa 36:11, 13.

69. So the MT. A few Heb. MSS and the Syr read *sibyām* (cf. Jer 30:10; 46:27; 2 Chr 6:37, 38).

70. H. Ringgren ("*kāsâ*," *TDOT* 7.263–64) discusses the use of the verb *kāsâ* in the sense of 'to forgive' within a cultic setting, referring to Neh 3:37; Ps 32:1, 85:3.

71. On the usage of *mḥh*, compare Gen 9:23; Exod 21:33; 26:13; 38:15; Num 4:9, 15; 22:5, 11; Deut 23:14; Josh 24:7; Judg 4:19; Ps 32:5; 40:11; 85:3; Job 9:24; 31:33; 36:30; Prov 10:18; 11:13; 17:9; 28:13 (*HALOT* 488a–b).

72. Williamson calls attention to Psalms 35, 58, 59, 69, 109, 137, and Jer 18:23: *Ezra, Nehemiah*, 217–18.

the same God as he did? His very imprecations seem to be predicated upon the assumption that his opponents were praying to the same deity that he was.[73] In this context, Nehemiah entreats the deity to listen to the plaintiff (and not to his opponents).

Conclusion

In explaining the disputes and divisions evident in the narratives of Ezra-Nehemiah, some scholars have spoken of two contradictory perspectives operative in the Persian-period Judahite community. Those who advocated the first point of view, the assimilationist perspective, argued that the people of Yehud needed to cooperate with their local neighbors in the southern Levant. Those who advocated the second point of view, the separatist perspective, argued that the people of Judah needed to maintain their own distinctive identity and pursue a more independent course. Neither of these parties advocated rebellion in the context of the larger Persian Empire, but each had its own way of dealing with the nations surrounding Judah. Both parties wished for the survival of the community but pursued different means to accomplish this goal in the context of changing circumstances in the Achaemenid Empire. One pushed for more integration, while the other pushed for more differentiation.

The distinction between assimilationists and separatists has its drawing points, but examination of the materials in the Nehemiah memoir suggests that there was at least one other kind of dispute operative within Yehud, one that involved the very identities of Judeans.[74] I speak of identities, rather than of a single ethnic identity, because there was more than one collective identity at stake in the struggles of Nehemiah with his opponents. The tensions one sees in the book of Ezra-Nehemiah in the confrontations between Nehemiah, on the one hand, and Sanballat and Tobiah, on the other hand, reveal that Yahwists in Judah, in Samaria, and in other regions had some different assumptions about their own ethnic identity and, just as importantly, about each others' identities. In this respect, the distinction between emic and etic classifications is helpful, because however arcane the debates may have appeared to outsiders, the insiders within the debates came to the issues with their own particular sets of assumptions, traditions, understandings, and commitments.

---

73. And therefore asking Yhwh to forgive their sins (e.g., Ps 32:5, 51:3).

74. This question of Israelite/Judahite identity inevitably complicated the other debate about integrationist versus independent policies.

One group identity that Nehemiah takes as primary is that of the people of Judah. In this collective definition, the patriarch Judah functions as the eponymous ancestor of the Judeans, although Nehemiah himself does not put things exactly in these terms. The other collective identity at stake is a larger one involving the entire people of Israel. In this identity, a variety of sodalities trace their ancestry to a single eponymous ancestor, Jacob. The members of these tribes may have their individual histories and be originally associated with separate territories, but they all affirm a primordial unity in spite of their differences.[75] By any definition, there was at least some overlap between the two collective identities, because the two societies were genetically linked in traditional lore.

In his work, Nehemiah all but collapses the distinction between the two identities. Inasmuch as he addresses the larger issue at all, he basically equates the Judeans with the Israelites. But there were others both outside his community and inside his community who clearly disagreed with him. From the first-person accounts of Nehemiah's battling his foes, one can see that he too had trouble at times, defending the lines he drew between himself and his opponents.

The so-called adversaries of Nehemiah who held onto a larger concept of Israel either were reluctant to embrace Nehemiah's program or actively opposed it. They could agree about the importance of blood, language, cultic rites, ties to the land, and social customs but avidly disagree with the Judean governor about the relative importance of these attributes and how each was to be construed and applied. Those who identified with the larger concept of Israel could affirm the need for exclusivity but debate Nehemiah about how exclusive exclusivity had to be. It is no wonder that the issues aroused such passion and such controversy. It could not be otherwise. Nehemiah was battling not only the enemy without, but also the enemy within.

---

75. By the same token, there could also be considerable diversity within the tribe of Judah itself. The "differences within sameness" motif that one sometimes finds in discussions of ethnicity is very much in evidence within the Chronistic lineages for Judah (1 Chr 2:4–4:23). Like the writers of Ezra-Nehemiah, the Chronicler works in the late Persian or early Hellenistic period but posits a great deal of diversity (including intermarriages with other peoples) in the course of the tribe's development. The contrasts between Ezra-Nehemiah and Chronicles suggest that important aspects of Judah's identity were the subject of serious debate during this era: G. N. Knoppers, "Intermarriage, Social Complexity, and Ethnic Diversity in the Genealogy of Judah," *JBL* 120 (2001) 15–30; idem, " 'Great among His Brothers', but Who Is He? Heterogeneity in the Composition of Judah," *JHS* 3/4 (2000), http:/www.purl.org/jhs.

A New Model for the Composition
of Ezra-Nehemiah

JACOB L. WRIGHT

Candler School of Theology, Emory University

The organizers of the conference invited me to discuss my recently published book, *Rebuilding Identity: The Nehemiah-Memoir and Its Earliest Readers*,[1] because it presents a new model for the composition of Ezra-Nehemiah (hereafter EN) that has direct consequences for the way one thinks about the fourth century in Judah. When I began working on this book, I had not planned to develop a new model for EN. My aim was simply to analyze the composition and historical ramifications of Nehemiah's first-person account, which, I had assumed with the majority of scholars, constituted an independent source that the compilers of EN combined with the other sources of the book. EN scholars agree that the book as a whole consists of independently transmitted sources that were composed in isolation from each other and that were aligned into the present narrative of the Restoration by a compiler working in the fourth century B.C.E.[2] However, as I continued my reading of EN, I began to doubt whether the conception of a plurality of sources and a minimum of compilers or editors was able to account adequately for the complexity of the work. These doubts grew more acute when I read T. Cohn Eskenazi's monograph.[3] In emphasizing the unity of EN and departing from the source-critical method, Eskenazi's work caused me seriously to question the conventional division of the

---

1. BZAW 348; Berlin: de Gruyter, 2004.

2. Opinion is however split between scholars such as J. Blenkinsopp (*Ezra-Nehemiah* [OTL; Philadelphia: Westminster, 1988] 40–47), who maintain that the Nehemiah Memoir was inserted later into an account consisting of Ezra 1–10 and Nehemiah 8, and scholars such as H. G. M. Williamson (*Ezra-Nehemiah* [WBC 16; Waco, TX: Word, 1985] xxxiv–xxxv, 8, 28–30, 201–2) who posit an original combination and rearrangement of the Ezra and Nehemiah Memoirs, to which the account of the construction of the temple in Ezra 1–6 was secondarily prefaced.

3. T. Cohn Eskenazi, *In An Age of Prose: A Literary Approach to Ezra-Nehemiah* (SBLMS 36; Atlanta: Scholars Press, 1988).

book's sources and paved the way for me to discover new ways of conceiving the literary development of the book. As I continued my research, I came to conclude that not only are the putative sources in dialogue with each other but also the composition of the whole represents a series of responses to the work of the earliest readers of Nehemiah's account, who transformed it from a brief report into a lengthy "memoir" recounting the Restoration of Judah after its destruction at the hands of the Babylonians.

In my view, the history of the rebuilding of Jerusalem and the consolidation of the province in the book of EN represents how generations of authors, beginning in the mid-Persian period and continuing into the Hasmonean period—long after the fourth century—struggled to define the political and ethnic boundaries between Judah and its neighbors. The concern with identity prevailing throughout the book takes its point of departure from the expanded editions of Nehemiah's account: after serving for many years in a prestigious office at the imperial court, the protagonist hears, in conversation with his brother and visitors from Judah, that their compatriots are in distress and reproach. This unexpected encounter forces Nehemiah to come to terms with his own identity, which he does in a lengthy period of mourning and prayer. As the story progresses, his confidence increases until he finally seizes the opportunity afforded by his position of advantage to bring about a number of radical changes to the political, social, and religious conditions of his people.[4]

According to my analysis, the earliest edition of Nehemiah's account was composed with subtlety and fine nuances, but it was also quite concise and was not yet explicitly concerned with the issue of identity. It began with a superscription consisting of the first and last lines in chap. 1: "These are the words of Nehemiah, the son of Hachaliah. I was a cupbearer to the king (vv. 1a, 11b). And it came to pass in the month of Nisan . . ." (Neh 2:1ff.). Not only does the account of the conversation

---

4. In attempting to show why Nehemiah's account was transmitted in a history of the Restoration, my approach to the work and person of this historical figure departs from the widespread tendency to view him with deep suspicion. The negative assessment of Nehemiah is all the more problematic if, as I argue, many of the passages that have been identified as the idiosyncratic views of a single man in Judah constitute the work of later generations of readers. Nehemiah represents, then, quite literally (or literarily), the views of a larger group over an extended period of time. Even if I am wrong and all of the first-person passages in Nehemiah 1–13 stem from the hand of the historical Nehemiah, my study has the merit of revealing several possibilities for why and how his work was read long after his death.

with the men from Judah and the lengthy prayer in Nehemiah 1 appear to have been inserted for various reasons that I shall discuss below, but the lines that remain, once we remove the narrative and the prayer, form a heading that we would expect in autobiographical texts. For example, Ahiqar's account begins with "these are the words of Ahiqar" and is followed by information regarding his profession ("a wise and ready scribe").[5] From the evidence of these analogies, it seems likely that not the conversation with men from Judah (1:1–4) but rather the conversation with Artaxerxes (2.1–6), set in the first month of his 20th year, was originally the opening scene of the account.[6] In this text, a statement that the king appointed Nehemiah to the position of governor (פחה) in Judah is conspicuously absent. The cupbearer is only granted a short leave and is required to return.[7] Note the wording of v. 6b: "But how long will you be gone and when will you come back?"

After arriving in Jerusalem and inspecting the condition of the city on his night ride (2:11–16), he addresses the people and convinces them to repair the ramparts of Jerusalem, promising them that this restoration project will remedy the political disgrace and reproach of the province (2:17). They agree and commence with the construction project (2:18b: "And they said, 'Let us arise and build.' And they strengthened their hands for the good work"). The notice of completion followed immediately thereafter in parts of 3:38 ("So we built the wall. . . . And the people had a heart to do the work") and in 6:15 ("And the wall was finished on the twenty-fifth day of Elul—in fifty-two days"). The rest of the first-person account, I maintain, represents the work of later authors.

Before dismissing this conclusion as hypercritical, one should first examine the wide range of tensions and contradictions indicating that the work is the product of a lengthy maturation process. One of the most important witnesses to the original brevity of Nehemiah's Memoir is the register of the builders in Neh 3:1–32. Indeed, it poses insurmountable problems for those who insist upon the unity of the work because it contradicts the surrounding narrative in many respects and presents the construction of identity in a much different way. Nehemiah 3 emphasizes the unity of the builders, depicting them

---

5. An accessible translation and discussion of the text is provided by J. M. Lindenberger, "The Words of Ahiqar," in *Pseudepigrapha of the Old Testament* (2 vols.; ed. James Charlesworth; Garden City, NY: Doubleday, 1985) 2:479–507.

6. See my discussion in *Rebuilding Identity*, 46–57.

7. For the relationship of Neh 2:1–6 and 5:14–19 and the issue of Nehemiah's governorship as a whole, see ibid., 171–79.

working in tandem and mapping the wall around Jerusalem by com-
memorating the names of the various groups and districts in Judah
that participated in the building project. In contrast, the surrounding
narrative portrays this unity and consolidation of Judah developing in
a sequence of building phases, each characterized by a particular problem. Here, the Judeans rebuild their identity by means of an us-*versus*-
them scheme. Depicting simultaneously the reconstruction of the wall
and the reaffirmation of group identity, the narrative progresses dia-
lectically. Nehemiah first reports an advancement in the restoration,
then the antagonism that it elicits, and finally his response or counter-
active measures.[8] I refer to this narrative structure as "the שמע-
schema," because each of these paragraphs is introduced with a variation of the expression "when P.N. *heard*" (cf. Neh 2:10, 19; 3:33; 4:1, 9;
5:6; 6:1, 16).[9]

Whereas the present shape of the account, structured by this שמע-
schema, portrays the work as proceeding in building phases, each characterized by distinct problems, the register of the builders in Nehemiah 3 recounts the completion of the *entire* wall one section after
another and without the interruptive maneuvers of the enemy. After
v. 32, the circumference of the wall has been erected, and the reader
expects Nehemiah to report the success of the building project. However, v. 33 disappoints these expectations by describing Sanballat's
response when he learned 'that we were building the wall' (כי־אנחנו
בונים את־החומה). Not until 6:15 do we hear that the wall was finished,
and the three chapters that separate this notice of completion from the
final line of the register recount at length what occurred during the 52
days of building: instead of working in peace and harmony, the builders both are threatened with an attack from the surrounding nations
(4:1ff.) and voice their dissatisfaction with the work (4:4–5). The wall is
built first and then Nehemiah himself hangs the doors in the gates (cf.
6:1 and 7:1).

In contrast to this, the list depicts the work as beginning with the
construction of the gates and the hanging of the doors (3:1, etc.), and it
passes over Nehemiah in silence. The remaining account repeatedly
identifies the builders as the "rulers, nobles, and the rest of the people."

---

8. In the third and final movement of each sequence, the builders gain a starker profile and renewed strength as the adversary is rebuffed. Before the narrative achieves
its climax in 6:16, where the enemies acknowledge their failure and the builders' success, the reader has learned of Nehemiah's approach to various problems related to the
Restoration.

9. See the table in ibid, 28.

However, the list never refers to these groups; instead it speaks of the Judean 'princes' (the term שׂר appears eight times in this chapter). Finally, we know from the surrounding passages that both the high priest Eliashib, who in the list initiates the building, and many other nobles were related to Sanballat and Tobiah by marriage and commercial alliances. Thus, when read against the backdrop of the list, passages such as Neh 4:1–2 portray Sanballat and Tobiah as planning to attack their own business partners and children.[10]

Because of the close correspondence of the list to the account of the expansion of the holiness of the temple into the city as a whole in Nehemiah 11 and 12, I submit that the list was inserted into the building account at a very advanced stage.[11] Nevertheless, the placement of this text, which presents the building project as complete, constitutes important evidence for the original brevity of the building account. According to the next notice on the progress of the wall in Neh 3:38, the wall is only half finished. Why did not the redactor who inserted the list divide it into two halves and place the second part before the notice of completion in 6:15? The solution I propose to this problem is that 3:38 has been reworked. It originally reported the completion of the building and was connected to the notice in Neh 6:15, as Hurowitz has proposed in analogy to several building inscriptions.[12] Other scholars have noticed that Neh 3:38 forms the continuation of 2:17–18, where Nehemiah pleads, 'Let us build the wall of Jerusalem' (ונבנה את־חומת ירושלם, 2:17).[13] When the expression ונבה את־החומה recurs in 3:38, we are led to

---

10. For a detailed discussion of the list in its context, see ibid., 109–20.

11. Here, I have revised my earlier conclusions. Although I considered the possibility that the list was late as I was writing my book, I ascribed it to an early revision of Nehemiah's account. That the list was inserted at an advanced stage in the composition of EN makes sense not only of the priority it assigns to the priesthood and the emphasis on the city's holiness that it shares with Nehemiah 11 (compare vv. 1 and 18) and 12 (in Nehemiah 3, the priests begin the building by sanctifying the gates; see Neh 12:30) but also of the appearance of the שׂרים, who are the ones who circumambulate the walls in Nehemiah 12. That the account of the dedication of the wall in Nehemiah 12 represents a late addition to the book is argued in ibid., 273–87.

12. V. A. Hurowitz, *I Have Built You an Exalted House: Temple Building in the Bible in Light of Mesopotamian and Northwest Semitic Writings* (JSOTSup 115; Sheffield: Sheffield Academic Press, 1992) 122–23.

13. See J. Wellhausen, "Die Rückkehr der Juden aus dem babylonischen Exil," *Nachrichten von der Kgl. Gesellschaft der Wissenschaften zu Göttingen* (1895) 166–86; here p. 168; L. W. Batten, *The Books of Ezra and Nehemiah* (ICC; Edinburgh: T. & T. Clark, 1913) 224; K. Galling, *Die Bücher der Chronik, Esra, Nehemia* (ATD 12; Göttingen: Vandenhoeck & Ruprecht, 1954) 220; and R. G. Kratz, *The Composition of the Narrative Books of the Old Testament* (London: T. & T. Clark/Continuum, 2005) 64–67.

think that the work had not merely begun but was actually finished. That this was indeed the case is suggested by the next paragraph (4:1–3), which portrays Judah's neighbors as mobilizing an attack when they hear כי־עלתה ארוכה לחומת ירושלם 'that the walls of Jerusalem had been (fully) restored' (4:1).[14]

Before the insertion of the list, the building account referred to the construction only in passing. Nonetheless, I maintain that the concentration on the antagonism elicited by the building (and the attention devoted to the reforms) is not an integral feature of Nehemiah's account. Rather, it is due to the work of later authors, who drastically amplified his originally brief report. Instead of merely describing how the wall was built, they employed the building report and Nehemiah's influential name both to criticize their enemies and to present their ideas of what Judah's Restoration entailed.

The work of these earliest readers of Nehemiah's account can be divided into two groups. The first consists of the paragraphs just discussed that report the reactions of Sanballat, Tobiah, and Geshem to the progress on the wall (2:10, 19–20; 3:33–37; 4:1–17; 6:1–9). Although these paragraphs may contain bits of historical information, we cannot be sure to what extent Nehemiah stood in outspoken opposition to these figures. Based on his own account, as well as other sources (from the fourth century B.C.E. and the Hellenistic period), we know that there were many important figures from the aristocratic strata in Judah who adopted the practice of *connubium et commercium* with the Sanballatids and Tobiads and who had much to lose if the hardliners succeeded in centralizing the province and instituting their isolationist policies. By describing the machinations of Sanballat and his cohorts as supposedly conspiring to obstruct the Restoration of Jerusalem and cause physical and political harm to the Judeans, the authors of these notices allow Nehemiah, as a pivotal figure in the history of Judah, to warn later generations of his readers about the dangers inherent in cooperative efforts with the surrounding nations.[15]

After the completion of the building project and the concomitant consolidation of the builders into a work force, a process that recognized the need not just for a physical wall of protection around Jerusa-

---

14. This statement has been expanded with a second כי-clause: 'that the breaches were *beginning* to be stopped up' (כי־החלו הפרצים להסתם). In using חלל *Hiphil* to correct the first כי-clause and emphasize that the breaches were only in the *process* of being repaired, the redactional character of this line is difficult to deny (see my *Rebuilding Identity*, 121–22).

15. This point is treated more fully in ibid., 133–37 and 153–59.

lem but also an ethnic wall around all Judah, the authors of the second group of expansions turned to portraying the way that Nehemiah addressed "intramural" problems to buttress his wall. This second group of texts includes the introduction to the account, Neh 1:1b–4; the passages traditionally described as Nehemiah's reforms in chaps. 5 and 13; and finally, two other short passages in chap. 6. Many scholars, following the views of Williamson, assign the greater part of these passages to Nehemiah, who is said to have drafted an account of his reforms instituted many years after building the wall.[16] To be sure, chap. 5 and the three paragraphs in chap. 13 share much in common. All conclude with a prayer for remembrance (or זכרה־לי prayer), all omit mention of the wall, and all criticize the priesthood and the aristocracy.[17]

Nevertheless, I find Williamson's thesis problematic. If chap. 5 was drafted after chap. 6, then one must explain why 6:10–14, a paragraph that does not mention the wall and that criticizes the prophets, presupposes chap. 5 in its present location: The prayer for remembrance concluding chap. 5, just like the prayers at the end of each of the paragraphs in chap. 13, reads: זכרה־לי אלהי לטובה. The prayer concluding 6:10–14 reads: זכרה אלהי לטוביה. This pun on the name Tobiah indicates not only that a significant portion of chap. 6 was added after the composition of chap. 5 but also that Nehemiah's instituting a radical financial reform, presented in chap. 5, occurred during the 52 days of work on the wall.[18]

This historical incongruity is augmented by the likelihood that the three paragraphs in chap. 13 originally presented Nehemiah as also undertaking his other socioreligious reforms during this short time period. As many scholars agree, the statement in 13:6 that dates these reforms to the 32nd year of Artaxerxes was probably added by a redactor. To understand when the original authors of chap. 13 presented Nehemiah as introducing the reforms, note that the introduction of v. 4 (ולפני מזה 'but before this') contains an important clue. By process of elimination, we find that this expression must refer to the final passage

---

16. Williamson, *Ezra-Nehemiah*, xxxviii; M. Throntveit, *Ezra-Nehemiah* (International Biblical Commentary; Louisville: John Knox, 1992) 122–25; C. Karrer, *Ringen um die Verfassung Judas: Eine Studie zu den theologisch-politischen Vorstellungen im Esra-Nehemia-Buch* (BZAW 308; Berlin: de Gruyter, 2001) 145–47; and T. Reinmuth, *Der Bericht Nehemias: Zur literarischen Eigenart, traditionsgeschichtlichen Prägung und innerbiblischen Rezeption des Ich-Berichts Nehemias* (OBO 183; Göttingen: Vandenhoeck & Ruprecht, 2002) 328–30.

17. For a table presenting these passages synoptically, see my *Rebuilding Identity*, 166. A lengthy assessment of Williamson's thesis is provided on pp. 153–60 and 165–71.

18. For more on this point, see ibid., 149.

of chap. 6, where Nehemiah recalls that the Judean nobles and priests were actively corresponding with Tobiah. That they were exchanging letters means that Tobiah was not present in Jerusalem. In 13:4–9, Nehemiah speaks of an incident that occurred "before this." When he came to Jerusalem (13:6b), he saw that Eliashib had provided Tobiah with a chamber in the temple precincts. Enraged, he took radical action, requiring that Tobiah forfeit his *pied-à-terre* in the capital of Judah. This initiative forced the Judean nobility to pursue their relations with Tobiah through written correspondence.[19]

The theory that Neh 6:17–19 and 13:4ff. originally formed a single unit before they were separated by the gradual insertion of material in chaps. 7:1–13:3 is supported by the fact that 6:17–19 begins with the expression "and in those days." After being rejoined with 13:4–14, this passage also would have concluded with a זכרה־לי prayer. Here, a new narrative structure emerges: both the units (chap. 5 and 6:1–14) preceding the notice about completion in 6:15–16 conclude with a זכרה־לי prayer. Moreover, the three units (6:17–19 + 13:4–14, 13:15–22, and 13:23–31) following the notice of completion conclude with a זכרה־לי prayer yet also begin with the expression "in those days."[20] Because this expression in 6:17–19 clearly refers to the 52 days of work on the wall referred to in the immediately preceding notice of completion, the use of the same expression to introduce the remaining two units in chap. 13 requires that we read all these texts, just as we read the portrayal of the financial reform in chap. 5, as reports of Nehemiah's "extramural" activities during the time he was organizing the construction of the wall.

This presentation is historically improbable. Not only would Nehemiah not have had time during those 52 days to concern himself with such complex issues as financial, cultic, Sabbath, language, and marital reforms but also, in taking the people to task for all sorts of social and religious delinquencies, his modus operandi would have run at cross-purposes with his aim in the remaining (and probably earlier) texts of consolidating the Judeans into a unified group of builders. Instead of dismissing the texts as simply unhistorical, one should seek to appreciate the editorial intention in composing them. In 2:17, Nehemiah motivates the Judeans to accept his building proposal by promising that the repairs to the ramparts would redress Judah's situation of disgrace or distress (רעה) and reproach (חרפה). Because the authors of

---

19. On Neh 13:4, see ibid., 191–97.

20. The narrative structure emerging when 13:4–9 is read in sequence with 6:17–19 is discussed in ibid., 149. For the problems caused by 13:15–22, see ibid., 221–41.

this second group of texts noticed that this political situation persisted, although the building project had long since been completed and succeeding generations were initiating new building projects in Jerusalem, they updated Nehemiah's account and depicted the heroic builder in the midst of the work on the wall as recognizing the need for a radical intramural reformation.

All of these texts employ the two key terms of Nehemiah's motivational speech in 2:17 and attribute responsibility for the רעה and חרפה to the behavior of the aristocracy. In chap. 5, Nehemiah appeals to the חרפה of the nations in order to impress upon the nobility the necessity of recognizing the kinship of all the Judeans and discontinuing their conventional credit policies. In 6:10–14, the corrupt prophets attempt to bring reproach (חרפה) upon Nehemiah himself. In 13:4–14, the priests and officials were guilty of wrongdoing (רעה) in cultic affairs. In 13:15–22, the failure of the nobles and their ancestors to keep Shabbat is the very reason why the רעה had befallen Jerusalem in the first place. In 13:23ff., the Judean men committed רעה in their loose connubial practices, which led to a situation in which the children no longer were able to speak "Yehudit." The expression "in those days" that introduces all the paragraphs in chap. 13 serves to attach them like footnotes to the notice of completion in 6:15. Accordingly, the 25th of Elul is the date of completion not only for Jerusalem's physical wall but also Judah's ethnic wall, for the province had undergone a deep transformation.[21]

As the building account reached these literary proportions, it became necessary to provide the narrative with a new introduction in 1:1b–4. This text, like all the others in the second group of additions, distinguishes the problem of the ramparts from the רעה and חרפה of Judah: "The survivors . . . are in great distress (רעה) and reproach (חרפה). And the wall of Jerusalem is broken down" (1:3). Second, by using terms such as הנשארים and הפליטה, this text explicitly links Nehemiah's work with the Restoration of Judah after the Babylonian catastrophe. And third, in 1:4 Nehemiah's reaction to the state of affairs in the province is introduced with the expression "when I heard," preparing the reader for the passage introduced with "when they heard" (4:1), in which Sanballat, Tobiah, and Geshem react negatively to Nehemiah's efforts to redress this situation.[22] At a subsequent stage, the authors of the confession in 1:5–11a created the textual space that

---

21. On the significance of the notice of completion, see ibid., 158–59.
22. These points are elaborated in ibid., 57–65.

allowed Nehemiah to espouse a sophisticated theological interpretation of his later work.[23]

At this point (before the gradual expansion of the material in Neh 7:1–13:3), the composition of the book of EN begins. If it were not for the efforts of Nehemiah's earliest readers to draw out the implications of his succinct message, his account would probably not have prompted later authors to write this book. But once Nehemiah presents his building project as the Restoration of Judah after the catastrophe of 586 B.C.E. and exposes widespread corruption in the temple, Priestly authors take it upon themselves to set the historical record straight.

In line with the pro-Priestly register of the builders in Nehemiah 3, these authors begin the composition of the book with the account of the construction of the temple in Ezra 1–6. Here, the authors correct the expanded versions of Nehemiah's account by affirming that the Restoration did not begin in the 20th year of Artaxerxes' reign but in the coronation year of the first Persian ruler. And instead of simply granting a courtier such as Nehemiah a leave of absence to build the temple for his own reasons, Cyrus—in his role as king and appointed by God—builds the temple himself and for his own kingdom. Later this royal prerogative is transferred to the Judean people and their leaders. Furthermore, whereas Nehemiah simply "comes" to Jerusalem, the first group of builders makes *aliyah*.[24] Neh 1:1–4 identifies the survivors of the captivity with those who remained in the land (הנשארים) and is seemingly oblivious of a return from captivity. Ezra 1 and 2 reinterprets these protagonists in Nehemiah's account in terms

---

23. For the function of the prayer as a preface to all of Nehemiah 1–13, see ibid., 14–23.

24. Compare ואבוא in Neh 2:11 with the use of the root עלה 16 times in Ezra 1–6 (1:3, 5, 11; 2:1, 59; 3:2, 3, 4, 5, 6; 4:2). In employing both the *Qal* and *Hiphal*, the authors integrate the "going up" of the exiles with the "going up" of the sacrifices that the exiles offer once they arrive in Jerusalem. The purpose of the return is thus not simply to build but also to sacrifice. Other terms used to express the point that the protagonists of the Restoration were returnees from the Diaspora are גולה (1:11; 2:1; 4:1; 6:19, 20–21) and שבי (2:1, 3:8). The exilic emphasis is equally emphasized in the Aramaic portions of Ezra 1–6 (compare the Aramaic term סלק in 4:12 and the historical depiction in 5:12–16). The depiction of the returnees as arriving in Judah already united in their determination to build contrasts sharply with Nehemiah's account, in which groups that had long resided in Judah must be motivated to build. Nehemiah's depiction may be compared with the autochthonous conception of Israel's origins as expressed in the Patriarchal traditions and 1–2 Samuel, whereas the view of EN as a whole parallels the allochthonous notion promoted especially by the Exodus Conquest account in the books of Exodus–Joshua. For an explanation of Neh 7:4–6 in which Nehemiah espouses the Golah-oriented view, see my *Rebuilding Identity*, 298–307.

of the עלים ('the returnees'). Indeed, the authors of Ezra 1–6, in contrast to Nehemiah, do not acknowledge the existence of Judeans who were left in the province.[25] For example, Ezra 4 clearly links עם־יהודה ('the people of Judah') with בני־הגולה ('the children of the captivity') and עם־הארץ ('the people of the land') are the צרי יהודה ובנימן ('the adversaries of Judah and Benjamin'), not a group of previous residents who had escaped the captivity (cf. Neh 1:2–3).

Ezra 4 is significant for several more reasons: First, it emphasizes the harmonious dyarchy established by the high priest Joshua and the lay leader Zerubbabel in contrast to the malevolent relationship between Nehemiah and Eliashib. Second, it draws upon many features of Nehemiah's account (for example, the שמע-schema and the response to Sanballat in Neh 2:19–20) to present the animosity between Judah and its neighbors, beginning with the construction of the temple, not the wall.[26] Third, the Artaxerxes correspondence portrays the wall both as being built before the advent of Nehemiah and as being the cause for the court's consternation. Because Jerusalem is a "rebellious and wicked" city, Artaxerxes commands the work on the wall to cease until he "issues a decree" (4:21).[27]

Before he does this, as implied in Nehemiah 2, the temple has been built (Ezra 5–6), and he has sent a priest and scribe by the name of Ezra with papers in hand assuring him of unlimited funds from the royal treasuries to 'beautify' (לפאר) the temple (Ezra 7:27). According to my model, the earliest Ezra material is found in Ezra 7–8, and it was composed in the second compositional stage of the book as a literary bridge connecting the contents and *Tendenz* of the third-person temple-building account in Ezra 1–6 to the form and time period of the first-person wall-building account in Nehemiah 1–13*. That Ezra 7–8 was composed as a continuation of Ezra 1–6 seems at first implausible, yet the view that it is older than the temple-building narrative presupposes that the authors of EN totally revamped the original introduction to Ezra's account. If the authors were prepared to make such radical changes, why did they not also edit and rewrite—instead of just expanding—the introduction to Nehemiah's account? Of the two memoirs, it is Nehemiah's that would have been the first candidate for editorial work, because it portrays—from the perspective of Ezra 1–6—an unorthodox

---

25. See ibid., 62–66.

26. For a detailed comparison of these texts, see ibid., 323–24.

27. For the literary function of the Artaxerxes correspondence in Ezra 4, see ibid., 31–43.

view of the Restoration. On the other hand, Ezra 7–8 meshes very well
with the aims of Ezra 1–6; indeed, these chapters may be described as
nothing more than a variation on the theme of the temple-building account. Although this material may contain an older core with some historical basis (for example, chap. 8, which is dated simply to the "reign
of Artaxerxes, king of Babylon"), it serves for the most part to over-
shadow Nehemiah's subtle depiction of his good relations with the
king. Just as in Ezra 1, the initiative to beautify the temple proceeds
from the king, who does not need to be petitioned for permission as in
Nehemiah 2. On his own volition, he grants Ezra a document guaranteeing him full imperial support. However, years later he seems to have
forgotten about the beneficence he manifested to the priest of the Jerusalem temple, and now Nehemiah must even ask him for letters of safe
delivery.[28]

With the addition of Ezra 9, the third stage of composition, the book
treats Nehemiah's work much more positively. After the situation in
the province takes a turn for the worse (Ezra 9:1–2), the erection of the
wall, rather than being depreciated, is recognized as the only solution.
The notice in 8:35–36 concludes chaps. 7–8 with the same third-person
style with which it began, yet in chap. 9 Ezra resumes his account and
portrays a deficiency in a manner that strikingly resembles the first and
final passages of Nehemiah's work (chap. 1 and 13:23ff.). In both Ezra 9
and Nehemiah 1, groups report problems to the protagonists. Likewise,
both Ezra and Nehemiah react to what they "hear" by sitting down,
mourning, and making lengthy confessions. While Ezra tears out his
own hair and beard, Nehemiah in chap. 13 tears out the hair of the of-
fenders. (Both passages employ the very rare lexeme מרט.) And just as
Ezra mourned because Israel had taken "the daughters (of the nations)
for themselves and their sons," Nehemiah in this final passage of the
book makes the Judeans swear: "You shall not give your daughters to
their sons, or take their daughters for your sons or for yourselves."[29]

The addition of Ezra 9 provides the framework for reading Nehemiah's account, making it plain that the Restoration was not complete
when the imperial court issued a number of decrees promoting the
temple. As long as "the people of Israel, the priests and Levites had not

---

28. I discuss Ezra 7–8 in ibid., 86–93.

29. Both passages modify Deut 7:3 in the same manner; see esp. Ezra 9:12. Both a
comparison of Ezra 9 with Nehemiah 1 and 13:23ff. and a discussion of the way that Ezra
9 prepares the reader for Nehemiah's account are found in ibid., 248–57.

separated themselves from the people of the land" (Ezra 9:1), there was still much to be done. But Ezra is (initially) not the one who does it. Before the late addition of Ezra 10 (which employs the third person and different language from the language of chap. 9), the next scene in the book transports the reader back to the court of Artaxerxes, where Nehemiah hears about the affliction and reproach of his compatriots. He petitions for a leave of absence, comes to the province, and repairs the ramparts of Jerusalem. At every step, he faces the interruptive tactics of Sanballat and Tobiah, with whom the priests and aristocracy are connubially allied. Before the wall is complete on the 25th of Elul, he has removed Tobiah from his foothold in the province (Neh 13:4ff.), commanded the city gates to be closed on the Sabbath to prohibit foreign merchants from continuing their trade with the nobles (13:15ff.), made the inhabitants of the province swear to abolish their contacts with foreigners (13:23ff.), "chased away" a descendant of the high priest who is the son-in-law of Sanballat (13:28–29), and "fenced us round with impregnable palisades and with walls of iron, to the end that we should mingle in no way with any other nations" (*Ep. Arist.* 139).

After Ezra (in chap. 9) assumes a positive stance vis-à-vis Nehemiah's wall by expanding the purview from the temple to the people and ascribing to them the holy status that formerly only the priests had enjoyed, the path is paved for the composition of Nehemiah 8–10, which depicts Ezra as teaming up with Nehemiah in a dyarchy for which Eliashib has proved himself unworthy. The composition of these latest layers of the book takes it point of departure from Nehemiah's discovery of Ezra 2, which he refers to as "the book of the genealogies of those who were the first to come back." Once this text is quoted and slightly revised in Nehemiah 7, the authors of Nehemiah 8–10 create further unmistakable parallels with Ezra 3. Both of these texts tell of assemblies in the sacred seventh month but, whereas Ezra 3 presents the people as gathering to erect the altar and reinitiate the sacrificial cult, Nehemiah 8–10 presents the people as gathering in a plaza far away from the temple in order to hear the Torah read. On the second day, all the leaders, priests, and Levites gather around Ezra, who represents the institution of the סופר. They discover in their study at this "place" a new way of celebrating Sukkot.

While Ezra 3 reports the expected sacrifices for this festival, Nehemiah 8 presents the people as building *sukkot*, first on the roofs and the courtyards of their houses and then in the temple courts and throughout the city. By the 24th of the month (chap. 9), they have learned to read for themselves. The following lengthy prayer, which recounts the history of Israel in detail, passes over the temple in silence, emphasizing the Torah in place of the temple as the condition for tenure in the land. In chap. 10, they respond to the call for political autonomy in the prayer by cutting a covenant (or אמנה) to keep the *mitzvot*. Before the general pledge to the Torah is expanded with individual stipulations, the reader presumes that the temple has passed into complete oblivion.[30]

Nehemiah 8–10 gives expression to a growing tension between temple and Torah in the Hellenistic age. In replacing the high priest, temple, and sacrifices with a scribe, the Torah, and confession, these chapters constitute the final stage in a long literary process that began with Nehemiah's struggle with the aristocracy and priesthood to consolidate the province and establish its political self-determination and ethnic distinctiveness by means of the wall. This process of centralization continued with the intramural building projects of the altar and temple in Ezra 1–6 and the beautification of the temple in Ezra 7–8. The holiness of the temple was then expanded to encompass the entire city and its residents, first in Nehemiah 11–12, later in Ezra 9, and finally in Nehemiah 8–10.

Although Nehemiah 8–10 belongs to the final stage of development of EN, the process—or conversation—that generated the book continued. For example, the authors of 1 Esdras, in a manner similar to the methodology of Chronicler, found it necessary to make the radical move from the technique of simply expanding the text to that of deleting large portions of it in order to substantiate their views. The material that they decided to cut completely out of the history of the Restoration was, significantly, Nehemiah's first-person account, the text that according to my model initiated the process that produced the book of EN.[31]

To conclude, a brief word about the dating of the book: in telling the history of Judah's successful relations with the Achaemenid Empire, the authors of EN illustrate the correct manner of interacting with the empires that succeeded the Achaemenids. That the composition of EN

---

30. For Nehemiah 8–9, see ibid., 315–39; and for Nehemiah 10, ibid., 212–20.

31. However, the authors did find a place for the first part of Nehemiah 8 but only after they had made serious changes to it in keeping with their pro-Priestly orientation. For a discussion of 1 Esdras and the influential view of D. Böhler (*Die heilige Stadt in Esdras α und Esra-Nehemia: Zwei Konzeptionen der Wiederherstellung Israels* [OBO 158; Freiburg: Universitätsverlag / Göttingen: Vandenhoeck & Ruprecht, 1997]), see my *Rebuilding Identity*, 39 and 322–24.

culminated in the mid-Hellenistic period—not in the fourth century, as commonly thought—would agree with the archaeological evidence for the reconstruction of Jerusalem, according to which the city was hardly occupied during the fourth century but underwent major expansions beginning in the third century. The largest building projects were carried out by the Hasmoneans.[32] This building activity corresponds to a centralization of the province—a process that was perhaps initiated by Nehemiah yet is presupposed in the final form of EN.

In addition to this, I should draw attention to several bits of evidence that support the relative dating of the book's layers.[33] According to my analysis, the latest additions to EN can be isolated in Neh 7:1–13:3; they sever the connection between 6:17–19 and 13:4–9. Significantly, 7:4–72, which quotes Ezra 2, appears to respond to apocalyptic notions that most likely do not predate the Hellenistic period.[34] The literary complex Neh 8:1–10:30, when read against the backdrop of Ezra 2–3, witnesses a growing division between temple and Torah in the Hellenistic period. Furthermore, the prayer in Nehemiah 9 employs a key expression, כרצונם 'at their pleasure' (9:37; cf. v. 24), which occurs elsewhere only in very late texts (Dan 8:4; 11:16, 36; Esth 1:8; 9:5). So too, the form of the pact in chap. 10 and the sequence formed by it and the prayer in chap. 9 resemble the instructions for ratifying a covenant in 1QS I 18–II 18 (the so-called *Manual of Discipline*).[35] The reference to the offering of 1/3 of a shekel in Neh 10:33 and the casting

---

32. See the discussion and bibliographical references cited by O. Lipschits in *The Fall and Rise of Jerusalem: Jerusalem under Babylonian Rule* (Winona Lake, IN: Eisenbrauns, 2005) 212–13. Recently D. Ussishkin treated the problem of the size of Jerusalem in the Persian period, and his conclusions regarding the original aim of Nehemiah's building project support my own suggestions (see, e.g., *Rebuilding Identity*, 152–53). Specifically, Ussishkin argues that this project was first and foremost a symbolic, national, political act rather than a purely military act. Following this, attempts were made to settle the vast intramural areas, but these attempts largely failed. Large regions of the walled city remained uninhabited, while the population concentrated around the City of David and the area of the Temple Mount. This was probably the appearance of the city encountered by Alexander the Great in 332 B.C.E., and it remained so until its period of renewed prosperity, which began in the late Hellenistic period, in the second century B.C.E. (Ussishkin, "The Borders and *De Facto* Size of Jerusalem in the Persian Period," in *Judah and the Judeans in the Persian Period* [ed. O. Lipschits and M. Oeming; Winona Lake, IN: Eisenbrauns, 2006] 147–66 [here, p. 164]).

33. More arguments are scattered throughout *Rebuilding Identity*, but see especially pp. 307–8.

34. On Nehemiah's discovery of a book of genealogies that he employs to repopulate the newly built Jerusalem, see ibid., 298–301 and 306–7.

35. See ibid., 220; and D. Baltzer, *Das Bundesformular* (WMANT 4; Neukirchen-Vluyn: Neukirchener Verlag, 1960) 51–55.

of lots for the delivery of wood in 10:35 are both very reminiscent of developments in Hasmonean times.[36] With regard to Nehemiah 11, the designation עיר הקדש in vv. 1 and 18 appears elsewhere only in very late texts.[37] Moreover, the mention of Joiarib in 12:6 and 19 should, according to scholarly consensus, be dated to the Hasmonean or Maccabean periods.[38] Similarly, works such as Ben Sira, 2 Maccabees, 1 Esdras, and *1 Enoch* indicate that Nehemiah's account was widely read in the second century B.C.E. That those who read it also amplified it in order to draw out the implications of its message for new situations is not only suggested by the evidence of the text itself but is also to be expected in view of what we know about the growth of biblical literature.

---

36. See M. Weinfeld, *Normative and Sectarian Judaism in the Second Temple Period* (Library of Second Temple Studies 54; London: T. & T. Clark, 2005) 233–34.

37. See the list in my *Rebuilding Identity*, 307.

38. Ibid., 308.

Who Knew What?
The Construction of the Monarchic Past in Chronicles and Implications for the Intellectual Setting of Chronicles

EHUD BEN ZVI

University of Alberta

Introduction

The starting point of this essay is the portrayal of major characters in Chronicles or a section thereof as people who (a) know a variety of texts, including texts that are explicitly set in a time later than the putative time of the speaker in Chronicles, or (b) exhibit knowledge about future events. These particular attributes of the characters are for the most part conveyed to the intended and primary rereaders of the book through the direct speech of the relevant character and, therefore, cannot be explained away as the interpretive comments of a narrator whose perspective stretches to centuries after the narrated events. Moreover, these crucial utterances by the speakers tend to appear in unexpected contexts in the narrative of the book. Thus the tension between the contents of the utterances and the explicit narrative setting in the book serves to draw special attention to the utterances and their meanings. This tension suggests to the intended readers that something of importance that is far beyond the basic narrative thrust of the book is being communicated through these utterances. Two main examples will be discussed below and their implications elaborated.

The Case of David

The intended and primary readers of the book are informed that David's fame spread into all lands and that YHWH brought the fear of him on all nations (1 Chr 14:17). They also learn that David's kingship was exalted for the sake of his people (1 Chr 14:2). Against this background, they vicariously learn and vicariously experienced through their reading a central point in their story about themselves. David has just brought the ark inside the tent he has pitched for it, offered burnt and peace offerings in the midst of a great celebration (1 Chr 16:1–3), and organized the service of the ark (1 Chr 16:4–7). David, through Asaph, appropriately sings YHWH's praises, as the song concludes. Asaph (that is, David)[1] asks or, better, commands the community that (in the world of the book) is participating in the event to implore YHWH (along with him, of course) with the following words:

הוֹשִׁיעֵנוּ אֱלֹהֵי יִשְׁעֵנוּ וְקַבְּצֵנוּ וְהַצִּילֵנוּ מִן־הַגּוֹיִם

Save us, O God of our salvation, and *gather and rescue us from among the nations.* (1 Chr 16:35)

The intended and primary readers of the book are unlikely to imagine that the implied author and communicator of the book (that is, the Chronicler) is asking them either to (a) imagine David as delusional or (b) to wonder who has been exiled and must be gathered from among the nations at this particular time in the narrative. There has been no reference to any exile of Israel at this time or previously and, even if one were to argue that some people were exiled among the Philistines after the Philistines' victory over Saul—something the text does not claim— David had already defeated the Philistines (1 Chr 14:6–16) within Chronicles' chronology. Instead, it seems highly likely that, from the perspective of the intended and primary readers of Chronicles, David is praying and asking the community of his days to pray for the return of exiles that have not *yet been exiled.* Given the historical circumstances of these readers and their discourses, it also seems highly likely that, from their perspective, this exile would have been associated with (though not necessarily limited to) the Babylonian Exile.

This being so, one has to conclude that these readers most likely imagined David as one who knew the future (even the far future, like Moses; see Deut 4:25–28, 31:16–18). Significantly, the reference to the future Exile is not advanced by David as new knowledge or as knowl-

---

1. The words are uttered by Asaph, the Levite. The context and David's central role in arranging the entire service make it abundantly clear to the intended, primary readers of the book that the main person to be associated with the song is not Asaph but David. (Significantly, none of the psalms included or alluded to in this song [see below] are characterized as "Psalms/Songs of Asaph" in the book of Psalms). As is well known, the term *discourse* can carry many different meanings. Without entering into the contested field of defining this concept, in this essay I do not use *discourse* in the sense of conversation, discussion, or the like but in the general sense of a system or cluster of interrelated ideas, ways of thinking, images, linguistic, or extralinguistic expressions that govern the ways in which particular sets of issues may (or may not) be thought, imagined, stated, or generally dealt with in some social group.

edge that is not widely shared by the community or that needs to be repeated as a warning[2] or as a contingent future development (cf. 1 Kgs 8:46–50, 2 Chr 6:36–40) that requires explanation; it is presented as a matter of fact. It bears noting that David's primary distinction is not so much related to the fact that the text requires the readers to imagine him as a person who knows of a turning point in the future of Israel. In fact, the text suggests that the readers should imagine the entire assembly in the story as knowing this event as well. David's main characterizing stroke at the conclusion of his psalm of thanksgiving is that he brings to the attention of the Israel of his time an awareness of a future exile. Thus, David in this depiction of a crucial, formative, celebratory event (the bringing of the ark) is portrayed as someone who identifies himself with, reflects, and reinforces the identification of the Israel of his time with postmonarchic Israel (notice the "gather and rescue *us*").

Conversely, from the perspective of these readers, the reference allows them to identify with David closely, especially with David's Israel and, accordingly, to participate vicariously and rejoice with the Israelites at the time of bringing the ark. The gap between the Israel for whom Chronicles was composed and the Israel of David's time is thus bridged. The two become closely interrelated, and for this to happen, exiled Israel *must* share some of their discourse and world of knowledge with preexilic Israel. Similarly, a turning point in the establishment of the proper cult becomes linked with both its destruction (the Exile) and the hope for its full restoration in terms of YHWH's gathering and rescuing Israel from among the nations. This restoration process from the perspective of the intended and primary readers of the book has begun in some way but has not yet been completely fulfilled (2 Chr 36:22–23).[3]

To be sure, the authors and target readers of Chronicles know very well that the David of 1 Chr 16:8–36 is essentially uttering a slightly modified version of Psalm 96 that is framed by an extensive selection from Psalm 105 (again with slight modifications) and a short concluding selection from Psalm 106.[4] Shaping new texts and meanings by

---

2. Contrast with Deut 4:25–28, 31:15–21. The image of a great figure of the past who is informed of the future judgment of Israel is a common *topos* in late Second Temple literature (e.g., 1Q22 [= 1QDM] col. 1; *T. Levi* 14–25; *Jub.* 1:7–14).

3. See E. Ben Zvi, *History, Literature and Theology in the Book of Chronicles* (London: Equinox, 2006) chap. 10.

4. To be more precise, 1 Chr 16:8–36 is based on Ps 105:1–15, 96:1–13, 106:1 (?), and 106:47–48. Of course, as a literary unit, it conveys a message of its own, which is shaped partly by the "intertextual" references in the repertoire of psalms accepted in the

citing portions of other texts in the accepted repertoire of the late Persian period is certainly a well-known device among the Yehudite literati—a device that is raised to quasi-burlesque proportions in Jonah 2:3–10. While it is certainly true that, on one level the newly crafted text carries a message of its own and is most often anchored in the surrounding narrative,[5] explicit references to other texts known by the community are also integral to the communication and creation of meaning through the reading and rereading of the new text. In the present case, the key phrase "Save us, O God of our salvation, and *gather and rescue us from among the nations*" points to the text of Ps 106:47. Psalm 106 is a postmonarchic psalm that explains exile, recalls the history of Israel, and provides hope for the future. This psalm was certainly understood by the readers as speaking to the postmonarchic situation, including the situation of the primary readerships of Chronicles. In other words, David is portrayed here not only as aware of and properly responding to the future Exile but as someone whose speech speaks to both (a) the formative circumstances in the world portrayed in the book and present in the social memory of the readers of Chronicles and (b) these readers' own times; and this is accomplished by using the readers' psalms.[6]

Keeping this in mind, we should note that the intended and primary readerships of Chronicles (and the implied author they construed) are also asked to imagine David as choosing to cite a slightly modified version of Psalm 96 on the very same occasion. Although less obvious than Psalm 106, Psalm 96 was most likely understood by these readers as speaking to their postmonarchic situation.[7] In fact, unlike the MT, the LXX attests a tradition of interpretation that associates

---

discourse of the readership of Chronicles. See G. N. Knoppers, *1 Chronicles 10–29* (AB 12A; New York: Doubleday, 2004) 644–61.

5. See, for instance, A. E. Hill, "Patchwork Poetry or Reasoned Verse? Connective Structure in 1 Chronicles XVI," *VT* 33 (1983) 97–100; T. C. Eskenazi, "A Literary Approach to the Chronicler's Ark Narrative in I Chronicles 13–16," in *Fortunate the Eyes That See: Essays in Honor of David Noel Freedman in Celebration of His Seventieth Birthday* (ed. A. B. Beck; Grand Rapids, MI: Eerdmans, 1995) 258–74; H. N. Wallace, "What Chronicles Has to Say about Psalms," in *The Chronicler as Author: Studies in Text and Texture* (ed. M. P. Graham and S. L. McKenzie; JSOTSup 263; Sheffield: Sheffield Academic Press, 1999) 267–91. Incidentally, the same holds true even when the text exhibits some hyperbole in the use of citations for rhetorical purposes (see Jonah 2:3–10).

6. Cf. T. C. Butler, "A Forgotten Passage from a Forgotten Era (1 Chr. XVI 8–36)," *VT* 28 (1978) 142–50.

7. On Psalm 96, see E. S. Gerstenberger, *Psalms, Part 2 and Lamentations* (FOTL 15; Grand Rapids, MI: Eerdmans, 2001) 187–91.

Psalm 96 *both* with the rebuilding of the temple after the Exile and with David.[8] Although it is impossible to know whether this tradition goes back to the time of the primary readerships of Chronicles or whether it is a tradition that derives from Chronicles,[9] it proves that ancient communities of readers could and did understand not only the text of Ps 106:47–48 (as demonstrated above) but also the idea that Psalm 96 pertained to both David and the Second Temple period.

It is exactly this fluidity of meanings that allows the target readership to engage deeply with the text and to negotiate their identity through the intertwining of the converging and mutually identifying tendencies communicated by the text without negating the differences between them, their leaders, and their circumstances on the one hand; and David, his people, and the circumstances around the transporting of the ark on the other hand. In fact, it was this fluidity of meanings that made the text powerful for the mentioned readerships.[10]

A related ambiguity enhances further the fluidity of these (complementary) meanings conveyed by the text. The target readerships could have imagined that David knew, cited, and slightly rephrased Psalm 96 and the portions of the other psalms (e.g., Ps 106:47–48), but if they read Chronicles with the grain rather than against the grain, they could have also imagined that the authors of the relevant psalms were aware of David's utterances. In either case, a sense of association between the authorship of the relevant Psalms and David would have been affirmed.

Significantly, not only associations but also differences are conveyed and stressed, because the minor differences between the words of David in 1 Chr 16:8–36 and the relevant texts in the Psalms suggest an authorship and readership mindful of differences. Certainly some of the variants are grounded in the different settings of the relevant texts. For

---

8. The superscription to the psalm in the LXX reads: "When the house was being rebuilt after the captivity. An Ode. Pertaining to Dauid." See A. Pietersma, *The Psalms* (NETS; New York: Oxford Univ. Press, 2000) 95.

9. The tradition is to be differentiated from the actual writing of the superscription itself, which is a different issue—an issue that also defies precise dating.

10. G. Knoppers (*1 Chronicles 10–29*, 648) writes, "if the superscription had been part of the Chronicler's source, it is unlikely that he would have quoted this psalm in the context of the presentation of David's life." Setting aside the fact that I prefer to talk about the implied author of Chronicles as understood by its intended and primary readerships than about the actual author/s of the book, I disagree with this statement. These readerships had to construe the authorial voice of the book as a voice that has no problem with portraying characters as being aware of later events and texts, and in fact, uses double understandings (such as in this case) to advance rhetorical and ideological aims.

instance, whereas Ps 96:6 reads במקדשו, David says במקומו in 1 Chr 16:27. After all, there was not temple at the time of David's utterances. Similarly, the absence of the long history of sin in Psalm 106 may be understood as reflecting a different rhetorical setting for David's words. It is precisely against this affirmation of difference between (a) the communities explicitly addressed in these psalms and the related literati for whom Chronicles was composed and (b) the people addressed by David when he brought the ark both in the world of the book and the social memory of the literati that the rhetorical power of "Save us, O God of our salvation, and *gather and rescue us from among the nations*" is far more salient, and along with it the mentioned fluidity of meanings that serves the readers to negotiate their identities in terms of convergence and divergence from David's Israel at its time of glory, of likeness and of lack thereof.

The Case of Azariah, the Son of Oded, and of References to Prophetic Literature

More than 70 years ago, von Rad published his famous essay on the Levitical sermon in Chronicles.[11] One of the things he discussed there was the references to prophetic books in Chronicles. About 30 years ago, Japhet wrote that "the many verses of classical prophecy quoted by the Chronicler particularly in his speeches prove his familiarity with this corpus." She referred to von Rad's essay and considered 2 Chr 16:9 (cf. Zech 4:10), 15:6 (cf. Zech 11:6), 15:7 (cf. Jer 31:16), and 20:20 (cf. Isa 7:9) to be "the most obvious" examples.[12] This trend has been noticed and discussed by more-recent scholars as well.[13] Although at times the obvious "anachronistic" character of these quotations is mentioned,[14] the focus of these studies has not been on the effect that these quotations have on the characterization of the relevant speakers or by implication the effect they have on the constructions of the past that

---

11. G. von Rad, "The Levitical Sermon in *I and II Chronicles*," *The Problem of the Hexateuch and Other Essays* (London: SCM, 1984) 267–80 (first published in German as "Die levitische Predigt in den Büchern der Chronik," in *Festschrift für Otto Procksch* [Leipzig, 1934] 113–24).

12. S. Japhet, *The Ideology of the Book of Chronicles and Its Place in Biblical Thought* (2nd ed.; BEATAJ 9; Frankfurt am Main: Peter Lang, 1997) 183.

13. See particularly P. Beentjes, "Prophets in the Book of Chronicles," in *The Elusive Prophet: The Prophet as a Historical Person, Literary Character and Anonymous Artist* (ed. J. C. de Moor; OtSt 45; Leiden: Brill, 2001) 45–53; idem, "Tradition and Transformation: Aspects of Innerbiblical Interpretation in 2 Chronicles 20," *Bib* 74 (1993) 258–68.

14. So, for example, ibid., 266.

confront the intended and primary rereaders of Chronicles and their ideological implications.[15]

Azariah's speech in 2 Chr 15:3–7 provides an excellent illustration of the possible contributions to be gained by shifting the focus of the inquiry. The speech attracts the attention of the readers by defamiliarizing the expectations created by the narrative. Following Asa's glorious victory over Zerah—which is described in superlative terms in Chronicles—and the celebrated peaceful period that immediately preceded it, the reader does not expect to hear: וְיָמִים רַבִּים לְיִשְׂרָאֵל לְלֹא אֱלֹהֵי אֱמֶת וּלְלֹא כֹּהֵן מוֹרֶה וּלְלֹא תוֹרָא ('For many days Israel was without the true God and without a teaching priest and without divine teaching', v. 3), or וּבָעִתִּים הָהֵם אֵין שָׁלוֹם לַיּוֹצֵא וְלַבָּא כִּי מְהוּמֹת רַבּוֹת עַל כָּל־יוֹשְׁבֵי הָאֲרָצוֹת ('In those times, there was no peace for people coming and going, for many disturbances affected all the inhabitants of the lands', v. 5), or וְכֻתְּתוּ גוֹי־בְגוֹי וְעִיר בְּעִיר כִּי־אֱלֹהִים הֲמָמָם בְּכָל־צָרָה ('Nation crushed nation and city crushed city, for God caused confusion among them by every kind of distress', v. 6).[16] To be sure, v. 7, וְאַתֶּם חִזְקוּ וְאַל־יִרְפּוּ יְדֵיכֶם כִּי יֵשׁ שָׂכָר לִפְעֻלַּתְכֶם ('But as for you, be strong and do not let your hands be weak, for there is reward for your work'), serves to attenuate the discrepancy between the wording of the speech up to this point and the circumstances in which it is uttered, but by doing so v. 7 confirms the odd contextual situation in which the words are set to begin with and further draws the attention of the intended and primary readers to the message/s conveyed by the speech of Azariah, the son of Oded.

The readers for whom this speech was crafted were literati of late Yehud. They would have easily recognized another "odd," salient feature of this speech. The words set in the mouth of Azariah strongly echoed prophetic texts set in periods later than Azariah and Asa. For instance, v. 3 (יְמִים רבים . . . לְלֹא . . . לְלֹא . . . לְלֹא) contains an echo of Hos 3:4 (. . . אֵין . . . אֵין . . . יְמִים רבים); v. 5 (אֵין שָׁלוֹם לַיּוֹצֵא וְלַבָּא) contains an echo of both Zech 8:10 (וְלַיּוֹצֵא אֵין־שָׁלוֹם) and Amos 3:9 (the only two instances of מְהוּמֹת רַבּוֹת in the Hebrew Bible; compare with Zech 14:13);

---

15. Lack of interest in these matters is partially due to a common tendency to focus on the world view, world of knowledge, and literary techniques of the proposed *actual* author or authors of the book. This tendency has contributed to a better understanding of the social and intellectual history in late-Persian Yehud. But, as this essay shows, a complementary approach that focuses on the ideological worlds implied, created, reinforced, and communicated through the social process of reading and rereading Chronicles by the literati for whom it was primarily intended sheds additional important, unique light on the social and intellectual history of late-Persian Yehud.

16. The text may have also connoted a sense of "nation will crush nation and city will crush city, for God caused confusion among them by every kind of distress." See below.

v. 7 (וְאַל־יִרְפּוּ יְדֵיכֶם) (וְאַל־יִרְפּוּ יָדֶיךָ) contains an echo of Zeph 3:16 (אַל־יִרְפּוּ יָדֶיךָ) and of Jer 31:16 (compare כִּי יֵשׁ שָׂכָר לִפְעֻלַּתְכֶם in Chronicles with כִּי יֵשׁ שָׂכָר לִפְעֻלָּתֵךְ in Jeremiah);[17] to which one may add (with Japhet) a close textual tie between v. 4 and Hos 5:15.[18] Although each of these can perhaps be dismissed as a simple coincidence, the cumulative rhetorical power of all these occurrences within the range of a few verses most likely carried considerable significance to the primary and intended readerships of the book.

An illustration of the interpretive influence of this observation is in order. Verse 4 suggests to the intended and primary readers that the negative circumstances portrayed in vv. 3–6 belong to an undefined past. At the same time, the clout of the explicit reference to the past in v. 4 for these readers' understanding of these verses is not negated but rhetorically balanced by the difficulty that they face if they try to associate the text with a particular time in the past.[19] To be sure, some aspects of the text may have suggested to the readers that Azariah referred to the period of the Judges (see v. 4) and that this is what the Chronicler wanted to convey. But other aspects (for example, the lack of reference to the period of the Judges in Chronicles) pointed in a different direction. Among these other aspects, the most noticeable is the explicit, repeated use of words that link this text to other texts in the repertoire of the reading communities, as mentioned above. For instance, as these readers ponder about the possible referents in their discourse of the circumstances portrayed in these verses, the seemingly at best connoted reference to the (eschatological?) future created by the reference to Zech 8:10 in v. 5 becomes far more salient. This is because the other references to prophetic books led the readers to assume that the Chronicler at least at one level of meaning asked them to approach the speech of Azariah from an intertextual perspective that by necessity goes beyond the surface meanings carried by the narrative about Asa's days. Significantly, some of the other references to

---

17. On these matters, see Beentjes, "Prophets in the Book of Chronicles," 51–52.

18. S. Japhet, *1 & 2 Chronicles* (OTL; Louisville: Westminster John Knox, 1993) 20.

19. For instance, should they understand the Chronicler as asking them to skip all the reported periods that precede the utterance (for example, the relevant portion of the reign of Asa, Abijah, and so on) in the story narrated by the Chronicler and recall the background of the period of the Judges, which is not even reported in the book? (See S. S. Tuell, *First and Second Chronicles* [Interpretation; Louisville: Westminster John Knox, 2001] 169–70.) Or should they understand the Chronicler as asking them to associate this particular review of the past with Northern Israel only, even if this is nowhere stated by the Chronicler? (See W. Johnstone, *1 & 2 Chronicles, Vol. 2: 2 Chronicles 10–36: Guilt and Atonement* [JSOTSup 254; Sheffield: Sheffield Academic Press, 1997] 65–66.)

prophetic texts also reinforce associations between the circumstances described here and historical contexts in the speaker's future. This is certainly true of the reference to Hos 3:4 in v 3.[20]

Of course, from the perspective of the intended readership, the intertextuality of the speech of Azariah cuts both ways. References to Hos 3:4 and Zech 8:10 contribute to the readers' association of the circumstances portrayed in the speech with future events; conversely, the speech of Azariah provides an intertextual viewpoint from which the primary readership may reread and reinterpret the meanings conveyed by Hos 3:4. As Seligman already noted, whereas Hosea speaks of king, officers, sacrifice, pillar, ephod, and teraphim, Azariah refers to the true deity, priests who teach, and divine teaching/torah.

The consistent shift from the original singular to plural in v. 7's citations of Zeph 3:16 and Jer 31:16 suggests an interpretive approach to these verses.[21] Moreover, the setting described in Zeph 3:16 and Jer 31:6 concerns a great future that will be manifested following the Exile and that in many ways could not have been considered fulfilled in the days of the primary readership of Chronicles. The text thus creates a multiple interpretive, cross-temporal links between the Israel of Asa's days and the future Israel; between the words of Azariah, son of Oded, and the words YHWH's diverse promises of restoration; between Azariah and the later voice that will be heard according to Zech 3:16; and between the intended and primary readerships that identify with and vicariously experience their own events through their reading as well as the events they are reading about.

As in the previous case of David's psalm, the text of Azariah's speech as experienced and understood through the reading and rereading of the literati for whom the book of Chronicles was composed carries a fluidity of meanings that allows them to engage with it deeply on multiple levels. They also can negotiate their identity through the intertwining of the converging and mutually identifying tendencies communicated by the text without negating the differences between them. After all, they identify on one level with the community addressed by Azariah in the world of the book of Chronicles, and they identify with all the other communities—including those in the future—to which this text clearly alludes and whose images it evokes. At the same time,

---

20. Compare Japhet, *1 & 2 Chronicles*, 719; and I. L. Seligman, "The Beginning of Midrash in Chronicles," *Tarbiz* 49 (1979–80) 21 [Hebrew].

21. The feminine singular in Zeph 3:15 refers to Jerusalem; the fem. sing. in Jer 31:16 refers to Rachel.

they certainly cannot ignore the difference in their location. Of course, for the text to carry all these meanings, Azariah has to be imagined as bearing the voices of multiple texts set later than his putative time. The obvious "chronism" on the narrative level that is implied in any historiographical work is not negated but is, by discursive and ideological necessity, counterbalanced with claims for cross-temporal connections.[22] The latter are supported by, and expressed, among others, in terms of worlds of knowledge (including precise wording of texts, awareness of exile, and of what constitutes a proper response to it) that are at times shared by communities and individuals that exist in different eras. This basic conceptual approach allows for cross-temporal identification as well as for intertextuality within a repertoire of works set in or associated with different periods. It also allows the Chronicler to take a stance as an interpreter of previous texts and to advance claims about their meanings.[23]

Given the precedent of David, it is reasonable to assume that the primary and intended readerships of Chronicles imagined Azariah as being aware of the texts he was quoting—that is, he was knowingly quoting them.[24] If this was the case, then texts that were explicitly associated with later periods (for example, Zechariah, Hosea, Jeremiah, Zephaniah) had to be conceived at some point or on some level as being known to a prophet before they were written. Significantly, this

---

22. I discussed elsewhere the central and ubiquitous role of balancing claims in Chronicles; see *History, Literature and Theology in the Book of Chronicles*, passim.

23. See, for instance, G. N. Knoppers, "Hierodules, Priests, or Janitors? The Levites in Chronicles and the History of the Israelite Priesthood," *JBL* 118 (1999) 49–72; E. Ben Zvi, "Revisiting 'Boiling in Fire' in 2 Chr 35:13 and Related Passover Questions: Text, Exegetical Needs and Concerns, and General Implications," *Biblical Interpretation in Judaism and Christianity* (ed. I. Kalimi and P. J. Haas; LHBOTS 439; London: T. & T. Clark, 2006) 238–50; and idem, *History, Literature and Theology in the Book of Chronicles*, chap. 7.

24. It goes without saying that any study of Chronicles' understanding of temporal dimensions and fluctuations in the (proper) knowledge of the divine teaching associated with Moses among Israelites raises a number of issues that are substantially different from the issues involved in the case of Azariah, the son of Oded (for one thing, Moses was set in a time period in the story of Israel that was construed as prior to rather than later than the time of any Israelite speaker in the monarchic period) and therefore are beyond the scope of this essay. These matters must be addressed at length in a separate essay. There is not doubt, however, that Chronicles contains allusions and references to pentateuchal texts and that many of the considerations advanced here about identity, fluidity of meanings, interxtextuality, the late Persian, Yehudite social background of the authorship and primary readership of Chronicles and its/their interpretive approaches are relevant to the study of the world views shaped and reflected by references to pentateuchal texts in Chronicles, from the viewpoint of the latter's intended and primary readerships.

line of thought is present in other works within the authoritative repertoire of the Yehudite literati. The most obvious example is Gen 26:5b, which asks the intended and primary readerships of Genesis to associate Abraham with Mosaic Torah (and compare Gen 26:5b with Deut 11:1), even though, obviously, Abraham preceded Moses.[25] The appearance of similar ideological approaches to the construction of the past and to the cross-temporal character of some texts in works other than Chronicles, within the general setting of the Persian period, is only to be expected. Chronicles is simply part and parcel of a range of ideological discourses that informed and shaped the world of the literati of the time.

It is worth noting, however, that if carried to its logical conclusion, this line of thought leads beyond the "moderate" approach mentioned above to the concept of preexisting texts, whether written or unwritten. The latter is actually attested in the literature of the late Second Temple and its aftermath (see *Jubilees* and *2 Bar.* 57:1–2) and may be compared with later concepts of a preexisting Torah, such as the concepts reflected in the beginning of *Genesis Rabbah*.

In any event, the attribution of knowledge of things or utterances that have not yet taken places to pious figures in Israel's past (For example, David and Israel when David transported the ark; the prophet Azariah) shades them with a bit of godly character (cf. Isa 46:10). Certainly, these attributions contribute to the later characterization of David as a prophet.[26]

This said, at least in some of their rereadings of the text, the primary and intended readerships of Chronicles could have also imagined Azariah as being unaware that his speech referred to texts that would later be included in the repertoire of Persian Yehud. If so, within these readings they had to imagine a providential hand guiding Azariah and making him utter the very precise words that would allow and shape the true and full meaning of his speech, as understood by these readerships. This line of thought, if carried to its logical conclusion, leads to

---

25. On this matter, see J. D. Levenson, "The Conversion of Abraham to Judaism, Christianity, and Islam," in *The Idea of Biblical Interpretation: Essays in Honor of James L. Kugel* (ed. H. Najman and J. H. Newman; Leiden: Brill, 2004) 3–40 (esp. pp. 20–21).

26. See the well-known case of Acts 2:30–31. Of course, the characterization of David as a prophet did not begin with the book of Acts. See 11Q5 (= 11QPs[a]) col. xxvii line 11. See also Josephus, *Ant.* 6.166 (cf. *Ant.* 8.109). On these matters, see J. A . Fitzmyer, "David, 'Being Therefore a Prophet' (Acts 2:30)," *CBQ* 34 (1972) 332–39; and recently, P. W. Flint, "The Prophet David at Qumran," in *Biblical Interpretation at Qumran* (ed. M. Henze; Grand Rapids, MI: Eerdmans, 2005) 158–67.

the concept of prophets who were unaware of and, in fact, essentially unable to understand the full meaning of what they were prophesying (compare Qumran pesharim, New Testament exegesis, and the use of biblical references in, for instance, 1 Macc 14:9, 12; and compare Zech 8:4–5 and Mic 4:4). Significantly, the text of Chronicles leaves all these interpretive paths open.

Conclusions

Rather than dismissing references to speakers who know later texts or events as anachronistic mistakes that a good historian should have avoided, I strongly suggest in this essay that these references served important purposes and for this reason were highlighted in the text. These references created a fluidity of meanings that was essential to the didactic, socializing function of the text and, above all, essential to the reading and rereading of the text by the communities for whom it was composed. This fluidity of meanings allowed the primary readers to shape their identity in terms of convergences and identification with other communities of Israel across time without negating differences among them. These references also allowed for the development of a substantial degree of intertextuality. To some extent they permitted the development of integration through interaction with diverse authoritative texts in the repertoire of the primary readership—including interaction with Chronicles. This discursive interaction is, of course, related to and somewhat a reflection of the actual social situation of the literati who constituted the primary readership of Chronicles and who read and reread other books in their authoritative repertoire besides Chronicles. Their interpretive viewpoint was strongly informed by the knowledge they used as they read and reread Chronicles. Finally, I suggest in this essay that Chronicles stood ambiguously before interpretive approaches to "Scripture" (including prophetic texts) that played major roles in the late Second Temple period; in fact, it was already pointing to them.

In this essay, I point out the potential for understanding the intellectual and ideological setting of the literati in (Jerusalem-centered) late Persian Yehud. This understanding can be clarified by studying the intellectual milieu of the monarchic past in Chronicles from the perspective of the late Persian period's ideological world, which was implied, created, reinforced, and communicated to the primary readers through the social process of reading and rereading Chronicles. Much more work on these matters awaits us.

"Those Doing the Work for the Service in the House of the Lord"

1 Chronicles 23:6–24:31 and the Sociohistorical Context of the Temple of Yahweh in Jerusalem in the Late Persian/Early Hellenistic Period

JOHN W. WRIGHT

Point Loma Nazarene University

The social history of fourth-century Yehud remains elusive. The era has not yielded sufficient data for precise historical construction. Recent analyses of archaeological data have given us a general picture of the demographic contours of the Persian and Hellenistic province of Yehud. Yehud was an impoverished province (Lipschits 2003; 2005; 2006; Stern 2001: 353–582). A small, poor Jerusalem stood at Yehud's social and cultural center; the Temple of Yahweh stood at the center of Jerusalem. Evidence from the books of Nehemiah and Malachi, however, suggests that this temple was anything but a thriving institution. In the late fifth century, Nehemiah had to use his authority as governor to keep the temple personnel in place due to a shortage of temple income; the prophet "Malachi" indicates that temple income remained a problem later on.

Two sources of data do suggest changes in the fourth-century social and economic context of Yehud. Newly published Idumean ostraca reveal economic transactions on Yehud's frontier (e.g., Eph'al and Naveh 1996; Lemaire 1996; 2000; 2002; 2004; 2006; Porten and Yardeni 2006) and the slow expansion of Idumeans into the southern Shephelah, with its own administrative center in the Persian palace at Lachish (Sapin 2004; Fantalkin and Tal 2006: 177–81). More significantly, a shift in coinage possibly reflects the early Hellenistic removal of the office of the governor from administrative significance in Yehud.[1] Unlike the

---

1. "An important fact about the Judean coins from the Macedonian (ca. 330–312 B.C.E.) and early Ptolemaic (ca. 300–283 B.C.E.) periods is that none of them has the name

Persians, the Ptolemies oversaw Yehud by means of the office of the high priest. The high priesthood itself became an office purchased from its colonial overlords for the social and economic control of the Jews.

If this is so, fourth-century Yehud appears as the geographical core of a dispersed ethnic group with socioeconomic incursions at its periphery and a struggle to sustain a viable socioeconomic life at its center. All data point to the elite Yehudians' struggle to sustain their version of Yehud's cultural, political, and economic heritage by means of the Temple of Yahweh in Jerusalem. From the context of the imperial need for the economic exploitation of Yehud to the necessity for the high priesthood to gain status from the purchase of the office to peasant resistance to sending agricultural income to the temple in Jerusalem—the general picture of the social history of Yehud shows the temple in Jerusalem to be a vital battleground, in reality, for fourth-century Jews.

Can we push beyond this general picture in our construction of the social history of Yehud? Joel Weinberg (1992) attempted to do so in his hypothesis of Judah as a civic and temple community in the Persian period. His construction has met with only limited acceptance (e.g., Blenkinsopp 1991; Bedford 1991; and Horsley 1991). Behind Weinberg's hypothesis was the work of the scholar G. C. Sarkisian, who described the social and economic structures of Babylonia in the Seleucid period as a "civil and temple community." However, Sarkisian's work itself has not stood the test of scholarly scrutiny. L. T. Doty writes:

> Sarkisian's hypothesis concerning the political structure of Seleucid Uruk is therefore not adequately supported by the documents themselves. The present evidence indicates that the use of cuneiform for business purposes was not restricted to any particular political or social group in Uruk. Of course the persons involved in these transactions had to own the relevant property, or have sufficient capital to buy it, but among those who were financially able to participate there appear to

---

of a governor stamped on it. Rappaport has concluded from this given that the political situation in Yehud/Yehudah had changed with the arrival of Hellenistic rule. The fact that the late Persian-period coins have the name of the governor on them but the Macedonian-Ptolemaic coins do not means for Rappaport that there was no longer a governor in Judah and that the high priest had, in the absence of such a political leader, become the local minting authority. The data are too meager to confirm his inference, but at least the extant evidence makes it an attractive possibility. If so, the implication would be that the high priests of the very earliest post-Persian decades exercised greater power in the crucial economic sphere of minting and coins. Ultimate sovereignty, of course, remained with the foreign overlord, but local control may have rested with the high priests" (VanderKam 2004: 123–24). See also Rooke 2000.

have been no restrictions. Most were native Babylonians, and this is to be expected in an ancient Babylonian city in which the population probably remained overwhelmingly Babylonian throughout the Seleucid period. But Greeks, as well as Hellenized Babylonians, did from time to time enter into transactions which were documented in cuneiform, and with no apparent restrictions. (Doty 1977: 159–60)

If Sarkisian's original construction does not hold for Seleucid Uruk, it becomes difficult to sustain Weinberg's derivative hypothesis of Yehud as a civic and temple community. Once again, we seem to be left with understanding the importance of the Temple of Yahweh in Jerusalem but not really grasping its precise socioeconomic mechanisms.

I suggest that, even if Weinberg's hypothesis has failed, he successfully points us in the right direction to understand the sociohistorical matrix of the Temple of Yahweh in fourth-century Jerusalem. Late Persian, early Seleucid-period temples in Babylonia, particularly in Uruk, possess intriguing similarities to and dissimilarities with the Temple of Yahweh in Jerusalem during the same period. We might find the way into the temple of Jerusalem by following those who had permission to enter it: the priests.

However, this way is itself fraught with conceptual danger. In antiquity, there was no single office called the "priesthood." Max Weber invented a universal concept of *priesthood* as a means of translating a variety of phenomena from antiquity and elsewhere into categories within his neo-Kantian, European political categories.[2] Weber argued that a priesthood develops through the evolutionary routinization of religion from its origins within a charismatic individual to a certain type of regularized pattern of social behavior. The priesthood requires the abstract social organization that Weber calls the "cult":

> It is more correct for our purpose, in order to do justice to the diverse and mixed manifestations of this phenomenon, to set up as the crucial feature of the priesthood the specialization of a particular group of persons in the continuous operation of a cultic enterprise, permanently associated with particular norms, places and times, and related to specific social groups. There can be no priesthood without a cult, although there may well be a cult without a specialized priesthood. (Weber 1963: 30)

---

2. "The most basic and broadest questions are raised in the work of Max Weber, who formulated a universal conception of priesthood, not restricted to any one society. In this he explicitly recognized that the defining features of priesthood were themselves a problem in view of 'the diverse and mixed manifestations of this phenomenon.' Weber's discussion of priesthood has been influential in many areas of religious history, but is problematic when applied to the ancient world" (Beard and North 1990: 4).

The priesthood becomes an ideal type, a unitary phenomenon within the rationalization of subjective values that can occur in the history of religions.

When one turns to Neo-Babylonian-, Achaemenid-, and Seleucid-era Mesopotamia, however, one immediately confronts a problem with Weber's unitary understanding of the priesthood. According to Amélie Kuhrt,

> the category "priests" as such in relation to Babylonia must be dropped —there is no term that defines priests in any general sense whatsoever. The upper echelons of the temple consisted primarily, it appears, of administrative officials, who functioned together with officers appointed by the king, from Nabonidus onwards, and who co-operated in some way with this "civil" authority; it is a vexed question how the two were separated and what might have been their respective spheres of competence. Cultic personnel and ritual experts together formed just one category, a poorly defined one, within the temple; the category included lamentation-singers, liturgy-singers, the *sange* of specific deities, exorcists and possibly, though the evidence is entirely inferential, astronomers, diviners and omen-experts. It is possible that this group of cultic personnel was in part known as the "temple-enterers" (*ēreb bīti*), but this is disputed as the term may be a general one, defining all those allowed to enter the temple in order to carry out a wide variety of duties. (Kuhrt 1990: 150–51)

The Weberian ideal type of a "priest" is an anachronism in late Persian, early Seleucid-period Babylonia. If there is no such office as "priest," we can also see that there is no such general phenomenon as "cult." Temples, the houses of the gods, were vastly different institutions in antiquity, even within the Mediterranean world.

Why then have Weber's categories exercised such influence, especially within the scholarly constructions of the history of early Judaism? Weber's concepts subtly offer modern Western political and economic categories as transcendental categories. Weber's conceptual scheme places all categories either into modernist, liberal political categories or finds them wanting. John Milbank's magisterial work *Theology and Social Theory* traces Weber's conceptuality to its origins with neo-Kantian thought:

> Religion is presented as more properly concerned with the supra-social, with a world of universal "personal" value. This is a new version of Kant's identification of true religion with true morality, where we have a practical . . . access, to the realm of "transcendental objects" or "things in themselves," . . . the "religious" and the "social" are conceived of as al-

ways and forever categorically separate realms. Thus history can be narrated as the story of the interaction between personal religious charisma and substantive value on the one hand, and the various public processes of routinization and instrumental reason on the other. (Milbank 1990: 76)

The Western European, modernist dichotomy between the public and the private, the rational and the irrational, the secular and the religious, the realm of the state and the realm of value, though connected, appear as distinct realms. Weber thereby "repeats the Kantian identification of religion with the private, the subjective and the evaluative, in contradiction to a public, natural or social realm of objective, but humanly meaningless fact" (Milbank 1990: 76).

Weber tells a colonial narrative that absorbs the "Oriental" into Western, liberal categories, or decries the phenomena as regressive or primitive. However, the evolutionary story that Weber tells has a profound problem:

> the third stage is really only exemplified in the case of the west. One has to make two moves to avoid the obvious conclusion that "rationalization" is just one event in western history that happens to have swamped the world, rather than an always latent phenomenon. The first move is an orientalist one. The questions are constantly posed: *why* no capitalism, bureaucratic nationalization, formal law, harmonic music, in the east? The east is defined as a lack, a *stasis* and a set of factors of retardation. The second move is to acclaim Christianity as the "most religious religion." If only the west has arrived at the universal goal, then Christianity must be in some sense the universal religion. What Christianity is supposed uniquely to achieve is the separating out of the religious value-sphere as a purely private matter to do with the will rather than the intellect. . . . Absolute, religious morality is an essentially private affair. (Milbank 1990: 93)

Protestant liberalism, accommodated to its colonialized existence in the West, becomes justified as the highest form of human expression amidst the highest form of politics, the liberal nation-state, accompanied, of course, by the economics of capitalism, itself built upon a "fact/value" distinction.

If this is so, then Weberian categories of the "priest" cannot help us to fill in the gaps to understand the social realia of fourth-century Yehud without absorbing Yehud anachronistically into European colonial categories. As Weinberg suggested, we must look East rather than West to understand the Temple of Yahweh in Jerusalem in the fourth century. We may cautiously use comparative data found in private archives concerning temple personnel from Hellenistic-era Uruk. A form-critical study of the temple duty roster in 1 Chr 23:6–24:31 indicates a socioeconomic matrix for the Temple of Yahweh in Jerusalem that was shared with temples in Uruk during the Seleucid period. These duty rosters presuppose a temple-allotment system for the distribution of agricultural goods for temple offices. The temples in Uruk employed personnel, such as gatekeepers and singers, that parallel temple personnel established by David in 1 Chronicles 23–27. The Chronicler pictures a socioeconomic administrative structure for the Jerusalem temple that was similar to the administrative structure of temples in Uruk.

However, the data also reveal at least one important difference. Uruk temples had sources of income outside the direct taxation of its citizenry, through its own temple lands and usufruct. Because the Temple of Yahweh in Jerusalem seems not to have possessed its own properties, it would have depended exclusively on direct taxation and voluntary gifts from Yehudian families' lands.[3]

The Temple of Yahweh in Jerusalem emerges as the central social and economic institution for the redistribution of wealth among the Jews in the fourth century. The Temple of Yahweh as it emerged during the early Hellenistic period with its taxation authority, its personnel structure, and economic distribution system established a social and economic matrix for the central historical struggles within early Judaism for the centuries that followed.

Late Babylonian Temple Duty Rosters: A Form-Critical Study of 1 Chronicles 23:6–24:31

It seems counterintuitive to begin a sociohistorical reconstruction of fourth-century Yehud with an investigation of 1 Chronicles 23–27. Compiled with a thoroughly Chronistic vocabulary, the passage is unique to Chronicles. The grammar itself has characteristics of what Robert Polzin (1976) has called Late Biblical Hebrew, yet the text purports to describe appointments made in the tenth century B.C.E. by David. Even these appointments are anachronistic. Instead of contemporaries of David, the text uses genealogies from the Torah for the purported Davidic-era temple duty rosters. The chronology of the passage

---

3. Joseph Blenkinsopp (2001) has argued for the possibility that the temple in Jerusalem had a means of acquiring its own land. As Blenkinsopp recognizes, evidence for this is very slight and speculative. Without more evidence, it seems more plausible to hold that the temple in Jerusalem did not own land in the Persian or early Hellenistic periods.

implodes. Obviously, the personnel of the text provide no help for the history of Yehud.

The passage presents a particular institutional social order for the temple in Jerusalem. Gary Knoppers states,

> One also reads about ties among the governance of the state, the governance of the military, and the governance of the cult within 1 Chr 23–27. Priest, Levites, judges, gatekeepers, military leaders, and tribal officers all make appearances as an inveterate David makes a series of appointments in anticipation of his successor's reign. When seen against the backdrop of the close ties that could exist between temple and state officials in the Neo-Babylonian and Achaemenid eras, the close ties posited between David and the assorted officials in his kingdom become more intriguing. (Knoppers 2004b: 788)

As Knoppers continues to observe:

> Most of the scholarship on these difficult chapters has not been focused, however, on these larger social, political, and religious issues. Rather commentators have wrestled with the fundamental question of authorship. Do these chapters—comprising lists of Levites, priests, officials, and gatekeepers—stem from sources in the Chronicler's employ, from the Chronicler himself, from later editors, or from anonymous glossators? (Knoppers 2004b: 788–89)

I would like to suggest that the compositional issue itself dissipates once we attend to the social setting presumed by the passage. The key is a form-critical analysis of the texts, particularly 1 Chr 23:6–24:31.

Although scholars have disputed the unity of 1 Chr 23:6–24:31, they have recognized its genre as a temple duty roster (e.g., De Vries 1989: 198–203). The text begins as David grants allotments, having already gathered Israel together: "And David apportioned them allotments (מחלקות)." A series of prepositional phrases, all beginning with ל, governs the structure of the passage. The text enumerates the general clans that receive David's attention:

> For the sons of Levi from Gershon, Kohath, and Merari (23:6b)
>> For the Gershonites (23:7a)
>> For the sons of Aaron, their allotments (24:1)
>> For the other sons of Levi, for the sons of Amran (24:20)

The list subdivides into three lists. The passage forms a simple ring structure. This literary structure commonly highlights the center portion within a series of three in Chronicles; for example, within the genealogical structure of the descendants of Judah, the descendants of Judah are highlighted at the center (e.g., Williamson 1982b; Kalimi 2005: 215–74). The list links but differentiates the Levites and the sons of Aaron according to specific temple duties; the sons of Aaron receive more-prestigious allotments for their assignments.

Each subdivision lists the names of the people in each roster; the text identifies the figures genealogically by their father and occasionally by their siblings. Each sublist concludes with a summary, more or less expansive, of their duties. The same brief formula begins each conclusion: "These are (אלה). . . ." The first list concludes with "these are the sons of Levi for the house of their fathers, the heads of the fathers, for their assignments in the registry of the names of their persons (אלה בני לוי לבית אבתיהם ראשי האבות לפקודיהם במספר שמות לגלגלתם), doing the administration for the work of the house of Yahweh (עשה המלאכה לעבדת בית יהוה)" (23:24). The conclusion to the second list, the sons of Aaron, is briefer, without the narrative expansions found in the summary of the first list: "These are their assignments for their work: to enter the house of Yahweh (אלה פקדתם לעבדתם לבוא לבית יהוה) according to the commandments in the hand of Aaron, their father, just as Yahweh, the God of Israel, commanded" (24:19). The final conclusion summarizes not just the last sublist but the combined list of Levites and the subdivision of the Levites, the sons of Aaron: "These are the sons of the Levites in relationship to the house of their fathers. And they also cast lots as their brothers, the sons of Aaron, did before David the king and Zadok and Ahimelek and the heads of the fathers of the priests and Levites, the heads of the fathers like the lesser brothers" (24:30b–31). Having described the duties of the sons of Levi and the sons of Aaron in the first two sublists, the final conclusion uses the casting of lots to bring the list to an end within the narrative.

The formal structure of the lists emerges. David's allotments for the sons of Levi become encoded as a temple duty roster: (1) a preposition (ל) introduces the group to be assigned; (2) a list of names follows in various forms but with a fundamentally genealogical structure; and (3) a conclusion to the names occurs, introduced by 'these' (אלה), which summarizes the duties of the people assigned and/or provides for an integration of the list within the narrative of Chronicles.

With the formal structure of 1 Chr 23:6–24:31 in mind, we may isolate its genre more exactly based on a Seleucid-era tablet from Uruk, BRM II 17. The text has been transliterated and translated by McEwan (1981: 50–51).[4] The document represents, to my knowledge, the sole

---

4. Akkadian specialists have discovered difficulties in McEwan's transcriptions and translations. See Stolper (1985) and Brinkman (1983) for reviews of the book, especially with respect to corrections of readings and translations. None of the challenged readings affects the argument of this essay.

Neo- or Late-Babylonian temple duty roster that has survived antiquity.[5] The tablet shares formal features and a specialized vocabulary with the temple duty roster found in 1 Chr 23:6–24:31.[6]

The document begins with the standard dating and introductory formula used in the late Babylonian tablets:

> (On 22) Siman, year 67, Seleucus king:
> When the builders appeared together . . . of the house of the gods and
> said. . . .

Following this introduction, the text gives the assignment for the people who will be listed in the roster that follows:

> For doing the work in the house of the gods
> *a-na epuš*[uš] *šá dul-lu ina bīt ilāni*[meš]

Two lists of names follow. The text introduces the first group:

> The servers of the palace ([lú]*arad ekallī*[meš]) who [are] to work (*i-pu-uš-ma*)
> from 22 Siman to 22 Du'uzu

Eleven names follow, usually identified genealogically by their father and, occasionally, also by their sibling:

> Kidin-Anu, son of Labaši
> Nana-Iddin, son of Kidin-Anu
> Illut-Anu, son of Anu-aba-uṣur
> Nana-iddin, son of Ana-rabuti-Anu
> Anu-ikṣur, his brother
> Anu-aḫḫe-iddin, son of Nidintu-Anu
> Arad-Reš, son of Nana-iddin
> Dummuq
> Anu-iqbi, son of Nidintu-Anu
> Ina-qibit-Anu, son of Kidin-Anu
> Šibqat-Anu, his brother

At this point, assignments for the immediately subsequent time period interrupt the list. Ten names appear in the second subunit of the duty roster:

> The other servers of the palace ([lú]*arad ekallī*[!meš]) who [are] to work
> (*i-pu-uš-ma*) from 22 Du'uzu to 22 Abu are:
> Anu-mukin-apli, son of Nidintu-Anu
> Anu-uballissu, son of Anu-aba-uṣur
> Sumuttu-Anu, his brother

---

5. For a catalog of the Uruk texts, see Krückmann 1931: 9–12.

6. Thanks to my colleague at Point Loma University, Brad Kelle, for his assistance in the translation of the Akkadian text transliterated by McEwan.

Uṣuršu-Anu, son of Riḫat-Ištar
Ina-qibit-Anu, son of Kidin-Anu, the sons,
Arad-Reš, son of Anu-aḫḫe-iddin
Anu-aḫḫe-iddin, son of Anu-aba-uter
Liblut, son of Kidin-Anu
Anu-zera-iddin, his brother
Nidintu-Ištar, son of Nidintu-Anu

A summary conclusion to the whole document reincorporates the two sublists into the common duties assigned by the tablet:

> These servers of the palace (^{lú}*arad ekallī* ^{meš} *šuᵓāti*) [are] to do service (*dullu i-pu-uš-ma*) monthly according to the roster of their names (*ḫb-bu-ú šá saṭari!^{a-ra} ina šumāti* ^{meš}*-šú-nu*), as much as there is work (*dullu*) in the house of the gods. Whosoever among them who does not come to do work according to the monthly roster of their names shall pay in full whatever the assembly (*puḫru*) imposes upon him.

The document ends with a closing formula and a list of witnesses:

> These are the head servers of the palace (*arad re-eš* ^{meš})[7] who [are] to do the work from 22 of year 67—as much work as there is in the house of the gods monthly for the whole year. Month and servers of the palace. Witness. . . .

The document follows a very distinct form with a very limited vocabulary in order to produce the list of workers whom the 'builders' (*itannu*) assign to work in the temples of Uruk. The whole group ultimately functions underneath the authority of the assembly, the *puḫru*.

The formal parallel to 1 Chr 23:6–24:31 becomes immediately apparent upon comparison. The lists share a common formal structure: an introductory phrase introduced by a preposition; a list of names, identified by genealogical relationships; and a conclusion that begins with "these are."[8] The addition of the word "remaining" or "other" to each new sublist of a duty roster that is a compilation of multiple lists is also evidence that the Chronicles list and the Uruk list are two distinct manifestations of a common genre. On these data alone, one can infer that the Chronicler had encountered a genre such as evidenced in

---

7. McEwan argues that "the text has *arad re-eš* ^{meš}, which is a mistake due to confusion with the common personal name Arad-Reš" (1981: 51 n. 164). However, the use of ראש in the parallel text in Chronicles suggests that it is McEwan, not the scribe, who is mistaken. If so, the Chronicles text helps translate and clarify a cuneiform tablet from the Hellenistic era!

8. Attempts to see the conclusions of the lists in Chronicles as later additions to an earlier text (Williamson 1979; De Vries 1989) lose their force when seen in light of BRM II 17.

this temple duty roster from Uruk. He incorporated the genre into his depiction of the end of the reign of David for his own purposes.

The parallels between the two duty rosters go beyond a shared formal structure to a shared vocabulary. The conclusion of the first sublist in 1 Chronicles (1 Chr 23:24–32) in light of BRM II 17 ties the Chronicler even closer to the genre of the tablet from Uruk. The tablet's conclusion initially states that those assigned are 'to do service [*dul-lu i-pu-uš-ma*] monthly according to the roster of their names (*ḫib-bu-ú šá šaṭari!ᵃ⁻ʳᵃ ina šumāti*ᵐᵉˢ], as much as there is work (*dullu*) in the house of the gods'. The first sentence of the conclusion to the first sublist in 1 Chronicles uses very similar phrases: the sons of Levi are enrolled "for their assignments in the roster of their names" (23:24). Each conclusion appears in the same location and refers to the names listed in the document as a 'roster' (*šaṭari!ᵃ⁻ʳᵃ*/מספר).

This linguistic parallel highlights one other linguistic parallel between the texts: the distinct phrases used to describe the assignment of the workers in the temple. BRM II 17 begins with a phrase that appears in similar forms throughout the document: 'For doing the work in the house of the gods' (*a-na epuš*ᵘˢ *šá dul-lu ina bīt ilāni*ᵐᵉˢ]. The grammatical structure of the Akkadian presents an interesting formula: preposition + infinitive construct + noun + genitive phrase. Similarly, the Hebrew in the conclusion speaks of 'doing the administration of the work of the house of Yahweh' (עשה המלאכה לעבדת בית יהוה).

The specific formal and linguistic relationships allow us to move beyond merely designating 1 Chr 23:6–24:31 a temple duty roster. The form-critical analysis indicates that 1 Chr 23:6–24:31 represents the genre of a late Babylonian/Hellenistic-era temple duty roster from Uruk. An analysis of this sort not only helps us understand the function of the passage in Chronicles, it allows us to hypothesize about the concrete sociohistorical location of Chronicles. The Chronicler shows himself to be immersed in a temple culture similar to fourth–third-century Babylon/Uruk.[9]

---

9. One must guard against hasty generalizations formed by moving too quickly to other sites in southern Babylonia because of differences in the relationships between temples and personnel in Babylon and Uruk. For instance, McEwan argues, "In the Uruk temples rations seem to have been given only to the lower levels of temple personnel, while the higher levels received prebend shares. In Babylon, on the other hand, rations seem to have been used as a source of payment for all levels of temple personnel. In Uruk these rations, like the prebends, could be alienated through sale, gift or testament" (McEwan 1981: 137).

Duty Rosters and Temple Allotments:
The Economics of the Late Babylonian Temple Sacrificial System in Uruk

The temple duty roster from Uruk represents an interrelated body of documents from family archives that together give at least a partial view of the social and economic dynamics of the distribution of goods in the temples in Uruk. The duty roster was necessary, not merely to cover the tasks required to sustain temple activities; the duty roster presupposed a particular allotment system for the distribution of the economic goods that passed into and through the temple to the people in the city. Whereas the precise extent, mechanisms, and distinctions of this system from Uruk remain unclear and controverted, we do know the general operation of this temple economic system that the duty roster presupposes.

The temple duty roster from Uruk directly relates to a specific manner of distributing goods through the temple system—the distribution primarily, though not exclusively, of prepared food. As reimbursement for assigned work and/or responsibilities, temple personnel received commensurate rations. The extent of the rations depended on two factors: (1) the status of the office and/or responsibility assigned; and (2) the particular days during which one held the office and/or responsibilities. Assignments during festival days, days of more intense temple activities, would result in higher income. In this manner, the sacrificial system of the temples at Uruk provided an economic distribution system. From a modern Western perspective, the temples represented something like a payroll department, restaurant/catering service, and grocery store for those who received allotments for duties performed. By granting specific duties/offices to individuals during precise times, the temple duty roster thus provided a means for the temple administration to distribute the temple goods to personnel based on the days and even the times of their assignments.

The amount of goods that moved through the temple was substantial. One receives an impression of the extent of the goods from extant materials. CT XLIX 150, lines 25–33 details the daily distribution of bread to the various temples for the four daily offerings:

> from 81 *seah* of barley flour and 27 *seah* of wheat flour, which the baker bakes into 243 *ṣibtu* loaves, from which for four meals at the table of Anu the baker gives 30 *ṣibtu* loaves, 8 apiece for the main and secondary meals of the morning and 7 apiece for the main and secondary meals of the afternoon the baker gives. 30 loaves before Antu, 30 before Ištar, 30 before Nana, 12 before the shrine of Anu and the house god of the cella

of Antu, 4 before the two crowns of Anu, 16 before the zuqqarrat, 16 before the wings (?) of the cela of Anu and Antu, in toto 168 ṣibtu loaves for
four meals the baker gives. (McEwan 1981: 42–43)

The number of goods would have been too great to consume on site
(not to mention the excess 75 loaves baked by the baker and not distributed to the gods!). The bread would have been distributed from
the gods to the personnel, extending the patronage of the gods to the
households and clients outside the temple, or to other nonsacrificial
personnel in the temple.

This situation becomes more apparent when we discover the amount
of meat that passed through the temples. One tablet, AO 6451 rev.
(RAcc. 78), details the regular butchering and preparation for the secondary meal of the afternoon: "The normal secondary afternoon meal
of Anu and Antu and the gods of their temples of the whole year: four
pure fattened sheep, which have eaten barley for two years, one regular offering lamb fattened on milk and five other sheep, which are
(served) after the others which have not eaten barley" (McEwan 1981:
135). The temples provided various qualities of meat, as well as an extensive amount—ten animals for one meal, not counting the bread and
the beer distributed with it. In a largely subsistence, agrarian economy
in a society without refrigeration, the temples were an economic and
culinary windfall for those who had access to its goods—food already
prepared for ease of distribution to workers or clients of the elite.

A system of allotments, prebends, and/or rations distributed these
goods to various temple personnel, whether holders of offices or labor-
ers. Contracts that sold or leased these offices/duties remain that provide evidence for the means of distribution. The offices could be and
often were combined, with the accumulation of wealth coming through
the accumulation of rights to goods distributed through the temple.[10]
The office of highest status, the temple-enterers (ērib bītūtu), received
extensive compensation, although their responsibilities seem minimal.
McEwan translated a document that illustrates the amount of goods
given to the ērib bītūtu from the temple sacrificial system at particular
times:

> Rubuttu, daughter of Anu-uballiṭ . . . has sold of her own free will—one
> thirtieth (?) of a day in one day from day 1 to day 5, one ninth of a day in

---

10. See the study of Doty (1977: especially pp. 150–307) for an analysis of the buying
and selling of temple offices and their accumulation within families in Uruk over the
span of several generations. Families would accumulate interrelated offices for special-
ization as part of an extended "portfolio" of investments.

one day from day 6 to (day . . .), her share of the *ērib bītūtu* prebend before Anu, Antu, Papsukkal, Ištar, the Mistress of the steppe and all the gods of their temples—one twelfth of a day in one day from day 1 to day 15, her share of the *ērib bītūtu* prebend before Enlil, Papsukkal, Nana, the Mistress of Reš and Šarraḫitu and all the gods of their temples—one fifth and one half in one eighteenth of a day in one day in days 23 and 24, her share in the *ērib bītūtu* prebend and butcher's prebend in Egalmaḫ, the temple of Gula, the temple which . . . upon the grounds of Eanna, before the Mistress of the land and all the gods of her temple—her portion of the two cuts of cooked or raw meat in day 1 and six cuts of cooked or raw meat in the days 10, 11, and 12, and one cut of cooked or raw meat in day 27 from the sheep which are brought up to the table of the Mistress of the Land, her portion of the hulled barley and the six *takkasû* pastries and the oil and 30 Tilmun dates and a leg of mutton in day 13, together with the back portion of the *pīt bābi* festival (?), which goes up to the table of Anu and Antu—her portion of one cut of cooked or raw meat in day 27 from the sheep which come up to the table of the Mistress of the steepe: Total three-fifths of them, i.e., of these cuts of meat—one half in a thigh from a lamb which comes up to the table of Ištar on day 3—her portion of one seventh in one fourth of the ducks which come up to the table of Nana on every *ešeššu* feast and her portion in one half of a sheep which comes up to the table of the statues of the kings on every *ešeššu* feast— these portions monthly for the whole year, the *guqqû* and *ešeššu* offerings and everything which appertains to these portions, which are held with all the brethern [*sic*] and shareholders—for one mina of pure silver in staters of Demetrius in good condition for the full price to Anu-zera-iddin, son of Anu-uballiṭ . . . (line 29ff.) . . . for a memorandum (of agreement) for these portions which Anu-zera-iddin purchased previously from Rabuttu by means of a parchment document. (McEwan 1981: 77–79)

Offices/duties were assigned by dates for the distribution of the goods. To own an office was to receive the allotment of largely perishable goods that the temple produced during those days. A duty roster such as BRM II 17 would provide the central temple administration with records that corresponded to the individual contracts that provided specific allotments, all seemingly under the authority of the Uruk assembly (*puḫru*). Not only did a system of this sort provide a means of recording the tasks necessary to sustain complex institutions such as the temples in Uruk, it also distributed goods to the elite of the society in order to maintain their status.

The Uruk temple duty roster therefore presupposes a temple economic system that the temple personnel produced and from which they received. For lower offices, the temple allotments most likely provided for the subsistence of the office-holders/workers. For higher-status offices, those with less-productive responsibilities in the temple, the food would have allowed the office-holders to entertain and support a wider patronage system—people who ate at their table. In eating at their table, all—the head of the household and family and patrons—ate in allegiance to the gods of Uruk. By monitoring the offices and exchanges in the temple economic system, the *puḫru* themselves maintained their power as the arbiters of the whole urban economic structure. The Uruk temple sacrificial system was a complex system of a distribution of goods that interacted with the status structure of the whole city through the various temples. The documents consistently treat the various deities of Uruk and their various temples as a whole in terms of offices and responsibilities; offices and responsibilities are provided for the temples of all the gods, rather than being limited to a particular deity. The gods—Anu, Antu, Papsukkal, Ištar, the Mistress of the steppe and all the other gods of their temples—represented the social structure of Uruk as a whole. A system of this sort presupposes the complete intertwining of what we who are shaped by Weberian sociology tend to call the social, economic, political, and religious realms.

If this is so, by using a genre from a social and economic setting of this sort, the Chronicler shows that he had extensive exposure to at least a similar temple economic system in the late Persian and/or Hellenistic era (or so we may hypothesize) and portrayed David as implementing this system in the temple in Jerusalem. Given this, it is not surprising that we find evidence of additional overlap between the temple personnel found in Chronicles and at Uruk.

Temple-Enterers, Gatekeepers, and Singers in Uruk and in 1 Chronicles 23–27

I have argued that the presence in Chronicles of a genre of a temple duty roster similar to the genre found at Uruk presupposes a temple economic system like the system in Uruk and in the regions over which it had jurisdiction. The temples and its offices and personnel unified all of life for those who lived in and around Uruk. Additional evidence suggests that the Chronicler envisioned his own social-historical reality in a similar manner. This evidence is apparent in the fact that personnel/offices assigned by David to the temple and Jerusalem in 1 Chronicles 23–26 were the same as the personnel/offices found in the cuneiform documents from Hellenistic Uruk. While these offices were not unique to Uruk or Yehud, the overlap of the material discussed above suggests that a similar social system in Uruk, rather than the broader Mediterranean environment, provides the precise context for understanding the work of the Chronicler in fourth-century Yehud.

The highest office in the temple structure was the "temple-enterer," and thus it appears first in the list. The Uruk tablets show the preeminence of this person, who was called the *ērib bīti*. "The *ērib bītūtu* prebend is the most frequently occurring prebend in the Uruk archives" (McEwan 1981: 75). According to Doty, "*Ērib-bīti* was a general term used to designate persons with various functions who, either because of their office or because of their job, needed to be admitted to parts of the temple off-limits to others" (Doty 1977: 124). The *ērib bītūtu u* office was compensated 100 times more than a gatekeeper, an *atutu*.[11] The temple-enterer seems to have had no responsibilities that required his/her presence in the temple except on certain festival days when the citizens paraded in the city with the gods. All holders of this office were traditionally from the same elite family of Uruk. The office was held by "certain high officials of the temple or city administration, notably the *šatammu*, the *šakin ṭēmi*, and the *šangu* . . . presumably because their duties brought them into the temple" (Doty 1977: 126).

In light of the importance of these figures as the pinnacle of the social-economic system of the temple, it is interesting to find a similar phrase used to describe the sons of Aaron in 1 Chr 24:19. In the conclusion to the duty roster of the sons of Aaron, David grants the sons of Aaron assignments, their groupings (פקדתם) for their work. This office or group, not their duties, was additionally designated by an infinitive phrase: 'to enter the house of Yahweh' [לבוא לבית יהוה]. The sons of Aaron, therefore, were designated the holders of the highest social office of the late Babylonian temple system. The temple duty roster of 1 Chr 23:6–24:31 defines the sons of Aaron as preeminent in the Temple of Yahweh in Jerusalem, not because of their "priestly duties" in the sacrificial system, but by virtue of their office, which is also found in the Uruk tablets: to 'enter the house of the Lord'.

The relationship between the Chronicler's depiction of the house of Aaron and the *ērib bītūtu* is strengthened by the fact that two other offices enumerated in 1 Chronicles 25–26 appear in significant numbers and roles in the tablets from Hellenistic Uruk. Singers (*nāru*) appear as a temple office, as they do in 1 Chr 25:1–19. Although a complete com-

---

11. In a chart by McEwan comparing the average allotments/prebends, the *atutu* received 3 shekels per diem, but the *ērib bītūtu* received 312 shekels per diem (see McEwan 1981: 110).

parison is beyond the purpose of this essay and beyond my expertise in the material, sufficient texts have been translated from Uruk to indicate the role of this office in the temples of the gods of Uruk.

Singers, *nāru*, appear occasionally as temple officials in the Uruk archives. According to McEwan,

> There is no direct evident for the existence of a singer's prebend (*nārūtu*), but on analogy with Ash. 1930.575 where we find the phrase *šā itti* ᴸᵘ*kutimmi*ᵐᵉˢ used as a circumlocution for the *kutimmūtu* prebend, we are perhaps justified in viewing the unnamed prebend in VS XV 19 which is said to be held with the singers (*ša itti* ᴸᵘ*nārī*ᵐᵉˢ) as evidence for the existence of a *nārūtu* prebend. This prebend, as far as we can tell from the meager evidence of the ill-preserved tablet, seems to have consisted of portions of beef which came from the Irigal, Reš and Akitu temples. . . . The purchaser, Anu-aba-uṣur/Nidintu-Anu/Ḫunzu and probably the seller, Labaši/Ina-qibit-Anu/. . . . are members of the clans of Uruk. (McEwan 1981: 89)

The *nāru* do appear in the texts, and seemingly, at least on some dates, provided musical background for the gods while the sacrifices were prepared and cooked:

> Tenth day of Tašrit (RAcc. 89,7)
> During the night *umun šermal-ankia* is recited for Anu and an *elum umma* for the gods as the *dīk bīti* in *Ubsuukinaki*.
> At dawn the gate is opened. The night vigil is ended.
> Water for the hands is brought in and oil is taken.
> The main morning meal comes, the singers sing and the main (meal) is removed.
> The second meal comes. The second meal is removed.
> The main afternoon comes, the singers sing (and the main afternoon meal is removed).
> (The second afternoon meal comes). The second afternoon meal is removed.
> The gate is locked. (McEwan 1981: 170)

It is thus interesting to note that the sons of Asaph, Jeduthun, and Heman receive positions "for the music in the house of Yahweh with cymbal, tambourine, and harp for the work of the house of God by the hand of the king" (1 Chr 25:6). The Chronicler portrays a personnel structure of the temple in Jerusalem with direct musical involvement to announce the sacrificial distribution of goods similar to that found in Hellenistic Uruk.

Third, 1 Chr 26:1–19 portrays the appointment of gatekeepers to positions in and around the temple and Jerusalem. This office too is well documented at Uruk. It represents a much lesser office with distinct responsibilities and smaller compensation. Several contracts for the sale of the office of gatekeeper remain extant from Uruk. BRM II 34 reads:

> Nidintu-šarri, son of Anu-aha-usabsi, son of Anu-aba-uter, has sold of his own free will (his share) from day 1 to day 6 a total of five days in the month, his porter's [gatekeeper's] duties in the storehouse of the temples in of Uruk and the rations and whatever appertains to this porter's allotment for all these days monthly and yearly for 15 shekels of pure silver in the staters of Antiochos in good condition for the full price to Dumqi-Anu, son of Arad-Res, son of Dumqi-Anu in perpetuity. . . .
> . . . this Dumqi-Anu will do the porter's [gatekeeper's] duties for all of these days and nothing will go out of the temples of Uruk. Dumqi-Anu will faithfully perform the service with reference to the *pānu* of these days in perpetuity. (lines 1–7, 16–19; McEwan 1981: 74–75)

One discovers here the security role that gatekeepers played within the economic exchange of the temple. The office was necessary to preserve the accumulation of wealth in the temple for its grandeur and redistribution. The security role and visibility of the gatekeepers at Uruk seemingly led to other roles for them as well. According to McEwan, "in texts from Uruk we find porters mainly as principals and witnesses in contracts" (McEwan 1981: 54). BRM II 40 records a gatekeeper, Idat-Anu, son of Dumqi-Anu, son of Arad-Reš, who purchased a butcher's allotment in addition to his office as "the porter of the storehouse of Anu" (McEwan 1981: 101).

1 Chr 26:1–19 likewise assigns gatekeepers as guardians over temple storehouses and temple and city gates and even appoints a head of the gatekeepers such as we find in Uruk, the *sukkal atutu*. The Chronicler seems to be portraying David's establishment of the temple personnel in ways that are very similar to the personnel and functions found in the cuneiform tablets from Uruk. Appointed by David and listed following the singers, as in Uruk, the gatekeepers have lower status than the singers in the temple complex.

Of course, other temple complexes in antiquity had such roles as singers and gatekeepers, as did Babylonian-type temples in other periods in history. However, one last datum from Chronicles points to a late-Babylonian type of temple system such as the system found at Uruk as normative in the imagination of the Chronicler. In 1 Chr 28:11, David grants 'his treasuries' (גנזכיו) to Solomon as part of his plan for the temple. The root is a Persian loanword, ultimately of Elamite origin. "From the texts of Uruk but one financial officer is known, viz., the *ganzabara* 'treasurer'" (McEwan 1981: 35). This terminological overlap could not have happened before the Persian period, although it would, of course, have been an overlap also during the time of the Seleucid control of the Babylonian region.

The convergence of these data with the genre of the temple duty roster discussed above suggests that the Chronicler painted his sociohistorical picture of the Temple of Yahweh in Jerusalem by borrowing descriptions of personnel, functions, temples, and economics from the region of Uruk. The late-Babylonian, Seleucid-era texts are of great import for understanding the Chronicler's portrait of the social realia of Judah and Jerusalem when he composed his history.

From Imagination to Historical Reality: Yehud Temple Economics and the Absence of Temple Lands

The move from imaginative portrayal to historical reality is a move fraught with danger. The Chronicler may have constructed his portrayal of a temple personnel system without any reference to his own social reality in Yehud; it could have been a purely imaginative depiction. Additionally, we cannot be sure of the exact time or place of the composition of Chronicles, even though the Davidic genealogy, the use of the term *daric*, and other factors show that the mid-fourth century to early third century in Jerusalem are currently the best hypotheses.[12]

While we cannot arrive at a one-to-one correspondence between Chronicles and Yehud,[13] I find it reasonable to posit at least some general overlap between the Chronicler's portrayal of the temple personnel and the social reality of Yehud. If so, our analysis so far would also indicate a temple economic structure within fourth-century Yehud.

The idea that the Chronicler's portrayal was a grandiose depiction of the historical reality of fourth-century Yehud receives credibility from what he does *not* present in Judah compared with Uruk: extensive temple lands. In Uruk, as traditionally within the Babylonian temple economies, temple lands, flocks, and personnel provided the backbone of wealth for the temple, and thus, city economy.[14] Temple lands di-

---

12. See Williamson (1982a: 15–17) and Knoppers (2004a: 101–17) for their discussions of issues of dating.

13. There obviously were not 38,000 Levites in the Temple of Yahweh in Jerusalem during the fourth and/or early third century!

14. See, for instance, the use of year-old male sheep in the sacrificial system of the Eanna temple (analyzed by Zawadzki 2003). The temple flocks actually increased due to their returning more ewes for reproductive purposes. This analysis suggests a similar reason for the use of one-year-old male sheep in the temple sacrificial system of the Torah. One-year-old male sheep are mature enough to provide meat and skins, yet a

rectly provided the temple and its personnel with the goods that were distributed. Overseen ultimately by the *puḫru*, the temple lands distributed the common wealth of the city to the people that tradition—and innovation—demanded. There was no need for vast collections from individual families; the temple lands themselves provided an economic stimulus for maintaining power within the city. It may even have been that, during the Seleucid era, this distribution of goods stood apart from the taxation system of the Seleucids. As Doty shows, the Seleucid-era cuneiform tablets from Uruk are very limited in what they describe regarding certain temple transactions; other types of transaction seemingly were done under the watchful eye of royal representatives.[15]

Whereas Greek lands suffered economically during the fourth and third century due to the ravages of financing and waging war, especially along the coast,[16] the Babylonian region seemingly evidences relative economic stability and even prosperity. The temple personnel and economic system of Uruk, based on the usufruct and land of the temples of the gods of Uruk, provided for the distribution of wealth by means of the city's elite. The temple and their personnel would have appeared as benefactors for distributing the economic goods of the

---

greater percentage may be slaughtered without endangering the long-term viability of the flock, as long as a few males are left alive.

15. Doty hypothesizes that "we must imagine the following situation at Seleucid Uruk. When two private persons entered into a business transaction there were two possible modes of documentation. One was the writing of a cuneiform tablet sealed by the witnesses and one or both principals. The other was the writing of a document in Greek or Aramaic on parchment or papyrus. If the transaction were subject in any way to regulation by the Greek administration, whether because of a tax on the transaction or the participation of a royal official in the conclusion of the transaction, the parties to that transaction had no choice. They were required to have the document written up on parchment or papyrus and officially registered with the royal records keeper. If the transactions were not subject to official registration—and only a few were not—the contracting parties had a choice. The document could be written on a clay tablet in the traditional Babylonian manner and either kept in a personal archive or deposited in the temple for safekeeping. If the transaction involved property associated in some way with the native temples there was probably a strong tendency to use cuneiform" (Doty 1977: 335).

16. "In my opinion it was the crisis in foreign commerce of Greece, together with the political conditions, that brought about the difficult economic situation in which Greece found herself at the end of the fourth century. The decline was gradual, not catastrophic. Greece was faced with the necessity of readjusting in some way her economic life" (Rostovtzeff 1941: 125). For the complete discussion, see the classic economic work by Rostovtzeff (1941), especially pp. 74–125.

gods to the rest of the population, ensuring the loyalty of the people to the gods and to the governing families in the process.

Chronicles presupposes a different economic structure for the house of Yahweh in Jerusalem. Chronicles never depicts the temple as possessing its own usufruct or its own lands—something that added to the honor and prestige of a temple in a Babylonian model. The absence of temple properties seems to have been the actual reality. Nehemiah records that temple personnel had abandoned their temple offices to care for their own farms due to a shortage of revenue in the temple. If so, we are left with a special socioeconomic situation in Yehud: the need for sufficient revenue to sustain a personnel structure for the Temple of Yahweh as in Uruk but no actual revenue sources available. Temple tithes and offerings collected from the families of Yehud were the sole source of supply for the centralized gathering and redistribution of goods. Without a temple endowment, the temple and its god in Jerusalem would have to achieve the primary place of allegiance for its Yehud constituency in order to sustain the cultural and economic life of Yehud. Temple personnel regulated the economic flow of goods and resulting status by means of their offices in the temple and their allotments.

I suggest that this scenario describes the historical reality of fourth- and early-third-century B.C.E. Yehud. As in a late Babylonian city built around the house of the gods, the house of Yahweh in Jerusalem provided a central patronage hub for kinship groups of Yehudian ancestry—the *ethnos*.[17] The Temple of Yahweh in Jerusalem as it emerged during the early Hellenistic period, with its taxation authority, its personnel structure, and its economic distribution system established the social and economic matrix for the central historical struggles of early Judaism during the following centuries. Once the temple in Jerusalem received legitimacy from the Yehudians, control of the temple would mean control of the ethnic group's economy. Power would be given to the temple personnel to mediate between the small province and the larger imperial forces during the centuries to come.

Conclusion

I have argued that we might understand the social and economic mechanisms of fourth-/early-third-century Jerusalem by studying the

---

17. See Wright (2006) for a description of the political and territorial formation of fourth-century Yehud as an ethnos.

social setting presupposed by the Chronicler when he used the genre of a late Babylonian temple duty roster. Assignment of a person to work in the temple was an assignment to receive temple goods. Jerusalem then became a centralized location for the redistribution of wealth from the agricultural Yehudian family lands to the small urban setting of Jerusalem. As part of the Persian province "Across the River," Yehud maintained its social ties to the east even while it was being absorbed into western empires, first under the Macedonians and then under the Ptolemies. The subsequent history of Jerusalem and the Temple of Yahweh there presupposes the establishment of this sort of socioeconomic situation. This is the social reality that emerges from the mists of the historical imagination of the Chronicler.

References

Beard, M., and North, J.
    1990   Introduction. Pp. 1–16 in *Pagan Priests: Religion and Power in the Ancient World*, ed. M. Beard and J. North. London: Duckworth.

Bedford, P. R.
    1991   On Models and Texts: A Response to Blenkinsopp and Petersen. Pp. 154–62 in *Second Temple Studies 1: Persian Period*, ed. P. R. Davies. JSOTSup 117. Sheffield: Sheffield Academic Press.

Blenkinsopp, J.
    1991   Temple and Society in Achaemenid Judah. Pp. 22–53 in *Second Temple Studies 1: Persian Period*, ed. P. R. Davies. JSOTSup 117. Sheffield: Sheffield Academic Press.

    2001   Did the Second Jerusalemite Temple Possess Land? *Transeu* 21: 61–68.

Brinkman, J. A.
    1983   Review of *Priest and Temple in Hellenistic Babylonia* by McEwan, Gilbert J. P. *JCS* 35: 229–43.

De Vries, S. J.
    1989   *1 and 2 Chronicles.* FOTL 11. Grand Rapids: Eerdmans.

Doty, Laurence T.
    1977   *Cuneiform Archives from Hellenistic Uruk.* Ph.D. dissertation. Yale University.

Eph'al, I., and Naveh, J.
    1996   *Aramaic Ostraca of the Fourth Century BC from Idumaea.* Jerusalem: Magnes.

Fantalkin, A., and Tal, O.
    2006   Redating Lachish Level I: Identifying Achaemenid Imperial Policy at the Southern Frontier of the Fifth Satrapy. Pp. 167–97 in *Judah and the Judeans in the Persian Period*, ed. O. Lipschits and M. Oeming. Winona Lake, IN: Eisenbrauns.

Horsley, R.
1991   Empire, Temple and Community—But No Bourgeoise! A Response to
        Blenkinsopp and Petersen. Pp. 163–74 in *Second Temple Studies 1: Per-
        sian Period*, ed. P. R. Davies. JSOTSup 117. Sheffield: Sheffield Aca-
        demic Press.
Kalimi, I.
2005   *The Reshaping of Ancient Israelite History in Chronicles.* Winona Lake,
        IN: Eisenbrauns.
Knoppers, G. N.
2004a   *1 Chronicles 1–9: A New Translation with Introduction and Commentary.*
        AB 12. New York: Doubleday.
2004b   *1 Chronicles 10–29: A New Translation with Introduction and Commentary.*
        AB 12a. New York: Doubleday.
Krückmann, O.
1931   *Babylonische rechts- und verwaltungsurkunden aus der zeit Alexanders und
        der Diadochen.* Weimar: Hof.
Kuhrt, A.
1990   Nabonidus and the Babylonian Priesthood. Pp. 119–55 in *Pagan Priests:
        Religion and Power in the Ancient World*, ed. M. Beard and J. North. Lon-
        don: Duckworth.
Lemaire, A.
1996   *Nouvelles inscriptions araméennes d'Idumée d'Israel.* Vol. 1. Paris: Gabalda.
2000   L'economie de l'Idumée d'après les nouveaux ostraca araméens.
        Transeu 19: 131–43.
2002   *Nouvelles inscriptions araméennes d'Idumée d'Israel.* Vol. 2. Paris: Gabalda.
2004   Taxes and impôt dans le sud de la Palestine (IVe s av. J.-C.). *Transeu* 28:
        133–42.
2006   New Aramaic Ostraca from Idumea and Their Historical Interpreta-
        tion. Pp. 413–56 in *Judah and the Judeans in the Persian Period.* ed. O. Lip-
        schits and M. Oeming. Winona Lake, IN: Eisenbrauns.
Lipschits, O.
2003   Demographic Changes in Judah between the Seventh and Fifth Cen-
        turies B.C.E. Pp. 323–76 in *Judah and the Judeans in the Neo-Babylonian
        Period*, ed. O. Lipschits and J. Blenkinsopp. Winona Lake, IN: Eisen-
        brauns.
2005   *The Fall and Rise of Jerusalem: Judah under Babylonian Rule.* Winona
        Lake, IN: Eisenbrauns.
2006   Achaemenid Imperial Policy, Settlement Processes in Palestine, and
        the Status of Jerusalem in the Middle of the Fifth Century B.C.E.
        Pp. 19–52 in *Judah and the Judeans in the Persian Period.* ed. O. Lipschits
        and M. Oeming. Winona Lake, IN: Eisenbrauns.
McEwan, G. J. P.
1981   *Priest and Temple in Hellenistic Babylonia.* Freiburger altorientalische
        Studien 4. Wiesbaden: Franz Steiner.
Milbank, J.
1990   *Theology and Social Theory: Beyond Secular Reason.* Oxford: Blackwell.

Polzin, R.
  1976 *Late Biblical Hebrew: Toward an Historical Typology of Biblical Hebrew Prose.* Missoula, MT: Scholars Press.
Porten, B., and Yardeni, A.
  2006 Social, Economic, and Onomastic Issues in the Aramaic Ostraca of the Fourth Century B.C.E. Pp. 457–88 in *Judah and the Judeans in the Persian Period*, ed. O. Lipschits and M. Oeming. Winona Lake, IN: Eisenbrauns.
Rooke, D. W.
  2000 *Zadok's Heirs: The Role and Development of the High Priesthood in Ancient Israel.* Oxford Theological Monographs. Oxford: Oxford University Press.
Rostovtzeff, M.
  1941 *Social and Economic History of the Hellenistic World.* Vol. 1. Oxford: Oxford University Press.
Sapin, J.
  2004 La 'frontière' judéo-iduméenne au IVe s. avant J.-C. *Transeu* 27: 109–54.
Stern, E.
  2001 *Archaeology of the Land of the Bible II: The Assyrian, Babylonian and Persian Periods, 722–332 B.C.E.* Garden City, NY: Doubleday.
Stolper, M.
  1985 Review of *Priest and Temple in Hellenistic Babylonia* by Gilbert J. P. McEwan. *JAOS* 105: 141–42.
VanderKam, J.
  2004 *From Joshua to Caiaphas: High Priests after the Exile.* Minneapolis: Fortress.
Weber, M.
  1963 *The Sociology of Religion*, trans. Ephraim Fischoff. Boston: Beacon.
Weinberg, J.
  1992 *The Citizen-Temple Community*, trans. Daniel Smith-Christopher. JSOTSup 151. Sheffield: JSOT Press.
Williamson, H. G. M.
  1979 Origins of the Twenty-Four Priestly Courses: A Study of 1 Chronicles XXIII–XXVII." *VT* 32: 251–68.
  1982a *1 and 2 Chronicles.* NCB. Grand Rapids: Eerdmans.
  1982b 'We are yours, O David': The Setting and Purpose of 1 Chronicles xii 1–23. *OtSt* 21: 164–76.
Wright, J. W.
  2006 Remapping Yehud: The Borders of Yehud and the Genealogies of Chronicles. Pp. 67–89 in *Judah and the Judeans in the Persian Period*, ed. O. Lipschits and M. Oeming. Winona Lake, IN: Eisenbrauns.
Zawadzki, S.
  2003 Bookkeeping Practices at the Eanna Temple in Uruk in the Light of Text NBC 4897 (1). *JCS* 55: 99–123.

The Development of Jewish Sectarianism from Nehemiah to the Hasidim

JOSEPH BLENKINSOPP

University of Notre Dame

*A historian does not roam about at random through the past, like a ragman in
search of bric-a-brac; rather he sets out with a specific plan in mind, a problem
to solve, a working hypothesis to test. . . . To describe what one sees is one thing;
but to see that which must be described, that is the hard part.*[1]

The Lost Century

The period covered by our conference, the fourth century B.C.E., corresponds to the second century of Persian rule followed by the Macedonian conquest and its aftermath—let us say from the accession of
Artaxerxes II in 404 to the first year of the Seleucid era in 312. As far as
Judaism is concerned, this could be described as the lost century. There
is hardly a single biblical text that can be located *with certainty* in this
century. Josephus, our principal source external to the Bible, is not well
informed on the Persian period, and he makes matters worse by a tendency to conflate the three rulers named Artaxerxes and the three
named Darius, thus drastically telescoping the two centuries of Persian rule. After his lengthy paraphrase of the book of Esther according
to the expanded Greek version (*Ant.* 11.184–296), which he regarded as
the last biblical book, he ran out of biblical source material. He seems
nevertheless to have had some independent information on the Jerusalemite high priests, but his account of the circumstances leading to the
establishment of the Samaritan sanctuary during the Macedonian
takeover, the most important event he records for this period (*Ant.*
11.302–5), is justifiably considered suspect. The *mariage de convenance*
between Manasseh, brother of the high priest Jaddua, and Nikaso,
daughter of Sanballat, governor of Samaria, leading to Sanballat's

---

1. Lucien Febvre, "Leçon d'ouverture au Collège de France, 13 décembre 1933." I
owe the quotation to Carlo Ginzburg, *The Judge and the Historian* (trans. A. Shugaar; London: Verso, 1999) 35–36.

building of a temple for Manasseh, is suspiciously close to an incident recorded in Neh 13:28–29 (Blenkinsopp 1988: 365). Furthermore, the Samaritan Chronicle knows of no priest with the name Manasseh; Josephus is therefore presumed to have confused this Sanballat with the opponent of Nehemiah who bore the same name (*Ant.* 11.302). The occurrence in the Samaria papyri of a Sanballat, father of the mid-fourth-century governor of Samaria, removes or at least alleviates this problem but does not necessarily authenticate Josephus's account (Tcherikover 1975: 44–45, 419–20, written prior to the discovery of the Samaria papyri; Schürer 1979: 17–19; VanderKam 2004: 63–85).

Josephus reports that Alexander granted permission for the construction of a sanctuary on Mount Gerizim, the one later destroyed by John Hyrcanus in 128 B.C.E. (*Ant.* 11.322–34), but no confirmation is available from the Samaritan Chronicle. However, one conclusion we can draw from what he does tell us is that the politicization and commercialization of the official priesthood, a significant factor in sect formation in the Seleucid and Hasmonean periods, was already underway in the fourth century. One example: during the reign of Artaxerxes II (404–359), the Persian general Bagohi (Bagōsēs in Josephus) promised the high priesthood to Jeshua, the brother of the current incumbent, leading to an altercation in the temple between the brothers, the murder of Jeshua, and seven years' oppression by the Persian authorities (*Ant.* 11.27–301).

The Greek historians who cover the period, principally Diodorus, Xenophon (to 362), and Ctesias (to 382), are concerned primarily with Greek-Persian relations and the western Mediterranean region. None of them so much as mentions the Jews or Judah. At the same time, we can hardly suppose that Judah was unaffected by the constant military activity in the region, given its position on or near the main routes from Egypt to the eastern Mediterranean and the Persian heartland. An Egyptian revolt was already underway before Artaxerxes II came to the throne, and disturbances from that quarter continued intermittently throughout his reign. Revolts also broke out in Cyprus (389–380) and the Phoenician cities (385–383). The failure of the Persians to subdue their erstwhile satrapy of Mudriya left the entire Transeuphrates satrapy, Judah included, open to Egyptian and Athenian infiltration. Egyptian support for the so-called "Revolt of the Satraps" in the 360s entailed another march from Egypt through Palestine–Syria with Greek mercenaries. The attempt to subdue Egypt continued under Artaxerxes III Ochus (359–338), at first unsuccessfully, but at length ending with Egypt brought back into the Persian fold, if only for the last decade of the Empire's existence. But the failure of Artaxerxes' initial campaign against Egypt (351–350) inspired another Phoenician revolt masterminded by Tennēs, ruler of Sidon, supported by Egypt under Nectanebo, and opposed by Belesys, satrap of the Transeuphrates region (Diodorus 16.42), perhaps identical with a Belšunu mentioned in cuneiform texts (Briant 1996: 618–19).

There is no evidence that Judah was directly involved in the revolt instigated by Tennēs, but the involvement of Nectanebo and Belesys on opposite sides could hardly have left it unaffected. The archaeological indications of destructions alleged to have happened about this time (Hazor stratum II, Megiddo stratum I, Tel Qasile VI, and others) are badly in need of further study and clarification (Barag 1966). The notice that many Jews were deported to Hyrcania, and perhaps also to Babylon, and that Jericho was destroyed about the same time, derive from late ecclesiastical writers who are not well informed on the Persian period and are without independent support (Schürer 1986: 6 n. 12).[2] At any rate, the revolt was eventually put down and Tennēs executed in 345. This endless series of "the disasters of war" continued throughout the reign of Artaxerxes III and into the reigns of his successors, Arses and Darius III. Then, following the Macedonian conquest, Josephus records the sufferings inflicted on the inhabitants of Judah during the interminable hostilities between the *diadochoi*. The country, he tells us, was devastated, Jerusalem was occupied more than once and was destroyed during the conquest of the country by Antiochus III (*Ant.* 12.138), and many Judean Jews were deported to Egypt (*Ant.* 12.1–10).

Any assessment of the internal affairs of the province, its parties, politics, and sects must surely take this endemic state of warfare, the passing back and forth of armies living off the land, and the consequent social and economic disruption into account. These conditions are compatible with the frequent complaints of inequality, poverty, and social abuses of different kinds in late biblical sources (e.g., Job 22:1–11, 24:1–25; Qoh 4:1–8; and some psalms of lamentation), certainly no improvement on "the social crisis of the fifth century" (Albertz 1994: 495–97). There would also be support from archaeological evidence if the destruction levels identified at several sites could be dated precisely enough or, even approximately enough, to correlate them with the known facts of political and military history. The careers of the

---

2. Several scholars read the fictional *Esther* against the backdrop of these events during the reign of Artaxerxes III (Schürer 1986: 217–18).

vastly wealthy Transjordanian Tobiads, descendants of the Tobiah who caused problems for Nehemiah, reveal the existence of a Jewish lay aristocracy not greatly concerned with either the Law or the Prophets (*Ant.* 12.160–236). Joseph and Hyrcanus went about their business as tycoons and tax collectors during the late third and early second century B.C.E., but the conditions that made their careers possible existed already during the last century of Persian rule. These conditions were calculated to encourage discontent, opposition to policies pursued by the assimilationist ruling classes, and the creation of dissident groups, not necessarily confined to the poorest strata of the population.

The title of this essay involves taking chronological liberties and therefore calls for a word of justification. Nehemiah began his tenure of office as governor of the province in the 20th year of Artaxerxes— more likely Artaxerxes I (therefore 445/444) than Artaxerxes II, therefore (385/384; see Neh 1:2). After serving for 12 years, he visited the Persian court in the 32nd year of Artaxerxes (therefore 433/432; see Neh 5:14) and returned to Judah where he continued to serve—for how long we are not told but certainly not beyond 424/423, the last year of Artaxerxes. As for our *terminus ad quem*, Josephus (*Ant.* 13.171–73) introduces the brief account of his three 'schools of thought' (*haireseis*) into the narrative of the activities of Jonathan Maccabee (160–142), which may suggest that he took this to be the time when they originated. This would provide a logical terminus for a discussion of sect formation but would take us well beyond the parameters set for our conference. But if we can agree at a minimum that the *asidaioi*, pietist conventicles of the devout (*ḥăsîdîm*) of the type mentioned in 1 Maccabees (2:42, 7:12–17), represented a movement with a history reaching back before the reign of Antiochus IV, we can take this "Hasidic" phenomenon, as it existed in the early Hellenistic period, as a convenient terminus for our discussion.

Reading History Backward

The dearth of information from the fourth century for any aspect of the social and religious history of Judaism obliges the historian to fall back on inference based on information available for the periods immediately subsequent and prior to the fourth century as I have delimited it. In other words, we have to fall back on the *faute de mieux* of reading history backward from the time when sectarianism had become a fully visible social reality and forward from the relevant Second Temple biblical texts in the hope of presenting a *plausible* account of developments in between. The forward-looking approach will involve, in the first instance, a reading of Ezra-Nehemiah as our main source for an early stage in the development of sectarianism and a view of the individuals Ezra and Nehemiah as points of reference for conflicting ideologies during the fourth century and later. These, then, are the constraints that determine the line of investigation I propose to follow.

We begin by looking backward from the situation in the late Second Temple period. A feature common to sectarian or quasi-sectarian texts from that time is the concern to link up with the Babylonian Exile as the decisive turning point in the religious history of the people and, in doing so, in effect, to cancel out the intervening centuries. In these texts, the eastern Diaspora appears to be the most fitting location for edifying and didactic narrative, and the period of the Exile the most fitting time for visions and revelations. Didactic narratives and novellas such as the Diaspora stories in Daniel 1–6, Tobit, Esther in the expanded Greek version, Susanna, and Bel and the Dragon are set in that place and at that time, and the Qumran *Apocryphon of Joseph* (4Q371–73) even puts the Joseph story in an exilic setting following the fall of Jerusalem. The vision reports in Daniel and *4 Ezra* are likewise backdated to the time immediately following the Exile. The Diaspora tales in Daniel 1–6 represent Daniel (Belteshazzar) and his companions at the Babylonian court as a small-scale model or prototype for the pietist group in which and for which the book of Daniel was written long after the Neo-Babylonian period. In these stories, Daniel's status vis-à-vis his companions corresponds to the status of the Danielic *maśkîl* vis-à-vis the *rabbîm* (Dan 12:3). The Daniel of chaps. 2, 4, and 5 also engages in the same kind of pesher-like interpretation as the visionary Daniel of chaps. 7–12 and, for that matter, the Qumran sectarians. The Danielic reading of Jeremiah's 70 years (Dan 9:1–2, 24–27), which eventuates in a sevenfold extension of the period of Exile and punishment and a basic reappraisal of the history of the Second Temple period, is a typical example of this kind of interpretation.

This drastic reinterpretation of the history from the Babylonian Exile onward is not confined to the book of Daniel. For the author of *Jubilees* (1:7–18; cf. 23:14–31), the Exile was the time when God hid his face from Israel. It was followed by a long period of neglect of the Law and corrupt temple worship that came to an end only when God raised up a "plant of righteousness," no doubt with reference to the pietist group from which the book derives. The pattern is reproduced in the Enochian "Animal Apocalypse" (*1 En.* 89:68–90:5), according to which worship in the temple of Zerubbabel was polluted from the beginning, and

from then on the entire age was one of spiritual blindness (*1 En.* 89:72–
90:5). In the final period, corresponding to the rule of the Seleucids, the
devout who opposed the prevalent corruption are represented as
lambs and, according to a common opinion, the slain lamb is the high
priest Onias III, who was murdered at the instigation of Menelaus in or
about 170 B.C.E. (*1 En.* 90:6–12). The "Apocalypse of Weeks" (*1 En.* 93:1–
10 + 91:12–17) uses the same symbolic-chronological system as the
book of Daniel. According to both of these texts, the entire period from
the Exile to the time of writing is a time of religious infidelity, a failed
history.

The *Testament of Levi* also organizes the religious history of Israel in
weeks of years or jubilees. During the fifth week, the exiles are repatriated and the temple rebuilt, and the seventh and last week witnesses,
once again, the corruption of the priesthood. The sixth week, corresponding to the entire Second Temple period down to the time of writing, is passed over in silence. A final example: the fragmentary Qumran
text 4Q*Pseudo-Moses* (4Q390) presents Moses, presumably *in articulo
mortis*, predicting the course of history, again set out in jubilees. At the
time of the Exile, the only ones to escape condemnation are "those
who were the first to go up from the land of their captivity to build the
temple." Moses then predicts that in the seventh and final jubilee evil
will be triumphant, God will hide his face, and only a few survivors
will escape annihilation.

The consistency with which this symbolic historiography is reproduced in writings from the second and first centuries B.C.E. points to
the existence of a common tradition, perhaps, as Philip Davies (1987:
107–34) suggests, deriving from the broader Essene movement in its
pre-Qumran phase. The politicization of the official priesthood, the assimilationist policies it pursued, and the consequent alienation of the
more traditional elements from the temple as the principal focus of religious life must have encouraged the formation of dissident groups
long before the Seleucid epoch. The theme of the Exile as the great divide in the national and ethnic history and as the rite of passage that
had to be traversed in order to belong to the gathered community of
the new age is most clearly and forcefully expressed in the *Damascus
Document*. In the first section of the Admonition (CD I 3; II 1), the Exile
is the time when God hid his face from Israel and its sanctuary, the
time of wrath.[3] At this point we come across the much-debated prob-

---

3. For the expression, *histîr pānîm*, with explicit reference to the Exile, see Isa 54:8; it
also occurs in *Jub.* 1:13; 4Q387a 3 III 4; 4Q390 1 I 9–10. With the expression *qēṣ ḥārôn* ('the

lem of the gap of 390 years between the 'return to Zion' (*šîbat ṣiyyôn*) and the emergence of the Damascus sect. Some commentators hold that this gap, deriving from Ezekiel's sign-act indicating a period of punishment for Israel (Ezek 4:4–5), is an insertion that breaks up the narrative logic and perhaps also the prosodic regularity of the text. This may be so, but because the historical survey goes on to speak of the origins or immediate prehistory of the sect—the 20 years of disorientation (groping), the appearance on the scene of the Teacher and his opponents—the insertion must have consisted of a thorough rewriting of the survey (Rabinowitz 1954: 12–15; Davies 1982: 61–72, 233–35; Knibb 1983: 112). What, at any rate, is clear is the intent to associate the Damascus sect with the few people who survived the Exile with their faith intact and returned to Judah, where they constituted the prophetic remnant and the nucleus of a new community.

The same point is made later in the Admonition: God made a covenant with the remnant, those who left the land of Judah, went into Exile, and eventually returned. There followed a long period when Israel was under the dominion of Belial, a period that lasted "until the number of those years was complete," that is, until the founding of the sect (CD III 12–IV 19). The connection with the exilic generation is made once again toward the end of the Admonition (V 20–VII 21). At the time of the destruction of the land (*ḥurban hāʾāreṣ*), there came into existence a group composed of priests and lay members who left Judah and lived in "Damascus," that is, the land of Exile, where they entered into a covenant and dedicated themselves to the study of the law under a leader known as "the Interpreter of the Law" (*dôrēš hattôrâ*).

The symbolic historiography of the *Damascus Document* raises the question of its possible correspondence to history in real time—that is, whether it is possible to detect historical and social continuities, which would span the fourth century, behind these symbolic and ideological constructions. There was certainly continuity during this "lost century" at the level of the interpretation of texts deemed to be authoritative; and because interpretation is not a disembodied activity but is carried forward by specific individuals and groups it can count, in some form, as continuity on the level of social realities as well (Blenkinsopp 1981). Theological constructs, for example the idea that the Exile continued down to the emergence of the Damascus sect (Knibb

---

time of wrath'), compare *yôm ḥārôn ʾappô*, Lam 1:12, also with reference to the destruction of Jerusalem and the deportations.

1976; 1983), need not be dissociated from an awareness of real, historical situations and continuities.

The question therefore arises: do the *Damascus Document* and other sectarian texts from the late Second Temple period provide any clues to the origins and prehistory of these movements? As far as I have been able to determine, Albright was the first to propose a Babylonian origin for the Essenes, the putative addressees of the *Damascus Document*. He maintained that this Judeo-Babylonian sect migrated to Judah, either inspired by the victories of the Maccabee brothers or to escape the Parthian invasion of Babylon some two decades later, in or about the year 140 B.C.E. (Albright 1957: 3, 21–22, 376; Albright and Mann 1969: 19). Not all the arguments presented by Albright have survived scrutiny, but it has been noted that the laws in the *Damascus Document* for people living in "camps" (VII 6) suggest a Gentile and therefore, plausibly, a diasporic environment (Davies 1982: 202–4).

For this reason and others, not least the repeated insistence in these sectarian texts on continuity with the "remnant" of the Babylonian Exile, the Babylonian origin of the sect has emerged as a serious though not undisputed alternative to the hypothesis of Palestinian origin and continuity with the *asidaioi* of 1–2 Maccabees. Murphy-O'Connor (1970; 1985), one of the principal proponents of Babylonian origins, followed Albright in positing a return to Palestine in the mid- to late second century B.C.E., adding that the eschatological beliefs of the Judeo-Babylonian group may have motivated them to return; for them, the *kairos* was at hand. This is plausible, but it would have to be added that, if there was a return at that time, it was not the first. The first to return from the eastern Diaspora to Judah during the early Persian period, known in the *Damascus Document* as the 'founding fathers' (*hārî'šônîm*; CD IV 6, 8) and the original 'plant root' (CD I 7), were the people referred to in Ezra-Nehemiah as the *běnê haggôlâ*, who established themselves in Judah as a self-segregating society. This was the first of several returns (see Zech 6:9–10, Ezra 7, Nehemiah 2) and may therefore represent the beginnings of a process that continued into the Hasmonean period, eventuating in the sectarianism explicitly attested in the second century B.C.E. Continuity of this kind over several centuries is not implausible. Sects (the Karaites, for example) can continue in existence for centuries and preserve their essential tenets while making adjustments to new situations as they arise. Communication between Judah and the eastern Diaspora must have been frequent throughout the period of the Second Temple. Josephus tells us that the Israelites as a whole remained in Babylon after Ezra's mission (*Ant.* 11.133). He

quotes Hecataeus to the effect that many Jews were deported to Babylon by the Persians (*Ag. Ap.* 1.194) and notes that Jews were repatriated
from Babylon during the reign of Antiochus III (*Ant.* 12.138). So the
idea of sectarian activity in Judah throughout the late Persian and
early Hellenistic period, originating among Babylonian Jews and retaining its association with its Babylonian matrix, is hardly farfetched.
In the following section, I will try to add substance to the hypothesis of
historical linkage between the Damascus sect and the self-segregating
Diaspora community of the early Persian period by bringing Ezra-
Nehemiah, Chronicles, and late prophetic texts into the argument.

Ezra-Nehemiah:
Witness to Early Sectarianism

First, then, the issue of dating. In his memoir, Nehemiah dates his
governorship from the 20th year of Artaxerxes (Neh 1:1, 2:1), probably
Artaxerxes I (nicknamed Long Hand; therefore 445/444), to the 32nd
year of the same ruler (therefore 433/432) After his return to the province, he continued in the same capacity for some time, but certainly no
later than the last year of Artaxerxes (therefore 425/424 at the latest).
Ezra's mission to the province is dated to the 7th year of Artaxerxes
(Ezra 7:1, 8), either Artaxerxes Long Hand (therefore 458) or Artaxerxes nicknamed Memory Man (therefore 398)—in my opinion, the
former rather than the latter (Blenkinsopp 1988: 139–44). If we accept
these data, we would have to add that the book itself is the product of
a considerably later time. The initial section, Ezra 1–6, the account of
the first foundations of the new commonwealth, has enough in common with Chronicles to justify deriving it from the circle of the Chronicler, an opinion widely accepted. The lists of temple personnel in
Nehemiah 12 take us well beyond the lifetime of Nehemiah himself,
beginning with the list of high priests concluding with Jaddua, incumbent at the time of the Macedonian conquest (Neh 12:10–11; cf. *Ant.*
11.325–29, 346–47). The list of Levites looks back to "the time of Nehemiah the governor and Ezra the priest and scribe" as to a not-too-
recent past (Neh 12:22–26). Practically all commentators agree that
Nehemiah's covenant must be later than Nehemiah himself, probably
much later (Rudolph [1949: 172–76] opts for the early fourth century).
Morton Smith proposed that Nehemiah's *'ămānâ* derives from Levites
in the early Hellenistic period who, as opponents of the dominant assimilationist party, attributed it to their hero Nehemiah; as such, it can

be described as "the first example of Jewish sectarianism" (M. Smith 1960–61: 347–60; 1971: 173–74).

One of the first scholars to comment on the sectarian character of the *běnê haggôlâ* as profiled in Ezra-Nehemiah was none other than W. F. Albright, who remarked a good number of years ago that "the Babylonian Exile, often described as the great watershed of Israel's history, may well have seen the first stirrings of classical Jewish sectarianism, and of this we get hints in the memoirs of Ezra and Nehemiah" (Albright and Mann 1969: 16). The *běnê haggôlâ* was a self-segregating group that constituted itself as a distinct *qāhāl*, exercised the right to excommunicate (Ezra 10:8), excluded people of mixed descent (Neh 13:3), and covenanted together as an in-group composed of "those who had separated themselves from the 'peoples of the land'" (Ezra 10:3–5, Neh 10:1–40). The same situation is reflected in Malachi (3:16–18), roughly contemporary with or shortly after the mission of Ezra, in which the God-fearers, who pact together and whose names are recorded in a *sēper zikkārôn*, are assured that they will be among the saved on the day of God's final intervention in human affairs. A similar type of covenant appears in Chronicles from the late Persian or early Hellenistic period, which reinforces the point about the dating of the covenanting in Ezra-Nehemiah. Asa's covenant, for example, involved a public gathering which, like the gathering convoked by Ezra, took place in or near the temple precincts, involved taking an oath by those present, and entailed severe punishment of absentees (2 Chr 15:8–15, Ezra 10:1–8).

A link between the *běnê haggôlâ* and the Damascus sectarians that can easily be overlooked is the list referred to but not reproduced in CD IV 2–12. The list consists of the priestly and lay founders of the Damascus sect (*hārî'šônîm*, IV 6, 8) together with the people who came after them. In the context of *Damascus Document* historiography, these founders are the *šābê yiśrā'el* 'those who returned (from Exile)' or 'the penitents of Israel', an ambiguity that I think is deliberate. Philip Davies pointed out that the way the contents of the list are described (it includes the length of their residence in Exile, their deeds, and tribulations) confers on it an eschatological and predestinarian character (Davies 1982: 95–96). This list may be juxtaposed with the list of the first arrivals in Judah from the eastern Diaspora (*hā'ôlîm bāri'šônâ miššěbî haggôlâ*) set out in full in Neh 7:5b–72a. We should ask why, in a generally succinct narrative such a long list, already present in Ezra 2:1–67, would be repeated in the course of the redaction of the book at this point. I suggest that it is there for a definite theological purpose: it marks the completion of the founding of a new commonwealth and encodes a kind of realized eschatology, a profile of the saved community. Moreover, both this list and the one referred to in the *Damascus Document* illustrate the common practice of collapsing later stages or developments into the point of origin, the founding events. The Damascus list refers to the founders and those who came after them, while the Nehemiah list is certainly not confined to the first batch of immigrants. Whatever its purpose, it may indicate that, during the period from the mid-fifth century onward, the principal source of recruits for the self-segregating *běnê haggôlâ* was the self-segregating home group in Babylonia.

While there are obvious structural and organizational differences between the Judeo-Babylonian entity to which Ezra and Nehemiah belonged and the Damascus sect, which I take to be the parent of the Qumran *yaḥad*, there are ideological affinities that imply some degree of continuity. The sectarian or quasi-sectarian self-understanding of the *běnê haggôlâ* is apparent in such self-descriptions as 'the holy seed' (*zeraʿ haqqōdeš*, Ezra 9:2), 'the seed of Israel', and 'the remnant of the people' (*šěʾar hāʿām*, Neh 10:29; 11:1, 20; *šěʾērît hāʿām*, Neh 7:71). One of the most frequent of these self-descriptions is *šěbî haggôlâ* 'those from the captivity of the gola' (Ezra 2:1, Neh 1:2–3, etc), which will at once bring to mind the *šābê yiśrāʾēl* or, differently parsed, *šābî yiśrāʾēl*, those who first returned to Judah from Babylon, with whom the Damascus sectarians aligned themselves (CD II 5; VI 5; VII 16 = XIX 29; XX 17).

The account in Ezra 9–10 of Ezra's attempt to ban exogamous marriage—that is, marriage outside the Judeo-Babylonian Diaspora community—reveals the existence of a core of adherents, to which Ezra himself very likely belonged, known as "they who tremble at the word of the God of Israel" (Ezra 9:4, 10:3). This nucleus of the ultra-observant, the religious elite, combined in typically sectarian fashion a rigorous interpretation of the laws with the kind of intense religious emotion implied in the title *ḥărēdîm* and well documented in the Qumran sectarian texts. The only other place in which these *ḥărēdîm* appear is Isa 66:5, where they have been expelled by their "brethren" on account of their eschatological beliefs. That this title occurs only in Ezra 9–10 and Isa 66:1–5 suggests that these two texts are viewing the same entity from different perspectives and probably also at different stages of development (Blenkinsopp 2003: 51–54, 299–300). We also note how, in Ezra 9–10, the incident unfolds in an atmosphere of fasting, mourning, penitential prayer, and night vigil not unlike the spiritual environment of the book of Daniel. In brief: it looks as if Ezra and his fellow-

"tremblers" came to Judah with a missionary agenda based on the legal and prophetic traditions of their home group in Babylonia.

Ezra and Nehemiah as
Emblematic of Contrasting Ideologies

We pass on now to some indications, admittedly obscure, that Ezra and Nehemiah came to serve as contrasting points of reference in the parties and politics of Judah during the late Persian and Greco-Roman periods. We begin with ben Sira, who omits Ezra, certainly not by oversight, and applauds Nehemiah as rebuilder of Jerusalem and co-founder of the new commonwealth together with Zerubbabel and the priest Joshua (Sir 49:11–13). As intrepid defender of the Jewish people, Nehemiah was adopted as patron by the Maccabees. Joiarib, ancestor of the Maccabees (1 Macc 2:1), was probably added to the list of priests in Neh 12:1–7 who were among the first ʿôlîm, thus providing the Maccabees with the best possible lineage going back to the beginnings. It therefore comes as no surprise that the pro-Hasmonean festal letter to Aristobulus and the Jews in Egypt in 2 Macc 1:1–2:18 backdates Nehemiah to the first return. A rabbinic tradition will take this further by identifying him with Zerubbabel, based on the fiction that Zerubbabel was his Babylonian name (*b. Sanh.* 38a). The festal letter further states that he and not Zerubbabel and Joshua set up the first altar and rebuilt the temple, and it hints that he and not Ezra preserved the sacred books (2 Macc 1:18, 2:13).

The "canonization" of Nehemiah by the Hasmoneans would, we suppose, have rendered him *persona non grata* with their sectarian opponents, including the Pharisees, a circumstance that may help to explain Nehemiah's low profile in rabbinic traditions. The rabbis accorded Ezra a quite different reception. He was elevated to the high priesthood, founded the first yeshiva, presided over the "Men of the Great Assembly," authored the Targum, and compiled the Mishnah. Above all, he was the restorer of the Law so that, if Moses had not preceded him, he would have been worthy to receive it directly from God (*b. Sanh.* 21b). The Ezra Apocalypse (2 Esdras) transmits a different but only slightly less-exalted profile, representing him as primarily prophet and apocalyptic sage. Under divine inspiration and fortified by a fiery liquid, he rewrote the sacred books lost during the first siege of Jerusalem, the exoteric 24 destined for all and sundry and the (presumably apocalyptic) esoteric 70 for "the wise among your people," an allusion to the *maśkîlîm* of the book of Daniel (2 Esd 14:19–48).

In this text from the first century C.E., Ezra alias Salathiel is back-dated to the first return from Exile (2 Esd 3:1, 29, etc.), as Nehemiah is in the festal letter. In this respect, the Ezra Apocalypse follows the lead of the biblical book, according to which Ezra was the son and successor of Seraiah, the last preexilic high priest executed by the Babylonians (Ezra 7:1–5, 2 Kgs 25:18–21). He is not described as high priest in the canonical book, but in 1 Esdras (*archiereus;* 1 Esd 9:39–40) and in Josephus he is the first priest (*prōtos hiereus; Ant.* 11.121).

There is clearly insufficient material here to enable us to join all the dots on an interpretive trajectory traversing the late Persian and early Hellenistic period, but perhaps enough to suggest that Ezra and Nehemiah, as profiled in the homonymous biblical book, came to serve as points of reference in opposing ideologies that eventuated in the break between the Hasmonean leadership and the well-known dissident groups, including the ones mentioned by Josephus. The practice of backdating—that is, collapsing later stages and personalities into the defining moment of the first return from Exile—is illustrated by the way in which Ezra and Nehemiah are presented and is fully in evidence in the symbolic historiography of the *Damascus Document* and other sectarian writings. These considerations permit the hypothesis that the activity of Ezra and his core group, the *ḥărēdîm,* represents an early stage in a process that was going on throughout the fourth century and forms an important part of the prehistory of late Second Temple sectarianism.

If this is so, a further and final suggestion may be permitted. Because the Damascus sect saw itself as the continuation of the 'founding fathers' (*hārî'šônîm*), and therefore of the *běnê haggôlâ* of Ezra-Nehemiah, Ezra could have served as model for the Teacher of Righteousness revered by the Qumran sectarians. Both were Zadokite priests (Ezra 7:1–5; Neh 8:9, 12:26; 4QpPs[a] III 15), both were teachers and scribes and at the same time prophetic figures (e.g., 1QpHab VII 4), and both espoused a rigorist interpretation of the laws. Above all, both were seen, and saw themselves, as primary or secondary founders of a community that understood itself to be the one and only authentic Israel.

From Prophetic Eschatology to
Sectarian Apocalyptic

In the previous section, I have been arguing that the perceived affinity between the Damascus sectarians and the *gôlâ*-community of Ezra and Nehemiah implies not just a modeling of the sectarians on the exilic returnees but a genetic-historical connection, however inadequately we are able to describe it. The amply attested practice of backdating or collapsing later developments into the initial emergence of the protosectarian community of the exilic age conceals developments that must have been going on throughout the later Persian period and beyond. What we know or can reasonably surmise about both the formation and the reception of the Ezra and Nehemiah traditions from the fifth to the first century B.C.E. confirms the existence of historical continuity and linkage between the *gôlâ*-community and the *ḥărēdîm* on the one hand and the Damascus sect and the Qumran *yaḥad* on the other. We now go on to ask whether some of the large areas of empty space in the picture can be filled in with the help of late biblical prophecy. Time and space permit only a brief outline of a large and complex research agenda.

We begin with the Book of the Twelve (*dōdekaprophētōn*). Ben Sira's allusion to "the bones of the twelve prophets" (Sir 49:10) tells us that this compilation was in existence in some shape or form no later than the early second century B.C.E. The last paragraph of Malachi (3:22–24) was probably appended to the collection by the final editors to serve as the conclusion to the prophetic corpus as a whole, perhaps as the conclusion to both Law and Prophets represented, respectively, by Moses and Elijah. In anticipating Elijah's return before "the great and terrible Day of Yahweh," the author recapitulates one of the central eschatological themes of the Twelve and the prophetic corpus as a whole (Wolfe 1935; Rendtorff 2000). The earliest interpretation of the finale, in Sir 48:10, understands the task of *Elias redivivus* as the final ingathering of dispersed Israel, an interpretation supported by the way in which it echoes the Isaianic Servant's mission: "to restore Jacob to him, so that Israel may be gathered to him . . . to raise up the tribes of Jacob, to bring back the survivors of Israel" (Isa 49:5–6), thus creating an intriguing link between the Elijah traditions and the ongoing interpretation of the Isaianic Servant.

A survey of the editorial history of the individual units of the *dōdeka prophētōn* will, I believe, confirm this movement from prophetic eschatology to apocalyptic eschatology. In the first part of Joel, the Day of Yahweh refers to a plague of locusts (1:15; 2:1–2, 11), but in the expanded version, the Day is the day of judgment in the valley of Jehoshaphat (4:1–3, 12–14). Its arrival will be signaled by portents in the sky (4:15–16), and it will conclude with the final ingathering (4:13), miraculous fertility (4:18), and the pouring out of the spirit with the revival of ecstatic prophecy (3:1–5). Here as elsewhere we have the intractable problem of dating, but the language and themes, together with the appropriation and reuse of prophetic motifs, point to the end of the biblical period. Bernhard Duhm (1911) derived the expansions from synagogue preaching as late as the Hasmonean period, but it seems more likely that this is sectarian doctrine of a somewhat earlier date though, unsurprisingly, opinions differ regarding the type of sectarianism it represents and the time of its composition. The fourth century certainly seems to be a safer estimate than Duhm's suggestion (Plöger 1968: 96–105; Redditt 1986). The Day of Yahweh is also a prominent theme in Zephaniah. A core series of sayings directed against both Judah and hostile nations is preceded and followed by the proclamation of universal judgment (1:2–6, 3:9–10) from which only a remnant, the "humble of the land," will be exempt (2:3, 3:12–13). This, too, is suggestive of a similar sectarian origin, though of uncertain date—in one view as late as the second century B.C.E. (Smith and Lacheman 1950).

The diverse material in Zechariah 9–14 has proved especially difficult to contextualize historically and socially. From the time of Eichhorn's celebrated *Einleitung* (1824, 4th ed.), most critical scholars have opted for the period from Alexander's conquests to the Maccabees. So, for example, the sayings against Syrian, Phoenician, and Philistine cities (Zech 9:1–8) have been interpreted against the backdrop of Alexander's progress down the Mediterranean coast after the battle of Issus, and "I will arouse your sons, O Zion, against your sons, O Greece" (9:13) is taken to predict the defeat of Alexander by divine intervention. The enigmatic allusion to a Pierced One in Zech 12:10, referred to Jesus in early Christian preaching, is often understood as a reference to the murder of Onias III in or about 170 B.C.E., though the comparison with the ritual mourning for a dying and rising god, the universal scope of the mourning, and mention of the House of David render this identification problematic. Inevitably, much or all of Zechariah 9–12 has been read as sectarian literature. In his *Dawn of Apocalyptic*, Paul Hanson (1975: 280–401; 1976: 33) assigned these chapters to a dissident prophetic-Levitical group in the first half of the fifth century, but in spite of the emphasis on the Day of Yahweh, especially in the final chapter, there is scant evidence for dissidence, group formation, and covenant making in this section. Malachi, on the other hand, generally taken to be roughly contemporary with Ezra and Nehemiah, refers to God-fearers who confer together, whose names are written in a "book of remembrance," and who await the day of Yahweh's decisive intervention when the distinction between the righteous and the reprobate, those who serve God and those who do not, will be as manifest to the rest of the world as it was to those whom we hear pacting together (Blenkinsopp 1990: 14–16).

The situation is different with Isaiah. Duhm (1922: 418), who was the first to identify Isaiah 56–66 as a distinct section in the book (*Tritojesaja*), read it as the production of a 'theocrat of the first water' (*ein Theokrater vom reinsten Wasser*) who wrote shortly before the time of Ezra and Nehemiah. Most critical scholars since Duhm are, however, convinced that the material in these chapters is too diverse to permit authorial unity, which of course complicates the issue of dating. In numerous studies on these 11 chapters, Odil Hannes Steck (1987; 1991: 278–79) argued for a theory of cumulative expansive comment (*Fortschreibung*), not to be considered apart from the formation of the book as a whole, and covering an extensive period from the sixth to the third century B.C.E. An initial edition of the book, concluding with the anticipated salvation of Jerusalem in 62:10–12, was progressively expanded with the execution of judgment on Edom in 63:1–6, followed by the community lament in 63:7–64:11 occasioned by Ptolemy I's capture of Jerusalem in the last year of the fourth century. This penultimate redaction was then further expanded with the addition of chaps. 65–66 sometime later.

Steck is one of a number of scholars writing over the last few decades who have plotted the cumulative and incremental process by which the book of Isaiah was transformed into something approaching an apocalyptic manual sometime in the late Persian or early Hellenistic period.[4] Steck was apparently not very interested in identifying the social coordinates of this redactional process and wrote about it as if it were comparable to the gradual buildup of barnacles on the keel of a ship. But it seems safe to say that the prophetic-apocalyptic world view reflected in these texts, and in other parts of Isaiah, especially the so-called "Isaian Apocalypse" (chaps. 24–27), is essentially the product of a group phenomenon. In his well-known *Theokratie und Eschatologie* (translated 1968), Otto Plöger outlined a trajectory from the prophetic

---

4. Examples: Claus Westermann (1969) picked out several *Zusätze* in the final stage of redaction: a last age in which sun and moon will no longer be necessary (Isa 60:19–20), new heavens, new earth (65:17, 66:22), peace in the animal kingdom (65:25), and a mission to the Gentiles before the end (66:18–19, 21); Jacques Vermeylen (1978: 471–89) set out six stages of formation ending in the third century with some final apocalyptic *retouches*; Wolfgang Lau (1994) traced the development of three circles of tradition (*Tradentenkreise*) around chaps. 60–62, the center of Trito-Isaiah. For other examples, see Blenkinsopp 2003: 20.

eschatology of the early postexilic period to the apocalyptic world view of the ḥăsîdîm (asidaioi) of the second century B.C.E. among whom, as he believed, the book of Daniel came into existence (Plöger 1968: passim).[5] The main points on this continuum were Joel 3 from the fourth century, Zechariah 12–14 the principal components of which date to the third century, and Isaiah 24–27. Plöger argued that these texts were produced by eschatologically oriented conventicles alienated from and marginalized by the official leadership, which of course included the priestly aristocracy. Plöger (1968: 48) added the interesting if controversial observation that these eschatological conventicles, in existence throughout the later Persian and early Hellenistic periods, "paved the way for the understandable but fatal attempt to translate the dualistic world view into terms of their own situation marked by opposition to the official community, and thus to convert cosmic dualism into an ecclesiastical and confessional dualism."

The surprising omission of Isaiah 56–66 from Plöger's trajectory was remedied (in apparent independence of Plöger) by Paul Hanson, whose attempt to trace the evolution of apocalyptic eschatology from its origins in the sixth century relies on Isaiah 34–35, 24–27, 56–66; Malachi; and Zechariah 9–14. The social situation corresponding to this textual continuum is identified as a progressive estrangement between marginalized prophetic groups allied with disenfranchised Levites on the one hand and the Zadokite priestly aristocracy on the other. The ideology of the Zadokite faction is said to be reflected in Haggai, Zechariah 1–8, and Ezekiel 40–48. Hanson's reading of these texts has provoked considerable criticism, much of it unfavorable (Carroll 1979; Grabbe 1992: 104–10; Schramm 1995), but because he dates none of the relevant texts later than the fifth century, his approach need concern us no further.

In Isaiah 56–66, the ḥărēdîm, those who tremble at the word of God, whom we encountered earlier in our discussion promoting the rigorous enforcement of Ezra's law, appear as a prophetic group hated and shunned by their "brethren" on account of their eschatological beliefs (Isa 66:5). They are associated with the poor and afflicted in spirit on whom God looks with favor in preference to the temple and its functionaries (66:1–4). Here, at least, there is no question but that we are

---

5. John Collins (1998: 112) takes Plöger to task for confusing the ḥăsîdîm with the maśkîlîm of Daniel, but we can say in Plöger's defense that "Hasidic" groups were probably not confined to those of 1 Macc 2:42, who actively supported the Maccabean revolt.

dealing with a group distinctive enough to be excommunicated, and there is good reason to identify them with "the servants of Yahweh," disciples of *the* Servant, who are destined to eat, drink, and rejoice in the end time, which they regarded as imminent, while their opponents suffer hunger and thirst and wail with anguish of spirit—the quintessential sectarian theme of eschatological reversal (65:13–16). Whether these ḥărēdîm and ʿăbādîm continued beyond the late fifth century into "the lost century" and whether, beyond that point, they can be considered the remote forebears of the Damascus sect are questions that, in the present state of our knowledge, or rather ignorance, cannot be answered with assurance.

By way of postscript, we may note that, since throughout the latter part of the Second Temple period Psalms was also regarded as prophetic material, allusion in several psalms to ʿăbādîm, ḥăsîdîm, and ṣaddîqîm as a collectivity, as forming a qāhāl or an ʿēdâ (Ps 1:5, 89:6, 111:1, 149:1), could reflect the existence of pietistic conventicles and therefore an incipient form of sectarianism. Christoph Levin (2003: 291–313) has recently proposed that the *Sitz im Leben* of Psalms in its final edition was not, as is generally thought, the temple liturgy but pietistic conventicles of the Greco-Roman period, in which it served as a book of prayer, study, and reflection. At that point, Psalm 1 was added as the introduction to the collection, several psalms were reformulated to express more clearly the polarity between the righteous and the reprobate (e.g., Ps 26:4–5), and external enemies of Israel were reinterpreted as internal opponents of the groups in question.

References

Albertz, R.
  1994 *History of Israelite Religion in the Old Testament Period*, trans. John Bowden. Vol. 2. Louisville: Westminster John Knox.
Albright, W. F.
  1957 *From the Stone Age to Christianity.* 2nd ed. Garden City, NY: Doubleday.
Albright, W. F., and Mann, C. S.
  1969 Qumran and the Essenes: Geography, Chronology, and the Identification of the Sect. Pp. 14–20 in *The Scrolls and the New Testament*, ed. M. Black. London: SPCK.
Barag, D.
  1966 The Effects of the Tennes Rebellion on Palestine. *BASOR* 183: 6–12.

Blenkinsopp, J.
1981 Interpretation and the Tendency to Sectarianism. Pp.1–26 in vol. 1 of *Jewish and Christian Self-Definition*, ed. E. P. Sanders and A. I. Baumgarten. Philadelphia: Fortress.
1988 *Ezra-Nehemiah: A Commentary.* OTL. Philadelphia: Westminster.
1990 A Jewish Sect of the Persian Period. *CBQ* 52: 5–20.
2003 *Isaiah 56–66: A New Translation with Introduction and Commentary.* AB 19B. New York: Doubleday.

Briant, P.
1996 *Histoire de l'empire perse de Cyrus à Alexandre.* Paris: Fayard. [ET: *From Cyrus to Alexander: A History of the Persian Empire*, trans. P. T. Daniels. Winona Lake, IN: Eisenbrauns, 2002.]

Carroll, R. P.
1979 Twilight of Prophecy or Dawn of Apocalyptic? *JSOT* 14: 3–35.

Collins, J. J.
1998 *The Apocalyptic Imagination: An Introduction to Jewish Apocalyptic Literature.* 2nd ed. Grand Rapids: Eerdmans.

Davies, P. R.
1982 *The Damascus Covenant.* JSOTSup 25. Sheffield: JSOT Press.
1987 *Behind the Essenes: History and Ideology in the Dead Sea Scrolls.* BJS 94. Atlanta: Scholars Press.

Duhm, B.
1911 Anmerkungen zu den Zwölf Propheten. *ZAW* 31: 161–204.
1922 *Das Buch Jesaia.* 4th ed. Göttinger Handkommentar zum Alten Testament 3. Göttingen: Vandenhoeck & Ruprecht.

Grabbe, L. L.
1992 *Judaism from Cyrus to Herod.* Vol. 1. Minneapolis: Fortress.

Hanson, P. D.
1975 *The Dawn of Apocalyptic.* Philadelphia: Fortress.
1976 Apocalypticism. Pp. 28–34 in *IDBSup.* Nashville: Abingdon.

Knibb, M. A.
1976 The Exile in the Literature of the Intertestamental Period. *HeyJ* 17: 253–72.
1983 Exile in the Damascus Document. *JSOT* 25: 99–117.

Lau, W.
1994 *Schriftgelehrte Prophetie in Jes. 56–66.* Berlin: de Gruyter.

Levin, C.
2003 *Fortschreibungen: Gesammelte Studien zum Alten Testament.* BZAW 316. Berlin: de Gruyter.

Murphy-O'Connor, J.
1970 An Essene Missionary Document. *RB* 77: 214–15.
1985 The Damascus Document Revisited. *RB* 92: 224–30.

Plöger, O.
1968 *Theocracy and Eschatology.* Atlanta: John Knox.

Rabinowitz, I.
  1954   A Reconsideration of "Damascus" and "390 Years" in the "Damascus" ("Zadokite") Fragments. *JBL* 73: 12–15.
Redditt, P. L.
  1986   The Book of Joel and Peripheral Prophecy. *CBQ* 48: 225–40.
Rendtorff, R.
  2000   How to Read the Book of the Twelve as a Theological Unity. Pp. 75–87 in *Reading and Hearing the Book of the Twelve*, ed. J. D. Nogalski and M. A. Sweeney. SBLSymS 15. Atlanta: Scholars Press.
Rudolph, W.
  1949   *Esra und Nehemia samt 3. Esra*. HAT 20. Tübingen: Mohr-Siebeck.
Schramm, B.
  1995   *The Opponents of Third Isaiah*. JSOTSup 193. Sheffield: Sheffield Academic Press.
Schürer, E.
  1979   *The History of the Jewish People in the Age of Jesus Christ*, vol. 2, rev. and ed. G. Vermes, F. Millar, and M. Black. Edinburgh: T. & T. Clark.
  1986   *The History of the Jewish People in the Age of Jesus Christ*, vol. 3/1, rev. and ed. G. Vermes, F. Millar, and M. Black. Edinburgh: T. & T. Clark.
Smith, L. P., and Lacheman, E. R.
  1950   The Authorship of the Book of Zephaniah. *JNES* 9: 137–42.
Smith, M.
  1960–61
The Dead Sea Sect in Relation to Ancient Judaism. *NTS* 7: 347–60.
  1971   *Palestinian Parties and Politics That Shaped the Old Testament*. New York: Columbia University Press.
Steck, O. H.
  1987   Beobachtungen zu Jesaja 56–59. *BZ* 31: 228–46.
  1991   *Studien zu Tritojesaja*. BZAW 203. Berlin: de Gruyter.
Tcherikover, V.
  1975   *Hellenistic Civilization and the Jews*. New York: Atheneum.
VanderKam, J. C.
  2004   *From Joshua to Caiphas: High Priests after the Exile*. Minneapolis: Fortress.
Vermeylen, J.
  1978   *Du prophète Isaïe à l'apocalyptique*. Vol. 2. EBib. Paris: Gabalda.
Westermann, C.
  1969   *Isaiah 40–66: A Commentary*, trans. D. M. G. Stalker. OTL. Philadelphia: Westminster.
Wolfe, R. E.
  1935   The Editing of the Book of the Twelve. *ZAW* 53: 103–4.

Index of Authors

Index of Scripture

New Testament

Apocrypha and Pseudepigrapha

Index of Sites

green
press
INITIATIVE

Eisenbrauns is committed to preserving ancient forests
and natural resources. We elected to print *Judah And The
Judeans In The Fourth Century B.C.E* on 50% post consumer
recycled paper, processed chlorine free. As a result, for this
printing, we have saved:

7 Trees (40' tall and 6-8" diameter)
2,789 Gallons of Wastewater
1,122 Kilowatt Hours of Electricity
307 Pounds of Solid Waste
604 Pounds of Greenhouse Gases

Eisenbrauns made this paper choice because our printer,
Thomson-Shore, Inc., is a member of Green Press Initiative,
a nonprofit program dedicated to supporting authors, pub-
lishers, and suppliers in their efforts to reduce their use of
fiber obtained from endangered forests.

For more information, visit www.greenpressinitiative.org